A History of Ottoman Political Thought up to the Early Nineteenth Century

Handbook of Oriental Studies

Handbuch der Orientalistik

SECTION ONE

The Near and Middle East

Edited by

Maribel Fierro (*Madrid*)
M. Şükrü Hanioğlu (*Princeton*)
Renata Holod (*University of Pennsylvania*)
Florian Schwarz (*Vienna*)

VOLUME 125

The titles published in this series are listed at *brill.com/ho1*

A History of Ottoman Political Thought up to the Early Nineteenth Century

By

Marinos Sariyannis

with a chapter by

E. Ekin Tuşalp Atiyas

BRILL

LEIDEN | BOSTON

Cover illustration: Illuminated manuscript, Five poems (quintet), Alexander the Great and the seven philosophers, Walters Art Museum Ms. W.610, fol. 345a.

Library of Congress Cataloging-in-Publication Data

Names: Sariyannis, Marinos, author. | Atiyas, E. Ekin Tuşalp, contributor.
Title: A history of Ottoman political thought up to the early nineteenth
century / By Marinos Sariyannis ; with a chapter by E. Ekin Tuşalp Atiyas.
Description: Leiden ; Boston : Brill, [2019] | Series: Handbook of Oriental
studies = Handbuch der Orientalistik. Section One, The Near and Middle
East, ISSN 0169-9423 ; Volume 125 | Includes bibliographical references
and index.
Identifiers: LCCN 2018038659 (print) | LCCN 2018040258 (ebook) |
ISBN 9789004385245 (ebook) | ISBN 9789004375598 (hardback : alk. paper)
Subjects: LCSH: Political science—Turkey.
Classification: LCC JA84.T9 (ebook) | LCC JA84.T9 S27 2019 (print) | DDC
320.0956/0903—dc23
LC record available at https://lccn.loc.gov/2018038659

Typeface for the Latin, Greek, and Cyrillic scripts: "Brill". See and download: brill.com/brill-typeface.

ISSN 0169-9423
ISBN 978-90-04-37559-8 (hardback)
ISBN 978-90-04-38524-5 (e-book)

Copyright 2019 by Koninklijke Brill NV, Leiden, The Netherlands.
Koninklijke Brill NV incorporates the imprints Brill, Brill Hes & De Graaf, Brill Nijhoff, Brill Rodopi, Brill Sense, Hotei Publishing, mentis Verlag, Verlag Ferdinand Schöningh and Wilhelm Fink Verlag.
All rights reserved. No part of this publication may be reproduced, translated, stored in a retrieval system, or transmitted in any form or by any means, electronic, mechanical, photocopying, recording or otherwise, without prior written permission from the publisher.
Authorization to photocopy items for internal or personal use is granted by Koninklijke Brill NV provided that the appropriate fees are paid directly to The Copyright Clearance Center, 222 Rosewood Drive, Suite 910, Danvers, MA 01923, USA. Fees are subject to change.

This book is printed on acid-free paper and produced in a sustainable manner.

Contents

Indices

Acknowledgments

In Ottoman moral philosophy, generosity (*sehâvet*) is one of the main virtues related to politics, and in our field one can do very little without the generosity of one's friends and colleagues, even though academic and socio-economic conditions do not favor this seemingly anti-productive virtue. Versions of some chapters were meticulously read by Antonis Anastasopoulos, Antonis Hadjikyriacou, and Ethan L. Menchinger; their remarks contributed much and prevented me from making numerous errors. My discussions with Boğaç Ergene, Gottfried Hagen, Güneş Işıksel, Katharina Ivanyi, Derin Terzioğlu, Baki Tezcan, Gülçin Tunalı, and Bilal Yurtoğlu were especially useful in illuminating various aspects of the subject. Several Ottoman manuscripts and a large portion of the modern bibliography were made accessible to me thanks to the generosity and help of Feride Akın, Cumhur Bekar, Günhan Börekçi, Melis Cankara, Lejla Demiri, Emrah Safa Gürkan, İrfan Kokdaş, Tijana Krstić, Dimitris Loupis, Vasileios Syros, and Özgün Deniz Yoldaşlar. I also have to thank Edith Gülçin Ambros, Tobias Heinzelmann, Elias Kolovos, Phokion Kotzageorgis, Christos Kyriakopoulos, Sophia Laiou, Andreas Lyberatos, Foivos Oikonomou, Nicolas Vatin, Yiannis Viskadouros, and Fr. Jason Welle O. F. M., for their magnanimous assistance whenever I asked for it. My thanks also go to Maurits van den Boogert, whose willingness and care were decisive for the present publication, as well as to Professor M. Şükrü Hanioğlu, whose opinion was key in this book being accepted for publication in the "Handbook of Oriental Studies" series, and who made important comments. The anonymous reader's remarks were of great help in rethinking the content of this book and restructuring its chapters in a, hopefully, more meaningful way. My poor English and some errors and points of confusion were amended by Alex Mallett, who meticulously edited the text and managed to make this book readable. I cannot ignore my debt to my teachers and mentors: apart from introducing me to Ottoman history and palaeography, John C. Alexander (Alexandropoulos) also taught me to formulate all my questions in terms of social history while, as well as making me as meticulous in care for details as she is, Elizabeth A. Zachariadou was the person primarily responsible for creating the ideal research environment in which the composition of this book took place.

Indeed, a major part of the research that led to this monograph was funded by the project "OTTPOL: A History of Early Modern Ottoman Political Thought, 15th to Early 19th Centuries", carried out at the Institute for Mediterranean Studies of the Foundation of Research and Technology—Hellas (Rethymno, Greece), within the action "Aristeia II" of the Greek General Secretariat for

Research and Technology, funded by Greece and the European Social Fund of the European Union under the Operational Program Education and Lifelong Learning (2007–13 Greek National Strategic Reference Framework).[1] For this project, I was lucky to have an excellent team of collaborators: E. Ekin Tuşalp Atiyas, post-doctoral researcher (who also authored chapter VI of this book); Marina Demetriadou, doctoral candidate; Michalis Georgellis, MA student; and Lemonia Argyriou, technical assistant. Words are not enough to describe how much I owe to their constant help and assistance; Ekin Tuşalp Atiyas, moreover, carefully read the first draft of this book and suggested numerous and valuable remarks and additions. I must also thank the-then director of the Institute for Mediterranean Studies, Christos Hadziiossif, who constantly encouraged me to continue with this project ever since I first thought of it, as well as to the administrative staff of the Institute (Georgia Papadaki, Valia Patramani) and especially its tireless accountants (Babis Flouris, Antonis Xidianos) for their support under the difficult circumstances prevailing in 2014–15. I wish to stress that the Institute for Mediterranean Studies, my home institution, provided the most creative and friendly environment possible, continuing a tradition of research in the humanities that often disappears under the pressure of financial and international constraints; I do hope it will continue to resist and provide the same steady conditions for serious research in the future.

My postgraduate students during the academic years 2013–14 (Kostis Kanakis, Ioanna Katsara, Yiannis Polychronopoulos, and Stavros Sfakiotakis) and 2014–15 (Petros Kastrinakis, Efthymis Machairas, Vuk Masić, Roger Meier, Rozalia Toulatou, Karmen Vourvachaki, and Dimitris Yagtzoglou) contributed much, even if it was without their knowledge.

Last but not least, I have to thank my parents for their continuous support and, of course, my family, Despoina Moschogianni and Anna, for whom the final months of the composition of this book must have meant a quasi-absence from almost every aspect of family life. Despoina, moreover, had been insisting for years that I write this book, although I never really understood why; many times I would have abandoned this project but for her insistence. Well—here it is now.

•••

Ekin Tuşalp Atiyas would like to thank Marinos Sariyannis, Marina Demetriadou, İzak Atiyas, and İlya Derin Atiyas for making Rethymno a paradise for work and fun. She would also like to thank Marinos Sariyannis and Derin Terzioğlu for their suggestions when writing chapter 6.

1 See also the project website: http://ottpol.ims.forth.gr/.

Note on Transliteration and Citations

The transliteration of Ottoman names and texts is always a thorny problem. For a book relying heavily on literary sources, the problem was even more acute, since its subject required the transliteration not only of Ottoman Turkish but also of Arabic and Persian phrases and the titles of works, some of which were not composed in an Ottoman environment. For reasons of consistency, we chose to use the Turkish alphabet and the generally-accepted modern Turkish orthography (with as few diacritical marks as possible); for the same reasons, we simplified published transliterations as well. As usual, terms that are now established in English, such as pasha for *paşa*, vizier for *vezir* or Sharia for *şeriat*, remain in their common forms. The names of Arab or Persian authors are transliterated using the system established by the *International Journal of Middle East Studies* (*IJMES*) (http://ijmes.chass.ncsu.edu/docs/TransChart.pdf). Titles of treatises in Arabic are given following the *IJMES* system when the works are in Arabic or Persian, too, and following Ottoman vocalization and transliteration when they are in Ottoman Turkish.

As the bulk of this book consists of detailed analysis of Ottoman texts, most of which have been published, I have tried to give the relevant page references as often as possible. In order not to encumber the book with innumerable footnotes, I have left these paginations in-line with a capital letter indicating the initial of the editor; the editions used are cited in footnotes whenever the text is first introduced.

Introduction

> One sees great things from the valley; only small things from the peak.
>
> G. K. CHESTERTON, "The Hammer of God"

∴

The idea for this book was first conceived back in the early 2000s, when I was translating Quentin Skinner's seminal *Foundations of Modern Political Thought* into Greek[1] while writing my doctoral thesis on marginal groups and criminality in seventeenth-century Istanbul. In the context of the latter I had already studied some of the major Ottoman political thinkers, seeking to explore their views on public order, the social "classes" and those who escaped from them, the rich vs. the poor, and so on. It struck me then that no-one had attempted to compose a comprehensive and detailed history of Ottoman political thought in the same way that Skinner (or even his predecessors) did decades ago for Western Europe; from that moment, I dreamt of being bold enough to take up the task of doing so.

Works on the history of Ottoman political thought have never, thus far, reached the length and scope of a monograph. True, some of the most important Ottoman texts were translated into modern languages fairly early: in the mid-nineteenth century, Walter Friedrich Adolf Behrnauer published three German translations, namely of Kâtib Çelebi's *Düstûrü'l-amel* and of Koçi Bey's first (whose French translation by François Pétis de la Croix had been published in 1725; a French translation of İbrahim Müteferrika's *Usûlü'l-hikem* had also appeared by 1769) and second *Risâle*;[2] Rudolph Tschudi published Lütfi Pasha's *Âsafnâme* in 1910, while Hasan Kâfi Akhisari's *Usûlü'l-hikem* was translated into German by Imre von Karácson and Ludwig von Thallóczy a year later.[3] However, the first attempts to study the subject as a whole were to appear comparatively late: in his still authoritative 1958 book on Islamic political thought, Erwin I. J. Rosenthal only used Behrnauer's translations as

1 Skinner 1978.

2 Kâtib Çelebi – Behrnauer 1857; Koçi Bey – Behrnauer 1861; Koçi Bey – Behrnauer 1864 (Behrnauer published Koçi Bey's second treatise as an "anonymous book of advice").

3 Lütfî Pasha – Tschudi 1910; Akhisari – Karácson 1911. Cf. Howard 2007, 142–143 on the European interest in Ottoman *nasihatname* literature.

© KONINKLIJKE BRILL NV, LEIDEN, 2019 | DOI:10.1163/9789004385245_002

the basis of his appendix on "some Turkish views on politics", which was the first comprehensive discussion of the subject in any non-Turkish language.[4] One year earlier, M. Tayyib Gökbilgin had published a pioneering article on the reform treatises up to Kâtib Çelebi, while a little later, in 1962, came Bernard Lewis's influential "Ottoman observers of Ottoman decline".[5] All these were mainly enumerations of the most important authors and summaries of their works, usually with an emphasis on the information they offered on the social and military situation of their era rather than their ideas on society, the state, or politics. An exception was Niyazi Berkes' and Şerif Mardin's attempts in the 1960s, but, as well as having their own, now somewhat outdated agendas, they focused on socio-political developments rather than political thought *per se*.[6]

While the emphasis on economic history had made the history of ideas somewhat obsolete by the 1970s (Lewis Thomas' book on Na'ima's work and ideas, published in 1972, was but an edition of his much earlier dissertation),[7] a second wave of interest arose in the 1980s and the 1990s. Articles like that by Hans Georg Majer on criticism of the ulemas (1980) and that by Ahmet Yaşar Ocak on Ottoman political ideology (1988) were accompanied by more comprehensive attempts to provide a broader overview of the subject, such as the influential 1986 article by Pál Fodor.[8] Previously unknown or neglected works were discovered, published, and/or analyzed: Andreas Tietze, Cornell H. Fleischer, and Jan Schmidt made Mustafa Ali's work a must-read for Ottomanists, Rhoads Murphey and Douglas Howard worked on the early seventeenth-century reform treatises, while Virginia Aksan and Kemal Beydilli highlighted the importance of some of the late eighteenth-century authors.[9] Almost simultaneously, Rifaat Ali Abou-El-Haj's controversial 1991 book on the Ottoman "early-modern state" made it clear that these texts should not be read at face value but rather in light of their authors' relative positions in the struggle between various strata of the ruling elite.[10]

The new millennium brought a new thrust to the study of Ottoman political literature: original texts are constantly being discovered and published,

4 Rosenthal 1958, 224–233.

5 Gökbilgin 1991; Lewis 1962. One should add the enumeration of political manuscripts in Levend 1962.

6 Berkes 1964; Mardin 1969a.

7 Thomas 1972.

8 Sivers 1971; Majer 1980; Fodor 1986; Ocak 1988; Herzog 1999.

9 Tietze 1982; Fleischer 1983; Fleischer 1986a; Schmidt 1991; Murphey 2009a; Murphey 2009b; Murphey 1981; Howard 1988; Howard 1996; Aksan 1993; Beydilli 1984; Beydilli 1999b.

10 Abou-El-Haj 2005 (in this second edition, the author has added an Afterword). See the detailed overview and commentary on the relevant literature in Yılmaz 2003b, 236–251.

while new approaches and methods of analysis are being applied while, at the same time, scholars have been trying to put forth a new agenda for the study of the topic.[11] In addition to the recent dissertations by Hüseyin Yılmaz and Heather L. Ferguson,[12] senior scholars are also turning their attention to this subject, which will arguably be one of the dominant themes of Ottoman studies in the years to come. An emphasis on the legitimization of power has prepared this trend somewhat,[13] while Ottoman economic thought, arguably a part of political theories and ideas, forms the subject of a very recent book.[14] Significantly, the Turkish journal *Türkiye Araştırmaları Literatür Dergisi* (Bilim ve Sanat Vakfı, 2003) dedicated an issue to "Turkish political history", with special emphasis placed on political treatises (among the articles therein, one should note that by Hüseyin Yılmaz, which is a superb survey of the state-of-the-field of the history of Ottoman political thought, its methodological problems, and the agenda for future research).[15] It must be stressed here that MA and PhD theses completed in Turkish universities (and often unduly overlooked by non-Turkish scholars) contain a remarkable wealth of material; these not only edit and transcribe sources but also contain thematic studies.

Still, the state of the field is deplorably poor. Suffice it to say that the most comprehensive survey of Ottoman political thought so far is to be found in the work of a non-Ottomanist, namely Anthony Black, which contains short sections on Ottoman political thought within its general framework (45 out of 352 pages), based on second-hand sources (translations and secondary literature) and with a rather weak assessment of Ottoman ideas on the subject. On the other hand, the most recent effort for a synthesis by an Ottomanist, Linda T. Darling's 2013 book, focuses only on the concept of justice, which is followed from Ancient Mesopotamia to modern times (out of 212 pages, no more than 40 concern the Ottoman Empire).[16] As for Hüseyin Yılmaz's *Caliphate Redefined: The Mystical Turn in Ottoman Political Thought*, which is to appear almost simultaneously with the present book (published by Princeton

11 Kafadar 2001; Ergene 2001; Yılmaz 2003a; Yılmaz 2003b; Howard 2007; Darling 2008; İnan 2009; Ferguson 2010.

12 Yılmaz 2005; Ferguson 2009.

13 See Karateke – Reinkowski 2005.

14 Ermiş 2014 (there was also the early attempt of Uğur 1995).

15 Yılmaz 2003b. The complete reference of the issue is *Türkiye Araştırmaları Literatür Dergisi*, 1/2 (2003): *Türk Siyaset Tarihi—Tanzimat'a kadar*.

16 Black 2011; Darling 2013c. Uğur 2001 (cf. also Uğur 1995) is a monograph, but in fact it contains little more than Levend 1962; cf. Douglas Howard's review in *Turkish Studies Association Bulletin* 13/2 (1989), 124–125.

University Press), while a fascinating description of Ottoman political ideology in the Süleymanic era, it does not go beyond the end of the sixteenth century.

Older overviews, published up to perhaps the beginnings of the 2000s, share two common disadvantages. The first is that they limit themselves to the major thinkers in much the same way that historians of early-modern European political thought used to focus only on innovative or imposing thinkers such as Aquinas, Thomas More, or Macchiavelli, and ignore the many others who made the background against which innovation could be seen or, in contrast, the foundations upon which innovation was built. As in the famous simile originally introduced by Niccolò Machiavelli,[17] they described only the top of the mountains while ignoring the valleys, thus giving a distorted view of the political landscape. In fact, the canon of Ottoman political thought established by most of the overviews contains almost exclusively only those works that happen to have been published. Furthermore, very few studies even mention the ethico-political treatises of the *ahlak* (*akhlâq*) tradition or the Sunna-minded authors of the seventeenth century, while (with the exception of specialized studies) the eighteenth century is usually neglected.

The second disadvantage might be attributed to a "local Orientalism": Oriental studies in the first half of the twentieth century emphasized the innovative and philosophical merits of the great medieval thinkers of the Near East, such as al-Farabi, al-Ghazali, and Ibn Khaldun. When Arabists like Bernard Lewis or Erwin I. J. Rosenthal turned their attention to Ottoman political authors, they tended to see either a sterile imitation of their great Arabian and Persian prototypes or a senseless series of concrete advice on military and administrative matters with no relevance for political theory; this was all the more so since the Islamic philosophers who were translated or imitated were mostly those considered to be insignificant (with the exception of Nasireddin Tusi, whose influence was long overlooked). The value of Ottoman political works was usually measured against the scale of their innovation compared to their medieval predecessors rather than the way they responded to specific problems of Ottoman society; or, in the words of Hüseyin Yılmaz, what was sought was the "worth" rather than the "meaning" of Ottoman political theories.[18] The traditional image of the "decline" of the empire after the mid-sixteenth century, which was virtually unchallenged until the early 1990s,

17 Machiavelli's quote ("those who make maps of countries place themselves low down in the plains to study the character of mountains and elevated lands, and place themselves high up on the mountains to get a better view of the plains") concerns the understanding of princes and people: Machiavelli – Thomson 1910, 5–6.

18 Yılmaz 2003b, 285.

played no small role in promoting this perspective. On a larger scale, one can also note the influence of the more general view of "post-classical" Islam as a period of intellectual decline, a view that has only recently begun to be challenged.[19]

1 What Is Ottoman Political Thought?

Strictly speaking, political thought (or philosophy) may be defined as the study of society, state, and politics with a view to describing aspects of a legitimate government, such as its form, function, and limits. Unlike medieval Islamic political philosophy, however, Ottoman authors who are considered to be political thinkers do not always fit into such a definition. True, there are those who proposed (be it original or not) a complete and coherent system of either moral values that should guide political decisions or historical laws that describe human society and the function of political power. On the other hand, writers such as Koçi Bey and other "Golden Age" advocates, and even more so Ayn Ali and other authors of "administrative manuals", cannot possibly be said to have had (or, more accurately, to have expressed) a vision for state and society or a coherent set of guiding principles. Yet a study of Ottoman political ideas that lacks these groups of thinkers, concentrating only on political philosophy or theory instead, would be only half a study. These authors may only have offered their advice *ad hoc* and on specific issues, such as army discipline or the tax system, but they undoubtedly had a general vision of what good government is (bluntly put, in their case, the kind of government prevailing in the early sixteenth century). Moreover, such concrete advice was considered part of a proper "book on politics" or "book of [political] advice" (*siyasetname, nasihatname*) by the Ottomans themselves. Political thought, in this respect, should not be identified with political theory or political philosophy; what is now called governance or statecraft was undoubtedly conceived as being a part of politics, indeed its very core.

On the other hand, the very notion of politics (as happens also with the notions of state or society) is a distinctly modern one: Karen Barkey defines modernity as "the constitution of a political arena increasingly defined by a struggle over the definition of the political".[20] Things get even more complicated when we talk of cultures, such as that of the Ottomans, which are not only pre-modern but also non-European, and thus use a very different notion

19 See e.g. Radtke 2000; El-Rouayheb 2008 and 2015; Ahmed 2016; Griffel 2017.

20 Barkey 2008, 206.

of politics, if they use one at all.[21] The definition of politics is even now an object of discussion, but one cannot deny that it has a strong connection with notions of power, control, and the state; it is in this sense (rather than a connection with the public sphere, which would create further problems for a premodern society)[22] that we consider all Ottoman texts and ideas pertaining to governance (which is a more accurate and less anachronistic term) to be political, whether they are specific or philosophical. This may be described (in the anthropological jargon) as an "emic" approach, i.e. a viewpoint from the perspective of the subject rather than of the observer (such as the one proposed by Clifford Geertz or Marshall Sahlins in anthropology).[23] After all, an "etic" approach to Islamicate political thought, i.e. one based on what European tradition considers to be political thought, would enlarge the scope of the study in disproportional dimensions, since almost all Islamic law would have to enter the equation. On the other hand, it must be noted that an "emic" paradigm often (as in the Indian case, in the words of Sheldon Pollock) "reproduces on [sic] order of domination and does so by excluding the oral, the subaltern, and (very largely) the vernacular".[24]

Less ambitious "etic" approaches have focused on an internal categorization of political literature: terms such as "mirrors for princes" (a quite vague category whose only definition—whenever used in Islamic context—is the similarity with late-medieval European *specula regis* or *Fürstenspiegel*) and "advice literature" have been proposed, and (in the Ottoman case) even more elaborate distinctions have been suggested (as, for instance, the term *ıslahatname* or "book of reforms", a term that does not appear in Ottoman texts).[25] A classification based on the "emic" viewpoint is that proposed by Ann K. S. Lambton. She distinguishes three broad categories or "formulations": jurists' works originating in *fıkh* (*fiqh*) and based on religion; the "formulation of philosophers", based on righteousness and knowledge; and finally the "administration manuals" or "the literary formulation", based on justice and influenced by Sassanid

21 Even now the issue of *Türkiye Araştırmaları Literatür Dergisi*, 1/2 (2003), which we mentioned above, was labeled "Turkish political history" (*Türk Siyaset Tarihi*) and contained articles on subjects as varied as Ottoman political thought, political history, diplomatic history, and even historical chronicles and modern-day general histories.

22 Cf. Mottahedeh – Stilt 2003 and Klein 2006, as well as the detailed and intriguing discussion of "civil society" in an Ottoman context by Anastasopoulos 2012. On the definition of politics cf. Palonen 2006.

23 Cf. e.g. Geertz 1983.

24 Pollock 2008, 541.

25 See e.g. Levend 1962; Uğur 2001, 4–7; Yılmaz 2003a. On the various classifications used for Arabic and Persian political literature, see the recent survey by Marlow 2009.

theories of government.[26] In a more genre-centered vocabulary, the latter two categories would correspond, respectively, to *ahlak* literature, which tries to combine a philosophical view of the world and society with individual and political morals, and to *adab* (lit. "etiquette, manners" or, more generally, the special knowledge required for a profession) literature that gives more concrete advice on government. Ethics are central to all three "formulations", but their origins and their connection to politics differ. However, even this distinction is precarious, since, as Lambton observes, not only does "a good deal of cross-fertilization" exist but also "some writers wrote now as jurists, now as philosophers, now as counsellors of kings".[27] As we are going to see, in the Ottoman case all three categories were present, while a more original genre was also developed from the mid-sixteenth century: a development of the *adab* or "mirrors for princes" category that focused on institutions rather than moral or practical advice. Usually labeled (more often by modern scholars than by their authors) *nasihatname*s or "books of advice", these texts constitute a specific Ottoman literary genre, with its own tropes and *leitmotifs*.[28] In this vein, the most recent categorization I am aware of, which seems a very plausible suggestion from a philological point of view, proposes four genres, namely *ahlak*, *fikh*, *tasawwuf* or Sufi perspective, and *ıslahat* or reform literature.[29]

In fact, one may perhaps speak of several parallel genres, each one influencing the others and yet having its own characteristics; it is hoped that the reader will recognize these sub-genres in the structure of most chapters. In this book, more emphasis will be placed on the content of Ottoman political works than on their form; on the other hand, it is hoped that the degree of detail with which these works are presented will give some idea of their literary structure. In fact, form and content are so closely interlinked that the theoretical or ideological trends that we will try to follow are usually coherent in their formal features as well: philosophical descriptions of society tend to take the form of moral treatises, authors speaking of decline and of the "Golden Era" tend to

26 Lambton 1974, 404–405; Lambton 1981, xvi–xvii. Interestingly, Lambton prefers to consider Ibn Khaldun in the context of the "theories of the jurists" (Lambton 1981, 152ff.; she had named Ibn Khaldun "sui generis" in Lambton 1974, 405). In another article of hers, Lambton prefers to divide the "literary formulation" into "administrative handbooks" and "mirrors for princes" (without explaining much about the former): Lambton 1962, 91–92.

27 Lambton 1981, xvii.

28 Douglas A. Howard identified some of these as the "prophetic voice" often assumed by the authors, the use of the memorandum or *telhis* form for advice, and the preoccupation with language: Howard 2007, 149–152. Cf. also the list of *siyasetname* topics drawn up by Levend 1962, 169–170.

29 Gündoğdu 2016.

write "mirrors for princes" (although such texts were usually aimed at viziers), and so forth.

Moreover, it must be noted that actual political thought is more than that expressed in texts such as those described above. J. G. A. Pocock's notion of "political language" (or, as he later termed it, "political discourse", which should be preferred to "political thought"), i.e. a set of "idioms, rhetorics, specialized vocabularies and grammars" integrated into a "community of discourse", fits into this aspect well.[30] In the same vein (and in what has been termed "the linguistic turn" in late twentieth-century history of ideas), the vocabulary itself is important. As Reinhart Koselleck and the other exponents of the German *Begriffsgeschichte* school have shown, concepts and how they are matched with words have their own historical development: theories, ideologies, mentalities, and even acts are articulated in terms of concepts, and their exact meaning and content in any given historical context, their broadening or changing, is of paramount importance for understanding intellectual history. To make sense, however, the inventories of concepts thus studied should be analyzed in their complex interdependencies within the framework of a "language" or "discourse", which in turn may be in conflict with another contemporary discourse.[31] Furthermore, Cemal Kafadar has remarked that, to understand political thought fully and correctly, we must take also into account non-textual sources such as behaviors, symbols, and rituals.[32] No matter how much I would like (or even tried) to include this aspect in this book, however, it will instead be the task of another scholar to add these dimensions.

2 Scope and Aims: the Quest for Innovation

In contrast to the dominant image of the Ottoman Empire, innovation and reform seem to have been constant features of its administration. Some authors, such as Na'ima in the early eighteenth century, did see the need for reform and so advocated it; others, such as Mustafa Ali in the late sixteenth century, perceived change to be a challenge to the traditional order and suggested a return to what was considered the "Golden Age" of the empire, the first half of the sixteenth century. It could be said that the process of transformation

30 See e.g. Pocock 1987; Pocock 1988. Alam 2004 may be said to be a proponent of this method in an Islamic context, but without any reference to Pocock's theoretical views.

31 Koselleck 1979; Richter 1987; Iggers 1995; Pocock 1996; Koselleck 2002.

32 Kafadar 2001, 27–28; cf. Iggers 1995, 567–568; Karateke – Reinkowski 2005; Faroqhi 2006 (= Faroqhi 2008, 53–85).

culminated in the first half of the nineteenth century, when a huge program of reforms was implemented, the well-known *Tanzimat*. The traditional view of this change places emphasis on its Westernizing aspects and attributes it to the influence of Western Europe. However, recent studies have emphasized the internal dynamics of early-modern Ottoman society and administration rather than external factors, treating the developments of the seventeenth and eighteenth centuries as a path towards modernity; these views have also, in turn, been described as biased since they should be studied in the context of the long discussion on relations between the Ottoman Empire and the West.[33] This book will seek to give some answers to, or at least to set the framework for answering, questions such as: Did Ottoman political thinkers precede administrators in proposing reform, or did political writers feel overtaken by developments with which they did not agree? What was the relationship between religiously-based ideological currents, such as the Kadızadeli movement in the mid-seventeenth century, and like-minded reforms in the tax and landholding systems, and how did traditionalist political thinkers react to those? Was there an observable belief in an urgent need for change within Ottoman political thinking in the eighteenth century, or were reforms such as the "New Army" (*Nizam-i cedid*) of Selim III in the 1790s or the massacre of janissaries by Mahmud II in 1826 initiatives of strong rulers and a small circle of advisors? What was the relationship between European (and/or Iranian) thought and Ottoman political developments, through immigrants and renegades? Were there internal dynamics, such as innovative political thinking in the second half of the eighteenth and the early nineteenth century, which led (or at least contributed, since one cannot deny the European influence) to the radical reforms of the Tanzimat period?

A few words on theory would not be out of place here. The approach this book tries to follow owes a lot to the so-called Cambridge school in the history of political thought. Scholars of this school, which famously includes Quentin Skinner, J. G. A. Pocock, John Dunn, and Richard Tuck, stressed that works of political theory must be seen as forms of political action; at the same time, they never lost sight of textual interrelation, tracing their interdependencies and their use of selected political vocabulary. In this context, the study of the social and intellectual climate (or "matrix") out of which major authors emerged is considered a prerequisite for understanding innovative ideas and ideological debates. The essence of this approach may be described as finding

33 See, for instance, the overview by Quataert 2000, 64ff. and 141–46; cf. the early thoughts by Berkes 1964, 26ff. and the more recent views of Abou-El-Haj 2005, 81ff.; Yılmaz 2008; Tezcan 2010a; Yılmaz 2015a.

a third way for the history of political thought, between the ahistorical study of a sequence of texts (the "textualists"), on the one hand, and strict, deterministic "contextualism" (i.e. the attribution of every text or idea to specific historical and/or social needs), on the other. Furthermore, these scholars tried to apply what was termed above an "emic" approach, placing emphasis on the questions and issues the political authors themselves were addressing rather than their relevance to present political science. In other words, the audience and its expectations must be given equal weight as the author.

Critics of this approach have contended that the "unintended consequences" of an author's work are (for the scholar) more important than his intentions, or that the method described above is irrelevant for present-day politics;[34] other criticisms focus on the "Orientalist" side of seeing political thought in history as culminating in modern-day European and/or Atlantic preoccupations.[35] The basis of this criticism is the issue of the relevance of the past for present-day problems, a central point in the arguments against the Cambridge School (Skinner refuted the idea that the history of political thought is the history of different approaches to humanity's "perennial questions", and thus was accused of "antiquarianism"). However, a reading of early-modern authors with a view to seeking allies or genealogies of modern trends or *problématiques* (such as, for example, liberalism, tolerance, or democracy, to cite the usual suspects of this method) runs the very real risk of ignoring the historical context and thus producing obvious anachronisms and misunderstandings.[36] After all, our aim here is to approach Ottoman political thought (or discourse) from the perspective of a historian rather than a political scientist, with no claims or attempts whatsoever to interpret modern-day eastern Mediterranean politics.

---

34 On the "Cambridge School" and its critics see Skinner 1969; Janssen 1985; Åsard 1987; Pocock 1987; Dunn 1996; Tuck 2001; Hellmuth – von Ehrenstein 2001; Ball 2007; Piterberg 2003, 60–62.

35 For instance, Christopher Goto-Jones recently accused the "Cambridge School" of Orientalism, arguing not only that these scholars neglected non-European history of ideas, but also that the very quest for "context" serves as a legitimization of Eurocentrism (even in the title of Skinner's famous work, which talks of the foundation of "modern political thought" rather than "European political thought"): Goto-Jones 2008, esp. 5–8. It is true that all the major exponents of the Cambridge school were specialized in the European history of ideas (which cannot be considered a disadvantage anyway); Dunn 1996, 14–16 spares some words for non-European political theories, while Pocock has written an article on ancient Chinese philosophy. On the other hand, similar criticism has been launched against the corpus or canon of what is generally considered "political thought" at large: Stuurman 2000, 154–155. For the problems of applying the methods of European intellectual history to non-European cultures cf. Pollock 2008.

36 Cf. Neguin Yavari's review of Alam 2004 in *Journal of the American Oriental Society* 129.2 (2009), 311–314.

Thus, the approach to Ottoman political thought that this book proposes differs from earlier (Ottomanist) approaches in three main ways. First, it seeks to examine more than the major classical political thinkers in order to establish contexts and currents, to locate innovation(s) and "secondary" trends, and so forth. Studies focusing only on the "major" authors, such as Kınalızade Ali Çelebi, Koçi Bey, and Na'ima, have the disadvantage of presenting the history of political theory as a series of great minds that either recapitulated the ideas of their predecessors, be they fellow-Ottomans or Persians, or departed from them. In contrast, research that also encompasses as many minor writers as possible would show the general trends of each period and consequently the degree to which a "major" thinker used commonly-employed mental tools or developed innovative ideas. Furthermore, it would track ideas that were current among lesser-known authors but which may not have been propagated by the major ones. Innovation, as well as tradition, can also be a collective effort, according to the dynamics of a society and the political and ideological climate of an era, and this can be shown only by extending the field of research to a vast number of authors and works rather than a few geniuses.[37]

Secondly, alongside traditional political treatises, other types of sources that could contain pieces of political theory or advice have been included in the corpus examined in this work. Such sources include moralist treatises, historiographical works, copybooks of protocol and official correspondence, administration manuals, literary works, treatises on theology and *kalam*, collections of legal opinions (*fetva*s), encyclopedic works, and so on.[38] This will help to locate the political thoughts and ideas that circulated within the broader context of both theory and practice as well as extending the arena of political ideas to a wider range of intellectual and administrative groups within the ruling elite. However, a word of caution may be useful here: as may be suggested by these two points, the current study would be enormous in size and almost limitless in terms of time and work. Thus, while I tried to accumulate

37 By no means, of course, do I pretend to have studied the whole array of Ottoman political literature. As noted in the Acknowledgments, part of this research was funded by the OTTPOL project; this had the side effect of setting a rather tight time limit on the completion of the present book. For lists of Ottoman political works see Levend 1962; Çolak 2003. The list gets even bigger if we consider that political thought is also contained in moral treatises (see the exhaustive list by Levend 1963).

38 Cf. the notes by Yılmaz 2003b, 253–258. For other efforts to incorporate such sources into the study of Ottoman political thought, see e.g. Tezcan 2001; Neumann 2000; Murphey 2005; Sariyannis 2008a; Riedlmayer 2008; Yılmaz 2006, 165ff.; Howard 2008; Holbrook 1999; Fazlıoğlu 2003; Al-Tikriti 2005a.

and accommodate as many authors and types of works as possible, I certainly do not claim that the present book fully covers the aims I gave myself.[39]

Thirdly, a history of Ottoman political thought cannot be limited to a simple enumeration of works and ideas. A concurrent task should be to explore recurring themes and their development across the period in question. Some scholars have, for instance, investigated the development and transformation of notions such as justice, world order, and the state.[40] It is necessary to proceed to a study of themes and notions, such as: the virtues demanded of the ruler; the place of the sultan within the state apparatus; the ideal structure of society; views on social mobility; debates between old laws (*kanun-ı kadim*) and innovation (*bid'at*); the place of religion; the shifting balance of power with (Western) Europe; and so on. In such a way, we may explore the political vocabulary of Ottoman theorists and state and conduct a comparative study of the extant political treatises, something that has, up to now, been limited to either limited periods of time or but a few authors.[41] In the conclusion, I examine some of these fundamental concepts in the form proposed by the German "conceptual history" or *Begriffsgeschichte*.[42] This is not meant to be a quest for perennial issues that are teleologically revealed during the course of human history: instead of looking for the genealogy of modern notions such as democracy or liberty, we will try to map the inventory of ideas and political terms and notions that the Ottomans inherited, created, or used themselves, with a view to understanding the development of such concepts and the socio-political changes behind them. This systematic study of Ottoman political texts ultimately seeks to place such texts within various identifiable ideological currents with a view to linking them to socio-political developments.

Yet I would like to underline that this does not seek to be a ground-breaking study; I do not claim to be proposing a totally new interpretation, to have found a new theory, or even to be applying an entirely new methodological approach within a seemingly well-known topic. It is, instead, a reference book, in the sense that it tries to map all available information on pre-modern Ottoman political ideas which have, up to now, been scattered across unpublished manuscripts, rare translations, editions in transcription, or in modern Turkish (and thus accessible only to a restricted audience of specialized

39 See also above, fn. 38.

40 Ergene 2001; Hagen 2005; Sigalas 2007; cf. also Sariyannis 2011a.

41 A similar, but incomplete, attempt at a comprehensive treatment is Lewis 1988; for the Tanzimat period, see Doganalp-Votzi – Römer 2008 and Topal 2017; see also Vatin 2012.

42 Koselleck 1979; Richter 1987; Koselleck 2002.

Ottomanists), and which have been studied only in short, article-length surveys and unpublished theses. As Colin Imber wrote recently,[43]

> There is always ... a temptation to try to catch up with whatever historians of Europe are doing by applying to the Ottoman Empire whatever is currently fashionable in the West. However, attempts to catch up and to follow fashion are usually doomed, since the requisite basis of knowledge is so often lacking.

The aim of this book is, precisely, to offer this "requisite basis of knowledge". As such, no elaborate textual analysis tools are used and there is little effort at comparative study; there is, instead, a detailed narrative of texts considered as political, which are placed together under the rubric of identifiable ideological currents with an effort to trace genealogies and affinities. This does not mean that new results do not appear: at the end of the conclusions section of this book, I try to gather some of these in order to show how the methodology described above has helped bring to light continuities, ruptures, and links that were not evident through previous methodological approaches.

Furthermore, we will only deal with the origins and influences of Ottoman political thought in passing. Literature on medieval Islamicate thought is abundant,[44] and continuities will be duly noted where necessary; on the other hand, the questions of the Central Asian origins of,[45] the relationship with contemporary Islamicate empires such as the Safavids of,[46] and the Byzantine influences on Ottoman political theories[47] will be left for another time and/or author. In the same vein, I am fully aware that any study of Ottoman ideas and culture would be incomplete if it did not cover the non-Turkish-speaking populations of the Empire, including Ottoman Arabs, Christians (Greek, Armenian,

---

43 Imber 2011, 8.

44 For example Rosenthal 1958; Lambton 1980; Lambton 1981; Black 2011; Darling 2013b; Boroujerdi 2013. Islamic ethics, on the other hand, is curiously understudied; see Donaldson 1963; Fouchécour 1986; Fakhry 1994. A detailed study of Ottoman translations of Arab and Persian treatises would be very useful, but as far as I know none has been carried out so far; one may consult the notes by Levend 1962, 176–183 (cf. the remarks by Hagen 2003b).

45 For two conflicting views on this issue, see İnalcık 1967 and Imber 2011, 173–200; cf. Kafadar 2001, Burak 2015. The major source is the eleventh-century *Kutadgu Bilig*, composed in the Karakhanid khanate in Transoxania (Yusuf Khass Hajib – Dankoff 1983).

46 See, for example, Lambton 1980 and esp. Lambton 1956b; Lambton 1981, 264–287; Mitchell 2009; Black 2011, 223ff.; cf. also the last section of the conclusion in the present book.

47 See Oktay 2001; Ahrweiler 1975 remains a classic of Byzantine political ideology; see also Paidas 2006; Odorico 2009; Syros 2010.

Slavic …), and Jews. Unfortunately, however, limitations of time and language made this task impossible within the scope of this book.[48] Nevertheless, the close relationship between Ottoman political thought and the Ottoman central government, and the almost exclusive Turkish-speaking Muslim character of the latter (at least until the Tanzimat period that constitutes the end of this study), perhaps make this particular lack less important than it would be in other fields of Ottoman culture. Having defined politics as the field of public life related to statecraft and power, it seems quite natural that, when we talk of Ottoman political thinking, we are mainly referring to thinking about the Ottoman state or, to put it another way, to attempts to influence state policy-making. That said, a study of the above-mentioned "other voices" would surely shed new light on the history of Ottoman political ideas as it is usually conceived.[49]

A collateral lacuna, which is impossible to fill due to the present state of the field, is the fact that, while we may know the history of translations (mainly from Arabic and Persian into Ottoman Turkish) of political works and, to a lesser extent, the diffusion of their copies over time, there is no scholarship (or, indeed, knowledge at all) on their commentaries. Indeed, this point may be expanded to original Ottoman texts as well. Thus, there is a serious lack of knowledge as to what the *reception* of both old and new political texts was for Ottoman audiences.[50]

3 A Note on "Modernity"—Early or Not

The working hypothesis is that the Ottoman state underwent a process similar to what has come to be called the formation of early-modern states in Western Europe and that this process should be reflected in various ways in the history

48 On the attitudes of Byzantine authors against the Ottomans after the fall of Constantinople see Moustakas 2011; on the Greek (and Romanian) Phanariot political (often historical-*cum*-political or moral-*cum*-political) literature, see Duţu 1971; Apostolopoulos 1976; Panou 2008; Costache 2010–2011; Stavrakopoulou 2012; Shapiro 2014. In 1808 a *nasihatname* in Ottoman Turkish was commissioned by Alexandros Mavrocordatos: Philliou 2011, 30.

49 Cf. the observations by Stuurman 2000, 156–157 on Western European thought.

50 Cf. the observations of Pollock 2009, 954–955: "The place of traditional commentaries in contemporary philological training illustrates one of the main things that has been wrong about the field … How different my first experience of reading Virgil would have been had I read him through Donatus-Servius rather than through Conington-Nettleship".

of its political ideas.[51] As such, I follow Rifaat Abou-El-Haj's suggestion that the late seventeenth century marks the transition of the Ottoman Empire into an early-modern state (with the state's autonomy from the ruler being the central feature); this view has recently been enhanced by Baki Tezcan, for whom the expansion of the political nation (i.e. the groups that can legitimately participate in state power) and the limiting of the sultan's authority by the ulema and the janissaries were such developments, and that they can be traced to the seventeenth and eighteenth centuries.[52] While it was emerging as an autonomous entity, the state gradually took more and more power from the hands of the sultan himself and, at the same time, became a field of contest for an extended "political nation", one which tried to gain control of state power instead of finding alternative loci of authority. This process may not have been entirely successful, as it was full of regressions and shortcomings, but it was at least evident in its degree of legitimization. The present book intends to focus on the Ottoman case, and therefore it departs from the generalizations of "Islamic political thought"; after all, the trend in Ottoman studies currently is to consider the Ottoman Empire an early-modern state comparable to contemporaneous European empires and states rather than (or, more correctly, as much as) a continuation of medieval Islamic political entities and traditions (not to mention the ongoing debate over what is "Islamic" or "Islamicate").[53] This view became popular in the late 1990s: we can quote Linda T. Darling, for instance, who argued in 1998 that "for most of the early modern period, Middle Eastern history followed a similar trajectory, not an opposite one, to that of the west"; almost simultaneously, Virginia Aksan, taking it as granted that the Ottomans were an "early modern empire" similar to the Habsburgs and the Romanovs, outlined the similarities and the common features those states shared with the Ottoman Empire, especially militarily.[54]

51 My discussions with Antonis Anastasopoulos, Christos Hadziiossif, and Antonis Hadjikyriacou were essential for writing this section.

52 Abou-El-Haj 2005; Tezcan 2010a. James E. Baldwin recently expanded this thought to Ottoman provincial history, analyzing a military uprising in Cairo and finding that "a public law emerged which ... was external to the Sultanate", as "the authority to define it no longer rested with the Sultan, and was instead claimed by other sections of the ruling class" (Baldwin 2015, 157). Interestingly, a similar interpretation was recently offered for the Byzantine Empire, where of course there can be no issue of "early modernity" (Kaldellis 2013 and esp. 2015).

53 Ahmed 2016; Griffel 2017.

54 Darling 1998, 241; Aksan 1999; a broader comparison (including the Mughals) was attempted by Subrahmanyam 2006. The term "early modern empires" may be seen as a wider form of Marshall Hodgson's "gunpowder empires".

Before proceeding to a fuller examination of the concepts of "modernity" and "early modernity", a note on periodization is not unnecessary; if there was such a radical transformation of the political institution *par excellence*, i.e. the state, it should be pivotal in our views of the course of Ottoman history. Periodization has been a debated issue in Ottoman history ever since Halil İnalcık's conceptualization of a "classical age" from c. 1300 to the end of the sixteenth century, followed by a long decline, was challenged in the the early 1990s by a group of scholars that included Suraiya Faroqhi (see also below, chapter IV).[55] In 1996, Jane Hathaway suggested that the period from 1453 to the conquest of Egypt in 1517 could be considered a transition to "a predominantly Muslim polity", and she also saw a process of decentralization that stretched from the late sixteenth century to Mahmud II's reign in the early nineteenth.[56] Half a decade later, Linda T. Darling proposed replacing the classical age/decline/reform paradigm with another set of three periods, namely expansion (1300–1550, with 1453 dividing it into pre-imperial and imperial phases), consolidation (1550–1718, with another two sub-periods separated by the late sixteenth-century socio-economic crisis), and transformation (1718–1923, i.e. beginning with the "Tulip period", with the first sub-period ending in 1839 when "resistance to transformation" ceased to hold the upper hand). Darling thus attempted to bring Ottoman chronology closer to that of both the West and other empires within the region, since the "consolidation period" corresponds roughly to the "gunpowder empires" concept and the "transformation" to the Enlightenment and colonialist modernity.[57] Recently, Rhoads Murphey has written of a "high imperial age" between 1480 and 1820, a period "when Ottoman traditions of sovereignty were formulated, elaborated and implemented as expressions of a unified and cohesive system of rule and political control".[58] As for Baki Tezcan, his concept of a "Second Empire" from ca. 1580 to 1826 is not so far from Hathaway's "decentralization", although in a much more "Istanbul-centric" vein.

The very concept of "early-modern", used so much in recent scholarship, is not without its problems. Traditionally, Ottoman society was labeled "premodern" for the period before the Tanzimat reforms. In the last few decades, however, a "grey zone" of "early modernity" has been increasingly introduced

55 On İnalcık's views see, among others, İnalcık 1972; İnalcık 1980. The literature against the "decline paradigm" is now large enough; some seminal titles are Kafadar 1993; Darling 1996; Barkey 1994; Faroqhi 1994; Quataert 2003.

56 Hathaway 1996.

57 Darling 2002.

58 Murphey 2008, 4–5. Elsewhere (ibid., 4) he speaks of the period 1450–1850 as "a single continuum" in terms of "the normal *modus operandi* of the state governing apparatus".

in order to describe those centuries that were previously labeled as "decline". It was Rifaat Abou-El-Haj who first developed the notion of "early-modern centralization", enumerating its characteristics as follows:

> the separation of public affairs from the personal affairs of the ruler and his family, the tendency to transform the zone frontier into a demarcated linear border, a growing specialization of function in some branches of the central administration, and finally, [the] rapid conversion of public lands into semiprivate property.[59]

More recently, Tezcan has argued that "the early modern and modern periods had two very significant sociopolitical developments in common—the expansion of the political nation and the limitation of royal authority".[60] Darling, on the other hand, identified modernity with the successful subordination of all sources of authority to the power of kings, thereby placing the beginning of this period back to what were traditionally considered to be the "classical" years".[61]

The usual criticism of the term "early-modern" is its Euro-centrism and teleological character. On the one hand, as Hathaway has remarked, "the standard equation of Europeanization with modernization and modernization with reform" makes the "(early) modernity" paradigm easy to fall into the trap of Orientalism;[62] among various responses to this critique, one could cite here M. Şükrü Hanioğlu's view of modernity as a reality of change, one to which *both* the Ottoman Empire and the European states had to adapt, rather than a Europe-driven procedure.[63] To quote Linda Darling again,

> The interrelations between European states ... can to some extent serve as a model for relations between Europe and the Middle East in the early modern period. For example, it is clear that European military and economic expansion resulted in increased competition between [European]

59 Abou-El-Haj 2005, 54.

60 Tezcan 2010a, 232.

61 Darling 2008, 506. Jocelyne Dakhlia finds elements of a "modernism" in the "universalisme politique" and the "conception a-religieuse du bon gouvernement" seen in late medieval Persian "mirrors for princes" (Dakhlia 2002).

62 Hathaway 1996, 30.

63 Hanioğlu 2008, 3. Cf. the remarks in Ortaylı 1995, 10ff. The discussions on an "Ottoman Orientalism", which arose together with modernity in the region and tended to see the Arab lands as a quasi-colonial area, are of some relevance here; see the survey and assessment in Kechriotis 2013.

> states … leading in most cases to a hardening of international boundaries, greater governmental efforts to mobilize people and resources for the state's purposes, and a rising sense of national identity … European relations with the east might well be examined in similar terms: not as the colonization of passive victims, but as an economic and political competition that led to changes on both sides and intensified the sense of difference.[64]

On the other hand, the very term "early-modern" presupposes modernity, seeing this period as an antechamber for the nineteenth century. To quote Palmira Brummett,

> the whole notion of the early modern as an era that anticipates the ideas, state formations, and hegemons of the nineteenth century suppresses a set of very powerful continuities that tie the sixteenth, seventeenth, and even eighteenth centuries to the long medieval era that preceded them.[65]

One might even say that post-1990 scholarship, while trying to oust "old-fashioned" Marxist unilinear stage-theory from the door, introduced a similar theory through the window.[66] Moreover, as I will try to explain below, by eliminating any concrete explanatory bases, Marx's theory was thus turned upside-down and made to stand on its head (once more), to make an ironic allusion to his famous quotation on Hegelian philosophy.[67]

Indeed, it could be argued that the term "early-modern" is in fact a self-explanatory theory that merely serves to compare meaningfully processes that were common in various contemporaneous societies. It has become almost

64 Darling 1998, 245.

65 Brummett 2015, 9. One should not forget that these terms are "modern" in another sense as well: they were coined in the period now termed "early-modern", when the general attitude among intellectuals was that they were living in an era radically differing from the past. We could note here that the respective terms in French literature are, for instance, *histoire moderne* for "early-modern history" and *histoire contemporaine* for "modern history".

66 On the genealogy of "early-modernism" with relation to the 1989–1990 political changes cf. Hadjikyriacou – Lappa (unpublished).

67 "The mystification which dialectic suffers in Hegel's hands, by no means prevents him from being the first to present its general form of working in a comprehensive and conscious manner. With him it is standing on its head. It must be turned right side up again, if you would discover the rational kernel within the mystical shell." The quotation comes from the afterword to the second German edition of the *Capital* (1873); see https://www.marxists.org/archive/marx/works/1867-c1/p3.htm#method (accessed September 2015).

axiomatic now, as has been mentioned, that similar forms of political organization and of intellectual developments were common in societies as different as France, England, and the Ottoman Empire in the period commonly designated as "early-modern", i.e. (in European terms) from the Renaissance up to the late eighteenth century. Moreover, the "early modernity" concept helps Ottomanists engage in a fruitful conversation with specialists of European history, and thus it has become somewhat fashionable to include this notion in any study of post-sixteenth-century Ottoman history; this follows earlier fashions such as the emphasis placed on "negotiation", "fluidity", and "pragmatism".[68]

However, a full explanation of why similar procedures of state-making did (or did not) happen over a wide geographical and cultural range during the period in question is still lacking. Current definitions of modernity do not offer any hints as to why and how this development occurs: all focus mainly on political aspects[69] and thus make it difficult to interpret "modern" developments in non-Western societies through reasons other than the influence of the West. But if "modernity" can be interpreted as the gradual expansion of the Western capitalist world into other economies and societies, "early modernity" cannot. In other words, if we wish to speak of "early-modern" developments in the Middle East before the nineteenth century, i.e. in a period when Western European political influence was insignificant, we have to explain them in terms of socio-economic developments. These changes may be attributed either to local developments in the economic sphere and socio-economic relations or to their integration into an increasingly global (and, arguably, already Europe-driven) economy. In this respect, the most comprehensive approaches to the notion of "early modernity" in an Ottoman context are those that go beyond the "political level". Dror Ze'evi spoke of an "institutional" and an "epistemological" facet of modernity, the latter encompassing changes in religion, cosmology, and culture in general (and here one may remember the recent German contributions to the idea of an autochthonous eighteenth-century "Islamic enlightenment", or the even more recent emphasis on "confessionalization");[70] as for Tezcan,

68 See the criticism of "Ottoman pragmatism" in Dağlı 2013 and of "fluidity" in Hadjikyriacou-Lappa (unpublished). For a review of post-World War II approaches to Ottoman "modernization" see Emrence 2007.

69 Even thus, definitions are controversial: Shmuel N. Eisenstadt speaks of "a conception of the future characterized by a number of possibilities realizable through autonomous human agency" (Eisenstadt 2000, 3) and Karen Barkey, similarly, of "the constitution of a political arena increasingly defined by a struggle over the definition of the political" (Barkey 2008, 206).

70 Ze'evi 2004, 76. On the debate concerning the "Islamic Enlightenment" (*islamische Aufklärung*) see Schulze 1996; Hagen – Seidenstricker 1998; Radtke 2000. On "confessionalization" in the Ottoman Empire see Krstić 2011; Terzioğlu 2012; Terzioğlu 2013. For

he departs from simple political definitions (although politics is his main field of analysis) and speaks of "a modern sensibility" in "artistic, sociocultural, and literary developments" (including the now famous "individualization"). Even more importantly, he does not avoid discussing the connections between "early modernity" and the "dissolution of the feudal structures" and between "modernity" and the rise of capitalism. He maintains that capitalism should be connected with modernity, but not necessarily with "early modernity", or, in his own words, that "capitalism and colonialism transformed early modernity to modernity" (in fact, these assessments may be seen as another rendering of Marx's "primitive accumulation of capital").[71] This view, in my opinion, is, thus far, the most satisfactory answer to the question of why "early-modern" political and cultural forms were observed in both Europe and the Ottoman Empire. In short, there is still nothing to successfully take the place of a traditional paradigm, one now generally viewed as both old-fashioned and (therefore) unfashionable: namely, the disintegration of medieval feudalism as a result of the monetarization process.

An alternative approach to the "modernity" paradigm may be based on Max Weber's theory of state and authority. Using this, the shift from charismatic to traditional/patrimonial and finally to legal authority, the three types of "legitimate rule" according to Weber,[72] may be seen in Ottoman developments: Halil İnalcık has described the "classical" period (i.e. roughly the fifteenth and sixteenth centuries) in terms of a Weberian "patrimonial state", while one may see a gradual transition to the "legal" state from the mid-seventeenth century onwards with the development of an autonomous rational bureaucracy that became increasingly independent of the ruler's wishes both in its decisions

a recent reconsideration of Ottoman intellectual life during this period, see El-Rouayheb 2015.

71 Tezcan 2010a, 19ff., 228–232. Ze'evi also stressed that modernity was "forged in tandem with colonialism" (Ze'evi 2004, 86ff.). Maxime Rodinson's definitions of the "capitalist mode of production" (*mode de production capitalistique*, i.e. production involving salaried labor and capital investment, even if it is not dominant in the society), "capitalist sector" (*secteur capitalistique*, i.e. a sector of the economy where the above means of production is dominant, even if this sector is still not dominant in the society) and "capitalist socio-economic formation" (*formation socio-économique capitaliste*, i.e. an economy and society fully dominated by capitalist production, with the relevant sociopolitical implications) are not irrelevant to this discussion, especially in its Islamic context; see Rodinson 1966.

72 Weber 1985; Spencer 1970; cf. Weber's views on the rise of rational bureaucracies (Weber 1978, 2:956ff.).

and in its reproduction.[73] If we want to place this periodization in terms of the "transition to modernity" paradigm (and in an effort to reconcile the different views on this paradigm cited above), we could consider the course towards modernity as having occurred in two separate stages. In the first stage, late fifteenth and early or mid-sixteenth-century sultans such as Mehmed II, Selim I, and Süleyman I successfully took control of the powers and sources of revenue that had remained in the hands of warlord- or ulema households in a manner reminiscent of the early Ottoman emirate. In the second, which seems to have started in the late seventeenth century, a state apparatus that reproduced itself through apprenticeships and patronage took over decision-making powers from both the palace and its recruits, especially in the financial administration.[74]

Of course, this Weberian approach offers no better explanation as to why similar transitions happened in different societies. Interesting as it may be, it still leaves the more or less simultaneous appearance of similar political features in different societies in a kind of socio-economic vacuum. "Modernity", and all the more so "early modernity", still continue to be heuristic models, by no means explanatory. Until we make a new reassessment of what happened within Ottoman society and its economy after the mid-sixteenth century, and why, the similarities with European developments may be highlighted but with no hope of providing any explanation for such similarities. Given such remarks, the occasional use of these terms in the present book may seem contradictory. Yet the main disadvantage of the "modernity" terminology, it could be said, is precisely the fact that concepts such as these (in whatever terms they are couched, Weberian or not) are restricted to the political and intellectual levels: types of government and of authority, political participation, and political actors' engagement in the public sphere, as well as rationalism or individuality. In a book concerning actors' views on state and government, and, more generally, intellectual history, the use of a paradigm focusing on a course toward "early-modern" and "modern" forms of rule may be less unseemly than my criticism above implies.

---

73 İnalcık 1992b; Sariyannis 2013, 105–107. I have also attempted to find similarities between the "fundamentalist" movements of mid-seventeenth-century Istanbul and Weber's "protestant ethic": Sariyannis 2012, 282–289. Weberian approaches have also focused on the study of the late-Ottoman administration: see Findley 1980, and cf. Bouquet 2015.

74 I tried to express this view, with more details, in Sariyannis 2013, esp. 84–87.

4 Trends and Currents: for a Thematic Description of Ottoman Political Thought

As mentioned, this book was conceived as a reference work, one that would amass as many of the available sources of Ottoman political thought as possible, place them into broader ideological currents, and seek to link them with socio-political developments. It is therefore structured into chapters that follow a roughly chronological order while mainly focusing on ideological currents. Thus, later texts may be dealt with in chapters focusing on earlier periods if they simply reproduce or develop an earlier tradition or thread of thought; the reader can refer to the timetable in the Appendix in order to study the chronological overlap of the chapters and the various trends. The descriptions of the texts will be as detailed as possible; although this method runs the risk of being tiresome, it also shows the literary structure of the various works and offers an analytical table of contents for texts that are otherwise difficult to read and understand.[75] Furthermore, it is precisely by citing as fully as possible the overall structure of such a text that the tropes and sub-divisions of the literary genre can be discerned. In this respect, the reader will perhaps observe that the ideological trends described in each chapter often correspond (albeit roughly) to literary sub-genres: thus, the neo-Aristotelian tradition described in chapter 2 is more often than not contained in *ahlak* treatises on ethics, while the "declinist" theories of chapter 5 are usually expressed in what modern scholars often call *ıslahatname*s (reform tracts) and in the more recognizable *kanunname*s, among others. Of course, the emphasis will be on the content of these works rather than their form, yet it is hoped that the degree of detail given will provide the reader with again the basis for analysis of form as well.

The first chapter attempts to survey the political ideas of the *gazi* circles which formed the nucleus of the early Ottoman state at the beginning of the fourteenth century. Of course, there is no way to find written sources originating from these environments; instead we can trace the survival of these ideas, mainly through later opposition to imperial policies toward the end of the fifteenth century. Thus, Yahşi Fakih's chronicle as incorporated in Aşıkpaşazade's history, as well as those parts of the latter written by Aşıkpaşazade himself, are studied as one example, together with other anti-imperial sources (such as by Yazıcıoğlu Ahmed Bican). The authors' emphasis on the need for the ruler to

75 More detailed summaries of most of the works analyzed here can be found online, on the database of the OTTPOL project of the Institute for Mediterranean Studies/FORTH (Rethymno): http://ottpol.ims.forth.gr/?q=works.

be generous to the soldiers, as well as the suspicious attitude towards every attempt to reinforce centralized power, are clear and unsurprising. After that, the first chapter deals with the introduction of imperial ideals by scholars born and trained in neighboring principalities and influenced by Persian culture during the fourteenth and the fifteenth centuries. Ahmedi's famous chronicle in verse, as well as early authors on ethics such as Şeyhoğlu Mustafa (who, like Ahmedi, came to the Ottoman court from Germiyan in the late 1380s) and Sinan Pasha, the bitter grand vizier of Mehmed II, brought onto the scene *adab* literature (the Persian "mirror for princes") and the notion of sultanly justice, which is more important than piety, according to the old motto which declares that a realm collapses due to injustice rather than infidelity. Finally, this chapter delves into the shifting methods of legitimization at this early stage of the Ottoman Empire.

The second chapter deals with the neo-Aristotelian tradition as inherited by Persian authors such as Nasir al-Din Tusi and Davvani, who combined Aristotle's analysis of the human soul with Plato's notion of the ideal state (via al-Farabi's tenth-century work). These authors conceived of humanity as a continuum, from the human soul to society, and their moral vision may be said to be a study in governance: from individual morals, i.e. governance of the self, through family and household governance, i.e. what the Ancient Greeks called economics (*οικονομία*: "regulation of the household"), to state theory and the governance of society. It is little known that the first introduction of such a theory to Ottoman literature dates from the early fifteenth century, when Ahmed Amasi, a contemporary of Ahmedi and Şeyhoğlu Mustafa, adapted two of the most famous Persian political works, Nasir al-Din Tusi's *Akhlâq-e Nâsirî* (also known as "The Nasirean ethics") and al-Ghazali's *Nasîha al-mulûk*. If Amasi's work passed relatively unnoticed, the blossoming of Persian ethico-political theory came in the time of Mehmed II with Tursun Beg's introduction to his history and Idris-i Bitlisi's treatise on ethics. Both works stress the cardinal virtues needed by the sultan, and both follow closely Jalal al-Din Davvani's *Akhlâq-e Jalâlî*, an improved and extended version of Tusi's ethical system. Kınalızade Ali's mid-sixteenth-century work, the most complete of its kind, will be studied in detail (with separate sections on the human soul and its faculties; political economy; and the beginning and principles of government) because a number of his ideas, such as the vision of society as composed of four orders (i.e. the men of the sword, the men of the pen, the peasants, and the merchants) remained relevant for many centuries to come.

In the third chapter, we will give an overview of the ideas prevailing in the field of juristic and political thought during the reign of Süleyman the Magnificent (1520–66) in order to detect the beginnings of later trends or the attitudes against which subsequent authors reacted. First, the basis of the Ottoman legal synthesis will be studied, with a focus on the work of the jurisconsult Ebussu'ud, who managed to reconcile the sultanly law with the sharia by expressing the former (especially in matters deemed of high importance, such as landholding) in terms of the latter. This endeavor was (somewhat unexpectedly) facilitated by the Ottoman reception of Ibn Taymiyya's work, traditionally considered the root of all fundamentalism. After that, the chapter will deal with what remained of the Iranian tradition, now in a more concrete and less theoretical form, often with strong religious and even messianic overtones. Although Kınalızade also belongs to this period, the main model for political writers at the time was Kâshifi's (rather than Davvani's) popularization of Tusi's system, which gave more weight to *adab* (concrete ethical and political advice) rather than *ahlak* (philosophical theory); this was expressed primarily by Celalzade Mustafa (d. 1567), Süleyman's chief counsellor. A special section will also be devoted to Lütfi Pasha (d. 1563) and his *Âsafnâme*, which marks the beginning of the Ottoman "mirror for princes" genre, with its stress on concrete advice and institutions rather than personal qualities, as well as being based on experience rather than authority. After a section highlighting new methods of sultanly legitimacy, showing how the idea of the Ottoman caliphate made its appearance after Selim I's reign, the rest of the chapter studies the reactions to the imperial vision and especially the ulema's opposition to the "Süleymanic synthesis". Following Şehzade Korkud (d. 1513), the unfortunate son of Bayezid II, and his views on the incompatibility of political power with true piety, we will study the fierce reaction to Ebussu'ud's efforts to legitimize "secular" law, primarily those of his predecessor Çivizade Efendi (d. 1542) and, of course, Birgivi Mehmed Efendi (d. 1573), whose immensely influential work was later conceived as the origin of seventeenth-century "fundamentalist" preaching.

The fourth chapter will examine the "decline" paradigm, i.e. the way in which Ottoman authors perceived the great social, political, and military crisis of the late sixteenth century. The recent discussion on the legitimacy of the term "decline" notwithstanding, it is interesting that this paradigm was first initiated by Ottoman thinkers themselves. Late sixteenth-century authors, however, did not specifically speak of a decline, i.e. some irreversible process towards disaster, nor did they give a central place to idealizing a glorious past (as their successors would do in the century after). Instead, following Lütfi Pasha, these authors gave concrete advice on and detailed complaints about various Ottoman institutions, rather than the virtues of individuals. This chapter first analyzes various anonymous works that stressed the departures from the "ideal" institutions of the early period of Süleyman's reign (e.g. *Kitâbu mesâlih;*

Hırzü'l-mülûk) before focusing on the enormous work by Gelibolulu Mustafa Ali (d. 1600), who expressed deep disappointment over what he considered to be the decay of knowledge and of the imperial institutions, combining it with an acute sense of Islamic history as a series of rising and falling dynasties. The chapter then examines some similar works and ideas by other late sixteenth-century authors, such as the historian Mustafa Selaniki and the Bosnian scholar Hasan Kâfi Akhisari. In so doing, it will demonstrate that their sometimes apocalyptic pessimism can be interpreted through the general climate of their time, which was seen as a period of crisis that had to be overcome.

In the fifth chapter, the "decline theorists" and the form their work took in the first decades of the seventeenth century (when the emphasis on institutions and the departure from an ideal state took a highly standardized form) will be further examined. These authors, while further deepening their predecessors' "Ottomanization" (by concentrating on specific Ottoman institutions and practices, rather than citing general ideas and advice), focused on the need to return to the glorious past: institutions of the early or mid-sixteenth century were idealized and strict adherence to the "old law" was advocated. On the one hand, we will examine works such as the anonymous *Kitâb-ı müstetâb* (ca. 1620), Koçi Bey's treatise (ca. 1630–1), the "Veliyyuddin *telhis*" (1632), and Aziz Efendi's essay (1633), all of which share the same view, namely that the present situation was a dangerous deviation from the rules of Süleyman's Golden Era and that the solution was to return to those rules; most of these authors seem to have been associated with Murad IV and his efforts to impose discipline and order on the janissary army after the upheavals of the 1620s. On the other hand, there is a set of authors who went a step further and, instead of comparing the shortcomings of the situation during their lives against the standards of a "Golden Age", they simply laid down rules they believed the government should follow. The normative role of lists and of *kanun* or "regulations" was clear by the late sixteenth century, but it reached a peak in the first decades of the seventeenth. These works include Koçi Bey's second treatise (1640), the anonymous *Kavânîn-ı yeniçeriyân* (1606), Ayn Ali's (ca. 1610) and Avni Ömer's (1642) descriptions of the janissary and timar system, and some general surveys of the empire, such as the majority of Hezarfen Hüseyin Efendi's compilation (1675) and the anonymous *Kavânîn-ı osmanî ve rabıta-ı Asitâne* (after 1688) as well as other, similar texts.

The sixth chapter (written by Ekin Tuşalp Atiyas) aims to follow the seventeenth-century conceptualizations of an ideal political order based on the double premise of the Sharia and the prophetic Sunna. A large part of the Ottoman seventeenth century has been viewed as having been dominated by three generations of "fundamentalist" preachers known as the Kadızadelis.

The debates of the seventeenth century cannot be simply described as the products of the antagonism between the Salafist legalism of the Kadızadelis and the heterodox reactions from its Sufi targets. A concern to uphold the Sharia was seen across the whole spectrum of the participants in these public debates, from the Halveti sheikhs to the Kadızadeli preachers. The chapter's main focus will be on whether there existed a distinct political and economic agenda parallel to these Sunna-minded tendencies. Based on such writings, this chapter seeks to investigate the boundaries of the incumbent political authorities promulgated by these authors, the standards of Sunna-abiding political conduct, the parameters of public administration and, more specifically, ideas surrounding relations between Muslims and non-Muslim, taxation, and the laws pertaining to ownership of land. With these priorities in mind, the chapter will first examine the writings of sixteenth-century figures such as Birgivi (d. 1573) and Münir-i Belgradi (d. 1620) before moving on to relevant treatises, correspondence, and panegyrics written by famous and not-so-famous preachers and sheikhs from both sides of the debate. These include such luminaries as Abdülmecid Sivasi (d. 1639), Kadızade Mehmed Efendi (d. 1636), Üstüvani Efendi (d. 1661), Abdülahad Nuri (d. 1648), Kadızade Mehmed İlmi (d. 1631–2), and Vani Efendi (d. 1687). Finally, the chapter will examine the echoes of the Sunna-based debates in the latter part of the seventeenth century. This is especially important because, while the Kadızadelis fizzled as a socially conservative movement and ceased to steer dynastic politics towards the end of the seventeenth century, the equally conservative political and economic mentality that they championed was preserved by a new generation of the Ottoman political elite that engaged in a series of administrative reforms that were unmistakably Sharia-based.

In the seventh chapter, the re-emergence of a more general and "philosophical" view of society from the mid-seventeenth century onwards will be examined. Some evidence of Ibn Khaldun's work can be discerned in Kınalızade's mid-sixteenth-century Nasirean masterpiece; from the mid-seventeenth century onwards, however, Ibn Khaldun's vision of rising and falling dynasties and general historical laws started to permeate Ottoman political thought increasingly intensely. First we will focus on Kâtib Çelebi's political and historical works, in which he uses a novel medical simile for human society (with the four classes compared to the four humors of the body rather than the four elements, thereby facilitating the view of society as a developing organism), a pioneering definition of the state (which he saw as inseparable from society), and the first systematic introduction of Ibn Khaldun's notion of the "state-stages" into the Ottoman philosophy of history. What was perhaps more important was Kâtib Çelebi's sense of innovation; more particularly, his admission that every kind (or stage) of society needs different measures and thus that any potential reformer should adopt a problem-oriented policy rather than revert to some idealized constitution(s) from the past. After surveying Kâtib Çelebi's influence on authors such as Hemdemi and Hüseyin Hezarfen (studied in part in chapter 5, too), this chapter will examine Mustafa Na'ima's (d. 1716) historiographical work, in the introduction to which Ibn Khaldun's theory is even more explicitly and faithfully presented: Na'ima retains the five stages of a dynasty, instead of the simplified three stages used by Kâtib Çelebi, and also introduces the nomadism vs. settled life distinction that was to become increasingly important in the second half of the eighteenth century. On the other hand, it will be shown that Na'ima's call for peace was paralleled in other early eighteenth-century works, such as those of the poet Nabi (d. 1712).

The final two chapters deal with the eighteenth-century authors and how they may have paved the way for the major reforms of the late eighteenth and nineteenth centuries. The eighth chapter first analyzes the "traditionalist" views of Bakkalzade Defterdar Sarı Mehmed Pasha (d. 1717) and his contemporary Nahifi Süleyman Efendi (d. 1738), as well as later authors who continued the "mirror for princes" eclectic tradition while adding original ideas on the reorganization of the army, the landholding system, or the economy. Such authors include Dürri Mehmed Efendi (d. 1794), Süleyman Penah Efendi (d. 1785), and Canikli Ali Pasha (d. 1785), all of whom had their political views enriched by their experiences in provincial or central administration, while, significantly, placing extraordinary emphasis on non-military matters, from economy to town-planning, in sharp contrast to the "Westernizers" who preferred to focus on army reforms. All these writers preferred concrete and specific advice rather than the theoretical musings of writers such as Kâtib Çelebi and Na'ima; however, they differ from their late sixteenth and early seventeenth-century predecessors insofar as they avoid any reference to "decline" or a "Golden Age". Furthermore, evidence from the late eighteenth- and nineteenth-century authors such as Ebubekir Ratıb Efendi, Ahmed Vasıf Efendi, Behic Efendi, and Ömer Faik Efendi shows that the "traditionalist" views and proposals were not in so sharp a conflict with the "Europeanist" ones as is generally believed. Some of these authors swiftly changed their attitude in accordance with government policies, while others effectively stood by Selim III's Westernizing reforms using "traditionalist" arguments. This is nicely illustrated in the traditionalist attitude of Şanizade, the copyist of Voltaire (1825).

Finally, the focus of the ninth chapter is on the second half of the eighteenth century, when emphasis on European-style military reforms was combined with a re-reading of Ibn Khaldun (whose work was translated into Ottoman Turkish in 1730). This began with İbrahim Müteferrika (d. 1745), who re-introduced Aristotelian ideas by speaking of the three possible constitutions (monarchy, aristocracy, and democracy) before then moving on to proposals for military reform (although he copied the discussion of Aristotelian governments from a translation of Kâtib Çelebi). Müteferrika's ideas clearly fitted into the intellectual climate of his era, reflected in the numerous translations of Aristotle's works and the emphasis on innovation in various scientific fields. On the other hand, the idea of the superiority of European military organization can also be found in other works from his time, often by making use of the concept of "reciprocity" (*mukabele bi'l-misl*) and of the idea that Europeans had first copied the Ottomans. In this context, the reader will follow the translation movement through the eighteenth century and Ahmed Resmî's call for peace and for a new understanding of international politics in the 1770s. We will also delve into the various viewpoints, some more traditionalist and others in a more "Westernizing" vein, of statesmen who formed the circle around Selim III and prepared his reforms. The chapter ends with the defenses of Selim III's reforms by "Koca Sekbanbaşı" (1804; probably to be identified with Vasıf Efendi) and Dihkanizade Kuşmani (1806), just before Mahmud II's major reforms that began with the 1826 massacre of the janissaries, an event which, in many ways, marks the beginning of modernity in Ottoman state history.

In the conclusion we will try to sketch the results of the abovementioned research and to clarify the links between Ottoman political ideas and the development of power politics in the Ottoman Empire. In addition, we will bring together material on the development of a number of fundamental concepts, such as justice, law, state, the world order, and so forth, in an attempt to initiate conceptual history within Ottoman studies. Finally, we will attempt to compare our findings with how political ideas developed in the other great Islamicate polities of the period, namely those that were flourishing in Persian and Indian lands. Two appendices will add a comparative timeline of historical events and political works, with reference to the chapters-*cum*-ideological categories as described above, and short samples of translated texts, thereby allowing the book to also be used as a textbook for Ottoman political thought.

CHAPTER 1

The Empire in the Making: Construction and Early Critiques

The emergence of what was to become the Ottoman Empire is one of the most fascinating stories of state-making we know, and discussions surrounding its features and character have been some of the liveliest in the Ottomanist field. Whatever the exact nature of the early Ottoman emirate, its development was, by any measure, spectacular.[1] The first emir, Osman son of Ertoğrul (d. 1324?), seems to have risen around the year 1299 to become a chieftain of settlers and raiders under vague Seljuk suzerainty in the region of Bithynia. Osman's success in raiding and in battle gave his son Orhan (d. 1362) a stable base from which he was able to conquer a number of important Byzantine towns in the region, including Proussa (Bursa, 1326), Nikaia (Iznik, 1331), and Nikomedia (Izmit, 1337). Moreover, Orhan's armies took advantage of an earthquake (at Kallipoli/Gelibolu, in 1354) to cross to Europe, where they played an active role in the struggles between the contenders to the Byzantine throne and, as a result, gained territories and towns such as Didymoteichon (Dimetoka, 1359 or 1361). Under Orhan's successor, Murad I (d. 1389), the state (by now increasingly endorsing the traditions and institutions of its Islamic predecessors) annexed territories of both the fellow-Muslim emirates of Anatolia (Germiyan, c. 1375; part of Karaman in 1387) and the Christian states of the Byzantine Empire (Adrianople/Edirne, c. 1369; Thessaloniki, 1387; Verroia, c. 1385) and Serbia (Nish, 1386). A major role in this process was played by warlords and the heads of large families, such as Evrenos and Mihaloğulları, who seem to have actually governed their own conquests in the Balkans, under Murad's nominal suzerainty. In the Ottoman victory at the decisive battle of Kosovo (1389) Murad was killed, but his son Bayezid I established Ottoman suzerainty in the area of the Balkans that had formed Bulgaria and southern Serbia (crushing a Hungarian-led crusade at Nicopolis in 1396) and then annexed many of the Turkoman principalities of Anatolia, occupying Konya (1397) and Sivas (1398). Bayezid, however, met his end at the hands of Timur; at the battle of Ankara (1402), his Anatolian vassals deserted him and he died a prisoner of

1 Among recent narratives of early Ottoman history are those by Mantran 1989, 15–80; Emecen 2001b, 3–20; Imber 2009, 7–24; Lindner 2009. On the *interregnum* after the battle of Ankara, see the now classic Kastritsis 2007.

© KONINKLIJKE BRILL NV, LEIDEN, 2019 | DOI:10.1163/9789004385245_003

the Chagatay conqueror. This looked like the end of the one-century old state, as Bayezid's four sons, Süleyman, Mehmed, İsa, and Musa engaged in a long civil war that only ended in 1413, with Mehmed as sole ruler of the remaining Ottoman territories. Following this, Mehmed managed to see off his Anatolian and Venetian enemies, as well as a much-debated series of internal revolts led by Musa's judge, Şeyh Bedreddin, and a millenarian preacher, Börklüce Mustafa. As a result of his successes, upon his death in 1421 the Ottoman borders were on the Danube in the north and the Adriatic in the west. His son and successor, Murad II, recovered all the Anatolian territories lost in the aftermath of the defeat at Ankara, captured Thessaloniki from Venice for a second time in 1430, and conquered new territories in Anatolia and on the Adriatic and Ionian coasts. Somewhat unexpectedly, he abdicated in 1444 in favor of his son Mehmed, but the perceived danger posed by a new crusade made him return only a few months later, defeating the Hungarians and their allies at Varna, on the Black Sea coast. After his death in 1451, he was again succeeded by his son, Mehmed II the Conqueror, almost the first act of whom was the conquest of Constantinople/Istanbul, which was to be the new capital of the empire. Mehmed's vision and state was very different to those of his fourteenth-century ancestors: what had begun as a semi-tribal confederation of warlords was now an organized settled state with a highly elaborate hierarchy and protocol and an apparatus formed of scholars and statesmen (who had already formed their own family dynasties) that was ready to articulate a theory of Mehmed's imperial vision.

The spectacular expansion of the early Ottomans demands an explanation, and many theories have been put forward. Originating as a small emirate in what used to be the Seljuk borderlands, the Ottomans had one significant advantage over the other emirates that filled the power vacuum created by the Mongol invasion of 1243: theirs was situated on the frontline with the lands of the infidels, Byzantium, and thus offered splendid prospects for a life of plundering, on the one hand, and religious fervor, on the other. And indeed, it is the precise nature of the balance between these two factors that forms the focus of much scholarly debate on the origins of the Ottomans. This debate, initiated by Fuad Köprülü (who was, in turn, answering the claims of Gibbons regarding the strong Byzantine character of the early Ottomans) and his face-value acceptance of the tribal origin of Osman's people from a branch of the Oğuz tribes, led to Paul Wittek's famous "*gazi* thesis". Wittek surmised that Osman's tribal nucleus gathered together a group of warriors of various backgrounds, all of whom were motivated by the spirit of *gaza* or "the Holy War", i.e. the prospect of war against the neighboring Byzantines. The ensuing debate might have been based on a misunderstanding, as if Wittek had meant a kind of Muslim group of crusaders;[2] most critics focused on the absence of religious zeal in the entourage of the first sultans and maintained instead that the early Ottoman emirate had mostly tribal (Rudi P. Lindner) or syncretistic (Heath Lowry) connotations. On the other hand, scholars closer to Wittek's thesis (Halil İnalcık, Cemal Kafadar) stressed that, for the nomadic or semi-nomadic warriors that formed the core of Osman's and Orhan's armies, *gaza* had a meaning closer to plunder than to "Holy War".[3] An Anatolian text on *gaza*, probably originating in the Karasi emirate, has recently been used to suggest that the frontier understanding of the term was different from the "more tolerant" *cihad* (*jihad*) of the ulema, making it more fitting for fourteenth-century freebooters. Colin Imber, however, analyzed the same text and showed that, in fact, it only recapitulated "the standard Hanafi rules of Holy War" and that *gaza* was never any different from *cihad*, always being one of the obligations imposed on the Muslim community.[4] However, Imber's interpretation may reinforce this alternative understanding of the *gazi*-thesis (one may call it the *akıncı*-thesis, since it stresses the role of raiders rather than holy warriors): the ulema were quick to try to embrace the heterogeneous freebooters of the Anatolian emirates and tried to instil the notion of *gaza* in order to proclaim the religious nature of their plundering the infidel.

Indeed, the nature of the emergence of the Ottoman state produced some peculiarities in the creation of its early intellectual elite, an elite that could articulate a fully-fledged political ideology. The very presence, let alone influence, of educated ulema and other individuals among the warrior entourage of the first decades of the fourteenth century, is an object of scholarly debate;[5] the same goes, even more so, for the ideas that motivated the warriors themselves. As noted above, it has been posited that their *Weltanschauung* was

2 I believe that Rudi P. Lindner, for instance, oversimplifies when he claims that Wittek's "extraordinary solution" can be reduced to "single-minded devotion to the holy war as a powerful engine of Ottoman history" (Lindner 2007, 10). In a way, the modern debate on "Wittek's thesis" has moved the subject from whether the unifying factor of the early Ottomans was their tribal unity or war opportunities to whether *gaza* meant religious fervor or just plundering the enemy. Wittek, however, never insisted on the religious character of the early Ottoman *gaza* (or, at any rate, never made this character his central argument). I find, for instance, that Heath Lowry's definition of the Ottoman *gaza* (Lowry 2003, 45ff.) is not as far from Kafadar's or even Wittek's as he considers it to be.

3 On the debate see the recent works of Kafadar 1995; Lowry 2003; Lindner 1983 and 2007; Imber 2011, 201ff.; Darling 2011.

4 Tekin 1989; Imber 2011, 59ff. and 201ff. On the other hand, Kate Fleet showed that *gazi* was not the *par excellence* title of early Ottoman sultans, as declared by Wittek and his followers (Fleet 2002).

5 Kafadar 1995, 109ff.; Lindner 2009, 120; Imber 2009, 212–214; Tuşalp Atiyas 2013, 43ff.

structured along the notion of Holy War or *gaza*; it has also been argued, in sharp contrast, that the concepts of Holy War and of the *gazi* warrior were imposed much later on a group of tribal soldiery with syncretistic mentality; still others have suggested that the notion of *gaza* had connotations more similar to plunder than to religion. Certainly, by Orhan's reign a settled economy, state-like administration, and layer of educated scholars offering their services in a competition with heterodox dervishes, had already emerged; among these scholars, Byzantine sources even record Jewish and Christian renegades able to engage in debates on the superiority of the Muslim faith.[6] One may certainly argue that the conflict between the old warriors who were trying to defend their interests, on the one hand, and incoming scholars seeking to impose the imperial visions of the Persian and Seljuk traditions, on the other, was the ideological representation of this political and social conflict between the *gazi* (or *akıncı*, if one prefers this term) military environment and the expanding imperial hierarchy, which was becoming increasingly powerful in the Ottoman state at the time.

As such, the first section of this chapter seeks to detect the political ideas of the former in a somewhat reversed way, by examining the opposition to Mehmed II's imperial plans after the capture of Constantinople. Indeed, in the plethora of general histories composed during the reign of his successor, Bayezid II, almost all bear the mark of this sultan's "reactionary" policy (the term belongs to Halil İnalcık); although none speak ill of Mehmed II, they tend to obliquely criticize his imperial policy and what they perceive to have been his "greediness", by which they mean his seizure of private and *vakf* (*waqf*) lands and their transformation into "state" land (*miri*).[7] These measures, as will be seen in the following chapter, harmed both the old warlords and the dervishes, i.e. exactly the groups that had emerged in the first period of the emirate and which were struggling to keep pace following the establishment of an administrative and ulema hierarchy.

---

6 Vryonis 1971, 426ff.; Zachariadou 1992; Balivet 1993.

7 İnalcık 1962, 164–165 (but cf. the cautionary remarks by Mengüç 2013). On this transformation see Özel 1999 (recapitulating the older literature), who argues that the reform had a fiscal rather than a land character. Özel also maintains, based on a register of the Amasya region, that the scope of the reform was much smaller than is usually thought, but admits (243) that the image may be different as far as it concerns the Western Anatolian and Balkan lands.

1 Opposition to Imperial Policies as an Indicator of *Gazi* Political Ideas

Apart from a few Byzantine authors, there are no contemporaneous sources for the first, formative years of the Ottoman Emirate, a lacuna that has led scholars such as Colin Imber to speak of "a black hole" concerning early Ottoman history.[8] With the exception of some anonymous chronicles (*takvim*), the oldest extant narrative of Ottoman history is the account by Yahşi Fakih, son of Orhan's imam. This deals with events up to the time of Bayezid I (1389–1402) and was incorporated into Aşıkpaşazade's Ottoman history, composed towards the end of the fifteenth century. Aşıkpaşazade included Yahşi Fakih's chronicle in his work (Aşıkpaşazade had been a guest in Yahşi Fakih's house in Geyve during an illness in 1413) and supplemented it with a continuation up to 1478, while around the same time Uruc Bey (as well as an anonymous "History of the House of Osman") seems to have used a summary of it, along with other sources (mainly folk narratives centered around specific *gazi*s or saints, *evliya* and *dede*), to compose his own chronicle. Aşıkpaşazade's and Oruç's additions, which cover most of the fifteenth century, seem to stem from different sets of sources, with the former more reliant on his own, personal experiences. On the other hand, Halil İnalcık showed that the second-earliest extant source, Ahmedi's *İskendernâme* (composed between 1403 and 1410), used another, now lost narrative, on which other mid- or late fifteenth-century authors such as Şükrullah, Ruhi, and Neşri also relied.[9]

1.1 *Yahşi Fakih and Aşıkpaşazade*

Thus, our first written sources for the ideas circulating during the early phase of the Ottoman Emirate are Yahşi Fakih's chronicle (as far as we can discern it from Aşıkpaşazade's history), on the one hand, and Ahmedi's versified history, on the other, both of which were composed soon after the defeat at Ankara. These sources are very different from each other, in regards to both the milieu in which they originated and their expected audience. The first is a product of the old generation of *gazi* fighters, and thus seeks to praise their role in the formation of the Ottoman Emirate and to cement their place in the structure of the empire-in-the-making, while the second is a product of a former courtier of another emirate (the Germiyan) who wished to secure his position in

8 Imber 1993.

9 On early Ottoman historiography see the detailed accounts by İnalcık 1962, Ménage 1962, and Ménage 1964.

the turbulent times that followed the defeat at Ankara, when he chose one of the wrong sides (that of Prince Süleyman Çelebi). Moreover, as Yahşi Fakih's chronicle was incorporated into Aşıkpaşazade's Ottoman history, one cannot be certain which part of the socio-political critique is his and which part is his copyist's. Nevertheless, the various layers of narratives and ideas superimposed (or coexisting, as in Kafadar's metaphor of a "garlic-like" rather than "onion-like" structure in early Ottoman historiography)[10] on Yahşi Fakih's text may be said to enrich rather than conceal the original spirit of the first warriors: both Yahşi Fakih and Aşıkpaşazade came from the same environment and do not seem to have been influenced by the Persian traditions on government that were circulating in neighboring emirates, as were other writers (such as Ahmedi or Şeyhoğlu). As will be seen below, although it is possible to detect ideas unique to Yahşi Fakih and Aşıkpaşazade, the pieces of political advice or evaluation expressed by both belong to the same set of ideas and emanate from the same milieu, thus enabling us to examine the text as a whole in this regard and to consider it a representative mirror of the *gazi* mentality. Thus, it might be appropriate to begin (somewhat paradoxically) with Aşıkpaşazade's work, even though it is not the earliest specimen of Ottoman thought and despite the fact that, in the long run, it came to represent an opposition to, rather than a description of, the imperial paradigm.

A descendant of the great early Ottoman mystic, Aşık Pasha, Aşıkpaşazade Derviş Ahmed was born around 1400 near Amasya. He took part in numerous campaigns and battles in Rumili during the reign of Murad II and the start of that of Mehmed II and, after 1453, he settled in Istanbul, where he began writing his chronicle. He seems to have died, almost a centenarian, in the last years of the fifteenth century (according to one tradition, in 1481). His chronicle (*Tevârîh-i Âl-i Osman*, "Stories of the House of Osman") goes up to 1478, while additions to 1502 contained in some manuscripts may have been made by a copyist belonging to the circle of Korkud, Bayezid II's son.[11]

Yahşi Fakih's chronicle, as preserved within Aşıkpaşazade's text,[12] contains some interesting insights on early Ottoman political practice and the way the

---

10 Kafadar 1995, 102: "… 'garlic' is a more apt metaphor for certain aspects of early Ottoman historiography than 'onion' because it recognizes a plurality of voices without assigning any of them, even the earliest, the monopoly over a 'core reality'".

11 Aşıkpaşazade – Atsız 1949, 82. Two different versions have been published, the second incorporating the first: Aşıkpaşazade – Giese 1929 and Aşıkpaşazade – Atsız 1949. On Aşıkpaşazade see Kafadar 1995, 96ff. and *passim*; İnalcık 1962 and 1994; Ménage 1962; Zachariadou 1995; Özdemir 2013. İnalcık 1994b, 139–143, considers the final part of the chronicle as original, as he argues that Aşıkpaşazade lived from 1392/3 to 1502.

12 On the parts attributed to him see Zachariadou 1995, and cf. Kafadar 1995, 99ff.

gazi milieu conceived it. An interesting feature is the constant use of the third-person plural to denote collective decisions. When his father Ertoğrul passed away, "they deemed Osman suitable" for his place (A94: *atasınun yerine layık gördiler*), and upon Murad I's death on the battlefield of Kosovo, "they" killed one of his sons, Yakub, and "they accepted Sultan Bayezid [II]" (A134: *Bayazıd Hanı kabul etdiler*).[13] In a similar vein, after Osman's death his two sons quietly discussed the question of who should be his successor, with Alaeddin insisting that Orhan should become the shepherd and that the territory rightfully belonged to him (A115: *bu vilayet hakkundur ... çobanlık dahı senündür*). A survey of other early chronicles, such as those of Mehmed Neşri and Kemalpaşazade, corroborates the conclusion that the succession of Ertoğrul by Osman around 1299 and of Osman by Orhan in 1324 were a process more of tribal election than merely hereditary succession from father to son. In contrast, authors closer to Mehmed II's imperial policies (such as Karamanlı Nişancı Mehmed Pasha) and later historians simply state that Osman and Orhan took the place of their fathers.[14] What is important for our aims here is not the tribal character of the first Ottomans but the fact that records of it remained valid throughout the fourtheenth and fifteenth centuries. In other words, the *gazi* worldview of a "society of warriors" with a ruler being *primus inter pares* was still alive (though, admittedly, in its swansong) even when sultans such as Bayezid I and Mehmed II were working hard to impose an imperial, autocratic model.

There are instances in which one cannot be sure whether a story or judgment originates from Yahşi Fakih or Aşıkpaşazade. For example, the famous passage relating the installation of a judge and the organization of the market in newly-conquered Karacahisar contains a story about a man from Germiyan who asked to buy the market toll:

> The community said: "Go to the ruler!" The man went to the ruler and made his request. Osman Ghazi said: "What is this market toll?" The man said: "I am to take money for everything that comes to the market". Osman Ghazi said: "Are the people of the market in debt to you, so that you want their money?" The man said: "My lord, it is a custom. In all countries,

13 On the other hand, a similar expression is used for the concealing of Murad II's death until the arrival of his successor Mehmed II, a part which cannot belong to Yahşi Fakih: *paşalar meyyiti kimseye bildürmediler. Divanlar etdiler. Tımarlar verdiler* (Aşıkpaşazade – Atsız 1949, 190–191). Here, however, the subject is clearly defined (the pashas). Cf. Vatin – Veinstein 2003, 82–83.

14 Cf. Lindner 1983, 21–23, for a description of tribal procedures of election as reflected in the early chronicles; and Sariyannis 2016, 36–39, for a more detailed analysis of such expressions in Ottoman historiography.

> whoever rules takes money". Osman Ghazi said: "Is this an order of God, or have rulers ordained it by themselves?" And again the man said: "It is a custom, my lord. It has been so from olden days". Osman Ghazi was very angry and said: "So one person's gain can belong to another person? No! It is his own property! What have I added to his property so that I may tell him 'give me money'? (A104: *bir kişi kim kazana, gayrınun mı olur? Kendünün mülki olur. Ben anun malında ne kodum ki bana akça ver deyem*). Go away and do not say such things to me again or you'll regret it".

However, when the community (*bu kavım*) continues to insist, on the grounds that market tolls are an old and established custom, the sultan consents, but stresses that whenever a person is given a timar, this cannot be taken from him without a good reason, and that upon that person's death the timar must be given to his son. Even if the story as a whole belongs to Yahşi Fakih, the reference to the inalienability of timars must be Aşıkpaşazade's addition because it is almost a direct criticism of Mehmed II's confiscating policies.[15] The same goes for the description of Osman's meager property as registered upon his death (A115). In contrast, the account of Orhan's dialogue with a dervish, who claims that God entrusted "the property of the world" to kings (A122: *Hak ... dünya mülkini sizün gibi hanlara ısmarladı*), seems to be Yahşi Fakih's own, as it is the opposite of the references mentioned above.

Bayezid I's defeat at Ankara, the one and only major defeat Ottoman chroniclers had to account for in this period, is the locus *par excellence* of the political critique they express.[16] Thus, we may attribute to Yahşi Fakih (his chronicle reaches Bayezid's reign, but we cannot be sure at which point it stopped) the justification of Bayezid's conquest of the Aydın, Saruhan, and Menteşe emirates as something done not out of oppression but justice (A135–36). In contrast, the libel against the ulema (A138–39), beginning with Çandarlı (Kara) Halil and Türk Rüstem (who previously, in Yahşi Fakih's chronicle, were held responsible for the institution of the janissaries: A128), must belong to Aşıkpaşazade.[17] Allegedly, in Bayezid's time the judges began to be corrupt; the sultan wanted to burn them all alive together, but they were saved due to the cunning intervention of Çandarlı Ali Pasha (Kara Halil's son; d. 1406). It was he who was

15 Lindner considers this story a "salutary legend" and a posterior addition to the chronicle; true, it shows an ulema influence incompatible in his view with the tribal realities of Osman's time, but the very fact that Karacahisar had belonged to the Germiyan emirate earlier may reinforce the authenticity of the story: see Kafadar 1995, 103–104 and cf. Lindner 2007, 79. On the Karacahisar incident cf. also Imber 2011, 187–188.

16 On the legitimization problems posed by the Ottoman defeat, see Kastritsis 2007, 195ff.

17 Cf. similar points in contemporary anonymous chronicles (Kafadar 1995, 111–114).

"the one that made the house of Osman succumb to sin" by bringing many Persian scholars to Ottoman lands. The main criticism against Bayezid, however, focuses on his alleged greed, i.e., an attitude similar to that attributed to Mehmed II by his critics, namely the allocation of revenues to the state rather than to the old military aristocracy. Thus, the description of the disastrous battle of Ankara in Aşıkpaşazade ends with a faithful servant accusing the sultan (A144): "You didn't spend your money. You put it all into your treasury, saying it is trust for your children". It is remarkable that, in his own chronicle, Nişancı Karamani Mehmed Pasha, a paragon of Mehmed II's administration (and vehemently criticized by Aşıkpaşazade), says only that the defeat in Ankara was due to "many reasons [he] cannot write in this book".[18]

Indeed, one could say that the core of Aşıkpaşazade's political advice lies in its refutation of Mehmed II's imperial policy. His side is clearly that of the old military aristocracy, of the free *gazi* warriors who found themselves marginalized by the imperial policies and the growing role of the janissary standing army.[19] He clearly tries to underestimate the janissaries' alleged relationship with the revered Hacı Bektaş (A238). Aşıkpaşazade puts the usual stress on the importance of justice, dictated, as shall be seen, by the whole tradition of political thought in his region and time, but then again justice is meant, in a sense, as synonymous with generosity and in contrast with greed. For instance, he observes that "the wishes and traditions of the House of Osman are founded on justice", noting that, upon his invasion of Karaman, Murad II did not extract the slightest amount from any subject of the emirate (A175). In the final part of Aşıkpaşazade's work, a list of the virtues of the Ottoman sultans emphasizes their generosity, to both the poor and dervishes, as well as their activity in charitable works and *vakf*s (A230–33). In a story where, once again, the Persian intruders play the role of corrupters, we read that Fazlullah Pasha, a Persian vizier of Murad II, advised him to collect obligatory alms (*zekat*), i.e. taxes, from his subjects in order to feed the army and fill the treasury. The just sultan replied that in his realm there are only three licit ways of collecting money, namely silver mines, the poll-tax from the infidels, and booty from the Holy War. "If the army is fed from sinful sources (*haram lokma*), it becomes sinful itself". This advice is followed by a special chapter entitled "What the end was of sultans who hoarded wealth" (A233–34), with Bayezid I as the first example: the only true wealth is that spent on charity, and the real treasury of a ruler is formed of the blessings showered on him by his subjects. This emphasis on the virtue of generosity and the underlying disapproval of the centralizing

18 Nişancı Mehmed Paşa – Konyalı 1949, 348.

19 See e.g. İnalcık 1994b, 144–147.

tendencies of the state is found in a wide range of Ottoman thinkers, as shall be seen.[20]

More direct criticism of Mehmed's policies is also evident, although always with a careful allotment of responsibility to bad counsellors. For instance, Aşıkpaşazade accuses Hakim Ya'kub Pasha of initiating "unprecedented innovations" (*işidilmedük ve görülmedük bid'atları*), and particularly of bringing Jews into the sultan's company (A244). More importantly, the renting of houses to Muslims in newly-conquered Istanbul for money (instead of granting them as full property) is severely condemned; Aşıkpaşazade attributes this measure to Rum Mehmed Pasha, allegedly a friend of the infidels who hoped thus to regain their city some day (A193; cf. A216).[21] Equally vehement is his attack on Nişancı (Karamani) Mehmed Pasha and the confiscations of private property and *vakf*s the latter instigated (A244–45), confiscations which Aşıkpaşazade describes as opposed to both the Sharia and the old practice—a *leitmotif* that recurs again and again in these texts, as mentioned above.

Advisors and officials may be blamed, therefore, but ultimate responsibility lies with the sultan: speaking of public kitchens and other charitable works, Aşıkpaşazade observes in the same vein that the purpose of such works is benefit in the next world (*ahret*), not in this one (*vilayet*). In this respect, the intention of viziers follows that of the sultan (*niyyetleri padişah niyyetine tabi olur*). He explains that viziers must follow the ulema and the dervishes (*vezirler ülemaya ve fukaraya tabilerdür*) because the sultan's purpose is manifest through his viziers; in turn, viziers depend on their stewards (*kethüda*), who are acquainted with some of the ulema, the poor, the common, and the ignorant (i.e. the people), and thus they may know who is in need. As such, any and all difficulties in such matters, and more generally problems in the world's order, come from the intervention of the viziers' stewards or of unsuitable trustees who refuse to feed and shelter every poor person as they ought to. Sultans send special investigators to the *vakıf*, who cut off expenditures and impose more burdens on the subjects in order to increase the wealth of the sultan's treasury (A246–47).

Thus, if we are to take these early chroniclers as representative of the ideas prevailing in the milieus of the *akıncı*s and *gazi*s, the social groups (together with the antinomian or, rather, rural Sufis) which constituted the early Ottomans *par excellence*, we would detect a strong commitment to a system of collective decision-making, to a kind of military democracy where the sultan was but *primus inter pares*. Every attempt to centralize power and revenue

20 Cf. on this Sariyannis 2011a.

21 On this issue cf. İnalcık 1969–1970, 242–45, and 1994, 145–146.

is condemned as a sign of greed and oppression; furthermore, a very negative attitude to the emerging strata of the ulema and the high officials of the court can be detected, especially when they are newcomers from Iran or the neighboring emirates. The army, meaning here the free raiders of the *gaza* and the early timariots, in contrast to the janissaries, is viewed as the spine of the Ottoman state; its protection is seen as almost the main task of a just ruler.

1.2 *Apocalyptic Literature as a Vehicle for Opposition*

Aşıkpaşazade's chronicle is not the only example of anti-imperial writing from the late fifteenth century.[22] One may see a similar attitude in various apocalyptic texts from that period, works which seek to demonstrate that their era has all the characteristics of the end-times, or at least that depravity is so dominant that it may have eschatological implications. Islamic apocalyptic imagery has a standard inventory of ideas connected with immorality, especially among women, decline in religious fervor, and dishonesty on the part of judges and other officials.[23] However, texts produced in the late fifteenth century have some features that show that they were primarily composed in order to criticize their own times and thereby to promote their own vision for what constituted an ideal society. For instance, some legendary histories of pre-Ottoman Constantinople, which circulated widely in this period, concentrate on tales of depravity and immorality that resulted in destruction, thereby implying (as shown by the late Stéphane Yérasimos) that the Ottomans should never make that city the seat of their empire and thus opposing the evolution of the military emirate into an empire with claims of universalism.[24] Interestingly, the same stories were re-told between the 1530s and the 1560s, when Süleyman I's plans for a universal empire brought the subject of imperial centralization into the middle political scene once more. This opposition may have reached a climax in calls for Edirne rather than Istanbul to be selected as the capital of the empire (or, at any rate, of the Ottoman state): there are early sixteenth-century legends on its founding, which place it as the polar opposite of Istanbul (created by the prophet Idris, or else predestined for the Muslim armies and inhabitants

22 The ideas that follow, as well as the part on Yazıcıoğlu, were first expounded in Sariyannis 2008a, 128–132.

23 Cf. Cook 2002, 13–14; Kurz 2011, 24–25. In the thirteenth century, this imagery was used against the Turks (*recte* Mongols): Peacock 2016, 294–295.

24 Yerasimos 1990, esp. 84–85, 154–59, 194ff., 201ff. Some of these legends continued to circulate during subsequent centuries as well, but we should not necessarily seek anti-imperial attitudes in the authors who incorporated them into their chronicles. See, e.g., Solakzade 1879, 201–209; Mahmud Efendi – Tunalı 2013, 167–174 and 351–353.

to come). One of these texts is the *Saltukname*, which celebrates a champion of the dervish warriors associated with Aşıkpaşazade's *gazi* environment.[25]

Sharp, though indirect, criticisms of contemporaneous social conditions can also be found in an encyclopedic work by Yazıcıoğlu Ahmed Bican (d. after 1466), a dervish and disciple of Hacı Bayram Sultan who lived all his life in his hometown of Gelibolu and who was part of the anti-imperial trend described above. Written in all probability shortly after 1453, *Dürr-i meknûn* ("Hidden Pearls") is a synopsis of Islamic cosmology and mythology, containing tales of the creation of the world, the form of the universe, the prophets, various mythical places, islands, and cities, attributes of the world's fauna and flora, etc.[26] Even at the beginning of his work, Yazıcıoğlu labels his own era "a time of disorder" (S19–20: *bu fitne zamanında*); later on he takes advantage of several opportunities to prove this claim, although he always does so while detailing societies distant in both time and place. In the seventeenth chapter of his book, Yazıcıoğlu enumerates the signs that will show that the end of the world is near. According to Yazıcıoğlu, the Prophet had said that these will start to occur after the 900th year of the Hegira, i.e. 1494/95. This reference shows clearly that Yazıcıoğlu wanted to speak of his own times.[27]

The first sign, as usual, is the clear decline in both morals and religiosity among the people (S122ff.):[28]

> The mosques will be many, but few people will pray, and even they will not be pious in their prayers, because they will not know the difference between legitimate and illegitimate (*helal ve haram*) in their gains ... Women will mount horses like chieftains (*beyler*) and they will dominate (*hükümet edeler*); boys will be like princes (*emir*) ... They will not esteem the pious and the spiritual, but the men of the world. Women will not stay bashful, women will sleep with women and men with men. There will be plenty of false sheikhs. Princes (*beyler*) will oppress in the name of justice; viziers will be jolly and treacherous fellows (*rind ve kalleş*); the ulema will be sinful (*fısk ede*); judges will take bribes. Adultery, sodomy and drinking will become manifest. Among the people, the wicked will become chieftains and the base will come to rule; people will rebel ... They will build high and magnificent houses like royal mansions ...

---

25 Yerasimos 1990, 207–210.

26 Yazıcıoğlu – Sakaoğlu 1999. Cf. Yerasimos 1990, 60–61; *Encyclopaedia of Islam*, 2nd ed., "Bîdjân, Ahmed" (V. L. Ménage). On the background of the genesis of the Bayrami order cf. Terzioğlu 2012, 91–92.

27 Cf. Yerasimos 1990, 195–196.

28 Cf. Yerasimos 1990, 195–196.

> Women will walk in the markets, gain money ... and resemble men. They [the people] will consume the property of orphans; they will not protect the poor. Princes will commend high business to mean persons ... The oppressed will not be heard. Judges will be dissolute and rulers (*ümera*) will be merchants (*tacir*) ... Sufism will be nothing but the external appearance (*tac ile hırkada kala*).

Particular emphasis is placed on the decline of market regulations:

> Merchants will cheat in their weights, and they will sell at whatever price [they like] (*türlü türlü narh ile satalar*); they will give full weight to the great and defective to the poor, and they will lie in their sales.

The ulema will also become depraved, issuing *fetva*s according to their own interests (*nefse kolay*), and finally:

> as innovation (or heresy, *bid'atleri*) will increase, they will restore the heresiarchs (*eshab-i bid'at*). The ulema will be begging [for favor] before the sultans' doors.

In the descriptions of Constantinople, similar immorality is said to have led to absolute destruction; such a city can only be doomed to destruction:[29]

> When they had completed all these [constructions], they [the ancient infidels] deported by force many households from every province ... They made every people of that era suffer, making them settle [in Constantinople] by force; and because all these people cursed the city ... they caused its destruction, as it became burdened with all these laments. This is why this city is destined to be ruined. They prayed for this, and their tears will never dry on the earth where they fell.

The criticism of Mehmed II's resettlement policy is clear. Things become even more explicit and straightforward when the anonymous author compares the old edifices to the new ones and states that the former were larger and more impressive, because[30]

29 Yerasimos 1990, 13 (the Ottoman text in the Turkish translation, 19–20).

30 Yerasimos 1990, 34 (the Ottoman text in the Turkish translation, 35–36).

> [a]t that time, edifices were not built by force. Everybody took their salaries. Nowadays, in order to build an edifice they tax the towns and provinces, and, moreover, they uproot and bring masons and builders from their places ... At the time of Sultan Murad, the son of a slave of the ruler could not become a slave of the ruler himself, and timars were not granted to such slaves. Nowadays, fiefs of these people are multiplied, and they look upon strangers with a better eye [than upon natives].

As for Yazıcıoğlu, he does not speak of Istanbul openly, yet he clearly agrees with the anonymous author that a city or state dominated by immorality and oppression has a gloomy destiny. The twelfth chapter of his book (S92ff.) deals with places destroyed by the wrath of God, and here Yazıcıoğlu is more specific about the responsibility of the ruler as opposed to that of the ruled. When God destroyed the sinful kingdom of Yemen, the angel Cebrail objected that among the inhabitants there were also devoted people. God responded by saying that they did not practice *emr-i maruf*, i.e. the command to do what is right and lawful, since the pious ones did not turn the impious away from sin, either with counsel (*nasihat*), coercion (*örf*), or even their loathing (*ikrah*). Yazıcıoğlu continues by reiterating the accusations mentioned above, among them that "present-day ulema lost their capacity to speak and their sight due to their fear of [losing their] offices (*mansıb korkusundan*)". Later on, speaking of the mythical destruction of pre-Islamic Basra and Khwarezm because of their oppressive rulers, Yazıcıoğlu observes:

> This people (*filan halk*) met [God's] wrath because of His revenge against this oppressor (*ol zalimin öcünden*) ... because they did not command what was lawful nor did they deny the unlawful (*emr-i maruf, nehy-i münker etmedikleri ecilden*) ... What is given to the oppressed is taken from the oppressor (*mazlumun dadını zalimlerden alıverir*), in both this and the next world ... The prayers of the oppressed in favor of the oppressor are acceptable ... So many oppressed met with misfortune in order for a tyrant to be punished, because they did not command what was lawful and deny what was unlawful. Thus, the sins committed by this oppressor are blamed on everyone (*cümlesinin boynundadır*).

•••

Yazıcıoğlu thus introduces the precept of "commanding right and forbidding wrong" (*emr-i ma'ruf ve nehy-i münker*), which was to play a major role in Ottoman politics some centuries later.[31] This traditional Islamic obligation was generally conceived as the obligation of each Muslim individual to impose (by deed, word, or at least thought) Islamic morality whenever it seemed to be neglected. Ibn Taymiyya's views (which were later to dominate the relevant Ottoman thought) tended to identify state officials rather than mere commoners as the main actors of this precept, and Ottoman jurists such as Taşköprüzade (d. 1561) and İsma'il Hakki Bursevi (d. 1725) downplayed whatever elements of the theory (e.g. in al-Ghazali's work) might be considered as an injunction to rebel.[32] The precept usually remained a tool in the hands of "fundamentalist" movements with a view to (re)installing orthodox life, such as the Hanbalis of Baghdad in the first half of the tenth century[33] and, as we will see, the Kadızadelis of Istanbul throughout the seventeenth. At any rate, it served as a commonplace for describing a corrupt society, one in which nobody (and the ruler least of all) is concerned with sin, and thus it was a useful tool in efforts to criticize state policies.

It should be noted that the army is absent from all signs listed as preludes to the Apocalypse and is not viewed as the cause of past disasters. It is merchants and, in particular, the ulema who are primarily blamed for the immorality of the times; the janissaries also have their place in the stories about Constantinople, where we also see enmity toward "strangers". One clearly recognizes the reaction of the early *gazis* and their descendants to the new imperial order imposed by Mehmed II. We should not think of these writers as "simple folk", as opposed to the sophisticated ulema and court officials (some of these authors clearly belonged to the elite of the day);[34] however, in a period where the notables of the past were bitterly reacting to the emergence of new elites, there is little doubt which side such works were on. The implied ideology is that morality and honesty, strict observance of religious rules, and a dominant role for free warriors who sustained themselves by raids or timars and who should have a share in state power, are the primary precepts an ideal society should follow. One could make two points here. Firstly, this predominantly moral interpretation of politics was not a feature of anti-imperial opposition exclusively; as will be seen, the imperial ideology of the fifteenth and early sixteenth centuries, imported from the Persianate emirates of Anatolia, was also

31 See the comprehensive and detailed study by Cook 2000.

32 Cook 2000, 151ff. (Ibn Taymiyya) and 316ff. (Ottoman Hanafism; cf. 427ff. and esp. 446 on al-Ghazali).

33 See Cook 2000, 114ff.

34 Cf. Kastritsis 2016, 252–253.

dominated by moral precepts and promoted an ethical interpretation of politics. Secondly, it is interesting to note that these same ideas, and especially the use of the apocalyptic imagery, were to have a significant revival throughout the seventeenth century and beyond (see below, chapter 6), again mostly as an oppositional tool, a reaction to contemporaneous political changes.

2 The Introduction of Imperial Ideals

As noted above, it was not only tribal warriors who filled the ranks of the first Ottomans throughout the fourteenth century. After all, the new state was not born into a cultural vacuum; on the contrary, the Seljuk sultanate of Konya and the emirates which had emerged in its place after the Mongol invasions of the mid-thirteenth century were flourishing centres of Persianate culture, absorbing cultural and political influences from both Iran and the thriving Mamluk lands of Egypt and Syria. Timur's invasion and the upheavals that followed, far from stopping the movement of people and ideas between these regions, actually enlarged the space of cultural exchange by adding to it the Timurid Empire and various Central Asian cities. The ideas and currents prevailing in this vast cultural space have only recently begun to be explored as a whole, and while Timurid and Mamluk culture are much more well known than they were in the past (when the splendor of pre-Mongol Islamic civilization left little space for them), the reverberations in Anatolia still await systematic investigation.[35] On the one hand, the emergence of a Turkish vernacular was reflected in a growing number of translations and original works, literary as well as religious and scientific. On the other, the unprecedented growth of mystical movements in the Persianate areas of Iran, Central Asia, and India found extremely fertile ground in Anatolia, with its various socio-cultural milieus and influences.

Statesmen and ulema from the neighboring emirates, which (being closer, both geographically and culturally, to the old Seljuk sultanate) had a higher degree of urban culture and closer ties to the Persian political traditions, soon began to settle in or around the Ottoman court, exerting their influence on the ongoing process of transforming it from a tribal emirate to a kingdom and an empire-to-be. A surviving document from 1324 and Ibn Battuta's 1331 description indicate that Orhan's entourage included scholars competent in

35 On intellectual life in the Anatolian cities under the Seljuks and successor emirates, see Vryonis 1971, 351ff.; Ocak 2009, 376ff. and esp. 394ff., 406–421; and the studies collected very recently in Peacock – Yıldız 2016.

both Persian and Arabic.[36] The antagonistic nature of this influx can be seen in the frequent accusations leveled against the "corrupt ulema" in the texts representing the earlier military aristocracy, as was seen above. A number of such scholars, individuals who had been educated in thriving cities such as Kütahya, Amasya, or even Cairo, were, quite early, writing works of political advice, direct or indirect, in an effort to establish their own position in the newly-born Ottoman apparatus. One of the first was Ahmed bin Hüsameddin Amasi, whose work will be examined in the next chapter, since it begins a tradition of translating Nasir al-Din Tusi's systematic moral and political theory. Most of the rest, however, turned to the more practical *adab* or "mirror for princes" literature.

Identifying *adab* with "mirrors for princes" might be somewhat misleading. *Adab* is a vague term that refers more to a genre than to a specific tradition: it comprises all literary works describing proper behavior and etiquette while also providing entertainment. In a sense, *adab* is everything an educated and witty person should know, and at the same time so is every literary work containing such information. As such, *adab* can also be conceived in a narrower sense, containing everything a specific professional, such as a scribe or a courtier, should know; and in this sense, "mirrors for princes" are the *adab* of rulers and follow the same literary rules (such as entertainment value, the widespread use of maxims, stories, and anecdotes, and elegance of style). As also noted in the introduction, on the other hand, "mirrors for princes" is a conventional term, borrowed from the European literary tradition, to designate a tradition of advice with a moral basis that sought to give concrete counsel for what is now called governance.[37]

At the time scholars from the Anatolian emirates began to enter Ottoman intellectual life, production of "mirrors for princes" was thriving in Anatolia. If we are to describe their basic aspects, there were two main models which could be followed, either independently or combined together. One was the Persian imperial tradition, as seen in Nizam al-Mulk's *Siyâsatnâme* ("Book of government") from the end of the eleventh century: focusing on practical aspects of kingship, such works gave detailed advice on the choice of one's courtiers and advisors, the use of spies, the administration of the army, the collection of taxes, and so forth, with particular emphasis on the importance of justice. The other most important works were those of al-Ghazali, and especially his *Ihyâ*

36 Kafadar 1995, 139; Lindner 2009, 120; Tuşalp Atiyas 2013, 43ff.

37 The literature on Islamic "mirrors for princes" is vast: see, for instance, Lambton 1971; Leder 1999; Dakhlia 2002; Aigle 2007; Marlow 2009; Black 2011, 91ff. and 111ff.; Darling 2013b; Yavari 2014.

al-'ulûm ("The revival of knowledge"), composed in the early twelfth century and representing a more Islamic version of kingship. Al-Ghazali also stressed justice as the necessary princely virtue, but he also argued that even an oppressive ruler (provided he is supported by force, *shawka*) must be obeyed for the sake of avoiding civil strife. On the other hand, he emphasized the moral qualities required by the ruler and employed much stronger religious bases compared to Nizam al-Mulk's Sassanian inheritance. In both traditions, the prevailing assumption is that the ruler has no innate sacred quality: his rule is clearly distinct from the cosmic rulership associated with the caliphate or with the mystic dimensions of Suhrawardi's illuminationism; he is an imperfect man who has to strive continuously in order to attain perfection for the sake of his subjects. Justice is the ruler's duty to both God and his subjects, and if justice is maintained then rulership will be maintained, too. The following synopsis will show clearly that these kinds of Persian-style "mirrors for princes", with their emphasis on justice and compassion and their strong pious and moralistic overtones, remained popular in both Ottoman and Persian lands until the rise of the "universal" empires necessitated the introduction of more comprehensive systems for interpreting society and history.

2.1 *Ahmedi and Other Persianate Works*

Of all the scholars who moved from the neighboring emirates to the Ottoman court the most famous is undoubtedly Taceddin İbrahim b. Hızır Ahmedi (c. 1334/5–1412), primarily because of the use of his work in the endless debate on Paul Wittek's *gazi* thesis. A native of Anatolia, Ahmedi moved to Cairo to study and then entered the service of the beg of Germiyan, Süleyman Şah. At an unknown time he joined the Ottoman court and, after the battle of Ankara, served under Süleyman Çelebi (d. 1411). Among his various poetical and moral works, the most important and well-known is his *İskendernâme* ("Book of Alexander"), since it includes a world history, the last part of which is the *Tevârîh-i Mülûk-i âl-i 'Osmân* ("The history of the rulers of the House of Osman"). This kind of versified chronicle covers the period from Ertoğrul up to Süleyman Çelebi; the latter is termed a "martyr", which means the work was perhaps completed after his death. Although Ahmedi chose the losing side during the Ottoman *interregnum*, his work was widely copied during the fifteenth century, though it was also strongly criticized during the next century as regards its poetical merits.[38]

38 Ahmedi – Silay 2004, xiv. We use here Silay's edition; other transcriptions or facsimiles include Ahmedi – Atsız 1949 and Ahmedi – Ünver 1983. On Ahmedi's work see İnalcık 1962,

The importance of the final part of Ahmedi's work as one of the first Ottoman chronicles has overshadowed the rest of his text, which in fact constitutes a universal history and a re-reading of the Alexander myth; the lack of a transliteration or translation of the *İskendername* in its entirety contributes to this.[39] It has been suggested that Ahmedi's work is more a "mirror for princes" than a historical epic.[40] At any rate, his political views can be seen scattered throughout his work, especially in the eulogies of the various sultans; they are influenced by the Persian tradition insofar they stress the importance of the personal virtues of the sultan, and especially of justice. We may single out the emphasis placed on the importance of the ulema (in contrast to their demonization by the more *gazi*-oriented authors) as well as the almost total absence of criticism of Bayezid I (a *topos* of the opposition).[41] Ahmedi's stress on justice can be interpreted as an affirmation of the role of the sultan: he is the dispenser of justice and it is his personal charisma that maintains the power of the dynasty. Unlike the infidel rulers who are doomed to fall, as described, for instance, by Yazıcıoğlu, Ahmedi's world admits the possibility of infidel or cruel kingship; all the more so, his presentation of the Mongol khans and of Timur suggests that, when justice is absent, only the utmost cruelty may keep a dynasty in power, especially when it is presented in the form of law (as in the Mongol case).[42] It was Timur's oppressive and devastating policy that overpowered Bayezid's piety and justice, not the latter's greed or neglect. On the other hand, one should note Heath Lowry's suggestion that Ahmedi wished that the young prince Süleyman would avoid the mistakes of his father, and thus implied that Bayezid's mistake was to turn against the Muslim rulers of Anatolia. Lowry points out, for instance, that the Anatolian conquests of Murad I are systematically downplayed, while Ahmedi stresses the religious zeal of the first glorious rulers to show that their success was linked to their struggle against the infidel.[43]

159–162; Ménage 1962, 169–170; Fodor 1984 and 1986, 221; Silay 1992; Sawyer 1997; Kastritsis 2007, 34–37; Kastritsis 2016; Turna 2009; Toutant 2016.

39 See Sawyer 1997; Kastritsis 2016; Toutant 2016.

40 Fodor 1984. There are parts in the epic, concerning Alexander's education by Aristotle, which show Ahmedi's familiarity with the neo-Aristotelian theories of the soul current in late medieval Persian philosophy (see below, chapter 2): Toutant 2016, 13–14.

41 It has been suggested that Bayezid's reaction, in Ahmedi's text, following the Mamluk sultan's death (he thought that Egypt would now be his instead of reflecting on death) is, in a way, conceived as hubris that resulted in his defeat at the hands of Timur (Sawyer 1997, 92–93; Ahmedi – Silay 2004, 21 [v. 280–282]).

42 On early Ottoman attitudes to the Mongols cf. Tezcan 2013; see also below, chapter 3.

43 Lowry 2003, 15ff.; cf. Kastritsis 2007, 36–37 and 197.

But if Ahmedi's work contains only scattered pieces of what may be reconstituted as his worldview, he had contemporaries who tried to transfer wholesale the Iranian "mirrors of princes" tradition into Ottoman culture. For one thing, translations of such texts into Anatolian Turkish appear quite early: the most striking example is Kay Ka'us (Keykavus) b. İskender's *Qâbûsnâme*, a famous book of moral advice composed in Persian in western Iran in the late eleventh century.[44] *Qabusname* was first translated as early as the mid-fourteenth century, while other translations date from the late fourteenth and early fifteenth centuries:[45] no less than five translations had been made by 1432. It is interesting to note that the first translation, or rather adaptation, was made by a pious individual who did not always agree with the sometimes libertine ideas of the original. Whereas, for instance, Kay Ka'us's advice is to divide one's wealth into three equal parts for household expenses, savings, and adornments or other luxuries, the translator replaces the last category with charity (*ahiret yolına*); additionally, he is "somewhat more negative to merchants" than the original.[46] Other popular works of this kind include Najm al-Din Razi's (known as Dâya; d. 1256) thirteenth-century *Mirshâd al-'ibâd*, which was translated several times during the fifteenth century.[47] Both were also translated by Şeyhoğlu Mustafa, another Germiyan courtier who changed sides (even earlier than Ahmedi) and brought with him all his knowledge of the Persian political tradition, which had, it seems, started to appeal to Bayezid I.

Şeyhoğlu seems to have been born in 1340 in the Germiyan emirate; he must have been a high official in the Germiyan court before moving to the Ottoman emirate following the death of Germiyanoğlu Süleyman Şah in 1387. His works include Turkish translations of Persian ethical works (*Kabusnâme, Marzubannâme*) and original works (*Hurşid-nâme* [1389], *Kenzü'l-kübera*), all of which concerned moral and political advice. It is this latter work (*Kenzü'l-küberâ ve mehekkü'l-ulemâ*, "Treasure of the great and touchstone of the learned"), completed in 1401 for some unspecified "Paşa Ağa bin Hoca Paşa", that may arguably be viewed as the first political treatise originally composed in Ottoman Turkish *stricto sensu* (Amasi's work, with which we will deal later, was to

44 On Kay Ka'us' work see Rosenthal 1958, 78–81; Fouchécour 1986, 179ff.; Black 2011, 131–132.

45 Kay Kaus – Birnbaum 1981, 4–7; Yılmaz 2005, 34–35. On the dating of the first translation see Kay Kaus – Birnbaum 1981, 9–30. The manuscript published by Birnbaum can be dated to sometime in the 1370s or early 1380s, but as it is not an autograph the translation must have been made a decade or two earlier.

46 Kay Kaus – Birnbaum 1981, 31.

47 Razi – Algar 1982; Yılmaz 2005, 35ff.; Peacock 2016; on Razi cf. Lambton 1956a, 138–139; Lambton 1962, 110–115; Black 2011, 136–137.

follow by half a decade).[48] Of course, the term "originally composed" must be taken *cum grano salis*, since the work is essentially a partial translation of Razi's *Mirsâd al-'ibâd* (1230–1) with additions by the author; in fact, from Razi's mostly Sufi treatment of the soul and spirit Şeyhoğlu adapted only the fifth and final part, concerning "the wayfaring of different classes of men" (and he omitted its last chapters, i.e. those concerning merchants, farmers etc., concentrating thus on governmental apparatus and the ulema).[49] However, given its early date and the fact that such works dominated the intellectual milieu of the late fourteenth and early fifteenth century, it seems appropriate to give here a description of the structure of the work, a large part of which consists of poetry and hadiths. It has four chapters. The first (Y40–66) deals with "sultans, kings, and beys" (*padişahlar ve melikler ve begler*), and the second (Y66–105), more specifically, with the three "situations" or "states" (*halet*) of the sultan, namely his relationship with himself, with his subjects, and with God. The third chapter (Y106–122) promises to speak of "the viziers, the men of the pen, and the other deputies", but in fact speaks almost exclusively of the former, discussing again the vizier's respective three "situations", this time in relation to God, to his king, and to the people and the army. As with the sultan, the main idea is that one must display certain virtues in all three situations: in the case of viziers, these virtues are honesty (*toğrılık*), loftiness (*yücelik*), perseverance (*sebat*), and forbearance (*tahammül*). Finally, the fourth chapter (Y122–153) deals with the ulema, *müftis*, judges, and preachers.

Şeyhoğlu's work, formulaic and commonplace as it may seem, represents a tradition of political thought that must have prevailed in ulema circles throughout the fifteenth century. One can see many of his ideas reiterated in other works of advice even in the sixteenth century; on the other hand, his political vocabulary is interesting, since some of the standard terms of Islamic ethico-political terminology were translated into Ottoman Turkish for the first time. Before leaving the Germiyan court, Şeyhoğlu had translated into Turkish (through a Persian translation by Sa'd al-Din al-Varâvinî) another work of this

48 Şeyhoğlu – Yavuz 1991. Very few scholars have studied Seyhoğlu's work from the point of view of political thought: Unan 2004, 313–352; Yılmaz 2005, 36; Darling 2013b, 238. I was not able to check Varlık 1979.

49 Razi – Algar 1982, 394ff. Razi's work was also translated into Ottoman Turkish in 1421/2 by Mevlana Kasım b. Mahmud Karahisari as *Kitâbu irşâdi'l-mürîd ile'l-murâd min-tercümeti kitâbi Mirsâdi'l-ibâd*. It is interesting to note that one of the few instances where Şeyhoğlu departs from his model is a reference to trade and fixed prices: bad judges, he says, take bribes, administer the *vakf* revenues for their own profit and even engage in trade, taking advantage of their privilege to draw the officially fixed prices (Y147: *narh*; cf. the relevant part in Razi – Algar 1982, 458).

kind, Marzuban b. Rustam's *Marzuban-name* (late tenth century).[50] The lasting popularity of such texts is shown by the fact that Şeyhoğlu's translation was adapted more than a century later under the title *Düstûrü'l-mülk vezîrü'l-melik bera-yı Sultan Süleyman Han* ("Rules of sovereignty, i.e. the vizier of the king, for Sultan Süleyman"), by a certain Fadlullah, a judge in Tabriz.[51] The only available information about the author is found in the title of the work, where he is described as *Fadlullah el-kadî bi't-Tebriz fi'l-Madî,* i.e. Fadlullah, a judge in Tabriz. Since Tabriz was briefly taken by the Ottomans twice in this period, for less than ten days in 1514 and for a number of months in 1534–35,[52] it is likely that he was some kind of temporary judge in the second period. However, we cannot exclude the possibility he was a Safavid judge who deserted to the Ottomans. Less structured and clear-cut than Şeyhoğlu's *Kenzü'l-küberâ,* this work consists mainly of stories and anecdotes: in the introduction, Kadı Fadlullah claims that he wanted to compile stories, advice, and words of wisdom that would help in the maintenance of the country and in praising a sultan's dominion (*vilayet ... baki ve ömrü devlet öğüş olmağa*), from various history books, so that the sultan may benefit and act accordingly. If he does so, his name and rule will last forever (A138). And indeed, the rest of his essay, which consists of ten chapters, is a collection of stories (each containing several sub-stories), mostly involving ancient kings (such as Ardashir), mythical creatures (such as Div Gâv-pây, "the demon with cow legs", from the time when demons lived among men), and animals, which were mainly of Iranian origin, illustrating the various *topoi* of good rulership.

Finally, we could end this survey with Sinaneddîn or Sinan Yusuf Pasha (also known as Hoca Pasha), an interesting and important personality who played an significant role in Ottoman intellectual life toward the end of the fifteenth century. In the trend we are describing, Sinan Pasha is clearly a follower of the moralistic, rather commonplace "mirror for princes"-style Persian tradition. His inclusion of political advice into an ethical system brings him near Tusian thinkers (with whom we will deal in the next chapter); his peculiar position in the Mehmed II vs. Bayezid II "conflict" (as well as his Sufi connections) created a link with the military and dervish-based opposition to the former, as seen in Aşıkpaşazade or Yazıcıoğlu's works, but overall he seems closer to the imperial model than to the "military democracy" dreamt of by these

50 Kadı Fadlullah – Altay 2008, 108–110. The edition of Şeyhoğlu's translation by Zeynep Korkmaz (Şeyhoğlu – Korkmaz 1973) was not accessible to me.

51 Kadı Fadlullah – Altay 2008.

52 Mid-July to spring: Uzunçarşılı 1949, 2:338–340. The MS is dated in 23 Muharem 946 (June 10, 1539); however, the author states that it was composed during the vizierate of Lütfi Pasha, which started in Safer 946 (beg. in June 18; see Uzunçarşılı, op.cit., 537).

contemporaneous authors. Furthermore, his descent from two prominent early Ottoman ulema families (his father was the first judge of Istanbul) has him closer to this scholarly milieu than to the older warlords.

Probably born ca. 1440 in Bursa, Sinan Pasha was a teacher in various *medreses* in Edirne and later in Mehmed II's *sahn-i semaniye*, while he also held the post of the sultan's *hoca*. In 1470 he became the vizier and in 1476 grand vizier. Within a year he was dismissed and imprisoned, but after a collective protest by members of the ulema (who allegedly threatened to burn their books and leave the realm), Mehmed II released him and sent him as a judge and teacher to Sivrihisar, where he stayed until the sultan's death. Bayezid II restored him as vizier and as a teacher in Edirne, and he died in 1486. Sinan Pasha wrote a number of legal and mathematical treatises, a voluminous work on *tasavvuf* (*Tazarru'-nâme*), and a collection of saints' biographies. The work that interests us here, *Ma'ârifnâme* ("Book of knowledge", also known as *Nasîhatnâme*, "Book of advice"), was completed during Bayezid's reign, i.e. after 1481, and is infused with his bitterness and lamentations about fate and the transitory nature of all worldly things.[53] Written in a mixture of prose, verse, and rhyming prose, a form that was to be perfected in the late sixteenth century, the *Ma'ârif-nâme*—written for "the commoners" who read Turkish—is a voluminous compendium of moral advice, one of the first in a long series of Ottoman ethical works.

2.2 *The Main Themes of Early Ottoman "Mirrors for Princes" Texts*

It has already been noted that, for the Persian authors and their Anatolian imitators of the fourteenth and fifteenth centuries, kingship was not a sacred quality. Instead of the mystic or even cosmic overtones it was to acquire later, in the sixteenth century, the position of the sultan was viewed as one of continuous moral strife. Thus, Şeyhoğlu may declare that the sultan is God's shadow upon earth, as if God was a huge bird whose shadow offers power and might on whoever befalls, and that perfect kingship approaches prophecy and (ultimate) knowledge, but on the other hand he stresses that the ruler must be just and generous and avoid oppressive and illegal acts by guarding his soul from evil qualities and wishes, such as lust for material things, calumny, or fornication. Real kingship (*has padişahlık*) is subjugation of one's body and heart and control of one's desires; on the other hand, though a good many may exert this "real kingship" only a few can exert the "general" one (*am*), i.e. worldly

53 *İslam Ansiklopedisi*, s.v. "Sinan Paşa, Hoca" (H. Mazıoğlu); Yılmaz 2005, 38–40; Darling 2013c, 131. His *Ma'ârifnâme* has been published in facsimile (Sinan Paşa – Ertaylan 1961) and recently in transcription and modern Turkish translation (Sinan Paşa – Tulum 2013).

rule, since the latter is something approaching prophecy (Y67–69). The sultan has to remember that his power is only transitory and that he must not seek it for himself; real power belongs to God (Y82–105). Should a ruler neglect these guidelines, his power is doomed: when the religious people forget their obligation to "command right and forbid wrong", when hypocrites and corrupted and oppressive people are the king's companions, when they increase taxes and impose innovations, take fees from travelers and merchants (Y77), and in general use their position to amass wealth from both licit and illicit sources (*halaldan ve haramdan*), then the sultan is doomed, if not in this world then surely in the next. Similarly, in a chapter praising God's rulership (T698ff, E262ff), Sinan Pasha names the sultan "God's caliph", but only in order to stress that this means he has to follow God's orders and administer justice; justice and the good morals of a sultan will make his realm prosper and his life be prolonged. Only Kadı Fadlullah seems to imply that the current rulership was similar to prophecy or the caliphate since he claims that "at first, kingship was upon the prophets, then it passed over to caliphs, and then to sultans" (A142: *evvel saltanat peygamberlerdeydi; andan hulafa andan padişahlar üstine düşdi*).

This emphasis on the dependence of rulership upon the ruler's ethical perfection also had a practical side: the ruler needed to achieve moral perfection and justice for the sake of his subjects and as the only way to keep his realm under control. In this regard, one might find a parallel with Aşıkpaşazade's or Yazıcıoğlu's opposition, where an unjust ruler risked not only his own downfall but also a disastrous collapse of the whole society he governed because his injustice was reflected in his subjects' corruption, and vice versa. A simile with the human body, very common across the history of Ottoman political ideas, helps Şeyhoğlu express the idea of interdependency between the ruler and his subjects: he is like the heart in the body, so if he is upright then the people will be upright, too. All the rest of his subjects are, in degrees (*tefafütince*), like the veins, sinews, bones, muscles, and hairs. Thus, as, in the human body, the limbs need the heart and vice versa, so are subjects, officers, and rulers interconnected and dependent on each other (Y92–93). Sinan Pasha expresses the same idea when he says that the king must treat his subjects with justice, neither punishing the innocent nor forgiving the guilty; his personal behavior reflects on the state of the realm. That is why the ancient kings of Greece and of Persia, whenever a powerful enemy or internal disorder seemed to be prevailing, first mended their own ways and abandoned entertainment (T692). Sultans should obey God's orders so that everybody will obey theirs (T720ff, E269ff).

Justice, then, is the key virtue that holds a realm together. For Ahmedi, Bayezid I established justice and equity in the country (*adl ü dad*) and, "since the people received that justice from him, whether big or small (*ulu kiçi ise*), they became industrious", and every piece of land became a sown field, a garden, or an orchard (v. 267–70). As for Sinan Pasha, he stresses that the sultan is urged to practise justice, as oppression is sure to lead to the destruction of his realm and of himself (T664, E250ff), while there is no stronger army for a king than justice. A just sultan respects the Holy Law and the ulema, protects the wealth of his subjects, ensures that cities and provinces are safe from thieves and robbers, is soft and merciful when necessary and severe when he has to be, abstains from excessive sexual pleasure (*kesret-i cima'*, T670) and the company of women, as well as from games and carousing (T672); he may have the occasional laugh, but only in moderation.

It is not clear what exactly these authors mean by "justice". There is the literal "judicial" meaning of dispensing justice with clemency and equity: Bayezid I in Ahmedi "knew that the judges were dispensers of injustice. Their deeds were bribery and corruption of the Holy Law". He assembled all of them and punished them as necessary (v. 273–78). Clemency is a necessary component of justice, and Şeyhoğlu argues that even proven culprits should be forgiven, for this is the virtue of mildness (*hilm*, Y54); a ruler should first try to mend the evildoers' ways by advice and persuasion rather than through the sword of the executioner (Y89). Sinan Pasha insists that if the ruler wants to use overwhelming force (*kahr*), i.e. the opposite of mildness, he should use it against his enemies as well as against hypocrites and "men of innovation". Moreover, a king should abstain as far as possible from ordering executions, as taking a person's life is, in general, God's prerogative (T706ff, E265ff); if he has to execute someone, he must be patient and avoid doing so while influenced by anger.

Furthermore, one might remark that, for our authors, another aspect of justice is equality, the primordiality of merit rather than of lineage or wealth. According to Ahmedi, Murad I did not hesitate to give high posts to destitute people, because "a padishah needs a vision such that dust and gold look the same in his presence". Repeating a *topos* of medieval poetry, Ahmedi notes here that even a mendicant can become king, if the Bird of Paradise happens to come over him (v. 136ff.). Sinan Pasha criticizes those who regard lineage (*neseb*) as more important than personal merit (*haseb*), noting that even the prophet Noah's children were rebels (T492ff, E189ff). One cannot help thinking that this attitude, albeit based on commonplace assumptions of medieval literature, corresponds to the emerging practice of *devşirme* recruitment (later described in the same light of meritocracy by several European authors, such as Busbecq);[54] on the other hand, both the ulema and court environment of the early Ottoman state offered plenty of opportunities for newcomers

54 Busbecq – Forster 1927, e.g. 59–61; Yapp 1992, 148–149.

from the Anatolian emirates or from even further away, regardless of their actual status.

Primarily, however, justice means the protection of the subjects, and especially the peasants, from oppression. In Şeyhoğlu's vision, the king must protect the weak and show the powerful their proper place (*hadd*). The subjects are to the sultan like relatives (*karabet yirinde*), and he must care for them as if they were his own household (*ehl-ü-iyal*). "Every good measure that was imposed in the process (*her sonradan konmış eylük*) to appease the burden of the subjects" will be counted in favor of the sultan, so he must follow the laws (*ol kanunca gide*) and avoid innovations, with the exception of good ones (*bid'at-i hasene*). If, on the contrary, he puts forth hard laws (*yavuz kanun*) and oppresses his subjects and the army, this will be counted against him in the Hereafter, even if he merely continues previous practices (Y71–73). The sultan must not forget that he is the shepherd of his subjects and that he must, therefore, protect them against the wolves, i.e. "tyrants and infidels"; as such, he must conduct the Holy War and be merciless against oppressive and dishonest officials and robbers (including *ahiler ve rindler*,[55] Y75). Justice is connected with abiding by the rules and laws by Ahmedi, too. He notes that kings before the Ottomans were infidels or showed cruelty; Mongol rulers, on the other hand, oppressed people with the law (*zulm itdiler veli kanunıla*), without painting their hands with blood, and "lawful oppression and confiscation are amenable to the people as a form of justice" (v. 7–8: *zulm kim kanun u zabtıla ola / adl gibi halka ol asan gele*). As with everything good, the Ottomans came in the end, just as God bestowed man with power, life, and intelligence (*kudret ü 'akl u hayat*), with the latter coming last as the most important of the three (v. 17–18). In another interesting passage, we read that, contrary to Bayezid I's piety and justice, Timur necessarily exhibited cruelty and tyranny since he lacked any justice at all (v. 295: *hiç adlı yoğıdı, lâcirem kim zulm ü cevri çoğıdı*).

Thus, in both Ahmedi's and Şeyhoğlu's mind justice is more than the sultan protecting the peasants like a benevolent father: there are rules that should ensure this protection, and these rules should be constituted as laws. In turn, these laws must be followed strictly, without alteration, and change (or, as the wording goes, innovation) is to be avoided, as it necessarily implies a weak power that suspends part of its protecting privileges in favor of the oppressing usurpers. A more nuanced view can be found in the writings of Sinan Pasha, who had been a vizier himself. He remarks that each place has its customary laws, and these should be respected (T684: *her memlekette bir 'örf olur ki onun*

55 On the *ahis*, a kind of urban artisanal fraternity attested in Anatolian cities in the thirteenth century, see e.g. Vryonis 1971, 396–402; Yıldırım 2013.

nizamı onunla olur ... ve her vilayette bir kanun olur ki mesalihi onunla düzülür). On the other hand, he also argues that a just ruler will abolish some of the "established innovations" (i.e. bad laws: *bida'-ı mu'tebere*) upon his accession to the throne.

As well as justice and clemency, a virtue that all these texts highlight (as did the "opposition" authors such as Aşıkpaşazade) is generosity. In Ahmedi's eulogies of the first sultans, generosity is praised as much as justice, culminating in his praise of Emir Süleyman [Çelebi] (v. 298ff.):

> Despite having troops and wealth, treasure and capability, still he does not fancy seizing domains (*likin itmez mülk almağa heves*) ... Necessarily, he should attain prosperity and glory. The kingdom and the sultan have an aspect of generosity. The one who gives his money to something will be like them (*nesneye nakdin viren eyle olur*). The one who does a job carelessly will go astray.

Ahmedi's urge against "fancying seizing domains" is interesting; Kadı Fadlullah also advises that a ruler should not covet the territories of other kings (A190); he must know the limits of his army's power, as well as that of his enemy. Sinan Pasha, too, emphasizes that the sultan should stay within the limits of religion, even risking a loss of wealth (T676: *hükm-i şer'den çıkmaya eğerçi bir mal-ı azime sebeb olursa*), just as he should not conquer castles by breaking a treaty or by breaking his word in any other way.

Just as Aşıkpaşazade and Yazıcıoğlu favoured a sultan who was generous to his army, so do these Persianate authors understand generosity as magnificence towards the ulema and the dervishes. A share in the treasury must be allocated to them, says Şeyhoğlu (Y70), whereas Kadı Fadlullah stresses the importance of thought and knowledge, which leads to the need for the pious (*dindar*) and the "friends of God" (A159: *Tanrı dostları*) to be respected and cared for. In the same vein, Sinan Pasha devotes a chapter to praising the sultans' generosity (*seha*: T686ff, E257ff). This is of two kinds: the lowest kind consists of not feasting on their subjects' wealth, the highest is being generous in one's own bestowals—provided, of course, that the royal wealth has not been acquired unjustly. A sultan, therefore, must respect the ulema and dervishes and be generous and humble; he must have four virtues, namely generosity, justice, honesty, and being firm in his decisions and awe-inspiring for his viziers. While Sinan Pasha does specifically refer to the army and the need to care for poor and valiant soldiers and their families, especially when they have been wounded or killed (T724ff, E271ff), his general attitude vis-à-vis the army can be seen as the precursor of later caution against giving the soldiers too much power: in order to avoid a rebellion against the sultan, the army should be kept from being unified, and one corps must be turned against another (T728: *bir bölüğünün şenaati bir bölük ile def' oluna*). Every group has its bad habits, and the bad habits of the army consist of their tendency to be disobedient. Here, Sinan Pasha enumerates the habits that lead each group to disaster: for soldiers, disobedience; for officers, immorality; for governors, powerless administration; for ulema, the desire to dominate; for judges, greed and favor toward the mighty (*meyl-i vülat*); and for rulers, the failure to protect (*za'f-ı humat*). At any rate, the authors within this group are much more favorably disposed towards the ulema, in contrast to the exponents of the *gazi* milieu we saw earlier. On the other hand, both groups share a common emphasis on justice and generosity, albeit with different content, as well as care for the moral welfare of both the ruler and the community of believers through the precept of "commanding right and forbidding wrong" (e.g. Şeyhoğlu, Y49).

The emphasis placed on a strong sultan can be seen in what these authors have to say about the delegation of power. Şeyhoğlu argues that the sultan must have power concentrated in his own hands and not give it to others (Y45), although, in order to keep himself informed of the affairs of the realm, he also needs a faithful, clever, and just vizier. A vizier, says Şeyhoğlu, is to the sultan as reason is to the heart (Y88); he should consult with him in all affairs, great and small, and learn every complaint and petition of his subjects, officers, and soldiers. He must take care to appoint honest and pious people to high offices and check their behavior, as his officers are like the senses of the body. The sultan must appoint a superintendent to look after pious foundations (Y100: *evkaf üzerine bir sahib-nazar*) and a pious and experienced chamberlain (*hacib*) to forward the petitions and complaints of the needy and the oppressed to him (a very Persian concept that seems to disappear later); in the same vein, he should appoint: a pious and courageous *bey* over the army, if his realm is next to an infidel realm (Y102); just governors (*şahne veya bir hakim*) over the provinces and towns; and wise, just, pious, and honest judges, who would not bear grudges, take bribes (which, Şeyhoğlu complains, happens very often in his times: Y104), or covet the properties of the *vakıf*s and orphans. If kingship is a tent, says Şeyhoğlu, the vizier is its pillar, officers (*begler ve sübaşılar*) are its ropes, and its piles are the sultan's justice. This means that the greater the number of viziers and officers, and the size of the army, the better. The vizier must have four virtues, namely honesty (*toğrılık*), loftiness (*yücelik*), perseverance (*sebat*), and forbearance (*tahammül*). Like the sultan, a vizier also has three "situations", in relation to God, to the ruler, and to the people and army, and in all these situations he must display these four virtues. As for Kadı Fadlullah, in his chapter on justice (A173–182) he emphasizes that the ruler should entrust his subjects to just and compassionate administrators, whom he, too, must honor. Sinan Pasha, with his more pessimistic view, describes careers in the sultan's service as full of anguish and strife (T496ff, E190ff), since viziers are almost doomed to practice oppression; the same happens with governors, who will have great difficulty in avoiding tyranny and arrogance and in observing their subjects' rights as they wish them to be observed (T504: *kendi hakkına muti' gerek ki kendi dahi muta' ola*). In Sinan Pasha's opinion, the sultan must not confer his power on officers, since, if they are unjust, his own justice is of no avail (T678), while he must choose them with care and ask them continually about the state of his realm. His governors should be competent and experienced, and he should ensure that the notables of his realm are trustworthy (T680: *zuaması sikat u ümena olalar*). However, as soon as he appoints such a governor, he should not interfere or dismiss him in the first instance as a governor must have time to learn the state of his province and acquire experience.

• • •

These ideas set the foundations underpinning most of Ottoman political thought until at least the mid-seventeenth century. The pre-eminence of justice is perhaps the most important of them. True, the concept of justice as a political virtue has a long history. Robert Dankoff summarized three major relevant strands in ancient political thought: in ancient Persia, the king was conceived as the embodiment of both justice and fortune; in ancient Greece, justice is social harmony, while the king is subject to fortune; and in the major religions of Europe and the Middle East (Judaism, Christianity, Islam), the ruler is subject to God's will (which replaces fortune) and his justice depends on his submitting to God's will.[56] Fortune or divine charisma also seems to have had a particular position in the Turkic political tradition of Inner Asia.[57] In early Islamic political thought, justice was not a central notion; as such, it belongs more to the Persian tradition—or, as Linda T. Darling has recently showed, to the Middle Eastern one from the ancient Mesopotamian civilizations.[58] According to Halil İnalcık, the Turkic tradition modified the Persian concept of justice, which was originally conceived of as a favor granted by the sultan. In texts such as *Kutadgu Bilig*, he argued, justice refers to keeping the law (*törü, yasa*);[59] one may notice this connection with legal rules in the

56 Yusuf Khass Hajib – Dankoff 1983, 6–7.
57 See Bombaci 1965–1966.
58 Darling 2013c; cf. Lambton 1962.
59 İnalcık 1967, 269; cf. İnalcık 1969a, 107–108; Mustafayev 2013.

works of fifteenth-century authors, as seen above, and it would acquire a much more important place in subsequent centuries.

Justice is combined with a whole array of other virtues, the most prominent of which are generosity and clemency. This reflection of the neo-Aristotelian theory of the soul had been fully elaborated previously by another newcomer from Amasya, Ahmed bin Hüsameddin Amasi, at the beginning of the fifteenth century, but it was to become most widely seen in the works of Bayezid II's eulogists at the turn of the sixteenth century and with Kınalızade Ali Çelebi in the middle of that century, as will be seen in the next chapter. At any rate, the central idea underpinning all fifteenth-century authors is that the ruler has a moral duty to strive for perfection; it is ethics, rather than power, mystic charisma, or (yet) obedience to rules, that was said to secure a ruler and the welfare of his state and subject. Eulogies of the Ottoman dynasty during this period still emphasized the justice and piety of its rulers, rather than divine favor. Let us take Ahmedi, for instance: Orhan was equitable and a dispenser of justice (*munsıfıdı Orhan u dadger*), his justice (*adl*) being so excellent that the justice of Caliph Ömer (Umar) was forgotten; he established mosques and public kitchens; he was a true believer and loved people of knowledge (v. 68ff.). His son Süleyman Pasha had all the qualities of leadership (*şart-ı serverlik*): courage (*şeca'at*), generosity (*sehavet*), administrative and ruling abilities (*hem siyaset hem riyaset ehlidi*), good judgment, and military ability (v. 94ff.). On the other hand, Ahmedi's and Şeyhoğlu's emphasis on laws cannot be ignored, especially as it is an element almost totally absent in previous literature and one which was to take a central place in the writings of later authors. It is important to remark here that a loathing of innovation, at least in principle, was something that these authors shared with the *gazi* opposition (as seen in the works of Aşıkpaşazade and Yazıcıoğlu). Innovation and the long-lasting debate around it would acquire a central place in Ottoman public discourse from the mid-sixteenth century onwards.

A slightly different tone dominates Sinan Pasha's work, permeated as it is with his bitterness over Mehmed II's behavior against him and with his mystic vision. For one thing, whereas Ahmedi's and Şeyhoğlu's works are structured around the personality of the sultan and his obligations vis-à-vis God and his subjects, Sinan Pasha seems to envisage a larger image of society, itself part of the cosmos. In his work there is a place for individual and social morality, the role of the "vain sciences" (T134ff: *ulumi'l-gayri'n-nafia*, a chapter actually stressing the importance of the Sharia and simple, pure faith as opposed to excessive philosophical explanation; cf. also T322ff), and glimpses of the Hereafter, the "friends of God" (T754ff), and especially the concealed ones (T770ff), pointing to the Sufi doctrine of the "pole" (*kutb*). If there is a general idea running through Sinan Pasha's work, it is the transitory and deceptive nature of this world; a *leitmotif* obviously linked to both his Sufi affiliation and his bitter experience as a result of Mehmed II's whims.[60] His integrated vision of things social and political is best seen in his chapter on those trying to secure the world order (T368ff, E142ff). Order and arrangement in the world (*cihanın nizamı ... ve alem intizamı*) is to be found when people respect and protect each other. Human beings are made to help and depend on each other; thus, everyone should try to benefit from the world order, serving either its esoteric or its worldly side. Certainly, one cannot equate the sultan with his servants, but everybody can be useful provided that their intentions are pure; even those choosing isolation save the world through their prayers (the chapter ends with a reference to the Sufi poles of the world).

It will be seen in the next chapter that Sinan Pasha's work stands somewhere between the more "naïve" and moralistic "mirror for princes" tradition, on the one hand, and the systematic exposion of a moral system based on a theory of the human soul, on the other. He cannot be termed a founder of this second trend, as there had been exponents before him (Amasi) and contemporary with him (Tursun Beg). Yet he stands at a point of transition, just as his era was an era of transition toward the claims for universal dominion put forth by Selim I and his successor, Süleyman the Magnificent.

3 Shifting Means of Legitimization

Simplistic as it may well be, the distinction made between the older generation of frontier warriors and the scholars who came from the neighboring emirates seems to follow the Ottoman history of ideas well into the fifteenth century. The images of the Ottoman dynasty created by these two traditions can be discerned in the different means of legitimization offered by the various authors of the period.[61] Earlier chronicles, such as Aşıkpaşazâde's and the various anonymous texts that express the culture of the early raiders, emphasize the religious spirit of the first *gazis*, even though they tend to ignore the inclusion of Christian warriors and notables in their ranks. Such texts are full of the legendary feats of saints and dervishes, stressing their high status in the

60 In a remark clearly addressed against Mehmed, he stresses the transitory nature of the world as follows: "every village that you considered yours, is now either a private property or a *vakf*" (T530: *her köy ki benim diye gezersin, geh mülk ü geh vakıf olup durur*).

61 All of what follows is based on the analytical study by Imber 1987; cf. also Imber 1995, 139–146.

entourage of the first sultans;[62] Oruç and other late fifteenth-century historians, more learned in Islamic traditions, even link Osman's genealogy with Ebu Muslim, the Abbasid champion and hero of an epic set in Horasan. But as the Ottoman dynasty became more and more settled and institutionalized, part of which involved developing a more regular army that replaced the now obsolete free warlords and raiders, the meaning of *gaza* was increasingly taken to refer to the proper Islamic meaning of Holy War instead of just looting and plundering, which seems to have been its understanding during the early Ottoman period. Ahmedi's emphasis on the *gazi* as an enemy of infidelity (an emphasis much discussed in the context of the Wittek thesis debate) falls into this reformulation of sultanly legitimacy: in later texts as well, the sultan increasingly becomes the champion of orthodox faith. The emphasis is on his personal charisma rather than on individual warriors and dervishes, and of course on the importance of faith rather than the loot acquired in the *gaza* raids. The sultans' prayers before important battles, and especially Murad I's prayer before the first battle of Kosovo, as recounted by Neşrî, nicely illustrate this point:[63]

> O God, possessions and slaves are yours; you give them to whom you will, and I am an insignificant, incapable slave of yours ... You know that my intention is not to gain property and riches. I did not come here for male or female slaves. I only genuinely and sincerely desire your approval.

Stories of dreams, where a saint or the Prophet himself invests the leader of the dynasty with divine grace, can also be placed in this tradition. On the other hand, emphasis on the personal charisma (*devlet*) of the sultan was very widely used during the civil strife that followed the battle of Ankara.[64]

Apart from religious justifications, however, there had to be a dynastic one as well. Different accounts of how the Seljuk sultan Alâ'eddin had granted the region of Söğüt to Osman's father, Ertoğrul, were systematized by Neşri, who polished away discrepancies of time and even put forward the suggestion that the Seljuk ruler had somehow bestowed his inheritance on Osman. Again Aşıkpaşazade's *gazi*-oriented version has Osman defying Ala'eddin and proclaiming himself independent, but Neşri's "legalist" version prevailed in the long run to the point that Feridun Bey's celebrated collection of chancery documents, issued in 1575, contains the alleged patents sent by Ala'eddin to

62 See e.g. Vryonis 1971, 392–396; Ocak 1993a; Ocak 1993b.

63 Neşri – Unat – Köymen 1987, I:287; Flemming 1994, esp. 66–67.

64 Kastritsis 2007, 206–207. On this notion cf. Sigalas 2007; Sariyannis 2013, 87–92.

Osman.[65] In the same vein, mythical genealogies celebrating the origin of Osman were created, beginning with Yazıcıoğlu Ali's (not to be confused with Yazıcıoğlu Ahmed Bican) adoption of Ibn Bibi's history of the Seljuks c. 1425.[66] These genealogies, in various forms, traced Ertoğrul's ancestors back to Oğuz (and thence back to Noah); again, the version favored by Neşri became definitive, as it provided both a grandfather with a king's name (Süleymanşah) for Osman and a lineage coming from the senior branch of the Oğuz family:[67]

> The experts in the knowledge of the foundations of the prophets and those who know the secrets of the meanings of the [human] works narrate that this great lineage [of the house of Osman] comes from Oğuz son of Kara Han, who was one of the children of Bulcas, son of Yafes, son of Noah, peace be upon him! As follows: Ertuğrul son of Süleyman Şah son of Kaya Alp son of Kızıl Buğa … son of Bulcas son of Yafes son of Noah.

Moreover, in Bayati's version, composed for Bayezid II's brother Cem in 1481, several ancestors (including Oğuz) are linked to prominent prophets of Islamic theology, thus combining legitimacy by descent and by Islam; indeed, it was this emphasis on true and orthodox Islam that would prevail as a tool of legitimization from the sixteenth century onwards:[68]

> Oğuz Han: He was given this name, which means "saint", in his childhood because he was seen as being on the right path [i.e. God's]. Because he recognized the Oneness of God he fought with his father, and Oğuz's army killed the latter. This happened during Prophet Abraham's times …
>
> Bozdoğan: He believed in the prophet David—peace be upon him—and belonged to the community of believers.
>
> Korkulu: He served under the prophet Solomon …
>
> Kara Han: When he became ruler, he believed in Islam and sent Korkut Dede to Medina, where he was enlightened by the light of Prophet

65 Imber 1987, 15; on Aşıkpaşazade's version cf. İnalcık 1994b, 152; on Feridun cf. Vatin 2010; Kastritsis 2013 and see below, chapter 3.

66 On the importance of genealogical trees for political legitimacy and the science of genealogy before the Ottomans, see Binbaş 2011.

67 Neşri – Unat – Köymen 1987, I:55–57.

68 Bayatlı – Kırzıoğlu 1949, 380–394 (he cites all Osman's ancestors, beginning not from Noah but from Adam); cf. Imber 1987, 19–20; Mustafayev 2013. A detailed discussion of these genealogies was made by Wittek 1925. On the afterlife of imperial genealogies in the sixteenth century see Flemming 1988.

> Muhammad's face—peace be upon him—and [returned to] teach the laws of Islam to the tribe of Oğuz …

On the other hand, different groups invented different stories; two texts of *kapıkulu* (janissary) origin, namely the *Historia Turchesca* and Constantine Mihailović's memories, preserve a tradition presenting either Osman or his father as peasants. Colin Imber notes insightfully that "it is conceivable that [this tradition] arose from the direct experience of the *devşirme* men who served in the *kapıkulu* corps".[69]

69 Imber 1994, 128, 136. The same tradition is also preserved in the chronicle of Oruç. On the presence of such legitimizing legends in Byzantine and post-Byzantine Greek chronicles see Moustakas 2011 and especially 2012.

CHAPTER 2

"Political Philosophy" and the Moralist Tradition

It may be argued whether certain elements of the "imperial vision" were present in the Ottoman state and ideology before the mid-fifteenth century; undoubtedly, however, it was during the reign of Mehmed II that the Ottomans became a fully-fledged empire with claims to universal dominion of some kind. As Dimitris Kastritsis notes, "Bayezid [I] … had anticipated in many ways Mehmed the Conqueror's centralizing imperial vision"[1] (and this explains why, as noted above, critics of the latter also dismissed the policy of the former). Yet the battle of Ankara was a major setback, and in the first years of the *interregnum* a vision of the prevailing prince as *primus inter pares* seems to have gained traction once more.[2] It took years for the Ottomans to recover militarily and politically, as well as ideologically, from this period of introverted self-reevaluation. Moreover, their conquest of Constantinople, an ancient Islamic dream foretold in the Quran and laden with apocalyptic and eschatological overtones, permitted the Ottomans to pursue an imperial policy aimed at creating a world empire.

The conquest of Constantinople in 1453 was only the first in a series of victories:[3] by 1458, Serbia (with its silver mines) was subjugated (partly due to the efforts of the grand vizier Mahmud Pasha Angelović, himself of Serbian origin), as were the Genoese colonies in western Anatolia and the north-eastern Aegean. What remained of the Byzantine Empire, namely the Peloponnese and the Black Sea coast, followed a few years later (with some setbacks at the beginning of the next decade). Mehmed's next targets were Wallachia, Bosnia, and Albania, where he gained considerable success (though not without some difficulties), while at the same time he consolidated his dominance over the Venetians in central Greece (notably with the conquest of Euboea in 1470). Moreover, the Ottomans had to cope with the Akkoyunlus in their eastern borders, under their ambitious ruler Uzun Hasan (an ally of the Venetians): the early years of the 1470s were dominated by the struggle for suzerainty over Karaman, i.e. central Anatolia, which ended in total Ottoman victory. The second half of the decade saw Mehmed establish his hold over the

1 Kastritsis 2007, 202 and 211ff.; see also Emecen 2014.

2 See Kastritsis 2007, 207–211.

3 For a concise chronology of Mehmed's, Bayezid's, and Selim's reign, see Emecen 2001b, 20–31; Imber 2009, 25ff.; for a more detailed exposition, see Mantran 1989, 81–116 and 139–145.

© KONINKLIJKE BRILL NV, LEIDEN, 2019 DOI:10.1163/9789004385245_004 western and northern coasts of the Black Sea, as well as over the Ionian and Adriatic coasts. Mehmed died in 1481, just after his vizier Gedik Ahmed Pasha had seized Otranto, leading to fears in Europe of a campaign against Rome.

Mehmed's confrontation with the Genoese and the Venetians, on the one hand, and his unabashed expansion over the Muslim states of eastern Anatolia, on the other, show his desire to create an empire with claims to universality. This imperial project, which had begun with the immediate transfer of the capital to newly-conquered Istanbul, was enhanced by his internal centralizing policies. Mehmed II's reforms concerning the land and revenue were referred to in the previous chapter;[4] in the administrative field he also abolished (or tried to abolish) the hereditary right of the old families to the vizierial posts (beginning with Çandarlı Halil's execution during the siege of Constantinople) and started using converts (such as members of the Byzantine imperial family)[5] and *devşirme* recruits (such as Mahmud Pasha) in these offices. His son Bayezid II's sultanate (1481–1512) seemed, at least in the beginning, to constitute a complete reversal of these policies: one of the new sultan's first acts was to reverse Mehmed's confiscation of private and *vakıf* revenues (an act which, as noted in the previous chapter, was hailed as a sign of generosity by the champions of the old warlord and dervish aristocracy). His sympathies with the dervish orders (all too happy to have their properties restored) earned him the surname Veli ("the saint"); upon his ascension to the throne, he brought to Istanbul a sheikh of the Halveti order with whom he had been on good terms during his governorship in Amasya; thus, he initiated the presence of this fraternity (which was to became one of utmost importance throughout the next centuries) in the Ottoman capital.[6]

As far as external policy was concerned, Bayezid was a markedly more peaceful sultan than his predecessor: part of this commitment to friendly relations with the West was due to the constant threat posed by his brother Cem, held as a hostage on Rhodes, Rome, and later in France, until Cem's death in 1495. To secure peace, Bayezid paid an annual tribute to Rome to ensure for his brother was held safe and quiet, while he also abandoned Otranto and concluded several truces with European states. However, Bayezid also waged

4 Oktay Özel (1999, 243) argues that the reform was small in extent and short-lived, and notes that "the claim that similar fiscal reforms were carried out to a lesser degree under Selim I and Suleiman the Magnificent ... should also be approached with caution"; however, one cannot ignore the fact that the huge territories conquered under these sultans, and especially Süleyman's Balkan conquests, were distributed as *miri* land to timariots, thereby diminishing the relative power of the warlords and dervishes reinstituted in their rights by Bayezid II.

5 Cf. İnalcık 1994a, 209–212; Lowry 2003, 115–130.

6 Clayer 1994, 18–19, 65–66, 154; Curry 2010, 68–72; cf. Terzioğlu 2012, 92–94; Karataş 2014.

campaigns, both in the west (annexing Hercegovina and parts of Moldavia by 1485) and the east (confronting the Mamluks, with little success, in south-eastern Anatolia); after Cem's death he felt more able to raid Hungary, Poland, and Venetian territories in the Adriatic. Peace with Venice and Hungary in 1503 permitted the Ottomans to concentrate on their eastern borders: by then, the Akkoyunlus had been replaced by a much more dangerous enemy, the Safavid dynasty of Iran under Shah Ismail, who claimed the allegiance of Shi'a sympathizers among the Turcoman tribes of Anatolia. Bayezid followed a rather timid policy against Ismail; however, Shah Kulu's rebellion in 1511 discredited both the sultan's power and his sons Korkud and Ahmed's ineffective administration. The following year, Bayezid's third son, Selim, headed an army rebellion and forced his father to abdicate in his favor.

One must not consider Bayezid's reign a period of stagnation and regression, as his external policy might imply. As well as the measures he took towards tighter control of the army, Bayezid (rather than Mehmed, as is often thought) initiated the codification of Ottoman laws in the *kanunname*s, the "books of law" describing the landholding, taxation, penal system, and administrative hierarchy of the empire. In this respect, his period may be seen as having laid the foundations for the spectacular military and administrative successes of his early sixteenth-century successors. It was upon these foundations that Selim I "the Grim" (1512–20) won his crushing victories over the Safavids, expelling them from most of eastern Anatolia. Selim gained the loyalty of the Kurdish chieftains of the region and also took tough measures against the Kızılbaş tribes who were prone to follow Shah Ismail's messianic claims.[7] Partly to avoid an alliance between the Safavids and the Mamluks of Egypt, Selim also campaigned against the latter with outstanding success. After the battle of Marj Dabik in 1516 the Ottomans annexed Syria and Palestine, and one year later conquered Egypt. Apart from formidably expanding the Ottoman Empire to almost double its territory, Selim's triumph over the Mamluks also made him the master of the three most holy cities of Islam, namely Jerusalem, Mecca, and Medina, thus enhancing even more the ecumenical scope of the imperial project. In the intellectual sphere, the conquest of Syria and Egypt further enhanced the continuum of scholarship between the Arab world and the Ottomans; on the other hand, the emergence of the Safavid state seems to have served as a barrier in communication with Central

7 It is reported that, in 1514, Selim ordered all Kızılbaş from seven to 70 years old to be registered and that accordingly up to 40,000 men were either slain or imprisoned. However, the massacre is not recorded in any contemporary source and the number may be highly exaggerated: see Emecen 2010, 95–100.

Asia and the Persian lands, although it also produced a new influx of Sunni scholars into Anatolia from Iran.

It is probably no coincidence that the rise of the Ottomans as a universal empire called for an ideology more elaborate than the "mirrors for princes" or *adab*-style eulogy of justice and piety (although translations or adaptations of works by Najm al-Din Razi and al-Ghazali by no means ceased during the sixteenth century[8] and despite a philosophical background on human psychology being evident in fifteenth-century *adab*-styled works, too[9]). An imperial project framing Constantinople, the promised land of Islam, and the holy cities of the Prophet, needed something more: a comprehensive theory that would encompass all of human society, raising the moral virtues demanded of a ruler to a universal system explaining both the individual and society at large. The Ottomans did not have to invent such a system: they had only to revert to an existing Persian tradition, drawn in turn from the Aristotelian concept of man, society, and state.[10] This was mainly provided by the thirteenth-century work by Nasir al-Din Tusi (*Akhlâq-e Nâsirî*, or "Nasirean ethics") and, later, his late fifteenth-century continuator Jalal al-Din Davvani (*Akhlâq-e Jalâlî*, or "Jalalean ethics"); both used al-Farabi's tenth-century synthesis of Aristotelian and neo-Platonic ethics and politics (together with Avicenna's and Ibn Miskawayh's views on economics and morals, respectively).[11] This kind of *ahlak* literature claimed a comprehensive view of the world as a unity, as it was developed in three escalating levels (individual, family, society), applying the same analytical tools (namely, the division of entities into components) in all three: i.e., speaking in turn of human ethics and the faculties of the soul, of household arrangements and more generally of the economy, and of the components of society and means of governance.

In some ways, this turn corresponds to a higher level of institutionalized education that permitted the acquaintance of Ottoman authors with these elaborate moral systems (after all, it was Mehmed II who established the

8 Yılmaz 2005, 24–25, notes two such translations by Ebu'l-Fazl Münşi and Kemal b. Hacı İlyas.

9 See, for example, Toutant 2016, 13–14 on Ahmedi.

10 On the itineraries of Aristotle's political ideas in the medieval Mediterranean and Middle East see the studies collected in Syros 2011.

11 On Tusi, see Lambton 1956a, 141–142; Donaldson 1963, 169–182; Madelung 1985; Fakhry 1994, 131–141; Black 2011, 149–157; on Davvani see Lambton 1956a, 146; Donaldson 1963, 182–184; Rosenthal 1958, 210–223; Anay 1994; Fakhry 1994, 143ff.; Black 2011, 188–189. On al-Farabi, see Rosenthal 1958, 113–142; al-Farabi – Walzer 1985; Fakhry 1994, 78–85; Fakhry 2000, 38–47; Black 2011, 57–74. Avicenna's economics were in their turn influenced by the Arabic translation of the work of a neo-Platonist author, Bryson: see the detailed edition and study by Swain 2013. On Ibn Miskawayh's moral theory, see Donaldson 1963, 121–133.

religious teaching institutions in Istanbul and organized the ulema hierarchy); on the other hand, just as had happened with the earlier introduction of the "mirror for princes" (*adab*) tradition, among the first to introduce these ideas were people educated near the old centers of Islamic scholarship and who had migrated to the new power. After all, Tusi's other—and in a sense more important—works (concerning astronomy, mathematics, and so on) were also translated and widely read in Ottoman medreses from almost the beginning of the fifteenth century, and some of them remained in use throughout the next three centuries.[12]

1 Works of Ethico-political Philosophy: from Amasi to Kınalızade

Ottoman literature did not need to wait until the conquest of Istanbul for someone to introduce the Persian moral and political systems (and, of course, elements of the Nasirean theory of soul can be found in earlier, more eclectic texts as well).[13] We already mentioned Ahmed bin Hüsameddin Amasi, a contemporary of both Ahmedi and Şeyhoğlu Mustafa but someone whose work started a much more "philosophical" tradition. Amasi, as revealed by his name, was a native of Amasya and came from a local family of scholars, Sufis, and officials, the Gümüşlüzade. Information on his life is very scarce; it seems that he was taken as a hostage to Shirvan by Timur, together with his uncle Pir İlyas Sücaeddin, the mufti of the city, and that they returned to Amasya after Timur's death in 1405.[14] It is not clear whether he is the same person as Şemseddin Ahmed Pasha from the same family, *nişancı* and later (1421) vizier. His work, *Kitab-ı mir'atü'l-mülûk* ("Book [that is] a mirror for rulers"),[15] was most probably submitted to Mehmed I in 1406, when the latter was re-establishing his base in Amasya.

Amasi used (or, indeed, translated—although he makes no references in his text) two famous sources of Persian political philosophy: the first was Tusi's *Akhlâq-e Nâsirî*, his outstanding systematization of Aristotelian and post-Aristotelian ethics; the second was al-Ghazali's *Nasîha al-mulûk*, the prototype of Sufi-oriented political thought, a reflection of which we saw earlier in Şeyhoğlu Mustafa's work. Amasi omitted or shortened the parts on theological,

12 See Aydüz 2011.

13 For instance, Kadı Fadlullah (A164) discusses the elements of the human soul, namely *ruh-i tabi'i, ruh-i hayvani*, and *ruh-i nefsani*.

14 Amasi – Yılmaz 1998, 1–3; cf. Kastritsis 2007, 72–73.

15 Amasi – Yılmaz 1998. Little has been written on Amasi's work: Fleischer 1983, 218 fn9 and 1990, 69fn.; Yılmaz 2005, 23–33; Darling 2013b, 238; Darling 2013c, 131.

social, and moral topics of both his sources in order to concentrate on the political theory part; as such, it is clear that he intended to enlighten the young ruler as to the virtues demanded of a prince rather than to give a full description of Persian ethical theory.

Amasi's work is divided into two parts of unequal length, based on his two sources: Tusi for the first and al-Ghazali for the second. The first part, designated a systematic treatise on morals (Y82–139), consists of three chapters, which deal with the main principles (*mebadi*), the purposes (*makasıd*), and the practical courses or measures (*tedbir*) of ethics. Thus, Amasi defines practical wisdom and its subdivisions (one's self, household, society) and describes the soul and its faculties, concluding with the four aspects of happiness, i.e. the four cardinal virtues (wisdom, courage, honesty, and justice). The second chapter (Y98–116) deals with the purposes of the science of ethics, further elaborating the cardinal virtues and their qualities and subdivisions. In the third chapter (Y116–139), Amasi moves on to the practical science of ethics (or, more accurately and according to his initial plan, the part of the practical science pertaining to associations); this, as he had stated previously, is divided into two "classes", namely the governance of the household and that of the "city". As for the second part of Amasi's work (Y139–156), based on al-Ghazali, it is programmatically devoted to "advice and stories" and thus belongs to the *adab* tradition, rather than to the *ahlak* as does the rest of his work. Indeed, this part is full of stories, mostly concerning Sassanian kings, that illustrate its meanings.[16] It is formed of three sections: on the duties of the sultan, on viziers, and on the "advice of the wise".

Amasi's work seems to have passed relatively unnoticed, both in Ottoman times (only two manuscripts are known) and in the study of Ottoman ideas. This is why most scholars consider Tursun Beg's introduction to his history of Mehmed II to be the first instance of Persian political-*cum*-moral theory in Ottoman literature. A member of an important family of the military class, Tursun Beg was born sometime after 1426. He seemingly had a *medrese* education, and was one of the initiators of Ottoman *münşi* or scribal literature;[17] he was a *protégé* of Grand Vizier Mahmud Pasha Angelović, probably entering his service in the mid-1450s. He served in various posts of the finance ministry for about 40 years, finally becoming a *defterdar*. Tursun Beg retired

16 In fact, some of them illustrate points in al-Ghazali's text that Amasi omits; see Amasi – Yılmaz 1998, 78. On al-Ghazali's ideas see Lambton 1954; Rosenthal 1958, 38–43; Donaldson 1963, 134–165; Laoust 1970, esp. (on the part used by Amasi) 148–152; Lambton 1981, 107–129; Fakhry 1994, 193ff.; Black 2011, 97–110. On the authorship of *Nasihat al-muluk* see Khismatulin 2015.

17 On this literature cf. Tuşalp Atiyas 2013, and cf. below, chapter 3.

to Bursa some time in the early 1480s, and he probably died there some time after 1488, since it was in that year that he commenced his *Târîh-i Ebu'l-Feth* ("History of the Conqueror"), a historical work covering the period 1451–88.[18] This work is preceded by a long introduction on the theory of state and rule (MI5a–25a, T10–30, B12–41), which is basically a synopsis of Tusi's ideas.[19] Interestingly, Tursun chooses to avoid discussing most of the "political" aspects of Tusi's theory; he prefers instead to focus on the theory of the princely virtues, emphasizing, as shall be seen, mildness (not a cardinal virtue in its own right) as embodied in his patron, Mahmud Pasha, who met his death under Mehmed II's executioners. Contrary to what the title of Tursun's history may imply, it is far from a hagiography of Mehmed II; rather, Tursun seems to have taken pains to criticize—discretely—his subject and instead eulogize the latter's successor Bayezid.

Indeed, the beginning of Tursun's introduction is essentially a paraphrase of Amasi's third chapter (on human associations). A uniqueness of his work is that, unlike other exponents of Tusian philosophy, he begins with political theory before examining the theory of the soul and its virtues. Of all the authors of this group, Tursun is also the only one who explicitly refers to events of his time: his special praise of mildness is perhaps a reference to the fate of his patron, Mahmud Pasha, executed by Mehmed II on account (it seems) of his hatred of Prince Mustafa,[20] and his account of generosity refers to Bayezid II's bestowing of the *vakıfs* and *mülks* confiscated by his father back on their previous owners (T22–23; cf. also T197–98).[21]

Next, Tursun Beg starts to describe his late patron, Mahmud Pasha; he was firm in his opinions and plans, intelligent and shrewd, had a pleasant nature, only spoke when necessary, and was condescending with his servants. When

18 This work has been published in transcription (Tursun Beg—Tulum 1977), in facsimile and extensive English summary (Tursun Beg – İnalcık – Murphey 1978), and recently in Italian translation (Tursun Bey – Berardi 2007). On Tursun's patron, Mahmud Pasha, see Stavrides 2001; on his political ideas see İnalcık 1977, 65ff; Tursun Beg – İnalcık – Murphey 1978, 20–24; Fodor 1986, 221–223; İnan 2003; İnan 2006; İnan 2009, 113–114; Yılmaz 2005, 40–41; Görgün 2014, 413–417.

19 Tusi's work is referred to explicitly (Tursun Beg – Tulum 1977, 16). Another source is the *Chahar maqala* by Nizamî-i 'Arudî-i Semerkandî (probably composed in 1156); see İnan 2006.

20 Mustafa died in 1473, just after Mahmud Pasha's dismissal from office and one year before his execution. There were other reasons as well, but it seems that the pasha's growing power also played a role (Stavrides 2001, 180–84, 329–355).

21 This identification of state appropriation with personal greed is significant, as it implies an identification of the state with the ruler; I have examined this subject in Sariyannis 2011a, 142–143 and Sariyannis 2013, 111–115.

once the question was raised as to how one could express the infinite gratitude owed to Sultan Mehmed II, Mahmud Pasha answered that the sultan also owes gratitude, to God, as recognition of His grace. The gratitude for the vastness of his lands would be to not covet the properties of the *reaya*; the gratitude for his highness (*bülendi*) would be to be merciful; for his innumerable treasuries, to give to charity and make charitable deeds; for his might, to pity the helpless; for his health, to heal the oppressed with a just law (*kanun-ı adl*); for his powerful army, to protect the lands of Islam from misfortunes; and for his court, castles, and gardens, to keep the property of his subjects free from oppression and torment (the reader may remember here similar ideas in the work of Sinan Pasha, another victim of Mehmed II's wrath). As well as the sultan, each of these expressions of gratitude should extend to all his subjects as well (T24–26). Mahmud Pasha also spoke against Mehmed II's excessive temper, although he noted that mildness, too, has a limit; the collection of money and treasure may be accepted, but only as long as it takes place with justice (*tarik-i şer' ve kanun-ı örf üzre ... hakk ile*).[22]

It is evident that Tursun used his patron's alleged words as the basis for his own political advice. One may even suspect that he did not care much for the elaborate ethical system he borrowed from Tusi: he begins with it so as to smoothly introduce Mahmud Pasha's encomium and his stress on mildness, for lack of which he suffered, as Tursun clearly implies. After Mehmed II's death, Mahmud Pasha had acquired the position of perfect statesman, both an exponent of Mehmed's imperial project and a victim of his centralization efforts and ruthless nature; the pasha's exaltation even reached the point of resulting in an anonymous hagiography, one which depicted him as a saint with supernatural powers. It is to be noted that copies of this legend were often grouped together with the anti-imperial texts on the "blessed Edirne" vs "cursed Constantinople", studied in the previous chapter.[23] Putting his political advice into the mouth of a deceased champion of the anti-Mehmed opposition, Tursun reinforced both his criticism of Mehmed's policies and his own position in the new environment following Bayezid's enthronement.

Slightly younger than Tursun but an equally important figure who also played a significant role in early sixteenth-century Ottoman writing was İdris b. Hüsameddin Bitlisî. Born in Bitlis some time between 1452 and 1457, he served under Uzun Hasan and his Akkoyunlu successors before joining Bayezid II in 1500 and living in the Ottoman state until his death in 1520. Bitlisi was thus

22 İnalcık and Murphey note that Tursun often makes allusions to the conquest as a process by which state revenues could be expanded (Tursun Beg – İnalcık – Murphey 1978, 17, 24).

23 See Stavrides 2001, 356ff. On the legend, particularly, see ibid. 369–396; Reindl-Kiel 2003.

part of an intellectual bureaucracy characterized by international mobility and a continuous shift in allegiances, like Amasi, Ahmedi, and Şeyhoğlu Mustafa (or, nearer to Bitlisi's own era, Musannifek, who came to Anatolia in 1444 from Herat and composed two works on government, for Mehmed II and for Tursun's patron Mahmud Pasha);[24] this "international class" seems to have played a major role in introducing Persian moral and political ideas into the Ottoman *milieu* and in shaping Ottoman institutions and ideas. An accomplished scholar and bureaucrat, as well as a noted Sufi, he became a not-so-successful courtier in Istanbul; he had more success under Selim I, who used him as an envoy and informant during the start of the Ottoman-Safavid conflict. In this role, Bitlisi was crucial in persuading the Kurdish chieftains to declare their allegience to Selim I.[25] He is best known, however, for his various historical and other works, among them the famous *Hesht bihisht*, i.e. the history of the Ottoman dynasty in Persian verse. In the epilogue of this work Bitlisi tries to justify Selim's takeover by stating that, during the later years of Bayezid II's reign, the world was full of disorder because the old sultan had abandoned all affairs to his officials or proxies (*nevvab*), believing that they would act for the best. He stresses that the sultan should possess the four cardinal virtues and argues that among Bayezid's children only Selim was suitable; his elder brother, Ahmed, is dismissed with the argument that, competent as he might have been, he had a similar disposition to his father's and thus was also favored by the (corrupt) officials.[26]

Bitlisi wrote another work which draws directly from the same tradition as Amasi or Tursun Beg. *Qanûn-i shehinshâhî* ("The imperial law") was also written in Persian, probably during the reign of Selim I, and is a typical treatise on moral and political virtues, based on previous similar literature.[27] After noting that the *hilafet* takes pride in the existence of the Ottoman dynasty, Bitlisi sets out to analyze the meaning of kingship, caliphate, and world order. Then, after studying the division of sciences and knowledge in order to specify the position of morals in kingship, he proceeds to describe some of the virtues that lead to right government (A18–21) and, more specifically, the cardinal and secondary virtues (A21–27). Next, in his third chapter (A27–38), the longest and the most practical of the essay, Bitlisi examines the practice of kingship.

24 Yılmaz 2005, 37–38.

25 Imber 2009, 39; for a comprehensive and insightful biography of Bitlisi see Sönmez 2012.

26 Bitlisi – Başaran 2000, 126ff.

27 Hasan Tavakkolî's edition and translation of the text (Bitlisi – Tavakkoli 1974) was inaccessible to me; I used the selective Turkish summary (omitting the non-political parts) in Akgündüz 1990–1996, 3:13–40 (and facs. of the Persian MS in 41–84). On Bitlisi's ideas see Yılmaz 2005, 82–86; Sönmez 2012.

This part of the work is closer to *adab* literature; however, there is a degree of abstraction not often found in other "mirrors for princes". The fourth and final chapter (A38–40), again close to the *adab* tradition, tries to link worldly kingship with the Hereafter.

Bitlisi's treatise constitutes a fully-fledged exposition of the Persian political and moral tradition. True, the discussion of governments (originating from al-Farabi), included by Amasi, is missing, in favor of a weightier place for individual ethics; but, on the other hand, this lack is replaced by an *adab*-styled discussion of concrete advice. Here we have both an account of the soul and virtues theory and one of the first instances of the dichotomy in the administrative apparatus, i.e. the antagonism between military and scribal services. In fact, Bitlisi's sources are two: on the one hand, his moral theory comes from Jalal al-Din Davvani's *Akhlâq-e Jalâlî*, an improved and extended version of Tusi's ethical system. On the other, for the last set of rules, with their emphasis on the conduct of imperial councils and care for the peasants, Bitlisi reverts to the famous *Siyâsetnâme* by Nizam al-Mulk (Nizamü'l-mülk), a work belonging more to the "mirror for princes" or *adab* genre. This kind of synthesis appears for the first time in Ottoman writings here: Amasi and Tursun only presented Tusi's philosophical system, while Şeyhoğlu or Sinan Pasha stressed either abstract moral advice for the ruler or a somewhat ethical reading of earlier *adab*. With Bitlisi, the literary unity of the Islamicate cultures that extended from Anatolia to Khorasan shows one of its last blossomings: his synthesis was a superb example of the fertile mobility of this international bureaucratic stratum to which he belonged; but, while Persian poetry continued to function as a model for Ottoman *literati*, political thought took (for the most part) a distinct path from then on, all the more since the heretical position of the Persian dynasty in Ottoman eyes made its political views reprehensible.

Amasi, Tursun, and Bitlisi's works did much to popularize this coupling of political advice with moral philosophy in a complete explanatory system, based mainly on Tusi's and Davvani's elaboration of al-Farabi and Avicenna's neo-Aristotelian theory. Their efforts, however, seem not to have been crowned with success: all three works were not very popular in their lifetimes, with very few manuscripts copied. Furthermore, as will be seen in the following chapters, the major political thinkers of the sixteenth century tended to abandon this approach in favor of a more down-to-earth, "mirror for princes" style. There were a few authors, mostly immigrants like Bitlisi, who (in a similarly unpopular way) tried to transfer the Tusian system: a contemporary of Bitlisi, Şemseddin Cahrami (Jahramî) likely came from Iran (Jahram is small town near Shiraz) and wrote his work, probably entitled *Siyâsiya berâ-ye Sultân Selîm* ("Government for Sultan Selim"), in 1513. The work is in three parts, concerning the administration of oneself or one's soul (*siyâsat-i nafs*), one's household (*siyâsat-i khâssa*), and the commons (*siyâsat-i 'âmma*). Cahrami considers a strong ruler necessary for good administration and presupposes that he has full control of his state; thus, he stresses the need for him to maintain not only high moral standards but also complete physical health, which is placed above the sultan's piety as the latter is permitted to drink wine. Like Bitlisi, Cahrami also produces a synthesis of Tusian ethical theory with the "mirror of princes" style of advice: he distinguishes the "ruling elite" (*khâssa*) into inner (*andarûn*) and outer (*bîrûn*); the latter, in turn, consists of ten governmental offices, for which the author gives specific principles. Further into the sixteenth century, Muzaffar b. Osman al-Barmaki, better known as Hızır Münşi (d. 1556), was serving at the court of a local dynasty in Azerbaijan before fleeing (probably because of Safavid interference and his own Sunni allegiances) first to Georgia in 1533 and then to Trabzon. His work (*Akhlâq al-atqıyâ wa sifât al-asfiyâ* or "The noblest ethics and the purest qualities", dedicated to Süleyman) was composed in an eclectic style, as it copies from different sources (including Tusi and al-Ghazali); its content covers the three areas of ethics (individual, household, politics) discussed by Tusi and his followers. What is interesting is that in his case (as, one may remember, in Tursun Beg's) the political part comes first, while subsequent parts mostly discuss the virtues of the individual.[28]

There was still to be a major expounder of the "philosophical trend", who was to be the most systematic and comprehensive of all, even if we consider his work to be the swansong rather than the heyday of this trend. The son of a kadi and poet, Kınalızade Ali Çelebi (1510–72) had a formidable education and a prodigious career. He studied in Istanbul and became an assistant (*mülazim*) to the *şeyhülislam* (1539–41) Çivizade (d. 1547, a strong opponent of Sufi thought and especially of Ibn Arabi, and who was dismissed for attacking a number of Sufi icons).[29] Having eventually submitted his works to the opponent of the latter, Ebussu'ud Efendi, Kınalızade was appointed as *müderris* in various medreses in Edirne, Bursa, Kütahya, and, finally, Istanbul. In 1563 he was sent as a judge to Damascus, then to Cairo, Bursa, and Edirne. In 1570 he was appointed judge of Istanbul, and next year Anadolu *kazaskeri*. His son, Kınalızade Hasan Çelebi, was the author of a famous collection of poets' biographies.

Kınalızade wrote various treatises on *fikh*, history, correspondence, and Islamic law. His most important work, however, is the famous *Ahlâk-ı Alâî* ("Sublime ethics"). Composed in 1563–65 when the author was a judge in Damascus (where he also discussed his work with Mustafa Ali, then *divan*

28 Yılmaz 2005, 104–107 (on Cahrami) and 101–104 (on Hızır Münşi).

29 On Çivizade and his views see Repp 1986, 244ff. and cf. below, chapter 3.

kâtibi of the beylerbey), it soon became a very widespread, popular, and influential work ("one of the 'bestsellers' of the Ottoman bookmarket from the 16th to the 18th centuries", as characterized by Baki Tezcan[30]). It constitutes an ambitious enterprise to encompass a full range of ethics at all three levels: individual ethics, or the governance of self, household economics (the governance of the family and the house), and political theory (the governance of the city, *recte* society). Kınalızade's analysis is primarily based on the well-known categories of ethics that were expounded by his predecessors. Kınalızade's account is, of course, much more analytical; as well as Tusi and Davvani, he also used al-Ghazali's philosophy and Avicenna's terminology.[31] The human condition is conceived as a continuum, from the human soul to society; Kınalızade's moral vision is in fact a study of government, in three escalating levels: from individual morality, i.e. governing the self, to the family and household maintenance, i.e. what the ancient Greeks called economics (*οικονομία*: "the regulation of the household"), and finally to political theory, i.e. the governance of society. For all three levels he employs the same analytical tools: the division of entities into components and the quest for the mean and for a balance, which can lead to harmony and order. As with his predecessors, the notion of the four cardinal virtues (wisdom, justice, honesty, and courage) and their subvirtues, with the respective vices, is central to his moral philosophy.

Kınalızade's voluminous treatise remained a classic for centuries afterwards; notions such as the "circle of equity (justice)" or the division of society into the four classes were to dominate or at least be present in almost every Ottoman treatise of political advice composed from the mid-sixteenth century onwards. On the other hand, his political ideas became increasingly marginalized. Even during his own lifetime, as we are going to see in chapter 3, Davvani's fashion had waned in favor of Kashifi's popularization, which gave more prominence to concrete ethical and political advice rather than philosophical theory; what is more important is that, in Kınalızade's time, the characteristically Ottoman "mirror for princes" genre, different from the previous mirrors thanks to its stress on concrete advice and on institutions rather than personal qualities, had already been started. Despite its tremendous popularity, therefore, *Ahlâk-ı Alâî* was the swansong rather than the beginning of a tradition.

30 Tezcan 2001, 110. Printed in Bulak in 1833, this major work was published in transcription only in 2007 (Kınalızade – Koç 2007; a modern Turkish version was also published in 1974 and 1975). Tezcan 1996, 65ff gives a detailed synopsis of the book, carefully noting the respective sources (Tusi and Davvani); cf. also the detailed analyses in Tezcan 2001; Oktay 2002; Unan 2004; Hagen 2013, 433–438; Ermiş 2014, 60–71 and 81–110.

31 See Tezcan 1996, 67, fn. 244, 81, fn. 294. On Kınalızade's philosophical and psychological ideas cf. also Yurtoğlu 2014.

2 Moral Philosophy as Political Theory

As has been noted, all these authors see political science as a part of moral philosophy. Amasi, for instance, states (Y82–98) that wisdom (*hikmet*) has its theoretical (*ilm*) and its practical (*amel*) aspects; he will explore the second, i.e. practical wisdom, something also divided up, into that which is related to the self alone and that which is related to common associations of men (*cema'ata müşareket ile*). The latter, in turn, may concern one's household or the "town and province and country" (*şehir ve vilayet ve iklim*). Thus, practical wisdom may, in fact, be divided into three kinds: the improvement of morals, the management of the household, and the administration of cities (*siyaset-i müdün*) or political wisdom (*hikmet-i medeni*). As this science discusses in essence the human soul, its principles belong to natural science (*ilm-i tabi'iyye*). This categorization, coming from Avicenna's work,[32] may be clearer with the following diagram:

Wisdom			
Theoretical	Practical		
	On self	On associations	
		On household	On society
	Improvement of morals	Management of the household	Administration of cities

Kınalızade further clarifies that the ethics of the first level, i.e. individual morals, is a simple (*müfred*) science, as opposed to the other two which are compound (*mürekkeb*) sciences since they concern groups rather than individuals (K97).

Bitlisi (A18) uses a different argument, one with a more religious basis. The Quran and the Sunna have two objects, namely theory and practice (*maksad-ı*

32 Avicenna, however, seems to have added a fourth sub-discipline on "prophetic legislation" to his later works. Although neither Tusi nor Davvani followed this categorization, a chain of commentators and continuators did, dividing political science into the governance of cities and the science of laws. See Kaya 2014, 272ff.

ilmi, maksad-ı ameli); each of these two can, in turn, be divided into two types, the serving and the served (*hadim, mahdum*). "Serving knowledge" or *ilm-i hadim* is any knowledge, such as Islamic law, that serves an aim, i.e. *ilm-i mahdum* or the knowledge of God. In the same way, "serving acts" (*amel-i hadim*) such as earning goods or improving oneself morally obey the "served act" (*amel-i mahdum*), namely the right guidance of people's affairs and looking after the world order. Here, Bitlisi refers to "spiritual" and "exoteric" kingship, saying that in some cases these two coincide, as with caliphs. In any case, the world cannot be deprived of one of these two at a time. Because Muslim kings are manifestations of divine power and knowledge, they have to gain knowledge of God, i.e. *ilm-i mahdum*; then, the prerequisite of this knowledge, as demonstrated above, is *ilm-i hadim*, i.e. the knowledge of Islamic law and other sacred regulations. In the same way, kings must improve themselves morally, i.e. exert the "serving act", since they are to exercise the "served act".

Moreover, Bitlisi states that God gave humanity the perfection of all virtues and capacities (A14–15). Because of this perfection, man is the substitute (*halife*) of God on earth; therefore, every perfect man can be regarded as a substitute. Furthermore, people such as holy men, prophets, imams, etc. can be named "spiritual rulers" even if they have no armies or viziers; such a naming is symbolic and temporary, just as is the king in the game of chess. In order for the workings of divinity to be visible, both knowledge and power must be manifest; these two virtues can be seen in the function of rulership, and especially in the life of the Prophet (A15–18).

At any rate, individual morality is conceived as a quality that is teachable, rather than innate. Amasi is at pains to demonstrate that one's morals may change, as there are ephemeral and constant features of the soul, the former prone to formation through education, punishment, example, and even miracles (Y98ff). Kınalızade, in turn, devotes a whole chapter (K149–154) to acquiring virtues, discussing whether they come by nature or by teaching; he argues that one is first taught the virtues, through the science of ethics, and then has to instruct one's nature accordingly. Similarly, there are ways (such as avoiding bad company) in which virtues, once acquired, can be preserved by the individual (K155–168). The teachability of virtue, as well as its composition from the four cardinal virtues, is based on an elaborate theory about the human soul. According to Kınalızade's analysis, the rational soul (*ruh, nefs-i natıka*) has three components, namely the "vegetable soul" or spirit of growth (*nefs-i nebati*), the "animal soul" or spirit of life (*nefs-i hayvani*), and the "human soul" (*nefs-i insani*), all with their respective "powers" or faculties (K47–94). The human soul, he goes on, contains two powers, that of perception (*kuvvet-i müdrike*), which pertains to the mind and comprises both the theoretical (*kuvvet-i nazari*) and the practical (*kuvvet-i amelî*) powers, and that of motion (*kuvvet-i muharrike*), which pertains to the body and comprises the power of sensuality or lust (*kuvvet-i şehevani*) and the power of wrath or passion (*kuvvet-i sebu'i, kuvvet-i gazabi*). If any of these powers functions in a prudent and moderate manner (*hadd-i i'tidal*) it becomes a virtue, while when it is used in excess or deficiency it becomes a vice.

Thus, the four cardinal virtues are defined as the use of one specific power in moderation:[33] the theoretical power produces wisdom (*hikmet*); the practical, justice (*'adalet*); the sensual, honesty (*'iffet*); and the power of passion, courage (*şeca'at*). Likewise, an excess or deficiency of such powers produces various vices; only justice has no excess or deficiency, rather its contrary, namely injustice or oppression (*cevr*). The below table shows this:

Soul / Human reason			
Power of perception		Power of motion	
Theoretical power	Practical power	Sensual power	Passion
(if moderated produce:)			
Wisdom	Justice	Honesty	Courage

Kınalızade notes here that, according to some authors, justice is the combination of the other virtues, but this has no logical sense; thus, he presents another definition of virtues and vices as well, based on a tripartite division of the soul into the angelic soul (*nefs-i meleki*), the soul (or faculty) of passion (*nefs-i şebu'i*), and that of lust or appetite (*nefs-i behimi*).[34] In Amasi's version (Y86–88), these three faculties are that of reason (*nutk*), which is peculiar to humanity and can be either the theoretical (*akl-ı nazari*) or the practical mind (*akl-i 'ameli*), and the faculties of appetite (*kuvvet-i şehevi*) and passion (*kuvvet-i gazabi*), which are also found in animals other than man. Moderation (*i'tidal*), excess, or deficiency of the three faculties produce the same four virtues and

33 On the theory of virtues in Kınalızade see some more details in Sariyannis 2011a, 126–128.

34 In al-Ghazali's ethical philosophy, the two latter powers are considered among man's vicious insticts (Laoust 1970, 217–218, 331). On Islamic theories on reason see Grunebaum 1962.

their related vices, but with justice now being a combination of wisdom, courage, and honesty. This three-fold formulation[35] (which was preferred by Tursun, T16–17, and Bitlisi) is shown in the table below:

Human soul		
Angel soul (faculty of reason)	Faculty of passion	Faculty of lust
(if moderated by intelligence produce:)		
Wisdom	Courage	Honesty
(if moderated produce:)		
	Justice	

Subdivisions of each virtue often differ slightly,[36] but it is important to note mildness (*hilm*) and public spirit (*hamiyyet*, defined by Kınalızade as being at pains "to protect the community and to defend one's self and dignity", *himayet-i hima-yı millet ve hiraset-i harim-i nefs ü hürmet*: K108),[37] which are included in the general virtue of courage, and generosity (*seha*), which is included in honesty. Now, generosity, as was also seen in chapter 1, has a special place. Amasi (Y100) claims that the faculty of appetite or lust, when moderated,

35 This second theory originated with Ibn Miskawayh and was further elaborated by Tusi (Donaldson 1963, 125–126 and 173–174). The first (four-fold) theory seems to be an elaboration by Davvani, whom Kınalızade here copies verbatim (Dawwani – Thompson 1839, 52ff.; Dawwani – Deen 1939, 21ff.).

36 Thus, for Amasi (Y98–116), wisdom comprises intelligence, quick understanding, easiness in learning, memory, and remembrance; courage includes zeal, endurance, humility, public spiritedness [*hamiyyet*], and compassion; as for honesty, bashfulness, suavity, patience, contentment, dignity, chastity, freedom, and generosity; finally, justice comprises faithfulness, familiarity, loyalty, compassion, fair retribution, compliance with Godly rules, resignation to God, and piety. For Bitlisi (A21–27; see also Sariyannis 2011a, 125–126), honesty comprises generosity and modesty; courage is zeal, clemency, and perseverance; wisdom is perspicacity and remembrance; and justice is faithfulness and fidelity.

37 This particular virtue, which Amasi cites without any explanation, is not Khaldunian as it may seem; see Dawwani – Thompson 1839, 71 (translated as "stateliness", i.e. "that into enmities or hostilities which may be necessary to protect the honor of faith or worship, or the dignity of life or feeling, no levity be allowed to enter"); Dawwani – Deen 1939, 32.

generates the virtue of honesty and, through this, generosity; thus, he even inverts the usual scheme, where honesty is the cardinal virtue and generosity the secondary. Tursun Beg, in a manner reminiscent of the opposition to Mehmed II, gives as an example the generosity of Bayezid II in bestowing the *vakfs* and *mülks* confiscated by his father back to their previous owners (T 22–23; cf. also T 197–98). Finally, for Kınalızade, generosity is so important that he proceeds to define its main components, such as beneficence, forgiveness, munificence, magnanimity, and so on; in various parts of his work (e.g. K125–133), generosity is always examined together with the cardinal virtues, thus making five rather than four of them.

Justice, the most important virtue of all, is subdivided into faithfulness (*sadakat*), familiarity, loyalty, compassion, visiting one's relatives, fair retribution, fidelity in friendship, justice in human relationships (*hüsn-i kaza*), affection, compliance with God's rules, acquiescence to God, and piety. In Tursun's words, justice is necessary for the integrity of the various classes (*temamet-i tavayif-i muhtelife*); for example, thieves and robbers must be suppressed. Without justice, a balance cannot be attained, the sword cannot be good, the word is not worthy, knowledge gives no results, and the ruler cannot be stable (T17–18). According to Aristotle, says Amasi, justice differs from the other virtues because both its excess and lack is the same, namely oppression: if, through an excess of justice, someone is granted more than he deserves, in consequence someone else is oppressed. Kınalızade agrees that justice also seems to have its excess, tyranny (*zulm*), and its deficiency, the acceptance of tyranny (*inzilam*). Some say that both these vices are oppression (*cevr*), of others or of oneself, while others accept only the former, namely tyranny, as a vice; Kınalızade is inclined towards the first opinion (K115–123; cf. K146, where he boldly criticizes none other than Nasir al-Din Tusi on this matter).

Amasi (Y104–107) and Kınalızade (K135) specify that justice can be of three kinds, namely equity in distributing property or social rank (*keramet ü mertebe*), justice in financial transactions, and justice in punishment. In all three kinds, justice is defined as the proportional treatment of all parts (*tenasüb-i ri'ayet*, K135); it means knowing and determining the middle way (*evsat*) through being guided by the law of God (*namus-ı ilahi*). What is more, justice is directly linked to the creation of political society. Both Amasi (Y104–107) and Kınalızade (K135–139) explain that mankind, unlike animals, needs a variety of artefacts to survive, such as clothes, weapons, and so on, all of which cannot be produced by one man alone. Thus, the formation of societies arises as a necessity, and man is sociable by nature (*insan medeniyyün bi't-tab'dır*, K136). But in order for justice and equality to exist (*tâ ki ta'adül ve müsavat ola*), inevitably there must be an intermediary (*vasıta*), and this is money, which is the indispensable means of exchanging goods equally and justly. This leads to the need for a supreme power to suppress tyranny and determine the value of money. Thus, three things are needed for the preservation of justice in society: the law of God (*namus-ı rabbani*), a human ruler (*hakim-i insani*), and weighed (i.e., defined) money (*dinar-ı mizani*); all three together, Kınalızade remarks, were named by the Greek sages *nâmûs* (*νόμος*), which corresponds to *siyaset*. First comes the law of God, which the ruler must obey, while he, in turn, is the regulator of money. Inversely, the extent of the oppression is greatest when the oppressor disobeys the law of God, medium when he does not comply with the ruler, and smallest when he disrespects the function of money. The third oppression leads to robbery and plundering, but the oppression resulting from ignoring the first two requirements is the greatest. Some sages, Amasi explains, divide justice into three parts: submission to God; respect for rulers, for the rights of other people (*hukuk-ı ebna-i cins*), and for just transactions; and submission to law and order (*eda-ı hukuk ve infaz-i vasaya*). We will return to the origins of political society and the justifications of power later on, but it is important to note here the close relationship of human associations with justice, which further explains its designation as the central political virtue.

2.1 *A Political Economy*

The second level of ethical practice, which in Amasi's model is part of the practical science pertaining to associations and in Kınalızade's expression it is the governance of one's household (*ilm-i tedbirü'l-menzil*), is strongly influenced by the ancient Greek *Οικονομικός* genre and especially by the Neoplatonist Bryson.[38] A large part of the relevant chapters in these works concerns the family, the marriage, the education of children, the relationship with one's servants and so forth; what interests us more is the fact that theories about wealth and economics appear in this context as well. Tursun and Bitlisi have little to say in this respect, but both Amasi (Y116–127) and Kınalızade (K325–405)[39] deal extensively with the issue.

As seen above, the sociability of mankind is attributed to the need for mutual assistance: man needs food, and neither agriculture nor husbandry can be done by one man alone, so people must collaborate with one another. Furthermore, a place is needed for rest and protection; a wife to bear and raise one's offspring; and servants to help. Thus, the five pillars of the house are the father, the mother, the child, the servant, and the means of sustenance (*kut*). Moving now to economics as a source of sustenance (and skipping

38 Plessner 1928; Swain 2013.

39 Cf. Ermiş 2014, 81ff.

the wealth of advice on domestic matters both authors have to offer), these can be viewed in three ways, from the point of view of: revenue; keeping hold of the former; and its expenditure. Concerning the first, the sources of revenue, there are several categories: one is bipartite, i.e. revenue that comes by gain and by choice (e.g. trade or craft) vs. revenue that comes incidentally, such as gifts or inheritance. Amasi's treatment of the subject stops here, but Kınalızade then describes another, more "economic" theory, namely revenue from commerce, craftsmanship, and agriculture. A third view sees four methods of revenue, adding leadership (*emaret*), by which is meant the pensions and salaries (*vezayif ü ulufat*) that come from the ruler (K335–36):

> Some have divided the ways to acquire property into three categories: commerce, craftsmanship, agriculture. And some have increased these modes of revenue to four, adding leadership. Because pensions and salaries come from the ruler's rank (*mertebe-i emaret kısmından add olunmakla*), this is a true categorization.

This addition seems to be Kınalızade's own (although it can also be found in Ibn Khaldun's work)[40] and is quite apt for an empire such as the Ottoman. Speaking of the ancient controversy on which is the best way, the author notes that (K336)[41]

> later authorities argued that so many illegal practices invaded commercial transactions that distrust on the origin of the fortunes arose; thus, agriculture should have precedence over commerce. In the acquisition of wealth, one should refrain first from oppression and injustice; secondly from shameful activities, and thirdly from disgraceful or dirty occupations (K336).

40 See Kunt 1977, 208; Tezcan 1996, 83–84; and cf. Davvani's text in Dawwani – Thompson 1839, 252; Dawwani – Deen 1939, 129. Ibn Khaldun's text (Ibn Khaldun – Rosenthal 1958, 2:316; cf. Ermiş 2014, 92) reads: "Certain thorough men of letters and philosophers, such as al-Hariri and others ... said: 'A living is made by (exercising) political power (*imarah*), through commerce, agriculture, or the crafts.' (The exercise of) political power is not a natural way of making a living. We do not have to mention it here. Something was said before ... about governmental tax collection and the people in charge of it. Agriculture, the crafts, and commerce, on the other hand, are natural ways of making a living." However, as Rosenthal notes (l.c., note 16) this is not found in the famous al-Hariri's works. I deal with this issue in more detail in Sariyannis (forthcoming).

41 Here in Halil İnalcık's slightly shortened translation: İnalcık 1994a, 44 (see also Davvani's text in Dawwani – Thompson 1839, 252–3; Dawwani – Deen 1939, 129). Cf. İnalcık 1969b, 98–99. On the prehistory of this theory, cf. Laoust 1970, 313–314.

Kınalızade then proceeds to analyze craftsmanship (*sına'at*), yet in a broad sense, one that seems to include commerçe and agriculture. Craftsmanship, he argues, can be divided into three categories, namely noble (*şerif*), middle or neutral, and inferior. Noble crafts are those conducted by human reason (*nefs-i natıka*) rather than the body, and they are subdivided into three main types: the "art of leadership" (*san'at-ı vizaret*), which has to do with the well-being of the community and pertains to the mind; the art of the literati, scribes, and judges, which pertain to virtue, knowledge of manners (*edeb*), eloquence, medicine, mathematics, and so forth; and the art of the soldiery (*sipahilik*).[42] As for the inferior arts, they are also divided into three categories. Trades such as hoarding, witchcraft, libelling, and pimping, which are opposed to the righteous ways of living, are the professions of mischief-makers and evil-doers; others, such as singing and buffoonery, are not opposed to the right way of living but only to the virtue and generosity of the spirit; finally, professions such as sweepers, tanners, or cuppers, the crafts of the lowest, only produce bodily disgust in themselves; however, they cause no damage to the mind so cannot be considered improper. On the contrary, since everybody must make a living, it is necessary that these strata (i.e. the lowest) occupy themselves with such professions in order not to damage the world order (*nizam-ı alem*); if everybody followed only the noble professions, the world order would be destroyed (cf. also K368, 412). Finally, the middle or neutral crafts can be divided into those indispensable, such as agriculture, and those that are not always necessary, such as the profession of the goldsmith. Here, Kınalızade notes that (again in İnalcık's words) "a craftsman should endeavor to make the best product possible without being content merely to earn his livelihood. While it [is] necessary, he [adds], to please the consumer since his satisfaction and prayers are the source of prosperity and salvation in this world and hereafter, it is a waste of time to be too meticulous making luxury goods. It is far better for a Muslim to spend his time in prayers" or charity (K337).

As for keeping hold of wealth, doing so must neither deprive the members of the household of their means of subsistence, nor be at the expense of religious duties, nor lead to avarice. Kınalızade warns against meanness, but stresses that expenses must be kept lower than the income; it is not sinful to keep one's wealth hidden, he says, provided the canonical alms have been extracted. He also gives specific advice concerning how one should invest one's wealth

42 İnalcık (1994a, 44) sums it up as follows: "The professions of ulema, bureaucrats and soldiers are based in spiritual qualities such as reason, rhetoric and valor respectively and thus make up the noble professions", which is not very accurate. At any rate, the absence of the ulema in the text is puzzling.

in different ways (cash, estate etc.) in order to be better protected against adversity (K340). The same goes for spending one's wealth: the priority should be the expenditure ordered by God, e.g. canonical alms, and then should come the expenses showing generosity, such as various kinds of presents and gifts; the necessary expenses for food, clothing, and so forth should have only a low priority related to the other two categories. Expenditure is subdivided into those asked for, such as expenses for one's family or canonical alms, those showing generosity, such as gifts to friends or presents to poets and storytellers, and those one spends for himself.

One may note that this highly-sophisticated theory is again based on the essential unity of the human condition, as professions are classified according to the faculties of the soul. We should be cautious as to the degree to which such assumptions, mostly formulaic and moralistic, actually shaped Ottoman economic attitudes and policies. True, the high place peasants and agriculture occupy in the realm of Ottoman economy and taxation, as well as a general distrust of large-scale commerce,[43] seems to corroborate Halil İnalcık's assertion that Kınalızade's ideas "cannot be altogether dismissed as purely theoretical and ethical advice, since they actually influenced the mind and behavior of the Ottoman elite and populace".[44] Yet, for the most part these ideas (the primordiality of agriculture over trade included) are not Amasi's or Kınalızade's but originate in Persian political thought of the preceding centuries, and they may have remained common for a long time even after actual attitudes and policies had changed. Let us note here that Bitlisi (A35–36) shows a slightly more favorable attitude toward commerce: although he has the usual eulogy for agriculture, which he considers the greatest treasury of the world, he also stresses that merchants should not be taxed excessively with dues and customs; the rich and important ones, especially, must be looked upon with favor, since they yield more profit for the state than they received in benefits bestowed on them.

Nonetheless, Kınalızade's addition to Davvani's text concerning leadership (*emaret*) as a source for revenue must be noted. As seen, this addition may have come from Ibn Khaldun's work; however, whereas the Tunisian scholar understands this revenue as the ruler's income, Kınalızade clearly meant pensions and salaries coming *from* the ruler. We might see here a sense of 'state' closer to its modern notion, i.e., as a self-reproductive mechanism which is clearly distinct from the person of the ruler: for Ibn Khaldun, the revenue from taxes belongs to the ruler, while for Kınalızade the state produces revenue for

43 Cf. İnalcık 1969b, 103–107; Faroqhi 2002 (= Faroqhi 2008, 119–148).

44 İnalcık 1994a, 45.

its employees.[45] It is highly illuminating to use these ideas (inherited as they were by one treatise from another for many generations) as a setting against which one can measure the innovative aspects of various exponents of eighteenth-century Ottoman economic thought, writers who developed a kind of mercantilism with an emphasis not only on commerce but also on state-driven production (see below, chapter 8).

2.2 *The Beginning and Principles of Government*

The need for the government of cities (*medine*, a term that originates from al-Farabi's terminology and in this context denotes society at large) and the rules thereof are conceived within the same frame of a continuum uniting an individual soul with wider associations. In order to demonstrate mankind's need for settlement (*temeddün*), both Amasi (Y127–130) and Kınalızade (K405–450) draw a philosophical distinction between simple and complex bodies; the latter reach their perfection from their complexity, and this is attained by various means. Man also needs help not only from the material sources of the world (such as fire, wood, etc.) but also from his fellow-men, since no one person can produce all the goods needed for their own subsistence. In Tursun's words, man has become civilized due to his moral qualities in order to promote his health and living resources (*emr-i inti'aşında ve ahkam-ı ma'aşında*), thereby creating societies (which "according to our customs" are called town, village, and nomad camp: *ki ana temeddün dirler ki, örfümüzce ana şehr ve köy ve oba dinilür*; T12–14). Every individual, Kınalızade says, needs to help and socialize with others, starting from the basic couple of a man and woman, needed for reproduction, then proceeding to the wider family, and finally to societies (*içtima'*), since one person cannot produce all the goods needed; as he had explained before, God's wisdom leads people to choose all kinds of profession, even inferior ones. Moreover, the existence of poor and rich is likewise justified, since if everybody were poor (or rich) nobody would serve anyone; while, with the existence of rich and poor, the servants get a living from the served and the latter get help, leading to the satisfaction of everyone's aims and to order in the world (K410–412). Thus, in Amasi's words (Y128),

> the human race is naturally in need of society, and this kind of need is called civilization (*temeddün*); this term derives from the word 'city' (*medine*), which is defined as every locality where people gather and help each other with the various professions in order to procure their means of living.

---

45 Sariyannis (forthcoming); cf. Sariyannis 2013.

However, the aims of each person in this association vary, and this can lead to a situation where the more powerful enslave the weaker. As such, there must be a power (*tedbir*) that keeps everybody to their own houses, ranks, and limits, preventing tyranny and oppression; this power is called governance (*siyaset*), and it can be procured either by a wise law (*kanun-i hikmet*), called then divine governance (*siyaset-i ilahi*), or by other means. A law of God (*namus-ı ilahi*) is needed,[46] together with a ruler and coinage (as seen above). Here, Kınalızade discusses a possible objection (to which we will revert in the next chapter), which, as we saw, had been troubling Ottoman authors ever since Ahmedi: what about Cengiz Han, for instance, who had imposed his own law (*yasa*) instead of God's? The answer he gives is that such a state is subject to continuous changes of fortune, and so its law is prone to collapse (K413–414).

Thus, in the field of the regulating principles (*takdir-i evza'*), a person has to be placed higher than others by the inspiration of God (*ilham-i ilahiyle ayruklardan mumtaz ola*). This person was called by the ancient sages *namus* (Greek *νόμος*, "law") and his orders *namus-ı ilahi*; respectively law-giver (*şari'*) and Sharia by the Muslim ones. Similarly, when it comes to issuing orders (*takrir-ı ahkam*) a person also has to be exalted with God's confirmation (*te'yid-i ilahiyle*); the ancient Greeks called him "the absolute king" (*melik-i ale'l-ıtlak, hakim ale'l-ıtlak*) and the Muslims *imam*. This is the classical formulation, as found, for example, in Amasi (Y129); Kınalızade, writing after the establishment of the Safavid state in the east, adds that this ruler is named *caliph* by the Muslims and *imam* by the Shi'a. The arrangement produced by the ruler's government is called divine government (*siyaset-i İlahi*) if it is made according to necessity and wisdom; then, its driving force (*vazı'*) is law (*namus*). Tursun notes here that these names are used by wise people (*ehl-i hikmet*), while religious people (*ehl-i şer'*) call them "Holy Law" and "Prophet" respectively. If the arrangement cannot be as perfect as that, it must be regulated in the manner of pure reason (*mücerred tavr-ı akl üzere*) and is called kingly government or kingly law (*siyaset-i sultani ve yasağ-ı padişahî dirler ki, örfümüzce ana örf dirler*). Although a prophet is not necessary in every country, a king is; if the king's power dies, order dies, too.[47]

46 On the term *nâmûs* and its history see Rosenthal 1958, 116–118, 145 (on Avicenna's views) and 212–213 (on Tusi and Davvani), as well as the relevant entry ("Nâmûs") in the *Encyclopaedia of Islam* (2nd edition) by M. Plessner.

47 On this point, somewhat awkwardly (but always following his model, Davvani), Kınalızade inserts an excursus (K418–450) on love (*mahabbet*). There are two ways to avoid the dangers of oppression and fighting inherent to any human society, he says: on the one hand, rules of justice and kingly government, aimed at both high and low (*amme-i havass u avamm*); on the other, love, which is reserved only for special individuals (*havass u efrad*

These theories on the origin and character of political society and power originate, as do most of the ideas seen in this chapter, in Tusi and Davvani's adaptation of ancient Greek theories.[48] As did most of their Muslim predecessors, Tusi, Davvani, and their Ottoman followers chose to emphasize the need for cooperation in order to achieve basic human needs as the motivating factor behind the origins of society. Although they sometimes referred to the idea that, without a regulating power, conflict and oppression would arise, society was always seen as a field of natural cooperation rather than strife. On the other hand, different views had begun to permeate Islamic political thought from the thirteenth century onwards, in the aftermath of the Mongol invasions. As will be seen in more detail in the conclusion, an emphasis on man's natural tendency to dominate and oppress one another was to become increasingly apparent during the seventeenth and eighteenth centuries. For the moment, however, the optimistic view of a growing, pious empire that would visibly bring security and peace probably favored an analogous view of political society.

Having established the origins of political society, the moral philosophers describe the forms of government in an Aristotelian model ultimately derived from al-Farabi. Amasi uses Tusi's formulation, distinguishing between the "virtuous government" (*siyaset-i fazıla*), also called the imamate, where the *imam* sees his subjects as friends and treats them with justice, and the "imperfect" one (*siyaset-i nakısa*), also called tyranny (*tagallüb*), where a tyrant, himself a slave of his own appetites, turns his subjects into his servants and slaves (Y130–135). Justice, therefore, is the sole element differentiating the various kinds of government. A more elaborate distinction, between the virtuous and the imperfect state (*medine-i fazıla, medine-i gayr-ı fazıla*), is to be found in Kınalızade (K451–459), who closely follows Davvani and the Platonic interpolations he made in Tusi's theory.[49] There is only one kind of virtuous state, while imperfect ones have three forms: in the "ignorant state" (*medine-i cahile*) it is bodily powers rather than the faculty of reason that lie behind the need for association (accordingly, there can be the "irascible ignorant state" or

ve a'yan u ahad). If love prevails in a given group (*cema'at*), justice is not necessary, as there are no conflicting wishes (K419). In the rest of the chapter, Kınalızade explores at length the various types of love, its causes and features; among the types of love, he also discusses briefly that of the subjects (*re'aya*) for the sultan (K441–442). This chapter was incorporated into Davvani's and Tusi's works from Ibn Miskawayh: Tezcan 1996, 94. Cf. also. Donaldson 1963, 130; Unan 2004, 121ff. On the importance of love or attraction for social unity in Kınalızade's vision see Hagen 2013, 438.

48 Yücesoy 2011; Syros 2012a.

49 On the supplementation of Tusi's system in Davvani's work see Rosenthal 1958, 217ff.

the "appetitive ignorant state", *medine-i cahile-i sebu'iyye* and *medine-i cahile-i behimiyye*); in the vicious or wicked state (*medine-i fasıka*) the faculty of reason exists among the people, but faculties of the body prevail; finally, in the "erroneous state" (*medine-i dalle*) people use their reason but consider wrong as being right (K450–51). The "erroneous state" can be either infidel, like the Frankish or Russian states, or Muslim, like the Kızılbaş (*Sürh-ser*, meaning Safavid Iran). Such deviations can be explained by the fact that humans vary enormously in terms of intelligence and morality. In the "virtuous state", the ruler may initially adhere to justice, and thus gain the hearts of the subjects, while in the "imperfect" one he uses oppression and fear, often prohibiting the subjects from using luxury goods, among others (K461). The explanation for the existence of impious and tyrannical but successful states, as seen, for instance, in Ahmedi's description of the Mongols, finds here its theoretical consummation.

Moving now to the "virtuous state", Kınalızade explains that its citizens (if we can translate *ehl* thus) are of five classes (*tayife*): (a) the "superiors" (*efadıl*), on whom the good arrangement of state affairs depends—these are the judges and ulema (*hukema-i kâmil ve ulema-yı amil*); (b) the "possessors of languages" (*zevi'l-elsine*), who advise people on what is good and right; (c) the "estimators" (*mukaddir*), who look after weights and measures and have knowledge of geometry and mathematics; (d) the warriors (*gaziler ve mücahid, sipahilik*), who protect the state against external threats; and (e) the "men of property" (*erbab-ı emval*), who produce the goods that people need. These are the "pillars of the state" (*erkân-ı medine*). However, as well as them, there are also the "plants" or "weeds" (*nevabit*), those who are like thorns among useful trees (K457–8). Furthermore, Kınalızade divides these "weeds" into another five classes (in a slight alteration from al-Farabi):[50] the "hypocrites", who follow the right path externally but are vicious in their hearts; the "distorters", whose beliefs are opposed to those of the virtuous and tend to prefer the "ignorant state" and so they interpret the laws of the virtuous state as they please; the "rebels" (*bagi*), who openly rise up against the ruler and wish to separate their own community from the state; the "apostates" (*marik*), who, unlike the "distorters", do not wish to misinterpret the laws but do so by mistake or misunderstanding; and the "sophists", who also deceive the people by distorting the laws. Kınalızade notes that, in contrast to Nasir al-Din Tusi's opinion, it is not possible to correct any of these people and they must, therefore be killed or exiled instead; he includes false witnesses, corrupt judges and professors, usurping sipahis, and profiteers, among others (K459).

50 Rosenthal 1958, 138.

An interesting point here is Kınalızade's account of the rise of states (K479–80):

> Let it be known that civilized societies (*temeddün*) are, in general, a composition and arrangement of various classes and communities. Every class has its appropriate degree [of power] and place, and professes its special activities ... The constitution of the world is based on the balance between these components ... For it is known that at the beginning of a state [or dynasty] a [certain] class comes to a unanimous agreement and its members support and help each other, like the members of a single body; because every person has a limited degree of power, but the power of many gathered together in one place is greater than the power of each individual. A small group [of people], when is united, prevails over a larger but fractured one. Is it not clear that any ruling class is not even one-tenth [in numbers] of its subjects? But they are united, and they prevail over the subjects because the latter are not ... Experience has shown that whenever such a ruling class has unity and mutual assistance it is safe from difficulties and deficiencies; but when, later, fractures and disagreements appear among this class, it starts to weaken and finally ends in ruins.

This passage comes, as usual, from Davvani's work, but Kınalızade has introduced a crucial difference: whereas Davvani had the traditional eulogy of unity and harmony among the various classes (enforced by the ruler's justice), our author stresses the unity of the ruling class (*her tayife ki bir devletin ashabıdır*), noting specifically that their numbers are very small in comparison to those of its subjects (*re'ayasına*).[51] Apart from the clear allusion to the Ottoman example, it is tempting to see here an echo of Ibn Khaldun's *asabiyya* or "esprit de corps", the solidarity that allows small nomadic tribes to prevail over large settled populations, only to fall in their turn when their members become too accustomed to luxury; all the more so since Kınalızade stresses that this solidarity characterizes "the beginning of a state" (or rather dynasty: *her devletin ibtidası*). Here, therefore, we might have the earliest recorded influence of Ibn Khaldun in Ottoman writings.[52]

---

51 Cf. Dawwani – Thompson 1839, 384–386; Dawwani – Deen 1939, 199–200.

52 Sariyannis (forthcoming). The similarity was also recently noticed by Doğan 2013, 205. Fleischer 1983, 201 showed that Kınalızade's formulation of the "circle of justice", a little later in the text, was not taken by Ibn Khaldun as Na'ima claimed more than a century after. Ibn Khaldun indeed cites the circle in the same way that Kınalızade did (Ibn Khaldun – Rosenthal 1958, 1:81 and 2:105; Ibn Khaldun – Rosenthal – Dawood 1969, 41),

This universal theory of society comes complete with a description of the four pillars (*erkân-ı erba'a*) or, as Kınalızade calls them, the four "elements of the body of the world" (K485–486: *anasır-ı beden-i alem*). These are: (a) the "men of the pen" (*ehl-i kalem*), meaning ulema, judges, scribes, doctors, poets, and the like, who are likened to the element water, since knowledge is vital for the life of the soul; (b) the "men of the sword" (*ehl-i şemşir*), likened to fire; (c) the class of merchants and craftsmen (*tayife-i tüccar u müstecliban-ı bizayi' ve erbab-ı hiref ü sanayi'*), likened to air since they bring ease and relaxation to the soul; and (d) the farmers (*zira'at-gerler ve ekinciler*), likened to earth because, while they work for the benefit of all, the other classes look down on them. Like the elements in the human body, these four classes must remain balanced; whenever a class grows excessively it hurts the others and thus the whole world; furthermore, each class must stick to its own occupation. For instance, if the majority of people become soldiers the number of merchants will diminish; if the military engage in trade and craftsmanship, disorder will ensue. One should also note here the somewhat "transitional" view of Bitlisi, who speaks of two classes of people (those on whom the sultan depends), the men of the sword and those of the pen; Bitlisi uses a simile related to the soul rather than the natural elements (A27–38).[53] In the long run, as will be seen, it was the four-fold distinction that prevailed.

• • •

If we are to specify one main characteristic of these works, it is their comprehensive character; or, to put it another way, their ambition to cover all manifestations of human activity. Political science is viewed as a branch of moral philosophy, and there is a continuum from oneself to wider society which is studied in the same light and with the same tools and concepts. After (in fact, even before) Kınalızade, this worldview waned in favor of more concrete, down-to-earth conceptualizations until the Khaldunist theories of Kâtib Çelebi

---

but it is easier to suppose that the latter used his Persian source (although this specific passage is his own addition to Davvani's text).

53 Thus, the king has the place of the head within the kingdom, and the place of the brain within the head. Now, the head and the brain constitute two separate powers, the first controlling perception and the second movement. The motive power (*kuvve-i muharrike*) corresponds to the army, the people of the sword, while the power of perception (*kuvve-i hassa*) corresponds to the people of the pen; these two powers must be kept in balance by the head and brain, i.e. the sultan. In the epilogue of another work of his, *Hesht Bihisht*, Bitlisi provides a different simile, saying that the sultan is the heart, his officers the powers, the army the limbs, and the people the hair and bones of the body politic: Bitlisi – Başaran 2000, 127.

in the mid-seventeenth century; however, there were some elements of Tusian political theory that were to be embedded in the foundations of Ottoman social and political thought for centuries. Contrary to a widely-supported assumption that Sunni Islamic political thought was not influenced by Avicenna and al-Farabi's Aristotelism, these ideas became commonplace for almost every Ottoman author, of *medrese* origin or not, even if he did not endorse the whole model of interpreting the world as a morality-driven continuum.[54]

Among the implications of the Tusian model, of special importance is its abstraction: as Gottfried Hagen remarks, in this model[55]

> the socio-political order is divinely ordained and therefore largely beyond human influence ... in other words, there is only one form of social order, not different ones for different states or periods ... [S]ocial groups and government are universal categories and in no way specific to any culture or nation, just as cultural, ethnic, religious or other differences among the subjects are not part of the theory, not even the distinction between nomads and sedentary folk so pervasive in other theories.

Consequently, this "world order", based on universal categories and extra-human arrangements, must be completely static, with the only possible differences being those resulting from varying degrees of justice or tyranny. This view is largely concomitant with the general aversion towards the idea of innovation, which was current in a large part (but not all) of Ottoman ideology until well into the seventeenth century. For most of this period, change would be ideologically acceptable only if it were done to the standards of another ideal form of the past—thus, again, within the same "world order", the only one existing and possible. While this idea may not have first entered the Ottoman world through Tursun or Kınalızade, their systematic exposition of such views contributed greatly to the crystallization and establishment of this underlying notion, namely that there is a perpetual and divinely-ordained social arrangement.

More specifically, there are three ideas that entered Ottoman political thought with Amasi's work and which were to be repeated by many authors

54 See Ahmed 2016, 127 and cf. ibid., 457ff. on Tusi, Davvani and some of their Ottoman continuators. On the dismissal of practical philosophy by a series of post-Classical commentators, on the grounds that the Sharia had attained the ultimate perfection of this branch, see Kaya 2014, 286–289.

55 Hagen 2013, 437.

subsequently, even if they did not adhere to the general "Tusian" trend being described in this chapter. The first of these was the quartet of the cardinal virtues, which played a central part in moral and political theory throughout the late fifteenth and sixteenth centuries.[56] The theory of virtues, based on a combination of Aristotle's and Plato's ethics, had been elaborated (together with the theory of the three-fold partition of the soul) in an Islamic context by al-Kindî in the ninth, Avicenna (Ibn Sina) in the tenth, and Ibn Miskawayh in the early eleventh century. It also played a major role in the later Middle Ages and Renaissance in Europe, as it was central to the definition of the ideal ruler until the reconsideration of *virtù* by Macchiavelli.[57] Fifteenth-century *adab* authors shared the idea that moral perfection is a prerequisite for rule, but the full elaboration of a complex system of virtues and their respective vices was developed by the authors who adapted Tusi's moral philosophy.

Secondly (and together with the preponderance of justice among the four virtues) is the idea of the "circle of justice", a recurring theme in Persian and Ottoman political ideology that was expressed by various formulations which differed from each other in various ways.[58] The basic idea of the "circle of justice" is that the ruler needs the army, the army needs wealth, wealth is produced by the peasants, and the peasants' welfare is secured by the ruler through justice. The elements of the circle may differ in number or description, but the essence is always that the ruler has to protect his subjects with justice in order to secure his own power. Here, too, earlier authors had also emphasized justice and its role in rulership, but it is Amasi who first quotes the famous "circle of justice" in Arabic (and so may be credited with the first appearance of it in Ottoman literature): "there is no religion without king, no king without an army, no army without wealth, no wealth without improvement of the cities, and no such improvements without justice" (Y142). From then on, not only was it only adherents of Tusian moral philosophy but practically every writer of political works in the sixteenth century who reiterated this pattern in various

56 On the cardinal virtues see Sariyannis 2011a; on the evolution of the idea in Islamic philosophy, see R. Walzer's detailed article in *Encyclopaedia of Islam*, 2nd ed. (s.v. "akhlak").

57 See Skinner 1978, 1:69ff. and esp. 128ff.; Bejczy – Nederman 2007. Cf. also the quite different perspective of Central Asia as represented in the four major characters in *Kutadgu Bilig*, namely justice, fortune, intellect/wisdom, and ascetic illumination (Yusuf Khass Hajib – Dankoff 1983, 3 and passim). On al-Kindi's adaption of Aristotle's metaphysics see Fakhry 1994, 67–70; Fakhry 2000, 22–29; on Avicenna's enumeration of the virtues, Donaldson 1963, 108; on Miskawayh, Donaldson 1963, 121–133; Fakhry 1994, 107–130.

58 This notion comes from a very old Iranian and Middle Eastern tradition (Darling 2008; Darling 2013c); it is also to be found in the Central Asian *Kutadgu Bilig* (İnalcık 1967, 263). A meticulous study of the development of the various formulations of this concept can be found in Kömbe 2013.

versions. A classic and complex formulation belongs to Kınalızade and constitutes the final part of his essay (K539). It consists of a cyclical border, inside which these verses are written:

> Justice is the cause of the righteousness of the world—The world is a garden; its wall is the state/power (*devlet*)—The Holy Law is what arranges the state (*devletin nâzımı*)—The only possible guardian of the Holy Law is sovereignty (*mülk*)—Only the army can give sovereignty a firm hold—Only wealth (*mal*) can bring together an army—The peasant is he who creates wealth (*malı kesb eyleyen ra'iyyettir*)—Justice makes the peasant faithful (*ra'iyyeti kul eder*) to the king of the world.

Third is the division of society into four classes and the related simile of the four elements, with the underlying idea that the balance between them is a prerequisite for the world order.[59] Although Plato's philosophy and Galenic medicine had put forth the need for balance in human society, the tripartite division of society found in Western political thought did not offer itself to a one-to-one simile; Iranian tradition, on the other hand, had developed the notion of a four-fold division. Whereas Tusi's main source, Avicenna, had kept Plato's three-fold division (also adapted in a similar form in medieval Europe) of rulers, artisans, and guardians,[60] it seems that the traditional division into warriors, priests, artisans and farmers appeared first in Firdawsi's early eleventh-century epic. This allowed Tusi to add the idea of a one-to-one correspondence of these classes with the four elements, in order to enhance the cosmic significance of this model and to inspire the idea of the need for balance; moreover, it was Tusi who first included merchants as well as the "artisan" class. Like the "circle of justice", the four-fold division of society soon became one of the more recurrent elements in Ottoman political thought. In fact, as will be seen in the conclusion of this book, it is exactly this model that is implied in the concept of "world order" (*nizam-i alem*), one of the most central notions in Ottoman thought.

2.3 *The* adab *Element in* ahlak *Literature*

Although the main characteristic of the *ahlak* philosophers is their highly theoretical description and normalization of human society and government, one should not think that they were devoid of more concrete advice in the style of *adab* or "mirrors for princes" that we studied in chapter 1. Indeed, they

59 On the pre-Ottoman genealogy of this idea cf. Syros 2013; Tezcan 1996, 121.

60 Rosenthal 1958, 152.

all contain a set of moral rules, either for personal improvement or for just and effective government, mainly but not exclusively elaborating the theory of virtues and vices, the latter being an excess or lack of the former, respectively. Yet what differentiates the relevant part of their work from other "mirrors for princes" (which took Nizam al-Mulk's *Siyasetname* as their main model) is the high degree of abstraction. Advice is usually given in lists: the seven virtues for those who seek kingship, the five categories of rules for government, the four principles concerning generosity, and so forth. We will see in chapters 3 and 4 how this obsession with lists became a typical feature of descriptions of society and the world by members of the Ottoman bureaucracy. More particularly, lists of virtues, of moral or wisdom prerequisites for good government, etc. were to form a large part of the late sixteenth-century decline theorists, who in this respect were, to some extent, popularizing the worldview of our Tusian authors.[61]

Thus, seven virtues are required of the king: high aspirations (*uluvv-i himmet*), resulting from control of his passions and lust (Kınalızade here illustrates the point with the example of Süleyman Çelebi, who kept indulging in entertainment and debauchery, thus leading himself to his doom);[62] solidity of opinion; determination and resolution; forbearance; wealth (so he does not covet his subjects' property); fidelity from the army and its commanders; and a noble lineage (*neseb*). This last point deserves some remarks, as it contrasts with fifteenth-century ideas as seen, for example, in the writings of Sinan Pasha. Kınalızade explains that "in most cases" a ruler's noble genealogy is useful for the order of the kingdom and the loyalty of his subjects; he illustrates this point with the negative example of the Mamluk dynasty. He hastens to add, of course, that the Ottoman dynasty is of noble lineage, and that the loyalty of its soldiers and officers is beyond any doubt, as nobody would even think of replacing the dynasty. He adds, however, that of all the virtues noted noble lineage is not obligatory, only very useful. Amasi, on the other hand, being much closer to an era in which the Ottomans could barely claim such a lineage, chose to ignore his model, Tusi, and to replace this virtue of the ruler with a fatherly attitude (*übüvvet*) that would make people love him (Y76).

Additionally, more "political" advice is forned of the conditions (or prerequisites, *şurut*) that ensure a ruler's justice. These are more directly linked to the worldview of moral philosophy, as they embody both the circle of justice and the four-fold division of society. A king should treat all people equally (*cümle*

61 For what follows, cf. Sariyannis 2011a, 124–128.

62 On this tradition and its role in the opposition to imperial projects, see Kastritsis 2007, 121–122 (and also 155–156).

halayıkı mütesavi tuta)—since men's relations with the world are like the four elements (K485–86)—and respect all four classes; the same principle must be kept when giving charities (*hayrât*). These charities are of three kinds, namely security (*selamet*), property (*emval*), and generosity (*keramet*; meaning high posts). (K492–94). As for people who are evil by nature, the ruler has several ways of dealing with them, including imprisonment, exile, and so on; if such measures do not lead to any improvement, some ulema proposed the person should be executed, but it seems better to resort to amputation when Islamic law does not prescribe capital punishment. Kınalızade here refutes the opinion of some "contemporary rulers" who claimed that the punishments of the Sharia did not suffice at that time, as there were large numbers of criminals (K489–90; Kınalızade, as will be seen at the end of the next chapter, might have had in mind his contemporary, Dede Cöngi Efendi, whose work embodied Ebussu'ud's spirit and the Ottoman *kanun* synthesis).

Lastly comes the normal amount of practical advice originating from Iranian "mirrors for princes", such as the need for the sultan to regularly listen to his subjects' complaints, the use of spies, the rules for military campaigns, acceptable behavior for the rulers' boon companions, and so on. The similarity with the works examined in chapter 1 is evident, for instance, in a section of Amasi's work (Y139–51) where he warns the sultan to be grateful for God's grace and urges him to follow uprighteousness in two ways: between himself and God, on the one hand, and between himself and the people, on the other. The latter corresponds to justice, and has several degrees. The first degree is recognizing God's rights over man and particularly over the sultanate. Among God's blessings (*nimet*), the second most important (after faith) is authority (*velayet*), as shown by various sayings of the Prophet; rulers, who are blessed thus, must be aware of their obligations. The second degree of justice is respect for the ulema; the ruler must listen to their advice and act accordingly. As for the third degree, it is that the sultan should not be satisfied with preventing his own injustice; he is also responsible for the misdeeds of his officials. Oppression of his subjects by them is to be credited to the ruler himself. One typical story (Y149) goes:

> They asked a king who had lost his power as to why power changed hands and why his realm went away. And he answered: "Because I was proud of my power and might, and haughty about my opinion, knowledge, and reason, so that I avoided consultation; because I handed over important affairs to small people, lost all opportunities in time, and was lazy and neglectful concerning the affairs of the people".

Departing slightly from Tusi's and Davvani's model, Bitlisi makes a distinction between innate and acquired virtues (A18–21): God presents gifts to man in two ways: either innate (*vehbi*), such as beauty, cleverness, and good fortune, or acquired (*kesbi*), such as gain through some trade. The second can be influenced by external factors, while the first cannot. The greatest of the gifts bestowed on man is the ordering of human affairs by divine guidance, *hilafet-i Rahmani*; this may be obtained via the "visible kingship" (*saltanat-ı suri*), with the "spiritual rule" (*hilafet-i manevi*), or with the "real caliphate" (*hilafet-i hakiki*), which combines the first two. It is sustained by a series of innate blessings, such as faith, good fortune, kindness in morals, good character,[63] and so forth. Bitlisi then proceeds to give pieces of advice, which vary from prerequisites that will ensure kings' eternal rule, i.e. their dwelling in Paradise (knowledge of and submission to God, and benevolence: A38–40), through types of entertainment the king must avoid, to rules concerning the collection of taxes, the cultivation of all arable land, even with state expenses, the protection of peasants, and so on.

What is interesting in Bitlisi's work is his use of the concept of rules to be followed by the sultan. Previously, when dealing with the cardinal and the secondary virtues (A21–27), he noted that the sultan must remember the rights of his subjects and military forces and stick to the laws ordained. And in the longest and most practical part of his essay (A27–38), he gives many pieces of advice (such as the need for the king's council to be accessible to every subject, the need for consultation with wise advisors, the tasks of the viziers, and so on) in the form of five categories of rules (*kanun*). The use of this very term is significant. Bitlisi uses it to denote law, rule, or custom,[64] and, of course, he was writing just when the culture of sultanly law or *kanun* was being established. Nevertheless, in this particular case, rules were for the sultan to follow, not to set. To see in Bitlisi a precursor of the seventeenth-century exponents of a "constitutionalism" binding the sultan to religious or secular rules (see below, chapter 5) would undoubtedly be far-fetched. However, one could return to our remark about Şeyhoğlu and other fifteenth-century authors, who had put kingship under the condition of moral perfection and just government rather than endowing the ruler with sacred charisma (let us

63 Here, like Amasi, Bitlisi delves into the issue of whether individual character can be changed or not. In his opinion, human disposition is by nature mild, so everybody is inclined to good morals, provided he has the right guidance. It is important to note that a king's good or bad morals have an effect on all of his subjects.

64 Tezcan 2000, 663, fn. 9.

remember, by the way, that Şeyhoğlu had explicitly referred to rules the sultan should follow: *ol kanunca gide*, Y72).

3 The Afterlife of a Genre

With Kınalızade's monumental work, Tusi and Davvani's development of neo-Aristotelian political and moral philosophy (mainly through al-Farabi's version) was finally popularized in Ottoman literature. In contrast to his predecessors (the works by Amasi, Tursun, and Bitlisi were copied only once or twice), Kınalızade's work enjoyed great popularity. Notions such as the "circle of equity" or the division of society into the four classes, especially, were to dominate or, at least, be present in almost every treatise of political advice composed from the mid-sixteenth century onwards. On another level, the Farabian notion of "the virtuous state" was incorporated by some sixteenth-century *ulema* authors, as, for instance, when Ahmed Taşköprüzade (1495–1561), one of the most celebrated Ottoman scholars of his time, presented "the science of government" (*ilm al-siyâsa*) in his encyclopedia (*Miftâh al-sa'âda wa misbâh al-siyâda fî mawzû'ât al-'ulûm*, or "The key to happiness and the guide to nobility in the objects of science", completed in 1557):[65]

> The science of government is the knowledge of what state and government entail, the condition of dignitaries, the situation of subjects, and the welfare of cities. This is a science which rulers need first, and then other people. Because man is by nature social. A person is required to reside in a virtuous city (*al-madînatü'l-fâdıla*) and migrate from an unvirtuous one, and to know how the residents of the virtuous city could benefit from him and how he could benefit from them.

Taşköprüzade, significantly, has this science as part of his section on ethics, and the authors he enumerates are pseudo-Aristotle, al-Farabi, Tusi, and Davvani. Like Amasi and Kınalızade, he does not ignore practical advice, which is contained in other parts of his encyclopedia, in special sections on manners for kings (*âdâb al-mulûk*) and viziers (*âdâb al-wizâra*), market inspection (*ihtisâb*), military administration, and so forth. A short note on his quite original categorization of science could be useful here: Taşköprüzade attempted to classify knowledgeable sciences along the stages of God's manifestation according to Sufi doctrine (universal spirit, intellect, nature, and

65 Taşköprüzade – Bakry – Abu'l-Nur 1968, 1:407–8 (as translated by Yılmaz 2005, 8).

man), which correspond to different stages of knowledge. Thus, he recognized: (a) the spiritual sciences, further divided into practical and theoretical and again subdivided into those based on reason and those based on religion[66] (what is described as the "science of government" above belongs to the practical and rational sciences); (b) the intellectual sciences (*makûlât-ı sâniyya*), such as logic, dialectics, and the art of debate; (c) the oral sciences (*ulûm-ı lafzıyya*), i.e. those pertaining to language; and (d) the written sciences (*ulûm-ı hattiyya*), i.e. calligraphy etc. Taşköprüzade's system is partly influenced by al-Ghazali and partly by the fourtheenth-century Avicennian encyclopedist Ibn al-Akfani, but does not follow any of the earlier categorizations.[67]

Yet Tusi's system must have seemed too elaborate or, perhaps more accurately, too abstract for the Ottoman authors. We have to wait until the mid-seventeenth century and Kâtib Çelebi to see another theorist with a tendency for general explanatory systems (and, this time, dynamic ones). It was, perhaps, the very static character of these descriptions of human society that made them sound somehow obsolete to the ears of late sixteenth-century authors, who were witnessing constant changes in fortunes, institutions, and moralities. Kınalızade, himself rather late in this respect (and the first after almost 50 years to take up a Tusian system in Ottoman literature), had no major followers, at least as far as the political part of his treatise is concerned.[68] In general, authors from the second half of the sixteenth century and the beginning of the seventeenth seem to have felt that concrete advice was more useful for their times, and so concrete advice was what they offered. On the other hand, and although the emphasis on the cardinal virtues faded away

66 This classification eventually produces four classes: (1) philosophical (or theoretical-rational) sciences (*ulûm-ı hikemiyya*), which include metaphysics (the science of man's soul), theology (angelology, prophetology etc.), natural sciences and medicine (including magic, alchemy, and the interpretation of dreams), mathematics and music; (2) practical philosophy (*hikmet-i ameliyya*) or the practical-rational sciences, i.e. ethics and administration (from the household to politics and the army); religious or theoretical-religious sciences (*ulûm-ı şer'iyya*), i.e. Quranic exegesis and jurisprudence; finally, esoteric or practical-religious sciences (*ulûm-ı bâtiniyya*), i.e. mysticism.

67 On Taşköprüzade's views see also Gökbilgin 1975–1976; Unan 1997; Yılmaz 2005, 93–99; Karabela 2010, 165–169; Hagen 2013, 409–411. On previous Islamicate categorizations of knowledge see Gardet– Anawati 1970, 101–124; Treiger 2011; Kaya 2014.

68 There have been some continuators but of a rather marginal importance: Sariyannis 2011a, 139; cf. also Yılmaz 2005, 30, fn. 13. We must also note that the notions of moral philosophy used in these works were also present in the *kelam* literature that formed the curriculum of Ottoman medreses (see Fazlıoğlu 2003). In general, however, Ottoman moral philosophy followed a more ethics-centered approach with Sufi connotations, discarding the political and economic part of the *felsefe* tradition: for an early example, see Ali Cemali Efendi – Kaplan – Yıldız 2013.

in the second half of the sixteenth century, the pattern of the "circle of justice" and the four-fold division of society, together with the emphasis on the need for balance, was to form the basic vocabulary of Ottoman political ideas until at least the middle of the seventeenth century. As for the underlying notion of a divinely ordained, universal "world order", this also continued to shape much of the Ottoman world vision, well into the eighteenth century.

CHAPTER 3

The Imperial Heyday: the Formation of the Ottoman System and Reactions to It

Süleyman began his outstanding reign in 1520 following the death of his father Selim I.[1] His situation was precarious: on the one hand, he ruled an empire that, within only eight years, had doubled in size and now included the three main Muslim holy cities and Egypt; on the other, a formidable new enemy had appeared in the East, Safavid Persia, both a menacing military power and a threat to the Ottomans' internal security, as the Turcoman origins of the Safavid dynasty and its emphasis on the Shi'i imamate appealed to large sections of the population of central and eastern Anatolia. However, the first, spectacular campaigns of the new sultan were orientated toward the West: Belgrade fell in 1521 and Rhodes two years later, while the Ottomans won a military triumph over the Hungarians at Mohács in 1526.

Initially, the Asian provinces called for the sultan's attention only due to successive revolts in Syria and Egypt, which ended—significantly—following the intervention of the all-powerful new grand vizier, Ibrahim Pasha (a childhood friend of the sultan), who—also significantly—drew up a new law-code for Egypt. However, Süleyman himself had to return urgently from Hungary in 1526 in order to deal with two rebellions in central Anatolia, before going back to intervene personally in the Hungarian dynastic conflicts, even laying siege to Vienna (1529) as a response to the Habsburgs short-lived conquest of Buda. The truce that followed enabled the Ottomans to launch their major campaign against Iran: by 1536, Baghdad and Erzurum had been annexed by the empire, while Tabriz was temporarily occupied. This campaign, however, also saw the execution of Ibrahim Pasha, who had almost scandalously risen to near-absolute power and thereby raised considerable jealousy and hatred (the two men, it seems, had believed they were to hasten the coming of the Messiah by capturing Rome).[2] In subsequent years, Süleyman made an alliance with France against the Habsburgs and planned to invade Italy, while the Ottoman navy under Hayreddin Barbaros captured Venetian fortresses in Greece and the Aegean. War in Hungary persisted until the signing of a treaty in 1547

1 On Süleyman's reign see Mantran 1989, 145–155 and 159ff.; Kunt – Woodhead 1995; Emecen 2001b, 31–39; Imber 2009, 42–53.
2 See Fleischer 2007 and cf. Flemming 1987.

© KONINKLIJKE BRILL NV, LEIDEN, 2019 | DOI:10.1163/9789004385245_005

(Süleyman profited by launching another campaign against the Safavids), only to be restarted in Transylvania, Hungary, and the western Mediterranean in the next few years. On yet another front, the conquest of Egypt had brought the Ottomans into contact with the Portuguese sphere of interest in the Indian Ocean: several naval campaigns resulted in the conquest of Basra and of Yemen, c. 1550, and in raids as far as Diu, in India. However, Süleyman's main interest remained Europe: after a short civil war between his two remaining sons, as will be seen in more detail in the following chapter, he launched his last campaign in person, dying only two days before the fortress he was laying siege to, Szigetvár, capitulated.

The discussion on whether Süleyman's reign was the "classical period" (whatever that means) of the Ottoman Empire notwithstanding, it was to form a yardstick for comparison in the following centuries. In this chapter, we will seek to give an overview of the ideas prevailing in juristic and political thought during his reign in order to try to detect the beginnings of trends that followed and the attitudes against which subsequent authors reacted.[3]

1 The Basis of the Ottoman Synthesis: Ebussuud and the Reception of Ibn Taymiyya

As shall also be seen in the next chapter, Süleyman's reign was generally regarded as the heyday of the Ottoman Empire; this view, however, rested more on his internal policies than on his conquests, which were no more spectacular than those of his father Selim. Süleyman was named *Kanunî*, "the Lawgiver", although he was not the first sultan to issue *kanunname*s, or books of laws and regulations.[4] His reputation rests primarily on his collaboration with the two major sixteenth-century *şeyhülislam*s, Kemalpaşazade (1525–34) and Ebussu'ud Efendi (1545–74). Both were outstanding scholars; the latter also organized the *şeyhülislam* office into a fully institutionalized quasi-governmental bureau, and was a paragon of what has been called the Ottoman synthesis of secular and sacred law.[5] "Secular" law itself was a synthesis, since in the preceding centuries the sultans had been issuing edicts that complemented customary laws and regulations; what Ebussu'ud primarily achieved was to locate the

3 This chapter owes much to Yılmaz 2005, who located and studied plenty of theretofore unknown minor sixteenth-century authors of political literature.

4 İnalcık 1969a; İnalcık 1992a. On *kanunnames* see also the bibliographical survey in Howard 1995/96.

5 Ebussuud – Düzdağ 1972; Repp 1986, 224ff. (on Kemalpaşazade) and 272ff. (on Ebussu'ud); Imber 1997.

areas of "secular" law that contradicted the Sharia (e.g. the concept of "state land" and the use of monetary fines) and reformulate them in terms of Hanafi jurisprudence so as to make them fit. The selection of the Hanafi school itself as the "official" school in Ottoman jurisprudence, or in other words the institutionalization of law and the firm connection of jurisprudence with the state (a process carried out through the institution of a state-appointed *şeyhülislam*, the formation of an imperial system of legal education, and ultimately the rise of an Ottoman canon of jurisprudence), was an Ottoman novelty—although, as shown recently by Guy Burak, it was a novelty shared in a common legal culture by other post-Mongol Islamicate dynasties of the region as well, such as the Timurids and the Mughals.[6] On the other hand, jurists (especially in the Arab provinces, it seems) kept having recourse to various schools of law in what was recently termed "pragmatic eclecticism"; in this context, with the adoption of the Hanafi school by the Ottomans, Hanafism acquired a "semi-default status" in practice, rather than an all-defining one (although Ottoman elites did try to enforce or at least promote Hanafi judges even in predominantly non-Hanafi provinces).[7]

As will be seen, Ebussu'ud followed a path that had already been taken in Mamluk Egypt,[8] yet the extent and efficiency to which he combined state priorities with Hanafi jurisprudence makes his synthesis, in a way, the work of Ottoman political thought *par excellence*. In other words, he gave a practical answer to the question that had occupied the minds of Muslim political thinkers for centuries, namely how to reconcile secular authority with the all-encompassing power of the Sharia in the absence of a legitimate caliph (although, as we shall see, there were also other ways to overcome the latter problem). It seems that, contrary to the common belief that Sunni jurists generally disregarded state laws, in the Ottoman case Ebussu'ud's enterprise was successful and Hanafi jurists incorporated Ottoman edicts (as well as archival practice) into their legal reasoning well into the eighteenth century.[9]

6 Burak 2013. The adoption of the Hanafi school by the Ottomans had started at the beginning of the fifteenth century, but was made clear in the Süleymanic years and especially after the conquest of Baghdad (1535), when Süleyman visited Abu Hanifa's tomb and ordered its reconstruction.

7 Ibrahim 2015. In the shift from *ijtihad* (interpretative freedom) to *taqlid* (legal conformism to an established corpus of jurisdictions), this eclecticism provided a flexibility necessary for the Muslim populations (in the same way, Christian subjects often had recourse to the Muslim courts in order to enjoy the same kind of flexibility). On the promotion of the Hanafi school by the Ottoman elite in Egypt see Hathaway 2003.

8 Johansen 1988; Ayoub 2016, 244–250.

9 Ayoub 2016; Burak 2016.

Ebussu'ud did not compose any major treatise explaining the grounds of his reformulation of the Ottoman sultanly-*cum*-customary law in Hanafi terms (his most influential treatise was a commentary on the Quran, which became fairly famous and highly-regarded).[10] He produced an extraordinary number of *fetvas*, which essentially formed Ottoman law in the Süleymanic era; furthermore, he also wrote commentaries on juristic issues and the Quran, as well as legal treatises. By the time Ebussu'ud became *şeyhülislam* there was already a huge amount of literature on *fikh* or Islamic jurisprudence regulating everyday aspects of the Sharia or Islamic law; on the other hand, Ottoman sultans from the late fifteenth century onwards had issued numerous law-codes (*kanunnames*), especially on land-holding, tax, and penal issues, which in various way departed from the precepts of the Sharia. Ebussu'ud's task, as mentioned, was to reconcile religious law with *kanun* or secular law in order to produce a coherent body of legal precepts that would respond to the needs of a quasi-feudal empire such as the Ottoman was in this period. In practice, what Ebussu'ud did was to create Islamic foundations for a secular legal system, i.e. to provide justifications based on Sharia-based stratagems and precepts for institutions and practices that had a clearly secular basis; the emphasis on the enhanced authority of the sultan was facilitated by Ebussu'ud's redesignation of the former as caliph. Moreover, Ebussu'ud's rulings often had clearly political goals, justifying the sultanly policies in various disputable issues (such as the executions of princes Mustafa in 1553 and Bayezid in 1559, or breaking the peace treaty with Venice in 1570).

With his legal devices, and in close collaboration with Süleyman (and perhaps, to a lesser extent, with his successor Selim II), Ebussu'ud legitimized current Ottoman practices under Islamic terms. In land-holding, Ebussu'ud established state ownership over the land (a key notion for the Ottoman feudal and taxing system), using an elaborate distinction between *dominium eminens*, possession and usufruct, and redefined the relevant terminology (and taxation) on the basis of traditional Hanafi theories on rent and loan. In order to justify the same practice, his predecessor Kemalpaşazade had used the Mamluk theory of "the death of the *kharaj* payer", i.e. of individual ownership being inherited by the public treasury and thus coming within the jurisdiction of dynastic law. Ebussu'ud tried another Mamluk idea, the concept of land tax as rent, before reverting to a subtler theory on the usufruct being delegated to the peasant. In another one of the main legal controversies that erupted in the mid-sixteenth century, that over religious endowments (*vakf*) and

10 On Ebussu'ud's Quranic commentary and its importance for Ottoman intellectual history, see Naguib 2013.

the legitimacy of endowing cash (on which he had to write a short treatise), Ebussu'ud argued that the sultan maintains ultimate control over the endowed land, but also defended the legitimacy of the donation of cash, i.e. of using money-lending with interest for charitable purposes. Ebussu'ud's arguments in this case are of special interest: he stressed, firstly, that such endowments had been legitimized by constant usage for centuries, and, secondly, that the possible annulment of these established endowments would jeopardize the welfare of the community. On this issue he embarked on a bitter debate not only with his predecessor Çivizade Efendi but also with Birgivî Mehmed b. Pir Ali (1523–73), a highly influential scholar who, as shall be seen, insisted that such endowments would constitute usury and should thus be condemned.[11] In this debate, Ebussu'ud clearly expressed the view of the majority of contemporaneous scholars, if only because the cash endowments supported most of their own activity; with the exception of Çivizade, more than one ex-*şeyhülislam* had supported this institution, including Ebussu'ud's immediate predecessor, Fenarizade Muhyiddin Efendi.[12] One of Ebussu'ud's supporters, a sheikh from Sofia named Bali Efendi (d. 1552), describes the central argument with formidable clarity:[13]

> The truth is, we know from the correctness of the cash *waqf* the strength of its argument. We know that it would be a great sin to prevent its practice ... This *waqf* supports the activities of Friday services. If it were lost ... Friday prayers would be abandoned ...
>
> God's legislation has no other purpose than to ease the way of His servants through the exigencies of the times. Some rules of the Sharia are overturned by changes through time, out of necessity and to ease difficulties ... There can be no doubt that the traditional citations for its [i.e., the cash *waqf*] inadmissibility have been abandoned in our time through the practice of the people opposed to it.

11 See Mandaville 1979 and Karataş 2010 (on cash-*vakfs*); Johansen 1988, 98ff., Imber 1997, 115ff. and Ivanyi 2012, 270ff. (on land tenure). On previous treatises on cash-*vakfs* see Kemalpaşazade – Özcan 2000, İnanır 2008, 252–256; on Kemalpaşazade's *fetvas* about land-holding and taxation, see İnanır 2008, 235–248.

12 Karataş 2010, 57–59. It is true that Fenarizade had bad personal relations with Çivizade; however, he had also been engaged in bitter conflicts (concerning the formulas of juristic documents, as well as the use of drugs!) with Kemalpaşazade, another supporter of the cash *vakf* institution: see Gel 2013a.

13 Mandaville 1979, 301–304.

1.1 *Dede Cöngi Efendi and the Legitimization of Kanun*

It is interesting that a justification of the right of the ruler to intervene in Islamic law precepts was sought and found in the work of Ibn Taymiyya (1263–1328), a strong opponent of Sufism and of "innovations" who (in the words of E. I. J. Rosenthal) advocated "a reform of the administration in the spirit of the ideal Sharia" and argued that "the welfare of a country depends on obedience to God and his Prophet, on condition that there is a properly constituted authority which 'commands the good and forbids the evil'".[14] Ibn Taymiyya's work became increasingly popular throughout the sixteenth century; the translation by Aşık Çelebi (d. 1572), a prolific translator (among other activities) of Arab political treatises such as those of al-Ghazali and of Husayn Vaiz Kashifi (Davvani's Timurid continuator), was widely read.[15] Ibn Taymiyya's ideas seem closer to those expounded by Mehmed Birgivi, the great opponent of Ebussu'ud and the precursor of the Kadızadeli movement in the seventeenth century, since he is generally seen as the forefather of Islamic fundamentalism. There were, however, points in his work that facilitated an Islamic justification of the Ottoman synthesis. Although he stressed the need for the ruler to follow the Sharia strictly as being the ultimate reason and object of his power, Ibn Taymiyya allowed him discretion over crimes and punishments not prescribed by the by it, such as bribery and abuses in administration; the same was valid for revenue sources provided the consensus of the ulema was not for prohibiting them.[16] In this respect, it is not surprising that, when translating Ibn Taymiyya, Aşık Çelebi added a section on the Ottoman landholding and taxation principles as set out by Ebussu'ud Efendi,[17]

> the *imam* and *şeyhülislam* of both ulema and commoners of our time, the consummation of jurisconsults and the upholder of the pious old virtues.

An interesting example of the affinity between the two jurists is the confiscation of the properties of Christian monasteries in 1568 on the pretext that they were not proper and legitimate *vakfs*, about a hundred years after the Mamluk authorities had done the same in Egypt following a similar *fetva* by Ibn Taymiyya. Furthermore, Ebussu'ud's assertion that monks should not pay the

---

14 On Ibn Taymiyya's work see Rosenthal 1958, 51–61; Lambton 1981, 143–151; Fakhry 2000, 101–104; Black 2011, 158–163.

15 See Yılmaz 2005, 55–56, and more particularly Terzioğlu 2007.

16 Black 2011, 161ff.

17 Terzioğlu 2007, 260 (and cf. ibid., 262 for another reference to Ebussu'ud).

poll-tax "provided they have no intercourse with other people at all" (*asla halk ile muhalatalarıyok ise*) is also strongly reminiscent of Ibn Taymiyya's views.[18]

A work adapting these ideas to the Ottoman context bore the same name as Ibn Taymiyya's treatise, namely *Risâla al-siyâsa al-shar'îya* ("Treatise on the government in accordance with the Sharia") or *Siyaset-i şer'iye* ("Government in accordance with the Sharia"). It was written in Arabic by Kemalüddin İbrahim b. Bahşi, known as Kara Dede or Dede Cöngî Efendi (d. 1565/6 or 1566/7); preserved in a number of manuscripts, since it became very popular in Ottoman medreses, it was translated into Turkish at least three times from the late seventeenth century.[19] An outstanding example of Ottoman social mobility, Dede Cöngi was an illiterate tanner before turning with great success to a career in the ulema, eventually becoming a *müderris* or teacher in various *medreses* in Bursa, Tire, Merzifon, Diyarbekir, Aleppo, and Iznik. In 1557, he became *müfti* of Kefe (Caffa); he retired in 1565 and died in Bursa.

Dede Cöngi's work is mainly a synopsis of the predominant views on Islamic administration and politics in his era. As Uriel Heyd notes, "[t]here is ... very little original thought in Dede Efendi's work[, as h]e mainly quotes various authorities in the field of public and especially penal law"; his sources are, among others, al-Mawardi, Ibn Taymiyya, and Ala' al-Din Ali b. Khalil al-Tarabulusi, a fifteenth-century Hanafi judge from Jerusalem and the author of *Mu'în al-hukkâm*.[20] In this respect, it is interesting that Dede Cöngi (like Ibn Taymiyya before him) employed ideas from different schools of law, especially the Hanafi and the Maliki, reflecting perhaps the new legal situation in the Ottoman Empire following the incorporation of the Kurdish and Arab territories; as expected of an Ottoman scholar, however, Hanafi thought is prevalent.

Dede Cöngi's treatise, full of references to *hadiths* and other authorities, sets out to demonstrate that one may justify, in terms of *fikh*, the existence of extracanonical rules, ones decreed by the ruler, which should be followed by both

18 On the Ottoman confiscation crisis see Fotić 1994; Alexander 1997; Kermeli 1997; on the *fetvas* regarding the poll-tax of the monks, Ebussuud – Düzdağ 1972, 103, nos 450–451; on Ibn Taymiyya and the Mamluks, Welle 2014.

19 Namely by Seyyid Sebzî Mehmed Efendi (d. 1680), İsmail Müfid Efendi (d. 1802), and Meşrebzâde Mehmed Arif Efendi (d. 1858). This last translation (printed as *Tercüme-i Siyâsetnâme*, Istanbul 1275/1858–9) was published (from a manuscript form) by Akgündüz 1990–1996, 4:127–173 (facs. follows). On this translation (not very accurate) see ibid., 4:124 and Heyd 1973, 198, fn. 5 ("rather free and enlarged"). Sabit Tuna (Dede Cöngi – Tuna 2011) provides his own Turkish translation; I preferred to follow it in cases of conflict. On Dede Çöngi's work see Akgündüz 1990–1996, 4:122–126; Heyd 1973, 198–203; Yılmaz 2005, 73–76; Black 2011, 215.

20 Heyd (1973, 199) notes that "in fact, most parts of Dede Efendi's treatise are merely shorter versions of some chapters of the *Mu'în*."

judges and the secular administrators of the realm. First (A132–46, T52–64), he examines the legitimacy of the extra-canonical authority of the ruler (*siyâsa*): not only, he contends, had the Prophet's companions punished evildoers without recourse to the Sharia in several cases but, also, present-day administrators have the ability to make decisions, and this does not contradict it. The causes of the need for such authority are many: first, widespread sedition; second, cases which pertain to the common good but for which there are no Quranic rules (such as the keeping of judicial registers, the mining of coins, and the creation of prisons); and third (A136–37, T56), divergences in the Sharia laws due to changes in necessary preconditions. The examples Dede Cöngi cites are of a rather narrow nature (e.g. problems in accepting women's testimony), but in a more general vein he notes that it is quite appropriate to obey and pay attention to the disputes of each period, which give rise to extensions of the competence of political authority. A fourth (and very similar) cause is that if mischief multiplies in society, broader measures need to be taken and so the competence of political authority has to be expanded. Whenever historical changes (*tağayyür-i zaman*) cause disputes and conflict, what was improper in an earlier period might be considered proper at present, and consequently extra-canonical authority could be properly extended (A139, T57). Furthermore, this expansion was made in accordance with the rules of the Sharia, and, furthermore (and this is the sixth cause), God himself granted such changes and expansions, as for instance when, through the Quran, He permitted practices previously prohibited. It is due to this reasoning that, for instance, the execution of habitual criminals (A142: *sa'i bi'l-fesad*) by sultanly order is deemed necessary. Dede Cöngi cites numerous authorities to the effect that this "execution for reason of state" or *siyaseten katl* is proper, and even obligatory. Here one could note the use of terms (*sa'i bi'l-fesad, siyaseten katl*) that played an extraordinary role in Ottoman penal law;[21] similarly, Dede Cöngi also deals with the various types of "discretional punishment" (*ta'zir*) with a view to justifying Ottoman practices such as monetary fines (A167, T88–89).

After establishing that the canonical legitimacy of extra-canonical punishment has been proven by means of Islamic jurisprudence, Dede Cöngi raises the question of whether it is proper for judges to act, in penal and other cases, according to these "political laws" (*ahkam-ı siyasiye*). He notes that, for the Hanafis, it is an open question whether judges may use "political laws". In a typical manner of *fikh* reasoning, he first cites the Maliki and Shafi'i (al-Mawardi's) opinion, namely that there are occasions in which things permissible for a secular governor (*wâlî*) are improper for a judge, only to reject all of them by

21 See Heyd 1973, 192–198, 261–262.

quoting Hanafi authorities, thereby reverting to the conclusion that judges are authorized to apply "political laws" (A146–151, T65–70). Judges, therefore, can use secular legislation; so may secular administrators, who (in a list of cases such as punishing an adulterous woman or a thief without waiting for proof according to the Sharia, according to al-Iraki and al-Mawardi) can act independently of Islamic judges and even surpass them (A152–57, T71–76). To justify this transgression, Dede Cöngi again uses Hanafi theory and practice (for instance, an administrator trusting his officers is analogous to a judge hearing a single witness of clear impartiality).

Providing further arguments in favor of permitting occasional transgressions of the strict prerequisites of the Sharia, Dede Cöngi stresses that criminals should never go unpunished due to lack of evidence, even if there is no canonical regulation on their imprisonment (A157–166, T77–87). The point of delegating authority to the administrator (A165: *mevzû'-ı velâyet-i vâlî*; T85) is to stop corruption and tyranny, and this cannot be done without punishment, while the judge's task is only to decide on the criminals' guilt; on the other hand, the competence of administrators (*ehl-i harb*) may cover that of judges, or vice versa, according to customs or circumstances (T85–86). Dede Cöngi also mentions the obligation to "command right" (A170, T97: *emr-i bi'l-ma'rûf*), perhaps as another reason for an administrator to yield power.

There is more than just the title of the work that connects it to Ibn Taymiyya: the emphasis on moral decay as a justification for the expansion of state authority to punish criminals, as well as the expansion of the coercive power of the state in order to re-establish the control of Muslim ethics over society, are aspects of Ibn Taymiyya's thought often distorted by present-day assumptions.[22] On the other hand, it is evident that not only the conclusions and underlying principles of Dede Cöngi's work, but also the specific examples and cases he cites, point to Ottoman realities, and particularly to the legal synthesis effectuated under Süleyman by Ebussu'ud. Especially telling is the emphasis he places on historical change and the need for the Sharia (or, at least, *fıkh*) to adapt to it. It was not for nothing that the ulema opposition relied heavily on the old aversion to innovation.

Another work by Dede Cöngi, composed again in Arabic, concerns the correct ways of distributing state expenses according to sources of income. The work, *Risâla fî amwâl bayt al-mâl* ("Treatise on the wealth of the public treasury") was presented to Prince Mustafa, Süleyman's son who was executed in 1553; it presents the established views of *fıkh* scholarship (again with abundant

22 Belhaj 2013.

quotations) on public finances.[23] Dede Cöngi first stresses the central role of the ruler in the administration and distribution of public revenue, noting that he is the administrator of the treasury rather than its proprietor (and here we might detect an idea of the state as an entity distinct from the ruler).[24] The treatise highlights the well-known division of the public treasury (*beytü'l-mal*) into four departments, each with its own income and expenses.[25] In Dede Cöngi's account of this traditional *fıkh* economic or, rather, financial theory, it is again clear that he took care to justify the Ottoman practices of his age. For instance, he refutes the idea that judges should not receive a salary from the public treasury (A229ff.); we will see below that Ebussu'ud's great opponent, Mehmed Birgivi Efendi, maintained that religious positions (including judgeships) should not be remunerated unless in the form of donations.[26] The final part of Dede Cöngi's treatise is of particular interest, since it deals with the rights of the sultan in regard to land (A234–35); he notes that land is like any other property in the public treasury and maintains that the sultan may grant unclaimed land for the general benefit of the Muslims. In a way similar to Ebussu'ud's arguments on cash-*vakf*s, Dede Cöngi claims that the very existence of universally-acclaimed medreses and other foundations based on landed property granted by rulers is proof of the legality of this practice.

1.2 *Between State and Legal Thought*

So far, reviews of Ottoman political thought have, surprisingly, ignored the Süleymanic synthesis. Historians of medieval Islamic political ideas, who are well aware of the debates on caliphal power and its limits, usually neglect the Ottoman period, while Ottomanists (often reluctant to use ulema authors when writing political history) tend to allocate such debates to the history of law. Yet Ebussu'ud's construction was, as seen, a major step in a long process of integrating secular power into the idea of a perfect Islamic community. Ottoman sultans contributed much to the institutional aspect of the process by creating the post of the *şeyhülislam* and by increasing state control over the judiciary. On the other hand, the continuity with Mamluk-era theorists such as Ibn Taymiyya, as well as the use of "pragmatist" arguments such as

23 Akgündüz 1990–1996, 4:213–236 (facs. follows, 236–254); Yılmaz 2005, 73.

24 Cf. Sariyannis 2013. Similar remarks can be made about Ibn Taymiyya's ideas on the ruler's authority (Black 2011, 161).

25 On the *fıkh* theories concerning public income and expenses, cf. *Encyclopaedia of Islam*, 2nd ed., s.v. "Bayt al-mâl" (N. J. Coulson, C. Cahen et al.). The actual organization of the financial departments did not follow these, neither in medieval Islamic empires nor in the Ottoman case; see, for example, Sahillioğlu 1985; Tabakoğlu 1985.

26 Ivanyi 2012, 258–262.

the acceptance of "changes through time", which can alter even the rules of the Sharia, show clearly the relationship of this reasoning with Islamic political thought. It is interesting to see that the arguments of the ulema who supported Ebussu'ud stand in a kind of balanced equilibrium between the notion of "established custom", which was to form a paragon of political concepts (in fact, it was already being used in the "decrees of justice" for mending oppressive practices),[27] and the affirmation of innovative change even in age-old and respected aspects of the Sharia, in order to adapt them to such "established customs". As will be seen, Ebussu'ud's opponents took advantage of this ambiguous position and harshly criticized him for "innovation".

On another level, it has been rightly argued that this "imperial", so to speak, trend in Hanafism was not purely state-driven, as there was a general tendency throughout the post-medieval era among the Hanafi ulema to recognize state authority in their legal reasoning.[28] Yet one cannot neglect the relationship of all these ulema with the state apparatus; furthermore, it may be argued that it was precisely the emergence of law-making ex-nomadic empires that necessitated this line of thought. Although dynastic claims to the caliphate continued to be raised, it is evident that, in the circumstances, there was a need for jurists to accept the ruler's legal capacity if they were to form part of it.

A different aspect of the tension between *kanun* and the Sharia was highlighted by Baki Tezcan, who argued that, in the process leading from a mostly feudal economy (such as prevailed until the mid-sixteenth century) to an increasingly monetarized one, *kanun* represented feudal law whereas the jurists' law (which arguably took over throughout the seventeenth century) was made by and for the interests of the emerging urban markets.[29] Though I generally adhere to his view of the socio-political transformation of the Ottoman Empire, Tezcan relies primarily on the example of cash-*vakf*s. Still, those ulema who argued in favor of this arrangement, fit for a monetary economy, also supported the legal justification of *miri* land, a paragon of Ottoman feudalism, which, significantly, was closely linked to the timar system and began to disintegrate because of monetarization and tax-farming.[30] One might talk here of a slight

27 İnalcık 1965; Sariyannis 2011a, 142.

28 See Burak 2013 (for a view that places emphasis on the dynastic actor); Ayoub 2016 (for a more ulema-centered view).

29 Tezcan 2010a, 19–45.

30 Tezcan tries to reconcile this contradiction by arguing that Ebussu'ud attempted to "bring the feudal customs … in line with jurists' law" (Tezcan 2010a, 43); I believe that it was vice-versa, at least from the jurists' own point of view. On the other hand, Ebussu'ud's opinion of *vakf*s could also be used in favor of endowing property rather than using it for increasing one's personal wealth: see an example in Gel 2013b.

confusion: the conflict between "secular" and "Islamic" law, between *kanun* and the Sharia, is one thing, and it concerned the jurists in as much as the two kinds of laws have different sources and different (or overlapping) executors. Within the "secular law" itself, on the other hand, there was a part based on customary law, which obviously preserves many of the feudal structures in use during the late Byzantine and the early Ottoman centuries, and another part associated with monetarization, as was the case with the monetary fines that replaced corporal punishment. We should also bear in mind that Ebussu'ud's legitimization of the notion of *miri* land did nothing to help impose the timar system (which presupposed this notion); it only reconfigured this system—one that had, by that time, been established for more than 70 years and which was perhaps already beginning to cede its place to monetized structures of taxation—and made it fit within an empire being presented as the champion of Sunni Islam and into a highly-sophisticated judicial system that professed a strict orthodoxy. In a sense, this is again an expression of the ambiguity surrounding legal structures in the turning point symbolized by Süleyman's reign. State ownership of the land was legitimized in terms of the "jurists' law" just when it was beginning to disrupt (as tithe and other taxes in kind waned away in favor of taxes in cash), and Ebussu'ud and his supporters were expressing this specific balance. Later, in chapter 6, how the legal arguments of their opponents were later used in order to undermine the feudal structure of land tenure will be shown—but, as is often the case, it was a structure that by then had suffered significant blows.

2 A New Legitimacy

At the end of chapter 1 we saw how Ottoman dynastic legitimization was developed during the fourteenth and fifteenth centuries, combining the religious fervor of the *gaza* (as seen by the ulema) with mythical genealogies linking Osman to noble ancestors and even prophets. As noted above, the fall of Constantinople had led to significant changes in the imperial image. A new emphasis on ceremonial and hierarchy, enhanced by the sultan's withdrawal from public appearances, was evident in court ritual and literature, as well as in the creation of a heavy and imposing style of art and architecture.[31]

31 Necipoğlu 1992.

In this new image, nobility of lineage, hereditary unity, and religious purity continued to play important roles in legitimizing the Ottoman sultans.[32] Furthermore, the emphasis on Holy War was renewed, as the sultan was presented as the champion of the faith against both the Christians and the Shi'a heretics of Iran.[33] The mystic identification of the sultan with the Messiah or with the "Pole of the world" does not seem to have lasted after the first decades of Süleyman's reign.[34] But a new factor was introduced by Selim I's conquest of the Hijaz (through the annexation of Mamluk Egypt) and thus of the holy cities of Mecca and Medina (1517). Almost simultaneously, the messianic claims of the Safavid shah, Ismail, posed a challenge for the Ottoman sultan that had to be answered, particularly so since a large part of the Anatolian population, being Alevi, was susceptible to these claims. This development created a new dimension in the issue of Ottoman legitimacy: was the Ottoman sultan also to claim the title of caliph, the protector of the holy cities? The rise of the Seljuks and, later, the fall of the Abbasids as a result of the Mongol invasion (1258) had led scholars such as al-Ghazali, Ibn Taymiyya, and Ibn Khaldun to accept a much more flexible interpretation of the requirements for the caliphate, essentially identifying the caliph as a ruler insofar as the latter followed the Sharia and executed its precepts.[35] Moreover, in practice the title of the caliph had acquired an embellishing, regional meaning that allowed for its use by regional rulers such as the early Ottomans and other dynasties in fifteenth-century Anatolia and Iran.[36]

It is not surprising, therefore, that Ottoman literature on the caliphate began to flourish at the beginning of the sixteenth century. Even before the conquest of Egypt (but after Shah Ismail's appearance), İdris-i Bitlisi had written, in 1514, an essay in Arabic entitled *Risâla fî al-khilâfa wa âdâb al-salâtîn* ("Treatise on the caliphate, and manners [i.e. advice] for sultans"), in which he discussed the issue of the potentially simultaneous existence of more than one caliph: his conclusion was that this is impossible, and to this effect he quoted hadiths stating that, if people acknowledged two caliphs, one of them should be killed. In his other works, he followed the idea that whoever carried out the right guidance of his people, the establishment of order, and the management

32 Flemming 1988. The same values played a major role in Idris-i Bitlisi's legitimization of the Kurdish chieftains as presented to the Ottoman side: Sönmez 2012, 72ff.

33 A number of treatises on the virtues of Holy War were translated or composed during Süleyman's reign: see Yılmaz 2005, 66 and fn. 125; cf. Imber 1995, 147–149.

34 Although Süleyman's Messianic claims had waned by the 1530s, a certain sense of historical moment did remain, as is also seen in imperial iconography; see Eryılmaz 2010.

35 See Rosenthal 1958, 38ff.; Sönmez 2012, 130ff.

36 Imber 1987 and 1992, 179; Sönmez 2012, 132–135.

of public affairs under the law of God, may be called God's elect for the caliphate; moreover, he stressed the nobility of the Ottomans' lineage, indirectly qualifying them for the designation of caliphs. While he refuted Shah Ismail's claims to descent from the Prophet, he was careful not to touch this subject as far as it concerned the Ottomans.[37] Fifteen years later, in 1529, writing a universal "History of the caliphs" for Ibrahim Pasha, Hüseyin b. Hasan al-Semerkandi impressively began the story of the Ottoman caliphate with Selim I, thereby showing that the latter was the heir of the caliphal lineage from the Mamluks by conquest.[38] Perhaps in the same vein and around the same period, Abdüsselam b. Şükrullah el-Amasi described the office of the imam and noted that he is the same as the caliph, substituting the Prophet in guiding the people in both religious and secular affairs (*din ve dünyada*). There are three ways for the imam to be chosen: appointment by the previous imam, a collective decision by the notables (*ehl-i ray ve sahib-i tedbir*) upon the death of the previous imam, and an appropriate person conquering the land with his army following the death of the previous imam. After designating the prerequisites for a person to become imam, stressing the value of knowledge, the author states that the present imam is Sultan Süleyman; one might suggest that what is implied is also succession by conquest.[39]

Unlike Bitlisi, the issue of descent was exactly what the ex-grand vizier Lütfi Pasha chose to tackle in 1554, probably hoping to gain Süleyman's favor again, in a treatise entitled *Halâs al-umma fî ma'rifat al-a'imma* ("Deliverance of the community on the knowledge of the imams").[40] Lütfi Pasha begins by praising Süleyman as "the Imam of the Age" who "has maintained the Shar'î laws in order and reformed the 'urfî dîwâns". His aim was to refute the arguments of those who maintained that a legitimate caliph should come from the tribe of Quraysh, i.e. have a blood relationship with the Prophet and his family. Presumably this had been a matter of debate at the time: Lütfi claims that he was asked the question by "certain of the noblest of the *aşrâf*". He quotes extensively from various collections of *fetvas* and hadiths, to the effect that:

37 Sönmez 2012, 139–162. Bitlisi also used regularly the term caliph for the Ottoman sultan in his *Heşt Bihist*: Bitlisi – Başaran 2000, 139 and *passim*.

38 Yılmaz 2005, 70; Kavak 2012, 98. It is to be noted that Semerkandi did not succumb to the Messianic literature revolving around Süleyman and Ibrahim at this time, since he reassures the reader that the End of Days is to come several centuries in the future.

39 Amasi – Coşar 2012, 140–145.

40 The treatise was partially translated in Lütfî Pasha – Gibb 1962; cf. Ocak 1988, 173–174; Fazlıoğlu 2003, 387–389.

> Likewise the authors of these books aforementioned permitted and applied the name of Imâm and Khalîfa to the sultan and the wâlî and the amîr. Our ulema ... have said, "What is meant by the Sultan is the Khalifa", and in another place "The Khalifa is the Imam above whom there is no [other] imam, and he is called the Sultan".

Then Lütfi defines first the sultan as the possessor of an oath of allegiance, a conquering power, and a power of compulsion, then the imam as one who maintains the faith and governs with justice, and finally the caliph as he who commands good and forbids evil (using the old precept of *emr-i ma'ruf ve nehy-i münker*). If all these qualifications apply to one person, he argues, then this person "is a sultan who has a just claim to the application of the names of imam and khalifa and wali and amir, without contradiction". The need for Qurayshi descent was a prerequisite only for the earliest times of Islam. Similarly, Lütfi rejects the opinion that no caliph is to be recognized after the first four, showing that this is a heretical opinion held by the Shi'a. After citing his sources extensively, he arrives at the conclusion that Süleyman "is the imam of [this] Age without dubiety":

> Then if it is asked "What is the proof of the necessity of being subject to him?", the answer is: 'If he or his like were not followed, there would not exist the regular ordering of the matters of temporal existence and the future life among mankind ... For the majority of the people of his age are his freedmen (*'utaqâ'*) and the freedmen of his fathers and ancestors ... since there is no possibility of banding together for the support of any other than the 'Otmânî, because the 'Otmânîs are blameless in respect of maintenance of the Faith and Equity and the Cihad. So if there is born a child of that lineage, he will follow the way of his fathers in maintaining the Faith and the Cihad ...

As Hamilton Gibb notes, Lütfi illustrates the *falasifa* theory of the caliphate, i.e. that "adopted universally by Muslim writers of the post-Abbasid age".[41] This may look as if Lütfi is at pains to prove a matter essentially solved; however, one must note that his very fervor in proving his point shows that the issue was still regarded as urgent and debatable at this time. As Colin Imber remarks, claims to universal sovereignty (always under a religious guise) were made by both of Süleyman's rivals, Charles V and Shah Tahmasp.[42]

41 Lütfî Pasha – Gibb 1962, 295.

42 Imber 1992, 179–180. On the afterlife of Ottoman claims to the caliphate cf. Gerber 2013.

On the other hand, Ebussu'ud had explicitly stated that Süleyman could exercise the right of the caliph to make definitive choices from different legal opinions, and in several cases quoted an imperial order together with—in fact, as the definitive answer to—authoritative jurisprudence.[43] An imperial decree issued in 1548 discusses the debate between Ebussu'ud and Çivizade (the former *şeyhülislam* who had been dismissed for his denunciation of prominent dervishes and who had died one year earlier) on the legality of cash *vakfs*; Süleyman takes a clear position on the grounds that their prohibition would be "the cause of a diminution in benefactions" and that most of the ulema asked favored Ebussu'ud's opinion:[44]

> Since it is my imperial custom and practice to advance the affairs of the Faith and to strengthen the true *shar'*, my decree has gone forth to this effect, that those benefactors who whish to make benefactions … on the basis of that which has been current practice in the Ottoman lands since olden times may establish their *wakfs*, choosing whether to do so with silver or with gold.

It is clear from the sultan's wording that he was practising his right, as described by Ebussu'ud, to decide on matters of jurisprudence, even when the issue at stake was relevant to the Sharia rather than the *kanun*.

3 Reactions to the Imperial Vision

Now, although it looked more and more majestically self-justified and inevitable, the imperial model did not cease to have its enemies. While Ebussu'ud and his adherents, such as Dede Çöngi, were trying to "Islamicize" the Ottoman synthesis, the strong religious connotations that the opposition had taken by Yazıcıoğlu's time became increasingly dominant. A cautionary remark seems useful here: there can be a tendency to revert to an oppositional, religious vs. secular understanding of the world in the post-Enlightenment sense. However, for the sixteenth-century Ottoman this opposition simply did not exist: one could place more emphasis on the Sharia's precepts, i.e. on the role of the ulema who would interprete and execute it, or on the sultan's right to complement the law, but all narratives would only move within a "religious" framework and inevitably use "religious" justifications.

43 Imber 1992; Imber 1995, 152–153.

44 Repp 1986, 255. On this decree cf. Tezcan 2010a, 31–34.

On the political level, a number of anti-imperial movements all took religious forms, mostly as mystical reactions based on Ibn Arabi's notion of "the pole of the world" (*kutb*): apart from the various rebellions of Anatolian sheikhs that rallied the heterodox Turcoman populations, one may mention the messianic movements around the Bayrami-Melami (and later Hamzevi, after the execution of the Bosnian Hamza Bali in 1561) dervishes of central Anatolia during the fifteenth century (1524, 1538, 1568) and numerous ulema and (mainly Gülşeni) dervishes accused of being heretics, who have been studied in an exemplary manner by Ahmet Yaşar Ocak.[45] It should be noted, however, that the *şeyhülislam* Çivizade Efendi, a strict defender of the Sharia and an opponent of Ebussu'ud's interpretations and syntheses, was dismissed in the early 1540s on account of (among others) his accusations not only against long-dead authorities of Sufism such as al-Ghazali, Ibn Arabi, and Jalal al-Din Rumi, but also against Sheikh İbrahim Gülşenî (d. 1534).[46] On the other hand, we will see below that eulogies for Süleyman such as the anonymous *al-Adliyya al-Süleymaniya* or Dizdar Mustafa's *Kitâb sulûk al-mulûk* used the same notion of the "Pole" to glorify the empire, as they identified this role with the Ottoman sultan.

A striking case, where opposition to the imperial project took the form of a total renunciation of secular power in the name of piety, is to be found (many years before Süleyman's accession) in the works of Şehzade (Prince) Korkud (c. 1468–1513), (most probably) the fifth son of Bayezid II. Having, even in his childhood, an inclination for scholarship, in his youth (and after sitting for two weeks on the throne as regent following the death of his grandfather, Mehmed II) he served as the governor of Manisa, where he was involved in naval conflicts with the French and Venetians (the siege of Lesvos, 1501), and then of Antalya, where he collaborated closely with Muslim corsairs. In 1509, perhaps seeing that he stood no chance against Selim, his competitor in the succession struggle, Korkud renounced his eligibility for succession and left for Cairo, where he spent more than a year at the court of the Mamluk sultan. He then returned home and became governor of Antalya and, later, Manisa. After the Şahkulu rebellion he recognized the accession of his brother Selim I; almost a year later, Korkud fled and was eventually executed near Bursa. During his adventurous life, he wrote many religio-political works in Turkish and Arabic, which mainly addressed the problem of the compromise of imperial authority with the precepts of the Sharia, as well as treatises on mysticism, music, etc. Among his most important works are: *Dawat al-nafs*

45 Ocak 1991 and 1998.
46 Repp 1986, 250–252; Gel 2010, 233ff.

al-taliha ila'l-amal al-saliha ("An errant soul's summons to virtuous works, through manifest signs and splendid proofs"); *Hâfiz al-insân 'an lâfiz al-imân wa Allâh al-hâdî ilâ sirât al-jinân* ("The individual's protector from faith's rejector, as God is the guide for the heavenly paths"), on apostasy (ca. 1508); *Hall ishqâl al-afkâr fi hill amwâl al-kuffâr* ("The solution for intellectual difficulties concerning the proper disposal of infidel properties"), on the correct distribution of holy war booty, with special reference to concubines (1509); and *Wasîlat al-ahbâb bi ijâz, ta'lîf walad harrakahu al-shavq li arz al-Hijâz* ("The means of the beloved for authorization, written by a son whom desire has driven to the land of the Hijaz"), on the importance of the Hajj, a work written in order to justify the author's self-imposed exile (1509).[47]

Dawat al-nafs, Korkud's most interesting work for our purposes, was completed in Arabic in 1508.[48] He composed it in Manisa and sent it to the court in order to ask his father to release him from his duties as a governor, as he no longer aspired to the throne and wished to follow a career in the ulema (or a kind of honorary retirement as *müteferrika*). This voluminous Arabic work, full of *hadiths*, Quranic quotations, and scholarly commentaries, is focused on demonstrating that being an effective ruler is incompatible with being a pious and proper Muslim, while also criticizing the imperial order being crystallized in the early period of the sixteenth century. Korkud's reasoning is heavily influenced by al-Ghazali's arguments against the ruler's revenues and on the advantages of seclusion.[49]

In his preface, addressed directly to his father Bayezid II, Korkud stresses the ephemeral quality of this world and the importance of salvation of the soul, as opposed to earthly power. He defines the *muflis* (the "bankrupt") as anyone who, despite following the precepts of religion, is doomed to hell because of his sins (T197–98). He then proceeds to enumerate the five main reasons he decided to resign his candidacy for the Ottoman throne. The necessity of administration (*urf*), he states, leads to: (a) committing murder not covered by the Sharia—Korkud explicitly refers to *siyaset* punishment, i.e. "administrative" execution, noting that the only case for permissible murder of a Muslim would be retaliation for murder, adultery, or apostasy, adding that, according to all the ulema, ordering someone else to commit murder is a grave sin even if the sinner does not commit the murder in person (T200);

47 On the last three works, see al-Tikriti 2005a; al-Tikriti 2004, 136–154 and al-Tikriti 2013; al-Tikriti 2005b, respectively.

48 Al-Tikriti 2004, 196ff gives an extensive English summary of the Arabic text. On Korkud's ideas, see also Fleischer 1990, 70ff.; al-Tikriti 2001; Ivanyi 2012, 112–116.

49 Cf. Laoust 1970, 95–104.

(b) seizing and spending illicit wealth—the author considers the various taxes a mixture (at best) of permissible and impermissible expropriations of wealth, admitting all the same that, were they abandoned, the ruler would have no resources whatsoever from his subjects. Even if the subjects accept paying their taxes, this does not invalidate the illegality of such extortions; moreover, the ways these revenues are spent are often sinful, such as when they support Sufis; (c) associating with sinners, for example Melami dervishes (a clear criticism of Bayezid's support for various Sufi orders); (d) abandoning one's spiritual "emptying of the heart", i.e. concentration on devotion to God and withdrawal from worldly affairs—to this effect, Korkud cites some historical anecdotes where princes and rulers abdicated to follow a sinless life; and, finally, (e) causing civil strife in the struggle for succession—because of the "emptiness of power" (T207: *khuluw al-imâra*), internal disputes and conflicts are inevitable and the Ottoman experience only proves this. Korkud further elaborates his argument on not associating with sinners in terms of the traditional complaint regarding the decline of the time (T211). From the time of the Prophet onwards, he argues, each generation is worse than the previous one, and he sees the society of his own days as especially guilty of material greed; moreover, living in a court causes jealousy in every possible facet of one's life, and jealousy and slander are grave sins. Korkud lists a number of ways to fight one's desire for alcohol, gluttony, sleep, and all kind of temptations inherent in court life; the only sure way, he concludes, is poverty and withdrawal from any governmental affair. Power and wealth inevitably give rise to enmity and envy.

These views clearly belong to an earlier trend of opposition; we may see their parallels in Kadı Fadlullah's adaptation of the *Marzuban-name* (see chapter 1)[50] and even (when discussing the inevitable character of internal strife) in Aşıkpaşazade's work.[51] However, there are points where Korkud's critique is more reminiscent of sixteenth-century debates. After lengthy discussions on the nature of knowledge and self-knowledge and on sin, guilt, and penitence, which aim to show that the only way to save his own soul was to withdraw immediately, i.e. before his death, from all worldly affairs (he also stresses that, for a ruler, this is even more obligatory: T227), Korkud embarks on an explicit attack on the emerging tendency to legitimize secular law: he

50 A story about Hüsrev's vizier who avoided killing his ruler's wife, as ordered, implies that committing a sin under the orders of one's ruler is a sin itself: Kadı Fadlullah – Altay 2008, 199.

51 For instance, when he speaks of fratricide (Aşıkpaşazade – Atsız 1949, 162): he has the officer who arrested and executed Murad II's brother admitting that he committed a grave sin, but that in this way the world was set to peace and a rule was laid for the future (*bizden öndin gelenler bu kanunı kurmışlar*).

condemns those ulema who consider *urf*, i.e. the imperial administrative practice, equal to the Sharia. Furthermore, he also sets out a series of specific grievances, which impressively foretell several tropes of sixteenth- and seventeenth-century Ottoman political writing: the material orientation and lack of discipline of the janissaries, the postal system that causes the harm to the peasants (this was to be a constant preoccupation for Ottoman political writers well into the eighteenth century), and the failure of the imperial administration to enforce the religious obligations of its Muslim subjects (T232).

Although Korkud's works were mostly not copied, they were read in the palace by high-ranking members of the ulema such as Kemalpaşazade (d. 1534), especially on the matter of apostasy as well as on his analysis of rulership.[52] The critique contained in the *Dawat al-nafs* against the mixture of Sharia and dynastic law, and especially against the use of capital punishment, on the other hand, was to become a central point in late sixteenth-century opposition, as shall be seen.

3.1 *The Ulema Opposition to the Süleymanic Synthesis*

Much more influential was the opposition to the *kanun* synthesis and its juristic exponents, i.e. Ebussu'ud, Dede Cöngi, and the like. Çivizade Efendi, the (not immediate) precursor of Ebussu'ud in the post of *şeyhülislam* (1539–42), was one of the paragons of this opposition.[53] The son of a respected *medrese* teacher, Çivizade also followed a teaching career, first in Edirne, then in Bursa, and finally Istanbul; he then moved into the higher posts of the judiciary, becoming judge of Egypt in 1530–1 and Anadolu *kazasker* in 1537. He was appointed *şeyhülislam* less than two years later, only to be dismissed from the office in 1542. It seems that the cause of his dismissal was his zealous commitment to Hanafi orthodoxy, which brought him into conflict with what seemed, then, the consensus of the Ottoman ulema. The issue at stake may seem irrelevant to imperial policy, as it concerned a subtle problem with the Islamic ritual (namely, whether one can perform the ablution wearing footwear); what seems to have played a more crucial role in his removal was Çivizade's rigid condemnation of Sufism, noted above. Çivizade returned to his old *medrese* post and later, when Ebussu'ud, then the *kazasker* of Rumili, was appointed *şeyhülislam* (1545), he took over the former's position and kept it until his death in 1547. It was during this period that he engaged in a legal dispute with Ebussu'ud on account of the latter validating religious endowments (*vakf*s) made by donating cash. Çivizade challenged Ebussu'ud's view and succeeded

52 Al-Tikriti 2004, 181–185 and 196.

53 On Çivizade see Repp 1986, 244–256; and the very analytical dissertation by Gel 2010.

in making the sultan accept his own view; however, and as Çivizade died soon after, Ebussu'ud rallied several retired and active high-ranking ulema and eventually had Süleyman issue an order permitting cash donations. Such foundations had been in use since the first decades of the fifteenth century, and were ratified by many famous and respected ulema during the course of the sixteenth century, including none other than Kemalpaşazade; Çivizade's argument was that this tradition was feeble (compared to the older Hanafi scholars) and that it opened the way to usury. Seemingly there was some public dispute on this issue, which shows that imperial policies were not accepted without some trouble.[54] In his traditionalist zeal, Çivizade seems to have even maintained that those dying after being hit by cannon or gunfire should not be considered martyrs.[55] It is to be noted that, in his attack on Ibn Arabi's Sufism, he used Ibn Taymiyya's arguments, being perhaps the first scholar to introduce these ideas into the "conservative" milieu (and long before they were used by Dede Cöngi to justify sultanly interference in legal matters).[56]

If Çivizade was a somewhat easy opponent for Ebussu'ud to fight, one cannot say the same for Birgivi Mehmed Efendi (1523–73), a widely respected and immensely influential scholar who vehemently challenged Ebussu'ud's legal strategems in favor of a strict interpretation of *fikh*. Birgivi was born in Balıkesir into a family of scholars and Sufis and, after receiving his initial education from his father, a prominent Sufi of that town, he went to Istanbul for further studies. He began to teach and became an army judge in 1551, following his former teacher's appointment as the *kazasker* of Rumili; around the same period he joined a Sufi fraternity, the Bayramiyye, only to leave it soon after for a professor's career in the small and distant town of Birgi, where he lived until his death. His work was both voluminous and widely-read; his most popular and influential treatises were the *Vasiyyetnâme* ("Testament"; also known as *Risâle-i Birgivî*, "Birgivi's treatise"), a catechism in Turkish, and its more complex Arabic counterpart, *al-Tarîqa al-Muhammadiyya* ("The Muhammadan way"); one should also note his legal essays dealing with issues such as the cash-*vakf* or the legitimacy of paying for religious services.[57] Another work of Birgivi's, *Zuhr al-mulûk*, is of a more directly "political" nature, since it is

54 Mandaville 1979, 297; Kemalpaşazade – Özcan 2000; Gel 2010, 211–230; Karataş 2010.

55 Gel 2010, 232–233. This was used as a counter-argument against Çivizade in the cash *vaqf* controversy: see Mandaville 1979, 303.

56 Gel 2010, 249–273. Among the issues related to this debate, one should note the question of Pharaoh's religion, which, according to Kâtib Çelebi, was also one of the issues raised by the seventeenth-century Kadızadeli movement.

57 On Birgivi's life and work, see Zilfi 1988, 143–146; Ocak 1991, 75–76; Radtke 2002; Ivanyi 2012; Yılmaz 2005, 76–82; Kurz 2011, 56ff.

addressed to the new ruler, Selim II, exhorting him to follow the precepts of the Sharia strictly and, particularly, to abolish the Ebussu'udic distortions of the Sharia in land tenure and taxation.[58]

In modern scholarship, Birgivi's name has become synonymous with Ottoman fundamentalism, representing the kind of zealot who condemned every innovation and argued for complete adherence to the Sharia.[59] This image, as will also be seen in chapter 6, was much influenced by Birgivi's association with the seventeenth-century Kadızadeli movement, as well as the misattribution to him of several polemical works against innovations by the late sixteenth- and early seventeenth-century scholar Ahmed al-Rumi al-Akhisari.[60] The influence of Ibn Taymiyya on the latter, in particular, has led many scholars to consider Birgivi a follower of Ibn Taymiyya as well, which is not the case: similarly uncompromising and strict as he may have been, Birgivi seems to have totally ignored Ibn Taymiyya's work, which during this period was mostly (and paradoxically) used by Ebussu'udic scholarship, as was seen in Dede Cöngi's case.[61] Birgivi's precursors should instead be found in Şehzade Korkud's treatises, and to a lesser degree in his own more or less contemporary "decline" literature (of which more in chapter 4). As Katharina Ivanyi remarks, Birgivi seems[62]

> a scholar immersed in "cases," ... rather than one concerned with "legal norms" ... he was concerned with concrete and hands-on advice on problems of everyday concern (rather than with what he would have considered abstract theorizing and high-brow conjecture).

One is tempted to correlate this remark with the general trend of Birgivi's contemporary and subsequent political thinkers (as will be seen below) to neglect the Tusi-styled quest for a philosophical foundation of society and politics in favor of more concrete and down-to-earth advice on specific institutions.

His polemical treatises against Ebussu'ud apart, Birgivi's main and most popular work remains *al-Tarîqa al-Muhammadiyya*.[63] It is divided into three

58 Ivanyi 2012, 43–45.

59 We will skip the very interesting discussion of whether he should be considered a precursor of the "Islamic Enlightenment" or "Puritanism" (Schulze 1996; Hagen – Seidenstricker 1998, 95ff.; Ivanyi 2012, 5–7), as it would necessitate a long digression from our subject.

60 On these works see Ivanyi 2012, 36–40; Sheikh 2016.

61 Radtke 2002; Ivanyi 2012, 79–82.

62 Ivanyi 2012, 72.

63 The most recent and comprehensive study of this important work is Ivanyi 2012. Radtke 2002, 161–170 gives a short synopsis and a detailed report of the sources used by Birgivi.

parts: on upholding the Sunna, on avoiding innovation, and on the importance of moderation (*iktisad*). Moderation, i.e. abstaining from excessive behavior that harms both body and soul, is for Birgivi the golden rule, corresponding to the Aristotelian mean and—interestingly—being nearer to Kâtib Çelebi's dismissal of the Kadızadeli theorists (Birgivi's seventeenth-century followers) than to the strict attitude of the latter (cf. below, chapter 7). But the emphasis on moderation apart, the general aim of the treatise is to violently attack and dismiss innovations; true, there are innovations which may be permitted or even recommended, such as the building of minarets, but in general innovation is a major threat to religion, closely resembling infidelity. His most important target is "innovation in custom" (*bid'a fi'l-'âda*), especially when committed by "the Sufis of our time" (although he never dismisses Sufism wholesale), such as dancing and music, issues which were to take on great significance in later debates. Birgivi discusses at length piety (*taqwâ*), focusing on trespasses against it: the sins or forbidden acts pertaining to the various parts of the body, including the heart (such as arrogance and hatred) an the tongue (such as blasphemy and lying). In this discussion he also reverts to the well-known theory of the soul and its faculties, as formulated by al-Ghazali and repeated in the Tusian theories of ethics.[64] Birgivi's central place in the opposition to the imperial legal synthesis can be seen in the fact that he felt it necessary to devote the last chapter of his *Tariqa* to the fiscal and land arrangements sanctified by Ebussu'ud.[65] Birgivi regarded money with great suspicion and considered the harmful characteristics of wealth as "overpowering", and in this vein, while showing the usual condemnation of both avarice and wastefulness, he adamantly denied the legitimacy of paying for any religious services (though he deemed gifts or donations permissible) and of monetary charitable endowments (as seen above). The denial of the latter was based on numerous different arguments, such as the disruption of the regular course of inheritance and the greediness of administrators, but mostly on the inevitable identification of such endowments with the strictly forbidden practice of usury. Moreover, Birgivi also challenged Ebussu'ud's formulation of Ottoman landholding; and, unlike the cash-*vakf* controversy, we have no evidence that this was an issue for debate after Mehmed II's "greediness".[66] Birgivi stressed the illegality of the land tax and the injustice caused to the heirs of the

64 Ivanyi 2012, 158ff.

65 For an analysis of this chapter, see Ivanyi 2012, 239ff. and especially 262–283. Cf. Mandaville 1979, 304–306; Mundy – Saumarez Smith 2007, 16–20.

66 A *fetva*, possibly dated to Süleyman's time, is similar to Birgivi's critique: Mundy – Saumarez Smith 2007, 244, fn. 42.

peasant; what he was opposing was not so much the concept of state ownership itself, which he accepted by necessity, but the function of the *tapu* system of tax and transfer of arable lands.

Birgivi's analysis of the soul's faculties and the virtues they produced brings him unexpectedly close to the *falasifa* tradition of the Tusian *ahlak* authors, and one may wonder whether this was pure coincidence. Towards the end of Süleyman's reign, the paragon of the Ottoman *ahlak* tradition, Kınalızade Ali Çelebi, was extremely vexed by the substitution of the Sharia by the *kanun*: the reader might remember his discussion of secular law, inserted into Tusi's and Davvani's theory on the formation of societies (K413–14):

> If you ask whether it is possible for an overpowering king to impose his government and apply his power in towns and men: as happened in the case of the Mongols, when Genghis Khan imposed laws (*siyasetler*) based on reason and intelligence [rather than God's inspiration], calling them *yasa*, and killed whoever did not follow them. And this law was accepted and executed by his children and adherents. We will answer that this may happen, as long as the power of this imposing king, his children, and followers lasts ... But when the shelter of kingship leaves this dynasty and the drums of rulership mark the time of another [dynasty], so must this law change and the foundations of its government and rules tremble.

It is evident that Kınalızade draws a simile between the sultanly law or *kanun* and Genghis Khan's arbitrary *yasa*, implying that the former may result in ruin as did the latter.[67] The difference with Ahmedi's pragmatic discussion of the same issue is telling: it will be remembered that the early fourteenth-century poet had remarked that Mongol rule ("lawful oppression") was amenable to the people; nearer to the time of our author, the geographer Aşık Mehmed insisted that the Mongols "produced mighty kings and powerful princes that ruled with justice and care for their subjects",[68] while one could also be

---

67 This section has been interpreted by Cornell Fleischer as a justification of the Ottoman *kanun*, which supports and derives from the Holy Law (Fleischer 1983, 208; 1986, 227); in contrast, Tezcan argued that Kınalızade instead sought to discredit *kanun* (Tezcan 2001, 118). On the challenges the Mongol invasions posed to Islamic legitimacy see Fleischer 1986a, 273–279; on the shift of meaning of the term *yasa* and *kanun* in the post-Mongol societies of the Middle East cf. Burak 2015.

68 Aşık Mehmed – Ak 2007, III:1858 (*Mogolân'dan padişahân-ı dad-küster ve husrevân-ı ra'iyyet-perver ve hakimân-ı ferman-reva ve emîrân-ı kişver-güşa bi-hadd ü bi-intiha zuhur itdi*). Aşık Mehmed (ca. 1556/57–1598), more than forty years younger than Kınalızade,

reminded of Celalzade's discussion of infidel but just kings. Interestingly, the defence of Ebussu'ud's legal synthesis by these authors fits well with Guy Burak's suggestion that Mongol rule was a major influence on this Ottoman development.[69] In this respect, Kınalızade's view may be seen as a precursor to the seventeenth-century reading of Ibn Taymiyya by "Sunna-minded" authors, which shall be examined in chapter 6 (note that Ibn Taymiyya's translator, Aşık Çelebi, was prone to accepting the possibility of non-*şer'î* success, in contrast to the text he was translating!).[70] In case he was not able to make himself clear, Kınalızade also added another point to Davvani's urge for minimal use of capital punishment (K489–90):[71]

> The devil seduces some rulers in the present day, to the effect that: "Nowadays, if one deems the sacred Sharia sufficient and stays within the limits and the orders of the Muhammedan way, the correction of the world becomes difficult, since wrong-doers, the, and robbers are so abundant!" And with this useless suggestion [these rulers] become drunk with the blood shed and spend their zeal in torturing people on the basis of imaginary and [unfounded] opinions.

Kınalızade could not have been clearer: this was exactly the point made by his contemporary Dede Cöngi Efendi in his effort to justify the legitimacy of the Ottoman *kanun* as a supplement to the Sharia, and it should also be remembered that Korkud had a similar criticism of this view. Might we attribute Kınalızade's taking of sides against Ebussu'ud Efendi's synthesis to his ulema education and career? It should be noted that he was a student and a *mülazim* (i.e. an appointed candidate for an ulema post) of Çivizade Efendi.[72] If the ulema were a rising class that was claiming a share in political power from the mid-sixteenth century onwards,[73] Kınalızade's position within that group may offer a context for his opposition to Süleyman's legal policy.

wrote a monumental cosmography which mainly draws on the medieval *ajaib* genre (Hagen 2013, 420–423); this particular passage, however, seems to belong to himself.

69 Burak 2013, 594–599.

70 See Terzioğlu 2007, 254–255.

71 Cf. Davvani's text in Dawwani – Thompson 1839, 395; Dawwani – Deen 1939, 206. Tezcan 2001, 119–120, also comments on this point.

72 Tezcan 1996, 16–17; Gel 2010, 89–91. Kınalızade's relations with Çivizade remained good after the latter's dismissal; on the other hand, Kınalızade's two brothers were students of Ebussu'ud, and one of them was dismissed by him.

73 This is the suggestion made by Tezcan 2010a, 30ff.

4 The Iranian Tradition Continued: Bureaucrats, Sufis, and Scholars

The sixteenth century was a period of translations: as the imperial capital attracted more and more intellectuals, mainly from the cities of Iran and Central Asia, its dependance on—or, more correctly, its close relationship with—Persian political ideas continued well into Süleyman's reign and beyond. Works such as al-Ghazali's *Nasîhat al-mulûk*, Hamadani's (d. 1385) *Zakhîrat al-mulûk* (influenced by al-Ghazali and Ibn Arabi's mystical ethics from a Sufi perspective), and Zamakhshari's (d. 1143) *Rabî al-abrâr* (an anthology of wisdom literature) were translated or adapted numerous times by leading Ottoman scholars; similarly, the pseudo-Aristotelian *Sirr al-asrar* ("Secret of secrets"), a medieval compilation of advice on government and ethics, as well as physiognomy and medical science, which exerted a major influence on Islamicate (as well as medieval European) thought, was translated in 1571 for the grand vizier Sokollu Mehmed Pasha.[74] At an unknown date during Süleyman's reign, Abdüsselam b. Şükrullah el-Amasi (not to be confused with the early fifteenth-century author) composed *Tuhfetü'l-ümerâ ve minhatü'l-vüzerâ* ("Gift for the commanders"), a translation of Jizri Mahmud b. Isma'il b. Ibrahim's (d. 1444) *Durrat al-garrâ fi nasayih al-mulûk wa al-wuzarâ*, which had been written in 1439 for the sultan of Egypt.[75] As was seen above, the work speaks of the *imam* or caliph, identifying him explicitly with Süleyman. Following the same model as Şeyhoğlu Mustafa in his fourteenth-century *Kenzü'l-küberâ* (based, in turn, on Najm al-Din Razi), Amasi structures his reasoning on the three "situations" (*hal*) of both the sultan (his relationship with himself, with his people, and with God) and the vizier (his relationship with God, with the sultan, and with the people and army). Not only were there translations, but original works in Arabic or Persian also kept being copied. For instance, İbrahim b. Muhammed, an Azeri author from the mid-fifteenth century, was copied by Mahmud b. Ahmed al-Kayseri in 1545, to be read by Sultan Süleyman. İbrahim's work is a typical *adab* text, making use of sources such as al-Ghazali and Zamakhshari; it also contains an interesting discussion of justice as a balance in all of nature, including in fauna and flora.[76]

---

74 On these translations see Yılmaz 2005, 44–62. On pseudo-Aristotle's text see Manzalaoui 1974; Grignaschi 1976; Forster 2006. A similar work (*Sîraj al-mulûk*) by Turtushi, a twelfth-century Egypt-based scholar, on principles of good government, was also very popular in its Ottoman translation (see Yılmaz 2005, 53–54).

75 The work was recently published as Amasi – Coşar 2012. Jizri Mahmud's work was also translated later by Mehmet b. Firuz (d. 1609) for Selim II.

76 İbrahim – Acar 2008 (on justice as balance see esp. 154ff.).

As well as these translations, the influx of foreign scholars produced original works as well. Among them, there were those transferring Tusi's neo-Aristotelism in one way or another, such as Bitlisi, Cahrami, and Barmaki, mentioned in the previous chapter. One important trend, enhanced by the Sunni vs. Shi'a aspect of the emerging Ottoman-Safavid conflict, emphasized the religious purity of the Ottoman sultan and the importance of the ulema. Muhammed b. Mehasin el-Ensari, probably an ulema from Syria, completed his *Tuhfa al-zamân ilâ al-malik al-muzaffar Sulaymân* ("The gift of time for Süleyman the victorious ruler") around 1524. His work seems to be unique in its emphasis on the legitimacy of Ottoman rule, probably due to his writing shortly after the suppression of the Egyptian rebellion by Ibrahim Pasha. The first chapter, as well as the preface, is devoted to proving this legitimacy and to showing that the subjects were to pay allegiance to the sultan according to the Sharia. Ensari stresses in particular the duties of the ulema: they are to urge the sultan to be just and benevolent and to warn him against oppression, thus being exalted even above the ruler (who has to adhere to their opinion). Writing some decades before Dede Cöngi, Ensari was one of the first Ottoman authors to include discussions of the public treasury in a treatise on government, focusing on the legitimacy of the various sources of revenue. Finally, he emphasizes that non-Muslims should not be employed in government; this was not a major issue for the Ottomans, but Ensari seems to have followed an Egyptian tradition of political thought, and especially Turtushi's *Sirâj al-mulûk*.[77]

Another work that stresses the religious role of the Ottoman ruler is the anonymous *Risâla fî mâ yalzim 'alâ al-mulûk* ("A treatise on what rulers need"), written in Arabic and dedicated to Süleyman. The author stresses that the sultan should conduct the Holy War (*jihâd, ghazw, mukâtala*) against "polytheists" and seditious people, as well as with a view to eliminating internal vice (*daf' al-sharr*) and disbelief (*izâla al-kufr*), while he also criticizes innovations (*bid'a*). Similar ideas, it should be noted here, can be found in Korkud's works: in his *Dawat al-nafs*, he criticizes what he views as the Ottoman concept of *jihad*, i.e. that focusing on its external, military dimension; the most important *jihad*, he argues, is seeking knowledge and truth rather than plunder (in his other works, too, he shows a concern for legal and political control of the *gaza* warriors, based on Shari'a norms). As well as advice on *jihad*, however, the author of *Risâla fî mâ yalzim* also gives instructions for people presenting themselves to the sultan (viziers and other statesmen and visitors): they

77 Mamluk influences are also evident in various other parts of the treatise: Yılmaz 2005, 70–73. On Turtushî see also above, fn. 74. The emphasis on not using non-Muslims in government is also seen in Nizam al-Mulk's famous "mirror for princes": Rosenthal 1958, 83.

should be careful to manage his temper so as to exhort him effectively regarding his duties. This exhortation is to be considered a duty in the framework of the "commanding right and forbidding wrong" precept, which is praised as the most virtuous form of Holy War. Finally, there is a long section on the personal life of statesmen and especially of the sultan: he is adamant that the sultan needs to avoid drinking wine, not so much because it is a sin but because[78]

> drinking would impair one's judgment in decision-making, lead to negligence in rulership, and cause failure to protect the realm, which might result in the loss of one's authority (*zavâl al-dawla*).

Another trend had much stronger Sufi connotations. As noted above, Ibn Arabi's theory of the "Pole of the world" (*kutb*), i.e. of a head of the mystic hierarchy who governs world affairs, whether secretly or not,[79] was used by dervish fraternities opposed to the imperial project. Other authors, however, relied heavily on this theory in order to imply that, in their era, this role belonged or at least was related to that of Süleyman (who, after all, was not immune from messianic claims himself, as has been seen). Dizdar Mustafa b. Abdullah, about whom we know only that he was the commander of the fortress of Çankırı, wrote in 1542 *Kitâb sulûk al-mulûk* ("Book on the paths of kings"), in which he tried to educate the ruler on the main principles of Sufi tradition. In this, he placed great emphasis on the notion of the "Pole of the world", exhorting the sultan to enhance his secular authority (*saltana, khilâfa, mulk*) via the spiritual one (*wilâya*). More bluntly, his contemporary, the anonymous author of *al-Adliyya al-Sulaymâniyya* ("Süleymanic justice"), who was probably an immigrant from the East, also extolled the role of the secret "Pole", urging Süleyman to cooperate with him. He assures Süleyman that, in his fight against the heretical Kızılbaş, he would be aided by the present Pole, who is now a Hanafi (previous ones had been Shafi'is; as Hüseyin Yılmaz notes, this is probably a reference to the Mamluk era). The author uses several passages from the Quran and the *hadith* tradition to show that the Ottoman dynasty is chosen by God; then, he exhorts the virtue of justice, urging the ruler to avoid oppression and to value compassion instead. He also stresses the need for consultation, illustrating his point with historical anecdotes. Furthermore, the sultan should follow the Sufi path in order to improve his level of devotion (*zuhd*) and piety

78 Yılmaz 2005, 65–67.

79 See İnalcık 1993, 211–212; Ocak 1991, 74–75.

(*taqvâ*); however, he has to remember that the real government of the world belongs to the hierarchy of the invisible saints and their head, the Pole.[80]

Another side of the traditional literature, mostly compiled from Iranian sources, was expressed in "encyclopedic" works, in which political theory was seen as a branch of human knowledge and science. Such works in this period had strong religious connotations and often used the notion of "duties", a concept with roots going back to medieval Persian literature (such as Najm al-Din Razi's work) and which was conceived as agreements between the ruler and God, as in the "situations" (*halet*) that were seen in Şeyhoğlu Mustafa's and Abdüsselam b. Şükrullah el-Amasi's works at the start of the fourteenth and the sixteenth century, respectively. For instance, the judge Hüseyin b. Hasan al-Semerkandi wrote his *Latâ'if al-afkâr wa kâshif al-asrâr* ("Fine thoughts and the revealer of secrets") in 1529 and dedicated it to Ibrahim Pasha.[81] The work was intended to provide the young grand vizier with a concise encyclopedia on government, morals, history, etc., and it draws from the ideas and vocabulary of *fikh* literature. It consists of three parts, namely on government (*siyasa*), the history of the caliphs, and miscellaneous topics (including manners, literature, moral qualities, stories about jinns and the creation of man, and, eventually, a concise geography of the *ajaib* genre). The first part consists of four chapters. In the first, Semerkandi speaks of the ruler's responsibilities and duties towards both God and his subjects: the sultan has to look after God's slaves (with the usual emphasis on the safety of property, roads, and the like) and uphold His orders. The author then enumerates several of the virtues required by the ruler, such as avoiding wrath and hasty punishment, having only appropriate pastimes (such as horse-riding), and consulting the right people. The second chapter discusses offices and their holders at all levels of government (*tabakâti'l-velâye*): Semerkandi analyzes the legal requirements and qualifications (which are of a quite high standard) for the five principal offices of government: the viziers (who are of two kinds, those who act as proxies for the ruler, *tefvîz*, and those who simply carry out his orders, *tenfîz*), the state offices (*mansıp*; these are the legal jurisprudence, the judicial system, and

80 Yılmaz 2005, 89–90 (on Dizdar Mustafa), 86–89 (on *al-Adliyya al-Süleymaniyya*). Among these Sufi-oriented treatises, we should probably include 'Ârifî Ma'rûf Efendi's (d. 1593) *Uqûd al-jawâhir li-zaha'ir al-ahâ'ir* ("Precious necklace for matchless treasures") of 1560, a book on the vizierate dedicated to Semiz Ali Pasha a year before his rise to the office of grand vizier (Yılmaz 2005, 91–93).

81 Semerkandi's work was first noticed by Yılmaz 2005, 68–70; for an extensive summary and analysis see Kavak 2012, who points out the strong connection of the work with the *fikh* milieus. The list of requirements for the various offices is an elaboration of a similar list by the Shafi'i jurist Ibn Jama'a (d. 1333): Rosenthal 1958, 49.

the market inspection—for this latter post, Semerkandi emphasizes its link with the well-known precept of "commanding right and forbidding wrong"), the chancery (*inşâ'*; among the qualities needed, the author stresses knowledge of the Quran and the *hadith*), the book-keeping (*dafâtîr*; in fact, on the keeping of army registers, a chapter somewhat outdated since it gives lengthy instructions on the recruitment of Arabs, on checking the Turks' religiosity, and so on), and the treasury (*amvâl*; the ruler's income must consist of canonical taxes and revenues only). As for the other two chapters, they discuss consultation (*müşâvere*) and justice, considering both indispensable principles to be followed in all the offices listed above.

In the previous chapter we examined another encyclopedist (and a major biographer of Ottoman scholars), Ahmed Taşköprüzade (1495–1561); it was seen how close he was to the Tusian model in his 1557 encyclopedia of knowledge. Taşköprüzade also wrote a specifically political treatise, *Risâla fi bayân asrâr al-khilâfa al-insâniyya wa al-saltana al-ma'nawiyya* ("Treatise explaining the mystery of man's caliphate and the spiritual sultanate"); this work is comprised of ten sections, on: the sultan and imam; the sultanate; subjects; parents; spouses; children; slaves; servants; and friends. Apart from the first section, they are all in the form of "rights" (*hukûk*): in order to attain the spiritual sultanate, the ruler must fulfil the rights of others; for example, fulfilling the rights of the sultanate means that the sultan must perform his duties as ordained by the concept of rulership; the rights of subjects correspond to the duty of the sultan to treat them with justice; and so on. Drawing on al-Ghazali and, especially, Hamadani, the author is careful to use Islamic rather than mythical anecdotes in order to illustrate his points.[82]

4.1 *The Scribal Tradition*

It was noted in the previous chapter that Kınalızade's monumental work was, in a way, a belated swansong of the Tusian theory. Even in his time, the fashion had shifted toward Kâshifi rather than Davvani's popularization of Tusi's system. Kashifi (d. 1504/5) wrote his work *Akhlâq-e Muhsinî* (1494/5) for a Timurid ruler, Abu'l-Muhsin.[83] As well as being more recent (and from Timurid culture, which had become the literary fashion in Ottoman circles), his work was a loose adaptation of Tusi and Davvani's books that gave much more weight

82 Yılmaz 2005, 94–96. Similar views on mutual duties can be seen in the early fourteenth-century Mosul historian Ibn al-Tiqtaqa (Rosenthal 1958, 65).

83 Kashifi – Keene 1850 (a partial translation focusing on the morality chapters). On Kashifi see Lambton 1956a, 147; Lambton 1962, 115–119; Donaldson 1963, 184–190; the special issue of *Iranian Studies* 36/4 (2003); and esp. Subtelny 2013.

to ethical advice (the style known as *adab*) rather than philosophical theory (known as *ahlak*); in other words, the vengeance of the "mirror for princes" tradition over the abstract interpretation of rulership. Kashifi removed the heavy philosophical systems of Tusi and Davvani's books and replaced them with historical anecdotes and poems. In Ottoman literature, Kashifi's work was both copied abundantly in its Persian original and translated four times during the sixteenth century (among the translations, one was made by Idris-i Bitlisi's son).[84]

The shift to Kashifi coincided with the rise of the scribal bureaucracy and its literary production, andit is perhaps no coincidence that Kashifi himself was an accomplished bureaucrat who played a major role in the development of scribal epistolary composition.[85] It was noted in chapter 1 that a bureaucratic structure, manned mostly by medrese-educated scholars from the neighboring emirates (as well as Islamicized Byzantines and Serbians, especially from the mid-fifteenth century onwards), was apparent even by the mid-fourteenth century, while the system for registering the land was in full use by the first decades of the fifteenth century. Tursun Bey and İdris-i Bitlisi, two of the most famous exponents of Tusi's and Davvani's political philosophy, were educated or had worked as scribes; however, the most representative literary genre produced by these bureaucrats was more closely connected to their everyday work, even though it may seem utterly rhetorical to the modern reader. The model prose, *münşeat* or *inşa*, quite similar to the contemporaneous epistolography of the Italian city-states, contained models and instructions with all the necessary ornaments for composing letters with a view to serving as the pattern for the day-to-day correspondence of the government.[86] Usually, such collections were compiled and used alongside collections of official documents, copies of registers and law regulations, and other useful texts; one of the earliest Turkish examples, *Teressül* ("Correspondence") by Kırımlu Hafız Hüsam (who was probably trained in the Germiyan court of Kütahya in the late fourteenth or early fifteenth century), contains general advice for letter-writing and

84 Yılmaz 2005, 45–47: in 1550 by Firâkî Abdurrahman Çelebi; around the same time by Ebu'l-Fazl Mehmed, son of Idris-i Bitlisi; in 1566 by Azmî Efendi, Mehmed III's tutor, as *Enîsü'l-kulûb*; toward the end of the century by Nevâlî Efendi, the successor of Azmi Efendi. Kınalızade (Kınalızade – Koç 2007, 38–39) refers to Kashifi's work, but does not seem to have used it.

85 Mitchell 2003.

86 On the evolution of scribal writing style and language, cf. Matuz 1970; Woodhead 1988; Riedlmayer 2008; Darling 2013a; Tuşalp Atiyas 2013, 138ff. On early Renaissance epistolography and its importance for the history of European political thought see Skinner 1978, I:28ff.

specific model phrases for letters addressed to governors, viziers, princes, various officials, and ulema, as well as to merchants, sheikhs, friends, and various relatives, including husbands and wives (as well as lovers, both male and female); model letters (and model answers to them) follow, together with model documents, mainly appointment diplomas for teachers, judges and officers.[87] As the palace bureaucracy was becoming an increasingly powerful and diversified apparatus,[88] such manuals kept being produced throughout the fifteenth and sixteenth centuries, culminating with Feridun Bey (d. 1583) and his famous collection of sultanly letters and treaties, *Münşe'âtü's-selâtîn* ("The correspondence of sultans"), completed in 1575. Feridun, the private secretary of the grand vizier Sokollu Mehmed Pasha, was given the position of *reisülküttab* or chief secretary in 1570 and that of *nişancı* in 1573–76, and again in 1581, holding it until his death. He also wrote a history of the Szigetvár campaign and a moral treatise, but his most well-known work was the aforementioned collection, which was presented to Murad III in 1575 and contains more than 500 documents, running from the first years of Islam until Murad's own time.[89] Not all these documents were genuine, and some were probably forged or invented by Feridun himself in order to legitimize the Ottoman dynasty and its worldview: as Dimitris Kastritsis has recently observed, the collection "was never intended as a practical chancery manual at all, but rather as a type of history writing".[90] This series of documents illustrated the rise of the Ottomans to the status of a world power, situated in the middle of an Islamicate world (those addressed to the "heretical" Safavid shahs are much more pompous than those to the "infidel" kings of Europe) but not ignoring Europe either: not surprisingly, Feridun had also commissioned the translation of a history of the kings of France.[91]

4.2 *Celalzade and the Glorification of the Empire*

Almost contemporary with Kınalızade, Celalzade Mustafa (c. 1490–1567) was a major exponent of the rising bureaucracy who followed a slightly different path, choosing to stand on the shoulders of Kashifi rather than Davvani or Tusi. The son of a middle-ranking kadi, he had a career similar to Feridun: he

87 Kırımlu Hafız Hüsam – Tekin 2008. The addresses to merchants (pp. 44 and 64) are of particular interest, as they stress their generosity and charity. The next known Ottoman manual, copied in 1479, has similar content: Yahya bin Mehmed – Tekin 1971; for an early sixteenth-century specimen, see Mesihi – Ménage 1988.

88 Fleischer 1986b; Darling 1996, 49–80; Sariyannis 2013, 105–107; Tuşalp Atiyas 2013, 55ff.

89 Feridun Bey 1848; Vatin 2010, 63ff.; Kastritsis 2013. There are two different printed Ottoman editions of this monumental work and a modern systematic study is highly needed.

90 Kastritsis 2013, 107.

91 Bacqué-Grammont 1997.

served in the Ottoman chancery first as a scribe in the *divan* (1516–25), then as *reisülküttab* (1525–34), and finally as *nişancı* or chancellor (1534–56). He then retired, only to return as *nişancı* upon Sultan Süleyman's death, a position he held until his own passing (1566–67). He is generally regarded as one of the main figures behind Süleyman's law-giving activity.[92] Celalzade was also a prolific writer, playing a prominent role in the development of the Ottoman "scribal" style, the *inşa*. He wrote poetry, translated a biography of the Prophet, and composed a history of Selim I's reign (*Selimnâme* or *Meâşir-i Selim Hânî*). However, what mainly interests us here are his Kashifi-influenced treatise *Mevâhibü'l-hallâk fi merâtibi'l-ahlâk* ("Talents bestowed by the Creator in the aspects of ethics") and his monumental chronicle covering the period 1520–57, *Tabakatü'l-memâlik ve derecâtü'l-mesâlik* ("Layers of kingdoms and levels of routes"). Both were completed after 1557, when Celalzade had retired from active service; more specifically, the composition of *Tabakat* must have begun in the early years of Süleyman's reign (certainly before 1534), while *Mevahib* was composed in 1564. They both seem to have been fairly popular, as each is preserved in more than twenty manuscripts.[93]

Celalzade's *Mevâhib ül-hallâk* is a work close to the "mirror for princes" genre, being a creative translation of Kashifi's *Akhlâq-e Muhsinî*.[94] In addition to his model, Celalzade added scattered pieces eulogizing the Ottoman lands and their excellence, as well as chapters on envy, calumny, and reason (*akl*); what is more significant is that he rewrote Kashifi's last chapter on "the servants of a ruler", dividing it into two: "On the vizierate", and "On the sultanate". He also added a long introductory chapter on the 99 names of God (*esma-i hüsna*: B27–34) and the way they can contribute to man's moral education. The main part of the work consists of 55 chapters on various moral virtues and vices, e.g. on faith, prayer, resignation, good manners, humility, justice, benevolence, purity, etc. (B24–26). The source of ethics, says Celalzade, is reason, which may guide people away from the "demonic" features of man (passion, lust, etc.) toward their "angel-like" characteristics (B37). Celalzade's emphasis on reason (which, he says, is the best vizier a sultan can employ) leads to him dividing

92 İnalcık 1969a, 115 and 138; Yılmaz 2006, 193ff and esp. 204–210; Şahin 2013, 228–30.

93 *Tabakat ül-memâlik* has been published in facsimile (Celalzade – Kappert 1981) and in an abridged Turkish translation (with omissions and misunderstandings: Celalzade – Yılmaz 2011). For *Mevahibü'l-hallak*, there is a detailed synopsis in Celalzade – Balcı 1996. On the manuscripts of the two works see Yılmaz 2006, 247–249 and Celalzade – Balcı 1996, 13–14 and 19–20; on their dating, Yılmaz 2006, 154 and Celalzade – Balcı 1996, 24. On Celalzade's work and ideas, see Fleischer 1990, 69 fn; Yılmaz 2006; Yılmaz 2007; Şahin 2013.

94 On the additions made by Celalzade to his model, see Şahin 2013, 196–197, 232. I used the detailed synopsis in Celalzade –Balcı 1996.

humanity into three groups, namely the intelligent (*akil*), fools (*ahmak*), and sinners (*facir*). A perfect individual exhibits a synthesis of knowledge (*ilm*), reason, and patience (*hilm*).[95] The degree of simplicity compared to the much more sophisticated psychology of Kınalızade or Tursun (and, in fact, as seen in Kashifi when compared to Tusi or Davvani) is evident. Other chapters deal with moral values and political principles, such as honesty (*sıdk*), courage (*şeca'at*), consultation (*meşveret*), and justice (*adalet*). The chapter on gratitude (*şükr*) contains an interesting description of the ruler's need to be grateful for God's blessings (which brings to mind the concept of mutual duties seen in the writings of Mustafa Şeyhoğlu and al-Semerkandî, as well as a similar passage in Tursun Beg): in return for his rulership, he must practise justice towards his subjects; in return for the extent of his territories, he should not covet his subjects' property; in return for his orders being followed, he has to recognize his subordinates' efforts; for being placed in such an exalted position, he has to be compassionate with those in low ones; for being rich, he must give to charity and distribute his favors to whomever deserves them; and so on (B54). In other chapters, Celalzade urges the sultan to be compassionate, generous, and mild, to care for the ulema, etc. Celalzade's system of values is one of mutual obligations (somewhat reminiscent of Taşköprüzade's similar adaptation in his *Asrar al-khilafa*): a chapter on the "duties to be obeyed" (*riayet-i hukuk*) lists the obligations one has towards others, including God, one's parents, relatives, teachers, neighbors, and guests, as well as the mutual obligations of people to their commanders, and vice versa (B82). This integration of individual morality with state politics can also be seen in the chapter on "governing" (B97: *siyaset*): governing can be either individual (*siyaset-i nefsi*), meaning a person's struggle against their own passions, helped by reason, or collective (*siyaset-i gayri*), i.e. administrators' awareness of any oppression or mischief among the people so that they may reform the perpetrators or punish them if necessary.

The chapters on the sultanate (B60–63) and the vizierate (B64–67) are among the longest in Celalzade's work (and also contain much original material). The sultan is "the soul for the body of justice, the eternal life for the body of the country"; kingship is necessary for societies, since its results are (B60)

> protection for the cities, safety for the people, security for their properties and ways of life, the promulgation of knowledge and faith, and the suppression of oppressors, evil-doers, and mischief-makers.

95 See also Şahin 2013, 234–238 for other examples of the importance Celalzade gives to reason.

Celalzade lists in detail the duties of a sultan, following the usual lines of "mirrors for princes", as did other authors of his time and earlier. As for the subjects, they may be divided into three categories: those who may believe anything, without being able to distinguish between right and wrong; those who may be guided to the right path through encouragement and intimidation; and those who are virtuous and behave according to reason (B62–63; reflecting, in a rougher style, Davvani's and Kınalızade's [K486ff.] division of men into five categories). Respect for the notables, compassion for the oppressed, help for those in need, the persecution of oppressors, and care for the security of the roads, are the five things that produce love for the sultan in his subjects' hearts (B63).

In the chapter on the vizierate, the author declares both the grand vizier and the divan scribes as being largely responsible for just administration. He provides a long list of the moral qualities viziers should possess, such as humbleness and patience, but also good manners, such as to answer the sultan's questions briefly and to look at him continuously (B65–67). As with other contemporaneous authors, it is in Celalzade's advice for the vizier (not the sultan) that we encounter the four cardinal virtues and their corrolaries (B67).[96] Moreover, Celalzade emphasizes the value of counsel; in fact, consultation (*meşveret*) is so important (and, one should note, so much based on reason rather than piety) that even the advice of intelligent infidels can be legitimately followed.[97]

Celalzade's ideas on kingship and law are best seen in his *Tabakatü'l-memâlik*, an original work in which he did not follow a specific model. There are some remnants of the Persian moralistic tradition (closer to *adab* than to *ahlak*), such as his praise of Rüstem Pasha (K502b–503a) for his six vizierial virtues, but the main focus is on the sultan and his power. Celalzade had planned it to be "a general panorama of the Ottoman enterprise", "meant to reflect the sixteenth-century *zeitgeist*".[98] What was eventually written, i.e. the history of the empire from 1520 to 1557,[99] would only be the last section or layer (*tabaka*) out of thirty. The first sections would describe the population and the empire (*memalik-i mahmiye tafsili*), speaking of the ulema and the learned men, the peasants, the soldiers, and the fortresses, lands, and regions, as well as the wealth and revenue of the empire (products, gems, mines etc.; K9a). More particularly, the work was conceived as follows (K10b–20b): the first section would

96 Cf. Yılmaz 2006, 159; Şahin 2013, 240.

97 Şahin 2013, 241.

98 Şahin 2013, 167, 169.

99 On the probable reasons of his stopping in 1557 see Şahin 2013, 177–178.

describe the salaried servants of the state (*erkân-ı devlet, ayan-ı saltanat*), with twenty subsections or levels (*derece*) on the palace personnel, the viziers (*vüzera ve erkân-ı devlet ve ayan-ı saltanat*), the janissaries, the sipahis, the palace porters, and the musicians and palace artisans. The second section would deal with the beylerbeyis and their provinces, with twenty-one subsections on each individual province; similarly, the next sections would enumerate the fortresses of the empire, the auxiliary troops, and the navy. Then, the work would deal with Istanbul and the twenty provinces of the empire, depicting the number and rules of their timars, their towns, villages, holy endowments, and population, all in subsections according to smaller administrative units. Finally, the thirtieth section would deal (and indeed deals) with Süleyman's reign.

This conception of the world demands some interpretation. The inclusion of history into a spatial description of an empire implies a worldview that regards the present as the consummation of history and as the perfection of the human condition.[100] In fact, the plan of Celalzade's book seems to come from the cosmographical tradition, which traditionally tried to encompass the world in a similar grid of lists: in Aşık Mehmed's (ca. 1556/57–1598) monumental work, for instance, and in the geographical part of his contemporary Mustafa Ali's history, geographical elements (seas, lakes, rivers, springs, wells, islands, mountains, flora and fauna, minerals, and finally cities) are arranged in lists according to their geographical region and alphabetical order.[101] Celalzade's plan is thus part of a tradition of describing the world through the use of lists, and one might argue that eventually this "empire of lists" became a typically scribal *Weltanschauung* for the Ottoman bureaucracy. In chapter 5 it will be seen that the list structure was used in a whole series of early seventeenth-century works, all composed by scribes and all proposing a normative description of the imperial institutions.

For Celalzade, the sultan is the ultimate source of the Ottoman *kanun*, and hence of the law. He places great emphasis on discretionary punishment by the sultan (*siyaset*), such as in the case of Molla Kabız (the highly-esteemed ulema who was executed for heresy in 1527, under Süleyman's personal pressure), or in the collective punishment of wrongdoers, much like Dede Çöngî.

100 Kaya Şahin finds it "neo-Platonic" and notes that it reflects Celalzade's desire "to represent the world within hierarchically/organizationally bound, recognizable, and also very bureaucratic categories[, a notion which] stems from the idea that every single part of the empire ... is tied together within a system in the middle of which sits the sultan, the ultimate lynchpin of a neo-Platonic universe": Şahin 2013, 174.

101 Aşık Mehmed – Ak 2007; Ali 1860–1868, 1:48–237; cf. Schmidt 1991, 49–50 and 289ff., Fleischer 1986a, 140–142, 241–52. This "list phenomenon" appears to have been common across Eurasia, according to Howard 2007, 156–157.

The sultan is thus above the law; unlimited power may eventually lead to oppression (*zulm*), but not in the case of the Ottoman sultan as he is "supported by God" and guided by "divine inspiration".[102] In contrast, when depicting Mamluk rule in Egypt he attributes their failure to their system of rulership, as they did not have an established dynasty; thus, they fell prey to the "fancy of kingship" (*sevda-yı saltanat ve malihülya-yı hilafet*),[103] which prevented them from seriously caring about the problems in their realm (K104b).

However, it is always justice that empowers the sultan and makes his realm prosper. Speaking of the Egyptian *kanunname*, in whose compilation he must also have played a role, Celalzade notes that it was (K127a)

> a moderate law (*i'tidal üzere miyane bir kanun*) ... in a way that does not cause any loss for the sultan's treasury and does not harm the tax-payers.

More on justice is to be found in the relevant chapter of Celalzade's *Mevâhib ül-hallâk* (B68–70). Celalzade defines justice as the equal treatment of various groups of people, without none of them being treated better or worse than any other. These groups, based on the four elements, are the men of the sword (governors and soldiers, under the element of fire), the men of the pen (viziers and scribes, under the element of air), artisans and merchants (under the element of water), and peasants (under the element of earth). Celalzade stresses that it is justice that causes the well-being of states and oppression that brings them down, giving a list of kings who, though infidels, were successful because of their justice (and, also, of Islamic dynasties that declined because they neglected justice: B70). Celalzade's formulation of "the circle of justice" is impressively original, since it introduces towns and cities in the classic series of dependences (B69):[104]

> With justice, a kingdom may last even if its master is an infidel, but with tyranny it cannot stand even if its master is a believer ... There is no king without an army, no army without wealth, no wealth without urban-dwellers, no urban-dwellers without peasants, and no peasants without justice; justice is the most important and necessary of all.

102 Yılmaz 2007, 199–200.

103 Celalzade adds that if only two Circassians remained in the world, one would be the king and the other would seek to dethrone him.

104 Also quoted in Yılmaz 2006, 159: *mülk adl ile kâyim olur sâhibi kâfir ise dahi, amma zulm ile durmaz viran olur sâhibi mümin olursa dahi ... melik 'askersiz, asker mâlsuz, mâl şehirlersüz, şehirler re'âyasuz, re'âya adlsüz olmaz adl cümleden mühim ve lâzım imiş.*

Elsewhere, a slightly different version of the "circle of justice" (a dynasty needs people to contribute their wealth) has justice replaced by compassion (*şefkat*), giving as an example Mehmed II's mild policy towards the inhabitants of conquered Istanbul (B81).

It may be noticed that, in Celalzade's description of the four elements of society, the ulema are absent, as the men of the pen include only viziers and scribes. Indeed, in Celalzade's work a special place is reserved for praise of the scribal career and the importance of the governmental bureaucracy. Recounting (in his *Selimname*) his own professional options in his youth, he argues that as a *medrese* teacher he would be financially insecure and as a judge prone to falling prey to unfortunate circumstances, while a scribe has peace of mind and ease (*rahat, huzur*). In the *Tabakat* (K, 259b–260b), Celalzade describes his highest office, that of *nişancı*, as

> the greatest among all offices and the noblest of all services ... [Because] all great sultans ... needed two types of servants to rule over vast lands: men of the pen and men of the sword (*erbab-ı tiğ ve kalem*). In fact, the sword and the pen are twins, one of them is the soul and the other is the body (*biri ten ve biri can*). But superiority of the pen has been proven. That is because the sword seeks to destroy whereas the pen aims to produce (*biri kati' biri nabitdir*) ... The rule of the sword devastates a country whereas the rule of the pen causes prosperity.

Furthermore, he goes on to say, it is difficult to find good scribes (unlike good soldiers), and scribes and chancelors busy themselves collecting revenue, while all other servants of the sultan are the cause of expenditure (due to their salaries).[105] In his *Mevâhib ül-hallâk*, Celalzade likens both the grand vizier and the divan scribes to the soul and heart, which give life to the body (B64). Not only is the divan scribe (*debir*) described alongside the grand vizier, but Celalzade even suggests that the grand vizier should be a man of the pen (*ehl-i kalem*) rather than a member of the military class (*ehl-i seyf*). A scribe is "the eye, ear, and hand of a sultan" (*padişahın görür gözü ve işidir kulağı ve tutar elidir*), while, furthermore, *kâtib* means "vizier" in Persian, which implies that the two titles are closely connected and even interchangeable. Celalzade's eulogy for the scribes shows their importance even in military affairs, as in

105 Trans. according to Yılmaz 2006, 89–90; cf. Şahin 2013, 222–223. Similar praise of the pen and the scribes can be found in Celalzade's work on the prophet Yusuf (Joseph): Şahin 2013, 240. Debates between the pen and the sword were quite popular in Arabic literature; see Gelder 1987.

their hands the pen becomes "an instrument of peace as well as of war". If there was any doubt which social group is represented by Celalzade's work, he took great care to dispel it.

5 Lütfi Pasha and the Beginning of the Ottoman "Mirror for Princes"

A possible side-effect of the move from Davvani's to Kashifi's influence (or, instead, a probable cause of it) was that Ottoman political treatises began to be more pragmatic. The quest for a unifying theory of human society emphasized the smooth functioning of state institutions. Initially, there were the ready-made models of Iranian "mirror for princes" literature, which emphasized the duty of the ruler to hold court regularly, use of spies, and so forth; until the mid-sixteenth century (and, sporadically, even later), Ottoman translations, adaptations, and original works repeated or expanded these tropes. Until the late sixteenth and even into the early seventeenth century, for instance, texts on using physiognomy as a means to select candidates with the proper moral qualities for posts either at the palace or in the army circulated widely.[106] Yet from the mid-sixteenth century onwards, the Ottoman authors were to develop their own style, focusing on institutions rather than the person of the sultan or the grand vizier. If the authors analyzed up to now had been transmitting the received Persian tradition, and occasionally making their own alterations or additions, this new trend, which began with Lütfi Pasha's *Âsafnâme*, inaugurated a distinctively Ottoman tradition.

Arguably, in this respect it is not a coincidence that Lütfi Pasha (1488–1563) was a product of the distinctively Ottoman system of recruitment. Of Albanian origin, he was recruited through the *devşirme* system and raised in the sultan's palace. He was first appointed the governor of Kastamonu, before then serving in various administrative posts and participating in many of Selim I's and Süleyman's campaigns, becoming a vizier in 1534/5 and ultimately the grand vizier in 1539 following the death of his predecessor, Ayas Pasha. He only served in this post for two years, as he was dismissed in 1541. He then retired to his farm in Dimetoka, where he died. During his retirement he wrote several books in Arabic and Ottoman Turkish, among which was a history of the Ottoman state (*Tevârîh-i âl-i Osmân*) and the treatise, examined in detail above, defending the right of the Ottoman sultan to claim the title of caliph. But the work he is most famous for is his *Âsafnâme*, on the duties of a grand vizier, probably

106 Lelić 2017.

completed after his historical work (i.e. after 1554).[107] *Âsafnâme* ("The book of Asaf", alluding to the mythical wise vizier of the prophet Solomon—the namesake of Süleyman!), despite being rather short compared to other treatises of the time, was a very popular and highly influential work; fifteen manuscripts are in Istanbul alone, and Evliya Çelebi records a copy kept in the library of the autonomous khan of Bitlis, in 1655;[108] as will be seen in the following chapters, it was partly or wholly incorporated into various treatises on government during subsequent centuries.

Âsafnâme is structured very loosely along the lines of Persian "mirrors for princes", containing four chapters: on the qualities of the grand vizier, on the army, on the treasury, and on the peasant subjects. There is no chapter on the sultan, and though this is nothing new, the emphasis on the grand vizier seems to have created a new tradition, as will be seen. The relevant chapter (T6–24) is, in many ways, the least original: it mainly contains the usual advice, such as that the grand vizier must not be malicious or selfish, that he must share his secrets with no-one but the sultan, that he must not spend his time carousing, and so forth. Yet the detail and the extent of concrete information on the functioning of the Ottoman (and not of any other Muslim) court is unprecedented. A few examples are telling: the advice that the grand vizier must take care of his people, raising the poor and powerless among them to various posts, is not original, but Lütfi goes on to specify that he should only grant timars, and not *ze'amet*s (greater timars), to his men. Lütfi was not the first to speak of restrictions in the system of couriers (*ulak*), yet he describes at some length the specific reforms he introduced during his own vizierate.[109] The grand vizier must appoint wise and experienced men at the head of the janissaries, and he must take special care of price regulations (*narh*), since they are one of the most important aspects of the world.

The same down-to-earth information can be seen when Lütfi Pasha describes the income of a vizier, and others in the hierarchy of state officials, from the *beylerbeyi*s, the provincial governors, down to the various administrative, judicial, and military offices. He specifies that only those who come from the imperial palace or are the sons of *beylerbeyi*s and *defterdar*s (provincial financial officers) can become salaried *müteferrika*s; similar premises must rule

107 Lütfi Pasha – Tschudi 1910; Lütfi Pasha – Kütükoğlu 1991; Akgündüz 1990–1996, 4:258–276 (facs. follows, 277–290). On Lutfi Pasha and his work, see Lewis 1962, 71–74; Fodor 1986, 223–224; Yılmaz 2003a, 302–303; Yılmaz 2005, 114–119.

108 Çolak 2003, 353; Evliya Çelebi – Dankoff 1990, 290.

109 Here Lütfi, as in other parts of his treatise as well, refers to specific reforms he introduced during his own vizierate. See *Encyclopaedia of Islam*, 2nd ed., s.v. "Lutfi Pasha" (C. H. Imber) and Yürük 2014.

the appointments of the district governors (*sancakbeyi*s), etc. The same level of detail is apparent in the chapter discussing the affairs of the army when on campaign (T25–35); issues such as the importance of logistical planning before the campaign starts, the spatial planning of a camp, and naval warfare (Lütfi was in charge of the fleet operating in the Adriatic and which besieged Corfu in 1537) show the author's experience but are also, for the first time, judged fit for a work of political advice, thus departing from both the morality-centered model of Tusi and his successors and the abstract advice of Persian "mirrors for princes".

Similar observations can be made regarding Lütfi's views on financial matters. He had already stressed that unclaimed inheritances must be kept guarded in the treasury for seven years, waiting for an heir to appear, because:

> the properties of people ought not to become the property of the sultan for no reason, since this leads to the death of his power (*emval-i halk bi-vech dahil-i mal-i padişahi olmak fena-yı devlet daldır*).

Again for the first time, a whole chapter (T35–40) deals with the treasury, and Lütfi stresses that (T35)

> the power of the king comes with the treasury, and the treasury comes with taking measures and not with oppression.

Afterwards, he once again recounts personal experience: when he became grand vizier, the treasury was in a desperate condition. Sometimes it had to be supplemented from the external old treasury (*taşrada mevcud olan eski hazine*; Lütfi must have meant the inner treasury);[110] this, he writes, is a disorder (*ihtilâl*), because revenues must always be greater than expenditure (but, later, Lütfi also notes that the revenue from Egypt belongs to the sultan personally as "pocket-money", *bi'z-zat ceb harclığı*). The grand vizier must take care of this issue in certain ways: first, by decreasing the number of the sultan's slaves, the *kul*s, and keeping their lists tidy and reliable (here the phrase *asker az gerek öz gerek*, "the army must be few in number and pure in essence", which was to be frequently cited in subsequent advice books); second, by appointing as *defterdar*s people with experience and wisdom, who know how to increase the revenues of the state, and who will not be led by greed and egotism. Salaries must not be increased, as far as possible, and pensions must be handled with care; here, Lütfi gives a list of the pensions that should be given to each retired

110 On the inner and outer treasury see Uzunçarşılı 1978, 73ff.; Sariyannis 2013, 112–114.

official in various ranks. It is better to give the *mukataas*, the public revenues, as government offices (*emanet ile*) rather than as tax-farming (T39). Every year, the budget must be checked in order to plan for the next.

Another striking novelty of Lütfi's treatise is his obsession with preventing peasant mobility. Somewhat awkwardly, he inserts a remark at the end of his chapter on the grand vizier stating that a *reaya* cannot be a *sipahi* if he is not a son or grandson of a *sipahi*, otherwise, everybody would want to be a *sipahi* and nobody would produce anything. He takes up this subject in detail in his fourth and final chapter (T40–44), which concerns the *reaya*. Instead of the usual emphasis on justice, here Lütfi prefers to stress the need to prevent peasant mobility. His specific concern is the unauthorized intrusion of peasants into the army's ranks. He emphasizes that only certain types of soldier (the *eşkinci, ellici* and *akıncı*) are to be recruited from the peasant population. The administrative tool permitting control of the *reaya* is the tax registers, he writes, which have to be conducted every 30 years and are kept in the imperial council. Whenever a *reaya* leaves one place for another due to oppression, the judge must send him back to avoid the ruin of the land (Lütfi makes no further reference to stopping the oppression!). Even the descendants of the Prophet must be controlled by their chief, who has to check for intruders. If a *reaya* obtains a fief for some reason, or becomes an ulema, his relatives must still remain taxable peasants. More generally, Lütfi argues that the *reaya* must not be encouraged (*re'ayete çok yüz virmemek gerekdür*); if they obtain large properties, they should not be oppressed, but they cannot dress in the manner of a *sipahi*. Thus, for Lütfi, strict compartmentalization is the essence of *reaya* administration. Everything he has to say regarding justice, of course, is again to do with specific Ottoman institutions and realities: namely, that extraordinary levies (*avariz*) must be collected at regular intervals and that oarsmen for the fleet are to be levied according to the empire's law and paid by the treasury.

•••

Lütfi, it seems, deliberately chose to avoid any theoretical or even moral musings, focusing instead on highlighting his day-to-day experience in the Ottoman administration in order to compile a manual for his successors. This does not mean, however, that there is no theory underlying his advice: the passages on the moral qualities of a vizier, on the importance of the imperial council, and—perhaps most importantly of all—on the strict compartmentalization of society between the taxable *reaya* and the untaxable administrative and military personnel (the *askeri*) clearly follow earlier trends (although the two-fold division of society according to taxation comes from Ottoman practice rather than any pre-existing political tradition). But on the whole, *Âsafnâme* stands out as an impressively original work, setting a new example for the genre that would be followed throughout the sixteenth century.

It is very interesting that Lütfi Pasha seems to have been considered ignorant in the eyes of educated bureaucrats such as Mustafa Ali and (perhaps) Celalzade, who looked with disdain upon *devşirme* recruits in high administrative positions.[111] As has been seen, however, he was perfectly capable of writing elaborate treatises in Arabic with quotations from *hadiths* and other medieval authorities, as he did in his essay on the caliphate. Yet the absence of any reference, quotation, or even of any real glimpse of earlier political philosophy in his *Âsafnâme* is striking. Not a single authority is mentioned. He does illustrate his points with stories, but they all come from his own experience under Selim and Süleyman: neither Muhammad nor the first caliphs, nor Anushirvan or Iskender/Alexander, are to be found. A reflection of the bureaucratic obsession with lists, mentioned above in relation to Celalzade, may perhaps be detected in his enumerations of posts, salaries, and pensions.

On a more political level, the emphasis placed by Lütfi Pasha (and, to a lesser extent, by Celalzade) on the vizier rather than the sultan himself is a sign of his times: even before Mehmed II, Ottoman sultans had begun to seclude themselves; they gradually ceased to appear very often in public and even to eat together with their officials, increasingly delegating their everyday powers to the viziers and the *kadiaskers*. The grand vizier started to be designated as the "absolute proxy" (*vekil-i mutlak*) of the sultan's power, and consequently to have a more important position in conducting political affairs.[112] While Selim I's grand viziers were short-lived and prone to immediate dismissal or even execution (hence the curse of the time, "may you become a vizier of Selim!"),[113] Süleyman and his successors relied extensively on their viziers (suffice it to mention the careers of Ibrahim Pasha and Sokollu Mehmed Pasha), each of whom adhered to specific policies and were allied with specific power parties. Lütfi may have not been the first or only author who wrote advice for viziers rather than sultans, but he had the authority to do so through experience,

111 Ali admits that, for a *devşirme* recruit, Lütfi's education was better than average, but he considers him as arrogant and having a high opinion of himself: Yılmaz 2006, 107–8.

112 Stavrides 2001, 30–37 (on the sultans' seclusion) and 56–59 (on the growing power of the viziers); Sariyannis 2011a, 129ff.; Yılmaz 2015a, 234–237. Stavrides' analysis is very reliant on the so-called "*kanunname* of Mehmed the Conqueror", which is, in fact, a much later product (see Imber 2011, 174–178), although this does not alter his central conclusions.

113 Ali, as quoted by Hammer 1963, 2:378; Çıpa 2014, 132.

and thus he managed to inaugurate a whole new style of treatises, one that was distinctively Ottoman.[114]

6 As a Conclusion: the Ideas at Hand, the Forces at Work

Instead of describing one specific line of thought, this chapter has offered a panorama of ideas and trends that were circulating in the mid-sixteenth century, an era that in the following century came to be considered as the heyday of the Ottoman Empire. Some of these trends were in fact the ends of long trains of thought, whose beginnings dated back to medieval times. These were, primarily, the morality-centered view of politics and the abstract advice given regarding rulership, which focused on ancient wisdom and the figure of the ideal king. Works that were part of this trend, such as those of Celalzade, often offered new insights (the glorification of the scribal bureaucracy, for instance) within an old genre without departing from traditional moral theory. Others were radical reconfigurations and calibrations of older debates and discussions, such as the *fikh* arguments on the relationship between the Sharia and secular government. Finally, with Lütfi Pasha's influential essay, there is the glorious beginning of a new tradition, one focusing on institutional rather than personal advice and on up-to-date information on the state and its functions.

At the same time, this era saw an array of social conflicts and of economic, social, and political developments that would soon radically transform the structure from which they had arisen. In many ways, Süleyman's reign was thus a time of balance between emerging and declining powers, emerging and declining genres and theories, and paths that would soon be abandoned and roads about to be followed. Of course, it would be somewhat naïve to say that there is a one-to-one correspondence between social groups and actors on the one hand, and genres or ideological currents on the other. Yet it is certainly possible to explore affinities and dependencies, and political thought has never been produced *in vitro*. Thus, Süleyman's era was probably the final time that the old feudal apparatus could feel confident and that it was the master of the socio-economic structure. Feudal relations had already begun to be disrupted, but there was still the grip of the state and the whole government apparatus was trying hard to keep these relations intact. One may see this confidence in the way Ebussu'ud used *fikh* in order to serve the purpose of keeping

114 Semerkandi's *Latâ'if al-Afkâr* (1529), Alayi b. Muhibbi al-Şirazi al-Şerif's *Düstûrü'l-vüzerâ* (1558; Şirazî – Dokuzlu 2012) and 'Ârifî Ma'ruf Efendi's *'Ukûd al-jawâhir* (1560) also discuss the vizier rather than the sultan (Yılmaz 2005, 68–70, 99–101, and 91–93, respectively).

the land-holding and tax systems in line with feudal practice. The emphasis of Lütfi Pasha on the rights of the *sipahi* and the need to check social mobility was a sign of his time: it means that he was worried by the rise of new mercantile strata and by the decline of the *sipahi* army, which, as will be seen, were to become a standard feature of the following decades. On the other hand, as the monetarization of the economy gradually created new opportunities to accumulate wealth, there were many urban groups that tried to fill the gap; among them, great pasha and ulema households, which, when needed, were to use tools from the same inventory (*fikh*, for instance) in order to justify their own practices.[115]

On another level, and unlike European feudalism, the Ottoman system of agrarian relations and the vassal-like fief-based military had to rely on a strong and absolute ruler, one who could distribute lands as if they were his own property and have ultimate control of legislation and administration. The messianic features of Süleyman's early reign and later claims to the caliphate later fit well into this need.[116] It is no coincidence that scribal political literature, the product of a governmental class whose power depended closely on the sultan's personal will and power, abandoned the view of the sultan as an individual who strived for moral perfection (see chapter 1) in favor of a more charismatic picture. One of the most striking features of Celalzade's work, apart from the glorification of his own scribal class, is the position he gives the sultan, above the law: inspired by God, the Ottoman sultan can never succumb to the temptation of tyranny even if he yields unlimited power. At the beginning of his *Tabakat*, Celalzade even described Süleyman as the Mahdi (K134b), whereas, in the preamble to the Egypt *kanunname*, he had compared Süleyman to the Prophet and to saints.[117] There were good reasons, therefore, why, when the sultan ceased to be the protector of the *sipahi* network and its supporting structures, theorists who favored the timariot forces tried to play down his omnipotence and bind him to the rules. As for the emerging societal groups, the tax-farmers on the one hand and the janissaries on the other, they had not yet found a voice in political literature (or, they did not yet need to; power comes first, justification follows).

115 See Gel 2013b; Tezcan 2010a, 36–40.

116 This trend was the culmination of a long process. Bayezid II was also seen as the renewer of his age at the turn of the Islamic century: see Şen 2017, esp. 604–605.

117 Yılmaz 2006, 205–206, and fn. 628 (cf. ibid., 200, fn 607); Şahin 2013, 56–57, 188–190.

CHAPTER 4

"Mirrors for Princes": the Decline Theorists

According to the view prevailing up to the early 1990s, it was during the Süleymanic era that signs of Ottoman decline started to appear.[1] Military victories were by no means absent, but no spectacular conquest like Selim's expansion in the Middle East or Süleyman's in Hungary was made after the 1540s; the new front against the Portuguese in the Indian Ocean was never very successful, although it continued to bring occasional victories until the 1580s. Moreover, Süleyman allegedly became a much more secluded and pious person after the execution of his vizier Ibrahim (this also seems to have been reflected in his patronage of poetry, with disillusionment of the literati being a secondary outcome).[2] The execution of the popular prince Mustafa in 1553 soon led to the rebellion of Süleyman's second son, Bayezid, who was trying to secure his place against his brother Selim. Bayezid raised an army consisting of peasants who had abandoned their lands; he was defeated near Konya in 1559 and fled to Iran, where he was held as a hostage before being executed by an Ottoman envoy. When Süleyman died during the siege of Szigetvár in Hungary, the grand vizier Sokollu Mehmed Pasha kept his death secret until Selim was informed and successfully enthroned.

Selim II (r. 1566–74) is generally considered an incompetent sultan who was lucky to have his father's major two statesmen, namely Ebussu'ud Efendi and Sokollu. The latter successfully suppressed a major revolt in Yemen and concluded a treaty with the Habsburgs. On both fronts he envisaged ambitious projects of building canals (in Suez and in the Volga—to fight in Astrakhan and the Caspian Sea), but none was effectively built. Finally, although at the beginning he was reluctant, it was under Sokollu's vizierate that Cyprus was conquered from the Venetians (1570–71), and it was through Sokollu's efforts that the major naval defeat of Lepanto (1571) had no lasting consequences for the Ottoman presence in the eastern Mediterranean. Sokollu remained in post after Selim's death as well, under Murad III (1574–95); however, the grand vizier's assassination in 1579 led to a change of policy. Sokollu's successors favored war rather than peace. Consequently, a long war against Safavid Iran started in 1578; after initial difficulties, successes, such as the occupation

1 For the chronology, again the most recent account is Imber 2009, 52ff.; see also Mantran 1989, 155–158; Emecen 2001b, 39–47.

2 Cf. Necipoğlu 1992; Andrews – Kalpaklı 2005.

© KONINKLIJKE BRILL NV, LEIDEN, 2019 | DOI:10.1163/9789004385245_006

of Tabriz in 1585 and the subjugation of Georgia two years later, led to further expansion of the Ottoman state eastwards with the treaty of 1590, which confirmed the conquest of the Caucasus, Kurdistan, and Azerbaijan. However, this expansion was only achieved at great cost, as both the state finances and the peasants were overburdened by the requirements of constant warfare.

In addition, almost as soon as peace with Iran had been concluded, another long war began, in 1593, this time on the Habsburg front. Serious defeats in Hungary and Wallachia proved that the era of uncontested Ottoman superiority had passed. After Murad's death, his son Mehmed III (r. 1595–1603) famously expelled his father's buffoons and dwarves from the palace, since they allegedly influenced the sultan's decisions,[3] and in 1596 he led the army in person against the Austrians. Mehmed did indeed (almost by mistake) win a major battle in Mező-Keresztes (Hacova), although his cavalry had fled the field (with far-reaching consequences, as will be seen). The Ottomans, however, could not take advantage of this victory and the war continued, with mixed results, until 1606. Meanwhile, a counter-attack by Shah Abbas I, beginning in 1603, cost the Ottomans Tabriz, Erevan, and Shirvan, making up for all the losses the Safavids had suffered during the previous war.

The usual emphasis on all things military notwithstanding, what mainly appeared to both contemporary and modern observers as a sign of decline was the internal situation of the empire. Janissary and sipahi rebellions, which were to form a recurrent feature of the following century, were first seen in 1589 with the "Beylerbey incident", when Istanbul janissaries revolted in protest over being paid with debased coins; monetary problems were especially acute in this period and played a major role in its perception as an age of disorder.[4] What seemed more important at the time, however, was the famous Celali rebellions.[5] Although they may be said to have been preceded by the "student (*softa, suhte*) revolts" of the 1570s and 1580s (when armed bands of provincial students roamed the countryside), Ottoman chroniclers considered the battle of Mező-Keresztes as their beginning: when, after the victory, the Ottoman commander ordered an inspection of the cavalry left in the field, he discovered that a large number of sipahis were missing, and accordingly deprived them of their timars. The now-dispossessed soldiers returned

3 On these categories of courtiers, cf. Dikici 2006 and Dikici 2013; see, in particular, Dikici 2006, 76ff. on the representation of dwarfs and mutes as the source of all evil by late sixteenth-century historians and political writers. The discussions on the advisors and favorites of the sultan partly reflect the struggle for control of information in decision-making; see Peksevgen 2004.

4 See Kafadar 1986 (esp. 76–80 on the Beylerbey incident); Kafadar 1991.

5 Barkey 1994; Özel 2012.

to Anatolia, where they joined armed bands of rebels. Peasants had already started to leave their plots and take up arms for a number of decades (they had made up the bulk of the army of Süleyman's son Bayezid), but in the final years of the sixteenth century these rebel bands, known as Celalis, almost reached the size of regular armies. Under leaders such as Karayazıcı, Deli Hasan, and Kalenderoğlu (the latter of whom also collaborated with a rebel governor of Aleppo, Canbuladoğlu Ali), they managed to defeat powerful Ottoman forces and virtually occupy most of eastern and central Anatolia, with occasional raids reaching as far as Izmir and Bursa, until they were co-opted or suppressed by successive imperial campaigns. Simultaneously, an enormous wave of migration of the peasants towards the big cities, and especially Istanbul (known as "the great flight", *büyük kaçgun*), contributed to a sharp decline in agricultural life within the countryside. It was not until 1609 that the Ottoman state regained firm control over the Anatolian countryside.

On the institutional level, the most striking feature of the late sixteenth century was the gradual waning of the timar system. As the use of lance-equipped cavalry was becoming obsolete in favor of infantry with firearms, so was the monetarization of the agricultural economy transforming the fief into a waste of resources from the state's point of view. The state needed cash to pay its infantry, both standing (the janissaries) and auxiliary (the mercenary militias known as *sekban* or *sarıca*). The latter were easy to recruit (by the state as well as by local governors who needed private guards) since more and more peasants' sons were leaving their lands, either because the military career was more lucrative (the "pull" factor) or because conditions in the agricultural villages were becoming ever more difficult (the "push" factor). The existence of dispossessed ex-sipahis (and such were being produced by the crisis of the timar system before and after the battle of Mező-Keresztes) added to this explosive mixture, and contributed to the collapse of sultanly legitimization in large parts of the Anatolian provinces. On the financial level, the need for ready cash led to the gradual expansion of the tax-farming system (*iltizam*): the state preferred auctioning and farming out taxes (as well as other revenue) rather than granting them as timars, a system that contributed to the enfeeblement of the sipahis and had a negative effect on the peasants' situation, as tax-farmers tried to gain most of their revenue.[6] Here we should note, however, that the use of this system had begun in the late fourteenth century, and that from the state's point of view it offered several advantages, namely the absence of risk and the minimal size of the tax-collecting apparatus.[7] On the other hand, one

6 The classic studies are İnalcık 1972 and İnalcık 1980.

7 Fleet 2003.

must be cautious in adopting wholesale the image described above, as in large part it originates from the Istanbul-based Ottoman authors; recently, Linda T. Darling has argued that a detailed inspection of archival sources would show that the timar system underwent a much less radical change from the 1580s onwards than we used to think. The timar cavalry ceased to be the backbone of the Ottoman army, but it remained useful for siege warfare, while timar-holders continued to belong to the rural elites. What changed was their relationship with the central elites, to whom most writers belonged.[8]

Other changes in the second half of the sixteenth century concerned the balance of power at the center itself: sultans were steadily withdrawing from actual politics, delegating more and more of their powers to the grand viziers. After the civil war between the sons of Süleyman, which eliminated all contenders to the throne, the eldest son of every reigning sultan was sent to be a provincial governor in order to gain experience. This meant there was no "competition" over his succession, and he was to develop his own household and prepare to rule. The sultan's household, including both his *harem* and his entourage, played an increasingly important role in government, while the ruler himself withdrew into a more symbolic and legitimizing role.[9] Furthermore, the sultan's slaves (i.e. the *kapıkulları*, who constituted not only the janissary army but also most of the administrative apparatus of the empire) began to reproduce themselves: the *devşirme* system of recruiting was gradually substituted by *protégés* rising from within the sultan's household.[10]

The perception of all these changes as constituting a visible "decline" has been seriously challenged by a series of studies since the early 1990s. Linda Darling has shown that the financial bureaucracy actually increased its capacity to deal with tax collection and the administration of public finances in the late sixteenth century. Karen Barkey has claimed (perhaps with some exaggeration) that the slow and intermittent suppression of the Celali revolts was due to a process of state-building (co-opting the rebels into its system, with French and English parallels) rather than state inefficiency. Jane Hathaway has addressed the issue of decentralization, arguing that it was, in fact, a process closely connected to the elites of the central government. Rifaat Abou-El-Haj and Suraiya Faroqhi have maintained that, while there undoubtedly was a crisis, what ensued was a transformation of the Ottoman system that led to another version of the imperial paradigm, one not necessarily inferior (if this

8 Darling 2014; Darling 2015.

9 These developments were studied in detail by Peirce 1993.

10 On the function of the palace household see Kunt 2012.

term can be applied) to the previous one.[11] Recently, Baki Tezcan has proposed a continuous conflict between what he called the "absolutist" and the "constitutionalist" trends; in the context of this conflict, Murad III's reign, universally considered by Ottoman authors (as will be seen in detail) as the actual beginning of decline, is interpreted as an effort by the sultan to take back the reins of actual power, until then held by his viziers and *kul*s.[12]

1 Ottoman Authors and the "Decline" Paradigm

For our purposes, however, it is important to note that the "decline" paradigm was first initiated by Ottoman authors.[13] Abou-El-Haj's critique of the modern adherents of this theory was based precisely on their taking the sixteenth- and seventeenth-century advice literature at face value, whereas in his view these works should be seen as expressing the anxieties of an old order that was losing its prerogatives. True, the *topos* of a declining world had been a *leitmotif* in Ottoman literature even before the Ottoman Empire was established: it will be remembered that even at the beginning of the fifteenth century, for instance, Şeyhoğlu Mustafa was complaining of a lack of wise ulema, disrespect for the Sharia, and so on, not to mention Aşıkpaşazade, Yazıcıoğlu, and the other exponents of the "anti-imperial" opposition. Furthermore, the notion of decline was also a literary convention, one which can be seen in several works dating from the first half of the sixteenth century.[14] It is true, however, that this notion takes on completely new dynamics from the middle of that century, and becomes a central point in almost every treatise dealing with government towards the end of it.

It is important to note that the Ottoman authors to be examined do not use terms that imply a full "decline", i.e. an irreversible process bound to lead to

11 See Kafadar 1993; Darling 1996; Darling 1997; Barkey 1994; Abou-El-Haj 2005; Faroqhi 1994; Hathaway 1996; Quataert 2003.

12 See Tezcan 2010a, 55ff. and 97–99; on signs of Murad III's absolutism in contemporary sources see Fleischer 1986a, 295. Tezcan also connects Murad's absolutism with the conflict between "traditional" and "rational" sciences and the flourishing of the latter during his reign (Tezcan 2010b). Tezcan's theory has met with a rather lukewarm and cautious reception by fellow Ottomanists; similar views were also expressed in Yılmaz 2008 and Yılmaz 2015a.

13 On the genealogy of the "decline" trope in Ottoman literature, see Howard 1988; Herzog 1999.

14 See, for instance, the poet Latifi's complaints (Latifi – Pekin 1977; Latifi – Yérasimos 2001), as well as several anecdotes in Lami'i Çelebi's (d. 1532) *Letâ'ifnâme*, compiled by his son (Lami'i-zade – Çalışkan 1997). For more details, see Sariyannis 2008a, 133–134 and 135–136.

an eventual fall or disaster. When they have to use a term, they usually prefer "corruption" (*fesad*) or, more often, "turmoil" (*ihtilal*).[15] The meaning of these is that things are not as good as they once had been; however, they also imply that the situation could improve if the sultan (or the grand vizier) follows the authors' advice. The idealization of a glorious past is clear, but does not yet play a central role in these authors' arguments—in chapter 5, it will be seen how such an idealization began to occupy that role in the first decades of the next century.

1.1 *In Lütfi Pasha's Footsteps*

In other respects, the late sixteenth-century texts generally follow the path forged by Lütfi Pasha's treatise: not only are most addressed to the grand vizier rather than to the sultan himself, they also tend to ignore older works, hardly mentioning authorities such as Davvani or al-Ghazali at all, and, most importantly, they scarcely describe the moral qualities required of high officials.[16] While they almost always stress that the vizier must choose honest subordinates, their main emphasis is on the function of the imperial institutions: the janissary system, the palace and the imperial council, the ulema hierarchy, and so on. For the most part, these are works written by Ottomans for Ottomans, and destined for Ottoman rather than universal usage. This current of "institutional advice" reached its zenith in the final decades of the sixteenth century. The political treatises composed in this period may not be numerically greater than those produced in Süleyman's era, but what distinguishes them from earlier literature is their emphasis on the shortcomings of their own era, although an emphasis on a past "Golden Era" would follow.

Yet the first work to bear all these characteristics appears to date from before the end of Süleyman's reign. It is an anonymous work, entitled *Kitâbu mesâlihi'l-müslimîn ve menâfi'i'l-mü'minîn* ("Book on the proper course to be followed by Muslims and on the interests of the faithful").[17] The date this text was composed has been the subject of much scholarly debate, but it seems that the text almost certainly originates from the decade before Süleyman's

15 As seen in the previous chapter, Mehmed Birgivi was also an adherent of this trend; cf. Ivanyi 2012, 74–75.

16 On the other hand, we must note that treatises describing the means to discern the moral qualities of prospective officials by way of their physical characteristics were aboundant even up to the beginning of the seventeenth century: Lelić 2017.

17 Yücel 1988, 49–142; facsimile follows (citations of the transcribed text). See also Tezcan 2000; Yılmaz 2003a, 303–304; Yılmaz 2005, 119–121; İnan 2009, 120; Tuşalp Atiyas 2013, 56–61.

death in 1566.[18] There are some indications that the author held some minor state offices; although Yaşar Yücel suggests that he may have belonged to the *ilmiye* class, it seems very probable that he served in the palace, since he is very well informed as to what each military body should wear, as well as on the function of the imperial kitchens (Y104, 119). Furthermore, the author seems to know much about the function of the palace bureaucracy: he laments the poverty of some lower clerks, who have to spend the whole day in the palace without having a meal (Y100–1), and is particularly sensitive to the intrusion of strangers into the scribal ranks (though he says nothing at all about strangers in the janissary ranks, a central point of later literature). He is also at great pains to show that those who have worked in a particular bureau, such as the financial service or the council secretariat, should remain there, and new posts should be given to the apprentices of elder clerks (Y111–12).

Kitâbu mesâlih, which was destined for "the present rulers" (*hakimü'l-vakt olanlara*: Y91; the plural term appears elsewhere as well) and especially for the grand vizier (as indicated in many places), is a rather incoherent work, having 52 chapters that contain various pieces of practical advice with no apparent structure. It clearly follows the same path as its contemporary, the *Âsafnâme*: our anonymous author does not care for a philosophical foundation of society and politics nor for the moral qualities required by the sultan or even the grand vizier (who, as the addressee of the treatise, is considered *a priori* receptive to good advice). Rather, he focuses on specific institutions and the ways their shortcomings could be mended. It does this with much more detail (and much

18 According to Yaşar Yücel, who published it, the *Kitâbu mesâlih* should be dated shortly after 1639: Yücel 1988, 59–62. Only one manuscript is known, dated earlier than 1643; Yücel's dating is based mainly on the identification of a certain Yahya Çelebi Efendi in Beşiktaş, mentioned in the text, with the famous *şeyhülislam* who died in 1644, and on the vague reference to some decisive victories of the sultan over the Safavids. Baki Tezcan argued that several pieces of external and internal evidence point to a much earlier date, between 1555 and 1566 (Tezcan 2000, 658–659). Tezcan argued that another Şeyh Yahya Çelebi, a Sufi, resided in Beşiktaş in the mid-sixteenth century, while, moreover, references to particular people (a physician, Hamunoğlu, who must be a famous doctor from Süleyman's era) and events (the conquest of Egypt) as having happened during the author's lifetime suggest that he was alive during Selim I's reign; other pieces of information (e.g. the number of palace ushers, *kapıcı*) also conflict with was is known of the early seventeenth century. Based on the same reference to the sultan's victories (which arguably implies that the victorious sultan is still alive), Tezcan concludes that we should date this text before the death of Süleyman (1566) and after the 1555 campaign. One may also add that if we dated the treatise to the late 1630s it would be a quite out-of-date, isolated specimen of old-fashioned scattered advice, ignoring all the major themes that were steadily reccuring in the early seventeenth-century texts (for instance, there is no reference at all to the number of the janissaries).

less coherence) than Lütfi Pasha, showing a deeper knowledge of the everyday function of the state apparatus; in fact, one might even say that here we have a "bottom-up" approach, with the text being the work of a lower official watching developments at his own level of government. This approach may also be seen in the variety of issues the author raises: as well as the usual problems of sultanly justice, the army, the ulema, and peasants' lives, we read chapters on every possible aspect of Ottoman life, from the provisioning of Istanbul and the duties of the *muhtesib* (Y102–3, 114–17, 119, 125–26) to the kitchens of the imperial palace (Y104, 119; in both cases with the note "although insolent [to propose], it is a good act", *eğerçi küstahlıkdur lakin sevabdur*), and from inspectors sent to the provinces (Y121–22) to architectural methods of avoiding fires in big cities (Y122; the author proposes the use of more stone masonry, rather than wood) and ways of making a strong impression on foreign ambassadors (Y127).

A further difference from Lütfi Pasha's model is the main feature of this group of texts, namely its emphasis on what is going wrong in the present, rather than on the ideal functioning of the institutions. A good example is *Hırzü'l-mülûk* ("Stronghold [or, Amulet] of the kings"), an anonymous essay (all that is known is that its author held a fief [*dirlik*]), it must have been composed around 1574, and it was dedicated to Murad III.[19] The author states that the work is divided into eight chapters, including sections on various palace and government officials, as well as "on Istanbul, other great cities, and the arsenal" and "on Venice and other infidel states" (Y173, A33). However, all manuscripts end with chapter four (most regrettably, since otherwise we would have one of the most comprehensive political treatises of that era).[20] In its current form, *Hırzü'l-mülûk* begins with a note on the importance of the post of grand vizier, and then speaks of the kingly virtues, the properties and qualities of the viziers, the military commanders, and the army, and the various high-ranking

19 This text was published by Yücel 1988, 171–201 and then by Akgündüz 1990–1996, 8:31–63 (both with facsimiles). See also Yılmaz 2003a, 306–307; İnan 2009, 115–116; Sariyannis 2011a, 130–131. The dating is based on two verses mentioning Sultan Murad, although a later note at the beginning of one manuscript states that the work was offered to Murad IV. Its editor, Yaşar Yücel, remarks that a reference to the practice of sending princes to govern provinces suggests that the sultan is Murad III (further evidence for this dating is the mention of four viziers). It seems that the treatise was presented to him as soon as (or maybe even before) he ascended to the throne, since a whole section of the work is dedicated to the first acts a sultan should take (Y179ff, A40ff).

20 Furthermore, the work is divided into chapters and parts (*fasl, cüz'*) with a certain inconsistency that shows we are dealing with something approaching a first draft. It is possible that the division into *cüz'* comes from the copying of the work on paper prepared for another manuscript; see esp. fols 38b, 48b in the manuscript published by Yücel 1988.

ulema, as well as the sheikhs and the descendants of the Prophet. The author mentions al-Ghazali's *İhyâ'-i 'ulûm* (Y176, A36) and various unspecified Persian and Arabic books (Y183, A43), while he also cites numerous anecdotes from Selim I's and Süleyman's reigns. In general, however, the treatise bears the distinctively Ottoman late sixteenth-century feature of specific criticisms of and detailed proposals for contemporaneous politics. One might remark, as Baki Tezcan did, that the emphasis of *Hırzü'l-mülûk* on the need for the sultan to yield actual power and to take back responsibilities that had been delegated to the grand vizier fits well with a treatise dedicated to Murad III, as this is exactly what that sultan tried to do.[21]

Although *Kitâbu mesâlih* lacks both the structural coherence and the sense of a past "Golden Age" that are apparent in *Hırzü'l-mülûk*, the two works share a common inventory of ideas, most of which were to have a long lifespan in the years to come, well into the seventeenth century. As noted, *Kitâbu mesâlih* has a strong "bottom-up" or "street-level" approach. Thus, it is only in *Hırzü'l-mülûk* that we can find advice on the qualities required of sultans and viziers: although it delves into the importance of the latter post, comparing the four viziers of the imperial council to the first four caliphs, the author favors strong sultanly power. He admits that it is difficult for the ruler to watch over the affairs of the world in person; however, if he willingly tries to deal with every issue in his realm, God will help him, and for that reason this work was written for and presented to the sultan (Y173–76, A33–36). Then the author describes the sultanly virtues (emphasizing the preparations a sultan should make just after, or even shortly before, his accession to the throne), like most traditional treatises. However, he departs sharply from the usual commonplaces to offer counsel directly from the Ottoman experience. For instance, he remarks that the sultan should not marry his daughters and sisters to viziers or *beylerbeyi*s, but rather to *sancakbeyi*s whose life-long fief (*hass*) ought to be in the *terra firma* (not in the borderlands) and reach 4–500,000 aspers (Y176–83, A36–43). The same is seen in the chapter on viziers: after drawing some moral and practical advice from the inventory of older "mirrors for princes", the author again proceeds to give advice specially adjusted for an Ottoman vizier. In this, he writes that a vizier must not grant fiefs to people who have never fought or to former bandits (*harami*) who escaped punishment, and he must not succumb to the infidel states' bribes in order to prevent conquests (the author cites here two examples from Süleyman's reign, namely Ayas Pasha on Corfu and Ali Pasha on Malta); as well as his *kethüda*, the vizier's men should be salaried from his own income (Y183–185, A43–46).

21 Tezcan 2010a, 55–56.

More generally, there is an evident distrust of viziers throughout *Hırzü'l-mülûk*: the author speaks explicitly against granting (*temlik*) 40 or 50 villages to a grand vizier, as he has no need of such large property. After describing in detail how viziers manipulate such grants and use them to enrich themselves, the author remarks that the aim of conquest is to enrich the public treasury, not that of the viziers. Ideally, no *temlik*s should be granted at all, but if they must be, they should not exceed one or two villages. In conclusion, the sultan should elect as viziers people with few or no children and relatives; lands granted to them should also be situated in the inner Anatolian provinces, not on the fertile coastline (Y177–79, A37–40).

Thus, we enter into the land problem, or rather into discussions about the disrupted structure of the timariot system. The army needs fiefs (*dirlik*) according to the soldiers' needs, yet while this arrangement requires that most of the towns and villages belong to the state as fiefs (*havass-ı hümayun ve ze'amet ve timarlar olmak lâzım iken*), most of them were private property (*mülk*) or belonged to *vakf*s. Of course, the sultan himself had every right to endow his own *vakf*s with lands he conquered, and he should administer very carefully the granting of properties for pious endowments in order not to waste state lands (Y176–177, A37). Such distrust for *vakf*s is also evident in *Kitâbu mesâlih*, which often points out that if the grand vizier were to follow the measures being proposed he would do better than creating new charitable foundations (*imaret*) and spend less (e.g. Y107). As well as *vakf*s, the author of *Hırzü'l-mülûk* also laments the disruption of the timariot system: he notes that vacant fiefs ought not to be annexed to other timars but instead distributed to sipahis' sons or lawful applicants. Their size must not surpass certain limits, which he gives accordingly. Following this, and inaugurating a long tradition, he notes that strangers (*ecnebi*) have acquired fiefs, while sipahis' sons remain destitute since they are too poor to bribe the beylerbeyis. This may be the first reference to the intrusion of "strangers" into the military ranks, although the emphasis is on the sipahis rather than the janissaries (as would be the case in later treatises). Beylerbeyis, in turn, claim that they act thus because they are obliged to send huge sums of money to the grand vizier, so they have to accept bribes in order to provide this money. Indeed, all officers have to send two-thirds of their income to the grand vizier. The only solution is for the sultan to elect personally the beylerbeyis, regardless of the opinion of the grand vizier. After all, "the pleasure of kingly power is equity and giving" (*saltanatun lezzeti dâd u dihiş iledir*); if the sultan accepts unquestionably the appointments made by the grand vizier, the appointees will owe their posts to the latter and behave accordingly (Y185–89, A46–50).

Like Lütfi Pasha, the author of *Hirzü'l-mülûk* has little to say on the peasants themselves. In fact, he says almost nothing except for the usual eulogy on justice and the commonplace advice that the sultan must accept all petitions (*ruk'a*) given to him by his subjects when he appears in public, because he must protect the *reaya* and because sultanly justice helps maintain security in his lands, and thus ensures the world order (Y182, A42–43; in a similar vein, the author also suggests that *müftis* should be appointed in the provinces so that the poor subjects do not have to travel all the way to Istanbul to obtain a *fetva*: Y194, A55). He also reiterates the guidelines, often seen in imperial decrees, on the need for governors to protect peasants from the oppression of local magnates and tax-collectors (Y185, A46). In contrast, *Kitâbu mesâlih* appears much more sensitive to the peasants' problems. While reiterating the same *leitmotif* of the Iranian tradition, i.e. access to the right of petition, its author gives a very down-to-earth version in very Ottoman terms: he insists that things should be made easier for illiterate people from the provinces coming to Istanbul to give a petition at the Imperial Council (Y127–28). A very interesting chapter in the same work argues that Muslim peasants must be allowed to bear arms in order to fight robbers (the specific references are to Christian robbers in the Balkans and "Arabs" in Thrace);[22] the old law against this is now useless (Y101–2). Furthermore, the distribution of alms to the poor and needy must be rationalized: all the needy must be registered and alms must be distributed in an orderly manner. Here, the phrasing is "the rich need the poor; without the latter, the former would not exist" (Y128–29).

This emphasis on the problems of the common taxpayer is evident in other parts of *Kitâbu mesâlih*. It stresses that taxes and dues must be collected fairly and take into account provincial realities (Y103–4, 107–8). The author argues that, for the benefit of travelers and merchants, weights and measures used in different provinces should be reformulated according to those in Istanbul, so that the whole empire would use the same ones, just like *hutbe* and coinage (Y94). Moreover, the various posts of *emin*s and *kâtib*s should be given to *kul*s and not to urban dwellers (*şehirlü*), because the latter are often corrupt and because the state would thereby spend less money in salaries (since janissaries will always get their wages, one way or another; Y109).

Landholding issues constitute one of the major problems for our authors; another one is the army. Here again, "Ottomanization" is clear. Janissaries and other military branches form the main object of suggestions and advice in *Kitâbu mesâlih*. Its author maintains that the *acemi oğlanları*, i.e. the *devşirme* recruits, must not be given to Turkish families (*türk ta'ifesine*) for ploughing, but should get a military education right from the start (Y 93–94). *Kitâbu mesâlih*

22 Here there is another argument against the dating of the treatise in the 1630s, as the author completely ignores the Celali rebellions in Anatolia.

also has specific counsel concerning *devşirme* (see Y106–7), while emphasizing the need for constant military training (Y99) and campaign organization (Y96, 101, 104, 118, 119–21) with special reference to the struggle against the Persians (Y122–25). The author also gives suggestions regarding the sipahis, such as that they should have armed servants and that they should not lose their fiefs if they are ill during campaigns (Y109–10). But his longest chapters concern sartorial limitations: soldiers must only wear what is ordained for them, which the author describes at length and in great detail (Y96–100, 112–14). This advice is not just restricted to soldiers: various remarks stress that different classes (*ekabir, edna*, but also Christians and Jews) should wear different clothes (Y 95, 117). As for *Hırzü'l-mülûk*, it devotes one of its four chapters to the army (Y185–89, A46–50); given the dating of the two texts, it is interesting that its author has little to say on the janissaries' discipline and organization. He is content to argue that the strict rules for their salary, defined in accordance with their position, must be applied universally and without exception; there must be an upper level to their wages that cannot be surpassed. Furthermore, provincial governors should scrutinize timariots in order to see whether they possess their fief lawfully (but this should not apply to those who have held a fief for more than ten years: Y185–86, A46).

Finally, another common concern of the two texts is the ulema. According to the author of *Kitâbu mesâlih*, it is this class that provides the world order (*nizam-i alem bunlarun iledir*: Y91). They must be guaranteed steady posts and short *mülazemet* periods (less than six months; this was a kind of waiting period, during which a candidate was out of work until a suitable vacant post appeared). The author complains that, while many educated ulema wait for years for a post, some judges and scholars take bribes and dress like sipahis; he suggests that the latter be given timars (and, he remarks, "the class of the sipahi would benefit if scholars were among them") so that posts open up for those waiting (Y91–92). This rather odd proposition stands out clearly, as the rest of the advice is more traditional: the ulema must feel powerful enough not to fear local military officers (Y91–92), they cannot be addicted to drugs (Y95),[23] preachers must go with the army on campaign (Y 125), and so on. Similarly, the chapter on the ulema in *Hırzü'l-mülûk* examines various ulema posts and ranks, complaining that people with no education or knowledge use bribery

23 While "in other professions, addiction not only is not shameful, it also increases the mastery of the addict" (cf. Sariyannis 2007, 312). The author has similar concerns about provincial governors (Y96), who should be experienced in war rather than in bureaucracy ("be them scribes of the treasury or of another office") or poetry ("they should not belong to the kind of wits, or to the kind of poets").

to become appointed as judges or *medrese* teachers, most of whom owe their posts to their fathers or their high connections. Furthermore, the author has various suggestions regarding the *şeyhülislam*, sheikhs (stressing the threat of revolt by their followers), and descendants of the Prophet (Y189–201, A50–63).

Thus, after Lütfi Pasha's treatise, which functioned as a sort of prologue, Ottoman "mirror for princes" entered maturity with these two works. While *Kitâbu mesâlih* was written in a haphazard and amateurish way, in *Hırzü'l-mülûk* the level of detail of the information and the knowledge of Ottoman realities is combined with a tight structure and a scholarly yet down-to-earth and administrative style. At the same time, both works clearly bring to mind the state of equilibrium mentioned in the previous chapter: some respect for old and established customs is evident, but, in general, the anonymous authors see nothing wrong in urging the vizier or sultan to impose new regulations if necessary. As may be expected, this is much clearer in the earlier one, *Kitâbu mesâlih*. Knowing that his proposal for changing the *devşirme* recruits' training and education could appear too innovative, the author has a clear and bold argument, one which would be repeated later (Y93–94):

> This rule is not something that has stayed until our times from the times of the Prophet, so that changing it would be considered a sin. It was instituted in the times of Karagöz Pasha or Hersekoğlu; they thought it appropriate, and it was done. Thank God his excellency the present grand vizier is a thousand times more intelligent and wise: it is not proper that he submits his sublime opinion to the ways of such common (*ümmî*) viziers.

The same reasoning is repeated concerning the post of *muhtesib* and some obligations of the villages near Istanbul (Y111, 118):

> Why, they say this is an old custom, but they do not ask whether this custom was set by a wise vizier or by a commoner such as Karagöz Pasha or Hersekoğlu.

Whether these personalities are real or are just made-up names used ironically is not completely clear; Tezcan identified them with real personalities from the beginnings of the sixteenth century, namely Karagöz Pasha, governor of Anadolu (d. 1511) and Hersekoğlu (or Hersek-zâde) Ahmed Pasha, who was grand vizier several times during the reigns of Bayezid II and Selim I. The latter, in particular, played an important role in the codification of Ottoman laws.[24] At any rate, these expressions show that, on the one hand, by the mid-sixteenth century the notion of "old custom" as an unbreakable rule had already begun to be developed and, on the other, that it was still challengeable.

The author of *Hirzü'l-mülûk* often displays a similar attitude. As he once remarks (Y175, A35),

> May the sultan know that, whenever Sultan Selim [I], from among his illustrious ancestors, ... [wished to act] in a manner beneficial to the dynasty and the religion, he never said "this is contrary to Ottoman law" (*bu kânûn-ı Osmanî'ye muhâliftir*); he issued his order at once declaring that "whatever the great sultans do, becomes law" (*selâtîn-i 'izâm her ne iderlerse kânûn olur*).

As already noted, this claim that the sultan should yield actual power may be relevant to the fact that the treatise is dedicated to Murad III, who tried to impose his will over viziers and ulema. There is more than the expression of Süleymanic-era equilibrium in the emphasis on the sultan's absolute power in these late sixteenth-century works. Both these texts, and others that preceded and followed them, are defending the feudal order, based on the welfare of a strong and landed *sipahi* class and on strict social compartmentalization, against the intrusion of newcomers into the timariot army and the administration of revenues. Why, then, do they not make recourse to the concept of "old law"? Although, as will be seen, its use as a binding and legitimizing framework was elaborated at the end of the century, the notion that justice consists of following the "old law" was already current in the "decrees of justice" or *adaletname*s during the reign of Selim I[25] (not to mention the attacks on "innovation", with their long history). Still, whereas conservative discourse from the end of the sixteenth century onwards was to take what Tezcan termed a "constitutionalist" form, *Kitâbu mesâlih* and *Hirzü'l-mülûk* formulate the same discourse from an "absolutist" point of view.

One possible answer is that our anonymous authors had not yet discovered the outstanding power of the "old law" argument—or that the use of the "innovation" argument by the anti-Ebussu'ud opposition was too recent to let them sanctify the Ebussu'udic synthesis as "old law" (although all authors of this trend appear to ignore such debates completely). Yet it is also plausible to assume that they were attributing the "innovations" disrupting the timariot

24 Tezcan 2000, 664, fn. 54. On Hersekoğlu Ahmed Pasha see İnalcık 1969a, 120–123; Lowry 2011.

25 See Sariyannis 2011a, 142.

system to earlier, unworthy viziers and that they wished to stress the rights of present-day viziers (in the case of *Kitâbu mesâlih*) or sultans (in *Hirzü'l-mülûk*) to mend not only departures from the tradition, but also shortcomings in the old system. When it became evident that even a sultan who tried to circumvent viziers and other officials and rule with absolute power, such as Murad III, would (or could) not enforce a radical re-establishment of the timariot system, those who were standing up for the old order began to appeal to the past as a sort of binding constitution.

At the same time, however, the very invocation of Selim I (or Mehmed II in other instances), which is seen several times in *Hirzü'l-mülûk*, offers a model from the past as a guideline to be followed, and for that matter a binding one. Unlike *Âsafnâme* or *Kitâbu mesâlih*, then, *Hirzü'l-mülûk* inaugurates a long series of texts that point to a "Golden Age" in the past, where all these institutions worked perfectly. We have to note that, in this case, the "Golden Age" is situated in Selim I's reign, rather than Süleyman's. For example, the practice of giving unjustified land grants to viziers dates from Süleyman's reign, when a hundred villages were granted to Mehmed Pasha, while an anecdote presenting Selim I denying a *temlik* to his vizier further illustrates the author's point.

For the sake of comparison, let us take a look at an apocalyptic work from 1557, *Rumûzü'l-künûz* (or perhaps rather *Rumûz-ı künûz*, "Treasures of ciphers").[26] Composed by a Bayrami sheikh, İlyas b. İsa Saruhani (d. 1559), it contains a series of prophesies about sultans, viziers, high officials, and events to come until the year 3000 A.H. on the basis of the occult science of letters. One may see pieces of political advice and social criticism scattered among the prophetic calculations: for instance, a just sultan would regularize

26 Saruhani – Özgül 2004. The date is given at the beginning and end of the manuscripts (cf. Ö72: "the present sultan Selim [II]"). However, it seems that, as the text was quite popular (to the ten MSS cited in Saruhani – Özgül 2004, 25–26, can be added Paris, Bibliothèque nationale, suppl. turc 1067), there were certain interpolations made later. In particular (at least in the MS published by Özgül), there is a mention of *celalis* (Ö74), which sounds premature for 1557, followed by a large section on tobacco, "prophesizing" with precision its introduction, prohibition, and eventual permission through the *fetva* of 1652: "In the year 940 of the hijra there will appear a black water named coffee; it will be considered alternatively sinful or not, until it will be deemed lawful with a fetva in the year 980. After the year 1000 there will also appear a smoke (*bir duhan*); the people of the world will become addicted; a Sultan will prohibit it and execute lots of people, but as it will prove impossible to extinguish it a *mufti* will declare it lawful after the year 1060". In the same part, after describing several luxurious caps of that time, the author of the interpolation speaks of "a preacher by the name of Kadızade will make the Sultan prohibit [such luxuries]; however this prohibition will not be respected ...". The first dated manuscript is from 1655, a date that sounds very plausible for the final form of the text, due to its proximity with the events "foretold".

appointments, show respect for ulema and dervishes, and so forth. One may perceive a "bottom-up" approach not unlike that of *Kitâbu mesâlih*: a large part deals with judges, with an emphasis on the fees paid to them by litigants and the system for remunerating their substitutes (the *naib*s), and suggests that strict control by the sultan will eliminate bribery and corruption. Interestingly, it also envisages a perfect legal book, to be composed by one Molla Ahmed, which will be a perfect *kanunname*, conform to the Sharia, and will be used for 700 years (Ö66–69).

In striking contrast to other treatises of the late sixteenth century, *Rumûzü'l-künûz* views the sipahis as exploiters of the peasants instead of lamenting the former's socio-economic decline. Saruhani proposes that less tax be allocated to timariot sipahis (1/10 in times of peace, 1/8 in times of campaign: Ö53) and has a whole chapter on "the sultans' slaves" (actually, on timars; Ö71–73), where he complains about viziers' fiefs being rented out, which results in heavy taxation on peasants (Ö71):

> In the time when this [treatise] was written, in the years of the just sultan, the sipahis of the land were selling their timars to some strongman, or otherwise made him a steward (*kethüda*), and he was overburdening the peasants; now this [practice] has moved from the sipahis to the viziers.

Saruhani shows himself vehemently opposed to the sipahis, who drive the peasants to despair with their continuous demand for taxes. All too traditionally, the solution he offers lies in the careful registering of lands and taxes.

2 Mustafa Ali and "the Politics of Cultural Despair"[27]

The paragon of the "declinist" political literature in this period was undoubtedly Gelibolulu Mustafa b. Ahmed (1541–1600), known by the pen-name 'Âlî, one of the most prolific and interesting writers of the sixteenth century.[28] Ali was born in Gelibolu (Gallipoli) and received his initial education in his native city before moving to live with his uncle in Istanbul, where he pursued a *medrese* education as a student of Ebussu'ud Efendi's son, Şemseddin Ahmed. At the same time, he was closely associated with the poetic circles of the capital, establishing friendly relations with many renowned poets as well as with

27 I am borrowing this term from Murphey 1989.

28 The standard work on Ali is Fleischer 1986a; on his historiographical work, see also Schmidt 1991.

Celalzade and his successor, Nişancı Ramazanzade. From 1561 onwards, he held various offices as a secretary attached to his patron, Lala Mustafa Pasha. He accompanied him to Damascus and Egypt and on various campaigns (Cyprus, the Caucasus) until the pasha's death (in the intervening periods, Ali had minor positions in Bosnia and Aleppo). Then, in 1583, he returned to Istanbul, where he engaged in writing poetical, historiographical, and *belles-lettres* works while serving in the mid-ranks of the financial bureaucracy or as the secretary to various pashas (in Erzurum, Baghdad, Sivas, and other Anatolian towns). Returning to Istanbul in 1589, he spent a number of years in bitter isolation, continuously sending treatises and literary works to viziers and sultans in an effort to be noticed; in 1592, he was appointed a secretary to the janissaries and then registrar of the Imperial Council (*defter emini*), only to be dismissed soon after. In 1595, after Murad III's death, he was made a provincial governor in Anatolia and, finally, governor of Jedda. On his way to this last post, Ali arrived in Cairo in 1599; he reached Jedda at the end of that year, only to die soon after.

Ali's work is vast in both scope and volume: from poetry to history and from Sufism to etiquette, it is an extraordinary specimen of high-blown *inşa* literature. However, Ali's high expectations met with the complex political alliances of late sixteenth-century Istanbul, with the result that he almost never gained the recognition he felt was owed to him. His formidable erudition combined with his mediocre career produced a work marked with bitterness and despair: living in a general milieu of declinist, even apocalyptic visions, he developed a strong sense of a world in decline, and he did his best to describe it. His haughty style makes even the slightest detail look lofty and part of a grander vision of the ideal government.

One may find Ali's political views scattered throughout his historiographical works. The monumental *Künhü'l-ahbâr* ("The essence of histories"), arguably his most important work, is a voluminous world history, whose composition began in 1591/2 and was completed almost ten years later.[29] The work is conceived in four "pillars"; the first a treatise on cosmology and geography, the second and the third on pre-Islamic and Islamic history, and the fourth on the Ottoman dynasty. There is a strong sense of decline in Ali's views of Ottoman history, as explicitly stated in his introduction as well as being evident in his accounts of the reigns of Süleyman's successors.[30] This sentiment is even more explicitly stated in his final book, *Füsûl-i hall ü akd ve usûl-i harc ü nakd* ("The seasons of sovereignty on the principles of critical expenditure"), a short

29 Ali 1860–1868; Ali – Çerci 2000; Ali – Şentürk 2003. Cf. Fleischer 1986a, 235–307; Schmidt 1991; Piterberg 2003, 38–42; Hagen 2013, 450–451.

30 See Fleischer 1986a, 258–259 and 293–307; Ali – Çerci 2000.

history of the Islamic world from 622 to 1592.[31] As Cornell Fleischer has shown, this work is a fine example of "dynastic cyclism": dynasties follow a pattern of rise and fall, as they acquire wealth and allow injustice to spread.[32] The difference with the Khaldunist version of such cyclical theories, which, as shall be seen, would be introduced some 50 years later, is that Ali does not use the notion of historical laws; instead, he prefers to stress the more traditional ideas of justice and piety. Ali himself stresses that he compiled the work in order to show how kingdoms can be corrupted and how their fall can be prevented (D60). After laying down some rules for government, based on medieval "mirrors for princes", he gives a summary of every Muslim dynasty, focusing on the causes of the decline of each. While some of these causes have to do with specific events, others pertain to his political views. Thus, the Ummayads declined because of their greed for earthly wealth and because they did not pay proper attention to the counsel of wise men; the Abbasids, because they did not protect their people from the Mongol invasions; the Ghaznavids, because they let women and eunuchs interfere in state affairs, changed their officials often, and let governors and high-ranking men become impoverished; the kings of Shirvan, because of their tyranny and oppression towards their subjects; and a large number of other dynasties, because of civil wars between brothers.

As far as it concerns political thought, however, Ali's main work is "Counsel for sultans" (*Nushatü's-selâtîn*, often quoted as *Nasîhatü's-selâtîn*). Completed in 1581, with minor additions added by 1586, it became fairly popular (with nine known manuscripts, among which one is dated 1627 and another 1698), while its publication by Andreas Tietze in 1979–82 must be seen as one of the most influential editions of Ottoman literary works in recent decades.[33] In the tradition of *Hirzü'l-mülûk* and other similar works, Ali uses his experience in the middle ranks of the financial and military bureaucracies, and especially his participation in the eastern campaigns, to provide practical advice. The structure of the work is interesting: it begins with a preface on the importance of justice and the responsibilities of sultans (T1:17/89–37/120), and an introduction (T1:37–40/121–25) showing God's special favors bestowed on the Ottoman dynasty. Then, following perhaps the *inşa'* model of lists, as seen in chapter 3, Ali organizes his chapters around such lists or items (the same model is followed in his *Künhü'l-ahbâr*). Thus, the first chapter (T1:41–65/126–62) discusses issues necessary for kings, as presented by previous Ottoman rulers or the

31 Ali – Demir 2006; cf. Fleischer 1986a, 177–178 and 301ff.; Şeker 1995.
32 Fleischer 1983, esp. 206–216.
33 Ali – Tietze 1979–1982. See also Fleischer 1986a, 95–105; Fodor 1986, 224–225; Gökbilgin 1991, 199–201; Yılmaz 2003a, 304–306; İnan 2009, 114–115; Black 2011, 260–262.

ancient caliphs. In the second chapter (T1:66–86/163–88), Ali deals with the disorder (*ihtilal*) of his time and the eight ways it happens, all of which are because of practices contrary to the old customs. The third chapter (T2:9–47/119–73) sounds quite similar, as it discusses "the weaknesses in the general situation (*ahval-i cumhur*) as caused by certain evil abuses"; these abuses, however, are not alterations of the old law, as are those in the previous chapter, but the misdeeds of established officers. The book ends with a kind of autobiography (T2:48–95/174–224), obviously with the main aims of stressing Ali's education and skills that allow him to give advice and of illustrating the state of decline described in the previous chapters. Here, he states explicitly his bitterness due to not achieving the high posts for which he was fit and which had been promised to him (T2:70ff/196ff). Finally, an epilogue (T2:96–109/225–46), divided into ten sections, gives various piece of advice, addressed not to kings and viziers but to their servants (throughout this epilogue, one may discern Ali's familiarity with Tusi-style moral treatises and especially with the sections on household economics). A simple comparison with earlier treatises shows how innovative is the very structure of *Nushatü's-selâtîn*: instead of dividing his treatise into parts on the sultan, viziers, the army, and so forth, Ali straightforwardly sets out to describe the present disorder, enumerating the weaknesses and shortcomings of the function of government against a standard set, in general, in the past.

Ali also discusses some of these issues, and especially advice for kings' and notables' servants, in one of his final books, *Mevâidü'n-nefâis fi kavâidi'l-mecâlis* ("Tables of delicacies concerning the rules for social gatherings"), composed in 1599–1600 while in Jedda and Mecca as a reworking and expansion of a book he had written in 1587.[34] An exceptionally fascinating work, *Mevâidü'n-nefâis* is a collection of rules, descriptions, and advice not only for "social gatherings", as stated in its title, but also on issues as diverse as rulership, travel, musical instruments, slaves, food, and Sufism.

2.1 *Innovations, Abuses, Disorders: the Ottoman World According to Ali*

Although his emphasis on the "old law" differentiates him from earlier defenders of the old order, Ali still shares with *Hirzü'l-mülûk* a distrust of viziers and their delegation of power. His urging of rulers not to give over the affairs of the state (*umur-i mülk*) to eunuchs, mutes, and other courtiers (T1:41/127) is a direct attack on Murad III, but in his general view regarding sultanly power

34 The work has been published in transcription (Ali – Şeker 1997) and English translation (Ali – Brookes 2003), though it has not yet drawn the scholarly attention it deserves (cf. Salgırlı 2003).

Ali appears, at first glance, to be nearer the absolutist tendencies of this sultan than he pretended to be. He notes that sultans must now rely on viziers as it is impossible for them to inspect their army and lands themselves. However,

> in this matter [of unqualified persons appointed to high posts] ignorance is by no means an excuse; unawareness of the situation of the viziers (*vükela*) will not count as a valid defense on the Day of Judgment.

The present sultan, like his predecessors, prefers isolation to mixing with the people and has delegated all power to untrustworthy administrators, even though it is his duty to protect his subjects against these administrators' oppression (T1:18–23/91–98, and ff.). Similar observations can be seen in *Mevâidü'n-nefâis*: "neither permission nor allowance is authorized for deputizing someone else in [the ruler's] place", he writes, adding that the system of appointing a vizier as a "virtual monarch" (*padişah-i manevi*) leads to disorder in public affairs (B82). Again, the seclusion of the sultan contributes to his isolation from his subjects. Earlier rulers used to take their meals together with their children, viziers, and companions; this custom stopped in the reign of Selim I.[35] Ali criticizes this new practice of seclusion with the verse: *Haughtiness does not suit a king whom I love* (B92–95). Yet this emphasis on the sultans' personal responsibility may be seen as nothing more than a way to blame them, and particularly to blame Murad III, for all shortcomings of the age. When describing the "events", meaning the perturbations introduced by Murad, in his *Künhü'l-ahbâr*, he criticizes him for something that earlier authors would have praised, namely his absolutist grasping of the reins of power. He accepted and read petitions of grievance himself, and he began controlling himself all appointments, which earlier had been regulated by vizierial rescripts; this, according to Ali, meant that all issues were influenced by the sultan's boon companions rather than experienced viziers and counsellors (Ç2:241–243).[36]

In addition, for Ali kingship does not necessarily have a charismatic power and it is always possible that a dynasty will fall if it fails to impose justice. Also in *Mevâidü'n-nefâis*, a special chapter (B43–46) is devoted to the behavior of

35 On this practice cf. Peirce 1993, 174; Ali – Brookes 2003, 93, fn. 585. See also Peksevgen 2004 on how such discussions reflected various views on the control of information and secrecy.

36 Cf. Fleischer 1986a, 295. I cannot agree with Fleischer that Ali supports the "indivisible authority" of the sultan (Fleischer 1986a, 301–302); rather, he stresses that a large part of his power should be delegated to his grand vizier, who ought to be chosen carefully and checked regularly.

kings ("men who conquer their way to power", *sahib-i zuhur*[37]). Ali stresses that "as for monarchs of any age, their being 'The Shadow of God' is determined by their conforming to the Sharia". Ali criticizes ignorant people who sometimes make an appearance among Turkmens or Tatars and think they can become kings "with the right to coin and sermon" (B45):

> Given that every realm has an established ruler, these people cannot maintain stability and power unless the possessor of a realm is utterly tyrannical … [o]r unless the claimant proves himself superior and more powerful than the established ruler, and in comparison to him takes more bribes, so that the non-Muslim and Muslim subjects and the army all turn against the ruler and dispatch a letter of invitation to someone who calls himself a *celali*.

Ruling dynasties each have a time-span allotted to them, one which will end due to the negligence that comes from wine-drinking (by the king), inclination to accumulate wealth, and falling into the wiles of women. The true treasury of a kingdom is its subjects, neglect of whom will surely lead to the king's destruction. A king's charisma is not in itself sufficient, as the selection of high-ranking officials can be destructive (B59).

> However, whenever the foundation of a state is damaged so that the great personages turn their thoughts to bribery; whenever kings and ministers toss aside the safeguarding of the law so that their intelligent subjects, who seek their rights without having to pay money, rot in corners, dismissed from office; whenever unworthy and unprincipled low-brows who know only how to count out the coinage of bribery are raised day by day to offices of lofty rank … then that waterwheel begins to fall and collapse.

Even Osman's family seem to be insufficient compared to other families of ancient warlords: in the charitable foundations endowed by the sultans, in sharp contrast to the establishments of Evrenos Beg in Rumili, the food is inedible due to misadministration (T27–28/144–145). Ali comments boldly that

37 "The manifest one", by which Ali means men not born into a ruling house but who rise to power by force of arms (n. by Ali – Brookes 2003, 43, fn. 267); cf. Fleischer 1986a, 280ff.).

> the sultans of the House of Osman have withdrawn with lack of interest whereas that afore-mentioned *beg* possesses the secret of sainthood and working miracles.

Ali's discussion of Ottoman power is remarkably relativist, as (in his *Künhü'l-ahbâr*) he carefully situates the house of Osman among other contemporaneous Islamic states and denies that the dynasty has power over "the conjunction of times" (*sahib-kıran*), which, however, he willingly grants to Timur, for instance.[38] For that matter, Ali's *Füsûl-i hall ü akd* was composed in order to show exactly how the most powerful dynasties could fall prey to their own injustice and oppression. Having described the rise and fall of almost every Islamic dynasty, as noted above, there is a supplement (D141–43) on the Ottomans, and here one may clearly discern how Ali set the tone for subsequent political treatises. The Ottomans differ from most previous dynasties, he asserts, because they did not obtain power by any stratagem or trick but by practising the Holy War, while other Anatolian states that eventually submitted to the Ottoman sultans declined because of their own tyranny and oppression. At any rate, God's special bestowals granted to the Ottoman dynasty, as described in *Nushatü's-selâtîn* (T1:37–40/121–25),[39] incur a strong responsibility to keep their lands just and in good order and do not guarantee immunity to decline.

A story related in *Füsûl-i hall ü akd*, in all probability invented by Ali, illustrates this "exceptionalism under conditions" that directly links dynastic longevity with maintenance of the "old law".[40] Mehmed II's vizier, Mahmud Pasha, proposed to him the promulgation of a legal code, a measure that no previous Muslim king had taken, and suggested that once this code was promulgated decline could not touch the Ottoman state, apart from under two specific circumstances: first, if any of Mehmed's successors decided to promulgate their own law; second, if strangers (*ecnebi*) intermingled with the army. Indeed, states Ali, when such strangers from Istanbul became accepted in the janissary army during the imperial festival of 1582 (a view which was to be repeated by Koçi Bey, as shall be seen in the following chapter), the decline can be said to have started. From this point onwards, the janissary corps started to

---

38 Fleischer 1986a, 277–283.

39 The special favors are: the excellence of the sultans' palace and retinue; their religious orthodoxy; their freedom from plague; their absolute power to appoint their own people as governors of far-flung provinces; their extraordinary military power; and the fine state of their finances.

40 Cf. Fleischer 1986a, 178; Tezcan 2010a, 57.

oppress the Muslims. Moreover, the granting of important posts, such as the scribes of the janissary *bölük*s or of the treasury, through bribery further corrupted the old law. Bribery reached such a degree that it was considered to be licit (*helal*), like the tithe from fiefs (D142–43).

Thus, another target of Ali's criticism is the use of "strangers" in the governmental apparatus. What he primarily has in mind is *kul*s, the product of the *devşirme* system; in the preface to *Nushatü's-selâtîn* he criticizes converted infidels attaining high posts, i.e. against the extensive use of *kul*s in the administration (T1:36–37/119). He complains that young men in royal service should not associate with people outside the palace, as was the case until the reign of Süleyman (B20); the same goes for the aghas of the palace (B20–21). Ali stresses once again that "ignorant products of the palace slave system … have infiltrated the ranks of the Divan scribes", taking positions that used to be given only to renowned ulemas (B23ff). As well as *kul*s, other foreigners should not be favored either. Ali stresses that the conduct of the divan secretaries (and particularly the removal of those addicted to drugs) is to be tightly controlled, with special attention given to the election of the *re'isülküttab* and the *tuğrakeşan* or *nişancı*; the sultan should not show excessive honor to those who come from other countries (and, especially, he should not give high offices to Turks or Kurds). Beginning a line of advice that would become commonplace in the centuries to come, he advises the ruler to offer safety in office to people who have not committed serious mistakes, as such people's positions must be "consolidated by perpetuation" (T1: 63–64/159–61).

Ali's attitude to mobility is often ambiguous. On the one hand, he urges sultans to appoint wise men to high office, not paying attention to their lineage (to illustrate this view, Ali quotes Selim I saying that "in selecting [the officials] [the grand vizier should] screen everybody in [the] glorious capital city down to the porters that carry loads on their backs"). Ali argues in this point that:

> against the selection of wise men and the employment of philosophers no-one should raise objections saying "This is not the old custom". Between persons of equal seniority but belonging to different classes one should clearly apply the familiar principle that their trading capital is the cash of intelligence and the capital of plans and hopes the jewel of a penetrating mind (T1:50–53/140–44).

Mobility is especially commendable in the case of the ulema. In his *Künhü'l-ahbâr*, too, Ali sharply criticizes the shortcomings of a medrese education, which in his view prevents "Turks" from following an ulema career and having adequate incentive to acquire knowledge (Ş80). And in *Mevâidü'n-nefâis*,

"Turks" entering the ulema ranks is regarded as a sign that the system is finely tuned:

> Whether [the graduates of the medreses] be a poor son of the Turks or a wealthy man, whether a lowly sort blessed with comprehension or one of the privileged, by following the orderly path they attained the rank permitting them to be called learned (B67–74).

After all, one should be able to get along well with both high and low, as people

> are all brothers in their humanity, friends in their familiarity and relations, neighbors in their closeness to one another, equals in their talents and capabilities, and kinsmen of body and soul in respect to their blood relationship (T2: 2:101–102/234–36).

On the other hand, at other points Ali appears much more adamant in favoring social and professional compartmentalization. Like the anonymous author of *Kitâbu mesâlîh*, Ali places great importance on sartorial signs and, more generally, on luxury as a marker of class differentiation. When criticizing the waste created by excessive use of gold thread in textiles (T2:41–42/164), he notes that, after all,

> if everybody would conduct himself according to his profits and income, high and low could be clearly distinguished from one another.

In a similar way, one should be cautious against an overabundance of food at banquets and excessive liberality in such meals; the same goes for furnishings, clothes, houses, and horses, when one is not in harmony with his rank (there are detailed descriptions in *Mevâidü'n-nefâis*: B137–139 and 143–144).[41] In making these normative descriptions, Ali divides society into four distinct classes, namely sultans and princes, viziers and governors, notables of the realm who are considered to be among the middling ranks, and, finally, artisans, merchants, and craftsmen (B137). He observes (B37–38) that

> God made members of the human race dependent upon one another through the diversity of crafts and abilities ... The sultans of the world ... absolutely need every single man of trade and must have recourse to them ... There is certainly a need for the kings and princes to assign

41 See also Tietze 1982.

> position and glory; for wealthy persons to expend property and goods for the public weal; certainly for craftsmen to display their artistry and mastery; and for farmers to harvest canonically lawful food from their plowed lands. Similarly, there is demand on all sides for the knowledge of scholars, for the benevolent prayers of the righteous, for the warring and raiding of men of combat.

All classes of people are necessary and their activities commendable, then, but this does not mean that they should intermingle with each other's vocation. Thus, when it comes to social mobility, Ali complains that "the scum (*edani*; here meaning "of lower origin") begins to gain power by lavishing money [in bribes]" and "the high classes (*e'ali*) are disappointed and stunned", while, more particularly, judges become directors of finances or provincial governors (T1:66/163). Such interlopers abound in the judicial class: provincial judges are often ignorants (even "Turks ... of the merchant class", *renc-ber tayifesinden*: T1:75–79/174–80).

Peasants, in particular, attract a great deal of Ali's attention. Firstly, he famously stresses that rulers ought to prevent peasants from leaving their homelands and moving to cities, or at least to collect the due tax (*çift-bozan resmi*; T1:57–58/150–51). As in Lütfi Pasha's case, one gets the impression that Ali's main concern is the functioning of the tax-collecting system rather than the actual welfare of the peasants. Elsewhere (in *Mevâidü'n-nefâis*), he stresses that the *reaya* should not mix with people in power and that "they should not become cross by thinking that extrajudicial taxes (*tekâlif-i örfiye*) are unprecedented when they are imposed". Although the corruption of judges and provincial governors has disrupted the order of the world, the people should not have permission to bar from their villages *beys* and judges whom they do not want, because thus low-born and wicked people "aveng[e] themselves on their rulers" (B170–72). This attitude extends to the urban dwellers, too: concerning the regulation of standard prices, Ali remarks that if this matter is not administered with equity, it "leads to the enrichment of the lower class and to the bankruptcy and distress of the military class" (and not, as one would expect, the further impoverishment of the poor). The farmers go to the big cities and "break out of the circle of poverty"; this leads their relatives from the provinces to follow their example, and ultimately to the ruin of the timariot soldiers, who lose their peasants and have to put up with constantly rising living costs (T2:25–27/141–44).

More generally, like all known authors of his age, Ali clearly stands on the side of the timariots. The misdeeds of the registrars of the land (*kâtibü l-vilâye*), he argues, concerning the evaluation of the value of the timars and their distribution, especially when "by and by they turn to do business with cash" (*nakdîye ile satu bâzâra mübâşeret idüb*), lead to the disintegration of public matters (*ihtilal-i cumhur*) (T2:20–25/135–41). And, after noting the shortcomings of financial agents (*ummal*) and tax-farmers (*mültezim*), he proposes the abolition of tax-farming (according, also, to the Sharia) and conferring the collection of *mukata'a*s to *sipahi*s by way of trusteeship and supervision (*emanet u nezaret*) (T2:43–44/167–69). In contrast, Ali's distrust of the *kul*s appears to extend to the janissary army. He maintains that the janissary cavalry (*bölük halkı*) must be sent to Egypt, rather than alowing them to go astray in Istanbul after departing the imperial palace (T1:54–55/146–48; cf. a similar passage in *Mevâidü'n-nefâis*, B18).[42] Yet while a large part of Ali's idea about the present decline is founded on departures from an ideal timariot system, we do not see the fully-fledged attack on the janissary army that is so clear a characteristic of seventeenth-century authors (see below, chapter 5). His comments often appear to be more on the side of unthinking janissaries, who must be protected from going astray, rather than focusing on their excessive numbers or insolent behavior:

> While staying at the Imperial Palace, the [janissary horsemen] are given lavish supplies and unlimited furnishings ... [Others] who had left the Palace before them and, under the influence of drinking wine and listening to harp and rebeck, had given themselves over to a life of passions, [now] like stirrups never budge from their side ... Being led astray and being seduced every day a little more, they soon reach the point where their cash runs out and their horse trappings and garments all go down the drain ... They withdraw from view ... and get married in one of the towns in the neighborhood of Istanbul ... Thus they too begin, like those who are living there, settling in that place with farming and ploughing ... and the possibility of the arms and the horse, which are the preconditions of a sipahi, moving farther and farther away.

Yet, the facts that Ali does not concern himself with the janissaries to any great extent and that there is plenty of advice concerning the army on campaign (usually in terms of logistics and appointing the right people) shows that he does not consider them a central and crucial part of the Ottoman military force. His description of the abuses connected with the *devşirme* system of collecting children for the janissaries is telling: not only does he deem it contrary to

42 Obviously Ali would have rewritten this passage after his stay in Cairo, since he denounces at some length the behavior of the imperial slaves stationed in Egypt (Ali – Tietze 1975).

the Sharia, he also attributes it to a need "to increase the number of Muslims" rather than to enhance the military power of the Ottomans (T2:30/148).[43]

On the other hand, we have to note here that, while Ali appears so demanding of the peasants when comparing them to the sipahis, he does favor them when he compares them with the rich urban merchants, whom he views with the same contempt as earlier moralists. Since the levy of army provisions (*nüzûl*) and extraordinary taxes (*avariz*) are not spent entirely on military purposes, Ali notes as a bizarre curiosity the fact that (T2:36–37/156)

> the necessities of the victory-bonding army are always provided by the miserable and poor in ceaseless sacrifice whereas in certain sea-ports and other cities and towns there are rich merchants ... The poor are moaning under the hardships of destitution while such rich blockheads thrive in pomp and power. While the burden of frustration weighs heavily on the weak, it is clear in many respects that the excess of world-enjoyment of the rich is counter to perfect wisdom and circumspect policy.

The same is valid for usurers. Such people, he writes, should be heavily taxed for the benefit of the army and the treasury, as happened during the reign of Mehmed II and Selim I. The corn-profiteers (*muhtekir*), who become rich by causing dearth and scarcity, among whom are greedy magistrates and governors, constitute another factor in the decline (T2:35–39/155–60). The distrust of wealth is rooted in a deep understanding of society as a whole, a system of interdependencies where everyone has a place and there is a duty for every benefit:

> It is seriously not in order that such a rich person does not perform any service to the army of Islam and that he does not every now and then assist the public treasury in its expenses although he has accumulated such profit and capital during the justice-guided reign of the Sultan.

We may see here a distant reflection of the idea of mutual duties, as seen, for instance, in Şeyhoğlu, al-Semerkandi, and even Celalzade (see chapters 2 and 3).

43 We must note that Ali, possibly of *devşirme* origin himself, has no prejudice whatsoever against this kind of Islamization; on the contrary, in his *Künhü'l-ahbâr* he considers the ethnic mixture of the Ottomans a great advantage for the dynasty. See Fleischer 1986a, 254–255.

An interesting point on which Ali departs from commonplace advice concerns his financial views.[44] He often speaks of the fixing of market prices, noting that if the sultans consider this matter trivial and leave it to judges, then lower-class people become rich and the army becomes poor (for instance in *Füsûl-i hall ü akd*, D56–57); his concern for standard measurements of textiles and the wasteful use of gold thread (with the result that the precious metal yields no benefit at all and loses its value) bears some resemblance to *Kitâbu mesâlîh* (T2:41–42/163–164). Like Lütfi Pasha, he also stresses the need for austerity in public finances, although in Ali's work such austerity initially concerns the sultan in person. For instance, the sultan should create charitable foundations only through his personal property, i.e. his share of the booty, and not the public treasury (*beytü'l-mal*; T1:54/146; he also condemns as hypocritical the construction of mosques, dervish lodges, etc. in a flourishing city, in *Mevâidü'n-nefâis*: B121).[45] Furthermore, the sultan should not consider the lavish spending of money as generosity (*saha vu kerem*) but rather as waste and dissipation (T1:58–59/151–53). Ali also condemns unnecessary expenditure, such as keeping numerous palaces in the same city, waste in the palace kitchen, and court artisans (T1:59–62/153–57). In contrast, a chapter in *Mevâidü'n-nefâis* (B162–65) speaks of kingly generosity and beneficence, specifying that a ruler should spend 1% of the annual income of his treasury on gifts. Ali calculates the gifts given by the Ottoman sultans and finds them rather stingy; this contradicts somewhat his urge for sultanly austerity, but one should note that here he talks of gifts granted to erudite men (among whom he, obviously, counts himself).

2.2 *Ali as a Landmark of Ottoman Thought*

Ali himself stresses that he wished to depart from the established practice of copying earlier advice books, which were destined for other states and problems. His *Nushatü's-selâtîn* ends with a series of short appendices and supplements (T2:110–16/246–56) in which he defends himself against accusations of self-interest and bias and emphasizes that the great merit of his book lies in the fact that it has examples and stories from his own experience that give reliable information on the present time. And indeed, exactly like Lütfi Pasha before him, Mustafa Ali chooses to ignore the neo-Aristotelian and/or neo-Platonic traditions of a philosophical foundation of political society. Again like Lütfi Pasha (whom Ali calls, with contempt, "an ignorant Albanian", by the way: B41), this is not due to him ignoring the Persian sources (Ali was an admirer of

44 On his views concerning monetary problems see Kafadar 1986, 84–93.

45 Such considerations did have an impact, as seen in the opposition to Ahmed I's decision to build his mosque (Rüstem 2016, 254–256).

Kınalızade's, with whom he had long discussions while both were serving in Damascus);[46] instead, it was a deliberate decision (T2:115/254):

> Every learned and cultured person ... is aware that the peculiar ways of this wisdom-filled book ... differ from the character of other serious books, among other things, inasmuch as their stories and the exemplifications, which include subjects related to the life stories of bygone generations, are based on [historical] reports and therefore, they clearly contain the possibilities of truthfulness and lie whereas the stories in this book are the exact portraits of the people of [our] time and its anecdotes which have been related to serve as counsels and warnings are the true descriptions of the behavior of the great and mighty.

The most striking feature of Ali's extraordinary work is the degree to which it deals with very specific problems, proposing equally specific measures. The above exposition of his ideas does not do justice to the extent and detail of his advice on numerous issues, from the division of administrative units in the provinces to the debasement of coinage, and from the quality of the scribes of the field marshal (*serdar*) to the situation of the salaried garrisons of the fortresses. As has been seen, in this Ali follows a fashion current in his age, but does so in a more detailed way than average. Of course, much of Ali's advice clearly has to do with his own personal grievances, such as when he complains of the honor shown to strangers at the expense of commited servants to the sultan (such as himself). His repeated attacks on the *kul*s, the sultan's slaves, are a good example. On the one hand, in more than one way Ali's attack targets the janissaries, whom he regards as unmanly and corrupt, while he praises the chivalry and valor of the free sipahis. This attack goes so far as to deny the legitimacy of the *devşirme*, an insitution going back to the first sultans and considered one of the foundations of Ottoman power (T2:30/148):

> In particular, the service assigned to them [of collecting boys for janissaries] is itself at variance with the Divine Law. It was only adopted in the past out of need as a means to increase the number of Muslims.

On the other hand, Ali is engaged in a struggle against unilinear promotion of palace recruits to administrative posts. For instance, at the end of his autobiography in the fourth chapter, he wonders whether it is just and wise for a sultan

46 Fleischer 1986a, 43. Ali refers to Kınalızâde in various parts of his work (e.g. Ali – Çerçi 2000, 2:58, 128–30).

to appoint unworthy men to high posts only because they were raised in his palace, while skilled and educated men remain without high positions solely because they have been brought up outside it. Such evil practice has been employed since "the early days of the reign of the late Sultan Süleyman" (T2:93–94/222–23). In general, this plea has often been interpreted as an appeal to meritocracy; in fact, it is more of an appeal for recruiting medrese graduates, rather than palace-raised *kul*s, in governmental posts and for stopping the blurring of career paths (judges should not jump into financial or administrative posts, and *kul*s should not enter the scribal bureaucracy). In fact, Ali is not unequivocally and in principle opposing this; rather, it is a specific blurring he has in mind, namely upstarts from the provincial administration making their way into the higher echelons of central government, or *kul*s taking the place of senior *ilmiye* graduates.[47] It is more than clear that Ali's complains stem from his own disappointment at his mediocre career: he perceived his failure to find a position worthy of his merit and knowledge as the result of palace recruits occupying almost all the higher administrative posts. However, it would be an oversimplification to consider all his remarks the result of personal bitterness. The view of the janissaries and of the *kul* system in general as a threat to the meritocracy, represented by sipahi cavalry and trained scholars, was to become a standard view of early seventeenth-century theorists.[48]

As in *Kitâbu mesâlih*, so in Ali's work can an ambiguous attitude vis-à-vis the "old law" be seen. At quite a few points, Ali, too, considers "old custom" an impediment to sound practice, or at least something not necessarily binding: for instance, he urges the sultan not to pay attention to objections such as "this is not the old custom" (*kanun-i kadim*) (T1:50/140). Elsewhere, he speaks of "beneficial innovations and laudable rules" (T1:41/126: *nev-ayin-i hasene*) or of "the laws of the House of Osman and the innovations of the monarchs" (T2:113/252: *kavanin-i al-i Osman ve nev-ayin-i şehriyarân*). Other points criticize the law of Mehmed II (which, in general, is for Ali the paragon of Ottoman tradition) on assigning ranks and degrees to the ulema, because the late sultan did not consider the fact that even accomplished high-ranking ulema could be corrupted with bribery (B67–68; the same regulations are highly praised in *Künhü'l-ahbâr*: §76–84).

However, one may detect an attitude against the "disorders of the times" that praises the old customs, or, in Ali's words, "the rules" (he speaks of disorder

47 See the detailed analysis by Fleischer 1986a, 201–213. There are points in *Künhü'l-ahbâr* where Ali complains of newcomers from the Iranian lands taking presidency over the products of the *kul* system (ÇFleischer 1986a, 300).

48 Cf. Abou Hadj 1988. On Ali's contempt for his fellow scribes see Tuşalp Atiyas 2013, 70–72.

"contrary to the rules", *hilaf-i kavanin*: T1:66/163),[49] upon whose "orderly maintenance ... depends the maintenance of good public order" (B72). In fact, the whole second chapter of *Nushatü's-selâtîn* focuses on these departures from established laws. Ali clearly considers the Ebussu'udic *kanun* a perfectly legitimate source of law; indeed, as a complementary equivalent of the Sharia. When speaking of the highest officials of the *divan* bureaucracy, the *reisülküttâb* and the *nişancı*, he asserts that these officials and, in particular, the "imperial cypher officials" (*tuğrakeşân-ı divan*) are "the jurisconsults of the imperial laws" (T1:50/140: *müftiyân-i kavanin-i padişahân olub*); the daring use of the sharia term *müftî* as a simile for the chief chancellor is more than telling. In this respect, there is a striking slip of tongue in his description of Ottoman rise and decline that is contained in his final work, *Füsûl-i hall ü akd*. Ali writes that, following Mahmud Pasha's proposal, Mehmed II "promulgated an old law" (*bir kanun-i kadim vaz' itmişlerdir*). Obviously, the law was not old at the time of its promulgation; its being sanctified thus shows the identification of "just law" with "established custom". This emphasis on the "old law" as almost synonymous with "justice" is not peculiar to political authors of the period: on the contrary, it seems that it had become a permanent feature of Ottoman political ideology throughout the sixteenth century.[50] A few decades had passed from the time scholars such as Dede Cöngi were speaking of the adjustment of the law to the needs of the time; once the law was adjusted, it had to remain unaltered.

3 Ali's Contemporaries, Facing the Millenium

Next to Mustafa Ali (whom he had met and admired), the other great chronicler of this period was Selaniki Mustafa Efendi (d. after 1600), an official who served in various government posts, mainly financial.[51] His work is characterized by frequent and extensive comments on the political situation, in a manner that was to become quite common in Ottoman historiography. Selaniki had no real reason to be personally bitter due to unfulfilled high expectations, as

49 Tietze (1:41) translates "the old customs".

50 Cf. Sariyannis 2011a, 141–142; Selaniki – İpşirli 1999, index s.v. "kanun-ı kadîm"; İnalcık 1965. Tezcan 2000, 658 shows that Ali systematically speaks of Mehmed II's *kanun* while he could not have seen the original text of the *kanunname*, or at least the text that was circulating as such (see also below, chapter 5).

51 Selaniki – İpşirli 1999, xii-xvii; *Encyclopaedia of Islam*, 2nd ed., s.v. 'Selânikî' (M. İpşirli). On the relations of Ali with Selaniki see Fleischer 1986a, 130–131. On Selaniki as social critic cf. also Schaendlinger 1992, 240. The following lines are based on Sariyannis 2008a, 137–140.

did Ali; however, his attitude is clearly similar despite their different characters (to use Christine Woodhead's words, "Ali, elderly, disappointed and cantankerous ... Selaniki, elderly, hardworking and conscientious").[52] For one thing, he constantly remarks on the moral decay of his times, from the soldiers who seek "the vanities of this world" to the rulers who "do not practice justice and equity". Here it is interesting to note that, contrary to Ali, Selaniki often uses the concept of "commanding right and forbidding wrong" (*emr-i ma'ruf ve nehy-i münker*), both for soldiers and for ulema and sheikhs. Apart from moral complaints, however, Selaniki is much more specific on several occasions, for example when describing the apocalyptic fears raised around the Hijra year 1000 (1591):[53] people of the lowest classes had started to farm taxes, while all the administrative staff (*erbab-i kalem ve küttâb*) had become devoted and attached to the mutes, dwarves, and eunuchs of the palace (an accusation common to all critics of Murad III),[54] buying their posts from them. Murad III is the target of harsh criticism: Selaniki stresses the monetary disorder caused by continuous wars, as well as the increase of prices. As the state's expenditure rose, due to the increase of the *kapukulu* and their wages, bribery became a common way to acquire posts in the military as well as the administrative hierarchy. As a result, general disorder arose and discipline waned. The misadministration of the customs, which fell into the hands of Jews, led to further disorder in the field of trade.[55]

After a detailed exposition of these matters, no doubt owing much to the financial training of Selaniki himself, the author proceeds to more general judgments. He cites from Islamic history in order to show that moral decline always led to destruction, as happened with Bayezid I's defeat at the hands of Timur. Faced with the decline of morals in every area of life, Murad III could not find any ulema or vizier suitable for state administration; he kept changing his high officials according to whim, resulting in constant defeat by the infidels. The military was corrupted as well: foreigners and lower-class people entered the janissaries, who in turn did not refrain from every kind of mutiny and sedition.

Selaniki's criticism continues well into Mehmed III's reign. He complains, on various occasions, of: bribery and usury; the corruption of "our leaders" (*hâkimlerimüzün*) and of the janissaries through injustice and innovative

52 Woodhead 2006, 159.

53 Ibid., 258. On the Islamic millenial fears cf. also below.

54 Cf. Selaniki – İpşirli 1999, 353, 441; from among later authors see, for example, Koçi Bey – Aksüt 1939, 23, 54, 60.

55 See also Kafadar 1986, 81–84 and 93–107, on Selaniki's views on monetary disorder, and 146–150, on his views on price regulation.

practices (*cevr ü bid'at*); the lack of efficient and competent officials; of greedy people coming to power; the excessive tax burdens imposed on the *reaya*; the fall of tax-farms into the hands of incompetent farmers; the corruption of bureaucrats and ulema; the intrusion of *çift-bozan* into the ranks of the janissaries (in short the violation of the holy law as seen above) (*emr-i ma'ruf ve nehy-i münker olmaz oldı*); the selling of high administrative posts (such as governorships, judgeships, *defterdar*-positions etc.) in the form of bribes and gifts (with the grim note that "in no state were bribes ever taken openly, without felicity turning to misfortune"); the disintegration of the monetary system and the excessive taking of taxes and custom fees due to the needy situation of the sipahis and the greed of the tax-farmers; and the increase in the number of viziers and other palace officials, with the subsequent granting of fiefs to the detriment of the treasury. This gloomy image leaves Selaniki with a very pessimistic view of the future of the Ottoman Empire.[56]

Although lacking systematic explanation, these ideas show an original approach; some of them, such as the need for a limited number of viziers or the disapproval of the "strangers' intrusion" into the janissary ranks were to dominate early seventeenth-century political treatises. Selaniki may well be the first exponent of such ideas, which were obviously current among the ranks of the scribal bureaucracy: both Selaniki and the early seventeenth-century authors, who form the subject of chapter 5, belonged to this class, one which seems to have considered departures from established institutional rules a major threat to the empire. On the other hand, it seems that, upon Murad III's death (or even during his reign), it had become quite common to criticize him for whimsical administration in public affairs. This is how Beyani Mustafa b. Carullah (d. 1597/8), a lower-class ulema who later retired to a Halveti dervish lodge in Istanbul and wrote a collection of poets' biographies, describes Murad III:[57]

> He did not pay attention to his people, causing the order of the administration to disintegrate ... In addition, because of his association with numerous women he had many children, resulting in an increase of expenditure and the opening of the gates of bribery. The state magnates also followed the same path, saying that "A vice approved by the sultan becomes a virtue". Whoever had a sheikh said "You reached God." Great and small, women and men, everybody sought to become rich ... Those who administrated the state were not content with [their stipends], but

56 Selaniki – İpşirli 1999, 458, 478–79, 504, 716–17, 784–85, 852–53. For the exact citations see Sariyannis 2008a, 137–140.

57 Beyani – Kutluk 1997, 28 (=17–19 of the Ottoman text); cf. Sariyannis 2008a, 140–141.

> started to trade; the magnates of the state took the foodstuff coming from the provinces for Istanbul and stocked it. Part of it was taken for the state, but its worth was not paid ... The cries of the oppressed reached the skies, but with no avail; the signs of the approaching doom became manifest ... People were desperate.

One may see some similarities with the quasi-Apocalyptic vision of Selaniki in a roughly contemporaneous text, which had a rich afterlife throughout the seventeenth century. *Papasnâme* ("The priest's book") was written by Derviş Mehmed, allegedly a Christian priest turned Muslim (and, indeed, he uses the Greek word *idolah* [εἴδωλα] for idols: S8b). It is recorded in at least seven manuscripts, all dated after the mid-seventeenth century (the first being dated to 1651).[58] The text, which can be classified as a "conversion narrative" according to Tijana Krstić, is essentially a prophetic vision (in many ways similar to Saruhani's *Rumûzü'l-künûz*, seen above) narrated by an alleged convert to Islam; his own conversion, all the more since he used to be a priest, illustrates the possibility of changes that would seem unbelievable.[59] Its dating is insecure; internal evidence could suggest that its original compilation should be dated to c. 1597/8, although one cannot exclude the possibility of additions or alterations during its long history of being copied.[60]

The author starts by wondering what will happen to the Muslim community, since bribery has created such disorder that the Ottoman dynasty itself may soon reach its end. With these grim thoughts, a dervish named Abdurrahman,

58 See Krstić 2011, 116–118. Here I use the MSS of Vienna, Österreichische Nationalbibliothek MS Mixt 689 (1651) and Istanbul, Süleymaniye Kütüphanesi, Saliha Hatun 112/2 (1685/6). The text is to be published by Günhan Börekçi and Tijana Krstić; I wish to thank them both for their permission and help.

59 On other "alternative histories" in addition to Saruhani's work analyzed above, cf. Reindl-Kiel 2002 and Reindl-Kiel 2003.

60 A terminus post quem concerns a sultan Murad's victories over the Persians (S5b). Most probably, this is Murad III and his victories in the Caucasus, Azerbaijan, and Tabriz, since the author seems to ignore Ottoman history after the rise of Mehmed III (1595–1603). Prophet Muhammad is mentioned as having "come to the world a thousand and six years ago" (S8b, V9a); according to this the text should be dated to 956/1550 (if we accept that Muhammad was 50 years old at the time of the Hijra; see *Encyclopaedia of Islam*, 2nd ed., "Muhammad"), which seems too early. If there is a misunderstanding by the author and he had the Hijra in mind, the date becomes 1597/8, which is much more sensible. A certain emphasis on Yemen adds to this hypothesis, since the province was lost in 1636. Moreover, the description of Mehmed as a champion against the Central European forces and a reference to the need to inspect the janissary and the sipahi registers (S23b–24a, V34a-b) could strengthen the dating of the original text to just after the battle of Mező Kerésztés (October 1596)

whom the author serves for four years, arrives and tells him that not only will the dynasty go on, but 70 sultans will follow; at the end of this series, the End of Days will come, the world will be misled by a pseudo-prophet, the infamous Deccal, only to see the final victory of the prophet Isa (Jesus). After a long discussion in which Abdurrahman tries to persuade Mehmed of the reality of this prophecy and admits that the ulema of his day are mostly corrupt, the vision begins (S10a, V12a) with the thirteenth sultan, Mehmed III, who is prophesied to take Wallachia, Poland, and Hungary. All 70 sultans to come (under traditional Ottoman royal names but also other ones such as Hasan, Edhem, Yusuf, Ali and so forth) follow, in various symbolic forms.[61]

Then, a fascinating story has one of the next sultans take Moscow and Vienna, and afterwards a complex course toward world conquest, including the fall of Spain, Germany, Rome (*Kızılelma*), France, England, and even China and the "New World" (which, the author notes, is not a new world *ad litteram*, but was so named because it was unknown to us before: S20b, V29a), as well as the death of the Pope at the hands of the Istanbul rabble (S21a, V29b); however, it also includes occasional setbacks due to either revolts by the infidels or various sultans who succumb to arrogance and tyranny. Among the deeds of the glorious sultans to come should be noted: the mass-killing of the Istanbul Jews and the prohibition of wine (S14a, V17a–b; the Jews are to come back many generations later, when the 44th sultan grants a low tax-rate to whomever wants to settle in the capital: S21a, V29b); the prohibition of narcotics (S14b, V18b); the prohibition of idleness (S18a, V25a: "those who practice no craft should be gathered and punished severely, and those whose mind is not fit for a craft should be directed to practise agriculture"); the granting of stipends to the elderly (S19b, V27a; also S24b, 35b); the abolition of both fratricide and the *kafes* practice, with the sultans' brothers being appointed viziers, admirals, or *müftis* (e.g. S21a, V30a); the compulsory freeing of slaves after seven years (S24b, V35a); and so on.

An interesting throwback to the sixteenth or seventeenth century comes in the story of the reign of the 56th Sultan, when he inspects the janissaries (now numbering 600,000) and the sipahis (400,000), erases the names of half of them from the registers and cuts the stipends of those remaining by half

61 The series seems to include Ahmed I, Osman II, Murad IV, and Ibrahim (whom a marginal note in the Vienna MS, copied in 1651, calls "the present sultan": V16a). However, this must be a coincidence, since Ahmed is to impose a tax on Malta and Osman is presented as an old man who will abolish bribery (S11a-b, V13a–14a; moreover, Mustafa is missing and Osman's anonymous successor is to capture Moscow).

("since there is no campaign"). The result is a revolt by both the soldiers, who wish to put the grand vizier on the throne, and the townspeople (*şehirli*), who kill the vizier. Subsequently, the sultan reduces the number of servants allowed to three for the common people, 25 for the viziers, and 50 for himself (S23b–24a, V34a–b). If the dating we propose (late sixteenth century) is correct, and if this description is viewed as a piece of indirect political advice, it would precede the first known reference to the need to inspect and reduce the numbers and salaries of the *kapıkulları* by more than two decades (the suggestion was first articulated in the anonymous *Kitâb-ı müstetâb*, c. 1620; see below, chapter 5). But then again, this specific description might be a later addition, since all known manuscripts are dated after the mid-seventeenth century.

One might draw a line connecting all these texts, including Ali's, with the Islamic millennium (1591/2), something that was seen as either an object of eschatological fear or marking the beginning of a new era. This is how Selaniki describes this climate:[62]

> As for the discussions prevailing among the people on the change of times, they were expecting for disorder and malice, saying "undoubtedly there will be great events in the year 1000". [But] with God's grace and assistance, every corner remained safe and secure.

This description may seem a bit too weak to be presented as the dominant intellectual mood of the period; however, the gloomy assessments by Ali and Selaniki seem to corroborate this view. In Cornell H. Fleischer's words,[63]

> The enthusiastic proposals for practical fiscal and administrative reform propounded by Ali in the *Counsel* embodied a hope that change and deterioration could be reversed by a return to Ottoman ideals and by strict observance of *kanun* in letter and spirit. In the year AH 1000 these hopes were replaced by a nostalgia for a past that could never come again, a golden era ... Ali's topical and practical outlook on Ottoman affairs gave way to a larger, more abstract view of history, a view that judged a society by its ideals and the extent to which it fulfilled them.

62 Selaniki – İpşirli 1999, 257. Cf. Fleischer 1986a, 112, 133–42, 244.

63 Fleischer 1986a, 139. For a contrast with the much more optimistic view at the turn of the previous Islamic century, during Bayezid II's reign, see Şen 2017, esp. 601–606.

If this applies to Ali's later works, and especially to his universal history of dynasties, texts such as Selaniki's history and the prophetic vision of Derviş Mehmed (as well as of Saruhani's *Rumûzü'l-künûz*, which was seen above) instead correspond to a worldview chronologically centered around the year 1000 as a starting point for either decline or rise; whichever is the case, they all convey a sense of urgency and of a crucial historical moment that has to be overcome. A "Golden Age", the *topos* of posterior literature, is already present, be it in the past or the distant future.

3.1 *Hasan Kâfi Akhisari, Üveysi*

Ali's name is often coupled with that of another late sixteenth-century author, Hasan Kâfî b. Turhan b. Davud b. Ya'kub ez-Zîbî el-Akhisarî el-Bosnavî. Akhisari, however, differed in many ways from his great contemporary, in both personality and work.[64] He was born in Bosnia in 1544, where he had a medrese education, which he continued in Istanbul from 1566 onwards. In 1575, he returned to Bosnia as a teacher; about a decade later, in 1583, he changed career path to become a judge in his native town, Akhisar. He was then appointed to other towns of the region, went on the Hajj, and joined the campaigns to Eğri (1596) and Estergon (1605). He died in 1616 in Akhisar, leaving behind him a large body of work on philology, *fikh*, theology, philosophy, and history. Among his numerous treatises, what interests us most is the *Usûlü'l-hikem fi nizâmi'l-âlem* ("Elements of wisdom for the order of the world"); Akhisari wrote it in 1596 in Arabic, and since it was very successful among various ulema and officials, he also translated it into Turkish. Akhisari's treatise was widely read; it was copied in numerous manuscripts, and gained a new lease of life in the nineteenth and early twentieth centuries, with many editions and translations.

Akhisari's essay is an unusual mixture of traditional "mirror for princes", with a strong Ottoman flavor, and an attempt to theorize on the human soul and society in the manner of the moralist *ahlak* authors. At the very beginning of his treatise, Akhisari states that it concerns the order of the world (*nizam-i alem*) and that it should be used by "the officials of the government and the experts of the sultanly court" (I248; elsewhere, he repeats that he meant "to reiterate the rules of the world order" [I250]). A world order, he explains, exists because God wanted the world and its people to survive until the End of Days. Propagation of mankind comes from social intercourse, which comes from

64 On his life and works see *Diyanet Vakfi İslam Ansiklopedisi*, s.v. (M. Aruçi); Fodor 1986, 225–227; Yılmaz 2003a, 307–308; İnan 2009, 116; Black 2011, 263–264. For the transcription of his *Üsulü'l-hikem* see Akhisari – İpşirli 1979–80; for an early twentieth-century German translation, see Akhisari – Karácson 1911.

property (*mal*), which comes from custom (*te'amül*), that is, dealing with other people (*mu'amele ve alış-viriş*). To attain this goal, certain rules are needed, so God divided people into four categories (*bölük, sınıf*): the men of the sword, the men of the pen, the cultivators, and, finally, the artisans and merchants. Then God ordained kings and rulers (*padişahlık ve beğlik itdiler*) to possess and control (*tasarruf idüp, zabt eylemeği*) these four categories. Kings and viziers, officials and soldiers belong to the first group; their purpose is to keep all four classes under control with justice and wise politics (*hüsn-i siyaset*), always with the counsel of religious and wise men (unfortunately, Akhisari does not elaborate on this somewhat awkward inclusion of kings within the first class, which they are supposed to govern). Another aim of this class is to keep the enemies at bay; kings and beys also have to take care of various other necessary things. The second class contains the ulema and other men of religion, who cannot fight. Their duty is to make sure that everyone follows the premises of the faith (*emr-i ma'ruf ve nehy-i münker*) and teach these to the other classes, especially to the king whose (spiritual) health is necessary for the health of the people. The third class "is now known as *re'aya ve beraya*", the peasants or flock. Their aim is to produce things, and thereby meet the needs of all the people; their work is superior to everyone else's, after knowledge and the holy war. Finally, the fourth class is composed of artisans and merchants, whose work is to produce and supply things that the people need.

Everybody has to belong to one of these categories in order not to be a burden to others. Men who are outside these classes must be forced to enter one of them; some philosophers even claim that people who do not work (*işsüz ve güçsüz kimesne*) must be killed. In olden days, sultans made annual surveys of such people and prohibited unemployed Arabs from passing into the Balkans (I252). Another point is that people should not cross these borders; everyone must occupy themselves with the work suitable to their class.

The allusion to Arabs in the Balkans apart, all this theory is a simplified version of the *ahlak* literature. Akhisari does not fail to cite the circle of justice, placing further emphasis on mildness or, more precisely, "mild government" (*hüsn-i siyaset*; I254). As usual with Ottoman "mirrors for princes", he also emphasizes generosity, as the ruler must practice his generosity equally to all classes, because he needs all of them: rulership comes through the support and collaboration of all social classes (*padişahlık cemi' esnaf ile olur*). Besides justice, mildness, and generosity, Akhisari also praises wisdom in a manner reminiscent of the Kashifi-influenced bureaucrat-moralists (see chapter 3, above): he has a whole chapter devoted to consultation, a practice that, as may be remembered, is deeply embedded in the long *fikh* and *inşa'* tradition, from Amasi to Semerkandi and Celalzade. At any rate, wisdom and intelligence is to be more highly valued than any other qualities;[65] in war, a stratagem is worth more than courage and might (I263–66).

Part of Akhisari's advice comes from his Persian models and belongs to traditional *adab* literature: for instance, he notes that the king should punish oppressors and collect taxes with justice, choose an able and wise vizier, esteem the ulema, respect and take care of his father and predecessor's friends and supporters in order not to make enemies, and so on. What differentiates *Usûlü'l-hikem* from previous similar works is the degree to which Akhisari manages to integrate the now almost commonplace ideas of "decline" within a traditional model, without the stylistic and structural innovations introduced by Ali. Thus, having described the world order, he claims that it has been turned upside-down. A nation (*kavm*) is not destroyed as long its deeds are governed by equity, justice, and uprightness; provided this happens, God Almighty does not change His favor contained in the order He has ordained (*nizam ve intizamlarında olan ni'met ve afiyetini*). So, Akhisari explains that he set out to examine all signs of "sedition and confusion" that had happened in the past ten years or more, since A.H. 980 (1572/3), in order to discover their causes and meaning. There are three of these: first, the negligence shown in governing with justice and mild administration (*hüsn-i siyaset*), due to unfit people having obtained high offices; second, that statesmen neglect taking counsel because their pride makes them despise the ulema; and third, that discipline and military ability have been waning in the army because the soldiers have no fear of their superiors. The ultimate source of these is twofold: greed for bribery and submission to the words of women.

Like Ali or Lütfi Pasha, Akhisari connects the compartmentalization of society with the maintenance of world order. One of the causes of the present-day disorder, he argues, is that since the year 1001 (1592/3) *reaya* and artisans from towns and villages were forced to join the army; as a result, the urban economy was ruined and prices increased tenfold. If the sultan is to care as in the old times, i.e. according to the Sharia, everyone should do only what is ordained to the class to which they belong, or else the dynasty will be weakened and power may even pass to another family. Furthermore, since disorder appeared in Ottoman lands, high positions started to be given to unfit persons, and he expresses his wish that the course of things would instead return to "the right manner and the old law" (*uslub-ı kavim ve kanun-i kadim*; I256–57). This emphasis on the "old law" is also a feature that differentiates Akhisari's advice from previous *adab*-style works.

---

65 It may be recalled here that Celalzade based consultation on reason rather than piety (Şahin 2013, 241).

Perhaps the field in which Akhisari's advice departs the most from his Persian models and becomes clearly "Ottomanized" is in his description of changes within the military strength of the empire.[66] Here, Akhisari provides one of his most original insights, namely that military technology has a role to play in the confrontation with the infidel and that faith and zeal are not sufficient factors for victory. First, he observes that Ottoman soldiers have lost their ability in battle because their chiefs fail to inspect and register them and their weapons, whereas in previous times the rulers themselves used to inspect their armies. Then he remarks that, 50 years ago (i.e., in the mid-1540s), the enemy started to use new weapons; if the Ottomans were to imitate the infidels in this respect, as they used to, they would surely beat them, but the Ottoman army neglected to do so and thus is constantly defeated. This impressive instance of comparison with the West stands alone for many years to come; on the particular subject of military technology, we have to wait until the early eighteenth century to find something similar. Still, there are some contemporary parallels: in Mustafa Ali's *Künhü'l-ahbâr* (Ç3:591–593) there is the story of a prisoner of the Habsburgs who reported that the enemy had four things that the Ottomans did not, namely: justice for the peasants, adequate provisions, timely payment of soldiers' salaries, and discipline.[67] As for Selaniki, he claims that "infidel rulers who are around and about us" were more careful than the Ottomans concerning monetary issues; "through the execution of [their] orders and punitive authority, they did not [let the currency] change [but] said: 'the Ottoman sultan is an example to us; see what kind of disorder will strike the state and the wealth of the land [if we follow their example]'".[68]

In his emphasis on army discipline and distrust of the janissaries, Akhisari agrees completely with the intellectual climate of his era; indeed, he sometimes foreshadows the major themes of subsequent political literature, as shall be seen in chapter 5. The king and his viziers, he writes, must prevent the soldiers from going to "innovations and needless whims" (*bid'atleri ve beyhude havalara*) such as coffeehouses; this can be done either through mild measures or suppression (*hüsn-i siyaset ve zabt ile*). Victory can be achieved with the help of God, but the officers must keep the army in good discipline, while the prayers and spiritual guidance of the ulema and sheikhs are very helpful. In

66 Among the instances where Akhisari provides original advice is his argument that the defeated enemy rulers should not be reinstated in their previous posts (for example, Christian notables from Thrace should be appointed as rulers in Wallachia and Moldavia).

67 Cf. Fleischer 1986a, 298.

68 Quoted in Kafadar 1986, 100–102, who remarks that "the intellectual roots of Ottoman Westernization lie in the earliest phases of Ottoman decline consciousness at the end of the sixteenth century".

the author's time, however, these groups are destitute and the *kapıkulu* make fun of them. Furthermore, Ottoman armies are defeated because the soldiers have become oppressors, and God must punish them. Three years before the completion of this treatise, Akhisari stresses, the soldiers in Rumili, and especially the janissaries, had started plundering the villages of Muslim *reaya*. All such sedition comes from greed and envy (*tam'-ı ham*).

Finally, in another pioneering set of ideas that forms the epilogue of his treatise, Akhisari defends peace (*sulh*) and agreeing treaties (*ahd*). War is difficult and full of bitterness, he writes, while peace brings safety and comfort. To make war with a nation that seeks peace is wrong. Additionally, it is a mistake and a great sin to break a treaty (I275–77). One may remark that, with Akhisari having lived most of his life in a frontier region himself, this might not be a coincidence; despite far from being a soldier himself, he knew very well the consequences of war.

In sum, Akhisari's treatise occupies a mixed position within the trends of his era. On the one hand, he seems more like a representative of the earlier generation, in the tradition of moralistic "mirror for princes" literature. As such, he refers explicitly (I250) to Qadi Bayzawi's (d. 1291) *Anwâr al-tanzîl wa asrâr al-ta'wîl*, a work widely read in Ottoman medreses, and to al-Zamakhshari's (d. 1143) *Rabî' al-abrâr*, which, as noted in chapter 3, was repeatedly translated in various versions, shortened or not, throughout the sixteenth century. In fact, it seems that his treatise is based on a shortened adaptation of Zamakhshari's work, entitled *Rawz al-ahyâr*, by Hatib Kasımoğlu Muhyiddin Mehmed (d. 1533/4), which was produced in the early years of Süleyman's reign. On the other hand, his use of the traditional *medrese* style to convey concrete opinions on contemporaneous problems, especially military ones, is typical of his age—all the more so since, as noted, he tended to present original criticisms and ideas, such as sections describing the weakness of women's advice in the chapter on consultation, the famous excerpt on European progress in military technology, the references to Bosnia, Wallachia, and Moldavia, and his disapproval of coffee. These ideas may have influenced political decisions, as Akhisari's work seems to have been widely read, though they do not seem to have found their way into his contemporaries' or his immediate successors' works, even though other *leitmotifs* of his treatise (such as the emphasis on consultation and the problems of coffeehouses) did.

For the sake of comparison, it will be useful to look at a very similar work with the same title (*Usûlü'l-hikem fi nizâmi'l-âlem*), written by Hasanbeyzade Ahmed Pasha (d. 1636/7). Known primarily for his chronicle, written in various stages between 1628 and 1635 and covering the period from the reign of Süleyman to that of Murad IV, Hasanbeyzade entered the palace bureaucracy in the early 1590s and served under various viziers and commanders, taking part in many campaigns on the Habsburg front. In 1600, he became *reisül-küttab* himself for a time, and then continued to serve in various financial posts in Istanbul and the provinces. His treatise was composed between 1619 and 1621 for Osman II's vizier (Güzelce) Ali Pasha and is preserved in two copies.[69] For his sources, Hasanbeyzade quotes "various books on ethics", and particularly Hatib Kasımoğlu Muhyiddin's *Rawż al-ahyâr*, claiming that he took many points concerning the world order and its arrangements from this treatise (IU2b). In fact, his work is a summary of *Rawz al-ahyâr*, but in a less detailed and creative way than is Akhisari's: Hasanbeyzade keeps some stories that Akhisari omits, and adds no original ideas, either his own or Akhisari's. The exact relationship between Hasanbeyzade's and Akhisari's works, and their common source, is still unclear.[70] What is clear, however, is that Akhisari added plenty of specific advice to his prototype, while Hasanbeyzade, writing in the second decade of the seventeenth century and following the popularity of Akhisari's work, was happy with a simple moralistic compilation. One particular point in Hasanbeyzade's treatise seems to have been added by the writer, since it is lacking in Akhisari's text: his emphasis on the need for the sultan to keep the army disciplined through mild measures (*hüsn-i siyaset*) and to show respect for the elder soldiers (İÜ 17a). If one knows the historical developments that happened soon after the completion of Hasanbeyzade's work, this remark gains a grim feeling of prophecy.

Such criticism became increasingly intense as the seventeenth century proceeded before taking a different form, one which will be studied in the next chapter. A famous poem entitled *Nasîhat-i İslâmbol* ("Counsel to Istanbul") was written sometime between 1624 and 1638 (since it mentions Baghdad as occupied by the Persians) by a certain Üveysi.[71] This *kaside* begins as an

69 Istanbul, Belediye Ktp. nr. o–49; İstanbul Üniversitesi Ktp. T 6944; here I consulted the latter manuscript. See Hasan Bey-zâde – Aykut 2004, XLIX–LV; Aykut seems to confuse the two copies; see p. LIV attributing the Belediye MS to the copyist of İstanbul Üniv. MS.

70 *Rawz al-ahyâr* was also translated into Turkish by Aşık Çelebi (whom we also encountered as the first translator of Ibn Taymiyya) for Selim II (d. 1574). Aykut (op. cit.) traces the use of Hasanbeyzade's source, which is selective: thus, Hasanbeyzade's first chapter corresponds to some parts of *Rawz al-ahyâr*'s third chapter; his second chapter, to the first and fifth chapter of his source; and so forth. One might conclude that Hasanbeyzade was, in fact, re-writing Akhisari's compilation or translating his Arabian version. On the other hand, his omissions from Akhisari's work must lead us to the conclusion that they both used an abridged form of *Rawz al-ahyâr*, possibly that written by Aşık Çelebi.

71 Üveysi – von Diez 1811; Gibb 1900–1909, 3:210–218; İz 1966, 1:117–119. The poet is often confused with his more or less contemporary Veysî (see next chapter). On the confusion between the two poets see Sariyannis 2008a, 143–145; Tezcan (forthcoming).

admonition to the inhabitants of the Ottoman capital (*ey kavm-i İslâmbol*); later on, however, the exclamation "Oh tyrant!" (*â zâlim*) seems to be addressed to the sultan himself, although in other parts of the text the author addresses the sultan with more respect. At the beginning of the poem, the prediction of the end time drawing near is reiterated, although this might be a rhetorical device rather than a real belief on the part of the author. After depicting the cries of the poor against oppression, the author accuses the sultan (or his administrators) of observing neither the Sharia nor the *kanun*, as he has abandoned the world to corruption by adopting unholy innovations (*ne şer'-i Allaha tabi'siz ne hod kanuna ka'ilsiz / cihsni dürlü bid'atla fesada verdiñiz billah*). The kadis are dismissed as corrupt, and the oppression and corruption of Istanbul's people has surpassed any known limits; vizierial posts are given to accursed Jews, while the sultan is surrounded by a crew of dwarves, mutes, and buffoons. Some criticism is more direct: instead of sword-fiefs (*kılıç tîmâr*), timars are given as shoe-money (*paşmaklık*) to viziers and sultanas, resulting in a natural reluctance of the *gazi*s to go to war, a situation exacerbated by the *sipahi*s' wages being far too low. Somewhat surprisingly, Üveysi seems to defend the simple janissaries ("If you talk about the janissaries, what can you tell of them? It is the pashas and the aghas that upset the world and cause corruption and anarchy"), keeping his wrath for major and minor officials, as well as for sheikhs, preachers, and dervishes. The sultan, Uveysî boldly continues, will be held responsible before God, though he will be saved in eternity if he decides to act in an upright and pious manner. Finally, it should be noted that, in one version of the poem (the one given by Fahir İz—see footnote), there is also an allusion to an eschatological just ruler who will redress the world order. One may see here a revival of the intellectual climate prevailing in the 1590s, as described above.

• • •

Thus, by the end of the sixteenth century, a specifically Ottoman genre, a version of *adab* or "mirrors for princes" in which advice was explicitly concrete, addressed to very specific problems, and which emphasized institutional rather than moral deficiencies, had reached maturity. Apart from these formal characteristics, the most striking feature of this genre was its view of the present as an era of disorder, a condition that could be mended only if certain shortcomings were addressed and, more often than not, departures from established custom were abolished. As for its social content, it is clear that all these works stood for the old feudal order, the timariot system; others spoke mostly from the point of view of the sipahi cavalry, while still more emphasized the problems created for the peasants by monetization and the disruption of the old tax and landholding system. In terms of political power, late sixteenth-century authors usually favored absolutism, as they urged the sultans to take back the reins of power from their viziers and take action. However, as shall be seen in the next chapter, it was inevitable that a more "constitutionalist" view would prevail. On the one hand, as the notion of the "old law" was increasingly sanctified and idealized while, at the same time, the person of the sultan was undergoing a continuous desacralization, "old law" was bound to form a sort of binding constitution that would claim to rule each individual sultan's whims. On the other hand, the rise of a new political force, the janissary army, was making the conditional power of the ruler a *de facto* standard feature of Ottoman politics. Even authors who wished to limit the janissaries' power had to admit this reality, and by then the argument for an old, sanctified order, one in which janissaries had been nothing more than faithful slaves, had become stronger than any appeal to the personal power and will of the sultan to repress them.

CHAPTER 5

The "Golden Age" as a Political Agenda: the Reform Literature

Ahmed I's reign, following the defeat of the last major Celali forces by Kuyucu Murad Pasha, seemed indeed to mark a new increase in Ottoman power—or, at least, a turning of the tide.[1] Ahmed, whose reign saw no other major victory, ordered the building of the Blue Mosque, the last of the great sultanly mosques of Istanbul, as a marker of what he considered to be a decisive move towards peace and imperial glorification.[2] However, this was little more than an illusion: the sizeable peasant armies that had imposed their rule over large parts of Anatolia may have been crushed, but local rebellions (which were also termed "Celali") did not cease. The governor of Aleppo, Canbuladoğlu Ali, had collaborated with the last major Celali leader, Kalenderoğlu Mehmed; other local leaders in the east, such as the Druze Fahreddin Ma'noğlu (whose rebellion lasted for two decades, until 1635), were even more successful. As for relations with other states, the Habsburg front remained quiet for more than half a century following the 1606 peace of Zsitva Törok (ratified in its final form only in 1612). On the other hand, a new European front was opened with the Cossack raids along the Black Sea coast, which lasted until almost the middle of the century and led to occasional crises with Poland. More seriously, the large Safavid counter-attack under Shah Abbas I continued, culminating in a major loss for the Ottomans, that of Baghdad in 1624.

Moreover, any optimism that had been left to Ottoman observers was to be harshly tested in the third decade of the seventeenth century: Ahmed I's brother and successor Mustafa proved to be mentally ill and, following a joint decision by the harem's chief agha, the *şeyhülislam*, and the grand vizier's *kaymmakam*, was replaced by Ahmed's eldest son, Osman, in 1618. Although almost still a child (he was only thirteen at the time), Osman was highly ambitious and began his reign by leading an army against Poland in person. Contrary to what contemporary chroniclers claimed, this campaign was far from successful, but the young sultan's next move was to prove fatal. Osman announced that he was going to go on the Hajj to Mecca, something no other sultan had

1 On the events of this period see Mantran 1989, 227–236; Emecen 2001b, 46–49.

2 Rüstem 2016. Cf. the encomium of Ahmed's almost supernatural forces, composed by his historian Mustafa Safi (Murphey 2005).

© KONINKLIJKE BRILL NV, LEIDEN, 2019 DOI:10.1163/9789004385245_007 done previously. Rumor had it that he intended to collect an army in the eastern territories of the empire and use it to suppress the unruly janissaries; the *şeyhülislam* declared that the pilgrimage was not an obligation for a sultan, but this was to no avail, and Osman insisted on carrying out his decision. This resulted in the first major janissary revolt of the seventeenth century: the rebels captured and eventually executed Osman, reinstating his uncle Mustafa in his place.[3] This regicide, preceding that of the English king Charles I (1649) by more than two decades, caused chaos, as Mustafa again showed his inability to rule, some factions of the army demanded justice, and another provincial governor, Abaza Mehmed Pasha, marched on Istanbul under the pretence that he was seeking vengeance for the sultan's blood. Soon after, in 1623, the fierce protests of various preachers and ulema led to the second deposition of Mustafa by the *şeyhülislam*, viziers, and other officials.

The new sultan, Murad IV, was only twelve years old, and power was effectively in the hands of his mother, Kösem Sultan. During his minority, the Ottoman armies managed to suppress various rebellions in the east and even gain some victories over the Safavids. However, after the popular grand vizier Hüsrev Pasha failed to recapture Baghdad in 1630, the sultan replaced him. Soon, a series of rebellions by the janissary and sipahi cavalry plunged the capital into chaos once more, as Murad twice had to concede to the rebels' demands. On a third occasion, however, in 1632, he did not succumb, and instead managed to convene separate councils of the various military and administrative bodies, making them swear an oath of allegiance. After suppressing the revolt with the help of his new grand vizier, Tabanıyassı Mehmed Pasha, Murad declared his decision not to give the soldiers any more privileges than they had had during Süleyman's reign. Furthermore, he started a program of iron discipline, often coupling it with the ideological project of Kadızade Mehmed Efendi, a preacher who found his way into the sultan's entourage and advocated a strict religious purification along the lines of Birgivi's teachings (as shall be seen in more detail in chapter 6). After a devastating fire in Istanbul in 1633, Murad imposed a ban on both tobacco and coffeehouses (the latter due to the role of these establishments in circulating rumors and instigating discontent) and renewed prohibitions on the rights of non-Muslims, pitilessly executing all law-breakers. On the military level, his harsh discipline had results: after imposing a peace upon Poland, the Ottoman armies under Murad's personal guidance captured Erivan (Yerevan) in 1635 and Baghdad in 1638; the ensuing peace of Kashr-i Shirin secured the new borders and put an end to almost

3 On Osman II's highly interesting reign and fall see Piterberg 2003, esp. 16–29; Tezcan 2010a, 115–175.

three decades of continuous warfare. Murad died in 1640, leaving behind a terrorizing reputation as a suppressor of janissary unrest and a strict keeper of religious order.

1 The Canonization of Decline

It was only natural that the events described (those culminating in Osman's murder) brought about an even more alarming sense of "decline" than that prevailing in the final decades of the sixteenth century. The comparison with the allegedly glorious times of the past became increasingly fashionable throughout the first half of the seventeenth century. While authors such as Mustafa Ali had spoken of "deviations" or "departures" from the institutional lines of old, they had not dismissed new ways of coping with the contemporaneous situation, nor had they made this comparison a central argument in their treatises. In contrast, the authors to be studied in this chapter, while further deepening their predecessors' "Ottomanization" (by concentrating on specifically Ottoman institutions and practices instead of copying general ideas and advice), also focused on the need to return to the glorious past: institutions of the early or mid-sixteenth century were idealized and strict adherence to their functional rules was advocated.

The concept of a "decline" presupposes that of a "rise"; in other words, of a "Golden Age" during which the institutions, power, and individual virtues of the Ottoman dynasty and state had reached their zenith. The placing of this era varied according to author. It may be remembered that the anonymous author of the *Hirzü'l-mülûk*, for instance, considered Mehmed II and Selim I as ideal rulers, and the same goes for Mustafa Ali, although they seem to have had different political aims (thus, *Hirzü'l-mülûk* stresses Mehmed II's absolutism, while Ali sees him as the founder of the "old law").[4] As shall be seen, while this remark remains valid for the first decades of the seventeenth century, by the early 1620s the decline was seen as beginning with Murad III's reign and the "Golden Age" was increasingly identified with Süleyman's era (although there are voices, most notably in Koçi Bey's work, blaming Süleyman for inaugurating administrative malpractices). Eventually, it was Süleyman's reign that came to be considered the "Golden Age" of the Ottoman Empire, even if most authors acknowledged that signs of what they perceived as "decline" had already started to appear. This "canonization" had begun long before Süleyman's death (for instance, in Celalzade's history, as well as in various commissioned

4 Cf. Tezcan 2010a, 57–58. On the image of Selim I in advice literature cf. also Çıpa 2014.

historiographical works such as Arif's 1558 *Süleymanname*), but reached its zenith in the seventeenth century, when a historian such as Solakzade could write (in the 1650s) that "in Süleyman's reign of justice the Ottoman state found its balance (*mizan*)".[5] This canonization of the past must have made its impact felt in practical terms as early as the start of the seventeenth century. We read that, in 1606, Ahmed I encountered the opposition of some ulema, who argued that things used to be conducted in a different way during Süleyman's reign; his answer was that "each period is different, those times cannot be compared with the present". Even eight decades later, in 1685, the same argument was used against the *şeyhülislam*, who had to remark:[6]

> Was Sultan Süleyman any prophet? Do his words have the status of a hadith? Such a rule was ordained for those times, but now it has to be abolished by present necessity.

A similar feeling may be deduced from a famous early seventeenth-century poem, the *Hâbnâme* ("Vision" or "Dream-book", mentioned also as *Vâkıʿa-nâme*) by Veysi (1561/2–1627/8), an ulema who held many judgeships during his life and died as *kadi* of Üsküb (Skopje).[7] In this work, composed in the early 1610s, Veysi sees Ahmed I meet Alexander the Great in a dream; when the former complains about his own time, Alexander points out that all the problems (such as factionalism and bloodshed) have always been present in the history of humanity: the world was never prosperous and thriving, at least no more than it is now. This view can be described as optimistic, as it places emphasis on historical parallels that show that the crisis can be overcome. Veysi stresses that continuous warfare, the disobedience of the *kul*s, and excessive taxation were the main causes for the difficulties of the Ottoman state; proposed remedies include more careful choosing of state officials and a stricter adherence to the Sharia. The ulema background of the author is evident in this way of thinking. Moreover, the author claims that the fault is in the subjects' sedition

5 Solakzade 1879, 4 (*bunun ayyam-ı adlında bu devlet buldı mizanı*), quoted in Woodhead 1995, 181. See ibid., 165 for other instances of late sixteenth- or seventeenth-century eulogies of Süleyman (Ali, Peçevi, Karaçelebizade); Kafadar 1993.

6 See the relevant references in Sariyannis 2008a, 142.

7 Veysi – Salimzjanova 1976; Veysi – Altun 2011. Cf. Gibb 1900–1909, 3:208–210; Fodor 1986, 227–228; Sariyannis 2008a, 143–144; Günay 2010; Şen 2011; Tezcan (forthcoming). On the confusion with his contemporary Üveysi see above, chapter 4. Sometimes (see e.g. Fleischer 1983, 199) it is asserted that Veysi was one of the first Ottomans to have acquired a manuscript of Ibn Khaldun's *Muqaddima* in Cairo (1598); however, we cannot identify with certainty the buyer of the manuscript as being this specific Veysi, although it seems quite probable.

rather than in their rulers' hopelessness. Obviously, Veysi was responding to an expanding sense of decline for which departures from the old law were mainly held responsible. It is noteworthy, too, that the work is fictional in character, especially since political discourse is placed into the sphere of dreams, not unlike the prophetic vision in *Papasnâme*.

According to Baki Tezcan's recent reading of seventeenth-century Ottoman history, this canonization of the "old law" was one of two ways in which the ongoing "constitutionalization" of Ottoman power was expressed. Tezcan spoke of "the second Empire", explained as "the expansion of the political nation and the limitation of royal authority", when "a much larger segment of the imperial administration came to consist of men whose social origins were among the commoners" and "[t]hus more and more men whose backgrounds were in finance and trade came to occupy significant positions in the government of the empire, replacing those military slaves and *civil*izing the imperial polity". In this process, various factions (ulemas, military groups, powerful households, etc.) began to challenge and legitimately limit (or claim to have the legitimacy to limit) royal authority from the beginning of the seventeenth century.[8] Islamic political theory, at any rate, had already been putting restraints on absolute rule, be they the religious (or legalist) approach favored by Ibn Taymiyya and (as seen, and as shall be seen later) Birgivi and his followers, or the need for justice stressed by Persian writers. What was originally Ottoman in all this is the cult of the "old law" and of the institutions of the "Golden Age" as well as the underlying notion that these rules and institutions served or were intended to serve as a kind of constitution, i.e. as binding rules for the sultan to follow.[9] It was seen in chapter 4 that, in a (perhaps deliberate) slip of the tongue, Mustafa Ali writes literally that Mehmed II "promulgated an old law" (*bir kanun-i kadim*), thus identifying the established rules with those that are just. It was in the early seventeenth century that this identification took on an elaborate and systematic form.

1.1 *"Constitutionalism" and Charismatic Rulership*

Somewhat paradoxically (if one keeps the association of the "old law" theorists with "Ottoman constitutionalism"), however, this kind of reasoning was, in more than one way, associated with Murad IV, seemingly one of the most autocratic sultans in Ottoman history. Indeed, the most famous expounder of the "Golden Age" idea, Koçi Bey, was also perhaps the most successful, as

8 Tezcan 2010a, *passim* (the citations are from pp. 232 and 10); cf. Vatin – Veinstein 2003, 84, 219; Yılmaz 2008; Sariyannis 2013; Yılmaz 2015a.

9 Tezcan 2010a, 48ff.

his advice is said to have been followed closely by Murad, to whom it was addressed. However, Koçi Bey's work by no means stands alone; a whole wave of similar texts, mostly of anonymous or contested authorship, shared the same view of the present situation as a dangerous deviation from the rules of Süleyman's Golden Age and of the solution lying in a return to those rules. In terms of form, these works were often composed as a continuation of earlier "mirrors for princes", such as Mustafa Ali's *Nushatü's-selâtîn*, which seems to have set the standard for the genre. On the other hand, the themes dominant in this ideological trend differ in many ways from Ali's ideas; for instance, while Ali was strongly critical of the *devşirme* system itself and favored the use of educated freemen in the administration, the writers to be examined now consider problematic the abandonment of the *devşirme* method of recruitment, focusing rather on its enhancement against the intrusion of "strangers" into the janissary ranks. The recurring themes of this trend show remarkable stability: redress of the timar system and of the economic basis of the timariot sipahis, discipline and control (in terms of numbers and salaries) of the janissaries, and suppression of bribery—these are the main lines that guide the reasoning of political literature from the 1620s through to the 1640s. It would, perhaps, be more fruitful to regard this trend as a reaction to the rise of the janissaries' power rather than as an expression of a "constitutionalist" argument against autocratic rule. Authors of this trend (closely associated with the government apparatus, as shall be seen) clearly considered the widening of the janissaries' social basis as an imminent threat to the social order and proposed a redressed sipahi nobility as a potential counterweight.

Moreover, the transformation of the sultan's power at a symbolic level reached its climax with Osman II's execution. Although eulogies of the Ottoman dynasty are still found in all political works from throughout this century, the personage of the sultan had undergone a rapid "desacralization" (to use Nicolas Vatin and Gilles Veinstein's words), one which reached a critical point with Mustafa I's deposition and continued right down to the early nineteenth century.[10] As has been seen, Ottoman political texts never (or almost never) made too much of the sultan's personal charisma: he had to be a mortal striving for perfection, and he could succumb at any moment to the temptation of injustice and thus bring about his downfall. The notable exception can be seen in various works authored during Süleyman's reign (for instance, Celalzade's) and is probably linked with Süleyman's own legitimizing endeavor, which, as has been seen, was based (during the first decades of his reign) on messianic and eschatological claims. Such claims continued on the part of individual sultans,

10 Vatin – Veinstein 2003, 66–68, 218–251.

notably Murad III, whose series of dreams and visions reveal that he believed in his own special, almost prophetic mission.[11] It appears that Ahmed I also tried to impose a similar image during his reign (it will be remembered that he denied the "old law" in 1606). His court historian (and royal imam), Mustafa Safi, endowed him with an almost supernatural aura,[12] while the building of his mosque in Istanbul (the Blue Mosque) in defiance of ulema and other forces in the court, and especially the closing of its central dome in 1617, was celebrated with unprecedented pomp, even having the unusual honor of being described in a specially-commissioned text.[13] Moreover, *Gencîne-i adâlet* ("The treasure of justice"), an adaptation of Hamadani's *Zakhîrat al-mulûk* (cf. above, chapter 3) that was dedicated to Ahmed I, not only equated the sultanate with the caliphate but also considered the caliph to be the shadow of God upon the earth (rather than the successor of the Prophet) and, most importantly, endowed him with prophetic power.[14]

All these self-glorifying efforts notwithstanding, however, the sacred character of the sultan seems to have had no appeal (even by the last decades of the sixteenth century; Selaniki's or Beyani's assessments of Murad III attest to this) for either authors of political tracts (even those from the sultans' entourage, such as Koçi Bey) or the major political actors in the capital, the ulema and the janissaries. From the late sixteenth century onwards (and especially after

11 Felek 2012; Murad III – Felek 2014. Cf. Hagen 2013, 455, who maintains (contrary to what I claim here) that "such claims, however covert, speak to a tendency towards extreme sacralisation of the persona of the sultan, by means of which Ottoman rule acquired universal and thus apocalyptic significance. We may assume that in the late sixteenth century Ottoman legitimacy no longer directly rested on justice in government and victory in war; rather, both had become secondary results of the sultan's sacred status granted by divine favor alone and therefore not in need of worldly justification". I suggest that such claims on the part of the sultans and their court notwithstanding, there was no such sacralisation in the public discourse by the last quarter of the sixteenth century.

12 Murphey 2005.

13 Rüstem 2016. It is worth quoting Ahmed's description in the introductory section: "that king of kings of the world, that heroic vanquisher of mortals, that protector of Muslims and monotheists and slayer of pagans and heretics, that possessor of wise viziers and benefactor of army-holding commanders, that patron of scholars and luminaries and succor of the righteous and the needy, that favorer of the most blessed lords of mankind [the descendants of the Prophet], the Shadow of God and the caliph of the world and of the age, by which I mean Sultan Ahmed Khan, son of Sultan Mehmed Khan, may God Almighty eternize his rule and perpetuate his sultanate till the revolutions [of the ages] cease and time ends, if God the All-Merciful thus wills" (ibid., 335).

14 Tezcan 2010a, 128–129. On the implications of the title "shadow of God" in Ali's less glorifying view, see Fleischer 1986a, 280–283.

Osman's execution), it was almost impossible to read such passages as those composed by Kemalpaşazade on the occasion of Mehmed II's death:[15]

> The permanent palace of the sultan of the world was devastated and in ruins, the pillars of the building were upside-down and, as a result, the heart of the people of Islam, nay, the very spine of all mankind had collapsed … The world was dressed in black and was mourning; the sky took off the sun's turban from its head and dropped it to the earth; taking off its luminous garments, it covered its shoulders with the fine cloth of obscurity.

True, the commitment to the dynasty created by Osman remained a fundamental feature of Ottoman self-image; even prophetical texts (as we saw in the case of *Papasnâme*) predicted no dynastic change until the End Times. The conception of Islamic history as a series of dynasties (as seen, for example, in Ali's *Füsûl-i hall ü akd*) and the implication that a fall of a dynasty would mean the disruption of the state, must have played a crucial role in this unique longevity of the royal family line.[16] In sharp contrast, individual rulers might be criticized and, by the early seventeenth century, eventually deposed or even executed. Charismatic rule may have remained a trope of political ideology, but it did not feature either in political theory or in practice.

2 The Landmarks of Declinist Literature

The heyday of these works was the beginning of Murad IV's reign, but the first specimen may well be the anonymous *Kitâb-i müstetâb* ("Approved [or, Agreeable] book"), which was composed around 1620 during the reign of Osman II (1617–22), to whom it must have been presented.[17] The anonymous author gives no information whatsoever about his life. From two passages of the work it seems that he was a *devşirme* recruit and that he was raised and educated in the palace; he shows detailed knowledge of the *kul* career system, and seems to be acquainted with Anatolia (e.g. Sivas) more than with Rumili. The author notes, as his sources, personal experience and conversations with

15 Quoted in Vatin – Veinstein 2003, 88.

16 In the few cases when other ruling families were envisaged (almost all dated after Osman II's execution), see Emecen 2001a.

17 The work was first published by Yücel 1988, 1–40 (transcription follows) and then by Akgündüz 1990–1996, 9:600–645 (facs. follows). Cf. Gökbilgin 1991, 206–209; Fodor 1986, 230–231; Yılmaz 2003a, 309–310; İnan 2009, 117–118.

"ulema and wise people" as well as "history books" (on the "circle of equity") and Yazıcıoğlu's *Muhammediye*, while (unlike Mustafa Ali) he writes favorably of Lütfi Pasha.

In the preface, the author states that he will enumerate the issues that have brought annoyance to the people and disturbed the world order before proposing ways of restoring the situation. The work is divided into twelve chapters, explicitly said to match the number of the months of the year and the signs of the zodiac, and in the first chapter he sets out to expound his general idea on the beginnings and characteristics of decline: until the beginnings of Murad III's reign, the viziers and officials administered justice and respected the Sharia and the *kanun* of the Ottoman dynasty. During Murad III's reign, however, the administrators started to neglect justice and acted contrary to the old laws (*kanun-ı kadim*); this is why villages and cultivated lands became deserted, the peasants dispersed, the expenses of the treasury surpassed its income, and strangers (*ecnebi*) entered the janissary corps. Moreover, viziers and officials turned on each other, started to occupy themselves only with personal affairs, factionalism, and bribery, and more generally abandoned the old laws (Y1–2, A601). After these introductory remarks, the author sets out to describe in detail these departures from the old customs and how to mend them.

To show the logic underlying the treatise, let us examine its "appendix", which poses seven questions the sultan has to ask of the viziers, the ulema, and the sipahi and janissary officials. These questions are: (1) How did the military victories of old turn into defeats and retreat, and is there any relation with the fact that sultans no longer lead campaigns in person? (2) Why can the army not repeat the victories of old, even though the numbers of janissaries and sipahis have increased so much? (3) This increase notwithstanding, in times of campaign very few soldiers appear in battle, since many of them are occupied with trade or other professions; what military use can be expected of such people? (4) In the old days, all military officials participated in the campaigns along with their retinue, which is not the case now; why have the old rules been neglected? (5) How is it that strangers, such as the sons of Turkish, Kurdish, Roma, and Iranian *reaya*, have entered the *kul* class? (6) Is it right that only janissaries get a full salary, while sipahis take false money and other *kul*s have fallen into the hands of Jewish and other infidel tax-farmers? (7) What happened to the sultanly fiefs (*havass-ı hümayun*), which used to yield considerable income, as now their peasants are scattered and their incomes lessened due to the oppression of the appointed agents (*voyvoda*)? (Y36–40, A641–45).[18]

18 Interestingly, in a late manuscript (copied in 1652/3) that omits this appendix, the copyist added *hadith*s and other material (A636–41); among them, notes on how Selim II used

Kitâb-ı müstetâb can be seen as the link between Ottoman *adab* literature, initiated by Lütfi Pasha and perfected by Mustafa Ali, and the canonization of the "Golden Age" vs. "decline" paradigm that was to follow. The emphasis placed on institutional functions rather than individual virtues and vices, a new stress on social compartmentalization, the sharp polarization between Süleyman's glorious reign and the deplorable past, and the localization of the causes of decline (disorder in the timar system, the intrusion of strangers into the janissary ranks and the swollen numbers and costs of the latter, and the destructive results of bribery at all levels) were all to dominate Ottoman political literature for decades to come.

2.1 *Murad IV's Counselors: Koçi Bey and His Circle*

The most famous expounder of the "Golden Age" trend is of course Koçi Bey. At the same time, he was also one of the most famous Ottoman political theorists, since he was translated into European languages very early and thus was much appreciated by early Turkish scholars.[19] In sharp contrast to his fame, very little is known about his life and career: of Albanian origin, he was recruited as a *devşirme* and served in the palace under Ahmed I and subsequent sultans, before he retired to his native city of Gorča (Görice) in the late 1640s. He seems to have been a close advisor to Murad IV and to his successor, Ibrahim I, for each of whom he wrote one of his two treatises.[20] Koçi Bey's first *Risâle* ("Treatise")

---

to perform imperial councils in the open in order for people to see that the sultan was not neglecting their affairs (A639), as well as a note on the classification of social groups (A640) which seems to come from Hasan Akhisari and perhaps resonates an ulema influence on the copyist. According to the note, God divided humanity into five groups, namely (a) kings, who practise justice and equity, (b) the ulema, who explain the Holy Law, (c) the military (*ehl-i silah*), who guard the state (*memleket*), (d) the *reaya*, by whom the treasury is filled, (e) the artisans (*ehl-i sanayi'*), by whose work all the world benefits. Eventually this peculiarity must be traced to Mahmud al-Zamakhsharî's *Rebî' al-abrâr*, Akhisari's main source, as the same classification is described by Hasanbeyzade who also translates Zamakhshari (see above, chapter 4 and cf. Sariyannis 2013, 102).

19 See Koçi Bey – Çakmakcıoğlu 2008, 18 for the various editions and translations. The text was mainly known in the West through Pétis de la Croix's French (1725) and W. F. A. Behrnauer's German (Koçi Bey – Behrnauer 1861) translations. Cf. Rosenthal 1958, 226–227; Black 2011, 264–265. On Koçi Bey's appreciation by nineteenth-century Orientalists and early scholars of the Turkish republic, suffice it to mention his being named "Turkish Montesquieu" in Hammer 1963, 3:489 (cf. Koçi Bey – Aksüt 1939, 11; repeated in Koçi Bey – Çakmakcıoğlu 2008, 9). Hammer even says that Koçi Bey deserves this title just as Ibn Khaldun had been awarded the title of "the Arab Montesquieu". On the use of the treatise in the mid-nineteenth century cf. Abou-El-Haj 2005, 79–80.

20 The most comprehensive biography is that by M. Çağatay Uluçay in *İslam Ansiklopedisi*, s.v. "Koçi Bey", supplemented by that of Ömer Faruk Akün in *Diyanet Vakfı İslam Ansiklopedisi*. Rifaat Abou-El-Haj has presented a detailed outline of Koçi Bey's first

was completed around 1630–31, probably in two versions.[21] As for his second treatise, which shall be examined below, it is a sort of short introduction to the practicalities of palace and government, written for Ibrahim I just after his enthronement.

The similarities of Koçi Bey's views with those of the anonymous *Kitab-ı müstetâb* are obvious; he takes up all the same issues tackled by the anonymous author and expands them, placing distinctive emphasis on the role of the grand vizier and on the need for long-term appointments in every rank and career line. As a matter of fact, it is highly probable that Koçi Bey's treatise was merely a compilation of several distinct memoranda submitted to Murad IV, either by himself or by a circle of middle-ranking clerks from the scribal bureaucracy. In 1979, Rhoads Murphey published ten such *telhis* ("Memoranda") from a copybook (*mecmua*) found in the Veliyuddin library, which bear numerous textual similarities to this treatise. Of the ten of them, three form part of Koçi Bey's treatise. According to Murphey, the form and style of the *telhis*, which in all probability were submitted to Murad IV in 1632, i.e. at the beginning of the reorganization efforts of the young sultan, show that, in all probability, they can be attributed to Koçi Bey. However, Douglas Howard questioned this authorship as "no more than speculative", and argued that the author of the *telhis* shows a more realistic attitude against timar-holders, accepting the possibility of granting fiefs to valiant peasants or officers at retirement.[22] At any rate, these texts are to be counted as part of a prolific production of memoranda by middle-ranking clerks, some of which were indeed read by the sultan, and which were to become *verbatim* imperial orders or otherwise contributed to Murad's actual policy. Apart from the three memoranda included in the final version of Koçi Bey's treatise, i.e. those tracing the beginnings of the decline to the reign of Süleyman, there are seven *telhis* that touch on various issues of the imperial administration, echoing and echoed by previous and subsequent texts of this genre.

---

treatise, re-organizing its features in order to show its internal logic, i.e. the ideal picture of the "Golden Era" versus the conditions prevailing in the author's time (Abou-El-Haj 2005, 101–111). On Koçi Bey's work see also Gökbilgin 1991, 209–211; Lewis 1962, 74–78; Murphey 1981; Murphey 2009a; Fodor 1986, 231–233; Yılmaz 2003a, 310–311; İnan 2009, 118–119.

21 Almost twenty MSS are known, some containing both treatises; three chapters were added to almost half of them, showing that the author wrote two versions: see Murphey 1981, 1096–97, and fn. 4.

22 Murphey 1981; Howard 1988, 65–68; İnan 2009, 119. The full text from the MS Istanbul, Bayezid Devlet Ktp., Veliyyuddin 3205 was published in Murphey 2009a.

These anonymous and short memoranda apart, another important product of the same period is the *Kânûnnâme-i sultânî* ("Book of sultanly laws and regulations") by Aziz Efendi; the very use of this title indicates the growing importance of the notion of *kanun* as a vehicle for political advice in what we call "declinist" literature. Aziz Efendi must have originated from the same milieu as Koçi Bey and the anonymous authors of the Veliyuddin memoranda: he describes himself as an "aged, distinguished, and loyal veteran in the sultan's service" who "is no longer capable of useful service" (M24). Various clues in his work imply that he had been a scribe in the chancellery, possibly of the Imperial Council. He had recourse to original registers and also the experience of making draft versions and outlines of imperial orders, which he incorporated into his treatise. He also refers to an older report, which he had submitted to the sultan "on the subject of the grand vizierate and other matters" (M4). It is of some importance to note that the scribal bureaucracy also formed Aziz Efendi's audience, if we can judge from the only existing copy, which was "bound into a volume intended as a learning manual for professional scribes".[23] According to the *termini ante et post quem*, the composition of the treatise can be placed with great accuracy between September 1632 and June 1633, i.e. just before Murad IV embarked on his great redressment project and in the wake of his successful suppressing of the sipahi rebellion. Aziz Efendi's treatise is made up of four chapters, of which the third is highly original as it deals with the Kurdish chiefs of the east, in the wake of Murad's Persian campaign and in view of the one to come (M12–18; cf. M:vii–viii and 52 n.56).[24]

2.2 *Decline and Redress*

The introduction of *Kitâb-ı müstetâb*, which declared that, from Murad III's reign onwards, the "old law" was abandoned and corruption dominated, was not openly repeated in the other works that followed this trend; however, this idea does form their underlying foundation. In his first chapter, Koçi Bey claims that sultans had had wise and experienced counselors (*nüdema ve*

23 Aziz Efendi – Murphey 1985, vii. The volume (Berlin, Preussischer Kulturbesitz Ms. or. quart. 1209) also includes geographical and historical notices, poetry, a collection of *fetvas* and regulations, a catalogue of administrative divisions, a list of taxes, instructions for official correspondence, and so forth. See Flemming 1968, 347.

24 Interestingly, part of his advice in this chapter concerns usury, as thoughtless policies in the late sixteenth century gave way to provincial governors distracting huge sums from them and alienating the Kurdish population from the Ottoman state. Aziz Efendi urges the sultan to appoint a respected ulema to solve the dispute between the Kurdish chiefs and the usurers; he should issue documents prohibiting interest and considering interest already collected by the money-lenders to be part-payment of the original sum.

mukarrebân) up to the beginnings of Murad III's sultanate. As long as Sokollu Mehmed Pasha was grand vizier (praise of Sokollu is another *topos* shared with *Kitâb-ı müstetâb*), eunuchs and other companions of the sultan did not interfere in state affairs and order reigned in the world (the same assertion is made for the grand viziers, who were undisturbed until Murad III's enthronement: A30; Ç41). Aziz Efendi, for his part, also puts the beginning of various detrimental practices (such as excessive number of viziers; M4–6) in Murad III's reign. In other parts of Koçi Bey's work, the beginning of the decline is placed later (for instance, timars were first given to strangers in 1584, at the same time that intruders entered the janissary ranks; dismissals of *şeyhülislam*s began in 1594); however, and in contrast to other authors (except perhaps Ali), he admits that signs of "decline" were apparent as early as the end of Süleyman's reign. In a couple of chapters (A61–64; Ç79–82) exactly composed to recapitulate his view of the Süleymanic era as the "Golden Age" of the state,[25] he in fact revises this assumption. After stating that, during Süleyman's reign, the empire had reached its fullest expansion and might and that the treasury was fuller than ever before, he observes that the roots of its decline ("the corruption of the world") also first appeared at this time (an idea first seen in Ali's *Künhü'l-ahbâr*).[26] This explains why, the title of the chapter notwithstanding ("On the perfection of the late Sultan Süleyman's era"), its content is a eulogy not of Süleyman but of his father, Selim I. Among other things, Selim paid attention to meritocracy and justice, and his respect for the Sharia was absolute: everybody was subject to the old Ottoman laws and abstained from any innovations (*bid'at*). Süleyman, in contrast, made various changes (e.g. he stopped attending imperial councils in person, he appointed his private servant İbrahim Pasha as grand vizier, etc.) that brought about decline and corruption.

There are three main fields in which these authors all agree that departures from the "old law" produced significant problems: the intrusion of strangers into the janissary ranks and the ensuing increase in their numbers; the disruption of the timariot system; and the functioning of the government at the highest level. As a general remark, it may be said that, whereas all three of these departures were described and criticized in earlier treatises as well, the level of detail as regards concrete information is, here, much fuller. The issue of the janissaries, however, is relatively new in Ottoman tracts: as has been seen, Ali

25 These final chapters, i.e. on the perfection and decline of the Süleymanic era and the subsequent digression on the "moral requirements" of a ruler (Koçi Bey – Aksüt 61–67) are missing in almost half the manuscripts of the treatise, showing that Koçi Bey wrote two versions (Murphey 1981, 1097).

26 See Fleischer 1986a, 258–259.

and Akhisari did speak of their oppressive practices (the former, particularly, more against the *kul*s in government than in the army), but this argument had never before had the central position it acquired in early seventeenth-century texts. In fact, one may speak of a bipolar conflict that characterizes these texts: on the one hand, we have the sipahis, virtuous and true soldiers who suffer from the abandonment of the old practices; on the other, the janissaries, full of intruders, who, by their number and oppressive behavior, have become a disrupting factor in Ottoman society and the military.[27]

Kitâb-ı müstetâb is probably the first treatise containing this kind of anti-janissary sentiment, inaugurating various *topoi* that were to be repeated for decades to come. The old custom, says the anonymous author, was that whenever the army gained a victory or conquered a castle, valiant soldiers were granted promotion or a fief, while those not participating were removed from their posts (Y2–4, A602–3). All changes in salaries and fiefs were reported to the sultan, who could either approve or reject them. Similarly, but in a more organized manner, Koçi Bey first describes how the system had functioned in the past, noting that janissaries were collected through *devşirme* alone, from among Albanians, Bosnians, Greeks, Bulgarians, and Armenians, and that they only lived in the Istanbul – Edirne – Bursa triangle. They used to be bachelors (marriage being permitted only following retirement) and lived in barracks. Their sons would start as *acem oğlanları* (janissary apprentices), while their officers served for at least seven or eight years (A27–29, Ç37–40).

Beginning with the Iranian campaign of Murad III, however, these rules started to be abandoned: the commanders of the army took liberties by granting promotions and fiefs at will, and as a result of bribery, we read in *Kitâb-ı müstetâb*, even as soon as a campaign starts. Thus, Turks, Kurds, Roma, and Iranians of *reaya* origin infiltrated the army (at another point, the author claims that nine out of ten *kul* recruits are "city boys"[28] from Istanbul, being Turks, Armenians, or Roma: Y25–27, A625–26). Koçi Bey locates the beginning of this entry of strangers into the corps to the early 1580s,[29] when some people who had kept the crowds at Mehmed III's circumcision festival under control were accepted into the ranks of the janissaries as *ağa çırakları*. Other innovations (*sipahi oğulları, becayiş*) further increased the number of such strangers; Aziz Efendi describes these tricks, recruiting apprentices (*ağa çırağı*) or

27 On this bipolar contrast see Abou Hadj 1988.

28 On this expression, which in this period signified unattached urban strata before taking a more moral meaning toward the end of the seventeenth century, see Sariyannis 2005, 4–8.

29 On this dating, which is written 909/1503 in the MS, see Koçi Bey – Çakmakcıoğlu 2008, 58, fn. 1. The reader may remember that Mustafa Ali (Ali – Demir 2006, 142) was also of the same view, giving the date 1582.

sipahis' sons (*ferzend-i sipahi*), as well as concealing the death of a soldier and selling his pay-ticket to "a shepherd, an agriculturist, or even a robber" (*becayeş*), in even greater detail (M6–8). As a result, a multitude of the ignorant and good-for-nothing are now paid from the treasury, including (in Koçi Bey's own words)

> city boys of unknown origin, Turks, Roma, Persians, Kurds, strangers, Laz, Yörüks, camel drivers, porters, robbers, and pickpockets.

Koçi Bey notes that were this number of soldiers needed by sultans in the past, they would recruit them in times of campaign and dismiss them afterwards ("the tailor, the grocer, the barber, each back to their job") instead of giving them timars and steady pay. And yet this would not be an army proper: an army consists of soldiers and the sons of soldiers, not laborers and petty artisans (*bakkal çakkal ile iş bitmez*). The author of *Kitâb-ı müstetâb* agrees that soldiers in the past were few in number but large in quality (*az idi lakin öz idi*; the expression dates at least from Lütfi Pasha), having spent their whole career on campaign and in battle. Nowadays, he says, a peasant (*reaya*) can sell a pair of oxen and become a sipahi or a janissary; strangers have become more numerous than the genuine *kul*s; some of them do not even know Istanbul, let alone the whereabouts of the sultan's court (Y5–9, A605–8). Furthermore, retired but salaried members have increased, but few among them are actually old or invalid; the rest have paid bribes in order to enter the payrolls as retired or rural watchmen (Y9–13, A608–12).

The results, he says, are detrimental for both the peasants and the treasury. All authors enumerate in detail the numbers of the janissaries (and of the salaried cavalry) and their salaries, showing the swelling of their ranks since the beginning of Murad III's reign (almost three times the numbers of 1574, according to Koçi Bey). Expenses increased abruptly and that is why the janissaries came to be paid in bad coinage, writes the author of *Kitâb-ı müstetâb*; Celalis and other rebels appeared, peasants' lives deteriorated, and the janissaries started to mutiny. Aziz Efendi describes two results: on the one hand, the army was swollen with useless a rabble that fled their provinces and thus threw their own tax-burden onto the rest of the peasantry; on the other, the constant need for revenue to cover increased expenditure led to increased oppression and thereby increased ruin of the land (M6–8).

Moving now to the other side of the equation, the timariots, our authors agree that alterations of the same kind also afflicted the timar system (and Aziz Efendi begins his treatise by praising Murad IV for having restored the proper status of the timar lands that had been held "captive and languishing ...

for the past sixty years": M3). *Kitâb-ı müstetâb* notes that fiefs are now granted by viziers and magnates (*ekâbir*); even a scribe can ascribe fiefs to his servants, children, and slaves, and thus collect the income, while the real timariot army becomes smaller and poorer—in fact, says the author, low-ranking and low-paid sipahis now constitute only a small part of the Ottoman army, whereas the rest consists of Turkish, Roma, and ex-Celali followers of the *sancabeyi*s, along with the janissaries who form its bulk (Y15–17, A614–16). Koçi Bey also considers the timariot sipahis the fundamental factor in the past sultans' victories (A24–26; Ç32–36): at that time, he says, there were no strangers among them, no peasants or "city boys"; they all were soldiers (sipahis or slaves, *kul*) or the sons of soldiers, with the latters' ancestry having to be proved by between two and ten witnesses. Moreover, they were not promoted in rank and fief unless their service on campaign was outstanding; they had to stay in their provinces and remain ready for battle always. This system worked because neither would Istanbul grant a timar without a proposal from the provincial governor, nor would a governor give timars to people who were not entitled to them. To illustrate his point, Koçi Bey gives various examples and quotes the numbers of timars and timariots in each province, adding that sipahis would never dig trenches or take care of firearms since these were jobs for the infantry (*piyadegân*). As he remarks elsewhere, in the past every class knew its limits and did not depart from them (*her zümrenin hadd-ı muayyeni olup*), unlike in the present.

Having described the rules of the military as in times of glory, Koçi Bey sets out to explain the causes and features of the decline (A30ff.; Ç41ff. and A38ff.; Ç51ff.). Before Murad III's ascent to the throne (1574), he claims, grand viziers were undisturbed from any interference whatsoever and only had to deal with the sultan himself. But afterwards, the sultan's companions started to gain official posts and intervene in state affairs, causing the fall of virtuous viziers. More particularly, it was in 1584 that Özdemiroğlu Osman Pasha granted timars to a number of strangers who had fought valiantly on the Iranian front, and thus opened the way to all kinds of peasants and "city boys" gaining timars without being worthy of them. Thus gaining power, these companions (*iç halkı*) started to take timars and other revenues for themselves and then to distribute posts in the provincial administration to unworthy people who bribed them. From provincial governors to the viziers' officers, from scribes to mutes and dwarves, everybody started to grant timars to their servants and even to their slaves, sometimes many to one person. This situation is also described in some of the Veliyuddin *telhis*: the fourth memorandum complains of the granting of state land to palace officials and favorites as either private freehold (*mülk*) or *vakf*s, arguing that such properties would serve the state much better if they were allotted to sipahis as timars (this distrust of *vakf* endowment, which brings to mind similar remarks by Mustafa Ali, is also to be found in Koçi Bey's and Aziz Efendi's treatises)[30]; other memoranda of the same group complain again about the granting of timars to servants and slaves (M140: *bölük halkı hidmetkârlarına ve azadsız köleleri*).

This led to the destruction of the sipahi class and their oppression by salaried slaves (*ulufeli kul*); the sipahis came to be dependent on the *vükelâ*, i.e. the proxies of the local governors. But, Koçi Bey notes,

> whoever has a fief from the emperor has no place in the household of a slave *vekil*; slaves befit to slaves (*hünkâr dirliğine mütesarrıf olanlar vükelâ kapısında neyler? Kul kul gerektir*) (A32, Ç44).

This way, concludes Koçi Bey, the army was led astray: timariots started to wear luxury clothes instead of armor, and now only a very small percentage of the timariots called up in times of campaign are ready for battle: real sipahis became workers (*ırgad işin işleyüp*), and this is no way to win any war.

In line with older administrative language, the ruin of the timariot system is closely connected to the fate of the peasants. As explained by Koçi Bey, as the salaried slave-army increased, the same happened with the expenses of the treasury, and so the tax burden of the peasants increased several times. This became even more acute after the janissary cavalry took over tax collection, which only resulted in more oppression. Contrary to the law, imperial fiefs (*havass-ı hümayun*) were given as private property, *vakf*s, or honorable fiefs (*paşmaklık*). Koçi Bey states that no other date or place has ever seen such a terrible oppression as that imposed on the *reaya* in his days; and it is the sultan who will be judged responsible, not his representatives. The woes of the oppressed can destroy dynasties, because "world can be maintained with blasphemy, but not with tyranny" (*küfr ile dünya durur, zülmile durmaz*),[31] Koçi Bey concludes grimly (A48; Ç63). And indeed, as, from 1582 onwards, imperial

30 Koçi Bey writes that not all *vakf* endowments comply with the Holy Law; a proper *vakf* must be made for charitable reasons and from land acquired due to conquests or other services to the state, whereas now magnates take villages and lands as a gift just because they are close to the sultan, and then proceed to name these lands *vakf* in order to ensure a steady income for their children. Income from these properties, however, should belong to the warriors of the faith (A55–56; Ç71–73). As for Aziz Efendi, he stresses that villages that have been given to useless people who declared them as *vakıf*s, in opposition to the law, should be redistributed as timars to the army (M6).

31 This expression is very often used in Ottoman literature and comes from Nizam al-Mulk's *Siyasatname*: Hagen 2005, 71.

posts were granted on the basis of bribes rather than merit, and while timars started to be given to others than their natural holders, i.e. the fighting sipahis, the Ottomans started to experience serious losses on all fronts. The "Circle of Justice" has been totally disrupted, states Koçi Bey, as peasants, the treasury, and the army all are in a desperate position.

Both *Kitâb-ı müstetâb* and Koçi Bey attribute the rise of the Celalis to the disruption of timar relations: Koçi Bey remarks that all the servants of grand viziers and other high state officials used to be their own bought slaves, not salaried peasants or tradesmen. There are two reasons why the latter case is harmful: first, such servants would stop paying their taxes and thus reduce the income of the treasury and of the timariots; second, that a peasant who tastes riding horses and carrying weapons gets used to such habits and can no longer return to agriculture. Koçi Bey notes that most of the Celali rebels belonged to that sort. As for the author of *Kitâb-ı müstetâb*, after citing a story about Süleyman and Lütfi Pasha illustrating the point that what matters most is not the amount of money in the public treasury but the well-being of the subjects (Y17–23, A616–22), he observes that poor peasants end up praising brigands and Celalis, and the Celali rebellions would not have occurred were it not for the judges' oppressive behavior (Y23–25, A622–25). He also adds a philosophical digression: kingship (*saltanat*) needs three things in order to be perpetuated, namely peasants, a treasury, and an army. The treasury is fed by the peasants, the army is maintained by the treasury, and thus can defend the peasants against the enemy. These three things are secured through three means: (a) justice, (b) the granting of posts and fiefs according to the old laws (*kanun-ı kadim*), and (c) that the sultan does not consult servants, who are irrelevant for the government (*hükûmetde olmayan hademe*). This passage, we must note, is typical of the genre: from a general, commonplace version of the traditional circle of justice, the author jumps into concrete advice on particular Ottoman institutions. On the other hand, we should also remark that here we have a very rare example of abstract political theory in a treatise of this kind. Furthermore, this is also an occasion on which justice is explicitly identified with the "old laws", which effectively take up a position in the traditional circle.

If we are to seek the underlying assumptions behind these assessments, we will find the invisible yet heavy inheritance of moral philosophy as expressed by Tursun Beg or Kınalızade. The circle of justice, meaning that the sultanly power had absolute need of the peasants' welfare, the four-fold division of society, and the need for a balance between the classes, had remained an integral part of Ottoman political thought, even if they were not always articulated in such terms. It was only in Kâtib Çelebi's time, the mid-seventeenth century, that the balance among the classes would re-emerge, in order to justify the suggestion of restraining the power of the army; Kınalızade's similar theorizing was not used by Koçi Bey or the anonymous author of *Kitâb-ı müstetâb*. Yet we can clearly see this concept behind the early seventeenth-century emphasis on social compartmentalization; the aversion to social mobility, exhibited so eloquently in Koçi Bey's lament about ex-peasant intruders in the janissary army or of the sipahis having to take up agriculture, is founded on the concept of borderlines (*hadd*) defining every person's position and socio-political status. In the same way, just as did *Kitâbu mesâlih* earlier, the first of the Veliyuddin memoranda urges the sultan to impose clothing restrictions with a view to prohibiting ostentation (M131: *ve ziyneti ref' edüb herkese mikdarına ve meratibine göre bir hadd ta'yyin olunub*).

Coming now to the third field of the distortions of the "old law", the high echelons of government, at first glance it is difficult to see what differentiates these early seventeenth-century authors from their *adab* predecessors. The emphasis on wise and experienced viziers, however, here has certain features that are typical of the era. First of all, following a trend seen earlier, the main responsibility lies with the vizier, not the sultan. This is stated more explicitly in *Kitâb-ı müstetâb*, where we read that the only person responsible for the affairs of the state (*saltanata müte'allik umuru*) must be the grand vizier, and no-one else. Grand viziers used to be feared by everyone; now they themselves fear everyone who has access to or influence over the sultan (Y17–23, A616–22). The sultan is like "a glorious bird of the spirit of the world", whose body is the wise ulema; its right wing is the grand vizier, its left one the *kapu ağası* (chief eunuch) of the sultan's harem. Now, after the glorious years that saw members of the ulema such as Ebussu'ud, viziers such as Sokollu Mehmed Pasha, and *kapu ağaları* such as Mahmud Ağa, the situation is lamentable. The *kapu ağası* should be the left-hand vizier to the sultan and second only to the grand vizier; sultans are to consult with *kapu ağaları* on various serious matters. After the aforementioned Mahmud Ağa, however, things changed; instead of being a product of the *deşirme* system, educated and trained in the palace, *kapu ağaları* are now urban dwellers who, one way or another, find their way into the *kul* ranks. Now, if it was appropriate to employ such people in the palace, the glorious rulers of the past would not have ordained the *devşirme* system (Y25–27, A625–26). This multi-faceted view of power fits well with the names of people cited: from Sokollu to Ebussu'ud, they were all independent personalities who wrought actual power, counterbalancing the sultan's personal will.[32] The

32 The same applies for Mahmud Ağa: it appears that his successor, Gazanfer Ağa, was the first in a line of *kapı ağaları* who were the personal choices of the sultan to curb the extra-courtier power of the viziers: Tezcan 2010a, 101.

old law, the anonymous author continues, demands that the sultan appoint a grand vizier as "an agent of governing power" (*vekil-i saltanat*): the latter was to ensure justice and equity, punish oppression, and ensure that every subject enjoys peace and well-being. "The fish stinks from the head", they say; the sultan's not choosing a wise and honest vizier is the root of all present-day problems (Y31–35, A630–41). A short note here: *Kitâb-ı müstetâb* was presented to Osman II, but the urge to delegate power shows that its author did not advocate the absolutist plans of his sultan. Furthermore, his advice on military campaigns does not correspond to Osman's practices (the Khotin campaign) or plans (the scheduled Hajj);[33] he cautions against new campaigns (Y9–13, A608–12) and does not deem it necessary for the sultan to participate personally.[34] Even more important, he stresses that the highest officials and the standing army of the capital should stay with the sultan, whether he leads the campaign or stays at home (Y17, A616).

As for Koçi Bey, at a first glance he appears to favor a more absolutist point of view,[35] as he uses Süleyman's example to argue that it would be better if sultans were present in the imperial councils and conducted affairs of state in person. This, however, is only an introductory remark before he argues that grand viziers should be kept in their post for a long period and rule independently in their entire jurisdiction, free especially from any interference by the sultan's boon companions (A20–21, Ç27–28). The same applies to other officials, from provincial governors to government scribes, who should be kept in their posts for a long time and not be dismissed unless they are guilty of bribery or other crimes (cf. A59–60; Ç77–78; similar advice is found in the second and third of the Veliyuddin memoranda). In a similar vein, just as *Kitâb-ı müstetâb* had used Ebussu'ud's example, Koçi Bey also stresses that *şeyhülislam*s and other high-ranking ulema should have a secured, long tenure in their posts (A35, Ç48). The emphasis on the need for the vizier be a product of a long palace career instead of being chosen according the sultan's whim from among his friends and companions also demands an enhanced and independent position for the grand vizier (*Kitâb-ı müstetâb*: Y9–13, A608–12; Koçi Bey: A63, Ç81). The advice that the palace must be cleansed of "low, undesirable types and city boys" and

33 See Tezcan 2010a, 131–152.

34 The author reverts to this issue at the end of the essay as well, asking whether the failure of campaigns is due to the absence of the sultan or to other reasons pertaining to the state of the army (Y36, A641). On the topos of the sultan's personal participation in campaigns see Karateke 2012.

35 Abou-El-Haj claims that Koçi Bey's view of the sultan is that "he possesses charisma ... and runs public affairs from the center and in person without delegating authority to anyone" (Abou-El-Haj 2005, 29).

manned with Albanians, Bosnians, and others of slave origin (*kul cinsi*), as the ancient law ordains (in Aziz Efendi's words: M6), is also a common trope in Koçi Bey (A32, Ç44).

The views described above seem to point to a plea for an effective delegation of power to the grand vizier and to a more-or-less permanent government apparatus. Before moving on to conclusions, however, we must note that our authors often advocate what looks like the centralization of power. According to the author of *Kitâb-ı müstetâb*, it is not lawful (*kanun değüldür*) for viziers (or other high officials) to grant promotions in salary or fiefs without first submitting them to the sultan because this leads to undeserved appointments, unrest among the janissaries, and problems in the treasury (Y4–5, A603–4). Koçi Bey, for his part, often speaks against grand viziers who became too strong and turned their properties into *vakf*s, alienating them permanently from state control (e.g. A63, Ç81). As for the Veliyuddin memoranda, they are full of advice on controlling the posts of the viziers: the first (M129–31) stresses that the number of viziers should not exceed four and that the sultan should attend the council in person. This emphasis on the number of viziers is also an obsession of sorts for Aziz Efendi, who begins his treatise proper with a chapter on "the ancient law" on viziers. In olden days, he states, the sultan kept four viziers in office, with their respective stipend fiefs, their stewards who administered these fiefs, and their retinues. However, since the time of Murad III the number of the viziers has surpassed this limit; accordingly, imperial lands were distributed to them and these were farmed out by the viziers to their own household (*kapu kulları*). While the present sultan, i.e. Murad IV, reassigned the lands and suppressed the rebels and evildoers, instead of reducing the number of viziers, he added another three, ignoring the fact that "excess of ministers is the cause of the poverty of the treasury". Aziz Efendi's advice is that the number of viziers be reduced again to four, that the grand vizier be independent in his office, and that *defterdar*s lose the rank of a vizier (M4–6). Still, to return to the question of absolutism, one may claim that too many viziers leads to weak viziers, and therefore they are easier to control from the sultan's persepctive; stabilizing their number to four would contribute to a sort of permanent governing team, arguably with more independence from the sultan's personal power.

Finally, another common feature of all these works is the emphasis they place on bribery. For the author of *Kitâb-ı müstetâb*, it is the root of all problems in the system. It has infiltrated the system so much that bribes are given openly and people who do not use them are considered light-minded. Judges, in particular, become heavily indebted while waiting for their appointment, and then have to pay it back by illegally extorting money from the provinces to which they are appointed (Y23–25, A622–25). Furthermore, according to a story he relates, one of the things that can destroy a powerful state is that the gates of bribery open and posts start to be bought and sold (Y30, A630). Koçi Bey also considers bribery the root of all evil and corruption and argues that the first step toward its abolition is the independence of the grand vizier. Moreover, the allotment of positions in the ulema and bureaucracy must be free from bribery; the number of all these positions should be defined and those that surpass it should be given timars and serve as sipahis. If all positions and fiefs were given with honesty and uprightness, nobody would give or take bribes (A59–60; Ç77–78).

Bribery, it should be noted, had been a common feature of works complaining about societal problems ever since the beginnings of the Ottoman state. However, whereas older references placed more emphasis on the sinful use of bribes by judges and poor peasants, having to bribe officials in order to save their property, in these early seventeenth-century texts (following a trend seen earlier in Mustafa Ali and Selaniki) almost every reference to bribery concerns the buying and selling of posts, and especially of high-ranking ones. As in the case of Ali's grievances about a lack of meritocracy, here again there is probably a reaction against newcomers in the bureaucracy and administration: by this time, pasha households had begun to push their own men into provincial administration, as shown by Metin Kunt, and the ongoing monetization of the economy might have replaced old patterns of patronage (*intisab*) with a system of money-lending ties not dissimilar to tax-farming.[36] It has been remarked that similar procedures can also be seen in early-modern Europe and that, in any case, they were part and parcel of state formation rather than manifestations of decline.[37] It must be noted that, unlike Ali, who lamented the dominant position of *kul*s in administration and advocated a more medrese-oriented career path, these authors defend the palace-trained *kul* administration against the practice of recruiting newcomers from the emerging urban strata.

2.3 *The Sultan and His Government*

To sum up, it is clear that all these texts belong to a common trend, one quite distinct from but often using ideas that originated in earlier, late sixteenth-century "mirrors for princes". The general idea of a "Golden Age" vs. decline apart, they share a common set of ideas for the reorganization of the state apparatus along the lines that once led it to might and glory. We read that the viziers

36 On the development of the Ottoman administration at the turn of the seventeenth century see Kunt 1983; Kunt 2012; Faroqhi 1994, 570–572.

37 Abou-El-Haj 2005, 8–9 and 129–131 (n. 13).

should not be more than four in the first *telhis* and in Aziz Efendi (the same idea was implied in the anonymous *Hirzü'l-mülûk*, where the viziers are likened to the first four caliphs), and that the *defterdar* should not be one of them in Aziz Efendi and in the second *telhis*; that the coinage should be standardized in the earlier *Kitâbu mesâlih* and in the first *telhis*; the case against some specific types of ostentation, such as silver swords, in the first *telhis* and in Koçi Bey (A25);[38] the need for all assignments to be recorded, in *Hırzü'l-mülûk* and in the third *telhis*; and so on. The dominant element holding together the advice contained in all these texts, however, concerns the army-*cum*-landholding system. All authors stress that the number of salaried soldiers, either janissaries (infantry) or cavalry, had swollen from the late sixteenth century onwards, and that, conversely, the timariot cavalry had decayed due to the misallocation of the fiefs. Thus, they propose a two-fold reform that would secure the timar revenues and the proper distribution of the timars on the one hand, and check the ranks of the janissaries with a view to drastically reducing their number on the other. In practice, they all seem to agree that the reorganization of the timar system should happen first and that distribution of the land as military fiefs is the most profitable way of landholding.[39]

Furthermore, they propose very practical and political ways to gradually bring this reform into effect. *Kitâb-ı müstetâb* somewhat traditionally suggests that the sultan must find and appoint as grand vizier a God-fearing, pious Muslim who will follow the path of justice as his predecessors did, and who will deal with the malfunctions described. In so doing, all other improvements will inevitably follow (Y31–35, A630–41). The other texts, however, are much more precise and practical in their solutions. Koçi Bey remarks that the janissaries cannot be regulated by advice: even if they took all their salaries in advance, even if the treasury covered all their needs, even if the ulema and sheikhs spoke to them against rebellion, they could not be disciplined; like mankind in general, they can be controlled only through subjugation, not clemency (A51; Ç67: *beni adem kahrile zabtolunur, hilmile olmaz*).[40] Past sultans used the standing cavalry (*altı bölük*) to control the janissaries and vice versa, while the timariot army was used to control those two *kul* groups together. Now, it is written, the timariots have decayed and the *kul* disproportionately grown. The

38 Koçi Bey's attack on ostentation and excessive pageantry does not mention the concept of someone transgressing their "limits" or *hadd*, as later authors would do (cf. Sariyannis 2011a, 140–141).

39 On this idea and its precedents and parallels see Murphey 2009a, 134, fn. 19.

40 As was also seen in chapter 2 above, previous political authors had elevated clemency to being one of the highest virtues for a king, even though it is not one of the four cardinal virtues. Cf. Sariyannis 2011a, 143.

solution, therefore, is simple: the timariot army must be looked after and increased, while the salaried janissaries must be decreased: the army should be few in number and high in quality. The first step, thus, is to inspect those unassigned timars held by the powerful in order to redistribute them. This cannot be done in Istanbul, as it will result only in further injustice and favors. Instead, the governor of each province must make the inspections *in situ*, since at this local level the sipahis, their sons, and the usurpers would be widely known. In addition, villages from among the imperial *hass* could be granted as timars to salaried troops in place of cash; thus, not only would this money stay in the treasury, but the janissary class would also lose power. All private (*temlik*) and *vakf* villages should be inspected. Those that do not comply with the legal requirements must be given as timars to janissaries, transforming them into timariots. Koçi Bey estimates that the salaries of 40,000 to 50,000 janissaries might thus be saved for the treasury (A55–56; Ç71–73). He gives similar advice in various other parts of his essay (e.g. A59–60, 65–67; Ç77–78, 83–86) and concludes that goodness and prosperity can only be gained if the reforms proposed are implemented; that is, if bribery is abolished, if posts and offices are given to worthy people and for a long time, and if the timar system exclusively serves the sipahi army. The same methods, more or less, are suggested in the Veliyuddin memoranda, which also emphasize long appointments, suggesting (as in the third *telhis*) that all assignments must be recorded, their duration kept reasonable, and their number frozen. What is even more practical is that they propose specific drafts of imperial edicts in order to enhance the timariot army at the expense of the janissaries (the fifth, six, and seventh *telhis*): these would be orders to the Rumeli and Anadolu timariots securing their revenues and describing how the timars should be inspected and the legitimacy of their holders checked. The second order, moreover, proposes a gradual rather than an abrupt means of taking these measures, so that a strong force would be gradually assembled in order to secure the implementation of the reform as a whole against the expected negative reactions. Finally, in Aziz Efendi's work, this last policy reaches its perfection, as he presents a detailed road-map for the sultan, laying down drafts for imperial prescripts (and urging the sultan to keep the content of his treatise secret so he may proceed swiftly to take the measures proposed: M22–24). After a careful inspection of the fiefs available for reassignment, the sultan should summon some of the provincial governors to the capital with their forces. Then, he must summon the janissary commander and other officers, as "shareholder[s] in the fate of this noble state" (M8: *bu devlet-i aliyyeden hıssedâr*), and declare to them that he has decided to reduce the number of viziers to four, to reassign misappropriated military fiefs, and to chase out low-origin intruders in the palace. After this, he must ask them what should be done with people who belong to the military but are unfit for their role or are occupied in other professions. The officers being compelled to answer that they will follow the sultan's orders, he should ask them to summon all their soldiers. At the same time, the armies of the provincial governors summoned previously should occupy their posts in order to intimidate the janissaries who may consider rebelling. Thus, a proper inspection and investigation of the janissary pay-rolls will lead to keeping the honest and true soldiers and expel the unfit and the intruders. The same must be done for the salaried cavalry and rest of the salaried *kuls*[41] (M6–12).

Yet the relationship of these suggestions to the actual reforms of Murad IV, namely the realignment of the timar system, remains open to debate.[42] The extent to which Murad actually followed such advice (as well as imposing discipline and order) is questionable. While one gets the impression that he did make serious efforts to inspect the timar system and ensure that only those entitled to military fiefs could have them,[43] was this as a result of his advisors' counsel or did he just follow the general *zeitgeist* following the janissaries' role in Osman's deposition and death? Or, to quote Derin Terzioğlu:[44]

> Was the relatively modest background of these authors the result of an attempt by Murad IV to build alternative channels of influence and alliance against more powerful elites in this period (…)? Or was it rather indicative of the extent of social and political mobilization from the very top down to the peripheral elements? The possibilities need not be mutually exclusive; probably, there was an element of both.

In other words, how may we interpret the common background of these authors, anonymous or not? It will be seen that, throughout the first decades of the seventeenth century, it was the scribal bureaucracy who took the initiative of advocating reform, rather than discontent ulema or dispossessed officers. A possible interpretation may be based on the growing role of this bureaucracy in actual policy-making. Indeed, one may argue that the central governmental mechanisms were becoming increasingly autonomous and independent from both the provincial military administration and the pasha households

41 Murphey translates "the artisans [in the palace service]" (M11); I think that *cemi'-i esnafi* refers rather to the various groups of soldiers.

42 Some measures taken by Osman II before his deposition, such as inspections of the army (Tezcan 2010a, 174), may or may not have been the result of similar advice in *Kitâb-i müstetâb*.

43 See Murphey 1996, 334–335.

44 Terzioğlu 2010, 250.

throughout the seventeenth century, in what Rifaat Abou-El-Haj labelled "the tendency toward a progressive separation between the state and the ruling class".[45] By the late sixteenth century, the Ottoman bureaucracy enjoyed an exceptional longevity of term (in sharp contrast with other administrative apparatus), while its reproduction strategies ensured a continuity of mentality and perhaps ideology. As the bureaucratization of the empire required a large scribal apparatus, the old career lines (*ilmiye* education for the chancery, palace *kul*s for the financial branch) became inadequate and clerks began to use their own networks of *intisab* (patronage) to reproduce their skills.[46] The professionalization of the scribal class, which was to become even more intense from the late seventeenth century onwards, led to its increased visibility in both political theory and practice. It would be only natural, one may argue, that their voices would become increasingly distinct and visible in the political discourse. Having identified their interests with those of the central government, they perceived an enlarged political nation of janissaries-*cum*-"lumpenesnaf" (whom they called "intruding strangers") as a major threat, one which could be counterbalanced by a stronger sipahi army.

3 Administration Manuals: an Ottoman Genre

In order to understand better such political activity by the Ottoman bureaucrats, one must step back and go back in time somewhat. If a common source of "declinist" ideology can be traced in late sixteenth-century "mirrors for princes" such as Mustafa Ali's works, another lies at the very core of scribal literary-administrative production, namely the tendency for the codification of the law. In chapter 3 the obsession of bureaucrat authors (such as Celalzade) with lists was noted; and one may say that such lists (of janissary numbers, of timars, of provinces) had a normative role in the *Kitab-ı müstetâb* and in Koçi Bey's work. In fact, even before the 1630s, authors who shared Koçi Bey's (and his predecessors' and followers') views about the causes and solutions

45 Abou-El-Haj 2005, 7. My discussion here is based on Sariyannis 2013, 103–111; cf. also Tuşalp Atiyas 2013, 63ff.

46 This self-reproduction appears to have begun with the financial branch, whereas the chancery remained attached to the medrese tradition for slightly longer: Fleischer 1986a, 219. The story of the rise of the post of the *re'isülküttab*, the chief of scribes (as opposed to that of the *nişancı*, the chancellor), in combination with the former's short tenures, as narrated by Woodhead 2006, may be interpreted as the beginning of a similar autonomy and self-reproduction in the chancery branch during the last two decades of the sixteenth century.

to what they perceived as Ottoman decline had moved a step further. Instead of locating the shortcomings of the present situation against the standards of a "Golden Era", they simply laid down rules for the government to follow. It is no coincidence that most of the works that could be classified within this trend bear the title of *kanunname*, or "Book of laws". In the words of Douglas A. Howard, "[s]ome Ottoman authors of advice for kings did use the official government document as a form"; and Heather Ferguson's remark, that *kanunnames* were, by themselves, a "paradigm of governance", one which created order and control by being issued, is not out of place here.[47]

Even what is known as "the *kanunname* of Mehmed the Conqueror" might well be, according to Colin Imber's reasoning, an actual product of a historian and (not paradoxically) *divan* scribe, Koca Hüseyin: he included a copy in his history, claiming that he had "taken it out ... from the *kanunname* of the Divan" in 1614 (the earliest manuscript of Mehmed's *kanunname* to survive is dated 1620). This would explain several anachronisms, which show that, in its current form, the text cannot be dated earlier than 1574.[48] If Imber's suggestion is correct, the fact that Koca Hüseyin attributed his compilation to none other than Mehmed II, one of the sultans most celebrated by the "Golden Age" theorists, illustrates splendidly the political agenda of these "administrative manuals". At any rate, regardless of the authenticity of the *kanunname*, the fact is that copies began to circulate in the early seventeenth century, suggesting there was a need to legitimize these regulations by an appeal to the glorious past. This emphasis on the ideal form of institutions seems to have been expanded in juridical theory as well: an anthology of *fetvas* and petitions by Ebussu'ud, entitled *Ma'rûzât* ("Statements"), was compiled so as to be presented to an anonymous sultan, and Colin Imber has argued that the compiler might be identified with the *şeyhülislam* Mehmed Es'ad Efendi and the sultan with Murad IV.[49]

When stating that some pieces of political advice took the form of official documents, Howard focuses on the *telhis* form, used, for example, by Koçi Bey. And indeed, Koçi Bey's second *Risâle* ("Treatise") is one contribution to this category of "administration manuals"; at the same time, it illustrates very well the close relationship between this genre and the "declinist" advice studied

47 Howard 2007, 147; Ferguson 2008. See also Howard 1988, 59ff.

48 Akgündüz 1990–1996, 1:317; Imber 2011, 174–178; cf. Tezcan 2000, 662, fn. 1 and 2 for the rich literature on the authenticity of the *kanunname*. Vatin (forthcoming) suggests, for instance, that the law on fratricide was interpolated during the first years of Süleyman's reign.

49 Imber 1992, 180–81, and fn. 11. On this text see also Heyd 1973, 183–185 (Heyd tentatively dated the text to Selim II's ascension; the editor of the book, V. L. Ménage, suggested Murad III); Repp 1986, 280ff.

above.[50] This *Risâle* is a kind of memorandum submitted to Sultan Ibrahim as soon as the latter ascended to the throne in 1640, and it seems that he had asked for an exposition of the structure and function of state affairs, and especially of the palace. This time, Koçi Bey avoided giving advice of any sort and only summarized the duties and protocol of the palace, or more precisely what a sultan needed to know in order to function within it. It is quite clear that Koçi Bey considered Ibrahim wholly ignorant of any administrative matter: he even includes an explanation of the basic terminology of the timar and tax system (A112/ Ç139). However, one may still discern the author's political views in his urging the sultan to begin his reign by inspecting closely, first, the treasury books and the tax registers (cf. also A96/ Ç122) and, secondly, the janissary and sipahi registers. He must order his vizier to record these registers anew so that the present state of the treasury and the army may be known in every detail. These, says Koçi Bey, are the most important matters; all the rest are trivial in comparison (A78: *cüz'iyyât*). The remainder of the treatise deals with the harem, the numbers, ranks, and salaries of the palace officials, the procedure and requisites for writing orders, the income of every province, the judiciary system, relations with the khan of Crimea, the financial bureaucracy, the *vakf*s, and even the names of the provincial governors and of the imperial doorkeepers. Furthermore, he gives details on the regulation of prices and on merchant affairs (A114–15/ Ç141–42).[51] Scattered pieces of advice repeat the points Koçi Bey had made in his first treatise,[52] and the work ends with the usual praise of justice; Koçi Bey also stresses, somewhat excessively, the need for the sultan to keep secrets, so as not to cause enmity between his officials.

50 Koçi Bey – Aksüt 1939, 77–127; Koçi Bey – Çakmakcıoğlu 2008, 101–155; German translation by Koçi Bey – Behrnauer 1864. On its authorship see Uluçay 1950–1955 and Howard 1988, 64–65, fn. 32.

51 In a curious passage here, Koçi Bey refers to some blessed bread he sent to the sultan, and advises him to take physical exercise so he would not have any need of doctors (A115/ P142).

52 Thus, the sultan is the only one capable of granting fiefs (*dirlik*: A84/ Ç108); peasants or town-dwellers should not be made janissaries (A85/ Ç110); military campaigns should not be launched too often, lest the peasants become impoverished; instead, additional taxes should be abolished and, furthermore, the coinage should be restored (A86–87/ Ç111–112; on taxes cf. also A104–5/ Ç130–31). Advice on coinage is repeated elsewhere as well (A95/ Ç121–122 and especially A119–20/ Ç147–48): Koçi Bey urges the sultan, among others, to prohibit the use of silver by the jewellers and to close down the mints of Erzurum and Tokat, which tend to produce false coins.

3.1 *Sanctifying Janissary and Landholding Regulations: the Early Seventeenth Century*

This discussion began with Koçi Bey's second treatise in order to highlight the affinities between the "administration manuals" and the "decline" theorists; however, his was only one of the last in a long series of similar essays. Perhaps the first of these attempts to systematize and register the rules and numbers of the state mechanism was the anonymous *Kavânîn-i yeniçeriyân-ı dergâh-ı âlî* ("Rules of the imperial janissaries") of 1606, an effort to codify the structure of the janissary corps, and which was widely read and copied.[53] The author differs from later imitators in that he does not belong to the scribal class: he states that he served for a long time in the janissary corps, as did his grandfathers, one of whom was Saka Mahmud, *ağa* of Istanbul during Süleyman I's reign (A149, 239). The description he gives of the *yeniçeri kâtibi* and his registers (A243ff.) may imply that he had served in that office (which would also explain his detailed knowledge).

The anonymous author begins his treatise by stating that Ahmed I had inspected and implemented his ancestors' laws (A130: *ecdad-ı izamlarının kanun ve ka'idelerin yoklayub icra etmekle*), brought welfare to the people with his justice, and exterminated the Celali rebels, with the result that "the world is cheerful like it used to be and is bound to revolve around the pole of his will". He decided to write the rules of the janissary corps, he says, as he heard them from his grandfathers and as he found them himself. In various parts of the work the sultan is addressed in the second person singular (e.g. A251). The treatise is divided into nine chapters, explaining in every particular the history and structure of the janissaries: the creation of the corps, the procedure for collecting and training Christian youths, their uniforms (stressing again the historical dimension), their internal structure and officer ranks, both high and low, their *vakf*s (A178–80), their lodgings, their duties and salaries, their registers, and the means of keeping them relevant and useful. In all these regulations the reader recognizes the topoi of political advice, such as harm brought by

53 At least ten manuscripts are known. The work has been published in multiple editions and languages over the last few decades: Petrossian 1987; Fodor 1989; Akgündüz 1990–1996, 9:127–268 (facs. follows); Toroser 2011 (facs. follows). See also Fodor 1986, 228–230; Petrosjan 1987; Howard 1988, 70–71.

intruders,[54] the dangers of bribery, the need for discipline, and the prohibition against janissaries following a trade.[55]

What is interesting in this treatise, and which differentiates it somewhat from others of its genre, is the emphasis the author gives to the history of janissary institutions, since he presents them as dynamic and undergoing many changes over time. He usually finds recent innovations devastating, but there are exceptions (such as when he mentions that "it used to be a rule that janissaries do not marry", A154, 157; elsewhere, he specifies that they should not marry while young and without the sultan's permission, A173). He enumerates those innovations in the corps that are contrary to the (old) law and those that are not (*kanuna muhalif olan bid'atlar … ve kanun üzere olanlar*: A263–268). Moreover, the author often explains the reason for various arrangements, as if justification by "the old law" was not yet sufficient.[56] On the other hand, he constantly keeps note of innovations that, in one way or another, harm the quality of the corps and the public treasury. The law, significantly, was formulated after consultation with judges, ulemas, and "the pillars of the state" (A169: *erkân-ı devlet*), or just the *ocak ağaları* (A215; cf. A136, A142), and consequently must be followed even if they are contrary to a particular sultan's will. No less than Selim I, on one occasion, refused to listen to his vizier, Piri Pasha (A143: "are you to teach me the law?", *kanunu bana sen mi öğredirsin*), and recruited boys from Trabzon, which proved to be a mistake. Thus, *kanun*, mostly identified with what is described as late fifteenth-century practice, is conceived as binding even for the sultan. On the other hand, its precise aim was to keep the janissaries under the ruler's control: their elders (*korucu*) should be appointed by the sultan, again after consultation with the grand vizier, the ulema, and the elders of the corps (A206). The ordering of the janissaries and the sipahis, the author notes, is the only way for the world to be ordered (A206).

It seems that the last years of Ahmed I's reign, following the definitive defeat of the major Celali chieftains, were seen as an opportunity to reorganize the eastern provinces along the lines of the "classical" timar system. The internal

54 The author claims that the first innovation that should be abolished is the recruitment of the servants of the aghas (A145: *ağa çırağı*): all of them are Turks and similar (*Türk mürk*), and their recruitment led to the corruption of the *devşirme* system; the same goes for the sons of *sipahi*s and of other officials (A152: *ferzend-i sipahi*).

55 The point is that a craftsman would not campaign for a salary, as he can make as much from his craft, and estimates that "now most [janissaries] have become craftsmen" (A196).

56 For instance, he notes that the benefit of not recruiting Turkish boys (A138: *Türk evladı*) is that, in such a case, the recruits would oppress the peasants of their villages, evade taxes, and create confusion with the local officials; also, boys who have a craft (A139: *san'at ehli olan*) would not risk for a salary and would rather stay back with their profession, while those who have lived in Istanbul have "their eyes too open" (A139; cf. again 145, 155–56).

and external peace that had prevailed for a number of years must have caused the increased production of "administration manuals", like those just examined, which describe the rules of the state in their ideal form. Indeed, Ayn Ali's work (or rather two works), completed c. 1610,[57] is the main prototype for this "administration manuals" genre. Müezzinzâde (as Kâtib Çelebi calls him) Ayn Ali was a scribe in the *mukabele* bureau and the Imperial Council, while he also served as intendant of the imperial registry (*emin-i defter-i hakani*) in 1607. According to Bursalı Mehmed Tahir, he was also *defterdar* of Egypt in 1609. His two works, which were very popular and influential,[58] are *Kavânîn-i âl-ı Osmân der hulâsa-ı mezâmîn-i defter-i dîvân* ("Rules of the House of Osman summing up the contents of the registry of the Imperial Council") and *Risâle-i vazife-horân ve merâtib-i bendegân-i âl-i Osman* ("Treatise on the salaried people and the ranks of the slaves of the House of Osman").

At the beginning of his first treatise, *Kavânîn-i âl-ı Osmân* ... (AA2–81; T90–111; A28–68), Ayn Ali states his aim: to list the administrative and financial units of the empire, and the ranks and numbers of its officials and soldiers, with a view to describing the details of the timar system, because "it took a long time to search for all this information in various scattered registers". The work is formed of seven chapters and a conclusion. Ayn Ali lists in detail the *has* and *saliyane* lands, as well as the provinces (*beylerbeylik*) of the empire, the districts (*sancak*) and their rules, the fiefs of the *sancak* financial officials, the structure of the timars and their military output in each province, as well as the rules and terminology of the system: the terms and types of fiefs and the rules on their bestowal and allotment to various ranks of soldiers and officers. In the final chapter, which is primarily what differentiates Ayn Ali's work from other manuals, the author proposes some measures for redressing shortcomings and failures in the timar system (*zeamet ve timar hususunda olan ihtilal*). The causes for the present situation are two-fold, he says: on the one hand, the timariots do not care for their duties and, especially, for the soldiers they have to maintain, sending their servants and slaves (*hidmetkâr ve abd-i müştera*) on

57 The *Kavanin* is dedicated to Sultan Ahmed I and his grand vizier, Kuyucu Murad Pasha, so it must have been completed between 1606 and 1611. Ayn Ali describes himself as the "ex-*defter-i hakani emini*", so 1607 should be a terminus post quem. As for the *Risale-i vazife-horan*, it uses a register of 1609.

58 More than 40 MSS of the *Kavanin* survive, including two French translations made in the 1730s. One MS (Fatih 3497) seems to have been an earlier recension of the text by the author (Howard 2008, 88–89). There are numerous editions: Ayn Ali 1978; Ayn Ali – Tuncer 1962 (a very poor edition); Akgündüz 1990–1996, 9:28–126 (with facs.). On Ayn Ali's work, see Gökbilgin 1991, 203–206; Gökbilgin 1978; Howard 1988; Howard 2007, 152–166; Howard 2008.

campaign; on the other, the inspections due in each campaign are not conducted properly nor are their results registered and kept. Ayn Ali claims that, as *defter-i hakani emini*, he himself tried to correct this last practice, but generally it has been 20 or 30 years since an inspection was carried out or registered.

The second treatise, *Risâle-i vazife-horân* (AA82–104; T111–123; A89–106), seeks to register all the persons, high and low, who "take salaries from the imperial threshold" (AA85; T113; A91: *atebe-i aliyye-i padişahîde her ay vazife ve ... üç ayda bir mevacib ... alan havass ve avam*); as such, Ayn Ali collected and listed all the salaries paid in the final third of A.H. 1018 (1609) in order to present a full and detailed image of the palace personnel and standing army at that time. The treatise is divided into four parts, roughly following a course from the outer to the inner service of the palace. First, Ayn Ali lists the numbers and salaries of the janissary infantry and cavalry, then proceeds through the navy, the arsenal, and the palace military personnel, before reaching the inner services of the palace, including the scribes of the Imperial Council and the other services (in the epilogue, he also lists the salaries of the higher ulema, praising the Sultan for the care and respect he shows for this illustrious group).

Ayn Ali used imperial registers and *kanunname*s, and probably scribal manuals as well, and his work was widely imitated. It seems that after the early 1640s, i.e. after the outburst of "declinist" literature that coincided with Murad IV's reign, a number of treatises sought to describe in detail the (now dying) timar system, enumerating the provinces of the empire and their timariot structure and revenues, as well as analyzing the terminology and categories of the various timars. Two almost identical versions are the treatise copied by (and by some scholars attributed to) Sofyalı Ali Çavuş in 1653 and another similar description, copied the same year.[59] All these texts, including part of Ayn Ali's essay, seem to be based on a series of *kanunname* texts from the Süleymanic era, with corrections and amendations reflecting more or less minor changes in the structure of the empire.[60] As Douglas Howard has put it, Ayn Ali used such "scribal manuals" as "literary models", copying them with corrections and emendations and adding his own commentary and advice.[61]

Another version is Avni Ömer's treatise, *Kânûn-ı Osmânî mefhûm-i defter-i hakanî* ("Ottoman laws, or, the contents of the imperial register"), which also contains an introduction on landholding status in Ottoman lands.[62] Avnî

59 Hadžibegić 1947; Sertoğlu 1992; Ali Çavuş – Şahin 1979.

60 See Akgündüz 1990–1996, 4:455–527; Howard 2007, 156, fn 97; Howard 2008. Cf. also Howard 1996 for an overview of the timariotic *kanunnames*.

61 Howard 2008, 95–98.

62 Avni Ömer – Uzunçarşılı 1951. See also Gökbilgin 1991, 212; Howard 2008.

Ömer Efendi b. Mustafa also belonged to the bureaucracy: he was trained in the scribal service of the divan and attained the posts of *nişancı* and of *reisülküttâb* (probably during Ibrahim's reign). A disciple of the Halveti sheikh Cihangirî Hasan Efendi, he founded a mosque in Kabataş in 1652 in which he was buried after his death in 1659. His work is roughly contemporary with Koçi Bey's second treatise (there is one copy, probably not an autograph but with notes by the author, copied in 1642). The author starts by declaring that the timariot system was not functioning any more: he states that he wrote his treatise because issues such as which kind of tax should be paid for lands, and whether those who have the usufruct of a plot also have its freehold property, were not known and unspecified, so he decided to describe all matters pertaining to villages, peasants, landholdings, and land taxation in the domains "inserted in general to the circle of justice and belonging in the territory of [the sultan's] full dominion" (U384: *havza-i hükûmet-i tam ve daire-i adalet-i amlarında münderic olan memalik*). Then he explains in detail the landholding system (U384–86; this section, including the introduction above, is copied almost verbatim from the *kanunname* of Sivas, compiled in 1578, a few years after Ebussu'ud's death),[63] starting with a historical account of the creation of the two categories (*arz-ı haraciyye, arz-ı memleket*) and explaining that, in the second case (which in central Ottoman lands is called *miri*), the substance of the land (*rakabe*) belongs to the treasury. Avnî Ömer then lists the land categories in the Ottoman empire, i.e. the various kinds of fiefs, the lands granted as *mülk* by the Sultan, the *vakf* lands, the Christian timars, and so on, noting the tax status of each and the obligations of their holders. Finally, in the unpublished part of the treatise, the author gives an alphabetical list of the *kaza*s in Anadolu and Rumili.[64]

• • •

Thus, such texts abounded in the first quarter of the seventeenth century. It was obviously not coincidental that this outburst was contemporaneous with the period when treatises advocating a return to the "old law", in order to mend the present "decline", became the main form of political advice. Moreover, both trends seem to have originated from the same milieu of governmental scribes and bureaucrats. While it is true that, from one perspective, these "administration manuals" cannot be considered political treatises *stricto sensu*,

63 Akgündüz 1990–1996, 8:425–427. For the *kanunname*s used as source for the second part of the treatise (land categories and lists), see Akgündüz 1990–1996, 4:455–527.

64 Gökbilgin 1991, 212.

they certainly do pertain to political thought. Together with the "declinist" treatises, they represent the climax of a trend that dominated Ottoman policy planning (regardless of its success) from the last decades of the sixteenth until almost the mid-seventeenth century, a trend that sanctified not the will of the ruler but the old and tested practice, considering it a sort of constitution binding actual political action. Sultans who tried to circumvent these old rules were criticized and even (in Osman II's case) deposed, on the very grounds that they ignored this sanctified "old law". On another level, such ideas were partly aimed at fighting the causes of social forces, such as the timar-holders, who had vested interests in the continuation of the feudal relations and of the direct collection of rural taxes by this provincial military. On the other hand, they sought to use these forces, and the force of their ideas, as a counter-balance to the growing political power of the urban janissaries. In a way, therefore, these authors shared with the janissaries the concept of a constitutional system, one in which the sultan's decisions would be checked and regulated by a "political nation", the extent of which could vary (and in which the janissaries included themselves). Competition about who should be entitled to participate in and, ultimately, to dominate this "political nation" was fierce and would become even fiercer during the course of the century. By claiming the omnipotence of the "old law", the governmental bureaucracy (as its sole legitimate interpreter) in fact advocated its own supremacy in the political field.

4 The Afterlife of the Genre: Late Seventeenth-Century Manuals

Calls for a return to "the old laws" grew weaker during the rest of the seventeenth century, as will be seen in the next two chapters; however, the "administration manuals" genre, offering compilations of rules and lists of provinces and military guards or salaries, continued to flourish, with authors often copying each other. As will be seen in chapter 7, from the mid-seventeenth century onwards and Kâtib Çelebi's work new directions emerged, ones that constituted a complete vision for human society once more (this time influenced by Ibn Khaldun's ideas); therefore, the tendency to make compilations of older sources predominated in authors continuing the tradition of the "old law"—a cause which increasingly seemed lost.

A celebrated example of such late "administration manual" is Hüseyin Hezarfen's work. Hezârfen Hüseyin Efendi b. Ca'fer (c. 1611–91)[65] was educated

65 Hezarfen's birth and death dates are a matter of debate. Wurm (1971, 74 and 83) accepts 1611 (based on a Venetian account of his age) and 1691 (based on a marginal note recorded

in Istanbul and served in the financial bureaucracy, being a *protégé* of Köprülü Fazıl Ahmed Pasha. He was a polymath and an encyclopedist in the mold of Kâtib Çelebi, and he made extensive use of Greek and Latin sources for his historical works, with two dragomans as intermediaries (one of whom was the famous Panayiotis Nikousios); his company was frequented by various European orientalists, such as Antoine Galland and Count Marsigli. His works are numerous; among lexicographical, moralist, medical, and mystical treatises, his universal history (*Tenkîh-i tevârîh-i mülûk*), which included the history of Rome, Ancient Greece, Byzantium, China, and Indonesia should be especially noted, as should a narrative of the discovery of the Americas.[66] Hezarfen composed some old-style moral-political treatises (*Câmi'ü'l-hikâyât, Anîsü'l-'ârifîn ve mürşîdü's-sâlikîn*),[67] but his main "political" work was *Telhîsü'l-beyân bî kavânîn-i Âl-ı Osmân* ("Memorandum on the rules of the House of Osman").[68] Composed in all probability around 1675,[69] this remarkable treatise is supposed to be an exposition of the history, institutions, and rules of the Ottoman state in the model of Ayn Ali's work or of Koçi Bey's second treatise, and, indeed, the sources Hezarfen used include these authors, as well as other regulations and compilations of laws or *fetvas*. However, Hezarfen wished to give more than an exposition of various institutions: he copies verbatim large parts of Kâtib Çelebi's works and Feridun Bey's collection of correspondence, while he incorporates Lütfi Pasha's *Âsafnâme* both partially, i.e. scattered across various parts of his treatise, and as a whole.[70]

Hezarfen begins with a eulogy of Mehmed IV and explains that, because he had described in such detail the rules of the Mongols and the Chinese in his universal history, he was asked to do the same for the Ottoman state. His work is formed of thirteen chapters (*bab*), the first of which deals with the history of the Ottoman sultans, in short notices. The second chapter describes Istanbul and its history, drawing from Greek sources (and explaining at great length

---

by Flügel, corroborated by Antoine Galland who knew Hezarfen personally) respectively; İlgürel (Hezarfen – İlgürel 1998, 5 and 7–8) adopts Ménage's date (1600) for his birth and Mehmed Tahir's (1678) for his death. According to Wurm (ibid.), Marsigli's information that Hezarfen had died by 1685 must be a mistake.

66 On Hezarfen's life and work see Anhegger 1953; Wurm 1971; Hezarfen – İlgürel 1998, 4–13. On certain aspects of his universal history cf. Bekar 2011.

67 Wurm 1971, 87, 98, 107.

68 Hezarfen – İlgürel 1998; cf. Anhegger 1953 for an earlier partial publication. See also Lewis 1962, 81–82; Wurm 1971, 102–105; Fodor 1986, 235; Yılmaz 2003a, 313; İnan 2009, 121–122.

69 The exact dating of this text is not certain, since various suggestions have been made varying from A.H. 1080 (1669/70) up to A.H. 1086 (1675); see Hezarfen – İlgürel 1998, 13, fn. 47 and cf. Wurm 1971, 102.

70 See Hezarfen – İlgürel 1998, 21–29 for a detailed analysis of sources.

the etymology of the name Istanbul from *εις την Πόλιν*: I46); the mosques, schools, markets, and other foundations of the city are also enumerated, as are its guilds (in alphabetical order). Then, Hezarfen gives lengthy and detailed information on the protocol and internal workings of the palace, its scribal institutions, the feasts and ceremonies held therein, the grand vizier and his income (copying mainly the first chapter of Lütfi Pasha's work), and the various career lines in the palace hierarchy; after the palace, he moves on to the army, enumerating the soldiers' salaries; he talks about state finances (with an excursus on the difference between the solar and the lunar year), land-holding and taxation, as well as the rules of the timariot system (again mostly copied from Lütfi Pasha);[71] he enumerates in great detail the provincial administrative units of the empire and their timars (including newly-conquered Crete) and describes the janissary corps, the navy, and the imperial arsenal (stressing the importance of geography and hydrography, as "the victories of the infidels are the result of the care they show for the naval sciences and weapons": I160).[72] The final chapters concern the Crimean khans, as well as various pieces of information on the science of war, the ulema, and the *şeyhülislam*s. Finally, at the end of his treatise Hezarfen copies various legal texts: mining regulations, some *kanunname*s from Thrace, and Mehmed II's law code. To this he adds the whole text of Lütfi Pasha's *Âsafnâme* (I266–274) as well as two reports on the introduction of coffee and tobacco to the Ottoman Empire (copied from Kâtib Çelebi). Finally, the thirteenth chapter is devoted to a lengthy and very detailed description of the 1672 feast of the sultan in Edirne.

Most of Hezarfen's treatise can be viewed as the consummation of the "administration manual" genre: the extensive lists of provinces, salaries, and names (of grand viziers, for instance) are modeled upon the finest specimens of earlier manuals, enriched with commentaries and further information. One may even find a detailed budget of state income and expenses (for the year 1660/1; I86–104). Most of the information he copies is rather outdated, much more so than that of his predecessors: for instance, he inserts some *fetvas* on land-holding and taxation by Ebussu'ud Efendi and Kemalpaşazâde (I108–112), while he seems to ignore totally the land and land-tax reforms implemented experimentally in Crete at a time when he himself was present there.[73]

71 These rules stress the need to avoid the intrusion of peasants into the timariot ranks (I141), but Hezarfen notes pragmatically that this cannot be achieved in every period, in a remark which will be examined in more detail in chapter 7.

72 The same advice is contained in his universal history, obviously under Kâtib Çelebi's influence: Wurm 1971, 98; Hezarfen – İlgürel 1998, 10.

73 On the other hand, he does take into account the poll-tax reform, implemented in Crete at the same period. See Sariyannis 2011b and esp. 48–49.

Some of Hezarfen's comments are also very similar to advice contained in early seventeenth-century works, such as *Kitâb-i müstetâb* or Koçi Bey's treatise. For instance, he states that the sultan should appoint a wise grand vizier and give him independence (*istiklal vire*), so no-one else could interfere in his business (I73). Similar advice is contained in the section on the sultan's administration of power, where we can also see some remnants of "declinist" theories: the sultan, he says, must have few companions (*nedim*) and not let them interfere in state affairs. In the time of the sultans of old (until Süleyman's time), the capital was so full of wise and honest people that the rulers could intermingle with companions freely; these sultans were glorious, valiant, and just, and their viziers well-meaning and hard-working. However, by the middle of Süleyman's reign, when the sultan executed his son Mustafa, general corruption and unrest in the empire had begun (I182–85). Furthermore, the emphasis he places on strict punishment, rather than clemency, brings to mind the similar passage by Koçi Bey, who had written that people can be controlled only through subjugation, not clemency (see above). Hezarfen maintains that capital punishment (*siyaset*) is essential, since the lowest of the people must be kept fearful while the better ones must be kept safe (I114: *halkın erazili havf üzere, iyüleri emin üzere olmak gerek*).

At some points, however, Hezarfen departs from the "administration manual" genre and inserts lengthy diversions on political advice or even theoretical discussions. Sometimes, these discussions appear to originate in tropes first seen in the sixteenth century. For instance, the position he cedes to the sultan is remarkably high, and there is almost no trace at all of the binding status of the "old law". The sultan is simultaneously the supreme preacher, imam, and governor (I113–14: *imamet ve hitabet ve hükûmet cümle padişahındır*), and governors are his proxies. The somewhat old-fashioned emphasis placed on the personal responsibility of sultans for the oppression exerted by their proxies (*vekil*) is repeated in a similarly old-fashioned way, when Hezarfen copies a letter allegedly sent by the dying Murad I to Evrenos Bey (I205–7).[74] Still, we could also postulate that Hezarfen's vision for the sultan represents his own, original ideas and is more than a simple figure of speech or rather trope of political tradition. In a chapter dealing with the market and the regulation of prices,[75] Hezarfen argues that the ruler (*hâkim*) should control in person such small matters (*cüz'iyyât*) pertaining to the well-being of the world, such as the

74 This letter comes from Feridun Bey's collection of sultanly correspondance: see Anhegger 1953, 376–77, fn. 33.

75 As will be seen in chapter 7, Hezarfen had included this part in the conclusions of his universal history. On the prehistory of the *narh* debate in Islam see Ermiş 2014, 111–120.

regulation of fixed prices. In fact, he says, this matter is a public issue (*umur-ı külliye*); if the sultan or the viziers consider it a triviality (*cüz'î*) and leave it to a judge, the latter cannot regulate it by himself since it is outside his competence as a "matter of politics" (or: of the administrative branch, *emr-i siyaset*). If the prices are not regulated, only those who are of no use to the sultan's service and to the army benefit: they become rich and assume the position of notables (*a'yan-ı memleket*), and as a result the well-to-do honest people are impoverished (I248).[76]

To understand this passage, it must be borne in mind that, in 1691, some fifteen years after the composition of *Telhîsü'l-beyân*, there was an effort to abolish the system of fixed prices on the ideological grounds that it was incompatible with the Sharia (see below, chapter 6). Arguably, the use of Sharia-minded arguments for financial reform was current among scribal bureaucracy at the time Hezarfen was writing his treatise (a similar reform of taxation and landholding, as will be seen in the next chapter, was carried out in Crete, and the reader may remember that Hezarfen perhaps deliberately chose to ignore it in his text). If the "constitutionalist" argument among these milieus had already started to shift from the binding force of the "old law" to that of the Sharia, it is tempting to see in Hezarfen's rearguard action a reflection of this struggle. Reinforcing the sultan's and the vizier's freedom of action might be Hezarfen's response to the fact that "old law"-based reasoning had, by that time, lost its strength.[77]

In the same context, Hezarfen's discussion of the ulema (I196–207) is of some interest as well. First, he states that, among the "pillars of the state", the ulema are the highest and most honorable, using a medical simile that he takes from Kâtib Çelebi (this excerpt will be studied in detail in chapter 7). Following this, he divides them into two categories: the manifest or external ones (*ulema-ı zahir*) who follow "the way of the eye" (*tarik-ı nazar*), i.e. muftis, judges, teachers, and so on; and the internal ones (*ulema-ı batin*) who follow "the way of purification" (*tarik-ı tasfiye*), i.e. the dervishes (the author names explicitly the Nakşbendis and the Halvetis). What is particularly important here is that, as Hezarfen seeks to clarify, doctors, astrologers, and scribes of the divan are included in the first category, under the rubric "masters of sciences" (*ashab-ı fünun*). Thus, the scribal bureaucracy, long ago inserted into

---

76 An almost identical discussion of the problem can be found in Ali – Demir 2006, 56–57. The distinction between "important matters" or *külliye* and "particular issues" or *cüz'iyye* (also seen in Koçi Bey's second treatise) has its parallels in Islamic philosophy and legal theory: see below, chapter 8.

77 As will be see in chapter 7, Hezarfen also used Kâtib Çelebi's pro-innovation arguments.

the four-fold division of society as "people of the pen" in their own right, were now also considered part of the ulema, the same group whom Hezarfen was sanctifying as the highest pillar.[78] Moreover, along with bureaucrats, representatives of the rational sciences (medicine, astrology) were similarly elevated; it is tempting to see here not only the influence of Kâtib Çelebi's scientist culture (see below, chapter 7) but also a connection with Hezarfen's reaction to Sunna-minded juristic reform, as I argued before: the more the professional classes shared the same place as the ulema, the less the ulema would appear as the highest and sole guides for society.[79]

Now, the *şeyhülislam* is considered equal to, if not greater than, the grand vizier. Of course, notes Hezarfen, in certain matters the vizier's post is indeed higher, as he is the sultan's absolute proxy and has far-ranging powers within common affairs (I197: *hall u akd-i umur-ı cumhur*). But, in the eyes of the sultan, the post of *şeyhülislam* as "the absolute master in religious matters" (*umur-ı diniyede riyaset-i mutlaka sahibi*) is higher, because

> state affairs are founded on religion; in fact, religion is fundamental, while the state was established as its subdivision (*devlet umuru din üzerine bina olunur; din asıl, devlet anın fer'i gibi kurulmuşdur*). The *şeyhülislam* is the head of religion, the grand vizier the head of the state (*yalnız devlet re'isi*), and the sultan the head of both.

In light of the earlier remarks on Hezarfen's possible position against the Sunna-minded tendencies of his fellow bureaucrats, all this reasoning may sound contradictory. Yet it should by no means be taken for granted that the *şeyhülislam* would take the reformists' side (and one may remember that, in Ebussu'ud's case, it was precisely the *şeyhülislam* who actually advocated the sultan's ability to circumvent the Sharia). More importantly, Hezarfen's unification of ulema, scientists, and scribes somehow undermines the monopoly of the ulema's competence to produce authoritative opinions regarding the world and society. As for the distinction between state and religion, it could actually be interpreted as an attempt to rule out any ulema jurisdiction in state affairs, regardless of the higher place Hezarfen cedes to religion and them as its

78 Another instance of the high position Hezarfen grants to scribes is when he notes that, in the time of Süleyman, many-folded turbans were only used by soldiers, "so as to show that they were higher than the tradesmen" (*ehl-i sukdan mümtaz idi*), while afterwards this headgear was reserved for the members of the divan (I72).

79 On the role of rational sciences in the wider context of Ottoman political and intellectual life see Tezcan 2010b and Kurz 2011, 176–248.

representative.[80] Furthermore, the term he uses for the state, "subdivision" or, literally, "branch" (*fürû', fer'*), belongs to Islamic jurisprudence, where it signifies substantive or positive law in contrast to legal theory.[81] If this interpretation is correct, Hezarfen's treatise takes the form of a "administration manual", normally used to legitimize the "old law"; however, he uses it, in a highly eclectic fashion, to legitimize the sultan's and the viziers' power to circumvent both the "old law" and the Sunna, if necessary.

4.1 *Parallel Texts: Eyyubî Efendi, Kavânîn-i osmanî, Dımışkî*

Although only four copies of Hezarfen's treatise are extant, it seems that it had some degree of influence as a model compendium of Ottoman state regulations. A text bearing extreme similarities is a *Kânûnnâme* attributed to some Eyyubi Efendi, about whom we know nothing else.[82] Eyyubi's text is in fact a summary of Hezarfen's material; its editor, Abdülkadir Özcan, suggests that it is an abridgment of the *Telhîsü'l-beyân*, but one cannot exclude the possibility that Eyyubi was Hezarfen's predecessor. Eyyubi's work contains a large part of Hezarfen's treatise copied almost verbatim, but excluding the first (up to the palace servants) and the latter (from after the excursus on the Crimea) parts, as well as Hezarfen's more abstract thoughts. Both the 1660/1 budget and a list of the gifts bestowed at the time of Mehmed IV's enthronement (1648) are found in both texts; if Eyyubi is to be considered later, one could posit that he decided to copy those parts related to the enthronement of the next sultan, i.e. Süleyman II (1687). Be it as it may, Eyyubi's work is the "administration manual" version of the *Telhisü'l-beyân*, its raw material, so to speak; whether it is its source or its abridgment, it shows the close relationship between Hezarfen's work and the earlier tradition of Ayn Ali and his continuators. A similar work of the same period contains almost verbatim (but also simplified) the rules regarding viziers and provincial governors, the list of provinces and their revenues, and part of the laws on the timar system from Hezarfen's work.[83] There are some minor discrepancies, especially in some marginal notes and in

80 Cf. Sariyannis 2013, 91–92 and 104, on the significance of this passage concerning the concept of *devlet* as "state". Yılmaz 2015a, 238 stresses this claim as evidence for the growing importance of the *şeyhülislam* office, to the grand vizier's disadvantage. The expression about religion (as the foundation) and power (*mulk* or *sultan*, as its guardian) goes back to al-Ghazali (Laoust 1970, 197 and 237).

81 Hallaq 2002, 153.

82 Eyyubi – Özcan 1994.

83 London, British Library, Or. Mss. Harley 3370, ff. 23–79. The manuscript was copied by a certain Salomon Negri in 1709 under the title "Notitia Imperij Othomannici" from an original belonging to the interpreter of the French Ambassador in Istanbul. The relevant parts in *Telhisü'l-beyân* are Hezarfen – İlgürel 1998, 83–85, 114–140. Both works refer to Morea,

the position of Crete in the list (Hezarfen, writing just after its final conquest, had placed the island after the province of Anadolu, while the anonymous compiler has it registered between Cyprus and Anadolu), which show that the manuscript was intended to have some practical use.

Another late seventeenth-century work, *Kavânîn-i osmanî ve râbıta-ı Âsitâne* ("Ottoman rules and the orderly arrangement of Istanbul"), is essentially a selective reproduction of the *Telhisü'l-beyân*.[84] In general, the relationship of this text with Hezarfen's *Telhisü'l-beyân* makes any identification of the compiler uncertain; it is only known that the compilation was made after 1688, as Mehmed IV's reign is mentioned as something in the past.

The text begins with a note on the Imperial Council and the days of the week in which it hears cases, then describes the judges and deputy judges of Istanbul and the dues for various judicial and notary deeds. The author proceeds to describe briefly various aspects of city life (the bakeries of the city and their production, the numbers and prices of other manufactures and stores, the city's neighborhoods, etc.). Then, he describes in great detail the palace, its topography, services, and protocol (I14ff.): he stresses the procedure of the Imperial Council and of the daily meals of all palace officials. Following this, the procedure for paying the soldiers' salaries, the structure of the inner palace and various ceremonies, the appointment of provincial governors, the situation of the Crimean khans, the history and ceremonies of the janissaries (I24ff., with a long excursus on Hacı Bektaş-ı Veli) and (much more briefly) of the *kapu sipahileri* (I31), as well as the representatives of European states (with a note on the tributes from Hungary; I31–32), are described in turn.

Then, somewhat abruptly, the author jumps to the ulema (I32; again copying Hezarfen, but omitting the simile with the human body). Following, almost word-for-word, Hezarfen's analysis, the author divides the ulema into the manifest or external ones (including, like Hezarfen, scribes of the divan, "those who know Indian numbers and the *siyakat* script"—a phrase missing in Hezarfen) and the internal ones; he also copies (with some mistakes) Hezarfen's assessment of the relationship between the *şeyhülislam* and the grand vizier.[85]

Written at almost the same time as the *Kavânîn-i osmanî ve râbıta-ı Âsitâne*, another description of the empire was also primarily based on Hezarfen as far as it concerns the non-geographical parts: Ebu Bekr b. Bahram Dımışki's

which gives us a *terminus ante quem* (the loss of the province to the Venetians in 1685). I wish to thank Antonis Hadjikyriacou for bringing this manuscript to my attention.

84 The text was published in İpşirli 1994 (see 18, 19, 28 and elsewhere for the dating).

85 The anonymous author here writes that the vizier is the head of "his own state" (*kendi devlet re'isi*), instead of "head of the state" (*yalnız devlet re'isi*) as in Hezarfen – İlgürel 1998, 197. See Sariyannis 2013, 91.

El-fethü'r-rahmânî fî tarz-i devletü'l-Osmanî ("The divine gift on the form of the Ottoman state"), completed in 1689.[86] Dımışki (d. 1691) was born in Damascus, where he was educated. He seems to have been attached to Köprülüzade Fâzıl Ahmed Pasha while the latter was governor of Damascus and to have followed him to Istanbul in 1661. Being well versed in mathematics and geography, he completed his *medrese* curriculum in Istanbul and was a teacher (*müderris*) there for twenty years, beginning in 1669. In 1685 he played a pivotal role in completing the translation of Willem Janszoon Blaeuw's *Atlas Maior*, commisisioned in 1675 (he did not know Latin but he made several additions and improvements). He also completed Kâtib Çelebi's *Cihânnümâ*, providing additions as well as the maps that were later used in İbrahim Müteferrika's edition (1732).

El-fethü'r-rahmânî, on the other hand, is partly a reiteration or imitation of Hezarfen's description and partly a geographical compendium. Dımışki begins by stating that he designed his work in order for the sultan to be able to have full understanding of the Ottoman Empire (*devlet-i alîye*) quickly. He first describes, using numbers, the expansion of Ottoman territories, noting that because of some oppressive pashas and governors (2.B) some of them have been lost to the infidel. In the first part (3.A–4.A), Dımışki explains that God ordained kings who use either reason or the Sharia; the latter is the best but states fall because of injustice, not infidelity. He also stresses the importance of punishment (*siyaset*), as realms have order when their people oscillate between fear and hope (*halk beynü'l-havf ve'r-recâ olmağla saltanat nizam bulur*); this dismissal of clemency, also seen in Koçi Bey and Hezarfen, is typical of the genre. Then, Dımışki lays down some of the usual advice, such as the need to select a wise vizier whose independence should be secure. Another section (4.A–5B) speaks of the qualities needed by a vizier: among others, he should not grant *zeamet*s to his retinue; must not take bribes nor covet the public treasury; should appoint and consult with the right people; and should look after the price regulations (which are "the affairs of the poor"). Dımışkî also repeats Lütfi Pasha's warning against peasants turned soldiers. In the next section (5.B–11.A), Dımışki speaks of the army (*asker*), which he divides into two categories: the first, the state notables (*a'yân-ı devlet*), includes four elements or pillars (the viziers and pashas, the *şeyhülislam* and the judges, the governors, and the high-ranking scribes). The second category is the army proper (*asâkir-i osmaniye*), those salaried and the timariot who "have ordained shares in the lands of the empire" (6.A: *memalik-i mahrusa arazisinde hisse-i mu'ayeneleri*

86 Dımışkî – Dorogi – Hazai 2011–2014; cf. Hagen 2006, 232–233. Because of the different paginations, we use here the folios as indicated in the Dorogi – Hazai edition.

vardur). Then Dımışki proceeds to enumerate in detail the various corps and groups of the army, in a careful hierarchy of divisions and subdivisions; he begins with the palace personnel and describes at length the protocol of the imperial council. Then he speaks of the servants of the palace, giving detailed lists of their daily salaries. In the next section (16.B–20.B) Dımışki speaks of the ulema, closely following Hezarfen's categorizations (external and internal ulema) and his account of the relationship between the *şeyhülislam* and the grand vizier; as such, it seems that this addition to the genre by Hezarfen had, by then, become classic.

In the section on governors (20.B–22.B), Dımışki, always copying Hezarfen, stresses that the governor is the sultan's proxy (*vekil*) and points out several specific points regarding the governors' retinue, the timariots, and so on, before giving a detailed enumeration of the governorships, their revenue, and the number of soldiers owed by each one (22.B–23.B), as well as some rules on the bestowal of timars. The next sections (24.B–36.B) deal with the salaried army; here, Dımışki inserts an excursus on the creation of the janissaries (25.B–35.A), where he almost places the point of their decline at the very beginning of their existence: "Peasants heard this news and wanted to enlist in the sultan's service. Many men enlisted … and as time passed they began being seditious" (25.B–26.A). Allegedly, it was after this that the janissaries began to be recruited via the *devşirme*. After describing their rules and structure in detail, Dımışki describes the arsenal and the navy and summarizes the budget for the year A.H. 1090/1679, just as Hezarfen had done for 1660/1 (36.B–37.A). Next, he gives the rules and protocol for imperial campaigns, adding a short history of the great Ottoman conquests (37.A–43.A). The rest (and indeed the largest part) of Dımışki's treatise is a concise but full description of Ottoman territory, from Istanbul (43.B–49.B; with stories on its creation, conquest, buildings, and population) to Egypt (126.B–134.A).

• • •

Thus, "administration manuals" continued to be produced throughout the seventeenth century. However, their accuracy compared to the actual situation of the empire grew weaker and weaker over time. If early seventeenth-century texts were outdated or exaggerated, Hezarfen's treatise is extraordinarily so: his use of Lütfi Pasha, already 150 years old, for matters such as the function and income of viziers, and of Ebussu'ud Efendi for land-holding regulations, shows that his work was conceived more as a compilation than as an actual description or a political agenda. Why, then, should a late seventeenth-century author copy mining regulations almost two centuries old? The answer may be found in the heterogeneous nature of *Telhisü'l-beyân* itself: why should the same author also incorporate the history of coffee and tobacco? As Hezarfen himself explains, he intended to write a *description* of the Ottoman Empire as a supplement to his universal history, in which he had produced similar descriptions of the Central Asian empires.[87] In this respect, he may be compared to his great contemporary, the traveler Evliya Çelebi, whose volume on Istanbul (the first book of his *Seyahatnâme* or "Book of travels") consists of a similar mixture of history, topography, and institutional description. Compilations such as these were conceived and executed within a broader culture of authors copying each other; to a certain degree, it was not originality that mattered but rather an exhibition of polymathy (similar observations have been made on Ottoman lyric poetry). On the other hand, it should be kept in mind that such compilations also had entertainment value; as Robert Dankoff has suggested, Evliya Çelebi had "the traditional twin aims of *edeb*: to instruct and to entertain". In the first case, he may or may not have intended to deceive his audience, while in the second there was a kind of mutual understanding and agreement.[88] It is tempting to apply this observation to the texts studied above, too.

Moreover, by this time the *kanunname* genre seems to have lost any normative value. Indeed, Hezarfen's real advice can be found in scattered pieces of inserted commentary. On the other hand, the anachronistic framework of his description (in contrast with the fact that his lists are quite up-to-date—see, for instance, the reference to Crete) shows, perhaps, that the real significance of his work is to be found in these scattered comments, rather than in bringing the "administration manual" genre to perfection—all the more if the interpretation proposed for his theory regarding the ulema is valid.

At any rate, then, the genre had clearly changed in aim and scope after the mid-seventeenth century. Eyyubi Efendi and the anonymous copyist were belated specimens of this genre, whereas the anonymous author of *Kavânîn-i osmanî ve râbıta-ı Âsitâne*, with his emphasis on both ulema and janissaries, was, as shall be seen, more attuned to late seventeenth-century realities. As for Dımışkî, it seems he was more interested in the emerging science of geography than with giving political advice. It seems that, as will be argued in the next two chapters, from the 1650s onwards the issue of the "old law" had lost its urgency and relevance for policy-making. The central bureaucracy still held to the idea that they were entitled to a share of the power, but the "constitutional"

87 Hezarfen seems to have embarked on an encyclopedic project similar to that of his mentor, Kâtib Çelebi; one has the impression, however, that his fame rested more on his European acquaintances than with his actual work.

88 Dankoff 2006, 153–154.

forces now regarded the Sunna, rather than the "old law", as the main framework of binding rules. On the other side, among the same circles there arose a different current of thought, one that explicitly advocated, for the first time, innovation and change as a legitimate and even imperative demand. The two trends did not necessarily have different aims (and, for both sides, monetization and the decay of the timariot system were, by then, accepted facts), but they differed in their ideological framework and legitimizing argumentation. Hezarfen's work, with its sharp contrast between form and content, represents this balance nicely.

CHAPTER 6

The "Sunna-Minded" Trend

E. Ekin Tuşalp Atiyas

This chapter follows the seventeenth-century conceptualizations of an ideal political order based on the twin premises of the Sharia and the prophetic Sunna. One of the events that have come to define the Ottoman seventeenth century is the emergence of the three successive generations of "Salafist" preachers known as the Kadızadelis.[1] Recent studies on the Kadızadeli movement and the reactions to it have opened up a wide arena for discussions of the concepts of orthodoxy vs. heterodoxy, the multiple pillars of Sufism, the boundaries of religious belief, and its early-modern regulations in the Ottoman Empire.[2] What has become evident is that the debates of the seventeenth century cannot simply be described as the products of the antagonism between the "Salafist orthodoxy" of the Kadızadelis and the "heterodox" reactions to it by its Sufi targets. Concern for upholding the Sharia and "commanding right and forbidding wrong" in the administration of the Muslim public sphere was shared by the entire spectrum of the participants in the debates examined in this chapter, ranging from Sufi sheikhs to Kadızadeli preachers.

This chapter will focus on placing these "Sunna-minded trends" on the historical map of Ottoman political thought.[3] The agendas of the first half of the seventeenth century hardly seem political at first sight and seem to have evolved around the tenets of correct belief and the correct performance of religious duties. However, it will be seen that the authors examined in this

1 The term "Salafism" was coined to describe the social and ideological movements that upheld the practices of the first three generations of Muslims (*al-salaf al-salih*) at the expense of the rationalist and allegorical readings of Islamic scripture. For a recent discussion of the term see Lauzière 2010.

2 See Ocak 1979–1983; Öztürk 1981; Zilfi 1986; Zilfi 1988, 129–181; Çavuşoğlu 1990; Clayer 1994; Terzioğlu 1999; Le Gall 2004; Terzioğlu 2007; El-Rouayheb 2008; El-Rouayheb 2010; Curry 2010; Terzioğlu 2010; Terzioğlu 2012; Ivanyi 2012; Sariyannis 2012; Evstatiev 2013.

3 For instance, Derin Terzioğlu concludes that although the Kadızadelis did not include administrative matters such as taxation, appointments to public offices, and criminal law in their writings, they might have shared their opinions on these subjects orally or in writings that have simply been lost or overlooked. She also notes that, up until the "third stage" of the movement in the 1660s and 70s, several unsympathetic observers also picked on the Kadızadelis for focusing on "trivia" and for not having anything of substance to say on the "important" problems that faced the Ottoman state. See Terzioğlu 2010, 258.

© KONINKLIJKE BRILL NV, LEIDEN, 2019 | DOI:10.1163/9789004385245_008

chapter did indeed discuss the limits of political authority: the standards of Sunna-abiding political conduct and the parameters of public administration as applied to the relations between Muslims and non-Muslims, and laws about taxation and ownership of land.

The preceding chapters sought "political thought" in the works written either by the theoretically-minded moralists hailing from the Perso-Iranian traditions or by the practically-minded Ottoman bureaucrats who focused on the day-to-day problems affecting the Ottoman treasury. Most of the writers studied here, however, were sheikhs, preachers, disciples, and lower-ranking ulema, some of whom were willingly accommodated, others uncomfortably tolerated by the political establishment. The texts produced by this diverse group would defy any genre-related categorization. The reigns of Ahmed I (1603–17) and Murad IV (1623–40) both produced a wave of political treatises in the *nasihatname* style, addressed to the sultans.[4] Yet, more often than not, these works of advice transmitted the voices of the preachers who authored them, and lectured their readers on religious and moral duties. In that sense they resemble the catechistical *ilm-i hal* literature from the same period. Some even formulated issues in the form of questions and answers, similar to fatwa manuals.[5]

It would also be wrong to conclude that the Kadızadelis and their Sufi opponents monopolized intellectual discussion about the Sharia and the Sunna in the seventeenth century. There were participants in the debate from all across the Ottoman confessional spectrum, including bureaucratically-minded Melamis such as Sarı Abdullah Efendi (1584–1660) and radical Sufis such as Niyazi-i Mısri (1618–94).

1 The Controversy of the Century? The Kadızadelis

Salafism is the most widely-used generic term to describe a range of ideological/theological movements that emerged in the long period between the fourteenth and the nineteenth centuries. In spite of the much-disputed ambiguities and anachronisms it evokes, the term has three components that are crucial

4 For a discussion of the political literature produced by the Sufi sheikhs and preachers of the time, see Terzioğlu 2010, 247–250.

5 For a discussion of the seventeenth-century *ilm-i hal* literature and how it represented the religious counterpart of the political advice literature of the period, see Terzioğlu 2013. For the role of preachers and the tradition of preaching in medieval Islamic history, see Berkey 2001 and more recently Jones 2012. Another discussion on the genre-related categorizations of Ottoman "advice literature" can be found in Şen 2011.

in defining these diverse historical movements: the primacy of the prophetic Sunna as a model for public behavior; the inherent belief in the corruption of the times as a result of "innovations" (*bid'a*) that contradict the practices of the earliest Muslims (*ehl-i salaf*); and a strong demand for the Muslim authorities to regulate, discipline, and improve public morals and practices.

The Kadızadeli movement has been widely accepted as a manifestation of this "Salafi reformism."[6] One of the earliest sources to mention the contentions of "Birgivi followers" (*Birgivi hulefası*) in Istanbul is the fatwa collection of the chief mufti Esad Efendi (in office 1615–22 and 1623–25).[7] Other sources refer to the adherents of the Kadızade movement sometimes as the Kadızadeliler and sometimes, using a popular corruption of *faqih*, as "*fakılar*."[8] The message voiced by the Kadızadelis found many adherents among the ulema as well as some individual Sufis. However, those who most enthusiastically embraced the message were the mid-to-low ranking mosque preachers, public lecturers, and lesser religious functionaries.[9] The very public nature of their preaching and lecturing rendered the Kadızadeli cause highly visible and further augmented the impact of their message. As will be discussed in the following pages, they managed to attract a very mixed social group as followers. The heterogenous nature of their adherents must have magnified the Kadızadeli voice and carried it to audiences it would not otherwise have reached. As a result, the Kadızadeli controversy occupied a significant place in contemporary writings and continues to do so in modern scholarship, perhaps disproportionally to its actual historical importance. Nonetheless, it is true that the rift between the followers of Kadızade Mehmed Efendi and those of the Halveti Sheikh Abdülmecid Sivasi created a large degree of socio-political tension in the capital, one which could only be curbed by the interventions of the high-ranking ulema and other political dignitaries. While the degree of political violence created by this rift never matched that of the janissary and cavalry uprisings, the Ottoman court was subject to constant manipulation from each side, both of which successfully commissioned judicial opinions and decrees for a series of executions and banishments.

The entire Kadızadeli vs Halveti rift emerges in the sources as an issue-based controversy centered on contemporaneous socio-religious practices. One of the earliest issues that emerged on the Ottoman public scene was the legality of cash *vakfs* and Birgivi Mehmed Efendi's challenging of the chief

6 Terzioğlu 1999, 194.
7 Terzioğlu 1999, 200.
8 Öztürk 1981, 200.
9 Zilfi 1986; Terzioğlu 1999, 194.

mufti Ebussu'ud (in office 1545–73) over cash endowments, which involved usury—prohibited by Islamic law but, as seen in chapter 3, rationalized on the basis of customary practice and the public good. Kâtib Çelebi's *Mîzânü'l-hakk fi'l-ihtiyâri'l-ahakk* (see below, chapter 7) serves as an index of the practices whose permissibility was challenged by the Kadızadelis.[10] Among the most controversial were visiting tombs, using music and dance in Sufi ceremonies, drinking coffee, the existence of coffeehouses, the consumption of tobacco, and communal performances of supererogatory prayers on the nights of Regaib, Berat, and Kadir.

Here, a short outline of the Kadızadeli movement will be given, which should be read against the other political developments of the seventeenth century that are described at the beginning of chapters 5 and 7. The first protagonist of the seventeenth-century Salafist upsurge in the capital, Kadızade Mehmed, came from Balıkesir and arrived in Istanbul sometime before 1622. By 1633, he had gained the attention of Murad IV, who frequented the mosque where he preached to listen to his sermons and so invited him to the palace.[11] Murad IV wanted to control the increasingly unruly janissaries and the cavalry regiments in the capital and the Kadızadelis' anti-innovation ideology served as a good pretext to get rid of the coffeehouses where the disobedient elements usually congregated.[12]

Kadızade Mehmed Efendi was given extra doctrinal credit in contemporaneous scholarship for producing an expanded translation of *Siyasat al-Shariyya*, by the Hanbali scholar Ibn Taymiyya (d. 1328), who was regarded as one of the strictest authorities in Islamic legal thought. The work is entitled *Tâcü'r-resâ'il ve minhacü'l-vesâ'il* ("The crown of the epistles and the way of [proper] causes"). However, its authorship has convincingly been disputed, and the most recent conclusion is that it was penned not by Kadızade Mehmed but by a Halveti sheikh by the same name, Kadızade Mehmed İlmi (d. 1631/2), who also wrote two *nasihatname*s for Murad IV.[13]

The chronicles are silent about Kadızadeli activism during the reign of Ibrahim I (1640–48). However, following the accession of Mehmed IV to the throne in 1648, the second Kadızadeli wave began to affect the capital. The most prominent leader of the Kadızadeli clique at this time, Üstüvani Mehmed Efendi, had many followers, especially among the personnel of the palace, including the gardeners (*bostancı*), halberdiers (*baltacı*), gatekeepers (*kapucıs*),

10 Kâtib Çelebi 1888/89; Kâtib Chelebi – Lewis 1957.

11 Terzioğlu 1999, 194.

12 Terzioğlu 1999, 201.

13 See Terzioğlu 2007.

and sweetmakers (*helvacı*).[14] Some of the more influential ones among them introduced Üstüvani to the court, where he later came under the protection of a certain Reyhan Ağa, the sultan's tutor.[15] The Kadızadeli sympathizers, and especially those among the palace corps, proudly pointed out that the people of the palace had never before been so distinguished in their piety and religious learning. Though indirectly, they played a role in the elimination of Murad IV and Ibrahim's mother, Kösem, in 1650–51 by the latter's arch-rival Turhan Sultan (Mehmed IV's mother), who crafted an alliance with Kadızadeli supporters in the palace against the pro-Kösem palace aghas, whom they accused of draining the public treasury, and the corruption that had characterized Sultan Ibrahim's reign. Not surprisingly, Kösem and her clique had close ties with the Sufi establishment.[16]

Between 1650–51 and 1656, the Kadızadelis were able to force the grand vizier Melek Ahmed Pasha (d. 1662, v. 1651–53) to crack down on at least one Halveti lodge, in Demirkapı. The *müfti* Bahai Efendi, who, during his first term of office between 1649 and 1651, had declared tobacco permitted, banned two rebuttals of Birgivi Mehmed Efendi's much-esteemed work *al-Tariqa al-Muhammadiyya* ("The Muhammadan way"), deported its authors from the capital, and issued a fatwa declaring *devran* and *sema* (the use of dance and music in Sufi ceremonies) prohibited during his second term between 1652 and 1654.[17] It has been noted that the nature of the movement had undergone a fundamental change by this time. Under Kadızade Mehmed, the Kadızadelis had denounced all corruption and wanted a complete and total reformation of ethical attitudes. Under Üstüvani, the movement merely became an interest group vying for power and ready to exploit it for whatever it could bring in terms of material gain.[18] This increasingly pragmatic outlook might have played a role in the widening of their social appeal around the middle of the seventeenth century. According to contemporary sources, the economic situation in the capital indeed contributed to the widening of the Kadızadeli network, especially as Istanbul tradesmen felt that they were unjustly suppressed by the economic policies of the janissary aghas in the palace (see also below, chapter 7). This resentment would culminate in the revolt of the "people of the market" in 1651 against the aghas and their protector, grand vizier Melek Ahmed Pasha.[19] The chief mufti and historian Karaçelebizade Abdülaziz Efendi, who was fairly

14 Terzioğlu 1999, 201.
15 Öztürk 1981, 215, 222.
16 Terzioğlu 1999, 202–203; Sariyannis 2012, 271–278.
17 Terzioğlu 1999, 204.
18 Öztürk 1981, 257.
19 Sariyannis 2012, 271.

sympathetic to the Kadızadelis, described the policies implemented by the aghas as an "evil innovation" (*bidat-i seyyi'e*)" that "obstructed the movement of merchants".[20] It is not clear to what extent the Kadızadelis steered the course of the tradesmen's revolt. Neither do we know whether the market forces that took up the Kadızadeli cause belonged to the richer and more rooted mercantile elite or to the lower strata of new entrants into the mercantile class who were striving to make the most of the economic opportunities around them, and which included the janissaries.[21] However, there is no doubt that the Kadızadeli discourse manipulated the mundane woes of those who had been negatively impacted by the economic conditions of the period.

The infamous "plane tree incident" (when janissaries and sipahis put an end to the power of the harem aghas) of 4 March 1656 was a temporary setback for the Kadızadelis. As a result of this event, it appears that the Kadızadelis lost most of their protectors and close friends in the palace. Despite their much-weakened status in the palace and among government officials, they still had some influence over the designation of posts and offices. The defeat of the Ottoman navy in the Dardanelles by the Venetians provided the occasion for a stronger show of force by the Kadızadelis.[22] The mob that was whipped up by the Kadızadeli leaders included *medrese* students as well as traders and craftsmen. The escalation of events alarmed the newly-appointed grand vizier Köprülü Mehmed Pasha and he banished the three Kadızadeli leaders Üstüvani, Türk Ahmed, and Divane Mustafa from the capital.[23]

The movement maintained a low profile until the end of Köprülü Mehmed's grand vizierate. Yet this was not to last forever, since, immediately after he succeeded his father in 1661, Köprülü Mehmed's Köprülü Fazıl Ahmed Pasha (d. 1676, in office 1661–76), who already had a reputation within ulema circles for his scholarly bent, invited the preacher Vani Mehmed Efendi, whom he had first met in Erzurum, to the capital. The influence that Vani had over the grand vizier is documented by the collection of his letters that reflected the significant level of correspondence between them, especially when the grand vizier was away on military campaign.[24] Within a year of Fazıl Ahmed's assumption

20 Sariyannis 2012, 276.

21 Cemal Kafadar has described the Kadizadeli movement as a reaction to "the new urban reality", a reality which promoted the sociability of the "Janissary-affiliated social class" (Kafadar 2007). Sariyannis agrees with this conclusion and points to support from middle or even upper mercantile strata, rather than the lower echalons who were used as a fighting force by former, being their servants and apprentices (Sariyannis 2012, 277).

22 Öztürk 1981, 255–257; Terzioğlu 1999, 205.

23 Öztürk 1981, 263; Terzioğlu 1999, 205.

24 Vânî Efendi, *Münşe'ât*, Istanbul, Süleymaniye Ktp. Ayasofya MS 4308.

of office and Vani's arrival in Istanbul, the central government was issuing orders prohibiting the sale of tobacco, coffee, alcoholic drinks, and other means of "illicit" amusement, as well as calling for vigilance against the mixing of the sexes outside family circles.[25] In line with the spirit of the times, the mufti Minkarizade Yahya issued a *fetva* against *devran*, to be followed by a longer one against the *devran* of the Sufis and the Mevlevi *sema*. In 1670–71, it was decreed that all taverns had to be torn down. One of the most controversial measures that was believed to have been inspired by such Kadızadeli "vigilance" took place in 1681, when the *kazasker* of Rumili Beyazızade Ahmed Efendi (1634–87) declared death by public stoning (*recm*) to be the appropriate punishment for a married Muslim woman accused of adultery with a Jewish man. The punishment was carried out in the middle of the At Meydanı in Istanbul.[26] This was the first incident of public stoning in the Ottoman capital and aroused much criticism, yet it also showed the authorities' firm backing of the application of the Sharia.

In 1683, when the ambitions of the grand vizier Kara Mustafa Pasha to conquer Vienna were quashed, the entire Köprülüzade clan was forced to resign from their posts. A counselor to Kara Mustafa Pasha, Vani Efendi was left in the lurch without his protection.[27] Shortly after this change in government, there also took place a definite shift in official policy towards the Sufi orders, and influential Halveti and other sheikhs were received favorably at Mehmed IV's court.[28] Subsequently, in 1687, the government put a tax on tobacco and thus legalized it.

2 Beyond the Social History of the Controversy

Although this narrative neatly summarizes how the Kadızadelis polarized the Ottoman public in the seventeenth century, it also draws a very simplistic picture of the main targets of Kadızadeli vigilance and represents them as a homogenous "Sufi lot". While Sufi practices do seem to have preoccupied the Kadızadelis during this period, there was by no means a united social or ideological "Sufi" front in the reactions to the Kadızadelis.

---

25 Terzioğlu 1999, 106.
26 Defterdar – Özcan 1995, 114–115; Silahdar – Refik 1928, 1:731; Terzioğlu 1999, 173.
27 Terzioğlu 1999, 173, 174.
28 For the Mevlevi influence at Mehmed IV's court, see Terzioğlu 1999, 174 and Baer 2008, 69–70.

First of all, the Kadızadeli position towards the Sufis showed great variety during the seventeenth century.[29] Neither the Sharia-minded ideologues of the sixteenth century, such as Birgivi, nor the seventeenth-century advocates of the Kadızadeli cause rejected all aspects of Sufism indiscriminately. Quite a few of them actually experimented with it at certain points in their lives. Secondly, when the writings of famous Halveti sheikhs beginning from the late sixteenth century are examined, it becomes apparent that the discourses about correct belief and practice varied greatly from one Halveti branch to another, and they often openly disagreed with each other. In any case, strict espousal of the Sharia had always been an important part of being a respectable Sufi figure.[30] It has been argued that, by the ninth century AD, and certainly in the classical didactic manuals of Sufism of the tenth century, Sufism had already fully embraced the Sunna, and antinomian Sufis were, by and large, the exception to the rule.[31] Among the terms that modern scholars applied to this Sunna-oriented Sufism and Sufis are "orthodox Sufism", "Sharia-minded Sufism", "juridical Sufism", or "Sunnizing Sufis." Depending on the audience, most of the "Sufi" authors examined in this chapter expounded "a type of mysticism that is epistemologically subservient to the authority of religious law".[32] Finally, one should not exaggerate the influence of the Kadızadeli preachers on the courts of the Ottoman sultans since they had to share royal favors and commissions with a powerful network of the deeply-esteemed Halveti *tarikat*s (fraternities).[33]

The most adamant opponents of the Kadızadelis in the first stages of the controversy were themselves "Sunna-promoting Halvetis". The primary adversary of Kadızade Mehmed in the 1630s, Abdülmecid Sivasi, came from a family of Sufi sheikhs based in Sivas and received a thorough education in both the exoteric and esoteric sciences under the direction of his uncle, Şemseddin Sivasi (d. 1597), the founder of the Şemsi branch of the Halveti order. Abdülmecid followed his uncle to Istanbul after an invitation by Mehmed III (r. 1595–1603) and there launched a distinguished career as a Sufi sheikh and preacher. Among those who pledged allegiance to Abdülmecid Sivasi were some of the highest-ranking military officials, including the *reisülküttab* (chief secretary) La'li Efendi, the chief mufti Sun'ullah Efendi, and finally Sultan Ahmed I, who

29 Terzioğlu 1999, 200, 212; Le Gall 2004.
30 See Clayer 1994, 75–78.
31 See Radtke 1994, 302–307.
32 Ivanyi 2012, 92–93.
33 Curry 2010, 77, fn. 101.

was reported to have held the Sufi sheikh in such esteem and intimacy that he addressed him as "my father".[34]

After Sivasi's death, his disciples, who had taken over many of the city's lodges as well as preaching posts, continued to play an important role in the controversies at least for two decades more. Among them, Sivasi's nephew Abdülahad Nuri (d. 1651) was a particularly influential figure and, according to his disciple and biographer Nazmi Efendi, also the last Sivasi sheikh to have fought successfully against militant Kadızadelis.[35] Abdülahad Nuri witnessed the reigns of Mehmed III, Ahmed I, Mustafa I, Osman II, Murad IV, İbrahim, and the first two years of Mehmed IV's reign. Compared to his master Sivasi, he was more explicit in his denunciation of the Kadızadelis and called them "lowly idiots" (*ammi eblehler*).[36]

The Sivasi branch did not become a major player in the third and the last phase of the Kadızadeli wave at least until the 1680s.[37] Yet the appearance of such a relatively complaisant stance should not rule out the existence of uniquely dissident voices, such as that of Niyazi Misri, who criticized not only the content of the Kadızadeli message but also the loyalties the Kadızadelis managed to secure at the highest levels of the Ottoman political establishment.[38]

With these qualifications in mind, we can proceed to a discussion of how the Sunna-minded trend shaped Ottoman political thought in the seventeenth century. Yet one first has to look back at two late sixteenth-century figures, Münir-i Belgradi and Mehmed Birgivi, who were often mentioned in the writings of the seventeenth-century authors as the ultimate authorities on the correct Sunna.

2.1 *Münir-i Belgradi and Two Works for Two Distinct Audiences*

Known as Münir-i Belgradi, İbrahim b. İskender of Belgrade was one of the most important figures of Sufi biographical writing in the empire.[39] As was typical of most of the scholars of his generation, Belgradi received training from Halveti sheikhs, in Sofia and Istanbul, and through a *medrese* education. As well as the two works that will be discussed here (*Silsiletü'l-mukarrebin ve menakıbü'l-muttekin* and *Nisabü-l intisâb ve adabü'l-iktisâb*), he wrote on many

34 On Sivasi see Gündoğdu 2000; Terzioğlu 1999, 250–251.

35 Çavuşoğlu 1990, 118ff.; Terzioğlu 1999, 250–251; Nuri – Akkaya 2003.

36 Terzioğlu 1999, 264.

37 Terzioğlu 1999, 251–252.

38 For Mısri's critique of the entire Köprülü clan, see Terzioğlu 1999, 336–342.

39 Belgradi – Bitiçi 2001, 116; Clayer 2002; Fotić 2005, 59–60.

different subjects, ranging from his refutation of the Mevlevi *sema* to aspects of Islamic law (*furu*), until his death sometime in the period 1620–28, in Belgrade.[40]

The two works that will be discussed below represent what is most interesting about Münir-i Belgradi. In *Silsiletü'l-mukarrebin ve menakıbü'l-muttekin* ("The chain of those who are allowed to approach God and the heroic deeds of the pious"), which is a biographical dictionary of Sufi sheikhs, he introduced the Ottoman audience to deep historical lore on Sufism and mostly identified himself with the historical tradition woven around Sufi sheikhs and their miracles. *Nisabü-l intisâb ve adabü'l-iktisâb* ("The genealogy of allegiance and the manners of acquisition"), on the other hand, seems to have been intended for the internal consumption of a much more restricted audience, i.e. "the *fütüvvet ehli*", the sixteenth-century offshoots of the *akhi* brotherhoods organized around craft guilds. With respect to its relevance for our study of Ottoman political thought, the *Silsile* shows how a Sufi *alim* from the Balkans perceived his own time as a period of decline. Belgradi idealizes the troika of the sheikhs (*meşayih*) who flocked to Ottoman lands in the fourteenth and fifteenth centuries, the frontier warriors (*gazi*) who expanded it, and the people (*reaya*) whose well-being represented the "good old days" of the empire. He decried the decaying status of the *meşayih*, the corruption of the religious establishment (*ulema*), and the dissolution of the aspirations for holy war (*gaza*). In the *Nisab*, Belgradi's main concern seems to be steering the guilds away from what he saw as the corrupting influence of certain antinomian Sufi sects. He engaged in a very critical reading of the textual heritage of *fütüvvet*s and tried to bring an internal discipline to *fütüvvet* culture by confirming certain textual traditions and eliminating others. While the first work ordered and presented the Sufi historical tradition as an antidote to the corruption of his time, the second work problematized the current state of that very tradition and tried to "Sunnitize" it by stripping it of the voices that were viewed as heretical by the Ottoman religious establishment.

The work that sealed Belgradi's status as an authority on Sufi historiography was *Silsiletü'l-mukarrebin ve menakıbü'l-muttekin*. As its title suggests, it is a biographical work that aimed to reconstruct the genealogical chains (*silsile*) of the Sufi sheikhs and spiritual leaders (*pir*) going all the way back to Prophet Muhammed with critical attention given to the hierarchies between disciples and teachers, and to the stories of their miraculous deeds (*menkıbe*). Belgradi began the work by exploring the Sivasiyye, Üveysiyye, Hacı Bayram, Zeyniyye, Nakşibendi, and Baba Kemal Cundi branches, noting and correcting the inaccuracies in these chains. The first section covers the Sufis of the pre-Ottoman

40 See Belgradi – Bitiçi 2001, 20–24.

period; the second is devoted to the personalities who lived under Ottoman rule and covers the period up to 1612.[41]

As mentioned above, in addition to the breadth of the biographical information it offers, *Silsile* also contains significant criticism of the current state of affairs. Belgradi's criticisms constitute one of the earliest examples of the Sufi outlook on the Ottoman "decline", one which would be often echoed in the writings of seventeenth-century Ottoman Sufis. Moreover, these criticisms highlight the complexities of the Sufi identity by revealing the sensitivities and priorities of an early-modern Ottoman Sufi. Most of Belgradi's criticisms are embedded in the biographies of influential Sufi sheikhs. For example, the biography of the famous illuminationist scholar Suhrawardi (d. 1191) leads to the account of how respected sheikhs from Iranian and Arab lands arrived in the Ottoman Empire only to be disappointed by the corruption introduced by viziers and *defterdars*. Excessive inflation, the oppression of the *reaya*, and the desecration of imperial practice by a new, ignorant cadre of political elites who did not know what real religion was led to the eventual impoverishment and diminished status of the real *meşayih* who were marginalized by the new order of things (B117, 156). Belgradi gives an especially detailed account of the inflation that hit the markets from the time of Süleyman the Magnificent onwards, leading to the capture of this world by malice (*fesad*) and bribery (*rüşvet*) and leaving no room for the dervishes' modesty and the religiosity of the pious (B118). Timars were bought and sold, the *gazi*s could not be trusted anymore, the *ulema* was preoccupied with buying and selling posts instead of with *ilm*, impious people became judges, ignorant viziers engaged in bribery, and the poll-tax (*haraç*) registers were given to bums (B158). While discussing the life of Sheikh Mahmud Buhari (d. 1587), Belgradi broached the subject of the 1585 famine, which led to an excessive shortage of essential goods and therefore caused inflation. Mutes and dwarfs intervened in the business of the state, while the masters of the old custom were long gone (B181–186). While relating the miraculous deeds of Sheikh Sinan Efendi (d. 1601), he engaged in a long harangue against judges who were "clueless about the Sharia but knew the income that their posts generated quite well" (B205). In his biography of Sheikh Bali Efendi of Sofia (d. 1553), Belgradi compared the conquests of the old days with the absence of any concern for *gaza* in his own: "When campaign season arrives, everyone disappears". *Zeamet*s were distributed as pocket money (B209) and the janissary garrison, which used to be the garrison of the righteous ones working for religion and holy war, became totally corrupted (B213). Spread among these observations are several direct admonitions that

41 Belgradi – Bitiçi 2001, 32, 33.

Belgradi gave the sultan to wake up and reclaim his hold on the affairs of his realm (B214).

Belgradi's *Nisabü-l intisâb ve adabü'l-iktisâb* is a refutation of Seyyid Muhammed b. Seyyid Alâuddin el-Hüseyin er-Razavi's (d. after 1514) *Miftâhü'd-dakâ'ik fi beyâni'l-fütüvveti ve'l-hakâ'ik* (also known as the *Fütüvvetnâme-i kebîr*).[42] Although Belgradi quoted Seyyid Muhammed quite often in the work and called him a *müteseyyid* (a true descendant of the Prophet's family),[43] the *Nisab* is a strong critique of the *fütüvvetname* tradition that Seyyid Muhammed represented and which, according to Belgradi was "full of vanities, false claims, and lies".[44] Belgradi claimed that the guild masters showed him the *fütüvvetnames* they had in their hands and, when he pointed out to their errors, they asked him to compose a work correcting all of them. His criticism of Seyyid Muhammed targeted the nature of the latter's sources. According to Belgradi, Seyyid Muhammed resorted to books that were not respectable (*muteber olmayan*), i.e. the books that, in Belgradi's words, belonged to "illiterate Sufis", Hurufis, Batinis, and similar groups of "perversion", among others. These did not abide by the Sunna, and transmitted information from one another under the rubric of *marifa*. Belgradi's criticism of these sources led him to the conclusion that it was wrong to ascribe the spiritual ranking of *pir* to fictional characters like Selman-ı Farisi, who had been elevated to this status by these sources.[45] A similar historical refutation was applied to the claim that Ahi Devran was the *pir* of the leather makers (*debbağ*). Belgradi corrected this information and pointed out instead that he was simply a master leather maker who lived during the age of Sultan Orhan. The claim of spiritual mastery was concocted later during the reign of Bayezid II when a "liar" wrote a *fütüvvetname* for the leather-makers.[46]

Belgradi's criticisms went beyond textual analysis of the *fütüvvet* sources. Scholars studying the *fütüvve* organizations and Ottoman guilds have demonstrated that the close ties between the *fütüvvet* and the craft guilds gradually declined, meaning that the phenomenon of *ahilik* died off over the course of the second half of the fifteenth century. By the sixteenth century, *fütüvvet* principles had their audience primarily in various Sufi groups instead.[47] Belgradi must have been very well aware of this, since in the *Nisab* he warns the *fütüvvet*

42 Berlin, National Bibliothek no. Lanbd. 589; İstanbul Üniversitesi Kütüphanesi, Türkçe Yazmalar, MS 6803.

43 Sarıkaya 2010, 47.

44 Sarıkaya 2010, 54.

45 Sarıkaya 2010, 54, 55.

46 Sarıkaya 2010, 51.

47 Yıldırım 2011.

brotherhoods against *rafizilik* (schism, especially represented by the Shi'a) and perversion, criticizes the Melamis, Kalenderis, and the Haydariyye, and underlines the importance of belonging to the *sünnet ehli*, the people of the Sunna. He pointed out the hidden meanings behind the usual practices of the brotherhoods and warned them that their loyalties actually might have extended to the Kızılbaş and the Safavid shah. Belgradi's own definition of *fütüvvet* is completely devoid of such impurities and is centered around the concept of valor (*yiğitlik*), whereby one would work and exert oneself according to one's own strength.[48] In conclusion, Belgradi's *Nisab* exemplifies the centrality of the market people as a social force and how their ideological loyalties became a source of concern for the Sunnitizing Halveti establishment from the sixteenth century onwards.

2.2 *Imam Birgivi as the "Predecessor"*

The biography and main works of Şeyh Muhyiddin b. Pir Ali b. İskender el-Rûmî el-Birgivî (1523–73) were described in some detail in chapter 3, above. In Ottoman historiography, Birgivi has been many things at once: the founding father of Salafism in Ottoman lands, the predecessor of the Kadızadelis, and one of the first early-modern critiques of the Islamic tradition who opened the way to the much-debated eighteenth-century Islamic "enlightenment".[49] His image as a strictly orthodox scholar comes from his oft-quoted participation in the famous cash-*vakf* controversy of the sixteenth century, in which he refuted the cash-*vakf* formulations that the Ottoman chief mufti Ebussu'ud and judge Bilalzade came up with.[50] His major work, *al-Tarîqa al-Muhammadiyya wa al-sîrat al-Ahmadiyya* ("The Muhammadan way and the character of the most laudable [Prophet]") is an extensive Hanafi-Maturidi explication of the Sunna that became a crucial reference text in the context of the seventeenth-century Kadızadeli versus Sivasi controversy, while his *Vâsiyet-nâme* was extensively circulated in the later period as one of the most consulted books on Sunni catechism (*ilm-i hal*). Birgivi's strict interpretation of Islamic scripture in his writings on law and piety stems from his loyalty to the Hanafi legal tradition and its most important figures, including Abu Hanifa (d. 150/767), Abu Yusuf (d. 182/798), and Muhammad al-Shaybani (d. 189/805).[51]

---

48 Sarıkaya 2010, 61–62.

49 Works on Birgivi include Yüksel 1972; Martı 2008; Birgili – Duman 2000; Birinci 1996; Radtke 2002; Lekesiz 2007; Kaylı 2010: Ivanyi 2012. See also chapter 3, above.

50 *İnkâz al-hâlikîn*, *İnkâz al-naîmîn* and *Al-sayf al-sârim*. For more details on the cash-*vakf* controversy see chapter 3, above.

51 Ivanyi 2012, 65. In addition to Abu al-Layth and post-classical "fatāwā" handbooks, Birgivi also drew on a range of other Hanafī sources—both early and later ones. From among the

Birgivi's interpretation of the Sharia and Sunna informed much of the subsequent debates on law, piety, and public administration in the seventeenth century. There are two crucial aspects of his influence that have been recently emphasized by students of the Birgivi corpus. One is that, ideologically and intellectually, Birgivi's thought was too complex to be simply branded as ultraconservative and anti-Sufi. In terms of his intellectual sources, although he is frequently mentioned alongside Ibn Taymiyya, the textual evidence that is thought to have brought them together has proven to be dubious at its best.[52] Moreover, his relationship with Sufism was much more complicated than previously thought. On top of his brief rapprochement with the Bayramiyya in Istanbul, in his writings he advocated a type of Sufism that focused on sobriety and strict adherence to the law.[53] Instead of outright condemnation of the Sufi tenets of Islam, he believed in the possibility of spiritual advancement "in the assimilation of Muhammad's beautiful example".[54] In terms of social outreach, Birgivi's message reached far beyond the Kadızadeli ranks, holding many seventeenth-century Sufi intellectuals in its sway.

It is not possible here to capture how concern for the primacy of the Sharia permeated all aspects of Birgivi's critique of contemporaneous political practices.[55] Yet Birgivi's handling of the issue of Ottoman arrangements regarding land tenure and taxation in the penultimate chapter of *al-Tarîqa al-Muhammadiyya* was widely followed in seventeenth-century Ottoman policies and therefore deserves to be studied in detail here.

In the *Tarîqa*, Birgivi voiced his criticism of the contemporary practices of land distribution, land ownership, and taxation.[56] According to classical Hanafi jurisprudence, ownership of land was originally vested in the individual, arising

former, he frequently cites Muhammad al-Shaybani (d. 189/804), al-Sarakhsî (d. 544/1149) and Marghînânî (d. 593/1197) (Ivanyi 2012, 72).

52 Ivanyi argues that the spurious link between them goes back to Ahmed al-Rûmî al-Akhisârî and his *Risāla fī ziyārat al-qubūr*, which was mistakenly attributed to Birgivi (Ivanyi 2012, 81; on al-Akhisari's relationship to Ibn Taymiyya see also Sheikh 2016). In a similar vein, Khaled El-Rouayheb has also argued that, "it is important to stress that [other than for the Ziyāra] Birgiwî showed little traces of being influenced by Ibn Taymiyya or Ibn al-Qayyim". He likewise speculates that "the views of Birgiwî and his Kadızadeli followers may have been rooted, not in the thought of Ibn Taymiyya, but in an intolerant current within the Ḥanafī-Māturīdī school, represented by such scholars as 'Alā' al-Dīn al-Bukhārī (d. 1438), who famously declared both Ibn 'Arabī and Ibn Taymiyya unbelievers" (El-Rouayheb 2010, 303). The same observation has been made by Terzioğlu as well (Terzioğlu 1999, 216, fn. 61).

53 Ivanyi 2012, 92; Terzioğlu 1999, 214.

54 Ivanyi 2012, 110. For a discussion of Birgivi's stance towards Sufism see Ivanyi 2012, 82–110.

55 Cf. above, chapter 3.

56 See Ivanyi 2012, 179.

from recognition by the *imam* of those who possessed the lands at the time of their conquest. The religious status of the owners in the time of conquest defined the nature of the tax that had to be paid: *'ushr* in the case of Muslims; *kharaj* in the case of non-Muslims. The status of *kharaj* lands remained fixed, however, even when the owners later converted to Islam or when the lands were sold to Muslims. Thus, from a relatively early stage, the initial connection between the legal status of the owner and the land was severed. In any case, the basic understanding remained one of individual ownership, not ownership by the state.[57] The Ottomans, however, would usually designate the new lands they conquered as *miri* (i.e. "of the ruler"). Yet these lands also continued to remain in the hands of the unbelievers who had owned them before and would continue treating it as if it were their own property, renting and even selling it. According to Birgivi, since those who cultivated the land were technically not its owners, the *kharaj* could actually not be demanded of them. As seen in chapter 3, one of the legal stratagems that Ottoman jurists employed to adapt this new situation into a Sharia framework was to reformulate the relationship between cultivators and the treasury as rent (*ijara*) that the cultivators were paying to the ruler, one equal to the value of the *kharaj*. Yet even with this new formulation, Birgivi ruled out the application of common legal transactions pertaining to property, such as "sale", "inheritance", and "the right to pre-emption".[58]

The clearest repercussion of the insistence on the private property status of the newly-conquered lands was in the Cretan *kanunname* of 1670, something which was in line with "classical" Hanafi legal theory and rejected the conventional Ottoman interpretation of the land as *miri* ("of the ruler").[59] In fact, the Cretan *kanunname* is seen as one of the products of the Kadızadeli influence on late seventeenth-century administrative decisions.[60] In the following pages, we will discuss the tenacity of the links between Birgivi, the Kadızadelis, and the policies implemented in the latter part of the seventeenth century. Suffice it to say here that the Sharia-minded approach to public administration in Ottoman lands did not begin with Birgivi since it was not only followed in the seventeenth century by the Kadızadelis.[61]

57 Ivanyi 2012, 115–117.

58 Ivanyi 2012, 279–280.

59 Kolovos 2007; Ivanyi 2012, 140.

60 Greene 1996; Gülsoy 2001; Veinstein 2004; Kermeli 2008.

61 Birgivi was not the first Ottoman thinker to emphasize the primacy of the Sharia as an important tenet of the ideal Muslim rulership and society. As seen in chapter 3, Şehzade Korkud (d. 1513), the eldest son of Sultan Bayezid II and brother of Selim II "the Grim", introduced a strong Sharia stance in his *Da 'wat al-nafs al-tâliha ilâ al-a'mâl al-sâliha* and

As will be seen, arguments for compliance with the Sharia in decisions regarding public administration would be used in the seventeenth century to criticize the functioning of the economy and the state's dealing with it. Birgivi himself was aware of the spinoffs of corruption in the larger sphere of the economy:[62]

> The majority of the sales in our markets and contracts of rent are invalid, corrupted, or reprehensible, [due to the fact that] most merchants and craftsmen are ignorant of the law.

Birgivi considered their transactions as either unlawful or reprehensible. Unlike Münir-i Belgradi, who idealized the Ottoman past based on the glories of its now defunct social, military, and political functionaries, Birgivi discussed the problems of inflation and coin clipping mainly from the perspective of their legal validity and religious permissibility.

2.3 *Commanding Right and Forbidding Wrong*

The Quranic injunction of commanding right and forbidding wrong has come to be seen as the backbone of Salafist theologies and their Sharia-centered political consequences. Ottoman Hanafism, however, has been regarded in general as rooted in "the accommodationist tradition of the Samanid northeast" and therefore not particularly concerned with the question of how to command right and forbid wrong, at least on the doctrinal level. Moreover, it has been suggested that, even when this issue was discussed, it did not take on the overtly political character that it had had for Abu Hanifa's interlocutors in the pre-Ottoman period.[63] Birgivi mentions the duty in his catechistic treatise without elaborating on it greatly, but treats it more substantially in the *Tarîqat*. Apart from a section where he promotes martyrdom in the name of the act, Birgivi's treatment does not depart substantially from the conventional Hanafi take on the subject.[64]

---

criticizes Ottoman administrative practices for their non-compliance with the Sharia. Ivanyi points to a sixteenth-century *fetva* that is surprisingly similar to Birgivi's in its critique (see again chapter 3, above). In a similar vein she notes that Pargalı Ibrahim Pasha had already attempted to "purify" the *kanun* by imposing, among other things, the *cizye* on Vlachs and *martolos*es in the preamble to the Bosnian *kanunname* (Ivanyi 2012, 142, 143).

62 Ivanyi 2012, 199, 200.

63 Cook 2000, 316. See also chapter 1, above.

64 Cook 2000, 323- 325.

On the practical level, the three successive Kadızadeli waves gave ample opportunity for their proponents to implement this injunction in the seventeenth century, although the authenticity of their call and the sincerity of their actions were always doubted by contemporaries. The chief mufti Zekeriyazade Yahya Efendi (d. 1644) is quoted to have referred to the Kadızadelis as "hypocrites" (*müra'iler*) who were "courageous in forbidding wrong, and respected by the ignorant masses; so that although their hypocrisy was harmful to themselves, it could be expedient in respect of others".[65]

No clear doctrinal take on the duty seems to have emerged in seventeenth-century Ottoman sources either. This doctrinal lacuna partly stems from the fact that the most famous Kadızadeli preachers to be credited with it did not leave many written works behind, especially compared to their more prolific Halveti counterparts. Üstüvani's sermons were later brought together by one of his followers in a catechistical compilation.[66] Vani Mehmed Efendi expressed his views on the danger of religious innovations and the necessity of religious obligations in two treatises written in Arabic, *Risâla fî hakk al-farz wa al-sunna wa al-bid'a fî ba'z al-'amal* ("The truth of religious obligations and the practices of Muhammad and innovation in some practices") and *Risâla fî karâhat al-jahr bi al-zikr* ("The abomination of public recitals of God's praises").[67] Even when it was mentioned and endorsed in the writings of the Kadızadelis or the Halvetis, the Quranic injunction to command right and forbid wrong rarely appeared as a distinct theoretical issue. Rather, the call for the implementation of this injunction seems to have served as a rhetorical tool to support the decline and corruption diagnosis prevalent in the seventeenth-century sources and to legitimize the distinct policies that the authors were advocating.

So if neither the Kadızadelis nor any others were offering a brand-new theory on the injunction of commanding right and forbidding wrong in their writings, then where else one can look for the expression of Sunna-mindedness in the Ottoman intellectual world? The answer is that, in each of the works analyzed in this chapter, a Sharia- and Sunna-centred viewpoint emerges as embedded in the authors' prognoses about the decline of Ottoman politics, society, and morals. Each author emphasized a different aspect of the Ottoman decline. Among the most disputed dimensions of the Ottoman decline in the writings of the seventeenth-century polemicists were disregard for the Sharia, the pervasiveness of innovation, the absence of qualified consultation around the sultan, the corruption of the ulema, the prevalence of bribery, the erosion

65 Cook 2000, 329.
66 Üstüvani – Yurdaydın 1963.
67 Köprülü Library: Lala İsmail 685/1, Hacı Beşir Ağa 406/3.

of the rules that regulated non-Muslim behavior in the public sphere, the ethics of the market place, and the taxation and administration of land.

3 Ottoman Decline *à la* Sunna

The crucial social and intellectual link between Birgivi Mehmed Efendi and Kadızade Mehmed was constituted through Birgivi's son Şeyh Fazlullah Efendi (d. 1622), who was taught by his father in Birgi and came to Istanbul around 1611–12. He served as Friday preacher, first in the Sultan Selim Mosque then in the Beyazid mosque. In both positions, it was Kadızade Mehmed Efendi who succeeded him, first in the position in Sultan Selim mosque and later in Beyazid Mosque following Fazlullah's death.[68] It has been noted that the year of his second succession (1622–23) also marked a turning point in the dissemination of Birgivi's works. In the same year, two copies were made of Birgivi's works after four years of silence. What is more remarkable, however, is that within eight years of Kadızadeli Mehmed taking up his new position as the preacher of Beyazid Mosque, 26 copies were made of Birgivi's works on religious sciences, compared with only 17 that had been produced in the previous 41 years since Birgivi's death.[69] It must have been Kadızadeli Mehmed's preaching, presumably filled with references to Birgivi, which created a demand for Birgivi's works and mobilized the copyists to reproduce them in increasing quantities.

Although Kadızade Mehmed must have played a crucial role in the introduction of Birgivi's corpus to a wider audience, the recent association of the authorship of *Tacü'r-Resail* with Kadızade Mehmed İlmi instead of Kadızade Mehmed Efendi renders the examination of the latter's intellectual world problematic, since it leaves us without any major treatise penned by Kadızade Mehmed. Nevertheless, a small portion of Kadızade Mehmed's account of the plight of Ottoman society is available in the panegyric poems he wrote for Murad IV. In a *kaside* presented to that sultan in 1630, Kadızade Mehmed complained of what he called the disruption of the proper channels of appointment, the domination of the *millet* and the influential people by women—whom he saw as responsible for many kinds of innovations (*bid'a*)—the engagement of the notables in wine-drinking and sodomy, the preachers who were mischief-makers and liars and who transmitted lies and slanders from the pulpits, and

68 Kaylı 2010, 182.

69 Kaylı 2010, 187.

the very short duration of *beylerbeyi* appointments, which forced them to rebel upon quickly losing their office.[70]

Kadızade's chief rival Sivasi was more productive in his rendition of a similarly pessimistic account of the era. He wrote three works that were explicitly aimed at an imperial audience: *Letâ'ifü'l-ezhâr ve lezâ'izü'l-esmâr* ("Smart blossoms and delightful conversations", also known as *Nesayihü'l-müluk*, "Advice for kings"), *Tefsir-i suretü'l-fâtiha* ("Commentary on the Sura of Fatiha"), and *Dürer-i 'aka'id* ("The pearls of the articles of faith"). In *Dürer-i 'aka'id,* written sometime after 1611, Sivasi described his time as one in which "sedition and rebellion" (*fitne u bugyan*) had set in: the common people (*avamm-ı halk*) believed whatever they heard, and would rather listen to the "heretics" (*melahide, zenadık*) than to "the singing nightingales of the orchard of the heart". He denounced "the people of innovation" and urged all Muslims to struggle against them. Not only in the *Dürer* but also in the preamble to the *Tefsir-i Suretü'l-Fatiha,* dedicated to Sultan Osman II (r. 1618–22), he evoked the Quranic injunction to "command right and forbid wrong" as the most important duty of a Muslim ruler.[71]

While Kadızadeli Mehmed and Sivasi both resorted to the accusation of *bid'a* in their condemnation of contemporary practices, the subjects of the accusation were different. While Kadızadeli Mehmed's innovators seemed to be a rather mixed combination of women, Halveti preachers, and sodomites, in the *Letaif* Sivasi described his innovators on the basis of a more legal rationale. In his attacks on the Hamzevis, Idrisis, and Hurufis, Sivasi used the phrase "people of innovation" as a synonym for "infidels" or "heretics".[72] Yet elsewhere he noted that there were some innovations that would make their practitioner merely a "person of (blameworthy) innovation" (*mübtedi*), not a heretic.[73] Also worthy of condemnation, according to Sivasi, were Muslim rebels (*bagi*), whose killing was lawful, as was that of adulterers and apostates (p. 102). The way that Sivasi explains the rationale behind it is fairly straightforward. He first argues that the sultan was not required to perform the obligatory *sefer* prayers while en route to the provinces because the provinces were considered his domicile, not distant lands of campaign. Therefore, rebelling in the provinces was like rebelling in the sultan's own house (p. 104).

70 Öztürk 1981, 43.

71 Terzioğlu 1999, 258–260.

72 Abdülmecid Sivasî, *Letâ'ifü'l-ezhâr ve lezâ'izü'l-esmâr* (*Nesâyih-i Mülûk*): Süleymaniye Ktp., Laleli MS 1613, 40.

73 Terzioğlu 1999, 262.

Distinct from the Birgivi line of interpretation of the injunction "to command right and forbid wrong" that defined the duty incumbent on all Muslims (*farz-ı ayn*), the interpretation in Halveti circles was that it was a duty to be fulfilled only by some members of the Muslim community (*farz-ı kifaye*), something that was further qualified by their stating of who could actually carry it out. For example, in the *Letaif*, which devoted its opening chapters to the inseparability of belief (*iman*), intention (*niyet*), and practice (*amel*), Sivasi argued that telling people what is right and what is wrong is the duty of preachers, but it is valid only when carried out with pure intentions (p. 64). The *Letaif* states that not everyone is capable of carrying out this injunction, only the caliph and the possessors of power (*eshab-i iktidar*) who were entitled to punish those who opposed the Sharia (p. 190). In *Dürer*, Sivasi argued that preachers could not and should not try to carry out investigations (*tecessüs*) into the affairs of governors (*hükkam*) and sultans. He also added that if, by fulfilling this injunction, preachers were going to cause animosity and sedition among the people, or if the severity of their judgment could turn people away from the Sharia, it would be better for them to keep silent.[74]

Sivasi's most vocal disciple, Abdulahad Nuri, took a less idealistic approach in his analysis of illicit innovation. One of his arguments was that, whenever a new custom appeared among the Muslims, the first response of the ulema was to declare it prohibited, and then, when it became widely practised, to reverse that position on grounds of public good (*istihsan*), a principle that was particularly important in Hanafi law.[75] As will be seen in chapter 7, a similarly matter-of-fact interpretation was made by Katib Çelebi, who, in his *Mîzânü'l-hakk*, argued that forcing people to abandon long-held customs and beliefs, as did the Kadızadelis, was futile.

A slightly different analysis of commanding right emerges in the *Nasihatü'l-mülûk tergiban li-hüsn as-sülûk* ("Advice to rulers in anticipation of good ways"), which was written by the chief scribe Sarı Abdullah for Mehmed IV in 1059 (1649)—a year after his inauguration—in order to "protect statesmen from engaging in oppression and making mistakes".[76] In addition to his long

74 Terzioğlu 1999, 260–261.

75 Terzioğlu 1999, 265; on *istihsan* see also below, chapter 7.

76 It is composed of two sections. The first deals with the affairs of this world while the second looks rather like a catechists' manual, instructing its readers in matters of faith, worship, and the afterlife. More interestingly, it was revived in the early eighteenth century by the very popular satirist and *belle-lettrist* Osmanzade Taib Ahmed. He wrote an abridged version of it called *Talhis al-nasâ'ih*, which he presented to Ahmed III. Osmanzade's decision to resuscitate this work makes a lot of sense because, in the early eighteenth century, being associated with Melami circles was still very much in vogue among the

career in the Ottoman bureaucracy, Sarı Abdullah Efendi was also one of the most renowned Sufi intellectuals of his time and left behind a large corpus of works ranging from commentaries on the *Mesnevi* to conversations on the fundamental pillars of religious belief.[77] In this work, Sarı Abdullah wrote a long discussion about who is responsible for imposing *ihtisab*, or public morality, and asked whether *ihtisab* could be carried out, without the permission of the *imam*, by persons other than the *imam*. Sarı Abdullah informed his readers that the *ulema* assigned different degrees to commanding right and forbidding wrong.[78] At one end, there were those actions that can be met with simple mercy and compassion, the disciplining of which did not need the sultan's confirmation. At the other, there were the actions that can only be deterred by *siyaset* and punishment (*ukubet*), the exercise of which is exclusive to the sultan because if everyone dared to carry them out it would be a source of sedition (*fitne*) in the society. Against these actions, only the sultan was authorized to carry out *ihtisab*.

3.1 *Fighting Innovation through Consultation*

One theme common in the works studied in this chapter is the necessity of consultation as a means of imposing the Sharia and eradicating innovation. In the same *kaside* that Kadızade Mehmed submitted to Murad IV, he warned the sultan about his duties to God and his responsibilities to his subjects. He implored him to follow the Qur'an and the Sunna in order to eradicate innovation. He also urged him to hold an *ayak divanı* as had been the practice of previous rulers. Unless the sultan fulfilled his responsibilities to his people, Kadızade warned him that he was going to account for his actions in the

political elites of the capital. For example, two of the highest-ranking officials, the chief mufti Paşmakçızade Seyyid Ali Efendi (d. 1124/1714) and the grand vizier Şehid Ali Pasha (d. 1716, vizier 1713–1716) were identified as the two leading Melami-Bayramis of the period.

77 Sarı Abdullah Efendi was a member of Grand Vizier Halil Pasha's (d. 1629) retinue as his ink bearer and personal secretary. Later on he was appointed chief scribe during the eastern campaign against the rebellious Abaza Pasha, and in the aftermath of his patron's death, following a brief removal from public office, he returned to office as *reisülküttab* during Murad IV's Baghdad campaign. He was also an important member of the Bayrami-Melami circles in the capital. He was well known for his enormous commentary on the *Mesnevi*, the *Cevahir-i Bevahir-i Mesnevi*, and hence was given the epithet *şarihü'l-mesnevi*, "the commentator of the *mesnevi*" by his contemporaries. His commentary on the first volume of the *Mesnevi*, which he dedicated to Murad IV in 1631, is the largest *Mesnevi* commentary written in the seventeenth century.

78 *Nasihatü'l-mülük tergiban li-hüsni's-sülük*, Beyazıd Devlet Kütüphanesi, MS 1977.

Hereafter.[79] Kadızade advised him to employ people of good insight or correct judgment (*ehl-i furkan*) who were both religious and pious, but also stated that such people were unfortunately hard to find in every religion.[80]

One author who placed great emphasis on the importance of consultation in his works was the Halveti preacher Kadızade Mehmed İlmi (d. 1631–32), the translator of Ibn Taymiyya's *Siyasat al-shariyya*. In addition to his *Tacü'r-Resail*, he wrote two major *nasihatname*s, one of each of which were submitted to grand vizier Kuyucu Murad Pasha (d. 1611) and Murad IV. Mehmed İlmi claimed that the sermons he gave as a preacher caught the attention of some distinguished members in the audience, who later asked him to write them down in different *nasihatname* versions.[81]

The first work, *Nushu'l-hükkâm sebebü'n-nizâm* ("Counsel for rulers, grounds for order"), seems to have been written during the early days of Murad IV's reign when the sultan's infamous iron rule had not yet been established. The second work, *Mesmu'atü'n-nekayih mecmu'tü'n-nesa'ih* ("Tales for the convalescent, the compilation of counsels"), was written before the 1632 uprising and its suppression by Murad IV, a turning point in his reign. Both texts heralded the heavy-handed approach that Murad IV would take later in his reign.[82] Yet neither work treated the ills afflicting the empire as systematically as did other contemporaneous works of the advice genre. Scriptural and historical anecdotes, verses directly addressing the sultan regarding virtues and vices, and statements about different social classes seem to have been haphazardly intermingled with analysis of the empire and metaphors used to validate them. In that sense, both reflected on paper the performance of a preacher in his pulpit. Not only their style but also the content of their counsel reveals the emphasis placed on preaching and *nasihat*-giving as a means to amend the decay of the empire. Both works placed significant emphasis on the need for the sultan to consult with the right people.

79 Öztürk 1981, 44.

80 Öztürk 1981, 176–177.

81 Kuyucu Murad Paşa enjoyed *Nushu'l-hükkam sebebü'n-nizam* so much that he submitted another copy to the grand vizier as a gift. The chief mufti Esad Efendi, after listening to one his sermons in Ayasofya, commissioned Mehmed İlmi to write another *nasihatname* to be submitted to Sultan Murad IV. Yet when the chief mufti died, İlmi did not have the chance to write a new *nasihatname* and submitted the old version, with some changes in it, to Murad IV. The second version was completed after 1625, the year of Esad Efendi's death. See Terzioğlu 2007, 266.

82 Terzioğlu 2007, 267. Kadızade Mehmed İlmi, *Nushü'l-hükkâm sebebü'n-nizâm*, Süleymaniye Ktp. Aşir Ef. MS 327; *Mesmû'atü'n-nekâyih mecmû'atü'n-nesâyih*, Süleymaniye Ktp. Hüsrev Paşa, MS 629.

The ultimate aim of consultation with those whom Mehmed İlmi referred to as "beneficial guys" (*faydalı ademler*) or "masters of consultation" (*ehl-i daniş*) was to draw the sultan and other authorities back to the Sharia. The order of the universe was hidden inside the Quran and one had just to enquire in order to learn it (N4). In the same vein, it was incumbent upon all believers to proffer advice (N14). In order to illustrate the need for consultation, Mehmed İlmi used the metaphor of a sinking ship that could only be salvaged by the joint efforts of the *ulema* and the *hukema* (N14), the metaphor of a city fire that could not be put out by just two men (N28), and the metaphor of a galley which could not be steered by only two oarsmen (N14). The foundations on which the country was built and the continuation of the principles of the dynasty hinged on the rulers' consultation with the *ulema* (N21). Mehmed İlmi further justified his point by reference to precedent. For earlier Ottoman sultans, i.e. the ancestors of Murad IV, consultation was an ancient custom (*kanun-i kadim*). To employ in their service, they selected the beneficial, good, and righteous ones from among the ulema, sheikhs, janissaries, cavalry, and various others. They used them as agents and secretly communicated with them through the messages written by their private secretaries (*sır katibleri*). If the news coming from these sources was in accordance with each other, then the sultans ruled in compliance with them; if not, then they found out which source was true and eliminated the untruthful one(s) from their ranks. This was how they were informed of happenings in the lands of Rum and Anatolia (N23). Mehmed İlmi warned the sultan not to operate without accurate information, since if he happened to punish a community without enough information, he would later regret his decision (M52). He vouched for the existence of saintly (*veli*) people who would do away with *bid'at* and *fesad* in the country (M41), but, because of the slanders directed at them by those who were very close to the sultan, they remained in hiding (M41). At one point, Mehmed İlmi even raised the question of whether a newly-installed sultan should keep his father's advisors around him (N63). He quotes what he claimed to be the opinion shared by the ulema, who saw turning away from one's friends and bringing in new people to replace them as one of the reasons for the problems of the state. Finally, in one of the most analytical sections of the *Nushu'l-hükkam sebebü'n-nizam*, Kadızade Mehmed İlmi enumerated the causes of *ihtilal* (destructive change) in a society. In addition to the lack of any will to impose *siyaset* for justice and the disobedience of soldiers towards their commanders, the preacher claimed that not consulting with the ulema and the wise (*ukela*), not giving them the respect they are due, and heeding the words of women and fools would all wreak havoc with the order of the world (N56).

When compared to Sivasi, Mehmed İlmi's works clearly lacked the same intellectual authority and by no means exhibited a similar breadth of legal knowledge. Nevertheless, he managed to demonstrate that his ultimate aim in penning these *nasihatname*s was to uphold the primacy of the Sharia. Further dismantling the prototype of the heterodox Sufi sheikh, Mehmed İlmi exhibited his loyalty to correct belief and correct religious practices by referring to Birgivi as one of the most esteemed scholars of previous times. He reverently mentioned his *Vasiyetname* as obligatory reading for every believer and also talked about his *Tarikat* and the unjust reactions to it by Birgivi's contemporaries (M113). Among the prerequisites for rightful rulership, Mehmed İlmi emphasized the obligation of the sultan and other judicial authorities to judge, rule, and punish in proportion to the stipulations of the Sharia (M122). Proportionality in applying Sharia punishments (*hudud*) appeared to be an important concern for Mehmed İlmi, who disapproved not only of excessive sentences but also of inadequate ones that fell short of the Sharia's stipulations.

Around the same time, Eskici Hasan Dede (d. 1638/39), a Sufi of unknown affiliation who lived in a mosque that was to become a rallying center for the Kadizadelis, wrote a *Pendnâme* ("Book of advice"), presumably for consumption by the audience of his mosque.[83] Hasan's text gives us a glimpse into the ideas and views of the more popular Sufi preachers; it also departs from the more "heterodox" view of his Melami counterparts, as Hasan transcends the traditional conflict between the sultan, the worldly king, and the secret spiritual ruler, the "Pole of the world" or "Pole of the poles" (*kutb-ı aktâb*): for him, this Pole is nothing but the Quran and the Sharia, which should guide the sultan to the right path (T266). The author seems to identify himself with the expounder of these Poles, though, and, perhaps to enhance this view, he stresses that the sultan must practise consultation (*meşveret*), here with the meaning of taking the advice of experienced and pious counsellors in private.

Hasan begins his treatise by stressing the benefits the sultan would gain from reading texts like his; because the sultan did not give ear to the advice by old an experienced people, he says, the world fell to affliction and the sultan himself "almost lost kingship from his hands" (*az kaldı saltanat elden gideyazdı*, probably referring to the 1632 rebellion, which would then constitute a further *terminus post quem* for the composition of the treatise; cf. T262). Furthermore, there is an even more important rulership (*padişahlık*), and that is the eternal one; power and state (*devlet, saltanat*) are but a dream of this world. First of all, therefore, the sultan must be in control of his body; if he has not conquered

83 Terzioğlu 2010.

his body he cannot conquer the world, and if he does not know how to possess his body he merely has to humiliate himself in front of those who may inform him of body control, i.e. men of abstinence and purity. Then Hasan proceeds to his justification of the need for consultation. There are things that the sultan knows and things that he does not, since, however perfect it may be, a mind always has need of a guide; furthermore, the affairs of ruling are like the sea, too extensive and difficult for a single mind to perceive. That is why consultation is so important in various matters (*ba'zı umûrda bâ-husus meşveret sünnetdür*, T289). The sultan's consultants must not be young, but old and experienced people who had served his predecessors and who dare tell him the truth, however unpleasant may it be. Concrete advice starts from here, with an enumeration of the causes for the "destruction of the world". Hasan states straightforwardly that the primary reason was the sultan's doorkeepers, who prevent the poor and the weak from having direct access to him. The door of the caliphs, he argues, must be open. Another cause are ignorant judges: what makes judges oppressive is fear of losing their jobs, because steadiness in the office brings justice. This view will be seen again, below, as it is a central *leitmotif* in Hasan's thought. Ostentation (*şöhret*) is another means to oppression, and both the sultan and his servants must practice abstinence. Moreover, the sultan has absolute responsibility for his poor subjects (*ra'iyyecikler*). Very often dismissing officials from their posts is like giving a sword to robbers and telling them to destroy the world, argues Hasan, before delving into some commonplace advice in the "decline of the world" style: nobody listens to the old, the ignorant have risen to high posts, people chase whoever says something right, and so forth. Hasan claims that the sultan has gained not one faithful servant since his rise to the throne, and he adds that the real skill of government is not in executing people, but in finding the right people for the right posts (*hüner katl itmek degildür. Hüner er yerine er bulmakdur*).

After reiterating the need for consultation with pious people (and Hasan notes that it is not easy to discern them), it is stated that two classes (*ta'ife*) can either destroy or repair the world: judges and governors (*beg*). If these two classes were reformed, the repair of the world would be easy. And reform could occur through long-term appointments: judges and governors must serve at least for five or ten years as the sole way to prevent them oppressing the people. The sultan, stresses Hasan, must tell them that they should have no fear of being dismissed; if they oppress people, the sultan should cut off their head rather than dismiss them. The reason for this advice is that today's people do not think of tomorrow, as the Day of Judgment is nothing but a legend to them; that is why they are prone to oppression and immorality.

3.2 *Who Is to Blame? Ulema, Non-Muslims and Evil Merchants*

Despite the constant emphasis on the importance of *ilm* and *ulema* for diagnosing and treating the ills of the empire, the *ulema* of the times were also subjected to severe criticism in texts penned by both Kadızadelis and Halvetis. Bribery in appointments and judgements remained one of the most vilified practices of the time and the *nasihat*-givers unanimously called for its eradication. The prevalence of taking bribes led most of the authors to conclusions about the moral depravity of the clerical corps that exhibited itself as sheer perversion, ignorance, and worldly pursuits.

Abdülahad Nuri's *İnkazü't-talibin 'an-mehavi'l-gafilin* ("The deliverance of the seekers [of knowledge] from the crowds of the ignorant") addresses the dangers of engaging in *ilm* for worldly pursuits.[84] In the first section, Nuri condemns the discussions that were allegedly being carried out in the name of *ilm* (*münazara*) yet were actually aimed at improving one's social and material status in the eyes of political dignitaries; the Muslim scholars regarded practising *ilm* with expectations for material benefits as debauchery. The second chapter is devoted to criticism of those who fraternize with state officials without taking into consideration God's approval and disavowal. The scholars who, after a long period of scholarly education, fraternized with sultans were deemed worthy of hell. In the third section, Nuri argues that the purpose of scholarly education was its implementation; according to him, *'ilm* and *amel* must always go hand in hand. In the forth section, Nuri complains about the preachers whom he called "the most vicious ones in the Islamic community (*ümmet*)." They speak gibberish in order to be appreciated by the public, engage in vain acts, and are mere shadows of real legal scholars (*fakih taslağı*). At the pulpits of the mosques they engage in excessive boasting and deliberately stayed away from recounting the deeds of the real saints (*menkıbe*) that could awaken those in error. He quotes from al-Ghazali's *İhya* and mentions earlier scholars who concluded that the real harm to the world would come from sycophantic *ulema* and those who pretended to be truthful. In the final section, he attacks heretical sects and scholars, calling them satanic, and quotes from Bayzawi and Ebussu'ud, who also commented on such people during their own lifetimes.

The thing that most disturbed our Sharia-minded commentators about contemporary *ulema* practices was their disregard for the Sharia. Kadızade Mehmed İlmi devoted long sections of his work to diatribes against the ignorance of judges and their neglect of the Sharia and the word of religion.[85] Sivasi went one step further and included neglect of the Sharia in legal judgements

---

84 Nuri – Akkaya 2003, 103–104.

85 *Nushü'l-hükkâm*, 11, 13.

among the items that would render someone an infidel. One of the examples given by Sivasi included a judge who ignored the Sharia by disputing the soundness of a *müfti*'s decision in a *fetva* manual. A judge who pronounced that he would rule by *yasak* and *kanun*, not by Sharia, or who announced that what was not allowed by the Sharia would be allowed by *kanun*, would automatically become an infidel since these utterings amounted to ridiculing and denying Islam, the Sharia, and the consensus of the community.[86]

The treatment of non-Muslim subjects constituted another item in the agenda of the Sharia-minded reformists. The erosion of the public boundaries between Muslims and non-Muslims was a concern frequently expressed by seventeenth-century Ottomans writers. The heavy-handed measures introduced by the grand viziers and other policy-makers during the second half of the seventeenth century to deal with this concern did not come out of nowhere, and rested on at least half a century of previous discussions.

In his *Letâ'if*, Sivasi discussed a range of misconducts which he thought contaminated the Muslim public sphere. Among these were the building of new churches and synagogues in Istanbul, Muslims frequenting *zimmi* bakeries, the illegal addition of extra stories to non-Muslim houses, and the violation of dress codes (p. 77–79). In a similar vein, Sivasi listed non-compliance with *cizye* payments, adultery with Muslim women, and murdering Muslims among the acts requiring capital punishment according to the Sharia (p. 80, 81). However, one particular admonition that Sivasi made about Muslim and non-Muslim relations directly concerned the functioning of the Ottoman state: the employment of Christians and Jews in running the affairs of the state. Especially worrying for Sivasi was the employment of *ehl-i zimmet* as scribes in the chancellery and treasury for the conduct of Muslim affairs (p. 74–80). Sivasi backed his warning with anecdotes from early Islamic times that aimed to capture the problems relating to trusting the affairs of the state to non-Muslims. He even attempted to horrify the reader by claiming that Jews were so deeply engrossed in state affairs that they had infiltrated into the most intimate quarters of the palace where they secretly converted the most pious of *harem* women to Judaism.[87]

According to Sivasi, an even more direct impact of non-Muslims' interference in government and public administration was in matters of taxation. In the *Letaif*, Sivasi condemned the taxation of wine as one of the fifteen illicit payments that God condemned in the Quran. He objected to any money gathered

86 Abdülmecid Sivasî, *Letâ'ifü'l-ezhâr ve lezâ'izü'l-esmâr* (*Nesâyih-i Mülûk*): Süleymaniye Ktp., Laleli MS. 1613, 72–73.

87 Terzioğlu 1999, 319.

from the taxation of an item that was explicitly forbidden by the Quran and the Sunna flowing into the treasury of the "shah of Islam." He claimed that if the sultan did away with this practice, the treasury would prosper again for, according to the Prophet, when someone closes the door of the *haram*, God will surely open him a door to the *helal* (p. 47).

The Sharia-minded take on non-Muslims included not only the *zımmis* living under Ottoman rule but also other infidels living in the abode of war (*daru'l-harb*). *Tâcü'r-resâ'il* begins with praise for the *gaza*, fighting for the faith, and a fictitious account of the ransacking of Rome by the Ottomans.[88] In addition to the main section, the translation of Ibn Taymiyya's work, Kadızade Mehmed İlmi also considered the position of non-Muslim subjects and their rights in Islamic history, the *kharaj* and *jizya*, and mentioned a work by Aristotle on the arts of war and methods of fighting.[89] The last prominent Kadızadeli preacher, Vani Efendi, also expressed strong interest in the *gaza*, which is seen in his correspondence with grand vizier Köprülüzade Fazıl Ahmed.[90] He also authored an important Quran commentary in 1679–80 entitled *Ara'is al-Qur'an wa nafa'is al-furkan*, in which he declared that the Turks were divinely ordained to carry out *gaza* whereas the Arabs had previously failed in it.[91] Vani is also reported to have played an active role as one of the "war party" who pushed for the siege of Vienna.[92] This is important for understanding not only the ideological reasons behind the second siege of Vienna but also the motivations of the pro-war party that continued to influence Ottoman foreign policy until the signing of the Karlowitz Treaty in 1699 which, as shall be seen in chapters 7 and 8, brought such bellicose discourses to an end.

These ideas, promulgated by both the Kadızadelis and their opponents, no doubt constituted the doctrinal backdrop to the strict Sharia measures of the seventeenth century such as the public stoning incident of 1681. It is not known if the person behind the decision, Beyazızade Ahmed Efendi, was openly a Kadızadeli follower, but we know that later in his life he became a Nakşibendi, an order known for its strict interpretation of the Islamic canon.[93] In the same

88 Terzioğlu 1999, 321.

89 Öztürk 1981, 155.

90 Vani Efendi, *Münşe'ât*, Süleymaniye Ktp. Ayasofya MS 4308.

91 For a summary of this work, see Pazarbaşı 1997. Baer states that, in his summary translation of certain sections of the work, Pazarbaşı omits any references to Kurds found in the original (Baer 2008, 206–210).

92 Terzioğlu 1999, 287.

93 He was the son of Beyazi Hasan Efendi (d. 1653) from Bosnia, who had served as the judge of Mecca and Istanbul. Beyazızade was educated by famous ulema of the time and got his diploma in Edirne. After serving for 20 years as *müderris* in various Istanbul

year, Beyazızade gave another harsh and equally controversial sentence: the execution of a master scribe of daybooks (*ruznamçe hulefası*), Patburunzade Mehmed Halife, for allegedly making statements amounting to apostasy.[94] The historian Defterdar Sarı Mehmed Pasha described Beyazızade as someone known among his *ulema* peers and the people for his temper and harshness.[95] A quick examination of the corpus of works he left behind reveals that Hanafi law occupied a central place for Beyazızade, both for the practice of law and as a main doctrinal source. Among the works written by Beyazızade are a juridical *sakk* collection intended as a guidebook for novice judges, a Quranic commentary, a treatise on Abu Hanifa's legal method, and another one on the denunciation of infidels.[96] What is interesting is that, according to contemporaneous sources, in both the stoning case and the Patburunzade case Beyazızade ruled in favor of the application of strictly Shari sentences despite the inadequate number of witnesses as required by the same Shari stipulations.

Nonetheless, there were also dissenting voices against this increasing "Salafization" of the discourse concerning non-Muslims, those who were Ottoman subjects as well those living in the abode of war. For example, although he is known to have supported the aggressive *gaza* policy of the grand vizier Fazıl Ahmed Pasha, Niyazi Mısri was infuriated by the treatment of non-Muslims in the empire and reminded the authorities that it was the taxes paid by the non-Muslims that constituted the core of the tyrants' wealth and so the former's wealth, lives, honor (*ırz*), and blood had to be protected.[97] Mehmed İlmi, in the *Nüshat*, advised Murad IV not to take his enemies lightly, and even to prefer peace to war in certain situations.[98] He quoted several Quranic verses praising peace and warned the sultan that the biggest mistake

medreses, he was first appointed judge of Aleppo (1666), then of Bursa (1672), and of Istanbul (1672). He was appointed chief military judge of Rumili in 1680.

94 In his *Zübde-i vekaiyât*, Defterdar Sarı Mehmed related that other scribes at the day-book bureau informed the chief mufti of Patburunzade's words. The chief mufti, however, dismissed the case, citing the inadequacy of witnesses. Yet when Patburunzade publicly criticized Beyazızade's decision to sentence the aforementioned adulterers to public stoning, Beyazızade seized the opportunity to count the evidence as admissible and dragged Patburunzade to execution. While conceding that Patburunzade's loquaciousness could get him into trouble, Defterdar claims that his life actually conformed to Islamic norms. Defterdar – Özcan 1995, 115 and cf. Sariyannis 2005–2006.

95 Defterdar – Özcan 1995, 210.

96 Ahmed b. Hüsameddin Hasan b. Sinan el-Bosnevi Beyazizade, *al-Tahqiq fi al-radd ala al-zindiq*, Süleymaniye, Esad Efendi, MS 1468; *al-Usul al-munifa li al-imam Abu Hanifa*, Süleymaniye, Esad Efendi, MS 1140; *Sak*, Lala İsmail, MS 93. For a discussion of his place in the seventeenth-century Ottoman *kalam* circles, see Çelebi 1998.

97 Terzioğlu 1999, 318–320.

98 Kadızade Mehmed İlmi, *Nushü'l-hükkâm*, 69.

he could ever make was to continue with warfare when his opponent asked for peace. He added that sultans must always abide by the terms of peace treaties. In his *Nasihatü'l-müluk tergiban li-hüsn al-süluk*, written for Mehmed IV, Sarı Abdullah Efendi offered similar restraint in matters of war. In the section on the duties of the grand vizier, Sarı Abdullah argued that the vizier should prefer peace whenever possible and should not force the sultan to conduct warfare when it was not necessary since it would lead to the depletion of the treasury and the destruction of the country and the population.[99]

Another common thread in these Sharia-informed criticisms was the reaction to the functioning of the urban economy and its moral underpinnings. As stated previously, the seventeenth- and early eighteenth-century accounts of the Kadızadelis disapprovingly declared the lower-echalons of urban *esnaf* as being one of the most important constituents of the Kadızadeli movement. Therefore, it is crucial to understand if and how the leaders of the Kadızadeli movement, its opponents, and other participants in the debates interpreted the economic landscape around them. Sivasi, in the *Letaif*, enumerated the moral vices of the times. Among the moral crimes, he denounced such as staring at women and young boys with less than pure intentions, and not being content with what God offered one, thereby developing excessive ambitions to earn more. According to Sivasi, these were the two moral shortcomings of hoarders.[100] In the *kaside* he presented to Murad IV in 1630, Kadızade Mehmed defined the same problem, but in more exact terms: the richest members of the military had become shopkeepers and they certainly did not want to observe the officially-fixed price; thus, their own prices were altered.[101]

The most detailed statement about the partakers of the Ottoman urban economy comes from Hasan Efendi. His *Pendnâme* starts with a general admonition to readers to not become distracted by the affairs of this world. Hasan Efendi distinguished between the people of this world (*ehl-i dünya*) and the people who had metaphorically left this world (*terk-i dünya*), and constantly reminded his reader of the ephemeral nature of life and the inevitability of death. He warned his readers against the people of innovation (*ehl-i bidat*), the people of bribery (*ehl-i rüşvet*), and the people of this world (*ehl-i dünya*). Yet the main targets of his criticism of those in pursuit of wordly pleasures and goods were the Sufis themselves. He criticized the inherent hierarchy of

99 Sarı Abdullah dispensed similarly cool-headed advice in another *nasihat* work attributed to him, *Tedbir ün-neşeteyn ve ıslahı'n-nüshateyn*, where he addresses the caliph: "If you are attacked or threatened by an enemy who is stronger than you, try to make peace (*müdarat üzre sulh yüzün göster*). If he is weaker than you, then engage in warfare (*mukatele et*)."

100 Abdülmecid Sivasî, *Letâ'ifü'l-ezhâr*, 184.

101 Öztürk 1981, 41, 42.

Sufism, Sufis' blind adherence to their sheikhs, and their dependence on the public for economic benefits, and especially their embeddedness in the imperial *vakf* networks.[102] He urged his readers to abandon a sheikh if they felt that he was even slightly interested in the riches of this world, and expressed his own disappointment at not being able to find a single unambitious sheikh. This emphasis on earning one's livelihood, being satisfied with moderation, avoiding being dependent on people's blessings, and not borrowing money and food gave the work an almost Melami tone. In his praise for self-sufficiency, Hasan Efendi referred to the producers (*çiftçi*), whom he saw as the ideal examples of moderation in consumption.

A similar emphasis on the producers also appears in Kadızade Mehmed İlmi's *Nüshat*, where he deals with them not as a morally-idealized category but as part of his theory of social classes. Like many generations of Muslim theorists before him, İlmi saw the key to the order of the universe in the preservation of each class in its designated place. According to İlmi, ancient scholars organized Adam and his sons into four groups: one for the sword, one for the pen, one for planting and sowing, and one for manufacture and commerce. Governing or *padişahlık* meant making use of these four groups and, at the same time, controlling them (N57). The people of the sword were rulers, viziers, begs, and commanders. With justice, and with the advice of the scholars and the erudite people around them, their duty was to engage in warfare. The second rank was occupied by the people of the pen, i.e. the ulema and people of erudition. The duty of commanding right and forbidding wrong befell them. Informing all classes (*cümle esnaf ehline*) of the Sharia's rules (either in writing or orally) was their main duty. They should uphold religious values through their opinions and advice, and convince people to perform their religious duties. Those who were known as the *reaya* were the third rank, and should work to produce crops and feed livestock in order to meet the demands of all social classes. Those who were knowledgeable about crafts and commerce occupied the final category. Again, laboring towards production was their main purpose (N57–58). Those who fall outside these categories should not be left on their own and must be included in one of these categories. The infiltration of the *reaya* into the ranks of the people of the sword and the pen was what caused the internal strife afflicting the empire (N58).

102 *Pendnâme-i Hasan* (*Hikâyât-ı makbûle ve nazm-ı mergûb*): Köprülü Ktp. Ahmed Paşa MS 345.

4 Political Practice and Political Thought

The texts examined above at times verged on catechistic, often replicated the preaching voices of their authors, and mostly addressed a royal audience. Above all, they emphasized the primacy of the Sharia and the Sunna and saw the proper functioning of the imperial political order as a function of the moral and legal underpinnings provided by those two. The question that remains is whether one can trace the intellectual/ideological origins of the administrative policies carried out during the second half of the seventeenth century—policies which manifestly had strong Sharia coloring—to the ideas promoted by the authors of these Sunna-minded political texts.[103] While it is not possible to associate every major political decision with a specific text, it is possible to trace the social and intellectual networks through which a form of Sharia ideology was channeled towards the chancellery and financial arms of the Ottoman bureaucracy and the judicial corps that carried out its implementation. As will become evident below, the process of the Shariatization of Ottoman public policy was especially increased during the grand vizierates of the Köprülüs and their relatives and protégés.[104] It is no coincidence that the policies that created so much controversy during the second half of the seventeenth century had been already pronounced by our Sunna-minded authors in the first half of it.

103 Scholars took note of this new "administrative activism" and even emphasized the move away from the imperial *kanun* towards the Sharia as the underlying drive behind these measures (Murphey 1993). On the growing importance of the Sharia within the Ottoman legal system, see Gerber 1994; Peirce 2003; Buzov 2005.

104 The appointment of Köprülü Mehmed Pasha as the grand vizier in September 1656 marks the beginning of the period, which in Ottoman history is called the "rule of the grandees" or the "Köprülü restoration". After Köprülü Mehmed, who held the position of grand vizier until his death in 1661, the grand viziers were: his son Fazıl Ahmed (d. 1676); his son-in-law Merzifonlu Kara Mustafa Pasha (d. 1683); another son-in-law Siyavuş Pasha; his younger son Fazıl Mustafa (d. 1691); his nephew Amcazade Hüseyin Pasha (d. 1702), and finally Numan Pasha (d. 1719), the son of Fazıl Mustafa. On the Köprülü family see Behçeti İbrahim's (d. c. 1738) history: *Silsiletü'l-Asafiyye fi hakaniyyeti'l-devleti'l-Osmaniye*, Köprülü Kütüphanesi, Hafız Ahmed Paşa, nr. 212. This work includes the biographies of Köprülü Mehmed Pasha, Fazıl Ahmed Pasha, Fazıl Mustafa Pasha, Amcazade Hüseyin Pasha, Köprülüzade Numan Pasha, Köprülüzade Abdullah Pasha, and Köprülüzade Hafız Ahmed Pasha. Behçeti compiled the information on the first five Köprülü viziers from Naima's and Raşid's histories. The sections on Köprülüzade Abdullah Pasha and Köprülüzade Hafız Ahmed Pasha contain original information. For the secondary literature on the Köprülü grand viziers, see Kunt 1971; Kunt 1973; Kunt 1994; Yılmaz 2000b; Duman 2006; Aycibin 2011; Özkan 2006.

To begin with, the concerns that Sivasi expressed in his *nasihatname* about the erosion of the boundaries between the non-Muslim and Muslim subjects of the empire seem to have been shared by a wide circle of political elites from the mid-seventeenth century onwards. The 1660 fire in Istanbul that burned down most of the southern shores of the Golden Horn gave the regal matriarch Hadice Turhan Sultan (r. 1651–83) an excuse to reclaim the Jewish settlements in the area and complete the unfinished mosque project that Safiye Sultan (d. 1605) had started half a century earlier.[105] The building of the New Mosque (Yeni Camii) by driving the Jewish residents out of the area initiated another wave of anti-Jewish and anti-Christian policies that radically transformed the urban profile of Istanbul in the second half of the seventeenth century.[106] The first preacher of the newly-inaugurated mosque of Hadice Turhan was Vani Efendi. According to Rycaut, Vani persuaded the grand vizier, Fazıl Ahmed Pasha, that the fires and the plague that struck the city, as well as the military failures against Christians, were[107]

> so many parts of Divine Judgments thrown on the Musselmen or Believers, in vengeance of their too much Licence given to the Christian Religion, permitting Wine to be sold within the Walls of Constantinople, which polluted the Imperial City, and ensnared the faithful by temptation to what was unlawful.

Given his aforementioned statements about the Turks' obligation to conduct *gaza*, it seems that Vani saw an obvious connection between conquest or lack of it in the abode of war and compliance with Sharia in the abode of Islam.[108] This view actually predates Vani: when the Venetians captured the islands of Tenedos (Bozcaada) and Lemnos (Limni) in 1656, the Kadızadelis blamed the loss of the islands on the fact that grand vizier Boynueğri Mehmed Pasha was a Sufi.[109]

During the conquest of Crete, the Ottoman land administrative practices that Mehmed Birgivi took issue with in the sixteenth century were targeted by the administration itself.[110] In 1669, following the conquest of Kandiye

---

105 See Thys-Senocak 1998.

106 For anti-Jewish policies in this period see Thys-Senocak 1998 and Baer 2008, 86–96. For anti-Christian urban policies see Baer 2008, 96–102.

107 Baer 2008, 110.

108 Baer 2008, 172, 173.

109 Baer 2008, 71.

110 The first known land and population survey (*tahrir*) of the island was undertaken in 1647, although the register has not survived. After Yusuf Pasha conquered Chania, he

(Heraklion), Grand Vizier Fazıl Ahmed Pasha authorized Defterzade Mehmed Efendi, one of the scribes of the janissary corps, to carry out a survey of the entire island.[111] The 1670 Cretan *kanunname* accompanying the survey highlighted a Quranic verse (al-Imran, Q 3:87)[112] and banned all uncanonical taxes that had been previously collected from the *reaya* as being an illicit innovation.[113] It also stipulated that the *cizye* payments due on the *reaya* were to be calculated based on the Sharia ratios, as stated in the *fikh* manuals.[114] The *kanunname* also introduced a three-tiered system for *cizye* collection, dividing the non-Muslim population into three ranks according to their wealth, a policy that would be carried back to the mainland by the 1691 poll-tax regulation.[115] This survey and the law book departed radically from the classical Ottoman *tahrir* tradition since what was being registered was not the male population of the villages, as had been the case for centuries, but the land itself. Moreover, the conquerors of Crete used clearly Islamic terms such as *haraci* to define the lands and declared them to be the freehold (*mülk*) of their occupants, as stipulated by Hanafi law.[116]

The Cretan departure has been interpreted in various ways: as a reaction to the necessity of incorporating the previous Venetian practices of land administration and ownership;[117] as a result of the central administration's attempt to

authorized Hasan Efendi, from the men of the pen, to register Chania's foundations and immovable property such as land, shops, and other buildings. The first registrar that we have dates from 1650, when the governor of Chania, Mehmed Pasha, carried out another survey (Gülsoy 2001, 186).

111 Gülsoy 2001, 193.

112 "Those—their recompense will be that upon them is the curse of Allah and the angels and the people, all together".

113 These were called *divani* taxes, and included *ispençe, resm-i tapu, resm-i ağnam, resm-i küvvare, resm-i deştbani, resm-i otlak, kışlak ve yaylak, cürm-i cinayet, bad-ı heva, resm-i arus*, and *tarh-ı milh*. This would be reconfirmed in a later *kanunname* for Crete, dated c. 1705–06, which adds that not a single penny must be collected from the inhabitants of the island in contravention of the Holy Law. The *kanun* that laid down these fines and taxes was no longer mentioned. Similarly, the *kanunname* for the island of Midilli (Mytilene, Lesbos), in the cadastral register of 1709–08, abolished the fines and many *örfi* taxes. According to a note at the end of the *kanunname* these impositions had been left out of the "old register", probably that of 1082/1671–2 or earlier (Heyd 1973, 153).

114 The *akçe* of the time equaled 1/14 shari dirhems based on *fikh* books.

115 Gülsoy 2001; see also Yılmaz 2000b, 203–208; Sariyannis 2011b.

116 Gülsoy 2001, 194; Kolovos 2007; Veinstein 2008; Kermeli 2008, 17–48. Kermeli points to Ömer Lütfi Barkan's *XV. Ve XVI. Asırlarda Osmanlı İmparatorluğu'nda Zirai Ekonominin Hukuki ve Mali Esasları, Volume I: Kanunlar* as the first emphasis on the departure from Ebussu'ud's sixteenth-century legal interpretation of land.

117 Greene 1996, 78.

attract both Muslim and non-Muslim *reaya* to (re-)settle;[118] as a consequence of the general empire-wide transformation of the taxation system; as one of the legal loopholes deliberately created by the Köprülü households who wanted to siphon off revenues from the central treasury for their own benefit;[119] and as a result of the fiscal necessities imposed by the specifics of agricultural production on the islands.[120] It has also been suggested that the application of Sharia principles on post-conquest surveys had already been carried out on what were called the "insular *kannunnames*", that is, the legal regulations issued specifically for the Aegean and Mediterranean islands such as Lemnos and Cyprus.[121] One interesting detail is the similarity of the land taxation policies implemented in Crete to those of Basra, which was subjugated by the Ottomans in 1669; there, too, the Ottomans declared the lands that the urban and tribal elites had been cultivating to be private.[122] This similarity has rightly been interpreted as an indication of the fact that Grand Vizier Köprülü Fazıl Ahmed had the same model in mind for both cases.[123]

Although believed possible and widely debated as one of the most plausible explanations for the peculiarity of the Cretan *kanunname*, none of the studies on the Cretan *kanun*s has presented a clear link between the Shariatization of Ottoman land management and the Kadızadeli wave, especially the influence of Vani Efendi on the Köprülü administration.[124] Unfortunately, very few of the administrative texts produced by the Ottoman bureaucracy chose to reveal the intellectual provenance of the policies they espoused. Therefore, it is highly unlikely that neither Birgivi Mehmed's *Tariqa* nor any other Kadızadeli text would surface in the *kanunname*s as the ideological basis for the privatization of land-holding rights in Crete. However, it is possible to gauge the influence of Birgivi on the Kadızadelis who consulted the Köprülü grand viziers based on an analysis of the circulation of his works, especially the *Tariqa*.[125]

---

118 Kermeli 2008, 33. Kermeli mentions this possibility but concludes that "the choice to allow extensive private landed property on the island could not be merely the result of political manoeuvring and propaganda", and points out the wider transformation of timar land and taxation system in the empire.

119 Greene 2000, 27.

120 Veinstein 2004, 101–106.

121 Veinstein 2004, 102.

122 Khoury 2001, 316.

123 Kermeli 2008, 37.

124 Greene is skeptical about this, and rightly states that the Kadızadelis did not take any explicit stand on this matter (Greene 1996, 73); Veinstein expands on it in detail (Veinstein 2004, 101–106; Veinstein 2008).

125 See Kaylı 2010.

The fact that Kadızade Mehmed Efendi's lifetime was a turning point in the dissemination of Birgivi's religious works has already been mentioned. A recent study has meticulously examined how the number of *al-Tarîqa al-Muhammadiyya* copied steadily rose throughout the seventeenth century, reaching a peak of 49 between the years 1689 and 1717.[126] The details of the circulation of the Birgivi corpus notwithstanding, it is clear that the *Tariqa* was by no means a marginal text; it was widely recognized by the Ottoman political elite, including Fazıl Ahmed Pasha, as an important legal and political reference work.[127] Therefore, despite the dearth of any direct references, it would not be too far-fetched to claim that those who carried out the aforementioned legal reformulations in the spirit of the Sharia were familiar with how Birgivi dealt with the issue of the legal administration of land in his *Tariqa*.

An important source that might explain the changing attitudes towards the taxation of newly-conquered lands is a translation commissioned by the-then grand vizier, Merzifonlu Kara Mustafa Pasha (d. 1683).[128] When compared to both Fazıl Ahmed and Fazıl Mustafa, Kara Mustafa Pasha seems less "authentically Köprülü", not only due to his "in-law" status but also due to his less-than-scholarly credentials. Nonetheless, the translation that he initiated reveals that he was at least interested in the legal origins of his otherwise reckless political and military actions, and that he was surrounded by a scholarly entourage that guided him in such matters. The work in question is *Kitâb al-kharâj* ("Book of land tax") by the famous Hanafi jurist Abu Yusuf (d. 798), who studied under Abu Hanifa and rose to the seat of *qadı al-qudat* of Baghdad during the reign of the Abbasid caliph Harun al-Rashid (d. 809).[129]

126 Among Birgivi's other religious works, *al-Tarîqa al-Muhammadiyya* was the most popular, with its 296 manuscript copies followed by the *Vasiyetnâme*, which has 164 manuscripts; ibid., p. 163. The ratio of dated manuscripts to the total number of copies for *Tarîqa al-Muhammadiyya* is 157/296; for *Vasiyetnâme*, it is 55/164; Kaylı 2010, 167 and 171.

127 Ahmet Kaylı points out the collection of Fazıl Ahmed Paşa in the Köprülü library, which has Birgivi's works on Arabic grammar as well as a copy of his *Tarîqa*, copied in 1711 by Mustafa b. Ibrahim el-Bosnevi. Kaylı also mentions the fact that Fazıl Ahmed himself copied out some of Birgivi's works, including a volume in the collection of Mehmed Asım Bey in the Köprülü library that contains two texts of Birgivi (*Avâmil* and *Izhâr*): Kaylı 2010, 212–213.

128 The earliest manuscripts of the translation are: Rodosizade (Rodosluzade) Mehmed, *Terceme-i Kitab-i Harac-i Ebu Yusuf*, Süleymaniye, Şehid Ali Paşa MS 717 (1683); MS 718 (mentioned as an autograph copy); Halet Efendi MS 128 (1683); Lala İsmail MS 85 (1745/1746).

129 Abu Yusuf – Abbas 1985; Al-Manasir 1992. Ben Shemesh also studied it as part of the series *Taxation in Islamic Law*. See Shemesh 1958–1969.

Works of fiscal jurisprudence such as the *Kitâb al-kharaj* constituted a separate genre with origins in the eighth century.[130] This genre was the product of an effort to systematize the legal foundations of the Islamic state's power to collect the land tax. It was Caliph 'Umar I (r. 634–44) who decided to treat the lands of conquest collectively for the benefit of all Muslims, instead of dividing it among the Muslim warriors as Prophet Muhammad had done, and to use it as revenue for the state finances. The problem was the absence of any stipulations concerning land tax in either the Quran or *hadith*.[131] The concern about legitimacy in taxing the land grew increasingly important, especially as the Abbasid state started to rule over large swathes of territory and, moreover, became increasingly centralized.[132]

The person whom the grand vizier commissioned with the translation was a certain Rodosizade (Rodosluzade) Mehmed (d. 1701–2), who would become fairly well known for his literary skills and services in the latter part of the seventeenth century.[133] In the introduction to his translation, Rodosizade mentioned that Mustafa Pasha, who was always preoccupied with conquering countries (*feth-i bilad*), holy war, and improving the country (*ıslahkar-ı ibad*), asked for a book that dealt with all these issues.[134] The ulema in his circle brought to his attention a book that was written by Abu Yusuf and submitted to Harun al-Rashid. They explained to the grand vizier its contents and commented further on it. The work seems to have impressed the grand vizier sufficiently that he commissioned Rodosizade with the task of translating it from Arabic to Turkish.

The *Kitab al-kharaj* starts with an address to a prince and initially shows the characteristics of a work of advice and *adab* rather than *fikh*. The preamble is followed by *hadith* reports and other juristic material relating to the distribution of booty taken in battle, landholding, land taxes, and taxes on agricultural produce. The discussion of *kharaj* precedes discussions of other taxes such as *'ushr*, *zakat*, and *sadaqa*. *Kitâb al-kharaj* also discusses the poll-tax or *jizya*, applicable only to non-Muslims, together with discussion of the social status, rights, and obligations of non-Muslim citizens in Islamic territory. The last sections of the book relate to topics such as to how to deal with thieves, how to implement the prescribed *hudud* penalties, how to pay government

130 Heck 2002, 147.

131 Heck 2002, 158.

132 Heck 2002, 166–167.

133 Rodosizade completed the translation of Qazwini's *'Aja'ib al-makhluqat* in 1703 (Hagen 2000, 187).

134 Rodosizade (Rodosluzade) Mehmed, *Terceme-i kitabü'l-harac*, Halet Efendi MS 128, 4, 5.

officials, administer border crossings, and organize warfare with non-Muslim neighbours.[135]

The importance of the work in the wider sphere of Islamic fiscal jurisprudence has been summarized as follows:[136]

> Despite its name, Abu Yusuf's *Kitab al-kharaj* is not limited to the legal theory of the land-tax, but can be more accurately viewed as a development within the sub-genre of state literature, i.e. the law of nations, for its attention to issues of state administration in general and those related to non-Muslims in particular. Abu Yusuf's work, while lacking organization, is marked throughout with a concern for principles favorable to the authority of the state, especially as embodied in the Abbasid Harun al-Rashid. This interest in authority is operative on many levels, in its incorporation of material on the Islamic conquests, but most strikingly in its focus on the caliph himself as lawmaker. The work is actually presented as a conversation in which the jurist responds to the caliph's questions of matters of administration thus affirming a caliphal role in establishing the law and maintaining justice. This feature of the work is meant not to grant license to the caliph to act arbitrarily, but rather to draw upon the legal authority of the caliph as Imam of the Muslim community (*al-umma*) in order to given an air of legitimacy to state administration, especially tax-administration. Evidence for this exists in the author's introduction, where emphasis is placed on the imam-status of the Abbasid caliphs, and throughout the work in the tendency to attribute legal decision-making to caliphal judgment (*ra'y*) and authority. More than his predecessors in the genre, Abu Yusuf shows a concern for Islamic identity in his presentation of his material as reports (often with chains of transmission) describing the measures undertaken by the first Muslims (*al-salaf al-salih*). This inclusion of hadith consciousness was one way to associate principles of administration (and explanation of them) more directly with the Islamic heritage.

The new element that Abu Yusuf introduced into the literature on land taxation was proportional taxation. In the lands taken not by treaty but by force, the *kharaj* was previously expressed in terms of fixed sums in cash, in kind, or both, as imposed by Caliph 'Umar I. In the *Kitâb al-kharaj*, Abu Yusuf demonstrated the inefficiency of the fixed-rate system as imposed by 'Umar and

135 Calder 1993, 109.
136 Heck 2002, 171–172.

proposed that it be replaced by proportional taxation on produce (*muqasama*). The arguments in favor of proportional taxation were presented in such a way as to stress the rights of the *imam* to vary taxation according to (the *imam*'s) assessment of what the land could bear. In line with the work's general spirit of granting a wide legal space for caliphal adjudication, the arguments in the *Kitâb al-kharaj* concerning the imposition of the *kharaj* aimed to maximize the government's capacity to tax, at its discretion, through proportional taxation.[137]

This translation act definitely symbolizes the Ottoman political elite's search for legal precedents for the increasingly Sharia-influenced taxation and land policies. In that sense, it echoes the legal exercises that Birgivi carried out a century earlier in his *al-Tariqa al-Muhammadiyya*. Given the date of the work's translation, one can further speculate whether the Ottoman Turkish version of *Kitâb al-kharaj* was meant to lay the legal groundwork for Kara Mustafa Pasha's unrealized European conquests or whether it was a product of the efforts to introduce more fiscal laxity into the Ottoman taxation system, as would be attempted later by the 1691 life-long tax farming (*malikâne*) code. In any case, there is one important difference between Birgivi's interpretation and the resuscitation of the Abu Yusuf text: Birgivi stood clear of any contemporary interpretation that gave the sultan too much leverage through *kanun* or other *kanun*-minded manipulations of Hanafi law. However, in referencing one of the most basic texts of Hanafi law, Kara Mustafa Pasha and the ulema around him chose a text that gave a degree of flexibility in matters of taxation within the larger Sharia framework while maintaining the centrality of caliphal, or in the Ottoman case, sultanly discretion.

Although Rodosizade's *Kitâbü'l-harac* continued to circulate extensively in both manuscript and printed forms well into the nineteenth century, the introductory sections of later copies no longer mentioned Merzifonlu Kara Mustafa and left a blank space in lieu of his name. It is not surprising that he disappeared from the pages, since the Ottoman forces under his leadership had suffered a crushing defeat at the gates of Vienna at the hands of the Habsburg-Polish alliance led by the Polish commander Jan Sobieski in 1683. Following the execution of the grand vizier, who was held responsible for the failed siege of Vienna, members of the Köprülü family became subject to demotions and dismissals. So, too, did Vani Mehmed Efendi, who was sent back to his *çiftlik* in Bursa where he stayed until his death in 1685. In the meantime, the Venetian fleet conquered the Morean peninsula in 1686. The loss of Morea was followed by the loss of Budin and a string of strategic Hungarian castles, the loss of

137 Calder 1993, 118, 123–124.

Belgrade in 1688, and that of Niş in 1689. Among the critics of Mehmed IV's pastimes that allegedly prevented him from actively dealing with these military setbacks were both Sufis and Kadızadelis.[138]

Vani Mehmed had already disappeared from the political scene by the time Fazıl Mustafa became grand vizier. However, Fazıl Mustafa also proved to be less than flexible when it came to the matters of conquest and warfare. Although we do not know if he was rooting for an aggressive *gaza* policy for the same ideological reasons as were Kara Mustafa Pasha and Vani Mehmed Efendi, we do know, for instance, that he was very much against the diplomatic mission to Vienna, arranged by the-then grand vizier Bekri Mustafa.[139] Reportedly, Fazıl Mustafa Pasha, who had not yet become the grand vizier, was so enraged by the peace mission that he accused the members of the mission of infidelity.[140] Fazıl Mustafa was again lukewarm about any peace attempt in the wake of the Battle of Slankamen (1691), where he personally led the Ottoman army; the battle led to enormous losses on the Ottoman side, and cost Fazıl Mustafa his life.[141]

In addition to his fixation with *gaza*, another concern that Fazıl Mustafa inherited from the Sunna-minded discourses of the first half of the century was the legality of market operations. His elimination of the application of state-determined fixed prices on a daily basis (*narh-ı ruzi*) in the markets, citing the absence of any stipulations concerning price controls in *fikh* books, can be seen as one of the most emblematic pro-Sharia statements of the period.[142] What is known as *ta'sir* in Islamic legal terminology had been widely debated in early Islamic sources. The founding principle behind the rejection of *narh* emanates from an anecdote involving Prophet Muhammad. Once, when an increase in prices had occurred, a group of purchasers asked Muhammad to set a price in their favor, to which the Prophet replied:

138 Terzioğlu 1999, 175; Silahdar – Refik 1928, 2:245–248: among them were Halveti Sheikh Hacı Evhad Şeyhi Hüseyin Efendi, the Celveti Himmetzade Abdullah Efendi, Vani's son-in-law Mustafa Efendi who was a preacher at Valide Sultan Mosque.

139 On the grand vizier Bekri Mustafa's initiative, Alexandros Mavrokordatos and Zülfikar Efendi were sent to Vienna on a peace mission, only to be held captive there between 1688 and 1692. Jobst 1980; "Takrîr-i Mükamele" by Zülfikar Efendi in Silahdar – Refik 1928, 2:654–655; Zülfikar – Güler 2007.

140 Cantemir – Tindal 1734, 738.

141 The historian and bureaucrat Mevkufati blamed Fazıl Mustafa Paşa's hastiness for the defeat (Aycibin 2011, 70).

142 Defterdar – Özcan 1995, 388.

> God keeps, grants, expends, and sets prices, and I should like to find myself before my Lord without any of you complaining that he had been wronged by me whether in his blood or in his money.

Muhammad is also said to have stated that "prices depend upon the will of Allah, it is he who raises and lowers them."[143] Of course, this anecdote gave a strong ground to the Sunni jurists who categorically opposed price controls in markets. Nevertheless, there were always "cases" in which jurists condoned state intervention in market mechanisms, such as underselling and, especially, hoarding, which many authors studied above abhorred. Departing from the Hanafi doctrine they otherwise remained loyal to, the Ottomans were engaged in complex *narh* practices from the very beginning.[144] Additionally, the one legal authority whom one would assume could influence the Shariatization of the discourses on public administration the most actually offered the most flexible and permissive views concerning the application of *narh*. In his *al-Hisbat fi al-Islam*, Ibn Taymiyya condemned *tas'ir* but refused to make this condemnation an absolute principle by systematic reference to the categorical decision of the Prophet. Unlike the legal writers, who simply quoted the hadith of Muhammad, Ibn Taymiyya devoted considerable energy to exploring the context within which the Prophet's decision was made, examining the conditions that existed and had to be understood regarding that decision.[145]

At this point, attention should also be paid to the fact that the link between Fazıl Mustafa's action and his Sharia sensitivities was only made by contemporary historians, such as Defterdar Sarı Mehmed, who did not approve of the policy. Moreover, the seventeenth-century texts did not offer any explicit doctrinal or moral stand concerning the application of *narh*. Kadızade Mehmed, whom one may expect would take a strict stand against it, in fact condemned the *esnaf*-turned janissaries who did not want any price controls.[146] It was a well-known Sufi intellectual from the turn of the century, İsmail Hakkı Bursevi (1653–1724), who alone provided an argument on the issue. While initially he seems to have objected to official price-fixing, he later justified it by referring to the inequitable nature of the people of his time that made it necessary for the authorities to intervene.[147] The absence of any references to the Sharia as grounds for Fazıl Mustafa's elimination of *narh*, apart from in the accounts

143 Essid 1995, 152.
144 For *narh* regulations during the classical period see Kafadar 1986, 115–132.
145 Essid 1995, 165–167.
146 Öztürk 1981, 43.
147 Kafadar 1986, 136.

of disapproving contemporaneous historians at least, shows that there existed other economic pressures that led to this decision. In any case, the decision created so much confusion in the markets, alongside the unexpected rise in prices, that the grand vizier was forced to swiftly revoke it.[148]

No matter what the real causes for his policies were, almost every policy decision that Fazıl Mustafa made seems to have been deliberately legitimized by recourse to the Sharia. Immediately after he became the grand vizier, Fazıl Mustafa abolished the wine tax (*def-i hamr*) imposed on non-Muslims. Although contemporary histories do not extensively delve into this, they nevertheless mention that the officer responsible for the collection of the taxes levied on wine (*hamr emini*), Küfri Ahmed Efendi, was executed in front of the Üç Şerefeli Mosque in Edirne, where the Ottoman court was residing at the time. Perhaps not the policy of elimination but the rarely-witnessed act of executing a middle-ranking tax official shows how far Fazıl Mustafa could go in dressing his policies in Sharia colors. According to the historian Raşid, all the catastrophes the Ottomans faced on the military front were attributed by the ulema to neglect of the Sharia and laxity of its implementation. The selling of wine and rakı and their taxation by the state were deemed contrary to the founding principles of the Ottoman state. According to Raşid, it was the warnings of the ulema that resulted in the lifting of these "un-Islamic" taxes.[149] The same mentality can be seen in Fazıl Mustafa's annulling of the taxes levied on the non-Muslims with the exception of *cizye* and *harac*. Similar to the Cretan case, the decision implied that non-Muslims would be exempt from the taxes deemed to be extra-Sharia, such as *avarız*, *bedel-i nuzül*, and *sürsat*, and their remaining debts would be canceled.[150] One contemporary observer expressed his astonishment and claimed that the *mevkufat* registers were almost going to be set on fire.[151]

The death of Fazıl Mustafa at the battle of Slankamen did not bring an end to the implementation of Sharia guidelines in public administration. The next most influential character who had a significant impact on Ottoman politics

148 Defterdar – Özcan 1995, 387–389.

149 Raşid 1865, 2:101.

150 These taxes had been imposed in order to meet the war expenditures in the post-Vienna environment. See Defterdar – Özcan 1995, 221 and (for their elimination) 298–299.

151 Özcan 2000, 11. It was not always the case that non-Muslims benefitted from the Shariatization of the Ottoman tax system. While residing in the island of Lemnos following his banishment by Fazıl Ahmed Paşa, Niyazi Mısri was often visited by the priests from Imroz who consulted him about the legitimacy of the *harac* tax imposed on them. In his answer Mısri was reported to have implied that the person responsible was Fazıl Mustafa. Terzioğlu 1999, 177–178.

was the *şeyhülislam* Feyzullah Efendi (1638–1703, ş. 1695–1703), who was initially brought to Istanbul from his hometown of Erzurum by his father-in-law Vani Mehmed Efendi in 1664. A descendant of a renowned Halveti family from the Karabağ region of Azerbaijan, Feyzullah Efendi received a solid education in Islamic sciences in Erzurum.[152] He was also exposed to the Halveti tradition through his uncle Sheikh Mustafa Efendi, who was the head of the Halveti order in that town until his death in 1667, and his father Seyyid Mehmed (d. 1693), who took over the leadership of the order after that date. However, it was Vani Mehmed, at that time a resident of Erzurum, who had the biggest influence on the young Feyzullah. By then, Vani Mehmed had established himself as a famous scholar in Erzurum and became first the protégé of Feyzullah's uncle, Sheikh Mustafa Efendi, and, later, his son-in-law.[153] It was also Vani Mehmed who took him to Istanbul and let him participate in the scholarly discussions held in the sultan's presence, thus bringing him to the notice of the sultan.[154]

From his appointment as tutor to Prince Mustafa in 1669 until his tragic demise in the wake of the Edirne Incident of 1703, Feyzullah Efendi built an extensive household for himself which he bolstered by marriage alliances, *waqf* properties, and by placing his kin in lucrative *ilmiye* positions.[155] Although his relationship with the Köprülü clan was far from easy, Feyzullah Efendi was an important element in the preservation of the Köprülü mentality in terms of the preservation of their material and ideological heritage.[156]

The ascession of Mustafa II to the throne in 1695 resulted in Feyzullah being made not only head of the entire *ilmiye* hierarchy but also the sultan's senior advisor on state affairs. It was apparent right from the start that Mustafa II was going to be a very different ruler from his two uncles, Süleyman II and Ahmed II, who had ruled before him. Having escaped the long periods of palace captivity that they faced during much of their pre-adult lives, Mustafa experienced a more liberal palace atmosphere, as did his brother Ahmed (who

152 In his autobiography, Feyzullah says that he received lessons from his father and a relative named Molla Seyyid Abdülmümin, who taught him the Quran, Arabic and Persian, literature and poetry, and Islamic law. Later, he learned syntax, grammar, semantics, rhetorics, and flowery phraseology from his cousin Molla İbrahim Murtazazade, who was one of the best-known scholars in the area. Nizri 2014, 22.

153 Nizri 2014, 21–22.

154 Kaylı 2010, 221.

155 For an account of how Feyzullah settled his sons and relatives into lucrative *ilmiye* positions, see Nizri 2014, 92–95.

156 He was appointed as the overseer of the Köprülü's charitable endowments. See Abou-El-Haj 2005, 145, fn. 58. He also infiltrated the Köprülü household by arranging marriages between his and the Köprülü family, see Nizri 2014, 65.

would be enthroned after him as Ahmed III). Mustafa II was known for his zeal for renewing the tradition of his ancestors by leading *gaza* against the infidels.[157] Feyzullah was a central player in steering the imperial policy towards *gaza*, and between 1695 and 1697 participated in all three military campaigns against the Habsburgs, not as a passive member in the sultan's entourage but actively fighting in the army.[158] He was also instrumental in concocting an image of the sultan that employed a wholly Islamic vocabulary. Writing in 1699, Feyzullah declared Mustafa II the centennial renewer (*müceddid*) in a short treatise that was recorded by Uşşakizade in his history.[159] He also praised the sultan for shunning pleasure, entertainment, and every amusement and nonsensical involvement (*rahat, melahi, lağv ve bitalet*), very much echoing the moralist discourses of the Kadızadelis before him.[160]

The Sharia-centered vocabulary that governed the reign of Mustafa II found its most formal expression in an edict sent by the sultan to the deputy grand vizier in 1696 that ordained that fermans and decrees should, from then on, only refer to the "noble Sharia" and strictly advised against the coupling of the terms Sharia and *kanun*.[161] However, given our survey of the earlier espousals of Sharia ideals by both Halveti and Kadızadeli preachers, Mustafa II's prioritizing of the Sharia in lieu of the *kanun* should not seem unprecedented.

Mustafa II, Feyzullah Efendi, and the entire Feyzullah clique would soon be toppled by the Edirne Incident. However the discourses they had been championing went beyond merely the creation of the image of a *gazi* sultan: they penetrated the upper segments of the imperial bureaucracy, which thus began to emphasize its reverence to early Hanafi legal references in state administration. Such testimony to the continuing observation of the Sharia by the Ottoman political elites can even be found in an explicitly anti-Feyzullah source, the *Anonymous History* covering the period between 1688 and 1704. The person who commissioned it was probably the grand vizier Rami Mehmed

157 Nizri 2014, 103–104.

158 Nizri 2014, 110.

159 Kaylı 2010, 224; Uşşakizade – Gündoğdu 2005, 750–756.

160 Kaylı 2010, 224.

161 "Apart from the penalties (*hudud*) ordained by Allah and the penalties by the prophet no penalties are to be laid down and chosen (*ihtiyar*), and interference by anyone else in the commands of the illustrious sharia is null and is rejected. However, in some decrees which have the character of *kanun* [the term] noble sharia is followed by and connected with [the term] *kanun*. Not only is [the sharia thus] quoted in a place unbefitting it. It is also highly perilous and most sinful to juxtapose the [terms] sharia and *kanun*. Therefore in firmans and decrees all matters shall henceforth be based on the firm support of the noble sharia only … and warnings are given against the coupling of the [terms] noble sharia and kanun …" See Heyd 1973, 154–155.

Pasha (d. 1708). Rami Mehmed was scandalously elevated from the seat of the chief scribe to grand vizierate (a leap in career which had never been seen before) under the auspices of Feyzullah Efendi, yet later fell out with him. In a section praising Rami Mehmed's vizierial virtues, the anonymous author gives a long description of an imperial council (*divan*) meeting that took place on January 26, 1703.[162] It was Rami Mehmed Pasha who oversaw the *divan* as the grand vizier. The anonymous author described Rami Mehmed's *divan* as the best one in Ottoman history with regard to its efficiency in handling petitions and its conforming to correct legal procedure. An important detail about the operation of the grand vizier's council is that, during their free time, the scribes at the *divan* occupied themselves reading *Kitâb siyar al-kebir*, the famous work on the Islamic law of nations attributed to the Hanafi jurist al-Shaybani (d. 805) and widely known from al-Sarakhsi's late eleventh-century commentary.[163] The main interest of this work is in its detailing of Islamic law as regards non-Muslims living in both the domain of war (*dar al-harb*) and the domain of Islam. It is not possible to know exactly what part of the work was the most relevant for the officials at Rami Mehmed's *divan*. However, it must be emphasized that it continued the line of argument made by Abu Yusuf and Birgivi by defining the legal status of a land appropriated by conquest as a function of the status of the land rather than the personal status of those working it.[164] In highlighting the *Kitâb siyar al-kebir*'s place as the main intellectual reference for the Ottoman chancellery, the anonymous historian attests to the continuing efforts of the central administration to determine its treatment of state affairs according to Hanafi law and identity.

5 Conclusion

As has been argued by recent studies on Ottoman Sufism and Sunnism, certain genealogies that long defined the field have been overstated in scholarship. Neither Ibn Taymiyya nor Birgivi Mehmed served as the sole ideological basis

162 Özcan 2000, 197.

163 Al-Sarakhsi's definition of *siyar* is as follows: "… [Siyar] described the conduct of the believers in their relations with the unbelievers of enemy territory as well as the people with whom the believers had made treatises, who may have been temporarily (musta'mins) or permanently (Dhimmis) in Islamic lands; with apostates, who were the worst of the unbelievers, since they abjured after they accepted [Islam]; and with rebels (baghis), who were not counted as unbelievers, though they were ignorant and their understanding [of Islam] was false" (Shaybani – Khadduri 1966, 40).

164 Heck 2002, 169.

for the Salafist movements that emerged in the seventeenth century. Even in those cases where their influence was most visible, they were not confined to the Salafism of the Kadızadelis but captivated a wider audience, including the Halvetis. As for the Ottoman Sufis, again recent scholarship has dismantled the image of a united Sufi front and exposed the dynamics that differentiated Sufi communities from one another. The way Münir-i Belgradi shaped his works and his criticisms according to different audiences is the clearest proof of the diversity of ideological options available to Ottoman writers in the late sixteenth century. Amidst this diversity, as in the case of the relationship between Birgivi and his Kadızadeli successors, one cannot speak of a single ideological core that was passed from Belgradi to the seventeenth-century Halvetis. For one thing, the ideological production of the seventeenth-century Sunna-minded authors was much different in both form and content when compared to Birgivi and Belgradi. Birgivi and Belgradi's works exhibited a different type of knowledge, one which was built on meticulous analysis of legal traditions in the former's case and textual criticism in the latter's, whereas seventeenth-century Sunna-mindedness was first seen in the preachings of the Kadızadelis and Halvetis and was later transferred onto the pages of the advice works they authored. Therefore, Sunna-minded trends did not pose the same theoretical challenge as did the older genres of Ottoman political thought but instead served as a discursive field that covered as many issues as possible, ranging from promiscuity to the corruption of judges. Another characteristic of the seventeenth-century Sunna-centered writings is that their preachers-turned-authors did not belong solely to the high-ranking clerical and political elite but came from a variety of social backgrounds and addressed an audience equally diverse in social composition.

CHAPTER 7

Khaldunist Philosophy: Innovation Justified

The repercussions following Murad IV's death in 1640 did nothing to reinforce the optimism that his activity had undoubtedly aroused in the circles lamenting Ottoman decline.[1] His younger brother and successor, Ibrahim, was considered mad, or at least feeble-minded (as Colin Imber notes, it is no coincidence that Koçi Bey's second treatise, composed for him, was "written in appropriately uncomplicated language"[2]): he suffered from continuous headaches and soon fell under the influence of an exorcist, Cinci Hoca. After a few calm years at the beginning of his reign, trouble began: in 1645, the Ottomans launched the Cretan War, which, although quickly resulting in the conquest of almost all Crete, nevertheless stalled before the largest city, Candia (Kandiye), as the Venetians captured Tenedos and effected an intermittent blockade of the Dardanelles. In addition, the extravagance of Ibrahim pushed state expenditure to incalculable heights, while his anxiety about not having a male descendant led (or contributed) to an obsession with his harem, which was subsequently invested with more and more power. A revolt by the janissaries and high ulema led to his deposition and eventual execution (by *şeyhülislam*'s *fetva*) in 1648; his son Mehmed IV being still a minor, actual power passed to the valide sultan, Kösem Mahpeyker (Murad IV's and Ibrahim's mother).[3] The power of Kösem lay mostly in her networking activity: her *protégés* were promoted and she arranged marriages of princesses to pashas who were thus connected to the dynasty. The early years of Mehmed's reign were equally turbulent: a sipahi rebellion just after his accession was suppressed by the janissaries, while the Celali rebel Gürcü Nebî marched on Istanbul demanding the removal of the "regicide" *şeyhülislam*. The role of the janissaries in dealing with both revolts resulted in a "janissary junta" led by a triumvirate composed of Bektaş Ağa, Kara Çavuş, and *kul kethüdası* Mustafa Ağa (Çelebi Kethüda Beğ), which dominated both economic and political life in the capital. Economic and social problems intensified; a massive protest of the "people of the market" against the grand vizier Melek Ahmed Pasha in 1651 led only to his dismissal,[4] but

1 On the political and military events of the period see Imber 2009, 71–74; Mantran 1989, 236–264; Emecen 2001b, 49–55.

2 Imber 2009, 72.

3 On Kösem's formidable career, see Peirce 1993, 105ff., 236ff., 248–252 and *passim*.

4 See Yi 2004, 213–233; Sariyannis 2012, esp. 268–282, for an alternative interpretation of the 1651 revolt.

© KONINKLIJKE BRILL NV, LEIDEN, 2019 | DOI:10.1163/9789004385245_009

soon after a re-arrangement of factions in the palace itself would bring about the fall of Kösem Sultan, who was murdered upon the order of Mehmed IV's mother Turhan, and the subsequent fall of the janissary aghas as well. The grand vizier, Tarhuncu Ahmed Pasha, tried to reduce state expenditure, to farm out vacant timars, and to force well-to-do officials and subjects to contribute to the treasury, but he was dismissed and executed in 1653. Anarchy in the capital continued: the domination of the harem aghas, which had succeeded that of the janissaries, came to an end in 1656 after a joint revolt of the sipahis and janissaries (the so-called "plane-tree incident", *vak'a-ı çınar* or *vak'a-ı vakvakiye*; the harem aghas' bodies were suspended from a plane tree, hence the name), only to be replaced with a "sipahi junta".

Finally, Turhan was forced to name as grand vizier a *protégé* of hers, the aged pasha Mehmed Köprülü (1656–61). To assume this post, Köprülü explicitly laid down his terms, asking for almost absolute power in order to restore the empire. He suppressed rebellions in Istanbul and Anatolia, broke the Venetian blockade in the Dardanelles, and in general became so powerful that, upon his death, he was succeeded by his own son, Köprülüzade Fazıl Ahmed Pasha (1661–76), an unprecedented phenomenon in Ottoman politics. According to Rifaat Abou-El-Haj, the beginning of the Köprülü "dynasty" marked the rise of a new source of power, the vizier and pasha households (*kapı*): these officials and magnates promoted their own relatives, servants, and *protégés* to high administrative posts, gradually diminishing the percentage of people originating in the palace or the army. Metin Kunt, however, has argued that this process started much earlier, and that private households had been established by the beginning of the seventeenth century.[5]

The influence of the Kadızadeli movement in Köprülü internal policies was described in chapter 6; in other fields, Fazıl Ahmed was credited with the capture of Candia in 1669 (he went to Crete and led the campaign in person), as well as with victories in Transylvania and Podolia. Later campaigns were not so successful: the siege of Vienna in 1683 was a complete disaster, as a Polish army routed the Ottoman besiegers; in the aftermath, a Holy League uniting Austria, the papacy, Poland, and Venice conquered Buda (1686), while a little later Venetian armies took possession of the Peloponnese. An army revolt on the Habsburg front led, in 1687, to Mehmed IV's deposition and a short period

5 Abou-El-Haj 1984, 7–9, 89–91 and *passim*; Kunt 1983, xvii, 40, 46, 64–67 and *passim*; Kunt 2012; Hathaway 2013. For an example of such a career see the biography of Mahmud Paşa (d. 1685) in Silahdar – Refik 1928, 2:223 (Silahdar – Türkal 2012, 1019): initially an Istanbul merchant, he became agha of Kara Mustafa Paşa and managed to rise to hold the posts of vizier and deputy grand vizier.

of military domination in the capital, which was finally put to an end by the decisive reaction of the merchants of the city, something that met with the new sultan's approval and help.[6] Indeed, Mehmed's successor, Süleyman II (1687–91), made serious efforts to restore the sultan's personal powers. Despite this, however, the Habsburg forces continued their counter-attack, managing to reach the Danube and even capturing Belgrade. Süleyman tried to stop their offensive using both diplomatic and military means, but the enemy continued to march through Serbia and the Danube principalities. At this crucial point, the new grand vizier, Köprülü Fazıl Mustafa Pasha (the younger son of Mehmed Köprülü), managed to reorganize the army effectively, purging the janissary lists of soldiers unable to fight, and with the help of other factors (such as the French-Habsburg war) launched a successful counter-offensive in the autumn of 1690. The Ottomans recaptured Belgrade and the rest of Serbia, while Mustafa Pasha continued to reorganize the timar system and the army. However, in 1691 Süleyman died and Mustafa Pasha was killed at the front; battles continued throughout the reign of Ahmed II (1691–95) without clear gains or losses.

Ahmed's successor, Mustafa II (1695–1703), led some successful campaigns against the Austrians but his army was crushed at Zenta in 1697, soon after the Russians had captured Azov in the Crimea. After long negotiations, led by the new grand vizier, Amcazade Hüseyin Pasha (also a member of the Köprülü family), the war was officially ended with the Treaty of Karlowitz (1699), the first treaty to officially recognize a surrender of Ottoman territories to the infidels. Amcazade Hüseyin Pasha continued the reforming efforts of his predecessor; however, Mustafa, who was trying to resume the sultan's powers against the notable pasha and ulema households (he tried to reverse the trend and use people from his own household),[7] was increasingly reliant on his former teacher and confidant, the *şeyhülislam* Feyzullah Efendi, whose unchecked nepotism alienated the court and the sultan from the bulk of the ulema hierarchy. The retirement of Amcazade Hüseyin Pasha in 1702 made things no better; as Mustafa had actually moved to Edirne during the Karlowitz negotiations and showed no signs of returning to Istanbul, dismay grew there. In 1703, a small rebellion of some military troops soon rallied other soldiers, ulema, and craftsmen, eventually establishing a rival power in the capital with its own *şeyhülislam* and officials (the so-called "Edirne event" or *Edirne vakası*). Mustafa amassed an army in Edirne and marched against the rebels, but the latter had already built a large force and were slowly advancing towards Edirne.

6 See Yi 2011.

7 See the numbers studied by Abou-El-Haj 1984, 49.

When the two armies met, that of the sultan went over to the rebels. Mustafa had to resign and his brother, Ahmed III, was proclaimed sultan.[8]

1 The Social and Ideological Struggles: between Viziers and Janissaries

If we are to accept that the late sixteenth and the seventeenth century was a time of strife between sultanly absolutism and the growing power of groups such as the ulema and the janissaries (with the latter increasingly representing the urban Muslim strata empowered by the monetarization of the economy) then the whole second half of the seventeenth century (until the major upheaval of the "Edirne event") would be a temporary victory of the absolutists. The actual power of the sultans may not have reached that of Murad IV, for example, but the almost continuous rule of the Köprülü household marks the alliance of weak rulers with strong viziers in an effort to keep interference by the urban and military newcomers to a minimum.[9] Pasha households, on the other hand, increasingly began to gain power and a growing degree of participation in the central and provincial administration, gradually substituting the sultan's household during the late seventeenth and early eighteenth centuries.[10]

On the other hand, the gradual growth in the power and autonomy of the central bureaucracy continued steadily in the second half of the seventeenth century. Further systematization and rationalization of the tax-collecting services was effectuated under the Köprülü regime and led to an even more autonomous and self-confident functioning of the scribal apparatus.[11] Even on the symbolic level of political ceremony, the government apparatus saw its role and visibility elevated. Thus, while, for instance, the 1582 sultanly festival included meals offered to the ulema, preachers, various military groups, palace officials (including viziers), and the people of Istanbul, no place was reserved for palace clerks; in contrast, the eighth day (out of fifteen) of the 1675 festival was devoted to a feast offered to the bureaucracy officials (*reisülküttab, ruznameci, baş muhasebeci*).[12] As seen in chapter 6, financial bureaucrats introduced substantial reforms, such as the rationalization of poll-tax collection,

8 For a detailed narrative and interpretation of the "Edirne event" see Abou-El-Haj 1984. On Feyzullah see the recent study by Nizri 2014.

9 This is, in general, the thesis suggested by Tezcan 2010a.

10 Abou-El-Haj 2005; Kunt 1983; Kunt 2012; Hathaway 2013.

11 Darling 2006, 123–124.

12 Ali – Öztekin 1996, 58ff. and 232ff. (on the 1582 festival); Nutku 1987, 56, and Hezarfen – İlgürel 1998, 241 (on the 1675 festival). On the increased visibility and self-confidence of

experimental new landholding and cadastral methods based on private ownership of arable lands, and the extension of the tax-farming system to lifelong leases (*malikâne*).[13] On the ideological level, it was noted that these reforms were more often than not justified not in terms of the "old law" but of correct Sunna practice. On the social level, all these measures fully conformed to the needs of a by-then highly monetized economy, not only on the part of the state (which thus covered more and more of its needs in ready cash) but also on the part of a new group of elite entrepreneurs. Tax-farmers, money-lenders who now made loans to whole villages in order to render possible the payment of taxes, and real-estate profiteers—they all benefited from financial experiment, no matter what their legal justifications might be. As the "old law" argument was, from the beginning, connected to the old feudal relations, market-oriented reforms made recourse to the other prevalent juristic reasoning, the appeal to the principles of the Sunna.[14] Furthermore, these elite entrepreneurs were not only newcomers, Christian and Muslim; a large part of tax-farming and money lending was, by the late seventeenth century and increasingly so in the century to come, effectuated by the janissary units, who had their own funds and networks.[15] Besides, vizier and pasha households, always in dire need of cash in order to maintain their patronage networks, their retinue, and the ability to buy governmental posts for their clients, began to be increasingly actively engaged in the market (the famous example of Derviş Mehmed Pasha, so masterfully studied by Metin Kunt, will be examined in detail later).[16]

In chapter 6, Ekin Tuşalp Atiyas showed the role played by Köprülü viziers, such as Merzifonlu Kara Mustafa Pasha, in initiating some of these market-oriented reforms (including the short-lived abolition of *narh* or fixed prices—the reader might remember here Hezarfen's defence of this institution) in tandem with their Sunna-minded legitimization; she also remarked that this

the scribal bureaucracy, see also Sariyannis 2013, 103–111; on festivals and their symbolic role, cf. Faroqhi 2008, 74ff.; Murphey 2008, 175ff.

13 On the poll-tax reform cf. Darling 2006, 125 (who remarks that with such reforms it appears that "a greater portion of the financial burden of empire was transferred to a shrinking non-Muslim population") and Sariyannis 2011b; on the landholding-*cum*-taxation reforms, see Kolovos 2007; Kermeli 2008; Veinstein 2008; on the *malikâne* see Darling 2006, 126–129. The developments in the book-keeping of the imperial government attest to the growing specialization of the central bureaucracy throughout the seventeenth century, too: see Soyer 2007.

14 Cf. Sariyannis 2012.

15 Yi 2004, 132–143; Tezcan 2010a, 184–190, 198–212. Yannis Spyropoulos is currently undertaking a research project on these janissary networks.

16 Kunt 1977; Faroqhi 1994, 547–549. For an earlier instance of such entrepreneurial practices by a pasha, see Gel 2013b.

legitimization was carefully selected so as to leave space for the sultan's, or in fact (given the conditions of the era) the grand vizier's, discretion. Yet in the case of the Cretan reforms of the poll-tax and landholding, as may be remembered, this attempt at justification was made after the measures themselves had been implemented, which may imply that the financial bureaucracy had played a much more active role than the Köprülü viziers' personalities would make us think. Thus, it seems that after the mid-seventeenth century an alliance of this bureaucracy with the autocratic vizerial regime began to initiate market-oriented reforms using the inventory of Sunna-minded political thought. In this context, as noted in chapter 5, this alliance had to compete with the janissaries, or rather the military, who were increasingly cooperating with the lower-class artisans and traders and developing their own financial networks.

Throughout the first half of the seventeenth century the governmental apparatus used the "old law" as a tool for establishing its predominance in the political field against the army forces; as analyzed above, when the bureaucrats started to identify themselves with the monetized policies and relations they chose to turn to the Sunna as a binding justification of their power. In response, it appears that the janissaries gradually began to appropriate an argument that traditionally had been used against them: the "old law" and the abhorrence of institutional innovation. As will be made apparent in chapter 9, they ended up identifying themselves with the old and sanctified Ottoman constitution in order to block any attempt on the part of the court and the government to curb their own power and their legitimate claim of being shareholders in the state.

On the other side of the conflict, however, the Sharia-based model had its shortcomings. The failure of the *narh* reform, as well as the eventually short life of the landholding and surveyal experiments, showed that Sunna-minded arguments worked poorly when set against age-old practices. One may suggest that, because the janissaries successfully claimed for themselves the benefits of the "old law" reasoning, and because the Sunna-minded model was not strong enough when applied to state policies, a new trend emerged, one that broke the circle of constitutional reasoning to advocate innovation and change—or, eventually, the right of the state to apply innovation and change. Whereas scribal discourse of the previous decades was still trying to suggest that enhanced timariot forces would counterbalance the janissary threat,[17] from now

17 In a similar vein, *kapıkulu* sipahis, i.e. standing cavalry, had been effectively acting as a counterbalance to the janissary infantry throughout the first half of the seventeenth century. However, after the middle of the century the two groups tended to forge alliances together, and even participated in joint mutinies and revolts (1655, 1656, 1687–1688). On this

on they would appeal to a strong centralized state, one which would apply smart measures to impose discipline. It appears, as will be seen, that this trend was also born from within the scribal bureaucracy and that it had to struggle its way through the second half of the seventeenth century (as shown from Hezarfen's example) until its eventual, albeit precarious, ideological victory, as seen in Na'ima's ideas and their influence.

In this context, it is not surprising that, the continuation of earlier trends of political thought (as seen in the final section of chapter 5) notwithstanding, this trend tried to take a wider view of the problems and structure of Ottoman society, just as Bayezid I or Mehmed II's authoritarian rule had favored the introduction of Nasir al-Din Tusi's ethico-philosophical theories. On the other hand, it would be strange if the difficulties and setbacks dominating this period met with the same optimism as the grand imperial project of the earlier sultans. As seen in the previous chapters, Ottoman littérateurs had already developed an acute sense of decline, and it was only natural that it was Ibn Khaldun's bio-historical theories they turned to when they began to look for models for a new, elaborate theory of society. Whereas, as has been seen, Tusi and his followers' vision of a "world order" was universal and static, Ibn Khaldun's model offered the advantage of allowing, if not imposing, change according to local, historical, and cultural conditions. In chapter 2 we traced some echoes of Ibn Khaldun's work in Kınalızade's mid-sixteenth-century Tusian masterpiece; from the mid-seventeenth century onwards, however, Ibn Khaldun's vision of revolving dynasties and general historical laws started to permeate Ottoman political thought with increasing intensity.[18]

2 Kâtib Çelebi and Ottoman Khaldunism

Indeed, it was around the early 1650s that a more general and "philosophical" view of society began to reclaim its place in Ottoman letters after the torrent of concrete, institutional advice described in the previous chapters. And it was Kâtib Çelebi, the famous polymath, geographer, and encyclopedist of the first half of the seventeenth century who initiated this renaissance of political

standing cavalry, its growth, and its important role in earlier Istanbul revolts cf. Tezcan 2010a, 184–190.

18 The literature on Ibn Khaldun's philosophy of history is vast: see e.g. Rosenthal 1958, 84–109; Lambton 1981, 152–177; Fakhry 2000, 108–112; Black 2011, 169–185. On Khaldunism in Ottoman writings see Fındıkoğlu 1953; Fleischer 1983; Lewis 1986.

theory (rather than advice).[19] Mustafa b. Abdullah, known as Kâtib Çelebi or Hacı Halife (1609–57) was the son of a scribe in the fiscal bureaucracy (and, at the same time, an imperial guard raised in the palace); he became an apprentice in his father's office in 1622 and accompanied him on various campaigns soon after. After his father's death in 1626, Kâtib Çelebi continued his scribal career and his occasional military duties while at the same time studying under Kadızade Mehmed Efendi and other scholars. In 1635 he settled permanently in Istanbul, developing into a celebrated bibliophile and a "freelance" teacher of law and theology, as well as of mathematics and astronomy. He maintained a circle of intellectuals and close relations with various European renegades, who translated chronicles and geographical works from European languages for him. Kâtib Çelebi's output was vast in both volume and scope: he wrote bio-bibliographical encyclopedias (his *Kashf al-zunûn* is still a valuable source for authors and books now lost), historical works (like the famous *Fezleke*, one of our main sources for the early seventeenth century), political advice, and geographical compendiums (his *Cihânnümâ* was based on the latest European atlases), not to mention various treatises or collections on various matters. He seems to have embarked on what Gottfried Hagen termed his "Encyclopedic project" as he strongly believed that the diffusion of scientific knowledge would benefit greatly in coping with the current crisis. Thus, he produced what he considered reference works, focusing on history, letters, and geography; in this context, he also translated (with the help of his convert friends) works such as *Atlas Minor* and Byzantine and European chronicles. Kâtib Çelebi is generally credited with the introduction of European-style scientific geography and more generally with a major attempt to rationalize Ottoman science and worldview. Indeed, in an age where the "rational sciences" (e.g. logic or mathematics) seem to have had started to decline in favor of "transmitted" ones (i.e. theology, grammar, and law) in the *medrese* curriculum,[20] Kâtib Çelebi emphasized the need and usefulness of natural sciences, placing emphasis on geography and astronomy. However, one must not overestimate Kâtib Çelebi's rationalism: he was a product of his tradition, entrenched in the transmitted way of thinking inasmuch he was prone to unquestionably relate traditions or practices that would nowadays sound quite irrational. The innovations brought about by Kâtib Çelebi were his quest for unambiguity and the widening of

19 On Kâtib Çelebi's life and work see Gökyay 1991; Hagen 1995/96; Hagen 2003a; Yurtoğlu 2009; and the comprehensive article by Gottfried Hagen on the website "Historians of the Ottoman Empire": http://ottomanhistorians.uchicago.edu/en/historians/65 (accessed May 2015).

20 On this development, which might be an overestimation based on Kâtib Çelebi's writings, cf. El-Rouayheb 2008; Tezcan 2010b.

the array of usable sources. The translations of the *Atlas Minor* and of similar Western European texts served to enlarge the tradition and to enrich it with a new and, furthermore, a more authoritative source; but it was primarily the traditional textual criticism tools that Kâtib Çelebi applied to these widened sources.[21]

As will be seen, Kâtib Çelebi's teacher Kadızade Mehmed Efendi's legalist and literal reading of the Quran impressed him but did not lead him to adhere to revivalist ideas. His own political sympathies were more inclined towards the reformist viziers who tried to find a stronghold in the turbulent politics of 1650s Istanbul, such as Tarhuncu Ahmed Pasha and Köprülü Mehmed Pasha.[22] Apart from the favorable references in his chronicle, this is also clear in his major political work, *Düstûrü'l-amel li ıslahi'l-halel* ("Course of measures to redress the situation"), composed during the former's vizierate and just a few years before the rise of the latter.[23] As the author himself narrates (not only in this text but also in his historiographical *Fezleke*),[24] it was composed in 1653 following a meeting of the financial scribes under the *defterdar* on balancing the state budget in which he had taken part. Indeed, this short essay stresses financial reform; however, its main value lies in the exposition of Kâtib Çelebi's sociological ideas, which include a novel medical simile for human society, a pioneering definition of the state, and the first systematic introduction of the Khaldunian notion of the "state stages" into the Ottoman philosophy of history.

2.1 *A Theory of State and Society*

We do not know how Kâtib Çelebi came into contact with Ibn Khaldun's philosophy and sociology of history (in his bibliographical encyclopedia, *Kashf al-zunûn*, there is an entry on the *Muqaddima*), but he included a very detailed account of it in his concluding remarks to his *Takvîmü't-tevârîh* ("Chronicle of histories"), a world history chronicle compiled in 1648.[25]

Kâtib Çelebi begins with an assurance that God ordains caliphs and sultans to administer the affairs of the people. Among the tribes and races who have

21 Sariyannis 2015, 452–456 and 461–463; cf. Kurz 2011, 215.

22 Hagen 2003a, 62–64.

23 There are two known MSS (Nuruosmaniye Ktp. 4075; Murat Molla Ktp., Hamidiye, no. 1649, ff. 39b–47a). The treatise was published in Ottoman Turkish as an appendix to Ayn Ali 1978, 119–139; Turkish translation in Kâtib Çelebi – Gökyay 1968, 154–161; a German translation had appeared as Kâtib Çelebi – Behrnauer 1857. See also Gökbilgin 1991, 212–217; Lewis 1962, 78–81; Thomas 1972, 73–74; Fodor 1986, 233–235; İnan 2009, 121; Yurtoğlu 2009, 16–22; Black 2011, 265–267.

24 Kâtib Çelebi 1869–1871, 2:384–85.

25 Kâtib Çelebi 1733, 233–237; Turkish translation in Kâtib Çelebi – Gökyay 1968, 114–117; cf. Yurtoğlu 2009, 22–24; Al-Tikriti 2017.

appeared on earth since the beginning of time, it has been God's will that the changes and phases seen in human civilizations and societies (*nev'-i beşerden her sınıfın temeddün ve ictima'î halinde*) correspond to those seen in individuals according to their age. As the "natural" life of man is 120 years, so is the usual time-span of a society (*her ta'ifenin müddet-i ictima'î*), although it can vary according to its strength or weakness.[26] There are three stages in every state and society (*devlet ve cemi'yet*), corresponding to the three ages of man (growth, stagnation, and decline). Just as an individual needs their parents' care while still a child, in its early stages a state or a dynasty (*devlet*) is characterized by its members' "zeal and mutual assistance" (*ta'assub ve ta'avün-ı ricâl*). And just as self-governance comes to a growing person, so does a king lay down just laws and use his treasury to govern his state. The finances, the army, the power, and the population of a state grows continually in its early period, the way a man's limbs grow until maturity. In the same vein, a mature society has its most just rulers and more generally its heyday in every respect.

In the age of decline, just as an old body loses gradually its temperature and humidity (*hararet ve rütubet*) and consequently its powers and senses, so do statesmen (*vükela-yı devlet*, a state's temperature and humidity) lose their ability to think rightly and take proper measures; consequently, the people and the army (the powers and senses) start to go astray. Furthermore, those officials who try to mend such problems of decline in the same way they would have earlier are bound to fail, since each period requires its own measures. More specifically, now, the signs of decline are: a tendency of the magnates to imitate their rulers in wealth and pageantry, and more generally a tendency to continually increase levels of luxuries and pomp. The middle classes want to live like kings, and the military prefer ease and peace to fighting. After presenting this grim image, Kâtib Çelebi feels compelled to note that no matter how binding is this historical scheme, God is all-powerful and may allow it not to come about in such a way. For one thing, a dynasty that neglects its laws and turns to tyranny will decline earlier than is usual (just like a sick man who takes poison instead of medicine), while a dynasty that takes wise measures and uses insightful statesmen as doctors can extend its days, the same as an old man can live to the end of his days in good health.

---

26 Here one can discern a distant reading of Ibn Khaldun, who states that "the term of life of a dynasty does not normally exceed three generations [of 40 years each]". The three ages described by Kâtib Çelebi correspond to Ibn Khaldun's description of these three dynastic generations. See Ibn Khaldun – Rosenthal 1958, 1:343–346; Ibn Khaldun – Rosenthal – Dawood 1969, 136–138.

The rest is a reiteration of earlier *topoi* on good government: Good politicking (*siyaset*) is the prerequisite for the longevity and well-being of a state, and it can emanate either from reason (*aklî*), in which case it is a branch of philosophy, or from the Sharia. The latter has no need of the former; a Muslim king will either follow God's guidelines and gain this world and the next or succumb to his whims, become a tyrant, and inevitably be punished. Whenever infidel rulers govern their states successfully, this is due to them following governmental rules based on reason, which is the essence, observes Kâtib Çelebi, of the "Turkish proverb: the world is destroyed not through infidelity, but through oppression".[27] A government based on neither reason nor the Sharia is doomed to collapse. Here, Kâtib Çelebi hastens to add some more concrete examples and cases of bad government, namely: the interference of women in state affairs;[28] a ruler who does not spare his subjects' blood; a ruler who tends to cut off his subjects' daily bread; and a prince who kills his father to gain the throne. All this is given in the form of "laws of history" of sorts. For instance: a patricide has never survived more than a year in power; viziers or chieftains who opened a ruler's way to the throne have very often found their death at the latter's hands; and the sixth ruler in every dynasty lost his throne (which in the Ottoman case would relate to Murad II's abdication in favor of his son, Mehmed II).

As mentioned, Kâtib Çelebi's most celebrated political work, *Düstûrü'l-amel*, was composed some four years after *Takvîmü't-tevârîh*. Perhaps because of the more general audience he intended it for, he now chose to present a simplified version of Khaldunist sociology. The references to "zeal and mutual assistance" (i.e. Ibn Khaldun's famous *asabiyya*) and the detailed descriptions of the laws of decline and the time-spans of societies are missing, as are the universal laws of history Kâtib Çelebi had tried to explore in his chronicle. Instead, in *Düstûrü'l-amel*, again perhaps due to his need to explain things to an audience of statesmen, Kâtib Çelebi adds some elaborate explanations that complete his vision of society and politics: most importantly, the identification of the rising and declining entity, *devlet*, to society as a whole and his sophisticated medical simile on the basis of the four humors rather than the four elements.

At the beginning, the usual eulogy of God and the Prophet refers, somewhat misleadingly, to the

27 We have seen this proverb (which goes back to Nizam al-Mulk; see Fodor 1985, 219, fn 5) quoted many times before.

28 Kâtib Çelebi also dedicated a special chapter of his *Fezleke* to this issue: Kâtib Çelebi 1869–1871, 2:309–310.

> political therapies brought about by the Holy Law, which are sufficient for redressing the disposition of the kingdom and of the state, as well as for bringing the powers of the rules of the religious community into balance (*edviye-i siyaset-i şer'iyesi ıslah-ı mizac-ı mülk ü devlete kâfi ve ta'dil-i kuva-yı kava'id-i din ü millete vafidir*).

Old-fashioned as it sounds, this introductory remark mentions balance, a key concept in Kâtib Çelebi's vision. Now, in the introduction to his treatise (AA122–3; G155–156) he sets out to present his views on "the dispositions of the state" (*etvar-ı devlet*). First he defines this term, stating that:

> [the word] *devlet*, which [originally] meant *saltanat* and *mülk*, according to another view consists of human society (*ictima-ı beşeriyeden ibaretdir*).

In the whole history of the term, this is the first time it had taken on such a broad meaning. Ibn Khaldun had spoken of the rise and decline of *dawla*, meaning dynasties. In *Takvîmü't-tevârîh*, Kâtib Çelebi had somewhat vaguely referred to groups (*ta'ife*) and dynasties, sometimes coupling the latter with "communities" or "societies" (*devlet ve cemi'yet*). Yet now he explicitly defines his subject as society as a whole; this will help him localize the present shortcomings and, consequently, the future measures to be taken across the whole body politic, rather than only in certain state institutions. To make this leap, he reverts to the Tusian theory of the continuum of the human condition: there is the individual state of man and the social state, both of which are governed by the same natural laws.

Indeed, Kâtib Çelebi argues that the social condition of man (*insanın ictima'i hali*) resembles that of the individual. An individual's life is naturally divided into three stages, namely growth, stagnation, and physical decline (*nümüv, vukuf, inhitat*); the coming of each age in turn depends upon the disposition of the individual, so a strong man comes to old age later than a weak one. Similarly, now, runs the social state of man, i.e. society or *devlet* (*insanın devletden ibaret olan ictima'î hali*), which is also divided into three ages depending on its strength: this is why some societies (*cemi'yet*) reached decline quickly, while others, "like this exalted state", being strong in their construction and well-grounded, were late in joining the age of stagnation. Moreover, in both the individual and the social state of humanity, there are specific signs showing the coming of each age, and those who want to take measures to redress the conditions of the commonwealth (*umur-ı cumhur*) have to act according to these signs, just as, in medical practice, a cure for children should not be given to an adult.

So far, Kâtib Çelebi repeats Ibn Khaldun's stage theory, which he had already described in *Takvîmü't-tevârîh*. But then he proceeds to further elaborate on this simile in the first chapter of *Düstûrü'l-amel*, on the peasants or *reaya* (AA124–129; G156–158). Human disposition, he claims, consists of four elements or, more accurately, the four humors (blood, phlegm, yellow bile, and black bile), and through the senses and faculties it obeys human reason (*nefs-i natıka*). In the same way, the "social and human constitution" (*heyet-i ictimaiyye-i beşeriyye*) is composed of four pillars, namely the ulema, the military, the merchants, and the peasants or *reaya*; through the statesmen (*a'yan-ı devlet*) who act as its senses and faculties, society obeys the sultan, who is like the human's faculty of reason. From among the four pillars, the ulema correspond to the blood; the heart is the seat of the animal soul (*ruh-ı hayvani*), carried, via blood, throughout the limbs of a person's body; similarly, the Sharia and religious truth correspond to the animal soul and so give life to society, spread by the ulema. The military correspond to phlegm, merchants to yellow bile, and peasants to black bile. Just as the four humors must be kept balanced, with none exceeding its defined limits at the expense of the others, so must these four social classes profit from each other and coexist in moderation and temperance. Kâtib Çelebi extends his simile even further: after digesting each meal, the spleen sends black bile to the stomach so it will not stay empty, and in the same way the peasants have to give their money to the imperial treasury whenever it runs out of money. To accomplish this task, however, they have to prosper in their businesses; this is why the sultans of old always protected the peasants from all oppression with justice.[29]

In the same vein, the army is to be compared to phlegm (AA129–133; G158–159). Just as phlegm is necessary, but its excess can be harmful to the body, so it happens with the army in relation to society (*cem'iyet*). Here, again, the theory of stages combines with that of the humors: when man passes the age of maturity or stagnation into that of decline and old age, phlegm dominates the bodily dispositions and keeps being produced, while the other humors tend to turn into phlegm as well. Once one has reached a certain age, it is no use trying

29 Here Kâtib Çelebi profits from the occasion to move to the usual eulogy regarding the reign of Süleyman the Magnificent. Süleyman did not think it proper for the peasants to leave their villages, and so when he wished to increase the population of Istanbul he transferred there the inhabitants of the conquered city of Belgrade rather than rural populations. But after him, the condition of the state (or rather its age) began to stagnate, and, with the coming of the Celalis, peasants started to leave their farms and emigrate to the cities. The reason for this was the excessive taxes imposed and the fact that the state followed the axiom "sell to the highest bidder", and thus farmed out all revenues from one oppressor to the other.

to fight back and extract the phlegm. What can be done is to try to bring the predominance of the phlegm to a lesser, harmless degree. This metaphor may be applied to the social organism (*hey'et-i ictima'iyye*): Kâtib Çelebi narrates in detail how Kemankeş Mustafa Pasha had been trying to reduce the number of janissaries to the levels existing back in the Süleymanic era, but, whenever he applied such measures, the janissaries again increased in number soon after. Thus, just like the phlegm in an old man's disposition, it is impossible to keep salaried janissaries at very low levels; what can be done, however, is to try to increase the power of the other three social classes. After all, there is no harm in a large army. If the soldiers' number cannot be reduced, their salaries may be, according to the old rules, although this must be done slowly and gradually, with thoughtfulness and careful timing: such is Kâtib Çelebi's advice.

Another chapter (AA133–135; G159–160) concerns the treasury, and further elaborates the medical simile. After noting that

> the sultan is the human reason (*nefs-i natıka*), the vizier the power of intellect (*kuvvet-i akıle*), the *şeyhülislam* the power of perception ([*kuvvet-i*] *müdrike*), and the other classes the four humors,

Kâtib Çelebi compares the treasury with the stomach, the money-changers and coin-weighers (*saraf ve vezzan*) with the faculty of taste (*kuvvet-i zaika*), tax collectors with attracting power ([*kuvvet-i*] *cazibe*), treasurers with holding power ([*kuvvet-i*] *masike*), and finally ministers of finances and scribes with digesting power (*kuvvet-i hazıme*). In the human body, food is digested with the help of all these powers, after which it is distributed to the various limbs; similarly, in society, all classes benefit from the money after it has been collected in the treasury.[30] However, if black bile is overwhelmed by the other humors in the body, the stomach stays empty, and if these are not balanced,

30 There are some similarities between this description and an excerpt from the famous thirteenth-century Sufi treatise *Mirshad al-'ibâd* by Najm al-Din Razi, which, as we saw in chapters 1 and 3, was translated or adapted (e.g. by Şeyhoğlu Mustafa) into various Ottoman versions: "all the other officials ... are like the five senses (the eye, the ear, the tongue, the nose, and the tactile sense), common sense, and the human faculties (thinking, imagining, understanding, memorizing, remembering, and the other faculties). The army commanders are like the head, the hands, the feet, and the other main organs ... The deputies, the tax collectors, the marshals, and other officials are like the fingers, the joints, the intestines, and so forth; and the rest of the common soldiery and the subjects, with their different ranks, are like the veins, the nerves, the bones, the hairs, the muscles, and all else that goes to make up the body. Just as a human being needs all of these, so that if one member is lacking his whole person will be deficient, so too the king needs all these classes of men" (Razi – Algar 1982, 424).

the health of the stomach is endangered. Also in the same way, if the peasants are oppressed, the treasury will be emptied, and if the four classes envy and fight each other then it will be harmful for the health of the state. The human powers described above are active and strong until the end of the age of stagnation, after which they gradually become enfeebled, with the result that digestive problems start to appear; this coincides with other signs of old age. The signs of old age in societies consist mainly of the pomp and pageantry (*ziynet*) displayed by all classes: the notables (*a'yan ve erkân*) start to extend their titles and pageantry and then, gradually, the middle classes (*evasıt-ı nas*) imitate the rulers in both clothes and luxuries. As a result, the expenses of both individuals and society as a whole (*infirâd ve ictima'ın masrafı*) continuously increase; this is why, explains Kâtib Çelebi in detail, the expenses of the treasury also continuously increase, disproportionally to state income. Once this has happened, it is not easy to increase income and diminish expenses to make the budget balance; it is even considered impossible by men of experience, unless it is imposed by force (*bir kâsirin kasrı*). Until then, notes the author (and, it must be said, in something that sounds like wishful thinking), measures for a provisional moderation of the financial crisis would be useful.

These final observations lead Kâtib Çelebi to his conclusion (AA136–137; G160–61), in which he presents his proposal for the way successful reforms could proceed. There are many ways to correct things, he says, but some of them are impossible under the current circumstances. First of all, what is needed is a "man of the sword" (*sahib-i seyf*) who will "make people submit to the right way" (*halkı hakka münkad etdirir*). Secondly, the notables (*ayan-ı devlet*) must understand that the true sultan is God; the subjects, the treasury, and the army are His, and if they submit to Him they will act with truth and justice and will manage to administer state affairs effectively. Thirdly, the army has to obey experienced officers and, under their protection, defend the state against traitors and evil-doers, as they did in the past. Fourthly, the viziers (*vükela-yı devlet*) must act in unity and harmony to reduce expenses and use the power of the army as an instrument for conducting everyday affairs. Kâtib Çelebi hastens to note that these prerequisites seem easy but are, in fact, quite difficult to secure (*sehl-i mümteni*) since few people care for the state and for justice, most seeking pleasure instead. As such, a strong man should be found. In the meantime, he argues, in a second "conclusion of conclusions" (AA137–38; G161), that it must be accepted that peasants cannot afford to contribute anything more to the treasury. The sultan should grant one year's income to a trustworthy servant of his, who will promise to pay it back gradually from the income of the years to come. This grant will give him great power, which he will then use to gradually reduce the number of soldiers and bring in the soft measures, described above, of cutting taxes and reducing military salaries. As for the excessive expenses, those which are in the hands of government offices (*emanetlerde olan*) will be reduced and then their administration given to trustworthy, honest clerks. In such a way, the problem of excessive expenditure would be solved within a year or two. Finally, oppression of the peasants must be dealt with by significantly reducing their tax burden and giving the relevant offices to experienced people who will not accept bribes; moreover, these appointments must be guaranteed for a long time. And so Kâtib Çelebi's essay ends with a message of hope (AA139; G161), namely that, no matter how grim the situation may seem, historical experience shows that the Ottoman state has the power to redress itself after disasters, as happened after the defeat by Timur or the Celali rebellions. If the appropriate measures are taken, this crisis will also be overcome.

• • •

It is in *Düstûrü'l-amel* that Kâtib Çelebi's innovative spirit most shows itself. His analysis of human society as being composed of four classes is not exactly new, of course: we encountered it in Amasi's (drawing from Tusi), Kınalızade's (drawing from Davvani), and Celalzade's (drawing from Kashifi) works, and in fact it constitutes a very common *topos* of the Persian and Ottoman political tradition. Kâtib Çelebi's contribution is that, whereas all those authors justified the need for balance based on a simile of the four classes with the four elements, he introduced a more scientific perspective, speaking instead of the four humors of Galenic medicine. Although the coupling of the four humors with the four elements had been made in the antiquity, and although the association of the humors with social groups had its counterpart in Renaissance European thought as well (which, however, lacked a four-fold division of society and thus focused on the need for balance),[31] earlier Islamic similes stressed the correspondence of the various elements of government with the limbs and organs of the body, as has been seen (for instance in Bitlisi's case).[32] Neither Renaissance European authors nor medieval Islamic ones had made Kâtib Çelebi's one-to-one coupling of the bodily humors with the four traditional social groups, although it must be noted that medieval Islamic and Ottoman

31 On the genealogy of the theory of the four elements and its use in political thought see Syros 2013; on the relation between the elements and the humors cf. Ermiş 2014, 48ff. (who erroneously states that "the application of the theory to social contexts" was Na'ima's, rather than Kâtib Çelebi's, contribution: ibid., 49).

32 Cf. Sariyannis 2013, 97–100.

medicine was, in practice, based on the four elements rather than the humors.[33] Nevertheless, Kâtib Çelebi's medical simile shows his tendency to use science in all fields of knowledge and, furthermore, it enabled him to elaborate better on the need for balance. Even specific medical advice, such as the role of phlegm in old age and the usefulness of black bile for the stomach, provides a scientific foundation for expounding ideas on soldiers, peasants, and the treasury. Moreover, the simile fits with Kâtib Çelebi's vision of the *devlet*, the state, as something more than just a dynasty or an apparatus: it is society as a whole that he has in mind.[34] The whole of society is in crisis, not just the state's institutions. This was a very fitting perspective for Kâtib Çelebi's times, at least from his point of view (as will also be seen in his last work, the *Mîzânü'l-Hak*).

What is perhaps more important is that the medical vision of society serves as a bridge for the introduction of the Khaldunian notion of the "state stages" into the Ottoman philosophy of history: a society is like a man, with various ages and an unavoidable end. Nevertheless, Kâtib Çelebi wants to stress that old age may be extended and health restored, albeit temporarily. For this, two things are needed. First, a doctor, a "man of the sword" who will impose his will like the doctor prescribes medicine (Kâtib Çelebi's model was probably Murad IV, but he must have understood that this role was now to be taken by viziers; Tarhuncu eventually failed, but Köprülü was on his way). Secondly, this doctor must apply the specific medicine fit for the patient's age: i.e., a mid-seventeenth-century vizier cannot apply measures from the Süleymanic era. It is this defense of innovation, of the notion that different times need different policies, that is the greatest difference between Kâtib Çelebi and his predecessors. The reader may remember from chapter 6 that Kadızade Mehmed İlmî also shared this "doctor metaphor"; his envisaged doctors were the ulema, however, i.e. the men of the pen, while for Kâtib Çelebi it had to be a man of the sword.

2.2 *Kâtib Çelebi's Other Works: World Order as Diversity*

His knowledge of Ibn Khaldun's work apart, other sources and especially his encyclopedic project brought Kâtib Çelebi into close contact with the diversity

33 See Savage-Smith 2013; Shefer-Mossensohn 2009, 23–24. Shortly before Kâtib Çelebi's work, during the reign of Murad IV, Zeyn al-Din al-Abidin b. Halil had written an erudite treatise on diet, exposing the humoristic theory in great detail (Shefer-Mossensohn 2009, 29). Kâtib Çelebi himself used the theory of the elements rather than the humors when discussing the pros and cons of tobacco and coffee, actually criticizing the work of a famous doctor, Davud al-Antakî (d. 1599), whom he had praised in his bio-bibliographical encyclopaedia (Kâtib Chelebi – Lewis 1957, 54 and 61–62; cf. Yurtoğlu 2009, 452).

34 On Kâtib Çelebi's understanding of *devlet* cf. Sigalas 2007, 400–405; Sariyannis 2013, 92–93.

of cultures and institutions existing not only in the world in his own time but also throughout history. His translations of universal geographies and of chronicles of Byzantium and Rome must have helped him realize the inadequacy of the prevailing model of a static, timeless "world order" as described in the then traditional world visions of Kınalızade and Mustafa Ali. This novel view of the world is evident in the introductory sections of *Takvîmü't-tevârîh*, where he explains his vision of universal history in order to elucidate the different calendar systems used throughout history, which he tries to reconcile.[35] *Takvîmü't-tevârîh* has no account of European histories, but the numerous works Kâtib Çelebi had translated from Latin compensate for that. If Khaldunist stage theory allowed him to advocate the possibility of change over time, his knowledge of socio-cultural diversity in the world further promoted a new vision of "world order", one where different arrangements were thriving with equal success all around the globe. From there to admitting that such diversity could also legitimately prevail within a given society there was only one step, and the tense Kadızadeli conflict, which he followed very closely, pushed Kâtib Çelebi to theorize in favor of diversity and tolerance in the context of a Muslim society as well.

One should note here, somewhat *en passant*, a short treatise or, rather, translation that Kâtib Çelebi wrote in 1655, *İrşâdü'l-hayârâ ilâ tarîhi'l-Yûnân ve'r-Rûm ve'n-Nasârâ* ("A guide to the history of [Ancient] Greeks, Romans and Christians for the perplexed").[36] Using European sources once again, he endeavors to discuss the history of (Eastern) Christianity and of various European dynasties. What interests us in this rather neglected book is his discussion of the types of government, coming straight from Aristotelian political philosophy, although with some minor misunderstandings (in fact, it is a free adaptation and expansion of a much shorter passage in Mercator's *Atlas Minor*).[37] In the matter of rulership (*emr-i saltanatda*), he says, most philosophers follow the views of three great philosophers of old, namely: (i) Plato. According to Plato, people must submit to and obey a wise and just king. For a person to be established in such a position, a noble lineage (*neseb*) is necessary. Most states in the world administer their affairs in this way; Greek philosophers named

35 Al-Tikriti 2017, 130–132. However, we must not exaggerate this universal view, as a similar relativism concerning the Ottoman dynasty can be also found in Mustafa Ali's work; see Fleischer 1986a, 277–283.

36 Kâtib Çelebi – Yurtoğlu 2012 (see esp. 46). Cf. Gökyay 1991, 57; Ménage 1971, 421–422; Yurtoğlu 2009, 76–77.

37 See Mercator 1610, 194 (*De politico statu regni Galliae*; cf. also later, 198). Mercator's text lacks the references to specific philosophers, the examples from contemporaneous European states and the detailed description of "democracy".

this kind of state (*bu makule saltanat*) a "monarchy" (*munarhıyâ*); (ii) Aristotle. He said rulership must be in the hands of the magnates of the state (*saltanat tedbiri a'yan-ı devlet elinde olmak gerek*), who choose a head (*re'is ihtiyar olunub*) from among themselves. In this way, nobody is raised above the others by dint of lineage, and the head of this government cannot neglect justice by acting independently. This form of state is called an "aristocracy" (*aristokrâsiyâ*—from Aristotle's name, claims Kâtib Çelebi, since *krâsiyâ* means "government", *hükûmet*) or "rule of the magnates" (*amme-i tedbir-i ayan*); one such example is the state of Venice; (iii) Demokratis.[38] His view was that the administration should be in the hands of the people (*saltanat tedbiri re'ayanın olmak gerek*) so that they themselves may avoid oppression (*kendülerden zulmi def'e kâdir olalar*). In this form, government is conducted by election (*tarik-i tedbir ihtiyardır*): people from every village elect one or two whom they deem wise and experienced, and send them as representatives (*muhtar*) to the centre of the government (*mahall-ı hükûmet olub divan kurulan yerde*). In turn, these representatives elect one from among themselves, and in the end a council of ten elected people administers state affairs. These ten sit on the council for one year, after which another ten people are elected in the same way. They inspect the accounts of the previous year's government and punish anyone who has oppressed people. This form of state, called a "democracy" (*dîmukrâsiya*) or "rule of the elected" (*amme-i tedbir-i muhtarîn*), is used in England and the Netherlands. All nations and religions are, in general, governed according to one of these three forms of state. No matter how radical it might seem, this theoretical piece seems not to have influenced Kâtib Çelebi himself (although a little later on in the same work, he describes the Venetian system in the same terms, as a development from democracy to aristocracy, one which led to better order);[39] it left no trace in either his later works or those of his late seventeenth-century followers. What is more interesting is that it had a second life after İbrahim Müteferrika incorporated it into his own political treatise of 1732, though without naming his source, with the result that he is often credited with the introduction of political Aristotelianism *stricto sensu* into Ottoman writings (see below, chapter 9).

Finally, in his last work, *Mîzânü'l-hak fi ihtiyâri'l-âhak* ("The balance of truth for the selection of the truest [way]", 1656), Kâtib Çelebi participated in the

38 Of course, such a philosopher never existed, and it is not easy to say whether the author just made up an etymology for democracy or was confused with Democritus.

39 Kâtib Çelebi – Yurtoğlu 2012, 97–98 (*ol zamandan beru şehrin intizâmı eyû olub 'azîm kudrete vâsıl oldular*). On images of democratic constitutions in eighteenth-century Ottoman texts see below, chapter 9, and Sariyannis 2016, 45–50, for a more detailed discussion.

current "issue of the day", the conflict between the Kadızadeli preachers and the Halveti dervishes over the abolition of various "innovations" (cf. above, chapter 6).[40] Kâtib Çelebi tackles a variety of subjects on which the Kadızadelis had initiated controversy. These were as diverse as the legitimacy of singing or dancing, of using drugs, tobacco, and coffee, various questions of belief such as what was the religion of Abraham and whether the Pharaoh died an infidel, and folk practices such as shaking hands and visiting saints' tombs. *Mîzânü'l-hak* contains various pieces that further elaborate the author's views on politics and society, including his famous plea on behalf of philosophy and the rational sciences, which, he claimed, had been expunged from the curriculum of the medrese schools (KC4–15; L22–28).[41]

Though the main subject of the treatise is the list of "innovations" and issues raised by the Kadızadeli movement during the first decades of the seventeenth century, Kâtib Çelebi's primary reason for discussing them is to highlight the diversity of mankind, and more particularly the legitimacy of this diversity. He propounds the ideas that mankind has always been divided, that this division has its advantages, and that an intelligent polity will not interfere with what is in people's hearts. Moreover, such divisions are inherent in civilization and society (*mukteza-yı hikmet-i temeddün ve ictima'*) and a wise man should get to know the beliefs and tenets of every class of people in every country, rather than try to impose his own (KC15–17; L28–30). This basic tenet is repeated in many parts of the treatise: Kâtib Çelebi stresses that if one tries to deter people from practices that have become customary over time, he will only produce conflict and war, since "human nature does not accept easily any criticism of common usage" (KC36–37; L47–48; cf. KC75, L89–90). In such matters, "one should [only] see if there is any public evil or any breach of order" (*emr-i din ü dünyaya zarar-ı 'am ve nizama muhil ma'naları göreler*: KC89–90; L104). And, after all, all these conflicts are but a sign of the natural human tendency for "domination, individualism, and independence" (*riyaset ve taferrüd ve istiklal*). Even children show this tendency, as do the various classes of men: this applies to both worldly affairs and religious leadership, and is behind the behavior not only of rulers, but also of sheikhs and even prophets.

This reasoning is explicitly directed against the Kadızadeli preachers with whom Kâtib Çelebi was constantly at odds, despite his expressions of respect

40 Kâtib Çelebi 1888/89; an English translation by Geoffrey L. Lewis is in Kâtib Chelebi – Lewis 1957; cf. Gökbilgin 1971. Lewis' translation is fuller than the 1888 edition, which omits, for example, the eighth chapter of the text (on the parents of the Prophet). Lewis collated this edition with British Museum Add. 7904 (see Kâtib Chelebi – Lewis 1957, 13).

41 Cf. Tezcan 2010b, 146ff.

for his own teacher, Kadızade Mehmed Efendi. His general idea on the subject is that religion has its place in life but that place is restricted: "not every facet of behavior can be Sunna, you know" (*cümle ahval sünnet olacak değil ya*: KC87; L102). The chapter on innovation (*bid'at*), which touches upon a central argument in the Kadızadeli conflict, is of particular interest as it also indirectly touches upon the "old law" argument, which must still have been running in his circles (the last "administration manuals", Koçi Bey's second treatise and Avnî Ömer's *Kânûn-ı Osmânî*, were only fifteen years old, and works such as Eyyubi's *Kânûnnâme* were still to come). Following an old thread in *fıkh* reasoning, Kâtib Çelebi divides innovations into good and bad (*bid'at-ı hasene, bid'at-ı seyyiye*). The former includes what was unknown in the time of the Prophet but "which the leaders of the Faith have subsequently allowed as filling a need (*iktiza hasbıyle*)", such as "the building of minarets and the manufacture of books". Kâtib Çelebi declares directly that there is no point trying to abolish innovations, even bad ones, once they are established in a community, for "people will not abandon custom" (*halk adeti terk eylemez*). What is necessary for the rulers is only to protect the orderly condition of the Muslim people (*ehl-i İslam nizamı*) and the principles of Islam among the community, and not to force anyone to comply with them. After all, "scarcely any of the sayings or doings of any age are untainted by innovation" (KC74–76; L89–91). As for the other central tenet of the Kadızadelis, that of the obligation to "command right and forbid wrong" (*emr bi'l-ma'ruf ve nehy 'an al-münker*), Kâtib Çelebi states that "in matters obligatory or prohibited, [this tenet] is obligatory[, while] in matters merely disapproved or recommended, it is recommended [but not obligatory]". By laying down a number of rules that further define this duty and its prerequisites, he once again declares that violent interference in people's lives and customs only brings dissent and strife (KC91–96; L106–109).

It is interesting to see how, in this issue, as indeed in most of *Mîzânü'l-hak*, Kâtib Çelebi prefers to use *fıkh* arguments rather than the Khaldunist or medicine-inspired philosophy he had preferred in his other works (one reason might have been that he was reacting to a *fıkh*-oriented legalism using the latter's very own weapons).[42] Another fine example is his discussion of bribery, a common *topos* in Ottoman political literature from the sixteenth century onwards (KC115–120; L124–127). Unlike his predecessors (see above, chapter 5), Kâtib Çelebi focuses on bribery not as a means to gain high offices but as gifts given to judges or other officials to secure favorable verdicts (or, he adds, any

42 Only the discussion of Khidr's immortality contains almost verbatim the observations on the three stages of human life, as analyzed in Kâtib Çelebi's political essays (KC17–19; L33–34).

other desideratum). However, he clearly considers "a judge obtain[ing] his appointment by giving a bribe" as forbidden for both sides, i.e. both the donor and the recipient, although a bribe given to secure one's rights is permissible under certain circumstances. Stressing the judge's post, in these cases, seems to be relevant to the holiness of that office. However, afterwards, Kâtib Çelebi describes bribery as one of the customs that cannot be prohibited since "there is no aversion from bribery at the present time". As such, he recommends a legal stratagem (the "oath of hire" or *icare akdı*, i.e. a fictional hire of the recipient by the giver for a day) to legitimize bribes given in order to avert harm or secure an advantage, unless this is given to a judge. After all, he observes,

> that is how bribery is conducted nowadays in government departments in all matters except appointments to the office of judge.

After this quite unusual proposal, Kâtib Çelebi somehow hastens to add, of course, that rulers of the past were much more adamant in maintaining the spirit of the law since

> there are many actions which can be dressed in the garb of legality but are not acceptable to the reason, because of the manifold corruptions lurking beneath [the surface].

It is impossible not to note the striking resemblance of such remarks with the famous (or, for others, infamous) Jesuit casuistry of the same period. French Jesuits had a marked presence in Istanbul from 1609 onwards, despite a temporary suspension in 1628, and they played an active role in Christian education in the city from the 1580s onwards, and increasingly so in the 1610s and 1620s, teaching the children not only of Catholic but of Orthodox Christians as well.[43] Furthermore, it is highly likely that Kâtib Çelebi's main convert informant and translator, Mehmed İhlasî, had been a former Jesuit.[44]

As well as, or maybe rather than, a Jesuit influence, however, in Kâtib Çelebi's argument one may detect a perhaps excessive application of *istihsan* (the mainly Hanafi doctrine for reasoning on the basis of personal deliberation) and, even more, of *istislah* (the similar doctrine that stresses the public good or human welfare, i.e. *maslahat*). The reader may also remember that Abdulahad Nuri, Sivasi's disciple who was discussed in chapter 6, had also used *istihsan*

43 Frazee 1983, 72ff. and esp. 80–87; Dursteler 2004, 294–301; Ruiu 2014. On casuistry in Christian ethics, see Boarini 2009.

44 See Hagen 2003a, 278, and more generally 66–68 and 277–280 on İhlasî and his background.

in a similar way when he argued that every new custom is prohibited at first and then declared licit after it wins the people's hearts; in this respect, both Kâtib Çelebi and Abdulahad Nuri can be seen as heirs to the Ebussu'udic tradition. Kâtib Çelebi explicitly uses the work of the Egyptian jurist Ibn Nujaym (d. 1562/3), from whom he takes the "oath of hire" stratagem and the summary classifications of bribery before proceeding to his own position (admitting the difficulty of prohibiting bribes and recommending this "oath").[45] In fact, here again we see how Kâtib Çelebi exhibits his competence in *fikh* reasoning (even the understanding of bribery in connection with the judges, rather than buying governmental posts, belongs to the traditional *fikh* discussion of the issue) in order to argue for a pragmatic view, thereby excluding, in practice, a great part of everyday life from the jurists' remit.

However, Kâtib Çelebi's views on bribery (more than anything else) seem to go further than the usual practice of *istihsan* and *istislah* reasoning. For one thing, custom never acquired the dominant position within legal reasoning which he is so willing to grant it.[46] Furthemore, attention should be given to the "rigorously literal legalism" of the Kadızadelis (in the words of Cemal Kafadar), which "could be seen to embody some 'legal rationalism' that questioned the preponderant use of vague and subjective criteria such as *istihsan* and *örf*."[47] Kâtib Çelebi's flexible use of *istihsan* and *istislah* may be examined in the context of his rejection of Kadızadeli legalism, and if, as I argue elsewere, the latter can be seen as a parallel of European Reformation and Protestant ethics[48] then the similarity of Kâtib Çelebi's arguments with his Jesuit counterparts might point to a common intellectual climate across the Mediterranean. The question is difficult to answer, but intriguing all the same.

At any rate, if this extensive use of *istihsan* is combined with Kâtib Çelebi's plea for a "man of the sword" (as in *Düstûrü'l-amel*) who would redress Ottoman society, arguably by dynamically applying *istihsan* and *istislah* according to the "needs of the time" (here is the Khaldunist part), the vision described at the beginning of this chapter can be seen: a strong centralized state, led preferably by a powerful vizier who would impose discipline on the military and reclaim political power on behalf of the state apparatus and governmental bureaucracy.

45 Ibn Nüceym – Sahillioğlu 1966. I wish to thank Boğaç Ergene for bringing this point to my attention.

46 See Hallaq 2001, 215ff. Ebussu'ud himself was very careful to render his appeal to custom in strictly Hanafi terms.

47 Kafadar 2007, 121. On *istihsan* and *istislah* see *Encyclopaedia of Islam*, 2nd ed., s.v. "Istihsân and Istislâh" (R. Paret); Schacht 1964, 60–62, 204; Hallaq 2002, 107–113. The use of these notions significantly predates the usual emphasis on "Ottoman pragmatism" (cf. Dağlı 2013).

48 Sariyannis 2012, 282ff.

As for the timar system and the poor sipahis, they were scarcely mentioned any longer: in *Düstûrü'l-amel*, it may be remembered, thoughts about the military are restricted to the janissaries and other salaried standing troops.

3 Kâtib Çelebi's Immediate Influence: the Conciliation with Change

If there is one element from Kâtib Çelebi's writings that passed almost immediately into his contemporaries' works, it was his sense of innovation, and more particularly his admission that every kind (or stage) of society (or the state) requires a different approach, and thus that any potential reformer should adopt a problem-oriented policy rather than revert to some idealized constitutions of the past. His general vision of history (i.e. his Khaldunist conception of the laws of history) would take another 50 years to be adopted wholesale, but the conciliation with the idea that societies change and ideal policies change accordingly (again often using the simile of the human body) was integrated very soon into works otherwise belonging to totally different political traditions. Furthermore, in sharp contrast to the "declinist" literature studied in chapter 5, his followers ignored the timar problems, as he had, and focused on the military-administrative branch instead.

A good example is the *Nasîhatnâme* ("Book of advice") composed in 1652, i.e. almost simultaneously with Kâtib Çelebi's *Düstûrü'l-amel*;[49] one should presume that the similarities with Kâtib Çelebi's ideas must be attributed to personal acquaintance rather than textual transmission. The identity of the author is unclear; one of the two manuscripts is followed by some poems signed by Hemdemî, and they might well belong to the same author. On these grounds, Joseph von Hammer-Purgstall (followed by Rhoads Murphey, who nevertheless considers the identification "far from being definitely established") identified the author as Solakzade Mehmed (d. 1657/8), the well-known historian who also wrote poems under the pen-name Hemdemi. Little is known of Solakzade: he was an early recruit to the palace and was a "constant companion" of Murad IV, together with Evliya Çelebi; it seems that he remained in the palace under the next two sultans as well. Solakzade was a musician and composer of note, but his main work is the history of the Ottoman dynasty up to 1643, mainly a

49 There are two manuscripts, Berlin, Staatsbibliothek Or. Oct. 1598, ff. 125b–172b (copied together with Defterdar Sarı Mehmed Paşa's treatise) and Vienna, Österreichische Nationalbibliothek MS N.F. 283. Here I use the Vienna MS, 1b–38b (see Murphey 2009b, 46–47, for some differences; probably a copy). There is no study of this text other than Murphey 2009b.

compilation of older chronicles.[50] At this stage of research, we cannot be sure about this identification: overall, the *Nasîhatnâme* seems to lack the concrete historical references one would expect from a historian (apart from the usual locating of the beginning of decline in the year A.H. 1000 and some moralistic rather than historical anecdotes about Mehmed II, Selim I, and Süleyman I); on the other hand, it undoubtedly shows some signs of historical thought.

Certainly, this is not a work that claims originality: if we have to classify it, it would instead fall under the "mirror for princes" category, with a strong thread of Sunna-minded advice and an all-too-traditional emphasis on justice. Hemdemi's (if we accept this identification) main idea, around which the treatise is structured, is that state power (*devlet ve saltanat*) is like a dome based on ten pillars (*payanda*). These pillars are prerequisites for that power, and include the maintenance of fortresses, the use of spies, the summoning of regular imperial councils, and so on. Among them, it should be noted that the first pillar, a strong army, efficiently protects "the people constituting the realm" from both "injuries inflicted by each other" and surrounding enemies. Also worthy of note is the emphasis placed on the Sharia. Thus, honor, family, property, and reason are properly protected with the imposition of the canonical punishments (*hadd*; V6b–7b). In these times, he writes, every one of these pillars has deficiencies, with their respective reasons (such as that the sultan and his people are ostentatious and thus increase their expenses, or that unworthy people are used in the administration of important matters[51]), and Hemdemi embarks on the usual complaints against bribery, lack of consultation, the fact that incapable people are used in state service due to bribery, intercession, or affiliation to some great household (9b: *bir büyük yere intisab*), and so on. A strong Sunna-minded influence is evident, as when, for instance, Hemdemi praises consultation (he divides the people into three categories just as did Kadızade Mehmed İlmi; see above, chapter 6)[52] and decries the neglect of canonical punishments, such as cutting off hands for theft. All kinds of corruption, including military defeat, stem from the abandonment of the Sharia; the connection between neglect of religious precepts and military weakness is illustrated by several *hadith*s and Quranic phrases. Thus, the six unsuccessful

50 Solakzade 1879.

51 This expression (*mesalih-i kibarda rical-ı sıgar istihdam etmek*) is strikingly similar to Sinan Paşa – Tulum 2013, 680.

52 There are whole men (*bütün adem*), who have their own opinion and are open to consultation, half-men, who have their own opinion but do not put it into consultation, and non-men (*hiç adem*), who have neither opinion nor do they consult. In the same context, various examples against women's opinions illustrate the attitude of Hemdemi against the court politics of the early 1650s, as seen in the introduction of this chapter.

years of the Cretan campaign (V37b) are explained by the "love of the world" (*hubb-ι dünya*) that is now instilled in the hearts of men, and which resulted in neglect of the Sharia and the increase of tyranny.

There is also a strong sense of "declinism", showing that the spirit of the authors of previous decades was still alive: the sultan must follow the example of his ancestor, Süleyman the Magnificent, impose order, and ensure the safety and well-being of his poor subjects (V15b). He must check where the order imposed in Süleyman's times is not present and thus bring it back; most importantly, Süleyman stuck to the precepts of the Sharia and always consulted his müfti, Ebussu'ud. Furthermore, Hemdemi claims that, from A.H. 1000 (1591), the empire has been plagued by self-interested people who have changed provincial governorships up to six times.[53] Thus, the expenses of the sultan and his entourage should be gradually decreased in such a way that unnecessary burdens will be lifted from the subjects; the sultan is like any other man, so his expenses should not exceed his revenue.[54] Other advice is reminiscent of Koçi Bey and Aziz Efendi: Hemdemi stresses the negative effect of *reaya* joining the army and the need to check the military registers, the responsibility of the beylerbeyis and their *voyvoda*s to safeguard the roads, and so on.

The author proposes "cure by opposites" (*tedavi bi'l-ezdad*); just as doctors cure diseases due to cold by using heat and vice versa, so must any reform find the root of the disorder and resist with their opposite (V16a). Hemdemi goes back to the ten roots of evil, as he described earlier, and discusses them one by one, emphasizing that the wealth (from money to houses and gardens) produced by agriculture, manufacture, and trade depends on the ruler, who must guard these activities as he guards the apple of his eye. It is interesting to note here the unusual place of trade and manufacture in an otherwise traditional description of economic activities; this departure from tradition was, as has been noted, fully in line with the realities of the monetized economy of the seventeenth century.

Yet there is no doubt that Hemdemi's treatise is closely related to Kâtib Çelebi's ideas. For one thing, he also brings back the general view of the creation of political society in terms of social philosophy, and in this he follows

53 Hemdemi is cautious about the accuracy of this, but says he has heard of people who met up to 90 different governors when travelling from Baghdad to Istanbul (V17a), which means that he had no access to official records.

54 Here the author inserts a story about Selim I's vizier Piri Pasha, explaining that there are three treasuries: one known to himself, i.e. the peasants; one known to the *defterdar*, from which salaries and other expenses are paid; and one known to the sultan, i.e. the inner treasury (V17b–18a). On the inner treasury and its relation with the sultan as distinct from the state, cf. Sariyannis 2013, 112–114.

both earlier traditions and Kâtib Çelebi's re-introduction of it. God created the world and the tribes of men and settled them on earth with a caliph for their well-being (V1b–2a: *hilafet ile emaret etmeleriyçün iskân eyledi*). In order to help each other and procure their food, settlement, and clothing, men formed societies (*cemiyet*), cities, towns, and villages, as God inspired them to. Their worldly professions (*dünyevi nizam-i intizam hâlleri*) were organized into four groups, namely farmers (*ehl-i hiraset*), craftsmen (*ehl-i sana'at*), merchants (*ehl-i ticaret*, i.e. "those who carry and bring required goods from one country to another"), and statesmen (*ehl-i siyaset*, i.e. those who practise good administration [*hüsn-i zabt ile hâkim ve zabit eyleyüb*]) to prevent people from attacking one another according to their natural faculties of passion and lust.[55] For this reason, God facilitated the "arrangement of the rules of the state (*tertib-i kava'id-i devlet*)"; moreover, He sent religion and the Sharia, so humanity could arrange its otherworldly needs and conditions, and He sent the Prophet and made Muslim kingdoms and states rise, among which were "the Exalted State [i.e. the Ottoman Empire] and other Muslim states". Now, there are five classes of "the people constituting the realm": canonical judges (*hükkâm-ı şer'*), secular governors (*hükkâm-ı 'örf*), treasurers and collectors (*ümena ve ammal*), soldiers, and peasants (*re'aya*). In these unfortunate times, the majority of these groups think only of profiteering. As for the peasants, they are so overwhelmingly burdened with taxes that they are forced to leave their villages, with the result that many in Anatolia have been deserted, while villagers in Rumili flee to infidel countries, with those remaining finding it harder and harder to make a living (V8b). Those who deal with crafts and trade (*esnaf ve re'ayada tüccar*), on their part, see their money disappear and abandon their commercial activities, while those who are able to keep some of their money are also heavily indebted.

Then the author proceeds to what may be called a Khaldunist vision of states, one clearly strongly influenced by Kâtib Çelebi. States, says Hemdemi, are like patients: young and old ones require different treatments. A man is small (*taze*) until the age of seventeen, young (*yiğit*) until forty, and old until his death; similarly, a state/dynasty is fresh when it appears, and gradually increases its strength until it reaches the point where it can defend itself against both external enemies and the tensions between its members. Then begins the young stage, until the pomp and luxury of the ruler and his subordinates increases, as do expenses and salaries; this is the beginning of old age, which ends with the collapse of the state. However, in contrast with human death,

55 This strange division echoes Kınalızade's and Ibn Khaldun's division of professions (see above, chapter 2).

the author claims that the collapse of a state can be prevented, as God has granted his protection upon men, both high and low. If a sultan loves God, follows His commands, and practises justice, the same will happen in the hearts of "the tribe that makes the state", and eventually even rain will make all business flourish, and vice versa (V11a–11b).[56]

In an interesting excursus (V24a), the author repeats that the Ottoman state has passed through the age of youth into old age, as luxury and pomp have led to the expansion of bribery and corruption and, ultimately, of oppression. As a result, the Celali rebels appeared in Anatolia and the sultan expended much energy suppressing them. The main cause of this was the appointment of greedy men to governorships through bribery and affiliation, as well as (adds the author in a marginal note) the granting of timars, zeamets, *vakf*s, and *malikâne*s to such people, who in turn gave the revenues to any tax-farmer (*mültezim*) willing to offer five *dirhem*s more, thus making the peasants destitute.

Hemdemi's treatise is a strange specimen of the eclectic tendencies of Ottoman literature: alongside its clear emphasis on the Sharia (the author seems to ignore the *kanun* completely) and pieces of received wisdom regarding sultanly justice, there are signs of an acute understanding of contemporaneous realities (as in his stress on tax-farming and the role of household affiliation in obtaining administrative posts). Kâtib Çelebi's influence is strongly visible not only in the Khaldunist description of the rise and fall of dynasties and the simile of the human body (including the cautionary remark that each age needs different medicine) but also in Hemdemi's recurrent references to "the people constituting the realm" (*devlet ve saltanat müştemil olduğu kavmi*) which bring to mind Kâtib Çelebi's definition of *devlet*.

Hemdemi was very probably a friend or perhaps student of Kâtib Çelebi; the reader will also remember Hezarfen Hüseyin Efendi, whose work was studied in chapter 5 and who bore a striking resemblance to Kâtib Çelebi himself: Hezarfen, indeed, had a similar career, was likewise a polymath and encyclopedist, also used Greek and European sources in his work, and had close relations with European scholars active in Istanbul. In a way, both men also shared a new culture of learning: instead of teaching in *medrese*s, they preferred self-instruction and had their own scholarly circles (in some ways the equivalent of European *salons*) with whom they discussed and exchanged knowledge. Contrary to what is generally believed, however, Hezarfen was more of a

56 Hemdemi also uses other anthropomorphic metaphors, similar to those used, for example, by Bitlisi: a state (*devlet ve saltanat*) is like a man; the sultan is the head, the vizier the heart, the peasants the feet, and justice the soul (*ruh*) (V19a).

compiler and imitator of his mentor than an original spirit; they were probably acquainted (Hezarfen seems to have been almost the same age as Kâtib Çelebi, although he outlived him by almost forty years). His universal history (*Tenkîh-i tevârih-i mülûk*), incorporating material on China and Byzantium (a practice Kâtib Çelebi had initiated), also contained a conclusion on geography (again his mentor's favourite subject) and a "conclusion of conclusions", which is in fact a verbatim rendering of Kâtib Çelebi's conclusion in his own universal history.[57] The simile of the time-span of a society with man's natural life, the three ages of states and their characteristics, are all copied word for word, though Hezarfen seems to have been more selective in copying his predecessor's final advice. He also added a "warning" (*tenbih*) about the importance of price-regulation, which he also included in his *Telhîsü'l-beyân*, the "administration manual"-*cum*-political treatise studied in detail in chapter 5.[58]

In *Telhîsü'l-beyân*, a work very much belonging to an earlier and this time bygone tradition, there are also examples of Kâtib Çelebi's influence. For one thing, as was implied in chapter 5, Hezarfen's attempt to undermine the ulema's competence and to justify the sultan's and the grand vizier's freedom of action is concomitant with the political aims (an alliance between the central governmental bureaucracy and strong viziers in order to control the janissaries' political power) Kâtib Çelebi's ideas wished to promote. And indeed, there are both more and clearer signs of Kâtib Çelebi's influence within *Telhîsü'l-beyân*. In his chapter on the rules of the timar system, after copying Lütfi Pasha's advice for avoiding the intrusion of peasants, Hezarfen notes (in a free adaptation of Kâtib Çelebi's analysis) that in this world everybody has to follow a certain way of making one's living, and thus both polities and houses need to be well-governed (*tedbir-i medine ve tedbir-i menzil görülüp*). But this, i.e. each person staying in his proper place, is not achievable in every period: the stages of a state (*bir devletin asırlarına göre*) all have different arrangements (*daima nesk-ı vâhid üzere ola gelmemişdir*), for "this is the necessity of the natural stages of civilization and society" (*mukteza-ı etvar-ı tabi'at-ı temeddün ve ictima'*).[59]

Furthermore, Kâtib Çelebi's medical vision of the elements of society can be seen in Hezarfen's chapter concerning the ulema. Before proceeding to the division between the external and the internal, he states (drawing from the first chapter of *Düstûrü'l-amel*) that they are the most honorable and exalted of the pillars of the state, being like blood, the natural humor of the body

57 Hezarfen Hüseyin Efendi, *Tenkihü't-tevârîh*, Istanbul, Süleymaniye Kütüphanesi, Hekimoğlu 732, ff. 277b–279b.
58 Süleymaniye Kütüphanesi, Hekimoğlu 732, ff. 279a-b; Hezarfen – İlgürel 1998, 248.
59 Hezarfen – İlgürel 1998, 142.

(*hılt-ı mahmud*), surrounded by the other classes (*sair esnaf dahi baki ihata mu'adil düşmüşdür*). They are thus like the heart, the source of the "animal soul" (*kalb ki, menba'-ı ruh-ı hayvanidir*) and which distributes this soul to the limbs of the body via the blood. In Hezarfen's simile, the "animal soul" is knowledge of the Sharia and the ulema are the intermediaries who pass it on to the people; as the animal soul is the source of the well-being and the continuation of the body, so does the Sharia do so for society and the state (*cem'iyyet ve devlet*). If blood is corrupt, it only brings harm to the body, and needs to be cured or extracted.[60]

4 Na'ima: Stage Theory in the Service of Peace

Hemdemi and Hezarfen may have reflected Kâtib Çelebi's ideas, especially those promoting Ibn Khaldun's bio-historical theory of stages, but a fully-fledged introduction of the Tunisian scholar's ideas into the Ottoman framework would have to wait for half a century and the work of Na'ima, one of the most important Ottoman historians. Mustafa Na'îmâ (ca. 1665–1716) was the son of the janissary commander of Aleppo; he entered the palace service at a young age and was educated as a scribe, spending his whole career in the *divan* bureaucracy. Being a *protégé* of the grand vizier Amcazade Hüseyin Köprülü Pasha (seen earlier as the principal negotiator of the Treaty of Karlowitz), he was commissioned by him to write a history of the Ottoman Empire in order to complete a now-lost draft by Şarih al-Menarzâde (d. 1657). Na'ima started this task around 1698 and seems to have worked on it until 1704, when he was promoted to *Anadolu muhasebecisi*, or chief accountant of Anatolia. He then held various other posts, always in the financial bureaucracy and with several ups and downs (occasionally due to his preoccupation with astrology), before his death at Patras in 1716. Na'ima's history, *Ravzatü'l-Hüseyin fi hulâsât ahbâri'l-hâfikayn* ("Huseyin's garden, with a summary of news of the East and West"; commonly known as *Târîh-i Na'îmâ*), is based largely on Kâtib Çelebi's *Fezleke*, as well as other historians, oral transmission, and lost works; it covers events from A.H. 1000 (1591) until AD 1660, while a treatise on the 1703 "Edirne event" was added later (as a preface to the second part of his chronicle, which would have covered the period up to Na'ima's own days but was never written). Na'ima's history proved both popular (there are more than twenty manuscripts

60 Hezarfen – İlgürel 1998, 196.

in Istanbul alone, some transcribed from the printed edition) and reliable, as he used multiple sources carefully, with an eye for objectivity and truthfulness.[61]

Na'ima's philosophy of history and politics is mainly to be found in his two prefaces,[62] the first written after Amcazade Köprülü Hüseyin Pasha commissioned the writing of his history in 1698, the second intended as the preface to the second part of the work and mainly concerning the 1703 revolt (*Edirne vak'ası*). A fluent speaker of Arabic, Na'ima was a careful reader of Ibn Khaldun and transferred wholesale not only his theory on the laws of history and the rise and decline of dynasties but also on matters as diverse as education and the economy. On the other hand, he extensively used the political framework of Kâtib Çelebi's *Düstûrü'l-amel* (as he also did with his historiographical work *Fezleke*). In doing all this, and thereby writing the most extensive and detailed theoretical introduction an Ottoman historiographer had ever produced, he had one specific aim: to justify his patron's actions in negotiating the peace treaty of Karlowitz. Thus, apart from using specific arguments taken from the Islamic tradition, which were somewhat reminiscent of those used by Akhisari a century earlier (see above, chapter 4), Na'ima also emphasized that peace may allow a state in a Khaldunian stage of decline to restore its power and glory.[63]

In the first and most detailed preface, Na'ima starts with a long essay on history writing,[64] where he also speaks, like Kâtib Çelebi, of what may be called the laws of history. The study of history will show

> what are the causes and the bases of action that foretell and bring about decay and decline to the civilization of mankind and which show that a state, a society of men (*devlet-i ictima'iye*), is on the way to expiration and death.

61 It was first printed by İbrahim Müteferrika in 1733, while two six-volume editions were published during the nineteenth century (A.H. 1280/1863–64 and 1281/1864–66). A modern Turkish translation (Zuhuri Danışman, *Naima tarihi*, 6 vols) was published in 1967. The definitive edition is now Na'ima – İpşirli 2007 (based on the edition of A.H. 1280 and hence noting different pagination compared to the usual one, since most scholars have used the A.H. 1281 edition). On Na'ima's life and work there are fewer studies than one would wish or may expect: the classic and fullest so far is Thomas 1972 (originally written in the mid-1940s); cf. also Na'ima – İpşirli 2007, 1:XIII–XXXV.

62 Na'ima 1864–1866, 1:2–65 and 6:Appendix, 2–58; Na'ima – İpşirli 2007, 1:1–48 and 4:1858–1893; partial translations in Thomas 1972, 65–89.

63 Cf. Thomas 1972, 66ff.; Abou-El-Haj 1974.

64 Cf. Thomas 1972, 110–115.

Because, he explains, the history of particular incidents is subordinate to the inherent qualities of any one specific state in its maturity, an intelligent man who can grasp these qualities will understand that state's course and development. This beginning sets the scene for what will follow, i.e. the exposition of a theory of history where universal laws govern various societies and states.

One part of the first section of the preface is based almost verbatim on Kâtib Çelebi's *Düstûrü'l-amel*.[65] Omitting the specific evidence on the numbers of the Ottoman army and the development of the budget deficit, Na'ima copies, in a slightly shorter form, his predecessor's analytical analogy between the human body and society (*ictima'-i beşeriyye, devlet*), with the three ages of man corresponding to the rise and decline of any given state. In the same way, he copies Kâtib Çelebi's simile of the four humors of the body with the four classes or "columns" of society, namely the ulema, the military, the merchants, and the peasants.[66] For the latter, Na'ima expands the medical simile in a rather unexpected way, saying that just as "dry" diseases like melancholia and anxiety occur when black bile is dominant, so does the excessive ease and luxury of the peasants (*vüs'at-ı hal ve tereffüh-i re'aya i'tidalden birun olsa*) produce strife, disobedience, and rebellion. However, just as the amount of black bile is seldom changed in the body unless caused by other humors, the peasants also never harm the state on purpose (*re'ayadan memlekete zarar mutasavver değildir*); it is just that "sometimes they get excited and easily erupt with protests and proclamations".

Now, omitting Kâtib Çelebi's excursus on the situation of the peasants and the causes of their oppression, Na'ima embarks on a short analysis of the merchant class, the yellow bile of society. When balanced with the other three humors, yellow bile increases the appetite of the body; in the same way, merchants, in an average situation, cause order and well-being in society by trading and bringing forth an abundance of goods. But bile is harmful if there is less or more than normal; likewise, whenever "the merchants and the rich" become either oppressed or greedy and profiteering, they are detrimental to the harmony of society (*cemal-ı memleket*) because they weaken and impoverish the people. As for the military, Na'ima repeats Kâtib Çelebi's analysis, stressing explicitly that an army always swells in number when a state is in the age of decline; again, he follows his predecessor verbatim in his examination of finances (always using the medical simile) and of luxury and pomp as a sign of decline. As for Kâtib Çelebi's conclusions, Na'ima refers to the need for a skilled

65 Na'ima 1864–1866, 1:27–33; Na'ima – İpşirli 2007, 1:21–25; cf. Thomas 1972, 73–76, with a detailed concordance between the two texts.

66 On Na'ima's formulation of the humor theory cf. Ermiş 2014, 48–59.

doctor to cure society's ills but avoids requiring this to be "a man of the sword" (this had already happened at the beginning of the Köprülü dynasty of viziers, and Na'ima had another cure in mind, namely peace).

A large part of Na'ima's preface (N I:33–40; Ip I:26–30) is based directly on Ibn Khaldun's account of the dynastic stages in his *Muqaddima*. Just after describing the three ages of the state (according to Kâtib Çelebi's anthropomorphic theory), Na'ima sets about describing in detail five such stages, following now more closely the Arab historian. It is God's will, he explains, that every "state and community" (*devlet ü cem'iyyet*) passes through defined stages. The first is that of "victory" (*zafer vaktı*), in which the state struggles "to free itself from the hands of others and to secure [its] dominion". In this period, people are content with a simple way of life and obey the principle of solidarity and zealous cohesion (*asabiyyet*), which is the cause of might and victory; the people and the army (*kavm ve asker*) are united, share all the booty, and nobody wants to exalt themselves over anyone else. In the second stage, that of "independence" (*istiklal*), the victorious state consolidates itself; the ruler begins to alienate his people (*kavm*) from his affairs, to become independent in his decisions, and to grant his family wealth and power. Moreover, the ruler gathers slaves and uses them to punish those who, led by their whims, act wrongfully. The tribal power (*kuvvet-i aşiret*) and the zeal is only an "imaginary event" (*emr-i vehmi*) that makes the members of a tribe unanimous in their opinions and acts; on the other hand, slaves and purchased servants (or those friends of the ruler who choose enslavement as a sign of kindness and favor) are "metaphorically within the notion of solidarity" (*mecazâ asabiyet hükmünde dahil*) and reap the benefits of the tribal structure. Thus, while this common zeal is necessary in the appearance of a state, it naturally gives way to the state becoming a "private tribe of the ruler" (*kavm-i hass*) as the dynasty leaves nomadism behind completely and becomes settled. Consequently, the early companions of the ruler gradually lose their power and their commitment to the dynasty. In the Ottoman case, observes Na'ima, the companions and servants of the sultan, be they men of the sword or of the pen, have various origins, and thus differ from each other in their customs, habits, clothing, and etiquette. While most dynasties perish in this second stage because of the kind of internal strife described above, the Ottoman state has avoided such a fate because of this peculiarity.

The third stage is that of peace, ease, confidence, and security. It is a time of prosperity; promising youths find their way into the state apparatus and flourish, while soldiers and servants are paid on time and are always ready to defend the country. State offices become stable and officials begin to form dynasties for their offspring, defending them against opponents; thus, solidarity becomes unnecessary, as nobody doubts anyone else's subjection and obedience. In the fourth stage, however, that of contentment and tranquility (*kana'at ü müsaleme*), people are content with their ancestors' deeds and do nothing but imitate them. Those who hold high offices have established their posts for themselves and for their offspring. Furthermore, the army begins to become rebellious and ill-disciplined; sending them on campaign is the only way to keep them under control, with the result that the state has to pay a heavy burden constantly, both in men and wealth. A wise measure for these troubles, adds Na'ima, is to put a stop to campaigns and to try to reorganize state affairs instead. Again, the reference to the contemporaneous political situation and the allusion to the peace policy of his patron is evident, all the more so since he later claims that the Ottoman state reached the fourth stage during the time of the disastrous siege of Vienna in 1683, i.e. at the beginning of the long war-*cum*-rebellion to which the Treaty of Karlowitz put an end.

Finally, the fifth stage is that of prodigality, excessive expenditure, and eventual destruction. Unlike their predecessors, the people of this period become greedy and chase after luxurious houses and clothing. Even new taxes and dues cannot cover their expenses; as their needs grow, the state even has to resort to forced loans, which come very close to confiscation (*müsadere*). Here again, however, Na'ima feels compelled to argue that things can be mended even at this stage, provided campaigns come to a halt first.

As noted, Na'ima was not content with simply copying Kâtib Çelebi's remarks on the four classes in light of his medical simile of the body and its humors; instead, he added his own observations on the merchants. Having expounded the stage theory, moreover, he expands on these thoughts in this new light. A small chapter on "the men of the sword and of the pen" (N I: 49–52; Ip I: 37–39) stresses that at the beginning of a dynasty or state the need for the sword is greater, while the pen only serves to execute the king's orders. Similarly, in the last stages of a state there is again a great need for the sword, overpowering that for the pen. However, in the middle stages the dynasty, now at the height of its power, has to rely on the men of the pen rather than the army in order to control its income and expenses and to carry out its decisions.[67] In this period, kings and viziers respect and care for both the ulema and the scribes. Even an excess of respect for those classes cannot be detrimental to the state; only rarely do men of the pen transgress their limits. They are usually moderate in their manners, build houses appropriate to their rank, and, in general, only benefit the state. Men of the sword, on the contrary, while offering their lives and souls in war against the enemies of the state, tend to be dependent on

67 Again this is Ibn Khaldun: Ibn Khaldun – Rosenthal 1958, 2:46–47; Ibn Khaldun – Rosenthal – Dawood 1969, 213ff.

the money and gifts given to them by the dynasty. It is especially when these remunerations become excessive that soldiers become used to a comfortable life. They wish to imitate their superiors in luxury, with the result that they often end up in debt and poverty. On the other hand, if the state increases their salaries in order to match their expenses, its budget becomes overburdened and consequently the peasants, the primary source of state income, are impoverished. Thus, the men of the pen and of the sword should be kept balanced, with careful dispensing of gifts and remunerations to those worthy.

Some of Na'ima's more specific observations on human societies are again summaries and in many instances verbatim copies of sections of Ibn Khaldun's work. After the theory of stages that had been popularized by Kâtib Çelebi, Na'ima introduces Ibn Khaldun's notion of nomadism versus settled civilization (*buduv ü hazar*) as a factor influencing the course of history (N I:44–46; Ip I:33–34). The "savage peoples" (*ümem-i vahşiyye*) are stronger than others, he argues, as might and courage are stronger in a savage and nomadic existence; because they do not know the hindrances of ease and comfort, they subdue other peoples easily. However, when they gradually become familiar with pleasures and comforts, so does their valor and courage disappear, just like when wild beasts are domesticated by man. Gradually, men tend to forget their training in war and arms and start to entrust the protection of their souls and goods to rulers as their proxies (*müvekkel*), and fighting with their enemies to professional soldiers. As such, they stay inside castles and houses and make a living under the protection of their dynasty (*saye-i devlette*); they ignore both the power of the ease into which they have sunk and the value of the state under which they live comfortably, and so they gradually lose their courage, immersing themselves into the comforts of settled life (*refh-i hazaret*).

4.1 *Peace as a Means to Avoid Decline*

As already noted, Na'ima's main aim in his introductory remarks appears to have been to justify his patron's Hüseyin Pasha's much-criticized negotiations that ended in the Treaty of Karlowitz. To this end, he uses two kinds of arguments. One is traditional, referring to examples from Islamic history to show that the Prophet himself, as well as other celebrated figures of the past, concluded peace with the infidels in order to gain time and resources to later impose a decisive victory. As Lewis V. Thomas showed, Na'ima wanted to emphasize that peace with the infidels could be an option under some circumstances, and was not automatically a sign of treason or cowardice. This kind of reasoning must have aimed at those who were willing to use religion-based arguments against peace, or even an imagined "old law" of the Ottomans (but not, as Na'ima tries to show, of Islam in general): in all probability, these critics can be identified with the janissary circles.

Thus, in his foreword, Na'ima stresses the idea that God has taught mankind to use those means and courses of action that suit each age of history, sometimes declaring war, sometimes concluding peace. To prove his point, he narrates at length the story of the treaty of Hudaybiyya, i.e. the peace concluded with the Quraysh of Mecca by the Prophet Muhammad, even though he undoubtedly could have employed miraculous means to overpower them supernaturally (N I:12–26; Ip I:10–20). Another historical example comes after Na'ima's description of the "circle of justice".[68] Na'ima again stresses that military campaigns are the most serious factor leading to the disruption of this circle; when the finances are in a bad state and the soldiers are divided, many rulers of the past chose to make peace instead. To support his view, Na'ima recalls the history of the First Crusade, who benefited from the discord and strife among Muslim rulers of the Middle East. In Na'ima's version, the temporary peace that gave Jerusalem to the crusaders also gave the opportunity to the Islamic states to re-organize their power; once this had happened, Salah al-Din (Saladin) was able to recapture the Holy Land after first recovering financially and mobilizing a united army.[69]

The second line of argument Na'ima uses in his plea for peace is more philosophical and must have been addressed to his fellow-members of the governmental bureaucracy. He reverts to the stage theory in order to prove not only that unnecessary war is a sign of the stages of decline but also that a prolonged peace might be a way to break this circle of decline and thus extend the life of a dynasty. This assertion is best described in a long concluding chapter in which he tries to plan a road-map for ending a crisis, based on Khaldunian notions (N I: 52–65; Ip I:39–48). Copying Kâtib Çelebi's *Düstûrü'l-amel* almost

68 He cites Kınalızade, erroneously claiming that the latter had taken this scheme from Ibn Khaldun's *Muqaddima*, as Kınalızade's source was Davvani. However, a similar "circle of justice" can indeed be found in Ibn Khaldun's work: see Ibn Khaldun – Rosenthal 1958, 1:81 and 2:105; Ibn Khaldun – Rosenthal – Dawood 1969, 41; Fleischer 1983, 201; Tezcan 1996, 115, fn. 419.

69 Na'ima cites al-Maqrizi's *Kitâb al-sulûk li-ma'rifat duwal al-mulûk* and remarks that this success story and its prerequisites are described in Abd al-Rahman Shirazî's book, parts of which were translated by Mustafa Ali in his *Nüshatü'l-selatin*, whence Na'ima took them and, as he asserts, appended them to his history. There is no further sign of this work in both Ali and Na'ima; in his second preface, Na'ima speaks of a treatise by Ebünnecib that was used by Saladin and which he intended to translate into Turkish (Na'ima 1864–1866, 6:Appendix, 53–58; Na'ima – İpşirli 2007, 4:1890–1892; cf. Thomas 1972, 45–48). The book must be Abd al-Rahman b. Nasr b. Abdullah (al-Shayzari)'s *Nahj al-sulûk fi siyâsat al-mulûk*, eventually translated into Turkish during the reign of Abdülhamid I (1774–89): see Na'ima – İpşirli 2007, 1:XXV; Fleischer 1990, 68, fn 4. *Nahj al-sulûk* belongs to the *ahlak* tradition, resembling Kınalızade's ethico-political synthesis with "mirror for princes" overtones (see some specimens in Ermiş 2014, 33–34, 45–47).

verbatim (but, as usual, omitting the statistical data),[70] Na'ima argues that, as the age of a state's maturity and stagnation comes to an end (he further explains this as the fourth and fifth stages), the state's expenses tend to exceed its income. Balancing the budget is generally considered to be a very difficult task, and Na'ima agrees with Kâtib Çelebi that only the use of compelling force (*bir kâsirin kasrı*) can achieve it. But instead of following his predecessor's advice, which focused on gradually reducing military salaries by a powerful vizier, Na'ima prefers to stress once more the need for a temporary abandoning of war and campaigns until the state budget is balanced and the soldiers regain their power. During this peaceful period, the government must care for the re-ordering of the cities and the well-being of the subjects and especially the peasants. More specifically, a sum equal to one year's state payments must be collected by taking arrears from state property (*mal-ı miriden*), by which the expenses would be carefully reduced. Na'ima explains that the abundance of cash will be beneficial, since "as the saying goes, wise merchants gain not from buying but from selling".

An excursus emphasizing that these efforts at redressing must be made carefully and gradually brings to mind similar remarks by Kâtib Çelebi as well as the rich experiences of seventeenth-century politics available to Na'ima. Thus, he maintains that one should be careful not to remove the signs of splendor and grandeur (*esbab-ı ihtişam*) from kings and magnates: the abolition of customary usage can be difficult albeit beneficial, and wearing furs or using decorated weapons are now ordinary practices for the people. In the fourth and second stages of a state's life, such luxury and respect for the king replaces the solidarity and nomadism of earlier stages. Some may complain that without money no government is possible and thus that this policy is impossible, but the result of such advice would only be complaints and misery for the people. To this effect, Na'ima quotes Ibn Khaldun again: by nature, man seeks perfection and so people tend to imitate great men, not only in their behavior and views but also in their attire. Consequently, a wise administrator would first seek to inspire respect for himself and the law in the people so that, afterwards, they will follow him wholeheartedly in his decisions. Thus, any reduction in luxury and pomp must be gradual and careful, and should be executed according to rank and in moderation. Pomp can be tolerated in state officials (*erkân-ı devlet*) while luxury should distinguish between soldiers and the servants of the state, on the one hand, and commoners on the other.

The end of Na'ima's first preface culminates in another eulogy of peacemakers. He mentions Kara Mustafa Pasha's vizierate and the war he initiated with Hungary, while noting that the Ottomans were then in the fourth stage

70 Cf. Ayn Ali 1978, 134–135.

of the state; due to the peculiarities of that stage, the campaign and the consequent 1683 siege of Vienna were doomed to fail. More and more campaigns followed, all to no avail, and more and more money and manpower were expended for no reason. What Na'ima wishes to stress here once more is the need, in such conditions, for an interval of peace, a

> time for ease and security, during which good measures would re-impose order and prosperity ... the peasants would be at rest by the lightening of their tax burden, the treasury would be filled again as a result of diminishing expenses, and the army would be re-organized.

Finally, under the vizierate of Amcazade Köprülü Hüseyin Pasha, peace was restored—and here Na'ima praises at length and somewhat immoderately (to use Lewis Thomas' words) his mentor, as well as the *reisülküttab* Rami Mehmed Pasha, who conducted the negotiations at Karlowitz. Thus, somewhat abruptly, Na'ima brings his preface to an end, expressing his hope that this peace will give the Ottoman state the opportunity to restore its order and prosperity.

4.2 *Optimism Revisited: the Ulema as Destroyers of Peace*

The optimism of the first preface, composed between 1699 (when the Karlowitz treaty was signed) and 1702 (the year of Amcazade's deposition), gives way to a grimmer image in the second, written soon after the "Edirne event" of 1703.[71] Most of the second preface is dedicated to a narrative of the revolt, one aimed at praising the course of action followed by Ahmed III and his grand vizier (and Na'ima's new patron) Moralı Hasan Pasha. Na'ima describes the *şeyhülislam* Feyzullah Efendi's meteoric career and nepotistic practices and maintains that such appointments are acceptable when granted by the sultan's favor, but declares this must be done moderately and with regard to dignity and merit. Famous ulema dynasties did exist before, but they behaved with self-restraint and frugality; the Feyzullah family, on the other hand, sought to control every single appointment.[72] Another objection, adds Na'ima, is that the *şeyhülislam* has indeed

> the general superintendence of the affairs of both religion and state, of things general and particular ... and since the sultan himself trusts him in good faith, he enjoys the trust of the dynasty.

71 Na'ima 1864–1866, 6:Appendix, 2–58; Na'ima – İpşirli 2007, 4:1858–1892; partial translations in Thomas 1972, 42–48 and 83–89.

72 One should not forget here that it was the conflict with Feyzullah that had led Na'ima's first patron, Amcazade Hüseyin Paşa, losing his position.

Na'ima's answer is that kings may well have trusted people to supervise their administrators, so long as the latter do not harm the state; but this does not mean that the former may take over these affairs completely. The ulema's task is to guide the administrators (*vükela*) to the right path, not to impose their own interests; it is the grand vizier's duty, having the highest post of all those granted by the sultan, to administer all the affairs pertaining to the well-being of the subjects, the treasury, the army, etc., of the realm. Whenever any other official or companion of the sultan interferes with the grand vizier's work and is able to annul his decisions, state affairs no longer follow the natural order (*nizam-ı tabi'i*) and rebellion may be close at hand. Moreover, such a person may amass the properties and the services of a large number of people and so overwhelm the power of the grand vizier, the absolute proxy of the sultan; his rise and power may become so great that he will be considered to have the equivalent of the sultan's power (*cenab-ı saltanata müşareket haline varsa gerektir*). Inevitably, concludes Na'ima, this will lead to fear, hatred, and his ultimate destruction. Moreover, he adds, administration and politics require "recourse to stratagems and intrigue"; these behaviors, however, are unfit for the dignity of the ulema, and so it would be better if they stayed away from state affairs as much as possible.

Na'ima then continues by narrating the Edirne revolt, before reaching his conclusion (N VI App: 43–52; Ip IV:1883–87). He remarks once more that, in these (i.e. his own) days, when the Ottoman state has reached its fourth or even fifth stage, the number of salaried people and the scale of state expenditure have increased to such a degree that covering them is almost impossible. In such circumstances, argues Na'ima, it is very difficult for a king to stay in the capital (*darü'l-mülk*) and impose reforms; instead, he should instead go somewhere else, using some excuse (such as hunting, war preparations, or just a visit), and try to amend things from there. From such a place, Na'ima explains, it is easier to amass money in the treasury by taking secret measures to reduce expenditure and increase income, since if he does so from the capital the people are bound to revolt. This happens because the people of the capital are, by nature, settled (*hazariyyet rüsuh bulmuştur*) and are used to profiting from the state and living off its money. As such, they keep a close eye on palace activity and tend to circulate news about the palace and the dynasty, whether for good or bad; in consequence, merchants might raise their prices or ask to be paid accordingly. Only from a distance and in secret is it possible to take such measures, just as merchants use "legal stratagems" (*hiyel-i şer'iyye*) to increase their property. In the same way, a man whose financial situation is in dire straits should find an excuse to leave his house temporarily so he can fix his finances gradually, away from the pressure of his family and his debtors, who will give him a period of grace by necessity. The "human society" (*devlet-i ictima'iyye-i insaniyye*) functions in a similar way; that is why Abbasid caliphs and Byzantine emperors maintained palaces away from their capital cities. Such a stratagem must be practised in moderation, and the expenses of the sultan somewhere else should not exceed those when at his palace. Mustafa II almost seemed to have left Istanbul forever, adding an extra dimension to the revolt that overthrew him.

After this interesting note, Na'ima proceeds to his "conclusion of conclusions" (N VI App: 52–8; Ip IV:1887–92),[73] where, after noting that "we should abandon words that do not comport with the time in which we live" (*asra münasıb olmayan sözler metruk kalmakla*), he sets out the main principles for conducting public affairs; if these are followed, he claims, a state "will not thenceforth experience further change and disturbances". Among these, some are quite abstract (caring for the peasantry, balancing the finances without creating discontent) while others are more concrete (preventing the provincial *taslakçı* class from harming the state treasury and officials).[74] Na'ima does not fail to note that such measures may well seem impossible and contradictory, and also that they seem very difficult to implement effectively in a short time, but he points to historical precedents.

4.3 *Social Discipline and Political Economy*

As well as the two prefaces, which contain (especially in the first) his *stricto sensu* political theory, Na'ima also scatters all kinds of political advice throughout his voluminous history. Such scattered advice has been collected by Lewis Thomas and, for the most part, consists of ideas related to practical morals that were intended for the ear of the ruler or his grand vizier.[75] Among them, a remarkable passage praises Murad IV's harshness and reign of terror on the grounds that (N III: 170; Ip II:757)

> this was a pretext for the purpose of controlling the riff-raff and to frighten the common people in the interests of the state (*erazili te'dib ve avam-ı nası terhib maslahatı için*).

However, in general Na'ima does not seem to favor harshness and intimidation. At another point he advises against hasty executions, noting that enabling a

---

73 Translated in Thomas 1972, 87–88 and 45–48.

74 This class, that normally designates a type of candidate for the janissary corps, could also denote anyone who claimed to be a janissary without being recorded in the registers. See Uzunçarşılı 1988, 1:153, 491–493 and cf. Sariyannis 2008b, 261 and 266.

75 Thomas 1972, 89–110.

condemned man to flee "is in itself laudable" (*nefsinde bir memduh iştir*: N VI: 276; Ip IV: 1738). His esteem of Murad IV's policies might be attributed to the target of the sultan's harshness, namely the janissaries (rather than specific pashas and other officials). Another possible explanation is that Na'ima saw Murad's reign as a different stage of the course of the Ottoman empire, one closer to its heyday, compared with his own times. Such a conclusion (which reminds us of Kâtib Çelebi's motto that different times require different measures) can be extracted from part of Na'ima's first preface (N I:46–49; Ip I: 34–37), in which he sets out to show how tyrannical and harsh ministers (*ümera*) weaken the state's power to conquer and its ability to wage war successfully. For reproductive needs, men have a natural tendency to dominate others (*re'is bi't-tab olup*), whereas whenever they are overwhelmed by the power and dominion of others and are obliged to submit and obey, their sensual ardor wanes and they become sluggish.[76] Thus, the use of intimidatory and violent methods in politics is not deemed right, especially toward the end of the period of stagnation; when rulers and judges investigate people's lives too thoroughly and impose severe punishments for minor misdemeanors, people feel humiliated, become avaricious, start to lie and deceive, and so on. Instead, ministers (*vülat*) should persuade rather than impose in order to enhance solidarity among the people.[77] Na'ima maintains that in public affairs and social intercourse it is not proper to exhaust and weaken the people by investigating their slightest movements (it is tempting to see here a reflection of Kâtib Çelebi's *Mîzânü'l-hak*).

Finally, among this scattered advice, one may find interesting glimpses of Na'ima's economic thought, a subject which was generally neglected by Ottoman authors (with the notable exception of Kınalızade and Dede Cöngi, who mainly repeat earlier categorizations). An important passage is one where Na'ima again speaks of the proper way to reduce expenses (N VI:310–15; Ip IV:1762–65). As he observes, history has shown that whenever there was an effort to cut excessive salaries or stipends by striking names from the payrolls (*kat'-ı erzak*), this only led to the destruction of the one attempting the reforms. The only way to cut such stipends is to do so gradually, by making no new appointments (and thus waiting for their total number to fall through the deaths of assignees) and by strictly prohibiting their trade. In such a way, Na'ima describes the traditional pattern of correlating income to expenses, i.e. according to the authorities of old: income from charity (*sadaka*), which is now formed of

76 Here Na'ima copies Ibn Khaldun's views on education: Ibn Khaldun – Rosenthal 1958, 3:304; Ibn Khaldun – Rosenthal – Dawood 1969, 424.

77 A discussion of mildness and shrewdness here also comes from Ibn Khaldun: Ibn Khaldun – Rosenthal 1958, 1:383–384; Ibn Khaldun – Rosenthal – Dawood 1969, 153–154.

tolls from Muslim merchants (*gümrük namına alınan zekat*), has to be distributed to the poor and needy, as well as to the clerks of the treasury (*beytülmal hizmetinde olan*). Land taxes, the poll-tax, tolls from infidel merchants, and money extracted from infidel rulers in exchange for peace (i.e. the largest part of state income) must be devoted to maintaining the army, paying the salaries of the ulema, and constructing castles and mosques, and so on. Such a categorization is nothing new; in fact, it is less completed or detailed compared to Dede Cöngi's mid-sixteenth-century treatise (see above, chapter 3), but Na'ima again has some notes on the situation in his own time. He remarks that this division has altered with the passing of time and changing conditions; for instance, most of the ulema take their salaries from the income of their own posts so that they now represent no burden for the state budget (*taraf-ı miri*), while most other offices are paid through customs income.

Another piece of economic-*cum*-political thought can be found following the description of the death of Derviş Mehmed Pasha (1655) and the huge wealth he had amassed through various entrepreneurial activities, including commercial husbandry and the exploitation of bakeries.[78] Na'ima first quotes the pasha as saying that there are three natural ways of making a living (agriculture, commerce, and leadership [i.e. income from the ruler]), while others have also added craftsmanship. This formulation (it may be originally attributed to the pasha or to Na'ima himself) departs from Ibn Khaldun's similar expression, which was, as noted above (chapter 2), repeated by Kınalızade.[79] However, unlike his mentor, Na'ima accepts leadership as being a natural source of revenue, but thinks that craftsmanship can, in fact, be reduced to commerce, as the income of most craftsmen barely suffices for their living and therefore they have no real revenue. On the other hand, magnates and officials benefit from the merchants and the peasants, because the latter do not ask for immediate payment, thinking of their future prospects, while also conceding part of their profits out of fear. That is how the notables and magnates take for themselves about a quarter of the efforts of the people and consequently get rich quickly. Derviş Mehmed Pasha allegedly argued that, whenever administrators *cannot* increase their income and property by commerce or agriculture, they tend to commit two great sins: first, they steal the money and property of the people, thus becoming tyrants; and secondly, they are incapable of storing even this wealth, stolen from the people, since they spend it on luxury goods they consider indispensable; as such, they fall into the hands of usurers

78 Na'ima 1864–1866, 6:26–28; Na'ima – İpşirli 2007, 4:1571–1572. Cf. Kunt 1977; Faroqhi 1994, 547–549. On Ibn Khaldun's formulation see Ibn Khaldun – Rosenthal 1958, 2:315ff.

79 See the detailed analysis in Kunt 1977, 206–211, and cf. Ermiş 2014, 97–102.

and profiteers and, in the end, have nothing to show for it but committing a great sin.

Na'ima seems somewhat reluctant to adopt this perspective. He hastens to note that some treatises on morality consider commerce and agriculture totally prohibited for rulers, viziers, governors, and administrators. Such texts argue that occupation with such work is only for inferior people, since administrators who practise them in order to amass wealth prevent others from doing the same, thus making them oppressors. If they constantly trade to procure indispensable luxury goods then they forget the virtues of generosity and become stripped of their humanity. So, Na'ima concludes, it is much better for magnates, after they have taken care of their household, to spend their revenue on generous acts of piety and charity. However, it is to be noted that he generally seems positive, or at least more neutral than his predecessors, about Derviş Mehmed Pasha's practices (whom, at any rate, he judges rather favorably).

• • •

If we are to summarize Na'ima's theory, then we can say that it is an extension of Kâtib Çelebi's vision of the human body as a parable for the state-society continuum combined with a fully-fledged adaptation of Ibn Khaldun's ideas about the laws of historical decline, on which he carefully comments while stressing the particularities of the Ottoman case. If Kâtib Çelebi had seen the threat to the welfare of the state in the growing power of the janissaries, leaving aside the until-then dominant defense of the timar system, Na'ima in his time had every reason to avoid such criticisms: by the end of the seventeenth century, the janissary corps, far from being a simple military group, had encompassed much of the artisanal and small trader groups (either by letting them into the janissary ranks or by the janissaries themselves taking up market and trading activities) and was a major player in imperial politics. Writing in the aftermath of the 1688 rebellion and on the eve of that of 1704, Na'ima did his best to emphasize the dangers lurking in both the unlimited growth of janissary power and too harsh and violent an effort to curb it.

It is significant that Na'ima inserts his own medical similes concerning the peasants and the merchants in order to stress that none of them should enjoy "excessive luxury". This emphasis on balance between the four classes had been, as noted previously, a constant feature of Ottoman political thought ever since Amasi, although all Ottoman authors up to his time, without exception, had used the notion only against the army. It was, they believed, the military that should be checked, since its excessive growth was harmful to the other classes. Na'ima, therefore, was the first to use balance and the theory of the body politic in relation to the taxable subjects of the sultan. Peasants may succumb to excessive ease and thus rebel; merchants may become greedy profiteers and so impoverish the poor. On the other hand, his views on the economy do not reveal Na'ima to be an enemy of wealth in general; furthermore, while discussing the fifth stage of dynasties, he remarks that the constant demands of the state from rich people make them fear for their sustenance and consider going to Mecca or to Egypt to once more become wealthy, not realizing that even in foreign lands they are not safe (here, one could also add Na'ima's reluctance to condemn fully the pomp and luxury of state magnates). His digression on the role of a capital city and of its population, in the second preface, is, unsurprisingly, dictated by the "Edirne event"; on the other hand, if combined with his other ideas, it shows his distrust and suspiciousness of the janissary-affiliated urban strata who were playing an increasingly important role in public politics. His praise of Murad IV's harshness could be seen in the same context.

In this vein, advocating peace as a way out of the stages of decline is Na'ima's original contribution, and it must be noted that he inserts it very carefully into his general framework while at the same time giving very specific advice on how the state should use such a period of peace to recover. Kâtib Çelebi, half a century earlier, had seen the solution in a powerful "man of the sword"; Na'ima, his position in the court meaning he was much more keen to keep an elaborate balance, emphasized a long interval of peace in which the state apparatus (which he praised so much) could bring about the gradual and careful reforms he proposed. With Na'ima, the seventeenth century ends with a new world vision, well vested in both history and the outside—and widening—world. More particularly, there were two important legacies for subsequent political writing: legitimacy of change (following Kâtib Çelebi's reasoning), and justification of peace. From a different perspective, one which would become increasingly dominant, there was also the acknowledgment (for the first time since Akhisari) that the Ottomans' military might was no longer sufficient for supremacy on the battlefield, and that a step back to think and reorganize was needed.

5 Peace and Change: Preparing an Ideological Environment

One may find the political preoccupations of the period in several other works that belong to genres other than political writing. Evliya Çelebi's monumental *Seyahatnâme* ("Book of travels") contains a few scattered views on politics that represent, to a large degree, the *Weltanschauung* of the Ottoman elite as it was constituted towards Murad IV's reign (during which Evliya began his travels): a mixture of legitimizing discourse in favor of strong sultanly rule and religious optimism (although the concept of what he sees as Süleyman's "Golden Age" is not missing).[80] Yet this work, which only marginally pertains to politics, will be skipped here; rather, the new ideas that were introduced in the second half of the seventeenth century will be studied in detail instead. For instance, it is not surprising, in light of the wars and treaties of the first decades of the eighteenth century, that Na'ima's defence of peace was followed by various authors. As well as political thinkers such as Resmi Efendi, whose work will be examined in more detail in chapter 9, this advocacy for peace also found its way into poetry. A whole genre of lengthy poems in praise of peace, known as the *Sulhiyye*, flowered in the period between the treaties of Karlowitz (1699) and Passarowitz (1718).[81] Yusuf Nabi's (c. 1642–1712) *Sulhiyye* is also a eulogy of Amcazâde Hüseyin Pasha, who was Na'ima's mentor; Nabi states that, due to that pasha's efforts, "the world found again its order, with peace and soundness". People had tired of continuous war, and "without an anchor, the ship of the realm had almost sunk". The Karlowitz peace treaty was like a slave's manumission document: friendship succeeded hostility, love and ease took the place of hate and fear. Nabi likens the war to a disease that had made health invisible; in this, we may perhaps see a reflection of Na'ima's Khaldunist notion that peace is like medicine for a sick state. Another *Sulhiyye* composed for the same treaty, written by Alaeddin Sabit of Bosnia (d. 1712), goes on to say that

> with the *fetva* of the imam of Islam, the wine of war became canonically forbidden (*haram*) and the sweet drink of peace permitted (*helal*).

Another poet, Seyyid Vehbi (d. 1736), wrote two similar poems on the treaties of Passarowitz (1718) and of Istanbul (1724, with Persia), which praised the grand vizier Damad İbrahim Pasha. Like his predecessors, he stressed the difficulties of war with multiple enemies; on the other hand, he laments much more forcefully the distress of the Muslim army. Ahmed III, he says, sought peace because he was saddened by the disasters inflicted on his subjects by the Austrians. Vehbi wrote explicitly of his hopes that İbrahim Pasha would be able to reinstate the might of the empire, avoiding a repetition of Karlowitz (which he sees as a defeat). Praise of peace (rather than military might) is also

80 On Evliya's political views see Dankoff 2006, 83ff. and esp. 106–114; Balta 2006; Taştan 2012.

81 See Rahimguliyev 2007 (in the appendices of the thesis, the author presents the *Sulhiyyes* of Nabi, Sabit, and Vehbi: pp. 91–108). On Vehbi's first *Sulhiyye*, see ibid., 73–80. On early eighteenth-century views on peace see Menchinger 2014a, 122–124, who argues that "the very rarity of the *sulhiyye* also militates against using it as proof of major change".

repeated in a very interesting history of ancient Athens, composed by the *müfti* of that city around 1738 and based on Greek sources:[82]

> Since the way of the wise is based on peace (*hükema mesleği sulh u salah üzere olup*), they did not approve of tyranny and oppression … The town had conflicts with no-one, and they arranged their affairs in consultation with the community (*umurları cumhur müşaveresiyle olurdı*).

To return to Nabi, his most famous work, the moralistic poem *Hayriyye*, written in 1701/2, should also be mentioned.[83] *Hayriyye* was very popular and was being imitated as late as the beginning of the nineteenth century (by Sünbülzâde Vehbi). It contains moral advice, along with digressions on Istanbul, springtime, and poetry, comments on the disadvantages of various professions (following the old style of *hasbıhal*), and criticism of his own time. In describing various potential careers, Nabi accuses the provincial notables (*ayan*), corrupted by extensive bribery, of oppressing the people; in the *hasbıhal* tradition, moreover, nor are these notables free from anguish, as they can easily fall prey to gossip and calumny (P188ff). High officials are also not to be envied: the life of a pasha is full of trouble, since he always owes money, has difficulty in raising an army, and thus has no choice but to oppress the people. In an extraordinarily sharp voice, Nabi asserts that

> this kind of oppression [the excessive exploitation of the villagers] is unique in these [Ottoman] lands; it is not to be seen even in Uzbek, Indian, Christian, or Persian states.

The state must comply with the premises of the Sharia if it is to survive and flourish; Nabi ends his piece of political theory with a reiteration of the famous "circle of equity" (P167–183). In another similarity between Nabi's concerns and those of Na'ima, a lengthy excursus about the risks and difficulties of agriculture seems to be directed against members of the elite who follow such enterprises (P162–167; after all, it is evident that he did not expect his audience to include peasants):

82 Mahmud Efendi – Tunalı 2013, 180–181; see also the original in 251, 279.

83 Nabi – Pala 1989; Nabi – Kaplan 2008. Cf. Diriöz 1994; Sariyannis 2008a, 145–147; Kurz 2011, 249–268; Sariyannis 2012, 288; Tuşalp Atiyas 2013, 241–243.

> no matter whether you make a profit or a loss, you are not fit for this job (*ehli degülsin*) ... farming turns a man into a peasant (*şekl-i insanı ider dihkâni*).

Last but not least, an important aspect of his accusations concerns Sufi circles, perhaps due to the influence of the Kadızadeli movement that was active during the author's youth. In general, Nabi's ideal is a quiet life, one self-sufficient and calm; in Marlene Kurz's words, he wished for "a state undisturbed by pressures from without and untroubled by material concerns—thus a state which permitted people to pursue their scientific and literary interests".[84] Perhaps it would not be too far-fetched to generalize this image to a vision for the Ottoman state as well.

The need for peace, as shall be seen, became one of the major tropes of eighteenth-century political texts.[85] Another was the need for innovation and reform, based on the notion of universal historical laws governing the rise and development of various states and hence the idea that different times need different measures. As will be seen, after Na'ima and toward the end of the eighteenth century the notion of nomadic life as a sign of valor and solidarity, connected with the rise of empires, became the dominant element of the Khaldunist ideas that were circulating. Thus, Na'ima's more faithful rendering of the stage theory did not leave as many traces. On the other hand, it certainly seems that, eventually, Kâtib Çelebi successfully popularized a three-stage version of Ibn Khaldun's laws of imperial growth, one connected with his own simile of the human body, and, perhaps most importantly, the idea that the measures to be taken should be adapted to the specific needs of the age. In this respect, it may be said that Kâtib Çelebi set the foundations for all reformist discourse of the eighteenth century.

---

84 Kurz 2011, 255.

85 The historian Vasıf (d. 1806) generally follows Na'ima's allusion to the peace of Hudaybiya in order to justify late eighteenth-century decisions to make peace: Menchinger 2014a, 139.

CHAPTER 8

The Eighteenth Century: the Traditionalists

The 1703 Edirne event may have not ended in outright regicide, but it was one of the most spectacular Ottoman rebellions: that a rebel army occupied Istanbul and almost clashed with an army raised by the sultan, eventually overpowering the latter, was unprecedented and was to remain a unique incident in Ottoman history.[1] However, it soon became clear that no irreversible harm had been inflicted on the empire. Under the financial and military reforms (which mostly followed a traditional vein, i.e. along the lines of inspecting the army and redressing the timar system, with a more modernist approach to the navy) of the grand vizier, Çorlulu Ali Pasha, Ahmed III's army was able to stand against Peter the Great's invasion at the Pruth river and impose the terms of the treaty that followed (1711). In the immediate aftermath of this, the Ottomans launched a successful attack on the Venetians and managed to reconquer the Peloponnese; on the other hand, however, the Habsburg allies of Venice launched a campaign that reached as far as Belgrade, which they captured. Both conquests were ratified by the Treaty of Passarowitz (1718).

The period that followed, and which ended in another major revolt, was later (in the early twentieth century) named the "Tulip Period" as a result of the Istanbul urban strata's obsession with gardening and, especially, tulips. More particularly, the Tulip Period was perceived to have coincided with the vizierate of Nevşehirli Damad İbrahim Pasha (1718–30). Traditionally, this period has been regarded as one of the exhibition of excessive wealth by the palace elite, and it has also been connected with ideas of Westernization and a more tolerant stance in matters of religion and science; recent interpretations have focused on the emergence of a "mass consumer" culture (with the popularization of elite forms of entertainment), on the "luxury antagonism" that was imposed on the elite by the palace, as well as on the cultural features that bear similarities with the early period of the European Enlightenment, including cosmopolitanism, religious tolerance, and the valorization of natural philosophy and social mobility (what Shirine Hamadeh has termed the Ottoman *décloisonnement* or "the greater porosity of social and professional

1 On the events of the period up to Selim III, see Mantran 1989, 265–425; Emecen 2001b, 55–62; Beydilli 2001, 63–70.

© KONINKLIJKE BRILL NV, LEIDEN, 2019 | DOI:10.1163/9789004385245_010

boundaries").[2] Ambassadors were sent to the European capitals and İbrahim Müteferrika, a Hungarian convert who shall be examined in detail in the next chapter, set up the first Ottoman printing press in 1726.[3] On the other hand, it is usually neglected that this "Ottoman Enlightenment" maintained close ties and links with trends of thought, literature, and art that were prevailing in the other Islamicate empires, and especially Iran, at the time.[4] On the battlefield, the collapse of the Safavid dynasty in Persia led to an Ottoman campaign that succeeded in capturing large parts of its territories.

İbrahim Pasha's rule ended abruptly in 1730 with the so-called Patrona Halil revolt, named after one of its leaders, a low-level janissary. The revolt, in which janissaries, petty artisans, and dispossessed members of the elite participated, was supposedly a reaction to the extravagance and the "Frankish" manners of the court, but it seems that matters such as heavy taxation (the infamous "tax for campaign assistance", *imdad-ı seferiyye*, for the new Iranian campaign that had just begun, and other annual taxes imposed on the urban dwellers) and the blocking of all means of upward mobility by İbrahim Pasha's nepotism (as had happened in 1703 with Feyzullah Efendi) were among the main reasons. Moreover, the ongoing procedure of the identification of janissary power with the interests of the Muslim urban strata should not be neglected; it was said that thousands rushed to register themselves on the janissary lists after the rebellion and the subsequent change in janissary leadership.[5] In addition, a much understudied aspect of the military revolts is their effects in the provinces: it appears that, ostensibly through the janissary networks of trade and patronage, both the 1703 and the 1730 revolt can be related to concurrent rebellions in both Syria and Egypt.[6]

Ahmed III abdicated in favor of his cousin Mahmud I (r. 1730–54). Another rebellion, less than a year after Patrona Halil, was suppressed quickly and easily.[7] Mahmud, probably under the influence of İbrahim Müteferrika's advice, brought in Claude-Alexandre Comte de Bonneval (d. 1747), a French nobleman seeking employment: de Bonneval, after converting under the name

2 For a critique of the traditional representations and an attempt to formulate a new interpretation, see Karahasanoğlu 2009. See also Salzmann 2000; Sajdi 2007; Hamadeh 2008; Küçük 2012; Erginbaş 2014.

3 I use here "Ottoman" as "Ottoman Turkish", i.e. using the Arabic alphabet; Greek, Jewish, and Armenian printing houses had been established earlier in Istanbul; see the survey by Pektaş 2015.

4 Erimtan 2007; Kurz 2011, 55.

5 Karahasanoğlu 2009, 215–216.

6 Hathaway 2004, 32–33.

7 See Olson 1977. According to Olson's analysis, this rebellion bore the characteristics of a "food riot" rather than a redistribution of power.

of Humbaracı Ahmed Pasha, started to organize the bombardier corps along European lines, as well as a school of military engineers (*Hendeshane*); both institutions functioned intermittently (occasionally meeting with strong reactions) until 1750.[8] Wars in the east continued, with the Ottomans suffering heavy losses at the hands of the new Afshar dynasty of Iran, while war with Russia was resumed in 1736 and with Austria a year later. The Ottoman army managed to retake the Serbian and Bosnian lands that had earlier been lost to the Habsburgs, while the Russian campaigns ended in stalemate, rather than in Istanbul's favor, in 1739. A new and disastrous (for both sides) war with Iran merely resulted in the restoration of the old boundary in 1746. A long period of peace followed, lasting until 1768 (and thus covering the rest of the reign of Mahmud I, as well as that of Osman III [1754–57] and, partly, that of Mustafa III [1757–74]).

This period is among the least studied by Ottomanists: it is generally accepted that, with no imminent threat apparent, military and other reforms gradually came to a halt. Power in the provinces increasingly passed into the hands of the *ayan* and *derebey* families, i.e. dynasties of notables who had gained a certain degree of autonomy, mostly through tax-farming and the decentralized means of recruiting troops and supplies for the state. Among these families, the Çapanoğlu and the Karaosmanoğlu in central and western Anatolia respectively, the al-Azm in Damascus, and the Buşatlı in northern Albania may be mentioned.[9] During the vizierate of Koca Mehmed Ragıb Pasha, and especially from 1757 until his death in 1763, there was an effort to enforce the existing laws and regulations related to the legal system, tax-farming, and public order, but these had no great results or continuity. Ragıb Pasha tried to modernize some military segments, to impose discipline, and to inspect the army registers; one of these measures, it should be noted, was the decisive end to the extensive powers of the palace's chief eunuch, who was stripped of the administration of the sultanly *vakf*s in 1757.[10] In light of previous developments, it is tempting to see here an effort to enhance the autonomy of the governmental apparatus vis-à-vis the court.

That is not to say that we should view this period as one of stagnation or decay. For one thing, even if such characterizations are valid from the point of view of the state, they are influenced by a teleological approach that views

8 Bonneval also wrote two advice-style treatises (Yeşil 2011b); see below, chapter 9.

9 Salzmann 1993; McGowan 1994; Nagata 2005; Yaycıoğlu 2012.

10 Barnes 1987, 68–69. On the relationship between the great *vakf*s and the state, cf. Kunt 1994, 190; Sariyannis 2013, 114–115. On Rağıb Paşa see the article of Mesut Aydıner in *Diyanet Vakfı İslam Ansiklopedisi*.

(Europe-oriented) reform as progress and any other change as decline. From another pespective, the process of the janissaries turning into a large "third estate", in a stable alliance with the artisan guilds, had, by the early eighteenth century, culminated in a well-balanced sharing of power, one which may not have helped Ottoman warfare but which did offer much-needed internal peace. To quote Baki Tezcan, during this period, the empire[11]

> was functioning much more smoothly as the royal authority had finally accepted the power of the web that surrounded it ... [T]he eighteenth century was more peaceful *internally* than the [pre-1703] period ... What was most striking about it, however, was its political leadership ... Unlike most of their predecessors during the age of the patrimonial empire, these grand viziers ... came from the ranks of the socioeconomic elite.
>
> The relatively smooth functioning of the [Ottoman] Empire in the eighteenth century was the result of the fine balance that the various representatives of Ottoman social classes had reached after a long period of political struggles.
>
> ... In consequence, the eighteenth century was the most peaceful one in terms of political conflicts between the janissaries and the court; yet at the same time, it was also a century of major territorial losses, contributing to the long-term territorial decline. Not surprisingly, an army centered upon a public corporation of middle and lower middle class merchants and craftsmen failed to perform successfully as a professional military organization.

Warfare was resumed again in Poland in 1768, in an attempt to thwart Catherine the Great's Mediterranean ambitions. Soon the Russians occupied the Danubian principalities, while they also incited a rebellion in the Peloponnese (the "Orlov revolt" of 1770) and sent a fleet to the Aegean, destroying the Ottoman fleet in Çeşme. With the treaty of Küçük Kaynarca, in 1774, the Ottomans managed to keep much of the territory lost to Russia, but the latter imposed an immense war indemnity, made the Ottomans accept the independence of the Crimea, and claimed the position of protector of the Orthodox Christian subjects of the sultan. As shall be seen, this devastating war proved to be a turning point in the reform efforts of the Ottoman government. Mustafa's successor, Abdülhamid I (1774–89), was determined to import whatever knowledge was considered necessary to restore Ottoman military might. He assigned to Baron François de Tott, an advisor to his predecessor, the task of

11 Tezcan 2010a, 195–196 and 241; cf. Quataert 1993.

establishing a corps of rapid-fire artillery (*süratçı*); de Tott created a cannon foundry and a school of engineering, thus following in Bonneval's footsteps,[12] while similar measures were undertaken to aid the recovery of the Ottoman navy under the admiral Gazi Hasan Pasha. Furthermore, the grand vizier Halil Hamid Pasha (1782–85), previously (like Rağıb Pasha earlier) the chief of foreign affairs (*reisülküttab*), strengthened and broadened these attempts while at the same time seriously trying to prevent violations of the old timar and janissary regulations. Halil Hamid also encouraged Ottoman manufacturing, especially textile production, taking measures against the import of European and Indian cloth, while he also made efficient moves to revive Müteferrika's printing house.[13]

However, continuous internal tumult, factional strife inside the government, and external warfare did not allow any of these efforts to bear significant fruit. During the 1760s and 1770s the power of the provincial *ayan* and the centrifugal tendencies of the provinces continued to increase, with *ayan* in Syria, Egypt, Epirus (western Greece), and Baghdad increasing their power, while the Wahhabi revivalist movement in the Arabian peninsula also posed a serious threat to the sultan's rule in neighbouring lands. At the same time, dynastic upheavals in Iran, where the new Zand dynasty had succeeded Nader Shah, ultimately contributed to further the disintegration of Ottoman rule in Iraq. Moreover, after settling her internal problems—namely, Pugachev's major rural revolt—Catherine the Great profited from a local dynastic conflict to annex the Crimea in 1783, thereby leading to Halil Hamid's fall; his successor, the grand vizier Koca Yusuf Pasha, led the pro-war party in Istanbul in an attempt at revenge. This second war, which started in 1787 and ended in 1792, again saw Austria allying with Russia against the Ottomans, who often managed to resist their enemies. However, the destructive battle of Maçin in 1791, (which was marked by an unprecedented collective petition by the Ottoman army to the sultan, Selim III, declaring its inability to fight successfully against a disciplined and organized enemy),[14] together with Austrian troubles due to the French Revolution, led to the Treaty of Jassy (1792) and to the sultan recognizing Russian gains in the Crimea, Georgia, and some of the Danubian principalities. These territorial losses notwithstanding, this peace allowed Selim

12 Cf. Aksan 2001. One cannot overestimate the importance of Aksan's work for understanding Ottoman military power and reforms in the eighteenth century (most of the relevant articles can now be found in Aksan 2004); see also Ágoston 2011, 2014 (for a more general survey). On Abdülhamid's reign see also Sarıcaoğlu 2001.

13 Shaw 1976, 1:256–57; Uzunçarşılı 1936; Aksan 1995, 180–184; Sarıcaoğlu 2001, 147ff.; Menchinger 2017, 96–105.

14 Beydilli 1999b, 30; Menchinger 2014a, 141–147; Yıldız 2016; Menchinger 2017, 152–157.

to proceed with his ambitious Westernizing reforms of the army, the *Nizam-i Cedid*, which will be examined in the next chapter.

It seems that the eventual failure or, at least, poor results of the reform efforts was partly due to factionalism within the government, such as Halil Hamid's rivalry with Gazi Hasan Pasha. However, it must be noted that, throughout this period, reforms and adjustments were not only the result of determined grand viziers or military counselors. A series of experiments in tax-collection and other similar issues were introduced by the financial bureaucracy: as was also seen in chapters 6 and 7, such experimentation had been started in the final decades of the seventeenth century with the introduction of the three-grade poll tax (which, however, soon gave way to collective estimate of a lump sum) and to lifelong tax-farming (*malikâne*) in 1691. By the third quarter of the eighteenth century, the system was experimenting with various ways of allocating and, more importantly, collecting taxes and other types of revenue within the tax districts, as well as dividing the projected profit of a tax-farm into shares (*esham*) that were then sold on by the state to a number of shareholders. These developments may be seen as a deliberate policy to privatize state assets, being part of a course toward modernism and the nineteenth-century centralized state.[15] It is again important to stress that these appear to have been the result of autonomous policy-making from within government circles, as the chief statesmen concentrated more on the possibility of military reform. As has been seen, this development, i.e. the autonomy of the central bureaucracy, was not a new phenomenon, as it had its origins in the mid-seventeenth century at least. Throughout that century, this community had developed a common and self-conscious culture that praised its own role in the government of the empire, taking *inşa* literature one step further and connecting it explicitly to the bureaucrats' rank and importance (some aspects of this process were seen in chapter 6).[16] It may be argued that, having fostered an alliance with the loci of political power within the state, i.e. the sultan and the viziers, the bureaucracy had identified itself with the state. It was precisely in these years that the *kalemiye* or scribal career gradually became a stairway to the higher administrative and political echelons. The most illustrative example is that of Râmî Mehmed Efendi (d. 1708), the head Ottoman diplomat at Karlowitz and the first scribe to become grand vizier (see also above, chapter 6).[17]

15 Cf. Salzmann 1993; Salzmann 2004; Darling 2006, 129–130; McGowan 1994, 713–716; Genç 2000; Ursinus 2012; Tuşalp Atiyas 2013, 24–26.

16 Aksan 1995, 2–23; Tuşalp Atiyas 2013, 132–191.

17 Itzkowitz 1962; Tuşalp Atiyas 2013, 9–29 for Rami's biography and *passim* for the scribal culture of the late seventeenth and early eighteenth century. Another acquaintance of Rami's was the poet Nabi, whom was seen above as a supporter of the Karlowitz

The main obstacle and opponent for this new political pole remained the janissary corps, which, as seen, had by then been transformed into a socio-political formation with corporate features, and which was determined to keep its share in the "political nation" following the last great revolts at the beginning of eighteenth century. It was this complex system of alliances, conflicts, and interests that in many ways determined the struggle of political ideas throughout the rest of the eighteenth century.

1 The Eighteenth Century and Its Intellectual Climate: on Ottoman "Traditionalism"

From the perspective of political writing, the eighteenth century contains two blossomings of original works: one during Ahmed III's reign, either at its beginning or during the "Tulip Period", and one during and after the long and disastrous war with Russia in the last quarter of the century. The gap between the two groups, some forty years of almost total silence, is puzzling, although it roughly coincides with the long interval of peace, something which was so unusual for Ottoman history. Indeed, it seems as if eighteenth-century political authors increasingly concentrated on matters of warfare, as if they perceived military defeats as the only problem of the state. Moreover, at first glance, many texts written during the first of the two periods seem to constitute a retreat from the bold Khaldunism of Kâtib Çelebi or Na'ima (although Ibn Khaldun's work would continue to exert serious influence, especially after it was translated in 1730 by Pirizade Mehmed Sahib Efendi).[18] They give the impression of a simple continuation of the "mirror for princes" genre; one may even be tempted to say they constitute its swansong. They are devoted to giving concrete advice on specific institutions, with a clear emphasis on the army, which was bound to dominate Ottoman political thought throughout the century. However, while they omit wholesale any reference to a Golden Age, they differ from earlier works such as those by Mustafa Ali, Akhisari, and Koçi Bey. It looks like early and mid-eighteenth-century Ottomans had lost the feeling of urgency that dominated the work of their predecessors of the early seventeenth century, and this is all the more strange when set against the

treaty (ibid., 217–218 and 237–238). Interestingly, in 1700 Rami had copied Kâtib Çelebi's *Mizanü'l-hakk* (ibid., 28–29).

18 Ibn Haldun – Pirizade 2008. However, as Henning Sievert showed, it was primarily through Na'ima's adaptation, rather than Pirizade's translation, that Khaldunism permeated Ottoman thought during the eighteenth century: Sievert 2013, 179–180.

backdrop of the military difficulties and constant experimentation in military and financial politics described above. On the other hand, perhaps this experimentation and the repeated attempts to reform the army and the treasury had made old-style reform treatises obsolete (although there were still some authors who remained loyal to the "decline" paradigm, usually following Sunna-minded lines).[19] If we accept that the powers of the day, the bureaucracy and the janissary corps, were balanced for most of the eighteenth century, bureaucratic authors (as the majority of political writing continued to be produced in that milieu) would have had no reason to argue for a total reconfiguration of the administrative and economic structure of the empire: they merely had to proceed peacefully with their experiments.

Overall, it must be noted that by calling this trend "traditionalist" we are simply trying to distinguish them from another group of texts that will be studied in the next chapter, and which are marked by an urgent sense of the need to introduce European-style institutions and practices, usually pertaining to the army. It is important to note that the works classified here as "traditionalist" actually show (as will hopefully be seen in the rest of this chapter) a remarkable development, and thus are far from being mere imitations of sixteenth- or seventeenth-century "mirror for princes" literature. Not only are concrete measures proposed for the specific problems of the period, new concepts are also used, ones borrowed from contemporaneous Islamicate philosophy and theology, to discuss the new status of the Ottoman Empire vis-à-vis its neighbors and the possibility of restoring it to its former glory. In this respect, it is not surprising that those who may be called "Westernizing" ideologues were, in the last quarter of the eighteenth century, visibly engaged in a conversation with the "traditionalists" rather than in a blind confrontation (although ideological conflict was increasingly present); furthermore, occasionally a "traditionalist" thinker might advocate more "Europeanist" reforms when the sultan's government favored such a policy. For one thing, as seen in the previous chapter, Kâtib Çelebi's argument that every stage of society (or a state) requires different measures (and thus that the potential reformer should adopt a problem-oriented policy rather than revert to some idealized constitutions of the past) was very quickly integrated into works that otherwise belonged to totally different political traditions. The idea that the measures to be taken should be adapted to the needs of the age, just like a doctor adapts his medicine to the age of the patient, became increasingly employed from the late seventeenth century. In this respect, "traditionalist" thought was much less traditionalist than the label implies.

19 On such a case (Fazlızade Ali) see Kurz 2011; cf. also Yakubovych 2017.

One can see signs of this trend in many different texts, and not only political treatises. The courtier and historian Fındıklılı Silahdar Mehmed Ağa (1658–1726/27), for instance, described the reasons for the crushing defeat of the Ottoman campaign against Vienna, to which he was an eyewitness.[20] The first reason he gives is the presence of "numerous people of the *manav* kind, who had followed the army only for gain"; concerned about losing the wealth they had gained, they fled first and thus panicked the rest of the army. Silahdar suggests that the general should have inspected the army and put these idle and destitute people (*dirliksiz, bi-kâr herifleri*) away from the appointed army artisans (*defterlü orducu*).[21] Moreover (and here one may perhaps discern a Kadızadeli influence), the army did not keep the Islamic precepts and indulged in drinking and amusements, including adultery. Other reasons concern the use of trenches and provisioning the cavalry. In these remarks, Silahdar's effort to explain the defeat in military terms uses none of the well-known *topoi* about the intrusion of strangers into the janissary ranks or the need to inspect the sipahi lists; instead, he prefers to blame the non-military rabble that accompanied the army and various decisions mainly made by the campaign's hierarchy.

Silahdar's work is interesting in other ways, too: the nonchalant way in which he records successive discussions of the merits of each potential successor for the dying Sultan Süleyman II by high officials and ulema illustrates very well the declining political importance of the sultan as a person (although Silahdar was very close to Mustafa II, who seems to have tried to assume the role again).[22] He can also be credited with being perhaps the first Ottoman historian who openly justifies an army rebellion: speaking of the "plane-tree event" of 1656 and the execution of the harem aghas (see above, chapter 7), he remarks:[23]

> Sure, this incident, being an arbitrary intervention of the army against sultanly power (*tahakküm-i ale's-sultan yüzünden asker ikdam itdüği*), was an insolent act and thus contrary to correct manners (*tavr-ı edebden hâric olup*), and one cannot deny that one or two innocent men were lost without any reason. If we are going to see it with a just eye, however, this assembly (*tecemmü'*) certainly brought some profit to the Exalted State; indeed, the aghas of the imperial harem had obtained excessive power over the course of Mehmed IV's reign and thought that they could share the power with the sultan of the seven regions of the earth.

20 Silahdar – Refik 1928, 2:89–90; Silahdar – Türkal 2012, 882–884.
21 On the term *manav* cf. Sariyannis 2005, 4; on the *orducu* see Veinstein 1988.
22 Silahdar – Refik 1928, 2:567–69; Silahdar – Türkal 2012, 1355–1358.
23 Silahdar – Refik 1928, 1:33–34; Silahdar – Türkal 2012, 41.

Such an attitude toward revolt is also seen in other works of the period. Na'ima's discussion of the Edirne event, as seen in the previous chapter, appears rather distant; he places more blame on the *şeyhülislam* than on the rebels. Other descriptions of the same or other revolts also show a sort of benevolent attitude, for instance when an anonymous chronicler praises the discipline and order prevailing among the revolting crowd in 1703, or when Abdi Efendi vehemently blames the grand vizier and his entourage for the 1730 rebellion.[24]

2 Defterdar and His Circle

One of the major exponents of the "traditionalist" trend in the early eighteenth century was Bakkalzade Defterdar Sarı Mehmed Pasha (d. 1717). He started his career as an apprentice in the financial service of the palace (*ruznamçe-i evvel*) and gradually rose to serve as chief minister of finance, or *başdefterdar*, no less than seven times between 1703 and 1714. His first term began during the vizierate of Rami Mehmed Pasha and ended with the "Edirne event", during which time he was in Edirne, at Mustafa II's side. Afterwards, he was soon reinstated by Ahmed III. He also held other high bureaucratic and administrative posts; in 1716, he was appointed governor of Salonica, before being executed (because he was an opponent of the new grand vizier) in 1717. While he included some pieces of advice in his historical work, *Zübde-i vekayiât* ("The quintessence of events", which is extremely valuable for the history of the last quarter of the seventeenth century and the "Edirne event"),[25] his most important work from our perspective is his *Nesâ'ihü'l-vüzerâ ve'l-ümerâ veya Kitab-ı güldeste* ("Advice for viziers and statesmen, or a book containing a bouquet of flowers"), a fairly popular work (it is preserved in more than ten manuscripts, some in slightly different versions) that was probably completed between 1714 and 1717.[26] Some manuscripts contain two appendices (U155–165, W151–158), one on innovation (a very short recapitulation of *fikh* distinctions) and the other containing a detailed description of the timar system in the "administration manuals" genre (see chapter 5).

To a large extent, Defterdar's work may be called eclectic: he freely copied or adapted passages and ideas, mainly from Lütfi Pasha and Hezarfen, as well as moral treatises. His work may be seen as being a continuation of Hezarfen's

24 Özcan 2000, 230; Abdi – Unat 1999, 5–6, 26.

25 Defterdar – Özcan 1995.

26 Defterdar – Wright 1935 (Ottoman text and English translation); Defterdar – Uğural 1990 (transcription and modern Turkish translation). On this work see also Lewis 1962, 82; Yılmaz 2003a, 313–14; Aksan 1993, 55–56 (=Aksan 2004, 29–30); Defterdar – Özcan 1995, lxxxvii–lxxxix.

Telhisü'l-beyan since it combines copying traditional descriptions or rules with to-the-point advice on contemporaneous problems. However, Defterdar seems to have placed more emphasis on the second element, i.e. concrete answers to specific problems that he experienced during his administrative career. One should note the emphasis he placed on bribery and on the need for administrative and financial appointments to be made for long periods; if possible, for life. He often refers to older concepts, such as the circle of justice and the "old law". If his political allegiances are sought, it is tempting to see his attack on the 1670s–1690s financial policies (such as his indignation at the "Sharia-minded" abolition of price regulations by Fazıl Mustafa Pasha in 1691[27] and at the widespread farming-out of revenues) as an expression of a new team of policy-makers, one opposed to the Sunna-oriented policies (and discourse) of the Köprülü viziers. His criticism of Beyazizade Efendi (d. 1687), the Rumili *kazasker* whose actions appear to have been associated with Vani Efendi,[28] seems to corroborate this view. The fact that Defterdar was sympathetic to Mustafa II's autocratic policies is evident from his appointment as chief minister of finances one year before the sultan's downfall.

One may argue that his work represents the view of a particular group within the government apparatus. His work was largely imitated or, more probably, he had a circle of interlocutors who shared the same ideas and even copied each other. It seems that they were all part of the scribal bureaucracy, and this might account for both their similarity of interests and the common arguments they employed. After all, Defterdar and his circle were part of the new efendis-turned-pashas[29] environment: that is to say, they were following the scribal career just at the time it was beginning to allow access to the highest posts in the administration. Thus, the existence of a circle of like-minded bureaucrats associated with Mustafa II's policies is an interesting hypothesis that requires further research.

For one thing, a text of political and moral advice entitled *Ta'lîmâtnâme* ("Book of instructions") and attributed to Şehid Ali Pasha (d. 1716), the grand vizier (1713–16) who died during the campaign to reconquer Morea, is just a shortened version of Defterdar's *Nesâ'ihü'l-vüzerâ*; it is not impossible that the former text was also written by Defterdar himself, either as a sketch of

27 Defterdar – Özcan 1995, 387–389; cf. Sariyannis 2012, 289.

28 Defterdar – Özcan 1995, 123–124, 210. Cf. Sariyannis 2005–2006, 253; on Beyazizade's association with Vani, see Zilfi 1988, 202–204, 209. Defterdar's assessment of Vani's personality also seems rather negative, as he says that "he did not abstain from vilifying and slandering the state magnates" and that "he was a master of the science of attachment (*fenn-i intisab*)", i.e. a careerist: Defterdar – Özcan 1995, 210–211.

29 The category was dubbed thus by Itzkowitz 1962.

his more ambitious work or as a short memorandum to the young vizier, summarizing it.[30] More importantly, there is also a contemporary anonymous chronicle, the *Anonymous history 1688–1704*, written by a member of Rami Mehmed's entourage (as the author himself states).[31] In many ways the text is identical with Defterdar's *Zübde-i vekayiat*, due perhaps to both copying official reports. The same applies to the author's political advice on the occasion of Ali Pasha's removal (1692), in which there are recognizable reflections of Defterdar's *Nesâ'ihü'l-vüzerâ* (the author notes that his advice is based on many books in Arabic, Persian, and Turkish).[32]

Another author obviously very close to Defterdar, and who had a fairly similar career, was Nahifi Süleyman Efendi (1645?–1738). Son of a *va'iz* (preacher), he seems to have had a good education; he served in various posts in the scribal service (in a period that suggests he may have been a colleague of Defterdar) and was the scribe of Kavukçu Mehmed Pasha when the latter went to Iran as an imperial envoy in 1689. He also followed the second *defterdar*, İbrahim Ağa, during the peace negotiations of Passarowitz (1718). He retired in 1725, having also served as a second *defterdar* himself. He was the author of numerous poetic and literary works. What interests us here is his *Nasihatü'l-vüzerâ* ("Counsel for viziers"), probably completed after 1717, as the majority of the work seems to have been copied from Defterdar's *Nesâ'ihü'l-vüzerâ* and, in particular, its first part, i.e. on the office of grand vizier.[33] Indeed, in its largest part Nahifi's text is but a summary of Defterdar Mehmed Pasha's treatise, which in some cases he renders almost verbatim, although he usually excludes the moralist parts.[34]

2.1 *"Mirrors for Princes" Revisited*

All these authors give the impression of writing as if nothing had been produced in the field of political advice for over 60, or even 100, years. The only general vision of society given by the group can be found in Nahifi, who ends his essay, somewhat abruptly, with the usual description of human society

30 Özcan 1982.

31 Özcan 2000. In a later note, the chronicle is named "History of Sultan Süleyman [II]" (*Kitâb-i tevârih-i Sultan Süleyman*); however it also covers the reigns of Ahmed II and Mustafa II.

32 Özcan 2000, 37–39. Cf. Özcan 1982, 201; Sariyannis 2008a, 147–149; Tuşalp Atiyas 2013, 286–292 (cf. above, chapter 6).

33 Nahifi – İpşirli 1997. Cf. Yılmaz 2003a, 314.

34 Cf. for instance Nahifi – İpşirli 1997, 21 (on the virtues of the grand vizier), 23–24 (on the need for spies in the land, against bad innovations, and on the regulation of prices), 25–26 (on unregistered lands and on military affairs); Defterdar – Uğural 1990, 55–63, 29–31, 23, 101–121 respectively.

(I27) as being divided into four parts, according to their trade (*hirfet ve senayi' cihetinden*), each of which depends on every other. Without describing the fourth class (the soldiers), he concludes that none of these classes should have supremacy over the others.

Defterdar's essay in particular, the most complete and ambitious of the group (and probably the model for all the others), is a blend of political and ethical advice with no apparent logic in its structure, and lacks both the sociological and historical vision of Kâtib Çelebi or even Mustafa Ali and the moral philosophy of the soul as seen in Kınalızade and Celalzade. Among chapters of concrete advice on statecraft and warfare, one finds large sections on virtue, on the need to keep away from law courts and legal disputes (U47, W84), on pride and greed (U123–131, W133–136), and on the value of true friendship (U133–143, W137–141).[35] However, there is in fact less incoherence than a modern reader may suppose. For instance, the chapter on friendship follows one concerning (among others) the dangers of consultation (*meşveret*), thereby urging caution when selecting one's confidantes.

Thus, Defterdar's essay begins with a long section on the virtues of viziers (U9–53, W64–86; as does the *Anonymous history*, Ö37–39 and Nahifi), the absolute proxies of sultans (*vekil-i mutlak*). For the most part, these virtues are commonplace traditional advice (the vizier should not covet subjects' property,[36] must tell the sultan the truth, and so on). However, there are parts where one can discern Defterdar's long experience in financial administration, for instance concerning landholding. The timar system is the subject of the final chapter of the treatise (U145–153, W142–148), although here Defterdar seems more inclined to copy earlier and outdated advice than to use his own experience: he stresses, with regard to the distribution of timars, that "the ancient law must be respected" (U145, W143), complaining that timars are now granted to people whose name no-one knows and even to un-manumitted slaves, and remarks that a timar is of no use if it cannot produce able soldiers for campaigns. Significantly, as if he wished to underline that such advice concerns actualities long gone, he notes that inspections carried out in 1602/3 and in 1613/4 by Yemişçi Hasan Pasha and Nasuh Pasha had, even at that time, demonstrated

35 Defterdar notes that in his days very few high state officials can show genuine friendship and commitment, as he himself bitterly experienced during his terms as treasurer (U135, W138). Cf. Abou Hadj 1988, 21–22.

36 Defterdar here has an interesting formulation: the grand vizier should covet neither the private goods of the sultan nor the "public property" of the peasants and soldiers (U17, W69: *emval-ı hassa-ı padişah ve emval-ı amme-i re'aya ve sipah*). In the same vein, he stresses (copying almost verbatim the mid-seventeenth-century historian Kara Çelebi-zâde: Kara Çelebi-zâde – Kaya 2003, 218) that the imperial treasury should not be used for personal purposes (U73, W98–99). Cf. Sariyannis 2013, 103 and 114.

such distortions and malfunctions of the system, and that the situation had never been permanently corrected.

Similarly, he dwells on the question of fixed prices (*narh*). Partially copying Hüseyin Hezarfen's passage on *narh* (see above, chapter 5), he maintains that the grand vizier must not be content to assign that task to judges and *muhtesibs*: he must control prices in person, because it is a public matter (*umur-ı külliye*) and, as such, a matter of politics (or: of the administrative branch, *emr-i siyaset*), i.e. outside the competence of judges (U31).[37] In the same vein, Nahifi copies the same passage on fixed prices and remarks that handing over affairs to inappropriate people and tradesmen (I25: *ehl-i dekakin*) may cause great harm; allowing tradesmen and men of the market (*esnaf ve sukî*) into the line of service (*tarik*) is like allowing strangers into one's private apartments.

Taking up a subject popular in seventeenth-century political thinking, Defterdar speaks at length of bribery (U55–63, W87–93), which, unlike Kâtib Çelebi but similar to Koçi Bey and his circle, he sees mainly as connected with the buying of governmental posts (although he also criticizes bribes in judges' courts, noting that friendly gifts are acceptable only if nothing is asked in return: U61, W92). When a post is given to someone unworthy by bribery, it is as if he has been given permission to plunder the property of the *reaya*, as he is prone to extract from them the same amount of money that he gave in bribes to obtain his office. Bribery is the root of all evil in the state, Defterdar stresses; it inevitably leads to the ruin of agriculture and rural life, and of the income of the treasury. The solution he proposes is unique. On the one hand, provincial office-holders should be constantly checked by spies. On the other, however, it is not proper that a governor be removed due to one or two complaints (the same passage can be found in Nahifi); in the same vein, judges should stay in office for exactly as long as they were appointed. This emphasis on the duration of office-terms was inherited from the seventeenth century and was to be increasingly repeated in eighteenth-century texts. Similarly detailed is Defterdar's account of the treasury and the posts of the Imperial *divan*, a subject he knew very well (significantly, this chapter is almost entirely devoted to financial administration; U65–83, W94–109, and cf. Nahifi, I24). Here, again, the essence of his advice has to do with securing terms of long duration (U69, W96).

Defterdar's discussion of the *reaya* (U93–99, W116–120) is somewhat hasty and old-fashioned; significantly, earlier in his treatise he failed to even mention them when describing the "circle of justice" ("there is no state save with men of substance and no men of substance save with wealth": U9, W64), and he

37 Defterdar uses the same passage in his *Zübde-i vekayiat*, while criticizing Fazıl Mustafa Pasha's attempted *narh* reform of 1691 (Defterdar – Özcan 1995, 388).

appears to understand justice more as equal treatment (the vizier "must treat all and everyone in an equal way": U11, W66) rather than as protection of the peasants. He does, however, stress that any new taxes should not be imposed on peasants, as excessive taxation is like taking earth from the foundations of a house in order to build its roof. Nahifi is slightly more interested in the fate of peasants: he suggests that special salaried agents should report regularly on the affairs of the provinces, informing the vizier which places have been ruined because of excessive taxation or oppression, and that harsh measures should be taken against highway robbers, among others. According to Nahifi, special attention must be paid to "bad innovations" (I23: *muhdesat-ı zulmiye ve bid'at-ı seyyi'e*), i.e. illegal taxes and dues imposed on the peasants without being recorded in the registers. Defterdar, on the other hand, devotes much more of his chapter on the need to keep peasants in their place. Faithfully copying Lütfi Pasha, he stresses that peasant families should not be allowed to follow when one peasant is granted a timar or when he starts to follow a career in the ulema. Whenever a peasant flees from his land in order to escape oppression, the governor of the area to which he has fled should send him back and resettle him there according to the old law (U97, W119: *kanun-ı kadim üzre*).

What seems to radically differentiate Defterdar's advice from earlier "mirrors for princes" (bringing him closer to Kâtib Çelebi and Na'ima) is his attitude towards the janissaries. He states, as does practically every other author, that the janissary army must be small in size but always ready for battle. He uses his own personal experience to describe how bonuses were paid in 1703 (U79, W103–104); what is striking here is that he writes nothing about decreasing the numbers or salaries of the janissaries. Instead, money should be found to pay them their current salary. Moreover, in his chapter devoted to the janissary corps (U85–91, W110–115), which he considers the most important issue for the empire, he proceeds to give similarly cautious advice. Obviously bearing in mind the recent 1703 revolt (but also reflecting older advice, e.g. that of Kâtib Çelebi), Defterdar hastens to note that reforms in this matter should be made slowly and in close consultation with the officer corps. As did many previous theorists, Defterdar also notes the intrusion of many strangers into the janissary ranks (U87, W112); as such the pay-rolls must be checked, though such should be done in close collaboration with the corps' officers. The same caution against harsh interference should, perhaps, be seen in Nahifi's advice to the grand vizier not to investigate the concealed faults of the people (I19: *halkın uyub-ı hafiyyesin teftîş eylemeyeler*; however, this advice, strongly reminiscent of Kâtib Çelebi, is not found in Defterdar). Finally, in Defterdar's long and detailed discussion of military practicalities (U101–121, W121–132; Nahifi has an almost identical discussion) that inaugurated a long tradition that was to last for more than a century, the same caution can be seen: among other practical advice regarding the manning of fortresses, the preparation of campaigns, and the paying of garrisons, Defterdar maintains that a field marshal (*serasker*) should always consult with experienced people; this consultation (*meşveret*), however, must not be made with just anyone but only with trustworthy and well-meaning men, although (U115, W129)

> it sometimes happens that from an ignorant child or from a woman of imperfect understanding there comes forth a correct opinion or a wise answer that brings about good results.

As remarked earlier, the lengthy discourse on friendship that follows must be seen as a supplement to this advice on consultation.

•••

There are two points on which Defterdar and his circle differ significantly from their predecessors, although neither is stated openly: one must read between the lines to understand where these authors depart from simply reiterating advice that was either commonplace or too concrete. One such point, as already noted, is the changed attitude towards the janissaries. The corps is, of course, still described as having surpassed both the allotted numbers (and expenses) and the required discipline; there is practically no political text from the late sixteenth century onwards that does not contain such remarks. However, whereas earlier authors had suggested taking harsh measures against the janissaries, either by the sheer application of force or by cunning use of divisions within the military (as in the case of Aziz Efendi, for instance), Defterdar urges caution, slow action, and consultation with janissary officers:

> If reform be desired, there must be appointed a trustworthy and upright and devout and circumspect person from among the experienced and practical men who are managers of the corps ... But in this matter [the expulsion of intruders from the corps] also there is need, after counsel has been taken with the ministers of the government and well-wishers of the sultanate, after consultation and covenanted agreement with the spokesmen of the corps' officers, that imperial orders on behalf of the sultan be issued and carried out in accordance with their trustworthy opinion. If there be agreement of hearts, it is to be hoped that this also (with the help and aid of the Creator), will be slowly and deliberately accomplished. On the other hand, it is impossible to put an end to these

> conditions by action from outside the corps. Absolutely without question it can come about only through the trustworthiness and uprightness of the persons mentioned above ... But in this affair consultation and deliberateness are extremely essential. The corps in question is impatient both of being too much troubled and oppressed and of being treated with boundless kindness (U87–91, W113–115).

While Defterdar had seen with his own eyes what angry janissaries could do since he was present at the 1703 rebellion, as he writes more than a decade later, it is more probable that such caution and circumspection was more related to an acknowledgment of the newly-established reality: he was aware that the janissaries had, by then, their say in palace and government politics and that this situation was legitimate enough to be taken into account in political discourse as well as in practice.[38]

We postulated that Defterdar was sympathetic to Mustafa II's absolutism but that he preferred to suggest a sort of sharing of power with the very rebels who overthrew the sultan. The key to understanding this apparent contradiction appears to be the second point in which he differs from earlier advice, and this is his emphasis on the need for longevity in appointments. Although such a demand was a recurring issue in many seventeenth-century treatises,[39] in these early eighteenth-century works it forms a key theme: governors and governor-generals should keep their posts for life, judges should stick to their appointed term durations, and *defterdar*s and their clerks should feel secure in their posts. One may see a reflection of the bitterness our authors appear to have experienced as regards their careers: having complained that there is no longer any friendship in this world, Defterdar asserts that high offices are like hot baths, as those who enter want to leave them and those who leave want to enter (U49, W85; an almost contemporaneous echo of such thoughts can be seen in Nabi's *Hayriyye*). Similarly, Nahifi notes bitterly that there is no end to the villainies of this time, and gives several morality-based reasons. However, personal experiences aside, the emphasis on long terms in bureaucratic posts may be seen as a plea to link continuation of policies with continuation of personnel. The financial and tax reforms clearly followed the same lines as those of the last decades of the seventeenth and the beginning of the eighteenth century, despite viziers and other administrators continuously changing. Defterdar's shifting allegiances, therefore, conceal his belonging to a scribal tradition that was experiencing an extraordinary continuity along policy lines. It was only natural that they should also advocate stability in their directing

38 Cf. Tezcan 2010a, 224–225.

39 Terzioğlu 2010, 270–271, 307; Sariyannis 2013, 105–106, fn. 91.

posts, obviously combined with enhanced self-reproduction: after all, this was the era of efendis-turned-pashas, such as Rami Mehmed and Defterdar himself. We might perhaps see the same self-confidence displayed in the distrust of pashas' households found in the *Anonymous history*, when the author urges viziers not to make distinctions between their men and strangers in their house (Ö37).

Thus, there was a group of administrators and writers at the beginning of the eighteenth century who preferred to move away from the more theoretical and philosophical style of the post-Kâtib Çelebi Ottoman literature and to make very specific proposals out of their experiences instead. As will be seen in both this and the following chapter, such a focus on the concrete and the actual was to become a standard feature of eighteenth-century political advice, unprecedented from the time of the early seventeenth-century "declinists". As this feature was much more intense on the "traditionalist" side (Resmi Efendi of the "Westernizers" being a notable exception), one may say that they saw themselves as continuing the "Golden Age" theorists even if they hardly refer to a "Golden Age". It will become clear in the next chapter that the "Westernizing" side, on the contrary, based itself much more on Kâtib Çelebi's and Na'ima's paradigm. At any rate, the significant presence of detailed administrative advice in this group of texts reflects the increased role of the financial and other scribal bureaucracy in forming Ottoman policies from the late seventeenth century.

3 The Last of the Traditionalists

As has been remarked, while the time from the end of the "Tulip Period" to the Russo-Ottoman war in the late 1760s saw many attempts at reform, political literature remained rather neglected. On the other hand, it should be noted that the work of non-political essayists on quite specific administrative problems remains unstudied. A good example is the *defterdar* Atıf Mustafa Efendi (d. 1742) and his treatise on the *sıvış* years, i.e. the problems emanating from the discrepancy between solar and lunar years. In this work, Atıf Mustafa Efendi boldly proposes that payments should also be made according to the solar calendar, and characteristically bases his proposal on a number of Quranic quotations, ranging from the people's need for salaries to the legitimacy of the solar calendar.[40] The self-confidence that educated Ottomans seem to have

40 Âtıf Efendi – Gemici 2009; on the *sıvış* crises cf. Sahillioğlu 1968 and 1970. Efforts to make a compromise between the two systems, in order to ease this problem, had begun in 1710 (Sahillioğlu 1970, 246–247); cf. Küçük 2017, 8–11.

felt during this period is clearly illustrated by an episode in Nu'man Efendi's (d. after 1755) autobiographical work *Tedbîrât-i pesendîde* ("Agreeable measures"). A well-educated member of the ulema, he participated in the talks establishing the Austrian-Ottoman border following the Treaty of Belgrade (1739) and describes with pride how easily he understood (using an English telescope) and emulated the function of a surveying instrument, which the Austrians had just learnt and were keeping secret.[41]

It was noted above that the decades between the 1730 revolt and the 1768–74 war were marked by an internal peace of sorts, a kind of armistice between the central government, which pursued experiments in administration and finance, and the janissary army, which enjoyed its share in power since nobody interfered in its workings and since its own right to interfere in politics was *de facto* legitimized. The same years formed one of the rare periods in Ottoman history in which military action did not seem too urgent: after some wars against Russia and Austria in the 1730s, which were more successful than not, and especially after the peace with Persia in 1746, no campaign was waged and it might appear that the Ottomans were confident that they would be perfectly capable of winning the war against Russia when it finally erupted in 1768. However, the devastating results of that war appear to have created a renewed sense of urgency for reform; at least this is what the number and character of political tracts composed after it ended suggest.[42] The "Westernizing" authors aside (as they will be studied in the next chapter), this second outburst of eighteenth-century political thought was, in fact, the swansong of "traditionalist" reform. It should be stressed once more that this term does not imply that the treatises to be examined advocate any return to the "old law", as did early seventeenth-century authors (although they often used this term in an effort to couch their proposals in the traditional language of their predecessors); rather, in a similar manner to Defterdar and Nahifi, these works are formed of compilations of older pieces of advice that their authors deemed appropriate, combining "traditional" (i.e. older views on society and state) with a keen eye for specific measures. On the other hand, from among

41 Nu'man Efendi – Savaş 1999, 66–68, 89–90; Nu'man Efendi – Prokosch 1972, 40–50, 86–94; Kurz 2011, 197–199. The instrument in question could have been Jonathan Sisson's 1725 theodolite with telescopic sights, as it was supposed to have been invented by "a wise English monk" twenty-five years before (Nu'man Efendi – Savaş 1999, 84; Nu'man Efendi – Prokosch 1972, 80). According to Prokosch (ibid., 215–216, fn. 40 and 42), the surveying method used by the Austrians was invented by Johann Praetorius in the early seventeenth century and improved by Johann Jacob Marinoni in the early eighteenth century, and was not kept secret (the maps, on the contrary, were).

42 On the perception of this change cf. Menchinger 2017, 5–6 and 28–30.

the authors to be studied here, Dürri Mehmed Efendi may be described as a follower of Na'ima's vision for peace as a prerequisite for reform. As for Canikli Ali Pasha and Süleyman Penah Efendi, they both begin with a specific military situation of a provincial nature, which they describe in detail, before then trying to make the best of their own experiences and (in the case of Penah Efendi) their readings. Interestingly, they both place significant emphasis on non-military matters, from the economy to town-planning, in sharp contrast to the "Westernizers", who preferred to focus on army reforms. Penah Efendi even looks to the Spanish experience in the Americas for policy models, in another example of the blurred borders between "traditionalist" and "Westernizing" authors.

Dürri Mehmed Efendi was born around 1734 in Kayseri. In 1751 he entered the chancellery bureaucracy and served in various positions, and in 1774 he was in the retinue of Abdülkerim Efendi, who had been sent to Bucharest to negotiate the peace with Russia. He participated in another peace delegation in 1790–91, when he was sent, together with the *reisülküttab* Abdullah Birri Efendi, to a meeting between the envoys of Prussia, England, and the Netherlands to negotiate another peace with Austria. Dürri's career reached its zenith in 1794, when he was appointed *reisülküttab*, only to die the same year. His *Nuhbetü'l-emel fî tenkîhi'l-fesâdi ve'l-halel* ("Selected wishes for the emendation of mischief and disorder") was composed in early 1774 and is preserved in only one copy; interestingly, the same manuscript also contains various embassy reports (including the famous report of Ebubekir Ratıb Efendi; see below, chapter 9), Humbaracı Ahmed Pasha (Comte de Bonneval)'s treatise (see below, chapter 9), and even the translation of a letter by Louis XVI to the French National Assembly.[43] The very composition of the collection, therefore, highlights the blurred line between "traditionalist" and "Westernizing" authors. In Dürri's treatise, as will be seen, references to the "old law" sit alongside a critique of the tax-farming system and the emphasis on reordering the army that is typical of the eighteenth century.

Not all political treatises of the period were composed by bureaucrats. An outstanding example of an active *ayan* who was deeply involved in both war and politics and who also cared to record his views on the contemporary problems of the Ottoman Empire was Canikli Ali Pasha (1720/1–85). He was born in

43 Istanbul, Topkapı Sarayı Kütüphanesi, E.H. 1438, ff. 281b–296a. For a description of the manuscript (which, however, omits an account of Azmi's embassy, following Dürri's treatise) see Karatay 1961, 1:311 (no. 966). Atik 1998 gives a detailed synopsis of the text (with several mistakes in the identification of the manuscript, based on a faulty reading of Karatay's entry). On the treatise, cf. Menchinger 2014a, 124–126; Menchinger 2017, 85, 88–89.

Istanbul to a father who was an imperial *kapıcıbaşı*. He succeeded his brother as *derebey* of Canik (the province of Samsun in the Black Sea) and participated in the Russo-Ottoman war of 1768–74; during these years, he extended his dominions west to Trabzon, Sivas, and Erzurum. In 1778 his enmity with the neighboring *derebey* family of the Çapanoğulları cost him his office and his rank; he fled to the Crimea until he was reinstated in 1781. Canikli wrote *Tedâbîrü'l-gazavât* ("The expedients of war", which was also copied under the titles *Tedbîr-i nadir, tedbîr-i cedîd-i nadir, Canikli Ali Paşa'nın risalesi*, and *Nesayihü'l-mülûk*) in 1776, during his participation in campaigns in Iraq and the Crimea.[44] He begins by explaining how he came to write the treatise, in the context of his continuous efforts to improve the army and the welfare of his subjects, as a response to the short war waged by Zand Karim Khan, the new Persian ruler, against Baghdad, which necessitated "new measures". Composed in a rather awkward style, which implies an author more used to action than writing, Canikli's treatise is reminiscent of Defterdar and his copyists, as it essentially is a "mirror for princes" adjusted for the specific issues of its day. One should note the same emphasis on consultation, which would be increasingly marked throughout the rest of the century, the same suggestion for life-long appointments, and a similarly moralistic view on the virtues required of a vizier.

Finally, the work of Süleyman Penah Efendi constitutes one of the most original specimens of "traditionalist" political advice of the eighteenth century. In sharp contrast, and although it has been known since the early 1940s, modern scholarship had neglected it almost completely until recently. Like Canikli Ali Pasha, Penah Efendi was also connected to the provinces, although in a different way. The son of Ismail Efendi of Tripolitsa (the capital of Ottoman Peloponnese/Morea), he was born in Istanbul in 1740 and entered the scribal service, initially in the service of the grand vizier Küçük Mustafa Pasha. He worked as a scribe in various governmental branches and was present at the 1770 revolt in Morea. He died in Istanbul in 1785, the same year that he wrote his treatise variously known as *Süleyman Penah Efendi mecmuası* ("Süleyman Penah Efendi's manuscript"), *Mora ihtilâli tarihi*, or *Mora ihtilali tarihçesi* ("History of the upheavals in Morea").[45] As demonstrated by its title, the first third of Süleyman Penah Efendi's text is a narrative of the 1770 revolt in the

44 Canikli Ali Paşa – Özkaya 1969 (transcription pp. 135–173). On Canikli and his treatise cf. Cvetkova 1975; Schaendlinger 1992, 250–252; Aksan 2011; Menchinger 2017, 85–86.

45 The only edition of this work is Penah Efendi – Berker 1942–1943 (there is also a Greek translation and study: Penah Efendi – Sarris 1993). See also Cezar 1986, 142–145; Telci 1999; Sabev 2006, 313; Ermiş 2014, 122ff., esp. 126–128 and 140–144. For the part related to the Peloponnese cf. Alexander 1985, 47–49, 117; Gündoğdu 2012, 25–27, discovered an anonymous narrative of the 1770 revolt, which seems to have common sources with (or whose

Morea. After initially describing in detail the events of this revolt, to which he was an eyewitness, he continues his treatise on the "ordering of the countries" (*nizam-ı ekâlim*, B157).

The originality of both the thematic axes and the views themselves in Penah Efendi's work is striking; his emphasis on the economy (rather than finances) and town-planning, particularly, is almost unique in Ottoman literature. Although his treatise, just like that of Canikli, is written in a somewhat provincial style (his efforts to write in high-flown prose often renders his text obscure), Penah had clearly done his reading and profited from it. The use of books printed by Müteferrika's press is especially noteworthy (and reflected in Penah's high opinion of this press): apart from Na'ima's work, he must have read *Tarih-i Hind-i Garbî el-müsemmâ bi-hadîs-i nev* ("History of the West Indias as heard from new information", also known as *Kitâb-ı cedîd-i iklîm*), whence he must have drawn his knowledge of Spanish policies in the Americas.[46]

In contrast to his underestimation by modern scholarship, Penah Efendi's work was not as isolated as it may seem to have been. For one thing, many of his views, such as the beginning of military reform in the provinces for fear of the janissaries, were suggested by other late eighteenth-century reformers, as will be seen in the following chapter. Penah Efendi's son, incidentally, was Yusuf Agâh Efendi (d. 1824), a close collaborator of Selim III and the first permanent Ottoman ambassador to London (1793–96). Furthermore, reflections of some of Penah Efendi's ideas, such as the encouragement of local manufacture in the face of imports of European and Indian garments and the revival of İbrahim Müteferrika's printing press, can perhaps be seen in the reforms implemented during the vizierate of Halil Hamid Pasha (1782–85), who, however, was executed in the same year that Penah Efendi's treatise was completed and the author himself died. As he was *şehir emini* of Istanbul in roughly the same period during which Halil Hamid Pasha was *kethüda* to the grand vizier (1781) and then grand vizier himself, we cannot exclude the possibility that the two men knew each other and had, perhaps, discussed these measures.

3.1 *Traditional Forms, Reformist Content*

The first remark that may be made concerning this group of authors is that Kâtib Çelebi's and Na'ima's Khaldunist ideas had, by then, become standard reading for the Ottoman literati, mainly through the printing of their works

writer was aware of) Penah's report but which "is not that interested in advising the authorities about saving the empire".

46 This was one of the first books published by Müteferrika's press (1730): Sabev 2006, 192–196.

by Müteferrika's press. Dürri's introductory analysis of human society and historical laws is as telling as it is, in several ways, original. His concept of what constitutes society shows the influence of Kâtib Çelebi's biological similes, for example when he speaks of "what is like the four elements (*anasır-ı erba'a*), namely the viziers, the soldiers, the peasants, and the sultan's treasury" (282b). In his introduction (283a–286a), Dürri notes that the Ottomans had constant military success for over 250 years; however, it is a necessity of the divine wisdom that, just like the human individual (*efrad-ı nev'-i beşer*) has three ages, of growth, stagnation, and physical decline (*nümuv, vukuf, inhitat*), so do states (*devletler*) as well. The Ottoman state has reached the age of maturity or stagnation, but because it is the greatest of its peers in magnitude, wealth, and power, the experts in history did not discern the signs that it was entering this age and thus failed to give the appropriate counsel. The Ottoman state passed through the "three ages" (*kurun-ı selase*) in A.H. 950 (1543/44), 980 (1572/73), and 1000 (1591/92); these ages, being the "age of growth" (*senn-i nümuv*), were full of wars and victories. Afterwards, however, came the "age of stagnation" (*senn-i vukuf*), when people want peace and welfare rather than war and glory. This explains why, from then on, Ottoman wars ended in both victories and defeats. Continuous warfare brought severe damage to the treasury and the army, although wise officials kept seeing the problem and explaining it to the grand viziers, who occasionally managed to take some measures. When the war with Russia started, it wrought great damage on the peasants, the army, and the treasury; thus, peace was concluded in order for the state to have the time and ease to mend its shortcomings (*tedabir-i nizam*).

One may detect some confusion in this account of the stages, as the "three ages" soon became only a preface to the "age of stagnation" and, presumably, the final threat of the "age of decline". In a period when, as will be seen in the following chapter, another aspect of Khaldunist philosophy (namely, the distinction between settled and nomadic life) was becoming increasingly popular, Dürri combined the simile of human ageing and the "three ages" (stressed by Kâtib Çelebi) with the more elaborate model of the "five stages" (expounded by Na'ima), mainly to emphasize the need for peace in order to reform the state (again just like Na'ima, but also in the same vein as a whole series of works written during and after the Ottoman-Russian war). Indeed, Dürri later repeats his plea for peace (294b–296a), copying faithfully the relevant part of Na'ima's history: he maintains that if the measures he proposes are taken, Russia will eventually stop coveting Muslim territory, and especially the Crimea. For this, however, there must be absolutely no war in the near future. If, "as is the natural custom of states" (295a: *adet-i teba'i-i düvel üzre*), Russia or some other neighbor again shows greediness for a region, the Ottomans should not wage war unless they have been preparing for at least five years; if they are not ready, they should feign friendship and even capitulate to some of the enemy's demands. Dürri even copies Na'ima's use of Salah al-Din's example in order to advocate peace through an appeal to the glorious past of Islamic history.

While Canikli's treatise, which is much more in Defterdar's tradition, exhibits no sociological theory whatsoever, Penah Efendi also shows himself a fervent Khaldunist. He begins his essay with a detailed chapter on the "military class" (B157), and in this such influences are evident. In the beginnings of a state or dynasty, he says, the soldiers obey and display solidarity and unanimity when plundering the enemy and dividing the shares of the conquered land; officials and statesmen tend to ignore their failings. This is a feature of that period, however; when the state proceeds to the stage of consolidation (*kemal ve kudret*), the soldiers begin to pursue ease, comfort, and luxury; moreover, the inhabitants of the various towns and villages develop their own various manners and character, with the result that controlling them becomes difficult. When wise counselors perceive that, consequently, the state will be dispersed, they divide the population under their dominion into various classes or groups that have to obey certain rules, and in times of need they have to leave aside other important affairs and occupy themselves with the urgent matter in hand. However, order can only be obtained through calm, rational action, rather than by the use of measures such as execution, exile, or confiscation. Ideally, it will happen in such a smooth and natural way that the common people (*avam-ı nas*) will not understand how it was imposed, whereas, notes Penah Efendi, those who naively try to impose order in certain matters, while clearly showing their intentions from the start, succeeded only in making themselves the target of criticism.

The purpose of Penah's account of the historical stages is to advocate reform of the military class, rather than to advocate peace; and in this he resembles more Kâtib Çelebi than Na'ima. After a state surpasses the age of growth, he maintains, it becomes difficult to rule and control in just one way (*bir renk üzere*) its soldiers and the general population (*askeri taifesi ve ol devletin kavmı*). Men of understanding divide the army into several classes, so as to have one class supervise and check another. But as a prerequisite, the king alone can have the power to expel and transfer undisciplined soldiers; if this power is granted to his ministers (*vükela*), within a few years all discipline and respect will be lost once more. This is what happened with the janissaries, who lost their discipline. Here, Penah Efendi quotes Na'ima (B159) on the three ages of the state and the similarities with the human body. Like all Ottoman Khaldunists, however, he notes that, unlike people, states that obey their laws and adjust themselves to the changes that occur in the world (*dünya tarz-ı ahar oldukça esbabiyle hâkimâne hareket olunsa*) may avoid decline and fall. A state is like a man who has an income of 40 purses; if he is disciplined, he will prosper right up until his death, but if is not, he will die in poverty and misery.

The contrast with the previous authors, from Defterdar's circle, who hardly put forth any vision of society, is evident. What they share is an indifference to the *kanun* v. Sharia conflict, or even for the concept of the "old law" as a binding constitution. It seems that such discussions had become irrelevant as the claim for specific reforms was now universal (although, as will be seen in chapter 9, the debate on "innovation" would gain a new visibility at the end of the century). Dürri, more conservative among this group in several aspects, attributes the glory of the Ottoman state to its having followed the Sharia (283a) and claims that all revenues should be collected along Sharia lines (286a), while he also stresses that measures concerning the janissaries should be taken "according to the old law" and more particularly to Süleyman's regulations (the "old law" is mentioned in other places as well, usually in relation to matters military). In the same vein, Canikli seeks to ensure that everybody acts according to the law, holy or sultanly (*gerek şer'i ve gerek kanuni*; Ö143); similarly, he praises Süleyman I, the "master of laws" (*kanun sahibi*), for he always acted according to the Sharia and *kanun* (*şer'an ve kanunen*), and maintains that it is advisable for the sultan to respect them (*şer'e ve kanuna tatbik ideler*; Ö151–152; cf. Ö161). Nonetheless, and despite their general conservatism, neither Dürri nor Canikli seem to be have preoccupied with such old debates, save for a sort of stagnation in their political vocabulary. As for Penah Efendi, he does not mention the "old law" or *kanun* at all.

Coming now to the central and provincial administration, the emphasis on long terms of office continues: Canikli repeats almost verbatim Defterdar's advice that commanders should not be removed for minor matters (Ö146) and even argues that officers such as *defterdar* and the kapudan pasha should be appointed for life. Furthermore, the sultan must give the vizieral rank to worthy people regardless of their previous situation, having checked their background and behavior (especially their knowledge of the situation of the peasants and their ability in war) when they come from "outside" (*taşradan*; Ö154). In general, as far as the rank of vizier is concerned, people originating in the palace (*ocaklu*) must be given preference to those coming from outside, while people should be promoted along a single career line: for instance, an agha of the janissaries should not become vizier (Ö156). The same distrust of provincial backgrounds can be seen in Penah Efendi's excursus on the scribal bureaucracy (B400–474), on whose selection and training under the *reisülküttab* he places great importance; because, he adds, no matter what position they are given in the bureaucracy, provincial people (*taşra halkı*)[47] will still behave with jealousy and enmity as they did in their villages, remaining ignoramuses and thus useless for government.

In discussing provincial administration, the rise of the *ayan*s is clearly reflected in these texts. Canikli, a major *ayan* himself, remarks that judges take the *ayan* and the inspectors' (*mübaşir*) side against the *reaya*, describing the tricks used by the *ayan* of Rumili to hoard and profit from the task of collecting supplies for the army. If oppressive *ayan*s were executed or exiled to Cyprus every year, he concludes, the poor peasants would be saved from their hands (Ö148). Of course, this could be a concession to traditional *topoi* in order to present Canikli as being more impartial and unbiased than he really was; on the other hand, it is interesting to note that he accuses the Balkan notables specifically, while he was from among the Anatolian. As for Penah Efendi, he ignores his hostility to the custom of lifelong tax-farming or *malikâne* when he talks about Egypt, since he proposes dividing it into various *malikâne*s so that its landlords would not have too much power (B390–391). Besides, in a chapter on the Christian notables or *kocabaşı*s (B396–97), he accuses them of injustice and proposes that they be appointed for one year each.

As may be expected given the pre-history of political texts and the situation current in their era, authors writing after the 1770s concentrate on the problems of the army. Following Defterdar's tradition, much space is devoted to the practical problems of campaign and logistics: Canikli, for instance, dwells at length on the subject of *mübaaya*, or state purchase of army supplies (Ö146–150). Elaborate instructions for the proper purchase of army supplies focus on the need for the personal involvement of central government officials, without local intermediaries. Furthermore, Canikli gives detailed instructions for the order of an army while on campaign, the arrangement of camps, the order of battle, and so on, stressing that, nowadays, wars are based on artillery rather than sword-fighting (Ö169).

As well as such conventional, down-to-earth type of advice, the traditional criticism of the janissaries and the disruption of army regulations takes a distinctively new form. All authors agree that the excessive numbers of men enlisted in the payrolls do not correspond to actual power on the battlefield. In Dürri's words, the salaries of the soldiers (as well as the stipends of the reciters of prayers, *du'a-guyân*) had surpassed any moderate level (*hadd-ı i'tidal*) and they should be brought back under control order. First and foremost, they

47 This term could be translated as "people outside the palace", but from the context it is clear that what is meant are people from the provinces.

should only be given to those properly entitled. Dürri describes at length the selling and buying of payrolls (286b–289b); janissary officers should thus inspect the payrolls and remove the names of anyone who does not take part in campaigns (291b). Similarly, the provincial armies (*eyalet askerleri*) need to be restored to their old order. Dürri remarks that, around A.H. 1110 (1698/99), these troops were very orderly: according to "the old law", whenever a fief became vacant it was given to a soldier, on condition that he stayed in the province; strangers were not given fiefs. As long as this order was kept, there was no need for irregular troops (*levendât*) for 30 or 40 years (294a–294b). Similar advice is given by Canikli, who maintains that everybody, from petty traders (*bakkal ve çakkal*) to infidel *reaya,* had been enlisted in the army in exchange for bribes, and nobody actually goes on campaign. The reason for all these shortcomings was, it is claimed, the intrusion of inappropriate people, servants of the households of the great statesmen, and ulema (Ö162) into the ranks of the army. Canikli proposes strict interrogation of the officers by the sultan so that all intruders, of peasant or urban origin, would be excluded from the military.[48] More practically, Penah Efendi (after noting that peasants who want to be free of the interference of local officials enroll in the janissary ranks, making them no longer an army created by the will of the sultan, but one created by its own will: B158) stipulates that janissaries must be given roll titles (*esame*), in which are explicitly written their names, characteristics, and post. To this effect, janissaries must be registered anew and should stay in their defined post until their death, unless the needs of the state dictate they be transferred. When this new order (*nizam-ı cedid*; B228) prevails in the provincial garrisons, it will be easier to impose in Istanbul as well; Penah Efendi even gives a template for the imperial decree that would ordain the expulsion of any undisciplined or disobedient janissaries.

So far, such advice does not differ greatly from earlier attempts to curb the numbers of salaried soldiers. There are, however, a few new points that may be attributed to contact with European armies and which are common to all three authors. One such point is the idea of imposing uniforms of sorts on the army. In Dürri's treatise, this idea resembles similar older suggestions (for instance,

48 As if he wanted to lessen the harshness of these measures, following in the tracks of Defterdar's cautiousness, Canikli emphasizes the importance of consultation (*meşveret*), primarily for matters related to war (Ö158). He notes that in matters of war it is the ulema and the high-standing state officials (*rical-ı devlet*) who now give their opinion, rather than the military officers, whereas in the olden days the officials and viziers were asked about the order and protection of the imperial lands, the military about matters related to war, and the ulema about whether the advice given by the other two classes was compatible with the law (*şer'e ve kanuna mutabık*; Ö161).

in the sixteenth-century *Kitâbu mesâlih*; see chapter 4) that emphasize the notion of *hadd*, limits separating the different classes or estates of people. Thus, he proposes the use of various uniforms (*tenvi'-i libas*) in order to distinguish janissaries and other soldiers from peasants and artisans (288a, 291b). Yet this suggestion goes further than merely emphasising social markers and takes a Khaldunist characteristic once more. Dürri complains that scribes and other officials buy luxury goods in foreign coinage, often surpassing their income in so doing. Since the statesmen (*rical ve ümera ve vüzera*) are the unifying agent of the state (292b: *devlet-i aliyyenin asabiyeti*), this situation is to the detriment of state since, in time of war, they all have no money and are therefore unable to contribute to victory. Instead, Dürri argues, everyone should dress and spend according to their place (*haddine göre*), and this re-ordering (*tanzim*) of lifestyle should be imposed on all classes by imperial order. If it is imposed effectively in times of peace (*hazarda*), soldiers and statesmen will also be free of foolish expenditure in times of war as well, and thus will only think of matters related to war (292a–294a). In Penah Efendi, however, the suggestion of uniforms is much more clearly reminiscent of Westernizing attempts; not only does he claim that janissaries of the same group or rank should be dressed in similar uniforms and that every officer rank should have its own color (B229); he explains clearly that, to impose order, the Christian armies use what is called a "regiment" (*regmend*), which means that 1,000 soldiers or more go on military exercises in which real battles are imitated and they are made perfect in discipline and order (B158). Army rules must be printed and published in booklets (which Europeans call *fuyte* [*feuilleton*]) so as to be known to everyone (B232).[49]

What is really striking, however, is the attitude of these authors vis-à-vis the timariot cavalry. Despite being disrupted and marginalized long ago, their protection was still a *topos* of political advice; the reader may remember how Defterdar respectfully repeated obviously outdated information and rules about the timar system. More than half a century later, it appears that the abolition of the system had ceased to be the centuries-old taboo it had once been. As such, Dürri remarks that the term "taxable peasant" should be restricted to non-Muslims (*memalik-i mahrusede ra'iyyet nutkı hemen ehl-i zimmete hısr olunmak*) since the taxes of any given district are extracted from them alone; consequently, they become impoverished and destitute. The reason is that, in the provinces, every single Muslim has a claim to a fief; whenever a tax is demanded, they all claim to be janissaries or sipahis. Dürri stresses that the state should thus take action to reduce the number of fiefs (290b–291a). Much

49 Regular training, a three-year proving period and obligatory service at the borders "according to the old law" are also among Dürri's proposals (291b–292a).

more radically, Penah Efendi declares that the timar system should be abolished and a salaried cavalry should take the place of timariot sipahis; thus, the income from the timars would be profitable for the state and the cavalry would increase in number four-fold. Since this is impossible, however, Penah Efendi proposes several measures to administer the timars and maintain order and discipline in the sipahi army in the same vein as that of the janissaries; his main *leitmotif* is that the timariots must stay in their fiefs and care for the land (B233–35). A similar radical departure from the respected principles of the "old law" can be seen in his chapter on the *tapu* or title deed, or rather the practice of granting to farmers only possession and usufruct of state lands (B397–400). Penah starts boldly with the assertion that "this is another reason why the world cannot prosper". The *tapu* landholding system means that "the land, whose first cultivator was Adam, cannot be inherited"; this gives rise to tax farmers, destroying the "landholders" (*eshâb-ı arazî*; this term usually means the timariot, but here Penah Efendi seems to have the peasant-farmer in mind). All income from the treasury comes from the "landholder"-farmer, he notes; artisans and the people in general are at ease only with the landholder's well-being. Penah Efendi claims that he has seen personally several instances in which a notable or officer has seized the land of some girls after the death of their mothers, since *tapu* land cannot be inherited through female lineage. The Exalted State should thus abolish the *tapu* system and proclaim all arable land to be private property (*sahiplerine temellük buyurub*), just like gardens or vineyards, so that it can be inherited. Moreover, villages that have been seized as *çiftlik*s by local notables must again become independent, and if a villager dies without any heirs then his plot should be given to the whole population of his village (*karye veya çiftlik ahalilerine cümlesine virile*).

Penah Efendi's proposal to abolish the timar system and privatize the arable plots is outstandingly radical and more than half a century ahead of its time (given that private ownership of arable land, after a long process during the 1840s, was only established with the Land Law of 1858;[50] on the other hand, it should be noted that such proposals were indeed implemented in the late seventeenth century, as seen in chapter 6). However, if we take into account Dürri's distrust of fiefs, we may discern a realistic change of views in authors coming from the bureaucracy (as both of them do). Indeed, the timar system was hardly even mentioned in texts written after 1774.

In sharp contrast, Canikli adopts a fully supportive stance vis-à-vis the timariot sipahis: he laments their situation, observing that the sipahis had been forced to sell their horses out of financial need and obliged to serve in the

50 İnalcık 1955, 225–227; İnalcık 1973, 32–33; Hanioğlu 2008, 89–90.

retinue of magnates and viziers. Likewise, his advice is also quite traditional: the sultan should inspect the registers of the timar villages and the lists of provincial sipahis. Furthermore, these timars should be revived: the sipahis must be ordered to move there with their families and provide the peasants with oxen and seed. If they are not able to take part in campaigns they should give their timars to others. As for those officers and magnates who hold timar revenues without being entitled to them, they must be executed (Ö166–167). The suggestion of reviving the timar system is something quite exceptional for this period, and may stem from Canikli's provincial origins.

Finally, all these authors have the usual cry against oppression of the peasants (e.g. Dürri, 286a–286b; Penah, B312–314, 317, 391–393), combined with reports of specific injustices (such as the use of messengers: Dürri, 289b–290a). Whereas, in their denunciation of the timar system, Dürri and Penah Efendi were in accordance with their times, their analysis of taxation is rather old-fashioned in an era characterized by growing privatization of assets, as they all criticize the tax-farming system. Dürri remarks that the tax burden of the peasants (including *mukata'a*s, fiefs, and the poll-tax) increases every year because of tax-farming. The three-year leasing system leaves the peasants destitute and drives them out of their villages to towns and cities, where they become servants or idlers. Yet he does not advocate the abolition of tax farming, preferring to suggest the abolition of extraordinary taxes instead (290a–290b). Canikli's discussion of taxation is located within a peculiar section dealing with Istanbul (Ö170–173). Because of the continuous campaigns, the presence of robbers, and the greed of state officials, he maintains, peasants from the provinces have fled in huge numbers to the capital. Istanbul has grown to such a degree that it needs feeding from all four of its mouths, namely the Aegean Sea, the Black Sea, Anatolia, and Rumeli; as the transport of goods by both land and sea is difficult during the winter, profiteering merchants raise prices, while the inhabitants gather in barber-shops and coffeehouses.[51] Since viziers and other palace officials devote their time only to the affairs of the capital and ignore the provinces, the latter have decayed. As a result, everybody comes to Istanbul, thinking that life there is easy, with the side-effect that the peasants who remain in their *avariz-hane* (tax units) have to pay much more in taxes than they should; all the more so since the poll-tax is farmed out as a lump sum. This vicious circle results in more and more infidel peasants flowing into Istanbul. They find salaries and stipends from the custom-house or the

51 Migration to Istanbul indeed seems to have reached unprecedented levels during the eighteenth century, and control of it was considered a major problem by the time of Selim III's reign: Faroqhi 1998; Başaran 2014; Başaran – Kırlı 2015, 261–263.

janissaries, and thus further weaken the treasury. Moreover, with such a large population it is difficult to discern the good from the bad, which leads to the appointment of indecent people to various ranks and posts.

Canikli's attack on Istanbul, or rather his view of the relationship of the capital with the provinces as unbalanced, is extraordinary; perhaps his provincial origins, as in the case of the defense of the timariot system, should be taken into account. He proceeds by remarking that Istanbul is said to have 80,000 quarters, each having 100 to 500 houses; if each household was to give one *kuruş* for the needs of the army in times of campaign the treasury would be filled. Canikli seems persuaded that the inhabitants of the capital would not feel burdened by such a measure since they are all well-to-do: the magnates have practically given an appointment to everybody, as every one of them has assumed the role of protector of a quarter, and thus they do nothing but build nice houses and pass their time in coffeehouses. "I say that Istanbul is the place of the rich", he concludes. But if the sultan takes care of the provinces, the treasury will prosper and Istanbul will be less crowded. As for provincial taxation, Canikli suggests that offices such as the *voyvoda* or the tax-farmer should not be given to unknown persons but to individuals who have profound knowledge of a province and of its peasants; if this is not the case, there are various ways for such officers to fall prey to infidel usurers (Ö159–160). It is tempting here to think that, when Canikli advocates tax-farming to people who know the land, he clearly has the *ayan* like himself in mind.

As for Penah Efendi's view of taxation and the economy, it deserves special attention as it contains highly original suggestions for issues such as town planning, which are generally absent in earlier Ottoman texts. Of course, he also speaks against excessive taxation and more particularly tax-farming, especially *malikâne*s and the case of poll-tax and extraordinary levies, which he thinks should be administered by the central government (B317–387). Like Canikli, he also views the internal migration of peasants to an overpopulated Istanbul as a problem. The answer he proposes is two-fold. First, the borders of the quarters of greater Istanbul must be defined carefully and the building of houses outside them strictly controlled and, secondly, whenever a quarter is burnt new houses should be built under rules ensuring large gardens and therefore low density (B230). Penah Efendi states that immigration will thereby decrease and the underpopulated provinces will flourish again. To achieve this aim he has further advice: new towns should be founded with the promise of tax immunities (or, small towns should be upgraded administratively); such towns would, in turn, prosper and increase the state revenues with their manufacturing production (B231). More specifically, he proposes the founding of such new towns near Edirne, in Lepanto, and in Missolonghi. Furthermore, he has specific ideas for the development of certain places such as Gümülcüne (Komotini), Tekirdağ, and Montenegro, stressing the need for the creation of new administrative units (B393–96). Undercultivated areas, like those in the Danube that were being randomly used by Vlachs should be registered and granted to local peasants, as well as to new peasants from either Albania and other poor lands or Poland (attracted through spies). New cultivations should also be encouraged, according to the example of the French, who founded coffee plantations in America. In the same vein, the production of local goods should be encouraged: Kütahya, claims Penah Efendi, can produce far better pottery than Austria, and thus the money that now goes to Austria (to buy pottery) would stay in Ottoman lands (B398–400).

Penah Efendi's originality does not end with his town-planning proposals. Inaugurating a fashion of intense preoccupation with the economy and trade (in contrast, Canikli considers explicitly financial problems secondary, arguing that usually they are only a pretext to avoid action)[52] that was to emphasize the need to increase local production, he explains that most European countries bring goods to the Ottoman Empire and take money in exchange, but also leave this money or at least half of it there since they also buy local goods. Some other countries, however, only export goods to Ottoman lands, with the result that they take Ottoman money back to their home; such goods include furs (implying that one such country is Russia). The import of furs and expensive cloths should thus be strictly controlled and their use restricted to high officials; the same goes for silk clothing from India. Local production of exotic goods, says again Penah Efendi, should be encouraged: coffee could be planted in Egypt, Basra, or Palestine (just as the French did in America); headgear could be made from cotton produced in Rumeli and the Morea; shawls now imported from Tunis could be produced locally, and so on. In general, not only should the local production of currently imported goods be encouraged but the use of expensive imported clothing should also be prohibited (B474–76). In his next chapter (B476–79), Penah Efendi further elaborates on this argument. He explains that in the case of imported silk and cotton clothes the damage is restricted to the buyers, who give their money; however, in the case of the production of gold and silver thread and embroidery, the damage is general. Such production leads to a shortage of silver coinage since the gold and silver

52 He states that whenever an officer receives an order, his answer is invariably that there is no money, but this is only a pretext so that he can avoid doing the task. Mustafa III tried to win the 1768 war with money, to no avail, while all the conquests of old had been achieved because of valor and zeal rather than money (Ö160). If the sultan looks after his subjects, disciplines the army, and consults with the right people, he will have no need of the treasury.

used annually for such products is more than that produced from mines. The production of golden thread should be prohibited, and artisans making golden embroidery should make normal decorated clothes instead.[53] This leads Penah Efendi to another issue, that of coinage: he asserts that either the current value of the Ottoman golden coin, i.e. *zer-i mahbub*, should be increased or its gold content decreased, so that its value would not correspond to its content in gold (the same goes for silver coinage). In such circumstances, Ottoman coins would not be taken abroad. Furthemore, nobody would melt them down to make gold or silver thread or jewelry. If these measures are taken, and if the exchange rates for foreign gold coins are defined and controlled, he writes, then the Indian and Yemeni merchants will not be able to profit and those valuable metals will stay in Ottoman lands. Penah Efendi ends this chapter by repeating his loathing of foreign goods, and specifically Indian clothes and Saxon pottery, as well as of those who use them for sheer pomp.

Most of Penah Efendi's observations are explicitly given in connection with the author's bitter experience of the 1770 Morea revolt, and it is in this light that his next chapter, on the "properties of the Albanians" (B239–312), should be read.[54] He describes them as unruly and undisciplined plunderers who know nothing of trade and the arts, due to their dense population and the barrenness of their land. Nonetheless, he acknowledges that they also have some merits, such as their hospitality and their high sense of honor. Penah Efendi proposes the creation of orderly camps and local garrisons, well-ordered and registered, in the Albanian territories. Perhaps more interesting are his views on cultural assimilation: the Albanian language is rough (as seen, he argues, from a comparison between Greek-speaking and Albanian-speaking villages in the Morea) and when it comes to courtesy (*nevaziş*) its vocabulary is harsh and coarse. But if they learn Turkish, there will inevitably be a subsequent change in their behavior (*tebdil-i ahlak*) since "the good manners of a tribe depend on its learning the language of its dynasty" (*bir kavm terbiyesi bir devletin tekellüm itdiği lisanı tekellüme muhtacdır*) (B309).

If the sultan issues such orders and some esteemed ulema and sheikhs go to teach them, it would be only a few years before they finally speak Turkish instead of Albanian. Penah Efendi's inspiration comes from an unexpected model: when Spain conquered "New India", he explains, its inhabitants were even wilder than the Albanians. The Spanish brought Indian women to their

53 One may remember here Mustafa Ali and his suggestion that the use of gold thread is wasteful for the precious metal, since it yields no profit. See Ali – Tietze 1979–1982, 2:41–42.

54 Cf. Anastasopoulos 2007, 44–45.

country and had them married to Spanish men; their children, who spoke both languages, were sent back to America and served as interpreters, with the result that the natives soon forgot their own language and now speak only Spanish. Similarly, Russia takes youths (*uşak*) from the Aegean islands and the Morea to Moscow, where they are educated in order to prepare disorder and rebellion. So must the Ottoman state bring Albanian youngsters to Istanbul, and educate and train them in camps outside the city's walls, giving them food and teachers; conversely, artisans from various Balkan towns should be transferred to Albanian towns for three years in order to show the natives how to produce tissues and other products. Obviously, Penah Efendi was conscious that his unusual proposals would sound rather strange; thus, he embarks on an excursus on the effectiveness of decisive imperial orders, giving again as an example the West Indian tribes and their awe on seeing the Spanish cavalry, having never seen a horse before.

• • •

At first glance, there is no significant difference between these post-1774 authors and the early eighteenth-century ones. Canikli's emphasis on distinct career lines resembles Defterdar and his circle; Dürri and Penah Efendi's Khaldunism is a continuation of Kâtib Çelebi and Na'ima, and their ideas on military uniforms do not really deserve the title of innovation in political thought. More interesting is the abandonment of the timar system, which nevertheless is but a synchronization with the realities of their times. In fact, Dürri and Canikli belong more to the seventeenth century than to their own, since the former was a rather conservative member of the bureaucracy and the latter represents a view from the provinces (and an extraordinary case of an *ayan* and a pasha authoring a political treatise). In a way, Canikli's style of concrete advice, one adapted to contemporaneous realities (a style originating in the typically Ottoman "mirrors for princes" genre), shows the survival of a tradition flexible enough to change its content without altering either form or the general world-view based on Ottoman exceptionalism and patrimonial patterns of sovereignty. It is perhaps not coincidental that Canikli belonged to the provincial *ayan*-turned-pashas elite: significantly, a short essay with very similar priorities and structure, *Risâle-i terceme* ("Essay of explanation"), also appears to have been composed by an author familiar with Anatolia and perhaps based in the Danubian provinces.[55] A relatively late specimen of the genre, as it must have been written in the late 1780s or the 1790s, this text could

55 Orhonlu 1967.

also have been written much earlier, with the exception of its criticism of the *ayan* and notables, which are never seen in earlier treatises.

What is really striking is Penah Efendi's case: his preoccupation with economy and commerce, his general vision for Ottoman lands, and his bold recommendation of European tactics all constitute an impressive introduction to the political discourse that was to dominate the final decades of the eighteenth and the whole of the nineteenth century. On the other hand, his emphasis on everyday issues at "street level", such as town-planning with regard to measures against fires and various issues pertaining to poor peasants, bring to mind a slightly earlier chronicler, Mehmed Hâkim Efendi (d. 1770), who has been described as a "*mahalle* historian" with a "street-level line of vision".[56] Even more characteristic is Penah Efendi's stress on the benefits of culture and education. Like Müteferrika before him (as will be seen in the next chapter), Penah Efendi also speaks extensively of the benefits of geographical knowledge: a cheap edition of a printed universal geography, he says, should be made available to all subjects, rich and poor; more generally, there will only be benefit from the founding of more printing houses (B473–474). In addition, short notices at the end of Penah's treatise advocate the detailed popularization of imperial orders and the creation of medreses, libraries, and mosques in the provincial towns rather than in Istanbul (B479). As for his proposals for the Albanians' cultural assimilation, they are one of the most original ideas to be found in Ottoman political literature, as is his inspiration from the Spanish model for the exploitation of the Americas.

A comparison with the "Westernizing" tracts to be studied in the following chapter would show the gap between them and Penah Efendi: he never advocates the wholesale adaptation of the European military model, and in many ways his treatise can be considered a continuation of the paths opened by Kâtib Çelebi and Na'ima. Yet his reference to Western military tactics, his looking to Spain for policy models, and his dismissal of the classical timar and landholding systems show that this gap is not as radical as it may seem. After all, the reference to the organization of Christian armies with "regiments" (*regmend*) must have come (as seen in the next chapter) from İbrahim Müteferrika's own treatise, which is a clear example of the "Westernizing" trend.[57]

Unfortunately, current knowledge of the dynamics inside the imperial elites of the eighteenth century is not adequate to permit the location of these

56 Zilfi 1999.

57 On the other hand, Penah's reference to *fuyte* (*feuilleton*) or booklets containing the army rules is not found in Müteferrika's work and thus must be attributed either to his own experience or another source.

authors inside policy lobbies or social groups. It appears, at any rate, that during the first three quarters of the century there was no intense ideological conflict within the elite: the debates concerning the "old law" and innovation, as well as those concerning Sunna-based policies, seem to have given way to a smooth general consensus, at least as far as it concerned the balance between shareholders in power, and to a rather abstract acknowledgment of Kâtib Çelebi's motto that different times require different measures. In the next chapter, it will be seen that proposals for a fully-fledged imitation of European, i.e. infidel, military science and organization were current by the 1730s or so; however, the authors examined did not seem to feel as if they had to answer to such reasoning. It seems that ideological conflict was resumed from the mid-1780s, as Halil Hamid Pasha's efforts to impose clearly Westernizing reforms must have caused internal strife in the Ottoman government. A few decades later, the janissary system would also feel the threat of such policies and would begin to be more vocal in public discourse.

4 Traditional Reformers: Rivers in Confluence

As has already been stressed, the gap between the "traditionalist" views and the actual "Westernizing" reforms of the later part of the eighteenth century was much narrower than it might seem. Penah Efendi's work is a typical example, showing the mindset of an Ottoman reformer who would not stand for the wholesale adoption of European military rules but nor would he restrict himself to a "revival of the old laws". In other examples, the same person could move from "traditionalist" to more "Westernizing" viewpoints over the course of his lifetime. An important factor in such a shift was state agency: since they concerned military organization, Westernizing reforms could not be initiated quasi-independently by the governmental bureaucracy, as was the case with reforms and experiments in landholding or taxation. There were many more interests at stake: because of the prominent place of the janissary army—or, should we perhaps say, the janissary system—as a stakeholder in the political arena, such attempts touched directly upon the problem of power and thus could only be initiated by the state; that is to say, by a strong vizier, such as Halil Hamid Pasha, or by a resolute sultan, such as Selim III. Thus, the interplay between absolutism and "constitutionalism" would emerge once more, this time in more complex forms as the different sides borrowed freely arguments for a common inventory, one which had been formulated earlier and for a different context. The remainder of this chapter and the next will be devoted to this interplay.

4.1 *On the Eve of Nizam-i Cedid: Vasıf, Ratıb Efendi, Abdullah Halim*

Ahmed Vasıf Efendi (c. 1730–1806) was born in Baghdad and, after working in several private libraries of local magnates, served as secretary to the *serasker* Abaza Mehmed Pasha. He was captured by the Russians in 1771 during the Hotin campaign. After his liberation he entered the state bureaucracy (1772) and played a role in various diplomatic endeavors, including the negotiations for the peace of Küçük Kaynarca. Upon his return to Istanbul he directed the revival of Müteferrika's printing press under Halil Hamid Pasha's auspices, and in 1783 he was appointed *vakanüvis* or official historian (and again in 1789–91, 1793–94, and 1799–1805), before serving in various posts, one of which was ambassador to Spain in 1787–88. In 1805, shortly before his death, he became *reisülküttab*.[58] Apart from poetry, geography, and various minor works, Vasıf's main written work is his court chronicle, *Mehâsinü'l-âsâr ve hakâikü'l-ahbâr* ("The charms and truths of relics and annals"). He also wrote an account of his embassy to Spain (*Sefâretnâme*); most probably, as will be seen in the next chapter, he may have been the author of the strongly pro-reform *Koca Sekbanbaşı risalesi*, which was composed just before his death. In an earlier age, however, Vasıf was much less tolerant of imitation of European ways. As a historian, he criticized Şahin Giray's efforts to recruit new Muslim troops in the Crimea and to impose "Frankish" uniforms on them.[59] In another instance, Vasıf's political views were expressed in his *Risâle* ("Essay"), which was incorporated into his chronicle.[60] As stated there, in 1784 the Duke of Montmorency-Luxembourg sent a letter to Abdülhamid I in which he suggested that Ottoman defeats were due to their inadequate training in the science of war; he thus offered his help to instruct the Ottomans in the latest techniques in fortification and artillery as a token of French friendship. The sultan asked Vasıf to write an essay on these issues based on his experiences with the infidels.

In language steeped in religious imagery, Vasıf argues that infidel kings have indeed found an easy way to procure what they consider to be greatly beneficial: in their countries they have a special place where they collect orphans and illegitimate children and train them in the modern science of war (*fenn-i harbi vaz'-ı cedid*); the same is done with some of their peasant subjects (*reaya*),

58 Ethan L. Menchinger's unpublished thesis, developed now in a very recent book, is an excellent intellectual biography: Menchinger 2014a; Menchinger 2017. See also Vasıf – İlgürel 1978, xix-xlvii.

59 Şakul 2014a, 661.

60 Vasıf – İlgürel 1978, 150–152. See Mardin 1969b, 28–30; Menchinger 2014a, 71–80; Menchinger 2014b; Menchinger 2017, 96–98.

whom they recruit as if they were their slaves[61] and force them to serve as soldiers (*tahte'l-kahr*). In contrast, in Muslim countries it is impossible to compel people to become soldiers, although their zeal for Holy War makes them willing and efficient; even if they are defeated occasionally, they would never submit to having their enemies teaching them the military arts.

Thus, Vasıf maintains that even in his time the Ottoman army was naturally superior to the European ones. How, then, can the continuous victories of the infidels be explained? The answer he gives to this question is that the occasional victories of the infidels are a result of satanic hosts granting them temporary success (*müzavele-i şeytaniyye mülabesesiyle hasıl olan kuvvet-i istidrac*). This temporary success (*istidrac*), in fact a divine stratagem to lure the infidels onto the road to perdition,[62] cannot last long and is not durable. Moreover, the weapons of the infidels are no different from those already known: their eventual defeat is certain.

Vasıf then proceeds to provide a subtle theological distinction to support his argument. Victory and defeat depend upon God's will, although the Christians believe the opposite. More particularly, the infidels think that war belongs to the category of particular events (*umur-ı cüziyye*) with which—according to them—God has no connection (*medhali olmayup*). Thus, they claim that victory belongs to whoever is better prepared for combat (*tedarük-i esbab-ı münaveşe*), here meaning in terms of weapons, strategies, provisions, etc. To reject this claim, Vasıf gives examples from Ottoman history in which inadequate preparations of the Ottomans did not prevent them from beating the infidels. On the other hand, he writes, the Ottomans must strive to achieve these ends and, Vasıf says, this is now happening (presumably through the reforms initiated by Halil Hamid Pasha, his patron). Hence, these means will undoubtedly be perfected, as the grand vizier has been entrusted by the sultan with the task of preparing what is needed for the army, multiplying the number of soldiers, and reducing state expenses. On the contrary, the French proposals are not to be trusted, since there can be no trusting Christian countries. For instance, when asked where this proposed training would take place the French ambassador suggested Crete, so it is obvious that France wishes to gain a foothold on the island for its own reasons.

61 Significantly, Vasıf uses the same verb that was used for the collection of boys for the janissary corps: *abd-ı müşteraları gibi … devşirüp*.

62 Redhouse's dictionary defines *istidrac* as follows: "God's inciting a sinner to perdition little by little by granting success at the beginning of his sin"; cf. Menchinger 2014b, 147: "a theological concept whereby God gives unbelievers success, making them prideful, in order to lure them to damnation and test believers' fidelity".

This perception of "particular events" versus "universal" ones (*umur-ı külliye*) was in line with a major philosophical debate which was taking place in the eighteenth-century Ottoman intellectual world;[63] the reader may remember Hezarfen's use (copied by Defterdar and Nahifi) of the same terms (*cüz'iyyât*, *umur-ı külliye*) but with completely different meanings, as matters (e.g. the regulation of prices) that may or may not be the responsibility of the government (the sultan or his viziers) or of the judge. Far from being fatalistic,[64] Vasıf's conception of causality is in fact a call for reform, albeit with traditionalist overtones: his ideas for reform were influenced by his mentor, Halil Hamid Pasha, and thus can be said to belong to the same climate as those of Penah Efendi. In his later works, Vasıf further developed his analysis of "particular events", increasingly stressing the need for the Ottomans to secure the logistical and military strategies that are required for victory, while he continued to use the concept of the "temporary success [of their enemies]" or *istidrac* to explain their defeats at the hands of the Russians. If the secondary (or "particular") causes are secured, then God will help and eventually bring victory to the Muslim armies. However, a disobedient and undisciplined army that ignores these factors, i.e. careful preparations for war, cannot match the Russian and Austrian soldiers with their organization and scientific training. In describing the principles of political society, on the other hand, Vasıf uses the more traditional model of the *felsefe* authors, such as Kınalızade.[65]

A very similar attitude can be found in the early ideas of another personality closely associated with Selim III and his reforms, namely Ebubekir Ratıb Efendi (1750–99). Ratıb Efendi's career bears numerous similarities with Vasıf's: the son of a provincial ulema, he was trained in Istanbul by Âmedci Edhem Efendi and served in the financial bureaucracy. He became teacher of calligraphy to Prince Selim (III), in which capacity he assisted the prince in his correspondence with Louis XVI (see also below, chapter 9). Following the death of his mentor Edhem Efendi, Ratıb Efendi became affiliated with Halil

63 See the detailed discussion by Ethan L. Menchinger (Menchinger 2014a, 64–110; Menchinger 2014b; Menchinger 2017, 55–58, 74–75), and cf. Yakubovych 2017, 162–164. In this analysis, Vasıf sometimes follows Kâtib Çelebi verbatim; see Menchinger 2014b, 149 and 159, fn. 68. In some respects, this discussion shares common ground with the development of the argumentation theory (*ars disputandi*) during the eighteenth century: Ottoman logicians argued that the aim of argumentation "is to grasp the knowledge of particulars (*juz'*) even though the subject-matter of argumentation itself is universal (*kulli*)" (Karabela 2010, 208; cf. El-Rouayheb 2015, 217–219). On the use of the same terms in legal theory (where the distinction is of universal principles vs. particulars) see Hallaq 2002, 166–167.

64 This is how Vasıf's views are described in Mardin 1969b, 28–30; cf. Berkes 1964, 65–66.

65 Menchinger 2014a, 173ff.

Hamid Pasha, as did Vasıf, and he became *âmedci* in 1779. After Selim's rise to the throne (1789) he was sent as an ambassador to Vienna for about six months in 1792, and upon his return he resumed his career, becoming *reisülküttâb* in 1795. The next year, in the aftermath of the French invasion of Egypt (and apparently due to his enemies' defamation of him), he was dismissed, exiled, and finally executed in 1799.

Ratıb Efendi's most famous work is his account of Vienna, the most voluminous of all Ottoman ambassadorial accounts by that time, with which we are going to deal in the next chapter. But while this account may be read as a suggestion for European-style reform, an early letter of his to the future sultan, his charge Prince Selim, bears many similarities with Penah Efendi's and Vasıf Efendi's views.[66] The letter was written in 1787 in the context of Selim's correspondence with the king of France; it is in fact a copy of Louis XVI's answer, explained and commented on by Ratıb Efendi. He cleverly suggests (presenting it as an interpretation of the French king's words) that the Ottoman sultan can achieve no conquests and victories without the level of control of the janissaries, ulema, viziers, and other officials that his predecessors used to have; Selim should first impose such order and control within his realm before embarking on any campaigns. This should be done by renewing the old laws, but in accordance with the nature of his own time (Y260–1: *kavanin-i kadime bu asrın mizac ü tabiatına tatbik ile tecdid*). The young sultan should first imitate the European order and make an army and navy similar to those of the European states. Here Ratıb Efendi admits the danger of rebellion, since the people may start calling the sultan "a worshipper of Europe" (Y264: *Frenk-perest*); as such, the sultan should first make the commoners (*avam-ı nas*) trust him. Indeed, it is very important that the sultan is loved by both commoners and the elite (Y269: *gerek avam-ı nas ve gerek hasü'l-has*).

Ratıb Efendi straightforwardly presents two possible solutions: either the army should be given European training and order, or it should be reformed along the lines of the Ottomans' glorious ancestors. He openly admits that he is a scribe, not a military man, and thus cannot give an answer. One passage could be interpreted as meaning that he favored the latter path (he suggests to Selim that he should tell Louis that, for some time now, the Ottoman soldiers have been used to comfort and ease, and that strangers have entered their ranks, while a lack of discipline and worthiness has also contaminated the ulema and officials: Y267); like Vasıf, he also seems quite skeptical about the possibility of a dispatch of French officers to train the Ottoman army (Y269–70).

66 Ratıb Efendi – Yıldız 2013 (transcription pp. 259–271). On Ratıb Efendi see Karal 1960; Uzunçarşılı 1975; Yeşil 2011a and 2014.

Ratıb Efendi stresses that Ottomans had assisted France in the past; France is again rather weak, especially financially, and French kings lie when they claim friendship with the Ottomans since they usually act in accord with Austria and Russia. More generally, no European state is to be trusted, and Ratıb Efendi presents several examples of European treachery against the Ottoman Empire. Thus, Ratıb Efendi urges Selim to refuse both requests (Y271).[67]

Moreover, Ratıb Efendi goes into some depth on financial matters. He remarks that every state has its own laws (Y263: *her devletin bir kanunu, bir kaide ve töresi vardır*) and cannot be compared with any other, and he argues that Ottoman state expenses are constantly paid in arrears (*tedahül*). A wise doctor, i.e. a grand vizier such as Koca Mehmed Ragıb Pasha (whose efforts were mentioned at the beginning of this chapter), can manage to reverse this process and create surpluses only if he is appointed for life. Now, he writes, the Ottoman state has no debt and does not need raw materials such as iron or meat from other states; moreover, its religion gives it an advantage, due to zeal for Holy War. Ratıb Efendi's downplaying of the financial problems here is strongly reminiscent of Canikli Ali Pasha's similar views. Significantly, both Vasıf and Ratıb Efendi oppose "Westernizing" proposals without denying the absolute power of the sultan (or his delegate, the grand vizier), although Vasıf's praise of Ottoman soldiers who "cannot be compelled" might be seen as a concession to janissary power.

It is interesting that one of the most "traditional" treatises of this period also comes from a scholar closely associated with some of the most fervent supporters of Selim III. Abdullah Halim Efendi was born in 1742/43 to a father who was a *müderris* and imam. He had a good *ulema* education and served as imam, secretary, and steward (*kethüda*) under various officers, including the *şeyhülislam* Arabzâde Atâ Efendi, several close collaborators of Selim III, such as the *defterdar* Mehmed Şerif Efendi and Mustafa Reşid Efendi (*kethüda* of the grand vizier), and finally İzzet Mehmed Pasha (later grand vizier, in 1794), whose *kethüda* he had been for four years. In 1791 he composed *Seyfü'l-izzet ila hazreti sahibi'd-devlet* ("The sword of glory [or: Izzet's sword] for his excellency the lord of the state") upon his patron's request.[68]

The main part of this work is almost wholly a traditional *adab* essay, drawing heavily on *hadith*s and Islamic jurisprudence (including Dede Cöngi's *al-Siyâsa al-shar'iya*) and reminiscent of sixteenth-century literature. Halim answers the complaints of his patron regarding the difficulties of the vizierate, stressing that governing with justice is one of the most commendable acts,

---

67 On the international context of these remarks see the analysis in Ratıb Efendi – Yıldız 2013, 239–243.

68 Halim Efendi – Şahin 2009.

accuses greedy tax-collectors, and blames bribery for losing so much land to the Russians, enumerates the advantages of forgiveness, piety, and abstinence for rulers and viziers, and so on. Between such traditional advice, Halim interpolates pieces on extra-canonical authority (*siyaset*) as a branch of the Sharia (§118–123, 132–154) and on the duty for Holy War or *cihad* (§127–131).

Halim's views of the army and war are typical of his stance between tradition and modernity. He defends the occasional use of archery in battle with the reasoning that all weapons are useful and that a bow can sometimes be more fitting than a cannon (§131), which may be an indirect criticism of Westernizing military reforms, and maintains that soldiers should not occupy themselves with agriculture or commerce (§164), describing the four-fold division of society as found in earlier writings. Yet although he does not speak of uniforms, he does suggest that each group of soldiers is given its own symbols so that they can be discerned from one another (§159). As for his division of the army into three groups (§156: those paid from the tax of the infidels and the booty, *mal-ı harâc u ganâyimden*; the ordered army or *asâkir-i mürettibe*, paid by the public treasury and more particularly from the section for canonical alms or *sadaka*; and the volunteers), it sounds like a modernizing concession with a concealed reference to the now bygone timariot army (paid for by the infidels' taxes).

By far the most interesting part of the treatise, however, is its epilogue (§175–243). It is structured in the form of a dialogue that appears to present all the different views of the Ottoman crisis prevailing in the 1780s: Halim imagines that in the year of the composition of his work, due to the loss of the Crimea and other territories to Russia, the population of Istanbul was divided into twelve groups, each of which elected its most distinguished and experienced member to voice their opinion. This meeting is described in some detail, and in lively (often humorous) direct speech, with the interlocutors having names such as Zerdeçâv ("turmeric") Çelebi or Yumurtacı ("egg-seller") Receb. These speakers lament the large-scale intrusion of ignorant Turkish peasants into the cities, which has led to a general decline in the quality of statesmen and scribes. The ulema and bureaucrats have neglected knowledge because of their rush for wealth and material gain. Meanwhile, morals have deteriorated (in contrast with the "nice custom of Moscovy", where a chief keeps in order every ten persons, another every hundred and so on; although this view is vehemently attacked by the chief of the meeting: §195 and 197), judges oppress peasants, the soldiers are not paid on time, and the viziers are too many in number and prone to luxury.[69] The chief of the meeting, Hidayet ("right path") Çelebi,

69 One participant even suggests killing the infidels of Istanbul (§204: *İslambol'un re'ayası*), since they are becoming increasingly numerous and pay much less in tax than the Muslim peasants.

accuses every speaker of hypocrisy, as they all blame each other and ignore their own sins; when he is reminded of the glorious sultans of old (and especially Selim I), he answers that the people of old also avoided luxury and pomp, esteemed knowledge, and were displeased whenever peace was concluded with the infidel. If such things change, the Ottoman state may replenish "as is written in the conclusion of Ibn Khaldun's *Muqaddima*" (§192–193). Finally, after refuting the Sufi who was present in terms that resemble Birgivi's accusations (cult of the saints, dancing: §217ff.),[70] Hidayet Çelebi argues once more that the state would be restored if everyone reverts to the ancient zeal and piety, before finally revealing his identity as the author of the treatise (§241). Thus, Abdullah Halim Efendi ends his work by launching traditional attacks on corruption, ignorance, and moral decay (smokers and divinators are again among the main targets), while at the same time defending the sultan and his viziers, as he places final responsibility on the conscience of all Muslims. It is interesting to observe his use of the old dictum that things change from time to time not to advocate innovation but instead to show the difference between the zealous Muslims of old and corrupt contemporaries.

•••

In the works of all the authors examined above (and perhaps most of all in Abdullah Halim Efendi's), one may discern a shift toward a more individualistic interpretation of history. In the words of Virginia Aksan,[71]

> By pointing to the efficacy of rationalizing warfare, [Ottoman bureaucrats] were suggesting that the outcome of war could be influenced by man, though divine intervention remained the deciding factor. The ideology of the "ever-victorious-frontier" and "the circle of equity" was slowly being replaced with that of service to *din-ü-devlet* on the part of each individual ... [A]rguments in the Ottoman-Islamic context for the legitimacy of peace amongst equals, fixed and defensible boundaries, and European style discipline and training, by calling on one's duty to *din-ü-devlet*, may have been persuasive and could explain in part the apparent willingness of some of the ulema to accept fundamental changes to the traditional order.

70 In this vein the author rejects Kâtib Çelebi on the grounds that "he is not one of the older ulema, of the best of the posterior ones, or even of those given priority" (§221: *ulemâ-i mukaddimînden, fühûl-ı muteahhirînden ve ashâb-ı tercîhden hiç birinden değildir*).

71 Aksan 1993, 63–64 (=Aksan 2004, 43–44); cf. Şakul 2005, 120.

It is noteworthy that the emphasis on service to *din-ü-devlet* was to be repeated in the preambles to the first laws of Selim III, inaugurating the *Nizam-i Cedid* reforms (although one may remark that this could just be a legitimizing argument rather than a new approach).[72] In some ways, one might trace the origins of such individualism to the Kadızadelis' emphasis on individual will and freedom of choice (and thus, heavier personal responsibility)[73] as well as to the "enjoining good and forbidding evil" precept. Contrary to what one may think at first glance, the appeal to individual responsibility was not turned against sultanly authority: the abstract nature of that model, the lack of references to corporate entities, and the division of responsibility into countless shares was practically a perfect tool to enhance Selim III's (and before him, Abdülhamid I's) project to restore absolutism in Ottoman politics.

One may trace this process throughout the texts written during the eighteenth century, and thus establish another link connecting "traditionalist" views with the Westernizing reforms of the last decade; the gap, indeed, is narrower than it may seem. In the same way, throughout the century information about Europe was much more widespread than we usually think, while actual imitation was neither as servile nor as deep as one may expect.[74] On the other hand, continuities in Islamic scientific traditions were fairly strong, and were evident even in persons associated with the new trends; one of the most famous mathematicians of the era, İsmail Gelenbevi (d. 1791), who taught geometry and mathematics at the Naval Academy in Istanbul and was the author of a famous essay on logarithms, also wrote an innovative treatise on argumentation theory (*adab al-bahs*), a paragon of Islamicate logic.[75]

4.2 *Religious Zeal in the Service of Reform: Emin Behic and Ömer Faik Efendi*

In order to show the continuity of political ideas toward the end of the eighteenth century, another two outstanding cases will be studied here. They are both considered to be supporters of the *Nizam-i Cedid* reforms, and at least the first certainly was. Nevertheless, it will become clear that their ideas contain more of the "traditionalist" type of thought of Canikli Ali and Penah Efendi than of the Westernizing zeal of the authors to be examined in the next chapter.

72 See e.g. Koç – Yeşil 2012, 3.

73 Cf. Yakubovych 2017, 163.

74 See Aksan 2004, 13–23; Murphey 1999.

75 Karabela 2010, 184–189; El-Rouayheb 2015, 54–56, 89. He had begun his career as a typesetter in Halil Hamid Pasha's printing press (Menchinger 2017, 99–100). On Gelenbevi's life and work, see Bingöl 1988; on his non-mathematical works cf. Kiraz 2013.

Es-Seyyid Mehmed Emin Behic Efendi, for one thing, was a committed supporter of Selim III and a victim of the sultan's enemies. He was a member of the financial bureaucracy and the first director of the paper factory that was opened in Beykoz in 1804. In 1807, he became chief buyer (*mübayaacı*) for the army for the Danubian coast and thus came into contact with Bayrakdar Mustafa Pasha, the avenger-to-be of the soon afterwards deposed Selim, becoming a member of the "Ruşçuk committee" that supported him. Behic Efendi was killed by the janissaries in May 1809.[76] His *Sevanihü'l-levayih* ("Inspirational memoranda"), a quite exceptional text, was composed in 1802.[77] If Behic seems a bit outdated compared to the other authors of his time (as will be seen in the next chapter), Ömer Faik Efendi is an almost perfect specimen of another era. A palace scribe, he is known to have later followed the Nakşbendi order of dervishes (which, its religious conservatism notwithstanding, had been associated with sultans including Ahmed III and Selim III).[78] As he himself narrates, he decided to write his treatise, meaningfully entitled *Nizâmü'l-atîk* ("The old order"), in 1804, after a meeting in which he discussed the *Nizam-i Cedid* reforms with Selim III's secretary, Ahmed Efendi.[79] He divided his treatise into 32 sections, nine of them concerning "spiritual measures" (*tedbirât-ı ma'neviyye*), i.e. pertaining to the ulema and the dervishes' prayers, and 23 concerning "the apparent order" (*nizam-ı suriyye*), namely the role of courtiers and officials, the military, and the economy. Both Kemal Beydilli and Kahraman Şakul argue that he in fact supported *Nizam-i Cedid*, albeit with certain proposals for amendments and changes, and indeed some of his proposals were later implemented by Mahmud II, and there are some striking similarities with Behic Efendi's treatise. Overall, however, his views seem more like a critique of Selim's reforms than support.

Both authors take a religious perspective: Behic begins by lamenting the situation of Muslim knowledge and morals within the Ottoman Empire. Mosques and medreses are empty, while no justice is to be found in the courts since the provincial *ayan* use them to enhance their own interests. Alongside cheap education books, new regulations (*nizamname*) on the ulema and their

76 Cabi – Beyhan 2003, 168 (on his association with Bayraktar Mustafa Pasha), 482 (on his death), and index s.v. "Mehmed Emîn Behîc Efendi, Cihâdiye Defterdârı"; Süreyya – Akbayar 1996, 2:364; Shaw 1971, 397.

77 Behic – Çınar 1992; see also Beydilli 1999b, 42–53; Şakul 2005, 141–145.

78 Artan 2012, 379–380. On the relationship between the Nakşbendi order and Selim's reform team see Şakul 2005, 120–121; Yıldız 2008, 641–653. Butrus Abu-Manneh has studied the Nakşbendi influence on the 1839 Gülhane rescript (Abu-Manneh 1994).

79 Ömer Faik – Sarıkaya 1979. See also Özkul 1996, 329–333; Beydilli 1999b, 37–42; Şakul 2005, 145–148; Yıldız 2008, 183–184; Menchinger 2017, 214.

behavior should be printed and propagated by specially-appointed preachers and muftis, who should do this instead of frequenting the *ayan*'s banquets; in the same vein, the kazaskers should choose two supervisors (*nazır*) to inspect the provincial ulema at regular intervals. Similarly, but much more emphatically, Ömer Faik's main idea is that "spiritual recovery" (*ma'nevi kalkınma*) should have its place in the reform program. He stresses that the Ottoman state is in fact "the Muhammedan state" and Selim the "leader of the believers";[80] thus, it has to follow the Sharia and practise justice in order to gain victory against its enemies and welfare for its subjects. As an example of the arrangements that could be criticized, Ömer Faik cites no less a figure than Ebussu'ud Efendi. To achieve this goal, jurisprudence (*fıkh*) must be read in the mosques and the population illuminated in religious matters; this way, people will obey the dynasty and pray for the sultan. "Zeal for the religious sciences leads to reform of the world" (*ilm-i dine rağbet ıslah-ı aleme sebeb*), Ömer Faik notes. He suggests that dervishes and sheikhs should help with their prayers all over the Ottoman lands; imams serving in the houses of magnates should help the needy in secret, paying the debts of those imprisoned and so forth, in order to cause prayers in favor of the sultan; finally, in times of campaign, dervish sheikhs should be paid to pray until the final victory.[81] Ömer Faik describes in the grimmest colors the situation of the ulema: he claims that the number of medrese students has fallen dramatically over the last thirty years, as well as both the number and the quality of the lessons delivered in the sultanly mosques.

What is impressive in both authors, compared to earlier discussions of the ulema hierarchy, is their common ideas on state control of religious matters. The ulema hierarchy may have been under the indirect control of the sultan's power from time to time in previous centuries, but here Behic and Ömer Faik suggest that a fundamental unity of state, people, and ulema must be maintained. Ömer Faik's grand plan for recovery, in which "apparent" and spiritual measures are coupled, and where *fıkh* subtleties would be taught to the believers from the mosques (rather than being the monopoly of the learned), is not as different from Behic Efendi's state-regulated inspections of the ulema

80 Beydilli (1999b, 37) notes a similar assertion recorded by Cabi – Beyhan 2003, 1:84, as a mystic revelation to Cezzar Ahmed Pasha: "this state is neither the Exalted State nor the Ottoman State, it is called the Muhammedan State" (*bu devlet ne devlet-i aliyye ne de devlet-i osmaniyyedir, buna devlet-i muhammediyye derler*). In the famous *Sened-i ittifak*, which marks the *ayan*'s consent to the rise of Mahmud II, it is also stated that "the Exalted Ottoman State is in fact a Muhammedan realm" (Akyıldız 1998, 215: *Devlet-i Aliyye-i Osmaniyye Saltanat-ı Muhammediyye olup*).

81 A practice stopped by Selim III, as noted in Beydilli 1999b, 39.

and propagation of the religious fundamentals as it may seem at first glance. This similarity is even more evident if we consider the two authors' views on the popularization of knowledge: Behic proposes printing cheap treatises on logic and the Arabic language for the benefit of the ulema and students (noting at the same time the potential profits for the state printing house; Ç10, 13), but this idea is not restricted to religious literature. He also complains that sultanly orders, as well as being issued over trivial matters, are written in such a complex language that their addressees fail to understand them (Ç7), and so he proposes recodifying laws in simple language (Ç49–50). Impressively, Ömer Faik makes almost the same suggestions: he stresses that orders should be short and written in plain language, as ignorant judges often read out them in an incomprehensible manner and, furthermore, that sultanly orders should not be issued for trivial matters. In more than one way, these ideas meet Penah Efendi's emphasis on the importance of printing and of the popularization of knowledge. Moreover, Behic stresses the need for education in foreign languages. To this end, he proposes the foundation of a special school, making an explicit appeal to the precept of reciprocity (*mukabele bi'l-misl*: the axiom that a Muslim state should use the infidels' military principles against them; see below, chapter 9). He sees this as a way to create Muslim interpreters who could translate European books and be competent in international diplomacy (Ç38–39).

Another common element in these authors, which they also share with Penah Efendi, is the emphasis they place on local production. Ömer Faik urges statesmen to avoid ostentation and pomp; he celebrates local products and laments the extensive use of furs, which has produced much income for Russia. He criticizes the buying and presenting of gifts such as luxury goods ornamented with gold and precious stones, stressing instead that local production can very well meet the needs of the population. Much more analytically, Behic Efendi describes the economic reforms of Peter the Great as an incentive to reform the Ottoman economy: he claims that not only the civilized but also the nomadic Muslim (*medenisi şöyle dursun edna bedevisi*) is much more competent than the European; thus, the Ottomans could easily succeed where the Russians have succeeded, since the latter are "the most disgraced of all the European nations" (*cem'i-i milel-i efrenciyyenin erzeli*; Ç67–68).[82] Behic Efendi

82 Cf. Hanioğlu 2008, 42–43. Behic Efendi's argument is taken from İbrahim Müteferrika (see below, chapter 9) who also stresses that the Russians were the most despicable and useless country in Europe before they embarked on their modernization projects: Müteferrika – Şen 1995, 189–190. On the contempt felt by the Ottomans for Russia until the 1768–1774 war cf. Ortaylı 1994b, 221. For a comparative military history of Russia and the Ottoman Empire see Ágoston 2011.

finds his optimism corroborated by the quick progress the Ottomans made in fine arts, bringing examples from illustration of books and the fabrication of furniture. He proposes the appointment of one *defterdar* for every province, with the premise that he not be dismissed before three years have passed; these officials will see to it that local products (*yerli malı*), especially textiles, be used instead of ones imported from Europe or India. Officials up to the sultan himself should give the example to the population in this respect (Ç61–64). Behic gives a detailed list of goods that could be produced in the Ottoman lands, initially with the help of European technicians; he suggests that textile factories should be created in a number of towns,[83] while factories for goods such as watches, glassware, and jewelry should be created in Istanbul. Special manufacturers could be used to produce official uniforms for government clerks and ulema. These goods should bear the state seal and be sold at fixed prices; moreover, workers should be well paid, efficient ones should be given a rise, and those who discover new techniques should even have their own seal on their products. Behic predicts strong reactions by foreign merchants; he suggests that a special office (*nezaret*) be created and that new and specific regulations for trade and the guilds be introduced, always according to the needs of the times (Ç68–76).

Behic Efendi's and Ömer Faik's views on the state show a vision of centralized, absolutist power, with a highly rationalized state, with links to the sultan but distinct from society. Ömer Faik suggests that courtiers should not let the sultan be isolated, but instead unite "like one body" to assist him. Moreover, it should be forbidden for them (as well as to other officials, such as judges, scribes, and teachers) to meddle with the common people in coffeehouses and barber-shops, in order to avoid the spread of rumors. In turn, Behic claims that a major problem in the functioning of the government is the fact that the top offices of the financial and administrative bureaucracy are overburdened with work and overcrowded with visitors; he proposes a high committee of ten select people who would constitute the "heart of the state" (*kalb-ı devlet*). They would discuss all matters of government and, after agreeing upon some measures to be taken, they would present them to the grand vizier (Ç19). His proposals on provincial administration (Ç22) are of a similar nature: he suggests the appointment of two "general governors", one for Anatolia (based in Kütahya) and one for the Balkans (based in Manastir), who would act according to special regulations (*talimâtnâme*) and be aided by a small committee and a retinue trained in the new camps of the *Nizam-i Cedid* (the reader may

83 He suggests Bursa, Amasya, Ankara, and Köprü in Anatolia and Edirne, Filibe, Manastir, and the Danubian coasts in the Balkans.

remember another example of this administrative idea in Canikli Ali Pasha's work). Similarly, Ömer Faik suggests that statesmen should have farms around Istanbul: thus, they will be used as camps for military exercises and at the same time they will contribute to the prosperity of the surroundings of the capital. As for the financial bureaucracy, Behic (Ç26–39) laments the ignorance and greed of the clerks and proposes the strict selection of the most competent, their regular inspection, their organization into four distinct groups and their constant training. In special schools they should be regularly taught not only mathematics and book-keeping, but also geography, Arabic and Persian, literature, geography, politics, and the history of Europe and of Turkey (*tevarih-i Türkiyye*—this could also mean "histories in the Turkish language"; Ç37).

Behic Efendi's ideas on reorganizing the judicial system also point to the same, centralizing tendencies. As demonstrated, he proposes a recodification of the laws in simple language, as well as the establishment of a special court (*hakimler mahalli*) in the centre of Istanbul where criminal cases would be heard (Ç49–50). Behic also proposes, for the administration of Istanbul (Ç51–56), that the city must be cleansed of unemployed vagabonds and all inhabitants must be provided with a "permit to pass" (*mürur tezkiresi*), as in European cities. An "inspector of the city" (*şehir nazırı*) should be appointed, preferably a high-standing member of the ulema; he will be granted independent clerks and a special building. This official should then record all foreigners (artisans and merchants from the provinces, workers, the unemployed) and give them a special pass with their description. A similar verification of the population should be done at the neighborhood level by local imams, while control of the population would be supplemented by inn-keepers and a special system of spies (*casus*). It should be noted here that, in this view of population registration and control, Behic Efendi was quite attuned to the administration of his era.[84]

At the same time, both authors show their concern for civil officialdom as a means of social mobility. Ömer Faik laments the moral and financial situation of the scribes and seeks security of sorts for public servants: he speaks out against the confiscation (*müsadere*) of the properties of dead officials and argues that a substantial part of their property should always be left to the deceased's family. In the same vein, Behic argues that descendants of noble families (*kibar-zadeler*), who are well-educated, smart, and competent, do not dare enter public service because they fear arbitrary decisions on the part of the government (from dismissal to execution and confiscation of property). As

84 See Kırlı 2010; Başaran 2014; Başaran – Kırlı 2015.

a result, they prefer to follow the ulema career, and so the government remains open to the meanest of men (*esafile*; Ç36–37).

Finally, another feature the treatises by Behic Efendi and Ömer Faik have in common is that they do not seem to consider the army as the central point of the reform efforts. They thus differ from both their predecessors and the current debates on the *Nizam-i Cedid* in two ways: they give the dominant position to the reform of state mechanisms, especially those that sought to control society, and they write as if the issue of the new army was not the subject of a hot debate that would lead to a rebellion a few years later. True, Behic Efendi's chapter on the army is incomplete, as the manuscript stops abruptly in the middle of it (Ç77–82), but what remains seems strikingly different from his near-contemporaries Sekbanbaşı and Kuşmani (see chapter 9). Behic describes at length the defeats since the 1768–74 war, which he attributes to a lack of preparation and proper administration (rather than poor tactics or equipment), and praises Selim III's efforts in short, noting that imitation of European models is done in the context of reciprocity (*mukabele bi'l-misl*). Before the end of his manuscript, he stresses that no training and discipline can bear fruits if the officers are not chosen properly—which would have been the subject of his next, lost section. As for Ömer Faik, he almost completely ignores the *Nizam-i Cedid*: he only suggests the creation of smaller arsenals and naval bases on the Black Sea coasts, as well as in Çanakkale and Bozcaada (Tenedos), to protect the capital and the merchant routes from Russian attacks. Another problem he addresses is the logistics of the campaigns, which result in the destruction of the wealth of Muslims. Ömer Faik's suggestion is that the *vakf* income should be used for urgent state needs: a special treasury (*hazine*) should be created, and in times of need the government should be able to take loans from it after a relevant *fetva* from the *şeyhülislam*.

•••

Thus, in Behic Efendi's treatise one may see a committed supporter of Selim's reforms, but this commitment is more evident in his biography than in his treatise. One could believe it was written by Penah Efendi, as far as it concerns the section on the economy at least; even the comparison with Russia departs from the *topos* of "reciprocity", while the lengthy first part places emphasis on the *ilmiye* and their role that is not seen in the army-centred supporters of the *Nizam-i Cedid* that we are going to study in the next chapter. Penah Efendi's economic ideas on the need for the enhancement of local production are also present in Ömer Faik's work, who also shares with others of his era a concern for enhanced state control and an emphasis on the use of the popularization of knowledge as a means for individual responsibility. Most of his advice, however, is more reminiscent of Defterdar Mehmed Pasha, to say the least, than of his contemporaries; if he should indeed be counted amidst the reformists, it would be only to prove the thin line dividing the two trends.

This may be seen as a more general conclusion as well: the authors here named "traditionalists" do not have radically different points of departure compared to those advocating Western-style reforms. For one thing, they tend to have detailed advice for actual problems and to focus on the condition of the army—just as the Westernizers did. Their basic assumptions on the socio-political structure of the Ottoman Empire are the same; in fact, the most radical departure in these issues is from Penah Efendi (who proposes the abolition of the timar system and of the *miri* landholding principles), who never actually advocates radical reform along European lines (nor does he accept the idea that European armies have now surpassed Ottoman troops). Yet the blurred line dividing the two trends does not mean that we can neglect the existence of a conflict on Westernizing reform—a conflict that grew stronger and stronger toward the end of the century, both on ideological and political levels.

4.3 *An Author in the Crossroads: Şanizade's Views on History and Politics*

The persistence of anti-Westernizing ideas even on the eve of the Tanzimat reforms, irrespective of the exchange of information with Europe, is exceptionally well illustrated in the historical work of Şanizade Mehmed Atâ'ullah Efendi (ca. 1770–1826). Son of a well-to-do family that made its way from artisanate (the family name means "son of the comb-maker") to high ulema bureaucracy, Şanizade had a good education in religious studies, medicine, and mathematics, and knew quite a few European languages (including Greek), as well as the usual Arabic and Persian. He served as a teacher (*müderris*) in various medreses, as a judge in Eyyüb, and as an inspector of *vakf*s before being appointed official historian (*vak'anüvis*) in 1819. Upon the abolition of the janissary corps[85] he was exiled to Tire and died there two months later. Şanizade wrote various medical treatises (among them, a translation of an Austrian treatise), poetry, and translations of German and French military manuals, as well as of geographical and mathematical works. His chronicle, *Târîh* ("History"), completed

85 Perhaps also due to his participation in the "Scientific Society of Beşiktaş", *Beşiktaş İlmî Cemiyeti* or *Beşiktaş İ'tikadı*, a closed group of conversations and scientific lessons with allegedly close ties to the Bektaşi order and perhaps with Masonic influences: Şânizâde – Yılmazer 2008, XCVII–XCIX; Eldem 2014, 272; İhsanoğlu 1995/96, 167–168.

in 1825, covers the period from Mahmud II's ascension (1808) up to August 1821; his notes for subsequent years were used by his successor, Es'ad Efendi.[86]

The introduction of Şanizade's work is a long essay on historiography (Y14–24), which in fact copies (with slight alterations) an essay by Voltaire.[87] As well as in the introduction, Şanizade uses European newspapers and reports elsewhere as well, and not only when narrating contemporaneous events.[88] Indeed, Şanizade makes a serious effort to understand and describe European developments; however, his sources of terminology and theory continue to be distinctively and exclusively Ottoman. When narrating the Liberal Triennium in Spain (1820–23) he presents it as a demand for "Demokratis' law" (Y1155: *kanun-ı Dimukrâtî üzere*), obviously having in mind İbrahim Müteferrika's description of democratic government (see chapter 9; copied in turn from Kâtib Çelebi). In another part, Şanizade tries to explain the French victories under Napoleon (Y208–211), attributing the "perfection of the military arts" to the "national unity" (*ittifak-ı milliyye*) exhibited by the French: a tribe that had fallen into lethargy was made strong, enhanced by "patriotism, fraternity, equality, and liberty" (Y208: *mahabbet-i memleket ve uhuvvet ü müsavât ve serbestiyyet da'valariyle*), and under the motto "freedom or death". Elsewhere, he speaks once more of the French Revolution (Y624–627): because of the words of some philosophers (*feylesof*),[89] the inhabitants of Europe started to seek equality and parity (*tesavi vü i'tidal*) and thus threatened the safety of their old notables; everybody aimed to seize the life and property of everyone else. Drawn into the same imbroglio, the Ottoman state tried to imitate these developments, but the results were devastating: apart from the loss of more and more territory, the appointment of inappropriate persons led not only to a weakening of the Empire's military potential but also to an increase in its expenses.

It is to be noted that in the passage above, talking of the Ottoman imitation of French ways, the author uses the well-known concept of "reciprocity" (*mukabele bi'l-misl*). Here, however, the notion has acquired a negative meaning. In other places, too, Şanizade proves rather hostile to Selim's reforms (Y33–42):

86 Şânizâde – Yılmazer 2008. See also Lewis 1961, 84–85; Arıkan 1990, 93–94; Eldem 2014.

87 The discovery of this copying belongs to Eldem 2014, who examines in detail the differences and omissions between the two works. Cf. the very different prefaces by previous historiographers: Menchinger 2010.

88 Şânizâde – Yılmazer 2008, LXXII–LXXIII. See, for instance, a long note on the relationship of the Pope with the (Austrian) Emperor and on the various branches of Lutheranism, or his essay on fire prevention with examples from the London experience (ibid., 819–824 and 852–854).

89 He describes their works as "natural philosophy" (*makal-i tabi'i-mealleri*), as he would later do with Ibn Khaldun (Şânizâde – Yılmazer 2008, 1028).

he insists that no matter how close to the right course and even how preferable to the old law (Y37: *töre-i kadimeye*) a new regulation may be, there will always be ignorant ones who will revolt against it, preferring their own personal benefit to the common good. Every tribe or group has its own natural customs and traditions; those who are not trained in arms and military ways, who do not know the virtues of patriotism and national zeal (Y38: *hubb-ı vatan ve gayret-i milliyye*), who are accustomed to idleness, showing respect for neither agriculture nor trade; those who think that good alliances and society differ from the state itself (*gûya devlet başka ve ittifakât-ı hasene vü cem'iyyet başka*); in short, such ignorant people (and Şanizade seems to imply the janissaries) are easily incited to rebel and disobey. This was facilitated by Selim's bad counselors, about whose behavior Şanizade complains in detail (Y40–42). Elsewhere, he complains of the situation in the Ottoman army (Y85–87): he notes that love of one's country and national (or religious) zeal (*mahabbet-i memleket ve gayret-i milliyye*) are an innate part of human nature; mankind always sought to live "quiet and free" (*azade*). However, a lack of training and exercise led most nations to lethargy and disunity, causing them to be subdued by other tribes. Şanizade then jumps to the problem of reforms, observing that man first has to learn and understand before accepting an innovation: before changing a people's customs, one has to make them understand the benefits of the specific reform. The need for a re-ordering of the Ottoman army was still not understood by the commoners (*avam*) because they cannot understand even their own situation: the elite blame the commoners and vice versa, and thus the virtue (*haslet*) that discriminates the two fails to be understood, producing instead animosity and jealousy. That is why, concludes Şanizade, the creation of *Nizam-ı Cedid* should have been done gradually and with care for the people's feelings.

Şanizade admits that, in his days, due to the general changes of the time (*teceddüd-i eyyam ve tebeddül-i a'vam*), there arose the need for a re-ordering (*tekmil-i nizam*) that would deal with the general idleness and lethargy prevailing in all affairs. However, such measures met with strong opposition (Y404ff). The janissaries, being (because of their previous order) more united than the other classes, dominated the rest. In this way, however, whatever affluence and comfort had been obtained due to the power of social solidarity (*kuvvet-i ictima'iyye*) is now lost as a result of the conflict among the other classes. In a similar vein, elsewhere Şanizade uses the old pattern of the four pillars (Y481–482) which constitute every state (*devlet*). Men of the sword, he notes, have prevailed over the others for some time now, but, since they lack the necessary number of soldiers ready for battle, men from the other three classes are permitted to use the title of soldier.

One of Şanizade's most concrete and lengthy pieces of political thought is contained in his discussion of the 1821 Greek Revolution (Y1027–1046). He begins with the statement that, due to the neglect of good counsel, the rules of politics (*kava'id-i siyasiyye*) have been abandoned and the army in particular lost its discipline and started to oppress the other three pillars, with the result that the balance of society was ruined. There are people ready to exploit such situations and, since some of them cannot be reformed and must be dealt with by severe punishments, it is a rule of politics (*umur-ı siyasiyye*) that the statesman must imitate the doctor, who cuts away the limbs that may prove irrevocably dangerous for the body (Y1029). Şanizade then cites the late thirteenth-century author Fâzıl (Shams al-Din) Shahrazûrî, who talks of the four kinds of government "according to Aristotle":[90] tyranny (*siyasetü'l-galebeti*), which ends in the humble and ignorant taking over the country; aristocracy (*siyasetü'l-kerameti*), or the government of those seeking wealth and honor; government of communities (*siyasetü'l-cema'ati*), or "government according to a common law (*'ala vefkı'l-kanuni'n-namusiyyi'l-mevzu'i*) shared by various groups (*firak*)"; and monarchy (*siyasetü'l-meliki*), which is "the government of governments" and the state of the virtuous.[91]

All the more striking for a polyglot doctor and a reader of Voltaire is Şanizade's view on authority. Not only does he favor the sultan's rule over the *ayan*, he is also very suspicious of collective systems of decision and counsel. Thus, commenting on the 1808 signing of the *Sened-i ittifak* between the *ayan* and the sultan (Y74–75; see below, chapter 9), Şanizade launches an attack on the notables, which in itself is not inexplicable bearing in mind Mahmud II's policy against them. Later on (Y631–633), he describes the same pact as

> the paper called "document of alliance" by some ecstatic idiots, blinded by the dream of fortune and wanting to establish themselves as statesmen (*rical-i devlet*)

and he quotes Mahmud II saying that the authors of the document dared to oppose to the Ottoman sultanate "which is incapable of being shared" (*kabil-i iştirak olmayan*). In the same vein, Şanizade's analysis of consultation or

90 Pourjavady – Schmidtke 2006, 76–85. This citation comes from Shahrazuri's *Rasâ'il al-shajara* (Şânizâde – Yılmazer 2008, 1030 fn), which had influenced Davvani and was particularly popular among Ottoman philosophers (see Pourjavady – Schmidtke 2006, 79).

91 In fact, this is an interestingly incomplete repetition of al-Farabi's (ultimately Platonic) list of "imperfect states", namely timocracy (*madîna karâma*), tyranny (*taghallub*, corresponding to Shahrazûrî's *siyâsetü'l-galebeti*), and democracy (*madîna jamâ'iya*), while monarchy corresponds to his "virtuous state" (see Rosenthal 1958, 135–136).

meşveret (Y1093–1094), a notion usually glorified in Islamic thought, is a rare example of straightforward absolutism.[92]

The point is not that Şanizade glorifies Mahmud II's absolutism, which after all is natural (and Selim II's Westernizing attempts had nothing democratic about them, for that matter), but that his reasoning, from beginning to end, is articulated in a strictly traditional style, even though the notions he uses are distinctively modern ("majority", "patriotism", "national/religious zeal"). What is important for our point of view is the persistence of traditional vocabulary and ideas even on the eve of the Tanzimat reforms (which, as will be seen, were far from articulated in a European-style vocabulary). The trend we named here "traditionalist", after all, did not advocate any aversion to European influence nor did it promote the static image of "world order" that prevailed before the second half of the seventeenth century; Ömer Faik's "old order" was conceived of as a complement to Selim's "new order", and Penah Efendi's "new order" was perhaps more in line with Kâtib Çelebi's proposals than with Selim's new army.[93] Its difference from the "Westernizing" trend, which will form the subject of the following chapter, is that it did not endorse the need to imitate European state and military organization; whatever ameliorations these authors proposed were rooted (at least in theory) in the eighteenth-century Ottoman tradition of experimentation rather than in wholesale admission of the experience of the infidels. In a way, authors such as Penah or Behic Efendi favoured modernization without Westernization.

---

92 I delve into some of Şanizade's views on democracy and consultation at some length in Sariyannis 2016, 53–55 and 57–59.

93 On the concept of "new order" as a rupture with the older concept of "world order" see below, the conclusion, and Menchinger 2017, 166–168.

CHAPTER 9

The Eighteenth Century: the Westernizers

Unlike the preceding years, the final decade of the eighteenth century is one of the most studied periods in Ottoman history.[1] Selim III (1789–1807) succeeded Abdülhamid in the course of the war against Russia and was determined to enforce decisive reforms and restore Ottoman power. Even before his ascension, from 1786 on, he had been corresponding with the French king Louis XVI with the help of his tutor, Ebubekir Ratıb Efendi, as seen in the previous chapter, with a view to seeking advice and diplomatic support for his plans.[2] At the beginning of his reign, he called an enlarged council, consisting of more than 200 administrators and military and religious officials to ask their opinion on how to restore Ottoman power. It is interesting to note that this was not a novelty; such councils (*meşveret*) were regularly held at many administrative levels and they became increasingly important in the second half of the eighteenth century.[3] For instance, we have the minutes of the council called after the disaster at Maçin (1791), arguably the central event that set Selim's thoughts into action.[4] After the end of the 1787–92 war, Selim III asked a series of high administration officials to write memoranda on the situation of the army and the state and to propose reforms or amendments, and then set out to make radical changes, particularly in the military. In the janissary corps, administrative roles were allocated to special supervisors, while the former aghas were left with military tasks alone. What remained of the timariot system was rearranged, with special care given to producing a cavalry ready to fight during both summer and winter, thanks to a system of rotation; provincial governors were asked to recruit and train troops as reserves; the engineering schools, initiated by Bonneval and Tott earlier, were expanded and enhanced; and foreign advisors were invited to contribute their knowledge to drilling and training the janissaries and other soldiers. Most importantly, an entirely new corps was created, the *Nizam-i Cedid* or "New order". This was composed of youths recruited in Anatolia; they were trained and commanded by European officers and

1 On the events of this period, see Shaw 1971; Mantran 1989, 425–445; Beydilli 2001, 70–90; Hanioğlu 2008, 42–71.

2 Uzunçarşılı 1938; Ratıb Efendi – Yıldız 2013.

3 See Aksan 2004, 21–22, and cf. Yaycıoğlu 2008, 144ff.; Yılmaz 2015a, 255–258. The preambles of the *Nizam-i Cedid* regulations often stress that these decisions were taken unanimously (*ittifak-ı ara-yı ulema ve erbab-ı şura ile*); see, for example, Koç – Yeşil 2012, 3, 60, 79, 95.

4 Yıldız 2016, 150–156.

© KONINKLIJKE BRILL NV, LEIDEN, 2019 | DOI:10.1163/9789004385245_011

funded by specially allocated revenues, the *irad-i cedid* ("new revenues").[5] In addition, recent research has shown that, the new army apart, Selim's reforms also had a centralizing aspect, specializing in population control and what has been called the "statistical" state, which was very much in line with features of "modernity" without being introduced from the West.[6]

Unfortunately for Selim, earlier troubles did not cease. In the Balkans, the power of the provincial notables reached new heights with Ali Pasha in Yanya and Pasvanoğlu Osman Pasha in Vidin creating nearly autonomous territories. On the other hand, the rearrangement in European alliances brought about by the French Revolution soon reached the Ottoman Empire with Napoleon's invasion of Egypt (1798–1801), which ultimately resulted in enhanced power for provincial notables in Syria and Arabia and increased the role of Russia in the Balkans. What was perhaps more important was that the opposition to Selim's military reforms, led by dispossessed members of the janissary corps (which, by that time, had come to represent a huge number of urban dwellers),[7] finally brought about his demise. After a first conflict in Edirne in 1806, which ended with Selim dismissing the commanders of the new troops that he himself had selected, the following year a revolt erupted among the auxiliary forces of the janissaries (*yamak*) who were guarding the fortresses of the Bosphorus, under Kabakçı Mustafa.[8] As had happened before, the rebels were soon joined by janissaries, ulema, and urban dwellers; Selim was forced to dismantle the *Nizam-i Cedid* and soon after to abdicate in favor of his cousin Mustafa IV. In response, the *ayan* of Ruşçuk and a former opponent of Selim, Bayraktar (or Alemdar) Mustafa Pasha, marched on Istanbul; in 1808 he entered the city with his army, as the chief of a committee of notables. He did not manage to rescue Selim, who was killed in the palace, but he overthrew Mustafa IV and put on the throne the young prince Mahmud II (1808–39).

Mahmud's reign began with an impressive document, the famous *Sened-i ittifak* or "Deed of alliance" (1808), which was signed by the sultan, the representatives of the government, and a group of provincial *ayan*, officially described as "great families" (*hanedân*), who had assembled in Istanbul. With this document, the latter had their local powers guaranteed in exchange for their support for the dynasty, and thus for the first time had their role in imperial

5 On Selim's reforms see Shaw 1971; Karal 1988; Kenan 2010.

6 Başaran 2014, 82–105; Başaran – Kırlı 2015.

7 Quataert 1993; Sunar 2006; this process had begun in the mid-seventeenth century (Tezcan 2010a; Yılmaz Diko 2015).

8 On this rebellion see the detailed analysis in Yıldız 2008; Yıldız 2012. The analysis in Argun 2013, 271ff., argues that this was "much more about the collision of two rival elite cliques for apportion of human and material resources than that of reformist-conservative struggle".

power officially recognised.[9] Mahmud first had to carry on the war against Russia and Austria, begun during the last years of Selim's reign partly due to the first Serbian uprising (1804–13), and was obliged to cede territory in the Danube and the Caucasus as part of the Treaty of Bucharest (1812). Internally (after a second janissary revolt in 1809) he was more successful: the Ottoman government managed to subdue centrifugal trends in Epirus (Tepedelenli Ali Pasha, who effectively controlled most of the south-western Balkan peninsula) and the Arabian peninsula (although this was done through the governor of Egypt, Mehmet Ali Pasha, later a major centrifugal figure himself), as well as other provinces (e.g. Crete, where Mahmud's governors finally purged the powerful janissary aghas in the mid-1810s). On the other hand, the Ottomans had to deal with the first major breakaway from their rule, the Greek War of Independence (1821). The struggle of the Christian subjects for independence had been increasingly marked from the late eighteenth century due to several factors, among which one should not neglect (as pertaining to our subject) their alienation from state assets,[10] together with other, more well-known reasons such as the influence of the French Revolution, the rise of nationalism, economic factors, and so on.

Confronted with all these challenges, Mahmud resumed effectively the reform policies of Selim: the first step, which will also mark the end of the present book, was the notorious *Vak'a-i hayriyye* or "auspicious event", namely, the destruction of the janissaries in 1826; after initiating a military reform that seemed a timid effort to revive Selim's *Nizam-i Cedid*, Mahmud decisively suppressed an attempted janissary rebellion by virtually exterminating a large part of them with heavy artillery. The corps was abolished throughout the empire (as was the Bektaşi order of dervishes, which was associated with them) and a new regular army was created in their place. Arguably, this was the prerequisite for the beginning of the long Tanzimat (i.e. reforms) period, which is more usually associated with the clothing laws of 1829 (establishing a uniform headgear for all subjects, Christian and Muslim), the almost concurrent educational

9 See the full text and literature in Akyıldız 1998 (and the English translation in Akyıldız – Hanioğlu 2006), and cf. Berkes 1964, 90–92; Ortaylı 1995, 29–30; Salzmann 1993; Yaycıoğlu 2008, 428–466; Yaycıoğlu 2010, 700–707; Yaycıoğlu 2012, 449–450; Hanioğlu 2008, 57–58. A similar understanding of state power can be seen in the slightly earlier *Hüccet-i Şer'iyye* (1807; marking Selim III's fall), agreed upon by "firstly our lord the Sultan ... secondly by the high officials of the state" (Beydilli 2001, 45; cf. Yıldız 2008, 457–472).

10 More particularly, Baki Tezcan (Tezcan 2010a, 235–237) argues that while the earlier Ottoman power-holders were restricted to the military elite, with Muslim and Christian urban and rural delveers sharing the same fate as the *reaya*, the growing participation of a large Muslim strata in political power through the intermediary of janissary enrolment had the side-effect of alienating the Christian subjects.

reforms, the abolition of the timar landholding system, and of course the Hatt-ı Şerif of Gülhane of 1839 (issued immediately after Mahmud's death by Abdülmecid, his successor), which constituted a major ideological breach with the Sharia precepts on non-Muslim subjects (according equal rights and demanding equal responsibilities from all subjects). However, this survey will end in 1826, considering the paramount importance the janissary system had for both the socio-political organization of Istanbul politics and Ottoman political thought.[11]

1 The Precursors of *Nizam-i Cedid*: İbrahim Müteferrika and the Dialogue with the West

From the survey in the previous chapter, it may have been clear that Selim III's reforms were not an abrupt break with previous policies. Although his choice to create new troops, rather than reform the old, was applied at an unprecedented scale, it was an enhancement of previous efforts, such as those carried out by Bonneval and by Baron de Tott. Nor was this emphasis a breakthrough innovation at the ideological level (although similar attempts by fellow Muslim rulers, such as Şahin Giray in the Crimea in the late 1770s and Tipu Sultan in Mysore a decade later, had met with a rather unfavorable response from Istanbul):[12] as will be seen, the idea of importing military techniques from Europe had appeared more than half a century before Selim's ascent to the throne. And it was the creator of the first Ottoman Turkish printing press, İbrahim Müteferrika, who was practically the first to make this suggestion (and certainly the first to make it in an influential way).

Of Hungarian origin, Müteferrika (whose Christian name we ignore) was born in Koloszvár, Transylvania (in 1674 or before), and had a religious education in either a Calvinist or a Unitarian (as argued by Niyazi Berkes) college in his home city. During the Imre Tököly rebellion (1692–93) he was made a prisoner of the Ottomans and under obscure circumstances converted to Islam (Müteferrika himself writes that his conversion was a voluntary move in his Transylvanian years).[13] He obtained a solid training in Muslim theology and

11 For a more general view of the late eighteenth and early nineteenth century see Salzmann 2012.

12 Şakul 2014a. Cf. the unfavorable reception of Peter the Great's reforms by the historian Raşid upon the former's death: "he had tried to impose crazy new fashions on his people" (Ortaylı 1994b, 221).

13 For recent recapitulations of the relevant discussion see Sabev 2014, 102–108 and Erginbaş 2014, 61–66; on his role in transcultural exchange, see Barbarics-Hermanik 2013. On the

oriental languages and served as an interpreter and emissary, as well as holding various military posts during the wars of the late 1730s. In 1726 he managed to found the first Ottoman Turkish printing press, with the support of the grand vizier Nevşehirli İbrahim Pasha. Before he died in 1745, he published seventeen books on history (including several works of Kâtib Çelebi and Na'ima's history), geography (including a monumental edition of Kâtib Çelebi's *Cihânnümâ*, reworked and supplemented, as well as a description of the Americas), and language (among them a Turkish grammar in French). It is interesting to see the rationale used by Müteferrika for justifying the need for a press and to overcome the objections of some ulema: among his arguments (as published in the introduction of the first book he printed), he stresses that the multiplication of copies and the subsequent fall in book prices would bring knowledge to everyone, from the rich to the poorest students and even the inhabitants of provincial towns and villages.[14]

Among his own works, which include an essay on the benefits of printing, a treatise on magnetism, and translations of Latin geographical and historical works, *Usûlü'l-hikem fî nizâmi'l-ümem* ("Rational bases for the order of the countries") was written in 1731 and published in his printing house the following year.[15] The importance of *Usûlü'l-hikem* is two-fold, as is its structure, too: on the one hand, it introduces (or rather re-introduces, as in fact it copies a forgotten work by Kâtib Çelebi) to Ottoman literature the Aristotelian distinction of governments (and it remained the only such work for a long time); on the other, it was the first time that an Ottoman straightforwardly proposed military reforms based on an acknowledgment of the superiority of European armies. In the first respect, Müteferrika's work stands alone, as indeed is this theoretical part isolated and unexploited inside the *Usûlü'l-hikem* itself; in the second, it was to be followed throughout subsequent centuries not only by theorists but by government policies as well.

In his preface (Ş123–127), Müteferrika states quite boldly the reasons he wrote his treatise: the 1730 revolt, as well as the military defeats of the empire, led him to study books in Latin and other languages in order to discover the reasons for the decline and the means for restoration, especially concerning the military strength of the Ottomans. The book is composed of three chapters, the first and last of which are related to the "need for order in the army", the

treatise referring to Müteferrika's conversion see also Krstić 2011, 203; Tezcan 2014 (who rejects Berkes's arguments about his Unitarianism).

14 Gerçek 1939; Sabev 2006, 139–140; Küçük 2012, 165; Erginbaş 2014, 68.

15 Müteferrika – Şen 1995. See Berkes 1962; Berkes 1964, 36–45; Yılmaz 2003a, 315–16; Aksan 1993, 56 (=Aksan 2004, 30–31); Yılmaz 2000a; Sabev 2006 and 2014; Erginbaş 2014, 85–92.

middle one to the benefits of geographical knowledge. The first chapter, composed of five parts (*fasıl*), is more theoretical, indeed written with a degree of abstraction (and with strong Aristotelian overtones) quite rare in Müteferrika's time, as seen in the previous chapter, whereas the rest of the treatise follows a more practical thread, although again this is with a level of abstraction unusual for its time.[16]

Let us first delve into the theoretical part of *Usûlü'l-hikem*. In a manner reminiscent of Kınalızade and Kâtib Çelebi, Müteferrika states that, as shown by geometrical proofs composed by the wise, the world is round and hung in the void, inhabited all around by men, like a "watermelon full of ants". God created man as a naturally civilized being (*bi't-tab' zevatlarında medeniyyet merkuz kılınmağla*); men seek society (*talib-i ictima'*) and need each other either for sustenance or to reproduce and to continue their life. This need led to people living together and thus to the creation of societies. However, due to the differences of their dispositions and their customs and opinions, some men tend to use power and violence in order to dominate others and make them submit to serving them. Because of these injustices, the foundation of justice and laws and thus the existence of wise leaders are necessary. These leaders' task is to use their practical philosophy (*hikmet-i ameliyye*) and impose equity and "obedience to laws, which constitute the means of politics" (*medar-ı siyaset olan ri'ayet-i kunun*), so no-one oppresses anyone else.

It was the Prophet who lay down these rules; but after he left for the Hereafter, a just and powerful sultan must rule to secure the application of the religious and secular rules (*kavanin-i siyasete*) and to put the affairs of the Muslims in order. Thus, an administrator is necessary to rule people, who have been created as dependent from each other for their sustenance and as social by nature (*emr-i ma'aşında dahi gayr-ı müstakil, belki medeniyyün bi't-tab olub*). Because of God's love for His slaves, He sends them either a prophet or a just ruler. The various peoples submit to the wise rules, as they are naturally inclined to do, and every community is subject to a king. Thus, people have created various states (*devletler kurdılar*) and appointed rulers by various names—caliphs, sultans, kings, khans, kaisers or tsars (Ş128–130).

---

16 There is also a long chapter (Ş154–162) on a quite different subject, namely the advantages of the science of geography. One of the arguments is that Muslim people live outside Ottoman borders, ignorant of each other; if all Muslims were acquainted with each other they could unite and dispose of their infidel rulers, under the protection of the one and only sultan (Ş156–157). Besides, geography is indispensable for the comprehension of history, as well as for conducting diplomatic negotiations in order to divide conquered countries and to reshape borders.

Then, Müteferrika proceeds on what is usually deemed his most original and impressive contribution to Ottoman political theory; however, it is but an almost verbatim copying of part of Kâtib Çelebi's *İrşâdü'l-hayârâ*, which was seen in chapter 7 above (§130–131). As everyone knows, he says, the religion and disposition of rulers varies; the same applies for the forms that the administration of human affairs may take, and that is why the structures of states and societies (*bünyan-ı devlet ve bina'-ı cumhur-ı cem'iyyetleri*) differ from each other. In this matter, most philosophers follow the views of three great philosophers of old, namely (and from here on Müteferrika follows Kâtib Çelebi word for word) Plato's view, i.e. "monarchy" (*munârhıyâ*); Aristotle's view, i.e. that rulership must belong to the magnates of the state ("aristocracy" or *aristokrâsiyâ*, or "rule of the magnates", *amme-i tedbir-i ayan*), as in Venice; and finally Demokratis' view, i.e. that administration should be in the hands of the people (*saltanat tedbir-i re'ayanın olmak gerekdir*) by election (*tarik-i tedbir ihtiyardır*), a form called "democracy" (*dîmukrâsiya*) or "the rule of the elected" (*amme-i tedbir-i muhtarîn*), as in England and the Netherlands.

It should be noted that, since Müteferrika never quotes his source and Kâtib Çelebi's *İrşâdü'l-hayârâ* remained virtually unknown until its edition in 2012, in general Ottomanist scholarship still attributes the introduction of the Aristotelian theory on government and the first mention of democracy to Müteferrika himself, usually alluding to his Transylvanian education.[17] On the other hand, Müteferrika's European influences were integrated into a more traditional Islamicate framework with remarkable efficiency. If we were to look at Müteferrika's private library, we would encounter (among a multitude of other works on logic, history, science, and so on) Ottoman political works from earlier centuries, including Mustafa Ali's *Füsûl-i hall ü akd*, Kınalızade's *Ahlâk-ı Alâî*, and Kâtib Çelebi's *Mîzânü'l-hakk* and *İrşâdü'l-hayârâ* (but not *Düstûrü'l-amel*, his main political work).[18] From these treatises he took most of the ideas expressed in the first part of his work, such as the division of governments (itself quite marginal in Ottoman political thought before then) and the fourfold division of society (each of which play a minor role in Müteferrika's argument). On the other hand, the same library contained another three dozen books in "Latin" (which could mean any European language), some of which dealt with philosophy and military tactics.

17 See, for example, Berkes 1964, 42–43; Yılmaz 2000a, 307, or Sariyannis 2013, 94. On the use of Kâtib Çelebi's works by Müteferrika see the detailed analysis in Yurtoğlu 2009, 37ff. and esp. 72–78 on the copying of *İrşâdü'l-hayârâ*.

18 Sabev 2006, 110–127 and 345–364.

However, one should note that Müteferrika was not the only writer to rely on Aristotle during the "Tulip Period" and beyond. Yanyalı Es'ad Efendi (d. 1731), a major intellectual figure of the period and, significantly, one who spoke Greek and frequented Greek circles (which were themselves undergoing their own Aristotelian renaissance), had translated Aristotle's *Physics* (or rather, a Latin commentary of the ancient work) into Arabic. Furthermore, intellectual life during Ahmed III's reign was characterized by a regeneration of Aristotelian philosophy, with a marked tendancy to purge Aristotle's work of the neo-Platonic ideas added by Avicenna and al-Farabi.[19] Nor was this phenomenon exclusively or predominantly due to the impact of European influence: it was remarked earlier that Iranian influences were clearly present during the "Tulip Period" and that its "Westernizing" aspect has been overestimated.[20]

Es'ad Efendi's example shows that Müteferrika's breach with Ottoman political tradition was perhaps more than a simple result of his Christian origins. What is also important, as far as it concerns Müteferrika's novelties, is that authors of this period "often celebrated both natural philosophy and *bid'at*";[21] in this vein, Müteferrika's innovative ideas on reform, as well as his Aristotelian views on society and politics, would fit well together in the intellectual climate of early eighteenth-century Istanbul. The way he writes about the role of printed books in society is striking, considering the history of the term *bid'at*:[22]

> The ancients always made fine innovations (*ibd'â*). Modern scholars are no more hesitant than the ancients in coming up with new rules and laws by which to organize empires and nations. Writing has helped them preserve their histories and perpetuate their respective orders.

Furthermore, one should emphasize the role played in this trend by Greek scholars and magnates such as Chrysanthos Notaras (who was corresponding with Es'ad Efendi) and Nikolaos Mavrokordatos. Around the same time (c. 1740), even a provincial *müfti* such as Mahmud Efendi of Athens could write a detailed history of ancient Athens, based on a Greek historical treatise through Greek intermediaries.[23] It is interesting that he also describes

19 See Küçük 2012 and 2013; on translation activity during this period cf. Şeşen 2004. The role of Greek scholars in this trend has been also noted by Ortaylı 2001, 41.

20 Erimtan 2007.

21 Küçük 2013, 130, and fn. 20.

22 As translated by Küçük 2012, 164. The quotation comes from Müteferrika's *Vesiletü't-tıb'a* ("The virtues of printing"), the preface to the first book printed by his press (1729).

23 Tunalı Koç 2006; Mahmud Efendi – Tunalı 2013; Tunalı 2014.

democratic government in quite a positive light, while his grim description of Sparta is strongly reminiscent of concurrent criticisms of Ottoman society and the army:[24]

> The strange things introduced to Athens (*Atina'ya ihdas olunan umur-ı acibe*) at that time had never been seen in another country. Because nobody was in conflict or struggled anyone else and all affairs were carried out by consultation of the commonwealth (*cumhur müşaveresiyle*). Every day a new order was introduced with the vote of everyone (*cümle re'yle*) ... No class could imitate their superiors in clothing and food; everybody was happy with the quantity given to them and could not surpass it by any means ... Nobody could have priority over or oppose the police officers in the assembly places, no matter how powerful one was or what their family was. If they did, they were killed at once. Moreover, the commoners (*pespaye*) and poor could not oppose their superiors or the wealthy ... While the inhabitants of Athens were following these customs and rules, Athens became such a well-ordered city that its like was not seen anywhere in the world .... [On the contrary, in Sparta (*Mizistre*)] the military class dominated their officers ... the rich could not oppose the poor, [and] most merchants and decent people left the city since their word was not obeyed ... Gradually their income, which previously was increasing, became insufficient and their vain expenses increased.

However, it should be noted that this Aristotelian perception of political theory had no continuators for the rest of the century. On the contrary, Müteferrika's views on army reform, which will be examined in the following section, were widely read and heavily influenced both political thought and practice throughout the century.

1.1 *Westernization: the Early Proposals*

Müteferrika was not the only supporter of the superiority of European army organization. The first such instance might have been a text known as *Su'âl-i Osmânî ve cevâb-ı Nasrânî*, or a "Dialogue between an Ottoman and a Christian Officer". This was allegedly a record of a conversation between an Ottoman

24 Mahmud Efendi – Tunalı 2013, 279–281; cf. also 244, with the inhabitants of Athens deciding to have no king after Codrus' death and ti be governed by judges with communal participation (*bi'l-cümle re'y ve tedbiri ve ma'rifetiyle olup yalnız kendü re'yleriyle iş görmüş değiller idi*). Democratic government is described in more detail in pp. 287–289, while later the author stresses that low and base people, as well as women, did not take part in the assemblies (298–299).

statesman and a Christian officer, conducted before the Treaty of Passarowitz (1718); it was copied by the chronicler Es'ad Efendi (d. 1848), who notes that it was written "in the form of a discussion by some wise men" (*ba'z-ı erbab-ı ukulün muhakeme yollu kaleme alıp*) and "submitted to Ahmed III through the grand vizier Ibrahim Pasha".[25] According to the text, during the negotiations for the treaty a Christian officer (*zümre-i zabıtân-ı Nasara'dan bir şahs*) had some friendly discussions with a notable from the Ottoman army (*namdarân-ı asakir-i osmaniyyeden bir merd*). The text, which was submitted to the sultan, Ahmed III, because it was deemed useful for the arrangement of state affairs, is structured as a series of questions and answers on both sides. The Ottoman officer first asks how the Ottomans prevailed in all battles with the Austrians until the first siege of Vienna (1529), whereas from that time on victory has usually been on the Christian side. The Christian's answers describe the rules of war as developed in Europe, and finally give advice on the diplomatic moves the Ottomans should make, explaining the alliances and enmities in Europe.

This peculiar document has drawn the attention of scholars focusing on the "Westernization" or "secularization" of the Ottoman society. Its absence from any source other than Es'ad Efendi's chronicle (composed in the 1820s) is puzzling and makes its authorship even more disputed. Şerif Mardin attributed it to Damad Ibrahim Pasha himself, while Niyazi Berkes argued that it was "inspired by the recommendations of some European observers who happened to be in Turkey at the time" and suggested more specifically a French officer, De Rochefort, who, according to Hammer, had submitted a project to create an engineering corps to the Ottoman court in 1717. Berkes made the bold hypothesis that "the document was inspired, if not prepared, by Ibrahim [Müteferrika], perhaps with encouragement from his former compatriots, for submittal to his patron, the Sadrazam [Damad] Ibrahim Pasha".[26] However, in some ways the text seems to be closer to Es'ad Efendi's later era than to its alleged date. One recognizes Müteferrika's description of European military discipline and organization, but also Vasıf Efendi's ideas on *istidrac*, as well as Ahmed Resmî Efendi's ideas on the balance of powers (see below); finally, the idea of the Europeans copying the initial discipline and order of the Ottoman army reflects, as will be seen, similar passages in Müteferrika's treatise but also (much

25 Unat 1941; Esad Efendi – Yılmazer 2000, 586–606. See also Mardin 1969b, 26–27; Kafadar 1989, 133; Berkes 1964, 30–33; Schaendlinger 1992, 241–242 and 246–250.

26 Mardin 1969b, 26–27; Berkes 1964, 30–31 and 33; the suggestion of İbrahim Müteferrika's authorship of the text was also made by Unat 1941, 107 n. 3, and was also thought probable by Schaendlinger 1992, 242 and 250.

more powerfully resonant) in Ratıb Efendi's and "Koca Sekbanbaşı" (probably Vasıf)'s works, composed in the 1790s and 1800s.[27] In fact, it may be the first case of the axiom of reciprocity or "meeting like-for-like" (*mukabele bi'l-misl*), a major argument in the inventory of "Westernizers" that gained importance towards the end of the eighteenth century.[28] A manuscript dated 1719–20 proves that the original text was indeed composed in 1718; we do not know why, but it must have become more widely known toward the end of the century.[29]

Such "discussions" are a rather unusual form in Ottoman literature (although the genre has a long history in medieval Arabic letters), but there are parallels from the late seventeenth century. Interestingly, one of them, *Risâla feva'idü'l-mülûk* ("Treatise for the benefit of rulers"), is a dialogue between an Ottoman functionary and an Egyptian janissary, Süleyman, who allegedly had been a prisoner of the French and describes Paris and its hinterland, as well as French morals, their political system, and social life.[30] The manuscript is undated, but based on internal evidence we can date it to the mid-1690s.[31] After an introduction, in which Süleyman is introduced by another ex-prisoner of the Europeans, Mustafa Ağa, and having warned the interlocutors that he has often been criticized for praising the infidels (1b–4a), Süleyman begins his narrative in the form of questions (by Ahmed Ağa) and answers. He explains that he was taken prisoner during the Ottoman-Habsburg War in 1683 and that he

27 This final idea is to be found in Es'ad Efendi as well: Esad Efendi – Yılmazer 2000, LXXXVIII, 456, 569–570.

28 On this concept see Heyd 1961, 74–77; Özel 2005; Şakul 2005, 118–121; Menchinger 2014a, 225–233 and 242–260; Menchinger 2017, 87.

29 The manuscript is Topkapı Sarayı Kütüphanesi H. 1634; I did not have the opportunity to compare it in detail with Es'ad Efendi's version, but the incipit and the final pages are the same (I wish to thank Lejla Demiri for providing me with scans of these); cf. Hanioğlu 2008, 44, fn. 4. As Ethan Menchinger points out (Menchinger 2014a, 154), there are parts of the text which can be found verbatim in Vasıf, meaning that it was known to him in the early 1800s.

30 *Risâla fevâ'idü'l-mülûk*, Paris, Bibliothèque Nationale, ms. turc suppl. 221; this was first noted by Kafadar 1989, 132–133. Another apocryphal "discussion between the preacher Vani Efendi and the Chief Interpreter Panayiotis Nikousios" on matters pertaining to religion, astronomy, and the occult was circulating in Greek from the mid-1690s. See La Croix 1695, 381–401; Zervos 1992, 312–315; Kermeli-Ünal 2013.

31 Based on the description of the dynastic structure of France (fol. 43b), we can deduce 1690 as a *terminus post quem* (the author records the death of Louis XIV's daughter-in-law, Marie-Anne de Bavière) and 1711 as a *terminus ante quem* (Louis de France, Louis XIV's son, is mentioned as still alive). In fol. 33a (cf. also 7b) the allusion to the present wars (*bu seferlerde*) in which Spain, England, the Netherlands, and Austria are allied against France must refer to the Nine Years' War (The War of the Grand Alliance, 1688–97); if we take literally the sentence "they have not been able to stop the French army for six years now", then we can date the manuscript with safety to c. 1694.

was then in the service of a young French nobleman, who served as an architect for Louis XIV, for eight years. The unreserved admiration for France and especially the French king is evident throughout the text, and it is tempting to suggest that the text is a product of French intelligence to promote the prestige of France in the east (the detailed knowledge of the structure and current situation of the French dynasty, as well as an allusion to the ruins of ancient Heliopolis as "city of the sun", seem to support this suggestion).

Finally, there is also another text from the same period (i.e. the earlier part of the century) where we find the same ideas present. Comte de Bonneval, alias Humbaracı Ahmed Pasha, composed two short treatises (translated to Ottoman Turkish from French) during the 1730s.[32] In the first, he sought to explain how the Habsburg government had been organized "according to the rules of political rationalism" (*kava'id-i siyasiyye-i akliyye*, an expression actually pointing to the earlier Islamic distinction between the Sharia and the administration according to reason, with the latter also deemed potentially effective). The second treatise deals with the political history of Europe in the first three decades of the eighteenth century; Bonneval urges the sultan to seek a more active role in European international politics, giving as an example Süleyman I's alliance with France.

As with the introductory parts of his treatise, Müteferrika's discussion of military matters begins on a theoretical level, complying with the general style of his work. Rulers, he says, have created various states (*devlet*), as ordained by the Sharia or, more generally, by nature, civilization, and humanity (*iktiza-yı tabi'at ve medeniyyet ve beşeriyyet*), each one ruling over a defined piece of land. Now, just as an individual has to protect his property against trespassers, every state, no matter what its name or form may be, has to protect the lands it rules against others. To guard his position and people, every ruler has to form an army, that is, to take some of his own people or other men and shape them into a corps that is constantly ready for war. This army must be trained in military discipline and armed with suitable weapons; afterwards, it must be kept under strict control and discipline (Ş131–132). Furthermore, as if he wanted to give his credentials as a renegade, Müteferrika discusses war, saying that some wars were made simply to ensure worldly profits, while others were made in defense of the oppressions of others, but those who are commited to the faith (i.e. Islam) have a duty from the Sharia to fight the Holy War. Thus, every state is obliged to keep an army ready for war, with special uniforms and training (Ş132–133). Such general surveys of the army as an element of human society within history can also be found in *Su'âl-i Osmânî*: we read there (from the

32 Yeşil 2011b.

mouth of the Christian interlocutor) that all realms are governed either with justice or with oppression, and it is the task of wise men in one realm to be aware of the situation in others. The "Christian officer" himself had read histories of the Ottoman Empire from its very beginnings and knows that the sultan is wise and just and that he acts according to the law of wisdom (U110, E590: *kanun-ı hikmete muvafıktır*). Nonetheless, he finds it striking that Ottoman notables (*erkân-ı devlet ve a'yan-ı saltanat*) change continuously, while in other countries these posts are given for life or, at any rate, are taken back only because of serious offences. The answer is that there can be no comparison between the Ottoman and other states: in the latter, posts belong to the nobility and are hereditary, while the sultan grants offices to whoever is worthy (U111, E591). However, it is often difficult to distinguish between the worthy and unworthy; moreover, the Exalted State is like the human body, with the grand vizier being the head: if the head is lucid and wise, an injured limb may function, while if not the whole organism will be destroyed.

Continuing his review of military history, Müteferrika then proceeds to study the soldiers and battle tactics in the armies of old (Ş133–144). This lengthy chapter stresses that although states of old were very different in terms of religion, society, and form, their military and their weapons were very similar. Ottoman sultans were distinguished in establishing strict discipline and training within their armies, resulting in them being almost invincible. Now that European armies are evidently stronger on the battlefield, it is of the utmost necessity to study the reforms they had made and the new weapons they use. The old military order makes the army ill-disciplined, difficult to assemble in times of campaign, hard to direct and to control (with the corollary that it may depose its chiefs and even the sultan himself: Ş142), and easy to beat in battle. The present superiority of European armies is clear, Müteferrika notes, judging from the way these states have raised their power and captured various lands all over the world; this was due both to their use of the science of geography and the military reforms they planned and carried out. The Ottomans should learn the methods and innovations used in these new armies, which Müteferrika names "new order" (*nizam-ı cedid*); the disadvantages of the old military techniques are obvious from the outcome of many battles, and an Islamic state should not ignore or neglect out of laziness the need to reform its army according to the new systems (Ş144–148).

This is, it seems, the first appearance of the term *nizam-ı cedid* (which was to be adopted for Selim III's ambitious modernization project several decades later) in such a context. As for the argument that the Ottomans were the first to impose discipline on and training for the army, and thus that imitating the European model would not be an innovation but a reappropriation of tradition, this was also to gain pre-eminence in the context of "reciprocity" during late eighteenth-century debates. Müteferrika placed so much importance on this argument that he returned to it in more detail, justifying very carefully the need for reform in terms of Holy War and of the natural superiority of Muslim warriors (Ş162–169). Thus, he describes the military superiority of the early Ottomans, when war was based on swords and hand-to-hand combat rather than artillery, and concludes that the Christians were forced to concentrate on perfecting the order of their armies in order to resist the otherwise irresistible Muslim armies. The main advantage of the Ottomans, according to Müteferrika, is their courage, boldness, and commitment to the ideals of the Holy War. Lacking these, Europeans chose to reinforce their soldiers' armories to defend against the vehemence of their opponents. The Ottomans then had to either make swift assaults or exhaust the enemy by occupying strategic points and avoiding battle until he is weary and confused. Under such conditions, Ottoman defeats can be explained only by specific reasons, some of which pertain to the Ottomans themselves, namely their failure to study the situation of the enemy and the reasons for their own decline (*fesad*), others pertaining to the infidels (their order and discipline, and their commitment to the new order of warfare; Ş169–170).

The argument for Muslim precedence in discipline and training was not invented by Müteferrika; it had been used by the author of *Su'âl-i Osmânî*. Here, the Christian side observed that the Ottomans stopped observing the rules of the Holy Law, as well as their old laws (*kavanin-ı kadime*). Their officers used to be pious, valiant, and zealous, while the soldiers used neither to mix with agriculture and commerce nor to pillage the land. That is why the Austrians, knowing that they could not resist an Ottoman assault, started making trenches and using artillery; they began to practise discipline and training, to collect books on government (*umur-ı dahiliyye*), and to build warehouses. If the Ottomans did the same, they would be invincible, because the Austrians only know how to use guns and ignore combat with swords. Furthermore, the Austrian army has a high degree of organization, with a hierarchy of officers controlling each other in groups of hundreds and thousands, while every contingent has its own uniform so that deserters may be recognized. Moreover, they use their rifles in turn and in concert, so shooting never stops. There is no way for an undisciplined army to stand against these troops, all the more so since Ottoman ranks are filled with "Turks, Kurds, and other groups of corruption". Discipline and order are the basis of victory. A similar reasoning is found in Bonneval's first treatise: he stresses the existence of constant laws and regulations which are printed and diffused among the population (an assessment very much in line with Müteferrika's printing project), as well as (unsurprisingly) the discipline of soldiers that makes them fight as one person. Then he proceeds to the same argument about Muslim superiority: the Prophet himself had used discipline and order (*hüsn-i nizam*) in his armies, whereas the Christian nations learnt this art from their conflict with the Muslims of Spain. It is interesting to note that, trying to explain the status of the Austrian nobility, Bonneval compares it to the "freedom" (*serbestiyyet*) and "exempted state" (*mu'afiyyet*) of the sipahi class. As traditional weapons such as swords and arrows began to decline, he says, the Austrian emperors started to draw their troops from the commoners rather than the aristocrats with the parallel aim of safeguarding their "freedom".[33]

Yet the argument of Muslim precedent is not enough for Müteferrika, who describes at length the socio-economic benefits to be gained from military order and discipline (§148–154). The purpose of order and discipline, he argues, is, obviously, to be victorious against the enemy; when two armies of similar organization, numbers, and strength meet in battle, victory favors the more disciplined side. This is evident in the case of the wars between European states, which have more or less similar armies. Secondly, a state whose army is well-ordered and disciplined secures its internal peace and well-being, while rebellions and disquiet arise in a state whose army loses its order. Müteferrika mentions at length the example of the Roman Empire, which collapsed due to the disorder that appeared in its armies, with the result that even the mighty title of emperor (*imparator*) fell to into disrepute until the Habsburg emperors used it once more due to the power of their armies (§149–151). States that do not comply with the necessities of the new military systems are doomed to submit to others.

It appears that Müteferrika considered this connection of military power with state power and internal peace a particularly strong argument. He claims that if an army has a strict and disciplined hierarchy then the people of the state will lead a quiet and easy life; since the ordering of the military is based on scientific foundations, the soldiers keep their discipline even though they differ from one another in character and nature. A disciplined army can pass through a vineyard with no soldier touching a vine; thus, people feel secure and follow their occupations in peace. Indeed, notes Müteferrika, reverting to the well-known model of the four-fold division of society, people living in a

33 Yeşil 2011b, 215–216. On the contrary, the author of *Risâla feva'idü'l-mülûk* emphasizes the French army being composed of noblemen and the fact that, unlike the Ottomans, soldiers are not confused with their servants (14b–15a). Such passages point to my suggestion that the text must be seen as an advertisement of French power, rather than an indirect criticism of Ottoman realities.

state (*bir devletin saha-yı dairesinde mevcud efrad-ı nas*) should be divided into four classes under the administration of a ruler so that the body of the state (*beden-i devlet*) remains well-ordered, just as the four elements maintain the health of the human body (Ş152–153).

Moreover, a disciplined army benefits the treasury and prevents unnecessary expenditure, since its soldiers see to their duties night and day instead of looking for ways to profit privately. With a well-ordered army, it is clear who belongs to the military and who does not, and thus every person carries out his own duty. This way, no class interferes with the duties of any other (*bir sınıf aher sınıfın zimmetiyle*); for instance, soldiers are not forced to be cultivators and the latter are not obliged to fight (*sipah ra'iyyet ile ve re'aya cenk ile cebr-u-kerh olunmayub*; Ş154). Furthermore, the number of soldiers must be known at all times; soldiers and civilians should not be confused with each other, and soldiers ought to wear special uniforms that should be prohibited to non-soldiers, as the intermingling of soldiers and civilians has caused much trouble, both in war and in peace.

The practicalities of this "new order" are discussed in detail in most of these treatises. In the description of France in the *Risâla feva'idü'l-mülûk*, Louis XIV's army is the main topic: its numbers, its superiority to the Austrian (8a), its division into infantry, cavalry, and dragoons, the structure of the officers and their divisions, the willingness of the soldiers and officers to fight in order to gain honor (10a), the perfectness of their manoeuvres (11a-b), their uniforms and ways of promotion (12b and 25a–26a, 28a-b), and their training, etc. The French army is regularly inspected so the king has absolute knowledge and control of it at any given time; furthermore, military salaries are provided through a strictly regulated system and procedure. Soldiers and officers are prohibited from acts of sale (18b) and from any kind of oppression of the peasants (20b–21a); they train regularly via military exercises and virtual battles (27a). A large part of the text is also reserved for praising the French fleet (22a–24b) as well as to Vauban's system of fortresses (35b–36a). Similarly, Müteferrika gives a detailed description of what he calls "military order" or *nizam-ı asker*, which in fact describes European eighteenth-century warfare. Using numerous French words (*soldat, grenadier, dragon*, and so forth), which presumably he introduced into Ottoman vocabulary, he examines: the division of the armies into regiments under a strict hierarchy of officers; the use of uniforms for each regiment; the presence of rifle units in each infantry and cavalry body; the proper officer hierarchy and the importance of staff officers, as well as of regular training; the use of passwords; and, finally, the use of two lines of battle, fighting with strict discipline and in collaboration (Ş171–186).

The first concrete proposition for the creation of a special, European-trained corps comes from the author of *Su'âl-i Osmânî*. In case a peace treaty is not achieved, the Ottomans should inspire zeal in their ranks and punish undisciplined soldiers and deserters; yet the advice the Christian has to offer is that they protect their border with 20,000 or 30,000 trustworthy soldiers, trained by Christian officers (*tavaif-i nasaradan mürettep*), who would be paid with the money that should be used for war (U116, E599). Such an army should be collected through conscription, although it seems that this was always considered as voluntary. Bonneval notes peasant boys were fitter for conscription than urban dwellers, since they were used to hard work and patience from childhood. More cautiously, Müteferrika first suggests that the existing army could be reformed, and explains why this is possible: since human resources abound, in three or four months the existing armies could be transformed into disciplined bodies along European-style lines. In a kind of concession to the existing order, he adds that the Ottoman army is unique in giving generous pensions to old, retired, or ill soldiers and officers, which makes it highly probable that experienced European officers may defect to the Ottomans (Ş188). Müteferrika proposes various ways for encouraging such defections, such as generous salaries and respect for the defectors' religion. The Russian military reforms under Peter the Great are another encouraging example.

What is very typical of these works is the almost total absence of non-military advice. Müteferrika's praise of geography (influenced by his admiration for Kâtib Çelebi) apart, all his views on human society are traditional commonplace advice, or (in the case of his description of polities) inserted without any connection to the rest of the treatise. One may perhaps discern a slight stress on sultanly absolutism, which is of course much more evident in the praise of France found in the *Risâla feva'idü'l-mülûk*: the king has absolute control over justice (29a) and the administration, and he is his own vizier (33a–35b). As for the *Su'âl-i Osmânî*, we must note an interesting dimension, namely its link with the early eighteenth-century praise of peace, as seen in Na'ima's and Nabi's work. It is stated explicitly that, after the Treaty of Karlowitz, [Amcazade Köprülü] Hüseyin Pasha had justified himself (as the principal negotiator) on the grounds that peace was needed for the welfare of the towns and of the treasury and the multiplication of the troops for future revenge. The Ottoman interlocutor asks his Christian counterpart whether he also believes that an interval of peace would be useful for an army to reorganize its discipline and material, so as to be able to come back more powerful (U114, E596); the Christian agrees, but remarks that the victorious side will dictate its peace terms to the defeated.[34] He then stresses that, whereas soldiers may be disciplined in a short time, it requires a longer period for the officers to be trained in the sciences of war. The Ottoman insists that the goal is retaliation, and thus a long time of peace is needed so that order is restored, to which the Christian answers that there are two ways of campaigning, one with constant attack and besieging, the other having an army ready at the border to inspire fear in the enemy and make him spend unnecessarily. We must also make a final note about a concept that was much used later, as seen in chapter 8, and which seems to have been first mentioned in this text: temporary success or *istidrac* in order to explain the victories of infidels. The author gives the example of the Crusaders when they managed to capture Jerusalem (U119, E602–603).

• • •

It is easy to understand why Müteferrika's work marks the beginning of a quite new trend in Ottoman thought. Undoubtedly, much of his orientation came from his Christian background: for one thing, his detailed knowledge of contemporaneous European military science must have originated in his Transylvanian years, and perhaps it was due to the same intellectual origins that he chose to copy Kâtib Çelebi's translation of the Aristotelian concept of politics and government. He may not have been the first to express such ideas, but the fact that his book was printed and circulated widely among Ottoman litterati made it one of the most influential works in the eighteenth century—and especially in its later half. As well as the works examined earlier, which were composed independently of one another, Müteferrika's ideas were used and copied, sometimes verbatim, by numerous authors, one of whom was Süleyman Penah Efendi (see above, chapter 8). An anonymous and undated manuscript entitled *Nizâmiyye* ("[Treatise] on order"), for instance, copies or paraphrases large parts of Müteferrika's *Usûlü'l-hikem* to produce a treatise (addressed to an unnamed grand vizier) on two issues, the benefits of geography and the organization of the army.[35] The author interpolates a long section presenting the idea of printing detailed maps of the Ottoman Empire (something which is again reminiscent of Penah Efendi), which, being in Turkish, would sell at a profit not only in Arab and Persian lands but in Europe as well (7b); on the other hand, he omits certain parts of Müteferrika's description

34 A large part of the Dialogue is devoted to a detailed description of the diplomatic situation of the time and advice on the moves to be made to ensure a possible peace.

35 Paris, Bibliothèque nationale, suppl. turc 201. One is tempted to suggest that this might also be an early draft of Müteferrika's own work.

of European armies, perhaps because with their detail they might sound too "Westernizing". Interestingly, a copyist or collector noted on the title page that the work was authored by "a monk who was honored by the glory of Islam".

Clearly, a link can be established between the outburst of such Westernizing proposals and works and the "Tulip Period", which roughly coincided with them and are usually associated with a marked influence of European ways and ideas. Yet Bonneval's activity in the Ottoman Empire and his treatises (as well as Müteferrika's essay) date to after Patrona Halil's revolt. Furthermore, Müteferrika's ideas share much not only with contemporaneous authors and scientists such as Es'ad Efendi and Mahmud Efendi of Athens but also with Kâtib Çelebi, whom Müteferrika admired greatly, Na'ima, and Ebu Bekr Dımışkî (see chapter 5). The very notion of the need to imitate Western progress in military matters (what would later be termed *mukabele bi'l-misl* or reciprocity), was first found in Hasan Kâfi Akhisari (see chapter 4); the argument that Western technology and other innovations could be used by Muslims without restriction, as long as it did not touch religion, was also used by the famous Damascene scholar Abd al-Ghani al-Nabulusi (d. 1731) in 1682 (in order to defend the use of tobacco!).[36] Thus, the genealogy of this group of ideas goes far beyond Ahmed III's reign and the cultural openings to the West within it.

Of course, all these authors being European converts cannot be considered mere coincidence. It might also be the reason (or at least one of the reasons) their views went unnoticed for decades, as there were no other proposals for the imitation of Western models until the 1770s. Another reason may be sought in the socio-political balance established after 1703 and confirmed in 1730: the acceptance of the janissaries' share in power by the palace and the governmental bureaucracy, which was mentioned in the previous chapter, made any suggestion for a re-orientation of the standing army toward efficient warfare, and even more for the creation of a new army, very difficult to uphold and, of course, to apply. Osman II's ghost was still very much alive.

On the other hand, it is impressive how influential and long-lasting the arguments in these tracts were. For one thing, it appears that, its absence from mid-eighteenth-century political texts notwithstanding, the idea of European inventions being a rediscovery of earlier Islamic findings had permeated Ottoman culture. The 1740 example of Nu'man Efendi's pride at having copied

36 Grehan 2006, 1371. Interestingly, among those who accused the defenders of tobacco of using European sources (instead of logic) we find the Greek Phanariot Nikolaos Mavrokordatos (d. 1730), whom we saw above as a pioneer of Aristotelian philosophy during the "Tulip Period": see Kermeli 2014, 133.

the Austrian surveying instrument (see above, chapter 8) is telling. This is how he answers the Habsburg general, when the latter asks him how he did it:[37]

> Do not think that since we do not know these tricks we had to learn them by one of your engineers ... We know them through the science of geometry and its proven rules. We have compilations of geometry books and figures of theorems. Because in the Exalted State we do not pay attention to mapmaking, it has been neglected, but we [know] it all the same. The wise monk in the state of England who said "I invented this" had [in fact] studied the rules ... contained in the books of geometry that had passed to the hands of the Christian nations with the fall of Cordoba ... We do know this practice with its methods and proofs ... Did you think we are ignorant? Did you think the Exalted State chose us for such a task in vain?

The idea that military discipline and training was an invention of the Ottomans in the fourteenth or fifteenth century, which was then taken up by their European foes, proved especially strong, since it could surpass objections based either on the abhorring of innovation and the superiority of Islam. Combined with the principle of reciprocity, it made a mighty weapon in the hands of the factions promoting European-style military reforms. What differentiates the authors to be examined in this chapter from those called "traditionalists" who were analyzed in the previous one is exactly this notion of reciprocal imitation. True, Süleyman Penah Efendi often looks to Europe for models of military organization or cultural assimilation, but he looks for inspiration not at a nation that is already a step beyond and that should be taken as a model. This is the quintessence of *mukabele bi'l-misl*, the common feature of the works examined in this chapter.

1.2 *Ahmed Resmi Efendi and the Balance of Powers*

As noted in the previous chapter, there is a strange 40-year gap in notable works of political advice, roughly from the end of the "Tulip Period" until the Ottoman-Russian war. The growing emphasis of Ottoman political thought on military organization may (partly) account for this silence, since these four decades were peaceful ones, as if Na'ima, Nabi, and other advocates of peace had finally been heard by the administrators. Furthermore, both Na'ima and the anonymous Christian interlocutor in the 1718 dialogue had stressed that peace would be an opportunity for reorganization, with the eventual aim of fighting back against the infidel with a stronger army. And, indeed, personalities

37 Nu'man Efendi – Savaş 1999, 89–90; Nu'man Efendi – Prokosch 1972, 93–94.

such as Bonneval and Ragıb Pasha made serious efforts to reform the army, albeit in different ways. When war resumed, the issue of peace re-emerged, and with it the new understanding of international politics as seen, for example, in Bonneval's work.

The channels connecting Western European thought with Ottoman literary circles did not cease; on the contrary, they grew increasingly influential. To the works cited above should be added an Ottoman translation of Frederick the Great of Prussia's *Anti-Machiavel* (1740), a refutation of Machiavelli's *The Prince* (which also contains the Italian thinker's text) from an enlightened monarch's point of view.[38] The translation was probably made in the late 1750s; the spirit of Frederick's work fits quite well with traditional Ottoman political thought, since it opposes the view of the monarch as necessarily wicked, cruel, and devious while stating that the only appropriate way to act is with justice and kindness. Nevertheless, the translator had to cope with terms and ideas that were new to Ottoman political thought; the very fact that such a text exists shows that this period was indeed one of significant translation activity. To this should be added the multiplication of Ottoman envoys sent to European capitals and the proliferation of their reports (*sefaretname*), which were then often incorporated into official histories and thus made available to an even wider audience.[39] From among these ambassadors or rather, perhaps, envoys, one could highlight Yirmisekiz Mehmed Çelebi, who visited Paris in 1721 and whose son Said Efendi (who had accompanied his father) was a close friend and supporter of İbrahim Müteferrika (and his partner in the printing enterprise until 1731, when he began to be sent as an ambassador himself),[40] the historian Vasıf Efendi, envoy to Spain, and Ebubekir Ratıb Efendi, who was mentioned in the previous chapter and to whom we will return soon. Another such ambassador, Ahmed Resmî Efendi, was also the initiator of a new understanding of international politics, in the vein of the remarks by Bonneval or the anonymous author of the "Dialogue", which may be seen as a stage in the gradual "de-moralization" of the Ottoman conceptions surrounding external

38 Aydoğdu 2008. On the circulation of Machiavelli's ideas in late eighteenth-century Greek Ottoman circles, cf. Stavrakopoulou 2012, 44–45.

39 On such embassies and the relevant literature, see Berkes 1964, 33–36; Unat 1968; Ortaylı 2001, 40–41; Aksan 1995, 42–46; Aksan 2004, 15–16; Korkut 2003; Şakul 2005, 123–124 and fn. 22; Ermiş 2014, 152–157; on the changing Ottoman attitudes regarding diplomacy, cf. Işıksel 2010 and 2014. On Ottoman knowleedge of Europe in the mid-eighteenth century, see Aksan 1995, 34–42.

40 Sabev 2006, 154–156, 168.

policies and international relations (or, in other words, a retreat of the idea of Ottoman "exceptionalism").[41]

Ahmed Resmî Efendi (1700–83), of Cretan descent, was the first Ottoman ambassador to Prussia (1763), where he was shown a review of Frederick the Great's army (in turn, he wrote his own report or *sefaretname*). Throughout the Russian-Ottoman war (1768–74) he was the *kethüda* of the grand vizier, Halil Pasha, to whom he presented his first essay (1769) on military affairs, partly based on his experience in Berlin (the word "experience", *tecrübe*, is repeatedly mentioned in the preface of the essay).[42] At the beginning of this treatise, Resmi shows an attitude towards war somewhat rare for his time: he states that "God has ordained that the order of the earth and protection from corruption is achieved through war" (based on a Quranic quotation),[43] and attributes Ottoman defeats in war to the long period of peace and the subsequent neglect of proper military organization (1b–2a). He then enumerates some issues he feels the grand vizier should attend to, concerning the order of a campaign; he focuses on the need for discipline during the march and in the camp, stressing (just as Silahdar Fındıklılı Mehmed Ağa had done on the occasion of the defeat at Vienna) the unnecessary multitude of auxiliary followers and animals, especially among the troops from Anatolia (4a–7a). He also deals with the army's logistics, proposing ways to secure provisions for the army without oppressing the peasants of the areas through which the troops would have to march (8b–10a). Resmi also discusses price regulation (again with an eye on provisioning the army), exhibiting detailed knowledge of the price of basic goods (10a–12a). As for the janissaries, Ahmed Resmi stresses the well-known problem of *esame*, i.e. roll titles, whose number did not correspond to the actual soldiers and which were the object of illegal sale and corruption among the officers. As did many before him, he recommends a thorough inspection of the pay-rolls, which would show the real number of troops ready for the field, but, proceeding beyond this, he also proposes ("in case these measures do not bring about results") the creation of a special corps (8a). Such a corps should be formed by

> 2,000 men chosen from among the lowest ranks of the inhabitants of the Balkans and Anatolia (*edna mertebe iki tarafdan iki bin adem intihab*).

41 On this process see Beydilli 1999a. On Ahmed Resmi, the classic study is Aksan 1995.

42 İstanbul Üniversitesi Kütüphanesi, TY 419, 1b–12a; an English summary is in Aksan 1993, 57–58 (=Aksan 2004, 33–35); Aksan 1995, 188–195.

43 Quran 2:251: "And if it were not for Allah checking [some] people by means of others, the earth would have been corrupted".

After being registered in special lists, they should be reviewed and inspected every two or three days. This way, Resmi notes,

> even if they were not fit for major battles they would at least [be able to] serve in minor skirmishes (*vakt-ı hacetde külli omazsa bari umur-ı cüziyyede istihdamları mümkün olmak gerek*).

With this impressive proposal, modestly hidden in six lines out of 22 pages, Resmi proves himself another precursor of the *Nizam-i Cedid* reforms, although, it should be noted, such was the method of recruiting locally-raised irregulars, the *levend*, which were the bulk of the army by his time and which, as Virginia Aksan remarks, "ultimately serv[ed] as the model for Selim III's 'New Order' (*Nizam-i Cedid*) troops".[44]

In his second treatise, Resmi deals with international politics and more particularly tries to give (to quote the lengthy title)[45]

> a response to those who state that it is impossible for the Russian infidels to be expelled or to withdraw from the territories they have temporarily (*kuvve-i istidraciye ile*) occupied for three or four years now in Ukraine, Wallachia, and Moldavia.

We should note the use of the term *istidrac*, which was used in Vasıf Efendi's short essay as well as in the *Su'âl-i Osmânî*—and indeed, there are parts of the latter that show a striking resemblance to Resmi's treatise.

Completed in 1772, this work was requested by the-then grand vizier Muhsinzade Mehmed Pasha as well as (according to some manuscripts) the

---

44 Aksan 1998, 28. This model of provincially-recruited armies, with the consequent interdependence of the central state and the local elites, was to wholly prevail by the early nineteenth century: Şakul 2014b.

45 *Moskov keferesi kuvve-i istidraciye ile üç dört sene Bender ve Bucak ve Boğdan ve Eflak'ta yerleşib etraf ü eknafa tasallutta müstemir olmağın fi mâ-ba'd bu taife rızasıyla bu mahalden çekilmek müşkil ve zor ile ihracı muhal görünür diyenlere vech-i tecribeyi iraet ve ale'l-husus bu vahime ile perişan-hatır olan Sadrâzam Muhsınzâde Mehmed Paşa hazretlerine tevsi-i daire-i tesliyet ve tenvir-i basıra-ı mekanet için kaleme alınan makaledir.* Ahmed Resmi – Parmaksızoğlu 1983 (modern Turkish version with facsimile); see also Aksan 1993, 57–59 (=Aksan 2004, 35–36); Aksan 1995, 195–198. The MS is anonymous, but a comparison with other works by Ahmed Resmi clearly shows its authorship (see Ahmed Resmi – Parmaksızoğlu 1983, 527; also accepted by Aksan). Topkapı Sarayı Ktp. H. 375 (Karatay 1961, 1:508 no. 1553) seems to be a very short synopsis.

reisülküttab Abdürrezzak Efendi.[46] At the beginning, Resmi seems to use the same arguments he had employed in his first essay on the necessity of war; however, he manages to conclude, through a combination of Khaldunism and an exhibition of diplomatic knowledge, that peace is also necessary. He admits that, as God has ordained, when the long-lasting and famous states (*devlet*) approach their age of decline (*sinn-i inhitat*), they are known to be content within their own borders (*hat-ı mahsusalarına*). God has also ordained that the states and dynasties, on whom depend the order of the world and the safety of the people, have to continuously attack each other on the slightest grounds. Some sultans, being inexperienced, short-sighted, and lacking good advice, endanger their power and subjects by launching wars to expand their lands; thus, they destroy their treasury and sometimes lose even the territory they already possess.

In order to prove this thesis, Ahmed Resmi cites a series of historical examples from the preceding 50 or 60 years: Mir Üveys from Kandahar destroyed the Safavid state of Iran in 1729, as the necessities of the age had not permitted new states in the area for the previous two centuries (*taze devletler ihdası tabi'at-ı dehrden za'ildir*). Inevitably, this caused unrest in the social organism (*he'yet-i ictima'iyye*), and all the neighboring states (the Ottomans from the West, Nader Shah from the East, the Russians from the North) tried to conquer as much Iranian territory as they could. After 20 years of war, the borders merely returned to the *status quo ante*, with Nader Shah's state replacing Safavid Iran (and he himself died because of his own perpetual wars). In a similar way, Resmi describes the subsequent wars of Russia and Austria against the weakened Ottomans, of Prussia against Austria, of Poland against its Tatar neighbors, as well as the conquests of Genghis Khan.

Ahmed Resmi notes (P531) that the real reason for this sequence of war and peace is that, according to God's will, the surface of the earth was divided between various nations (*milel*) that are separated by physical borders (*hudud*) such as mountains, seas, and rivers, and which fight each other, while also having periods of friendship and peace. The fact that, for the past four years, Russia had continuously attacked the Ottoman borders is, for Resmi, a paradox (*galat-ı tabi'at*) and must be attributed to astrological conjectures. In a similar situation, he adds (P532), when the stars of Süleyman I were in their most beneficial position, the Ottomans managed to gain victories in both the Indian

46 He was Resmi's brother-in-law and (soon after) the chief negotiator with the Russians (Aksan 1995, 107, fn. 30), as well as Vasıf Efendi's patron (I wish to thank Ethan Metchinger for this information).

Ocean and the Mediterranean; soon, however, they had to retire from their possessions in the former.

Thus, concludes Resmi, the war efforts of Russia on various fronts (Poland, Georgia, and the Mediterranean) are doomed to fail, since they are like loading a camel with a greater burden than it can stand. Because of the devastating results of continuous warfare upon the production and the income of its subjects, love for their country (P534: *memleket-perverin maslahatı*) will be lost. Moreover, the difficulties that will arise in the affairs of the notables will incite its neighbors to wage another war against Russia. Therefore, if the Ottoman state avoids a new war and is content with defending its borders, argues Resmi, Russia will have to withdraw its armies and fleet and seek peace.

The pieces of advice contained in his final work, *Hülâsatü'l-i'tibâr* ("A summary of admonitions"), a chronicle of the disastrous Russian-Ottoman war of 1768–74,[47] are mostly taken from his 1769 treatise. Resmi Efendi repeats the idea that war and strife is the fate of the world since "the essence of the world order has been based upon antipathy", but then stresses that the prosperity and welfare of a realm depend on peace. Peace, he claims, is "desirable and orthodox according to the Sharia and reason"; Resmi cites a number of historical examples from the Islamic and Ottoman past, but also notes that "in the opinion of Christian states, this rule is at all times held as a guiding principle" and that they always prefer peace to war. It is interesting how Resmi reverts to his 1769 argument about a long period of peace, but uses it to emphasize that no-one remembers the dangers and consequences of war, rather than to lament the neglect of the army (M36, 66–69).[48] As for Russia's continuous wars and victories, he repeats his 1772 assertion that they are a historical paradox (*zuhurât-ı garibe*), like Selim I's and Süleyman's campaigns or like a flood or hurricane, and that they cannot last long (M85).

Similar ideas are expressed in another anonymous work, *Avrupa'ya mensûb olan mîzân-ı umûr-ı hâriciyye beyânındadır* ("On the balance of foreign affairs relating to Europe"), completed in 1774, just before negotiations for the peace treaty of Küçük Kaynarca; it is highly probable that it was authored by Resmi Efendi as well.[49] It begins with an interesting description of human statehood, characteristically treating the Ottoman Empire as just another state in an international community (Y5):

47 Ahmed Resmi – Menchinger 2011.

48 Resmi tries to justify his signing the Küçük Kaynarca Treaty and, to effect this, he blames the Tatars of the Crimea as "a mischief-making, ill-omened people who had burdened the Sublime State from of old" (Ahmed Resmi – Menchinger 2011, 77).

49 Yeşil 2012 (see some arguments on the authorship of the text in p. 1, fn. 4); see also Aksan 1993, 59–60 (=Aksan 2004, 36–38).

> In order for the various nations to settle into their respective places expanding in a great part of the inhabited world, every group (*güruh*) needs to set forth laws (*kanun*) [that are] useful and suitable to itself. Just like the law provided by Sultan Süleyman to the Exalted State, so are other societies (*güruh*) also bound to arrangements (*nizam*) particular and useful for themselves. And in order to treat their external affairs equally in respect to each other, there is a need for balance (*mizan*). This balance has appeared for some centuries now and is called the "balance of foreign affairs"; it presently rules the situation in Europe. Thus, whenever a king upsets this balance by encroaching on the properties and territories, or the freedom (*azadelik*),[50] of a weaker state, the other states do not tolerate this and, in one way or another, they try to bring things back to their original equilibrium (*i'tidal*).

This is not the first time such a view was expressed in Ottoman writings: a quarter of the century earlier, the anonymous author of *Su'âl-i Osmânî ve Cevâb-ı Nasrânî* had stated that Christian kings always seek to be equal to each other (*beynlerinde müsavat murad ederler*) since they know that when one kingdom prevails over another it will soon prevail over others as well. Thus, whenever a country shows itself to be stronger, all the others form an alliance against it; this is illustrated by numerous examples from recent European history.[51] However, *Mîzân-ı umûr-ı hâriciyye* is one of the first instances when the Ottoman state is included explicitly within this description.

The author illustrates this thesis with numerous examples from contemporaneous and historical Europe, noting, for instance, that France sometimes helped the Ottomans in order to check Austria's power rather than out of pure friendship. He then describes at length and rather grimly the present military and international status of the Ottoman Empire, remarking that with the change of sultan (with the recent accession of Abdülhamid I to the throne, in January 1774) statesmen changed too, with the result that the crucial question is now pending: what is to be done, and more specifically whether peace should be sought, and, if yes, which infidel state must be trusted for help. Now, in order to argue for the necessity of peace, the author uses Ibn Khaldun's authority on nomadism and its decline (Y11):

> According to Ibn Khaldun's *Muqaddima*, we must obey the necessities of the time and situation: because of the long and uninterrupted

50 Cf. the use of *serbestlik* for the Polish state, slightly later: Yeşil 2012, 8.

51 Unat 1941, 120; Esad Efendi – Yılmazer 2000, 604.

> continuation of settled life (*temadi-i hazar*), we have forgotten the arts of war and consequently we have not had a single victory for five years now.

Furthermore, he notes, constant war has damaged the treasury, while the international situation is not favorable either. After carefully blaming (the dead) Mustafa III's avarice (*buhl*) and his counselors' simple-mindedness, he concludes that peace would be acceptable and fit for the current needs of the state. However, the Ottomans also need to find another ally as a mediator in order to benefit from the balance of power among the European states. The author examines three potential candidates (France, England, and the Netherlands), analyzing the intentions and power of each in detail.[52] At any rate, he concludes, the Ottomans need to gain the attention of one of these three states in order to use it as negotiator; to this end, permanent ambassadors should be appointed to the European capitals. As if to refute himself and to comply with more traditional advice, the author ends his essay by stressing the need for statesmen to be pious, well-meaning, honest, and united.

While analyzing the relationship with France, the author remarks that a French "nobleman" (*beğzade*: meaning Baron de Tott) was sent to train Ottoman soldiers. Then, he reverts to the argument of Muslim precedence, as did Müteferrika and the contemporaneous *Su'âl-i Osmânî*: Westerners always knew that the advantage of the Ottomans laid in their zeal for martyrdom and that is why they chose to intensify the training and drilling of their own armies in order to match this religious fervor. It is somewhat odd that Ottomans now have to revert to European methods of training and, besides, the author finds that there is a tendency to consider every inexperienced and young European adventurer as an experienced officer to whom Ottoman veterans should bow (Y15–16).

---

52 France, apart from being an old friend of the Ottoman Empire, needs good relations with it because of trade. The increased French trade, however, is not self-evidently profitable for the Ottomans: no matter how inexperienced they are, the author explains, Ottoman Black Sea merchants leave their profits to the land (*memleketimizde*), except when they are useful to the navy. The French merchants, in contrast, will co-operate with them only to decrease their capacity and profits, like they also do in the Aegean Sea (Y13–14). England is a strong state, possessing territories in India and in America, and also has the advantage of being commercially necessary to the northern countries, thus being able to manipulate them. The author argues that if the Ottomans open the Black Sea to Russia, the English merchants will lose out (to the French). Finally, Netherlands is not so strong a nation as the other two, but it is very active in the maritime trade; on the other hand, the Dutch have financially supported Russia and so have to be considered a second-rate potential ally.

2 Selim III and the Reform Debate

There is no doubt that a vision such as Resmi's regarding the Ottoman state and its place in the international system made it easier for advocates of Western-style reforms to exert their influence, and the acquaintance of Resmi and other officials and intellectuals with the European courts, to which they were sent as envoys, further enhanced this trend. In chapter 8, we saw Ebubekir Ratıb Efendi's (1750–99) early views as reflected in his correspondence with his pupil, the young prince Selim. After Selim's rise to the throne, Ratıb Efendi was sent as ambassador to Vienna (1792); the monumental account of his embassy, known as as *Büyük Layıha*, is his most famous and important work, and a substantial change in its author's views can easily be discerned.[53]

This enormous and detailed account of Austrian government and manners bears elements of the older "administration manual" tradition (e.g. Hezarfen's work) but, as Carter Findley notes, it also "resembles French works of the period that have terms like *état général* or *tableau* in their titles, followed by the kind of taxonomic layout that such a title would seem to imply".[54] In the first part, which deals with the army, Ratıb Efendi takes up the well-known argument, seen for instance in the works of de Bonneval and others (including Ratib Efendi himself in his correspondence with Selim), that the Europeans first imitated the Ottomans. He states that it was in the third quarter of the seventeenth century that European, and especially Austrian and Prussian, forces started to exploit the science of engineering and follow a scientific organization of the army; he focuses on the Austrian Count Lacy's reforms (1766–74) as a "new order" (*nizam-ı cedid*). He stresses that the Ottomans were the first to lay down military regulations (*nizam u kavanin*) and argues that only after they saw the Ottomans' superior discipline in the 1683 siege of Vienna did the Austrians begin to imitate their enemies, and they were allegedly particularly impressed by the Ottoman method of recruiting peasants (*Osmanlunın ebna-yı reaya ve evlad-ı Türkten acemi oğlanı devşirdiklerine kıyasladır*). However, later sultans neglected to preserve these regulations or impose new ones when they were required.

Ratıb Efendi then proceeds to give very analytical descriptions, in eleven chapters, of the structure, education, regulations, reserves, and logistics of the

53 Ratıb Efendi – Arıkan 1996. Cf. also Unat 1968, 154–162; Stein 1985; Findley 1995; Ermiş 2014, 122ff. On Ratıb Efendi see also Karal 1960; Uzunçarşılı 1975; Yeşil 2011a and 2014; and chapter 8, above.

54 Findley 1995, 45ff. It seems that Ratıb Efendi was greatly helped by Ignatius Mouradgea d'Ohsson, whose *Tableau général de l'Empire othoman* has a very similar structure; cf. Beydilli 1984.

Austrian army. He somewhat misleadingly describes the Austrian measure of sending home a third of the soldiers and of manufacturing uniforms and weapons with the money that would otherwise be used for their salaries (one might discern a subtle suggestion for the janissaries). The "conclusion" of the first part concerns the military forces of other states (Russia, Prussia, and France). As for the second, much smaller part (about a fifth of the total text), this deals with the Austrian government; its only chapter concerns the administration of towns and villages, as well as taxation, and describes in less detail the judicial system, the medical institutions, the police, the mines, and other revenues of the Austrian state. The conclusion of the second part, however, continues by citing other types of revenue (posts, banknotes, stamps, and lotteries). In this part, Ratıb Efendi straightforwardly accuses the Ottomans of neglecting trade with their own subjects; while other states tax foreign merchants more than domestic ones, the Ottoman rulers, out of pride and generosity, granted exemptions to foreigners and increased the toll duties paid by Ottoman merchants, with the ruin of the latter being the result. Moreover, cloth and textiles are imported from India and Europe instead of being produced in Ottoman lands; Ratıb Efendi specifically proposes that cloth manufactuing centres be founded in the Ottoman Empire, assuring the reader that the overall profit will be more than the custom dues lost from imports. This emphasis on the importance of local production was, as seen in Penah Efendi's and, later, Behic Efendi's work, a recurrent theme of late eighteenth-century thought.

Ratıb Efendi's intention of using this description to promote his ideas on Ottoman reform is evident, particulary since another, more concise and private report on his embassy shows a different image of Austria, one much less well-ordered and prosperous.[55] However, Stanford J. Shaw's assertion that Ratıb Efendi "praised the freedom left to individuals to do what they wanted without restriction by the state" and that he was an advocate of secular justice seems to stem from an overestimation of Ratıb Efendi's observations, which, after all, end with the remark that "the European states are in such a form that they can no longer be called people of the book".[56] Carter V. Findley's assessment sounds more balanced, when he says that[57]

> he presented Ottoman policy and intentions in a way that reflected his adhesion to the new trends of Ottoman political thought in an age when men of scribal background, like himself, were beginning to introduce into

55 Findley 1995, 63–66.
56 Shaw 1971, 95–97.
57 Findley 1995, 54–55.

> Ottoman policy a new emphasis on peace abroad and on the pursuit of prosperity at home.

Although he is generally viewed as one the reformists around Selim III, Ratıb Efendi seems to have favored "traditionalist" reforms rather than the "modernist" ones his sultan attempted.[58] The blurred line between these two stances is perhaps most evident from the remarks at the end of the previous chapter and, as will be seen, it remained so even after Selim's reforms had begun in earnest.

A good example token of this multiplicity of stances can be found in the memoranda (*layiha*) on possible ways of reforming the state, which, as was seen, Selim asked for from all the members of the higher hierarchy of ulema and bureaucracy in 1792. Most of the authors belonged to the chancery, but there were also high ulema and palace officials (as well as Western envoys or employees, such as Mouradgea d'Ohsson, a close associate of Ratıb Efendi, and a certain Brentano); from these memoranda, an abridged treatise was compiled for the sultan containing the parts of the individual memoranda pertaining to army reform, brought together under thematic categories (army, military stipends, auxiliary forces and artillery, cavalry).[59] In more than one way, these memoranda can be viewed as a synopsis of all the ideas and debates prevailing in eighteenth-century Ottoman political thought.

Quite a few of the memoranda proposed the recruitment of a new army, trained in the European way. This idea had been indirectly put forth by Bonneval (alias Humbaracı Ahmed Pasha), and directly by Resmi Efendi as early as 1769, but this was the first time it was proposed with such vigor. Koca (Gürci) Yusuf Pasha (the grand vizier until 1791) suggests that 10,000 or 12,000 youths be recruited from the Muslim families of the Anatolian and Balkan provinces and trained in strict hierarchy and discipline (Ka415–417). Similarly, Abdullah Birri Efendi (then *reisülküttab*) stressed that the recruits to the army (*yazılacak asker*) should be young (between 11 and 25 years old) and of peasant stock. They should be drawn from the poor, orphans, and the needy, and,

58 Yeşil 2011a, 237; Ratıb Efendi – Yıldız 2013, 255–256.

59 The abridged treatise was published in Karal 1941–1943. For full editions see Öğreten 1989 and Çağman 1995. Individual memoranda have also been published: "Sultan Selim-i Salis devrinde nizam-ı devlet hakkında mütalaat", *Tarih-i Osmani Encümeni Mecmuası* 7/38 (A.H. 1332), 74–88; 7/41 (A.H. 1332), 321–346; 8/43 (A.H. 1333), 15–34 (Tatarcık Abdullah Efendi); and Çağman 1999 (Mehmed Şerif Efendi). On the memoranda, their authors, and their ideas see also Berkes 1964, 72–74; Karal 1988, 34–41; Aksan 1993, 62–63 (=Aksan 2004, 41–43); Özkul 1996, 146–164; Beydilli 1999b, 30–34; Şakul 2005; Ermiş 2014, 135ff. On D'Ohsson's memorandum, see Beydilli 1984, 257–269 and Özkul 1996, 169–174. On the identity of "Brentano" see Beydilli 1984, 264–266, fn. 85 and cf. Özkul 1996, 164–168. The most analytical presentation and discussion remains Shaw 1971, 86ff. and esp. 91–111.

after an elementary religious education, be trained by Prussian officers in the European rules of war (Ka424–425). A very similar proposal for the creation of a new army, trained in the European way, was made by Mustafa Reşid Efendi (*kethüda* of the grand vizier), "the most important of the reformers by far ... the Sultan's closest confidant and the power behind the throne in his reform efforts", as named by Shaw (Kb104–106, Kc344), as well as by Çavuşbaşı Mehmed Raşid Efendi (previously *reisülküttab*; Ka420–422). A slightly different proposal, suggesting a smooth passage from the existing decentralized system of temporary recruitment, was made by Mehmed Şerif Efendi (then *defterdar*):[60] he begins by repeating the now age-old suggestion that positions such as those of grand vizier and governor should be permanent, or at least long-term, and then stipulates that in such a way every vizier and pasha could have a retinue of soldiers that they would keep trained and ready for war. These troops would form the "winter army" and be continuously trained during the winter months, when war is suspended (Ka422–424). As for the expenses of the new army, the suggestion of Birri Efendi and of Mehmed Şerif Efendi (Ç226–227) that they be met by the surplus of the *vakıf* income (a proposal also made by Ömer Faik Efendi, as seen in chapter 8) should be noted. Other proposals (such as Hakkı Efendi's), more conservative, suggested that the new troops should be partly financed by the revenue of vacant timars, partly by the villages, partly by the governorship revenues, and partly by the state.

More careful advisers emphasized that the introduction of such a new army should be done gradually and carefully. Mustafa İffet Bey, for instance, suggested, like Mehmed Şerif Efendi, the European-style training of soldiers in the seats of provincial governors and their gradual introduction to Istanbul (Kb109–110). Similar mixed armies, to be prepared in the seats of provincial governors, were proposed by Hakkı Efendi (two armies, one for the winter composed of Balkan recruits and janissaries, and one for the summer composed of Anatolian soldiers; Kb110–111, Kc342, Kc350) and Hacı İbrahim Efendi (Kb106–107). Rasih Efendi (ex-*rikâb kethüdası*) and other officials also felt that a mixed system should be preferred, one continuing Baron de Tott's efforts and selecting part of the janissary army to train. Even Tatarcık Abdullah Efendi (a high ulema, twice kazasker, and a close supporter and collaborator of Selim), after a remark on the lack of discipline among the janissaries and their essential uselessness in battle, suggested that their chiefs should be summoned and urged to restore discipline and to study the European arts of war through translations of manuals by "friendly countries"; a special corps could be formed from among their ranks that would be trained with the help

60 His memorandum was published in full in Şerif Efendi – Çağman 1999.

of foreign advisors, as in the past under Baron de Tott. This should be done gradually and, preferably, in provincial cities to avoid an adverse reaction by the janissaries in the capital (Ka417–420).

Finally, a group of advisors, mainly from the ranks of the ulema, mainly repeated traditional advice, although they always took care regarding the concrete and the particular in a way (as we saw in the previous chapter) that was typical of the eighteenth century. Thus, there are the usual criticisms of corruption and the inability of janissary and artillery officers (Enveri Efendi, Kc348; Osman Efendi, Kd424–425), the lack of discipline (Veli Efendizade, Kb108–109), and so forth, as well as traditional proposals about the control of pay-rolls and registers (Salihzade Efendi, Kb108, Kc346; Firdevsi Efendi, Kc346–347; Enveri Efendi, Kd429–430). In contrast to the proposals suggesting the recruitment of new soldiers, Ali Raik Efendi noted that it is impossible to reform the army in a short period and that the recruitment of troops from the provincial towns and villages results only in pillage and ruin (Kb109); as for Sun'i Efendi, he rejects all reformist attempts by simply proposing the restoration of the old laws for the army (Kc348). As will be seen, however, this was not the opposition Selim should have been afraid of.

•••

The various ideas and proposals of the memoranda may be grouped around two poles, a reformist and a more conservative one, but these were always the poles and factions found within the palace and government elite (and the high ulema); cautionary remarks favoring consultation with the janissary officers may be seen as representing a defense of the status quo, of the balance among political powers in the capital, as in Defterdar Mehmed Pasha's case (see chapter 8). A careful analysis of the social and political backgrounds of the "reformists" may show that most of them had connections with the faction of Halil Hamid Pasha, the reformist grand vizier of Abdülhamid I and Süleyman Penah Efendi's protector.[61] What is more important for our purposes, however, is the argument behind their proposals. Not all memoranda care to expand on their reasoning, as they mostly have a strictly administrative character, but when they do they build on the foundations that had been prepared by reformist political thought ever since Müteferrika and the anonymous *Su'âl-i Osmânî*. Thus, they usually stress that what they propose is not a sterile imitation of infidel ways but rather a reappropriation of Islamic experience that had been unduly forgotten. Before proposing the creation of a new corps, Çavuşbaşı Mehmed

61 See the detailed analysis by Yıldız 2008, 612–630.

Raşid Efendi praises the old system of janissaries, with their recruitment from the provinces and their intensive training; he emphasizes that youths must be recruited in the same old way (*devşirilüp*), but be trained with discipline and order (Ka420–422). Similarly, Abdullah Birri Efendi remarks that, if someone should raise objections regarding the imitation of Frankish ways, one should remember that the Ottoman navy has been imitating its European counterparts from the very beginning, while the Russian army was created by imitating the Ottomans.[62] As for Mustafa Reşid Efendi, he remarks that Sultan Orhan had tried to recruit salaried soldiers from Anatolia but could not impose discipline over them, and thus created the janissaries, who fulfilled these precepts; however, he writes, it is evident that this advantage has been lost for 150 years.

A second line of argument shows the influence of Ibn Khaldun's theory about nomadic and settled states, as popularized by Na'ima. By the third quarter of the eighteenth century, as the reader may have noticed, these ideas were recurrent in the Ottoman intellectual milieu.[63] Mehmed Şerif Efendi bases his plea for continuous training and exercise on the distinction between nomadism and settled life: if soldiers are left to settle down, their military ability will fade away (Ka422–424). Advisers proposing more modest reforms, namely training the existing troops (rather than creating new ones), also used the parallels between the nomadic state and the continuous drilling of soldiers. Rasih Efendi, for instance, suggests the translation of European books on the arts of war and the continuous training of the army in order to "restore the nomadic conditions in the time of settled life", with the help of military emissaries from friendly European countries. Furthermore, the old regulations should be renewed and enforced according to the needs of the present, if necessary (Kb107–108). This last idea, which originates in Kâtib Çelebi's work, can also be found in Mustafa Reşid Efendi's memorandum. Before reverting to Sultan Orhan's example, he notes that the restoration of the old rules should take into account the needs of the age (*kavaid-i atikanın iadesi mizac-ı asra tatbik olunması*). Then, using historical examples and an explicitly Khaldunist vocabulary, he shows how unanimity and solidarity (*ittifakü'l-kelim, asabiyet*) secure the rule of the ruling class (administrators and soldiers) over the tenfold population of their subjects.

62 This idea was not so far from reality as it may seem, as far as it concerns earliest centuries: see Ágoston 2011, 291–298.

63 Ibn Khaldun's *Muqaddima*, as noted in the previous chapter, was translated into Ottoman Turkish in 1730 (Ibn Haldun – Pirizade 2008). On Ottoman Khaldunism see Sariyannis (forthcoming).

2.1 *For or against Reform? "Sekbanbaşı" and Kuşmanî's Libels*

Once the *Nizam-i Cedid* corps was created, the reactions against it were, of course, as expected. The janissaries' opposition was self-evident and led to the eventual failure of the reforms, as is well known. However, one should not underestimate popular support for this opposition, due to both a strong anti-elite feeling that was arguably evident in Istanbul society and the close relations of the janissary corps with the lower urban strata.[64] Moreover, it seems that various dervish affiliations (Nakşbendi for the ruling elite, Bektaşi for the opposition) strengthened group identities and the subsequent conflict, although their mutual hatred had more social than religious reasons.[65] The most important pieces of political writing advocating Selim's reforms are in fact polemical tracts, more propaganda than actual political theory, conceived specifically as answers to the opposition.

These works include two detailed descriptions of the new corps and regulations, written by Mahmud Raif Efendi and Seyyid Mustafa, translated into French and printed in Istanbul in 1798 and 1803 respectively, obviously with the aim of advertizing the reforms to a European audience.[66] The second treatise contains a very interesting introduction, where the author, himself a product of the *Nizam-i Cedid* schools, tries to prove (citing Pascal as an example) that science can be taught regardless of an individual's inclinations; furthermore, Seyyid Mustafa stresses that countries, men, and institutions are subject to continuous change (*bi'l-cümle milletler tagyir ü tebdil ve devletler usulü dahi tahvil olunur*), repeating the (by then old and established) argument that Europeans took the basics of military tactics from the early Ottomans, while the latter's successors forgot the axiom of "reciprocity" (*mukabele bi'l-misl*) and believed instead that courage and zeal could substitute discipline and science.

In a much more polemic mood, one has to note the so-called *Koca Sekbanbaşı risalesi* (Koca Sekbanbaşı's treatise) or, more accurately, *Hülâsatü'l-kelâm fi reddi'l-'avâmm* ("The summary of the discourse to refute the rabble"),

64 Cf. Sunar 2010; Yaycıoğlu 2010, 678–683; Başaran 2014, 133–167; Başaran – Kırlı 2015, 272.

65 Yıldız 2008, 641–653 and esp. 712–726; Yıldız 2012; cf. Abu-Manneh 1982, Abu-Manneh 1994, and Artan 2012, 378–380 on the association of reform with Nakşbendi conservatism. In the seventeenth century, Nakşbendi spirituality was associated with the Kadızadeli movement, as shown recently by Sheikh 2016 (cf. Le Gall 2004). Dihkanizade Kuşmani, an ardent pro-Selim dervish whom we will study in detail below, appears to have been a Nakşbendi as well (Kuşmanî – Yıldız 2007, 16).

66 Mahmud Raif Efendi – Beydilli – Şahin 2001, and Seyyid Mustafa – Beydilli 1987 (the Ottoman Turkish MS is transcribed on pp. 430–442, and the French edition is reproduced on pp. 447–479); see also Berkes 1964, 78–81; Özkul 1996, 255–260; Beydilli 1999b, 34–35; Şakul 2005, 125–131; Yıldız 2008, 164ff. (on the propaganda tracts of the *Nizam-i Cedid* in general).

composed c. 1804.[67] The authorship of this essay has been disputed; by his own account, Koca Sekbanbaşı (Çelebi Efendi) must have been born c. 1718/9 (he claims to have been 87 years old when composing his treatise). He had been participating in campaigns since 1733 and served continuously since 1768, while in his life he had been a prisoner of the Russians (W239). Based mainly on "Sekbanbaşı"'s claiming the authorship of the Maçin petition in 1791 (W261), Kemal Beydilli recently identified him with none other than Ahmed Vâsıf Efendi (d. 1806), the well-known diplomat and historiographer (also a captive of the Russians in 1771), thus making him another example of a radical change in attitude (considering his 1784 treatise).[68] It appears that Vasıf's attitude vis-à-vis Europe had changed radically after his embassy to Spain (1787–88), just as Ratıb Efendi had had a similar experience during his days in Vienna.[69] Beydilli's arguments seem convincing, although the propagandistic character of the tract seems very different from Vasıf's sober and complex thoughts in his earlier works. Yet as, the authorship of the treatise is still disputed, we will use the pseudonym "Sekbanbaşı" when analyzing it. The structure of the work is of special interest since it also reveals the arguments made by the opponents of reform: as also implied by its title, it was conceived of as an imaginary account of a discussion with calumniators, containing answers to a series of objections raised against the *Nizam-i Cedid* army. Sekbanbaşı maintains that, due to the long period of peace, most of the experienced warriors had died and most inhabitants of the Ottoman Empire had been living in ease and comfort; as a result, when war with Russia began there was a lack of discipline and subsequent "corruption and disorder" (here one may discern an echo of Resmi Efendi's first treatise). Furthermore, the rabble that gathered in the coffee-houses and taverns discussed and criticized the measures taken by the government; they were not punished immediately, as happened for instance in the times of Süleyman the Magnificent, because "the force of necessity obliges the government to overlook their faults" (W221). Sekbanbaşı was then summoned "from the high-

67 The treatise has been published twice in Turkish: *Hulâsat ül-kelâm fi redd il-avâm / Koca Sekban başi'nin idare-i devlet hakkinda yazdığı lâyiha dır*. Istanbul: Hilal Matbaasi [1332] [1916] (Supplement to *Tarih-i Osmani Encümeni Mecmuasi*); Abdullah Uçman (ed.), *Koca Sekbanbaşı risalesi*, Istanbul 1975. Unfortunately, none of these editions was accessible to me; here I used its English translation, in an appendix in Wilkinson 1820, 216–294. On the treatise see also Aksan 1993, 61–62 (=Aksan 2004, 38–41); Beydilli 2005; Şakul 2005, 131–135; Menchinger 2017, 238–240.

68 Beydilli 2005; cf. Menchinger 2017, 268–276, who summarizes the debate on the authorship of the text and also finds the attribution to Vasıf more than plausible.

69 Menchinger 2014a, 29–30 and 96–100; Menchinger 2014b; Menchinger 2017, 118–131. On other instances of Vasıf's change of attitude under Selim III see Menchinger 2014a, 248–262; Menchinger 2017, 201–205, and 215–216.

est quarter" to write a simple-styled essay rebutting the calumnies circulated by such people.

If Sekbanbaşı's criticisms of the janissaries were made from a mainly military point of view (and his pseudonym, "the old chief of irregulars", clearly meant to stress his experience), he had a more religious counterpoint, Dihkânîzade ("son of the villager") Ubeydullah Kuşmani, who tried to answer from the opposition's own standpoint. We know little about Kuşmani's life except for what he himself states in his own works. He describes himself as a "dervish traveler" and states that he started his voyages in the year of Selim III's ascension and that he arrived in Istanbul five years later. Kuşmani seems to have traveled in Russia (or near the Russian borders), too. Between 1803 and 1805 he was accused of being a spy of Tayyar Mahmud Pasha (an *ayan* of the Caniklizade family who had taken control of the regions of Trabzon and Amasya); he was imprisoned and then released. From the historian Cabî Efendi we learn that Kuşmani was exiled from Istanbul in 1808 because he had spoken harshly against the janissaries while preaching in a mosque, and this is the last information about him there is. His treatise, *Zebîre-i Kuşmânî fî ta'rîf-i nizâm-ı İlhâmî* ("The book by Kuşmani describing the order [or, army] by İlhâmî[70]"), was composed in 1806.[71] In a similar way to Sekbanbaşı's work, Kuşmani's treatise is mainly structured as a dialogue, with the janissaries' arguments refuted by the author in the second person plural.

Both tracts, in İbrahim Müteferrika's tradition, primarily justify Selim's reforms based on the need for a strong army to defend the Muslim realms. Sekbanbaşı starts his treatise by stating that God has created "an Emperor of the world, to administer with justice the affairs of the whole company of his servants, and to protect them from their enemies"; He also has "subjected the earth to government in such a manner that it is divided into many regions, each of them should have its own Sovereign", while each sovereign protects his country and "the servants of God whom [it] contain[s]" from hostile neighbours.[72] It is human nature that the strong are superior to the weak and

70 A play on words: İlhâmî means "inspiration-giving", but it was also the poetic pseudonym of Selim III.

71 Kuşmanî – İşbilir 2006. Other works by Kuşmani are a postscript (*zeyl*) to a narrative of the 1806 revolt (Kabakçı İsyanı; Kuşmanî – Yıldız 2007, 72–80 [modern Turkish translation] = 135–145 [transcription]), in which he repeats most of his arguments in *Zebîre*, a very short political essay (*Mevâ'iz-i Kuşmânî*, Millet Ktp. Ali Emîrî-Şer'iyye, nr. 591), and some other treatises that have been lost. See also Beydilli 1999b, 35–37; Şakul 2005, 135–138; Kuşmanî – Yıldız 2007, 15–19.

72 Cf. a similar remark by İbrahim Müteferrika: Müteferrika – Şen 1995, 131–132. Sekbanbaşı mentions Müteferrika's *Usûlü'l-hikem* in Wilkinson 1820, 245.

seek to destroy them, and thus those states that take no precautions end up being dependent on others. In Sekbanbaşı's version of the birth of *Nizam-i Cedid* (W227–239), in 1792 it became known that there was a Russian plot, with the help of "zealous partisans of the Greek nation" (W230), to capture Istanbul after destroying its water reservoirs. This would be very easy, since the Anatolian troops were "employed in cultivating the land and smoking their pipes", while those who inhabit Istanbul were "either busy carrying on various trades, or at least not subject to any good discipline". To confront this danger, the only possible method was to keep a body of infantry, one composed of trained and disciplined men (rather than boatmen, sellers of pastries, and other tradesmen), always ready for service in the capital. A first attempt to recruit them from among the janissaries was fruitless because "our bravoes who are engaged in the 32 trades" were unwilling to submit themselves to a daily program of drills and thus be prevented from caring for their private affairs. The government then had to recruit some *bostancıs* and settle them in camps day and night, where they would be drilled daily and in good discipline. By such measures the Russian threat was considerably weakened.

In a very similar way, Kuşmani describes Selim III's efforts to organize and train the army. According to him, the reforms were necessary due to the pitiful situation of the Ottoman armies because of their lack of experience after a prolonged period of peace, on the one hand, and because their Christian enemies, working day and night for the amelioration of their own armies, exceeded the Muslim ones. Kuşmani then describes the reforms, insisting that Selim "renovated the foundations of the state" (İ7: *esas-ı devleti tecdid eder*) and that for a new branch to bloom from an old root, the old branch must be broken (İ4–23).

Both authors deplore the situation of the janissary corps, using a vocabulary coming directly from the early seventeenth-century declinist tracts. Sekbanbaşı asks the janissaries how they can explain their being routed by the Russian troops in the 1768–74 war and even whether they may prove "that at any time, or in any place, [they] have rendered the least service" to the sultan; he blames them for losing the war, for the odious treaty that was imposed on the Ottomans, and for the loss of the Crimea. Mahmud I was about to institute regular exercises, using a treatise entitled "The origin of the institution of discipline" (Müteferrika's *Usûlü'l-hikem*), but he died before he could impose these reforms. Sekbanbaşı cites examples where the *Nizam-i Cedid* troops were much more effective against the French invaders of Egypt than the more numerous but undisciplined janissary forces, as well as of the inability of the latter to cope with modern weapons (W246–254). Furthermore, while admitting the discipline and effectiveness of the corps during Süleyman's time, Sekbanbaşı argues that the infidels found ways to introduce their own spies into the janissaries' ranks to corrupt them.[73] These spies incited the soldiers to seek comfort and to care only for their salaries. Sekbanbaşı illustrates this account with several examples from the recent wars with Russia, citing, among other things, the Maçin petition of 1791 (W254–278).

Kuşmani also embarks on a vehement and long libel against the janissaries (İ26ff.): they meddle with the rabble, stay at home, and avoid campaigns; they practice all kinds of humiliating professions (İ27: *ba'zınız bakkal u nakkal ve kiminiz hammal u cemmal ve ekseriniz dahi dihkâniyyet ve sa'ir sanayi'-i izafiyye ile*); their own uniform is useless in war; and their lack of discipline makes their large numbers a disadvantage against the enemy.

> If soldiers could be made by gaining money from lawful or unlawful trades, by worldly professions, or just by simple luxury and clothing, undoubtedly the Porte would produce five million soldiers with ease (İ29).

Thus, one argument Sekbanbaşı and Kuşmani provide in favor of the new army is its efficiency: Kuşmani stresses the example of the gunners corps, which shows that soldiers' training can bring results that are beneficial for the state. As for Sekbanbaşı, he praises the discipline of the *Nizam-i Cedid*, their organization and how it excludes any possibility of intrusion by enemy spies, their steadfastness and mastery of military stratagems in battle (showing that such stratagems are in no way incompatible with the Muslim tradition), and the use of uniforms and passwords (where one recognizes the echo of Müteferrika's descriptions) (W254–278).

The strongest and most pronounced argument is, as may by now be expected, the precedence of Muslims in using military innovation. In Sekbanbaşı's treatise, we read that the rapid use of artillery and the introduction of military exercises were a novelty of Süleyman's time, unknown to the Europeans; he even states that it was Süleyman who first created a regular army, i.e. the janissaries. As with what was happening with the *Nizam-i Cedid*, in Süleyman's time older soldiers (*sekban*) found the janissaries' attire ridiculous and their institution useless, discouraging new recruits. To deal with the problem Süleyman decided to bring Hacı Bektaş, "the polar star of the times", from Anatolia and make him pray for the recruits; the latter stopped deserting and started fighting with supreme discipline and effectiveness. To cope with this, European rulers adopted the Ottoman systems, namely prohibition of soldiers engaging in

73 In another section (W280–286), Sekbanbaşı reverts to the damage done by foreign spies, describing how easily they can introduce themselves into a group of undisciplined soldiers, with no uniforms or organization.

other trades and constant military drilling, and managed to make their own armies invincible due to them keeping compact lines and the superiority of their rapid-fire artillery (W240–246).

Kuşmani first remarks pointedly that such rules did not exist in the time of the old sultans, but nor did such idiocy exist since the beginning of Islam; thus, because the infidels have proceeded so much in the science of war, it would be foolish for the Muslims not to follow them. Then he repeats the same argument in a slightly different way, as he seems to consider all Selim's innovations to be merely reworkings of age-old Muslim practices (without reverting to the Europeans' having borrowed them). His first point is that both these innovations were in fact used long ago: the various elements of the uniform were traditionally used by the Balkan Muslims, while the trumpet is nothing but what the Arabs call *tabl-ı harb*, or war drums; moreover, its usefulness is self-evident, even more so since the janissaries themselves had been so many times defeated without trumpets (İ23–30).

After all, observes Kuşmani in one of his most original arguments (İ30), most weapons and tools are indeed innovations of the infidels.

> Because these accursed ones are all oriented toward this world (*salik-i dünya oldukları ecilden*), they always think of increasing their knowledge.

That is why they have the custom of keeping an apprentice until he manages to find some new and unknown knowledge and thus prove that he may become a master workman himself. Muslims, in contrast, regard the world as something temporary and transitory, so they tend to neglect worldly affairs and give more importance to religion and piety. However, Kuşmani notes, during Selim III's reign factories were created within the boundaries of the Ottoman Empire, and these contribute to the military supremacy of the New Army. One may draw a parallel with Vasıf Efendi's (who was probably, as we saw, the author of *Sekbanbaşı risâlesi*) assertions that the Europeans' "satanic insight" (*'ukul-ı şeytaniyye*) allows them to organize affairs efficiently and that they are willing to sacrifice family and kin for trifling gains.[74] Similar thoughts can be seen in Sekbanbaşı's relation of his alleged discussions with Russian officers during his captivity: they explained to him how Peter the Great "subjected the Russians, whether they would or not, to the restraints of discipline" and thus he and his successors managed to capture Ottoman territories one after another (W279–280).

74 Menchinger 2014a, 207.

When Kuşmani turns to the issue of training, his argument is closer to the reciprocity principle.[75] Nothing can be wrong with learning more arts and tricks, he claims, and there is no art that can be achieved without training; to send an untrained army against a well-trained and experienced enemy would be just like collecting a street-dog and sending it hunting. Moreover, tradition and old glories do not necessarily bring victories by themselves. Without training and discipline, the janissaries are doomed to be defeated, no matter how many they are in number, just as happened in Egypt. Kuşmani here narrates a didactic story, according to which the secret for beating one's enemies is to always be one step ahead of them, i.e. to know the science of war better. The French realized this and were victorious, while Ottoman sultans of old kept pace with the infidels and introduced their weapons and tactics in time (İ55). Later kings, on the contrary, succumbed to the temptations of comfort and ease, turned to drug use, and led their whole people to an idle way of life, with the result that their enemies surpassed them in the art of war. A kingdom (*her kankı saltanatın malik olduğu iklim*), says Kuşmani, is like a ship, being in grave danger if the captain cannot prevent its crew from drinking and amusing themselves instead of remaining alert (a similar simile is used by Sekbanbaşı; W250).[76]

Likewise, Kuşmani's further defense of innovation is made in philosophical terms. For one thing, he considers tradition worthy to follow only if it is still effective: answering the argument that the janissaries were organized and sanctified by Süleyman the Lawgiver, Kuşmani observes that he did not give them permission to become corrupted and to roam the streets like swashbucklers (İ41: *kaldırım kabadayısı*). Then, in order to refute the dismissal of innovations by his adversaries, he follows a more philosophical route (somewhat reminiscent of Vasıf Efendi's views, as seen in the previous chapter): those who neglect the "pursuit of the necessary efforts" (İ75: *teşebbüs-i esbab*) and claim that "things must be done as in the time of [their] forefathers" fall into the sect of fatalism (*kaderiyye/cebriyye mezhebi*). In contrast, each generation is responsible for its fate; one has to fulfil the necessary prerequisites for one's aims and then leave the final result in God's hands.

•••

75 In his text on the 1806 revolt, Kuşmani also refers explicitly to the *mukabele bi'l-misl* principle: Kuşmanî – Yıldız 2007, 72=136.

76 The ship simile was also used by Kuşmani in the speech that led to his exile in 1808: Cabi – Beyhan 2003, 1:257.

Thus, the continuity between the more traditional ideas discussed in chapter 8 and the ardent defenders of Selimian reform is evident. They drew on the same inventory of arguments, their only difference being the degree to which they were willing to accept imitation of Western models. Some of the recurrent themes of reformist thought are apparent in Sekbanbaşı's treatise: the depiction of the undisciplined and ineffective nature of the janissary corps, and of course the alleged origin of Western discipline from the Ottoman army of the Süleymanic era; while he also refers explicitly to Müteferrika's *Usûlü'l-hikem* and Mustafa Ali's *Füsûl-ı hall u akd*,[77] it is quite probable that he had read Resmi Efendi as well. He also introduces a new argument, or perhaps a variation of what we have called the Muslim precedence argument: the justification of new military stratagems by examples from the glorious Muslim past. Kuşmani's tract presents some of the most common reformist arguments (the need for reciprocity or *mukabele bi'l-misl*, and the claim that the *Nizam-i Cedid* contains no innovations) but also some quite original ones, such as the appropriation of a usually conservative precept ("commanding right and forbidding wrong": İ15–18, 80) and a vehement attack on Hacı Bektaş, the protector of the janissaries (İ33–41). The mixed attitude toward Western mentalities is quite noteworthy, as is an old-style attack on smoking (İ64–65) that brings to mind the "Sunna-minded" authors of the seventeenth and early eighteenth century: by Kuşmani's time (if not earlier), smoking and frequenting coffee-houses had become a trait of the janissary-*cum*-esnaf strata. As for his affinities with Vasıf Efendi's thoughts on the causes of European success and, more impressively, on predestination and the role of human agency, they show once more that, by the last quarter of the eighteenth century, there was an inventory of ideas (including Na'ima's Khaldunism and Kâtib Çelebi's theory about innovation) from which virtually every elite author could draw. The content of the arguments, i.e. the politics they would eventually be used for, could change, but the form remained the same, and there is no radical rupture, in terms of reasoning, associated with the Selimian reform.

2.2 *Janissary Views in the Mirror of Selimian Propaganda*

Nevertheless, this image is somewhat misleading since it does not take into account the bulk of the Istanbul population, namely the janissaries and all those associated with them.[78] Indeed, the image of a society divided into two fiercely

77 See Wilkinson 1820, 217, 232 (on Ali) and 245 (on Müteferrika); cf. Aksan 1993, 61 and 68, fn. 73 (=Aksan 2004, 39).

78 For an attempt to reconstruct the oppositions' arguments, see Yıldız 2008, 168–181. A document probably written by Mahmud Tayyar Pasha, a descendant of Canikli Ali Pasha

uncompromising factions is evident in these works. The invective launched against the janissaries by Sekbanbaşı and Kuşmani approaches the limits of calumny. Sekbanbaşı presents some janissaries as admitting that what they are really afraid of is that they will lose their pay if the *Nizam-i Cedid* troops increase in numbers;[79] on the other hand, others understand that if the *Nizam-i Cedid* is abolished the infidels will be able to impose increasingly humiliating conditions on the sultan, whereas if the new institution is strengthened and multiplied the safety of the empire will be guaranteed (W246–254). For his part, Kuşmani labels his opponents disobedient, fanatic bigots, ignorant, and even madmen; he also states that since there are only four classes, namely "the people of the sciences and of asceticism (*ehl-i ulum ü zehadet*), those who are real soldiers or scribes (*hakikaten askeri ve ehl-i kitabet*), the merchants and tradesmen, and the farmers", it is these people, who are not real soldiers but just people roaming about wearing military clothes, who should be persecuted and killed, as is the practice with those who "refuse to enter one of the four classes" (İ12–13). Reverting to an old argument that originated with the Sunna-minded authors of the seventeenth century (see above, chapter 6), Kuşmani also associates the janissaries with the use of drugs and other intoxicants, including coffee and tobacco. He accuses Ottoman soldiers of selling their arms in time of war in order to buy their coffee and opium, and discusses at length the various opinions on smoking, which he condemns on various moral, medical, and legal grounds (including that it is a bad innovation; İ64–65).

It is tempting to seek the views expressed by the janissary opposition through the counter-arguments raised by Sekbanbaşı and Kuşmani. There seem to have been some "political" objections, implying that the new system had no results and that it had, in fact, caused rebellions in the Balkans.[80] The most often heard and strongest arguments of the janissaries, however, seem to have focused on the innovation presented by the new corps, and especially—since "innovation" had lost by then a large part of its bad

and a leading figure of the opposition, stresses that Selim's real aim seems to be the conversion of Islam to another religion (*tecdid-i din-i aher*) and laments that all the soldiers became "Frenks wearing hats" (Yıldız 2008, 181–182). On the reactions of the ulema and their motives see Argun 2013.

79 The same accusation is also made by Kuşmani: Kuşmanî – Yıldız 2007, 73=137.

80 Sekbanbaşı answers that, on the contrary, similar troubles did exist in Anatolia, Egypt, and other provinces before the institution of the *Nizam-i Cedid*. Even in the present time, France is ravaged by disturbances which have turned the country "into a slaughterhouse for swine", and similar troubles are observed in India, China, and even the new world; Anatolia, on the other hand, has remained undisturbed for the time being, which shows that all these troubles stem "from the decrees of Providence" (W221–227). See also Menchinger 2017, 213.

reputation—on the fact that this innovation was actually an imitation of the infidel. Most of Sekbanbaşı's arguments appear to answer such claims, and Kuşmani explicitly cites (in order to refute it) the argument that "those who use the innovations of the infidel (*ihdas-ı küffar*) become like them", as well as that the glorious sultans of old did not use such "bad innovations" (*bid'at-ı bed*; İ10). We know that this argument was indeed used in the *Hüccet-i şeriyye* drawn after Selim's fall, and thus that it was actually the main weapon in the inventory of the opposition.[81] Another argument, which is addressed by Kuşmani, was again of a religious nature and emphasized the importance of the janissary corps not in terms of "old law" but of literal sanctity, namely that the New Army was accused of having no spiritual leader (*pir*), unlike the janissaries who had allegiance to Hacı Bektaş-ı Velî. Kuşmani's answer is also interesting: he notes that an army should obey no-one but the "master of the time" (*sahibü'l-vakt*), i.e. the sultan, and if they act in unity they will succeed. After all, Hacı Bektaş gave his blessing to Osman I and to his successors, not to the janissary corps; furthermore, according to another tradition, Bektaş (and not Hacı Bektaş) was just the name of the first agha of the janissaries, whereas Alâ'eddin Pasha, Osman's brother, founded the corps (İ33–41).

More generally, it appears that the janissaries, partly because they sincerely considered their position sanctified by age-old tradition and partly because they were pushed toward conservatist reasoning by the very naming of the reform as "the new order" or *Nizam-i Cedid*, reverted to all the ideas of the "old law" and the religious vocabulary and terminology that prevailed in seventeenth-century texts. If we are to believe Kuşmani, another argument of the opposition was based on the precept of "commanding right and forbidding wrong" (*emr-i ma'ruf ve nehy-i münker*), which was also present in the 1807 *Hüccet-i şeriyye*.[82] Allegedly, the argument claimed that if obeying the ruler's orders can be considered an act within "commanding right" then disobeying wrong can bring no harm (İ80), and wrong in this context is the fact that public money (*beytü'l-mal*) is spent on the new soldiers' training (to which Kuşmani answers that this applies only when a ruler spends public money for his personal whims, not for something necessary). It appears that protests had focused on the issue of the financing of the new army, since Sekbanbaşı also deals at

81 Heyd 1961, 69; Beydilli 2001, 42 (*nâ-mesbuk bir bid'at-ı azime … kefereye taklidden başka devlet-i aliyyeyi dahi düvel-i nasara kava'idine irca'*).

82 Beydilli 2001, 44.

length with the special revenues allocated to the *Nizam-i Cedid* (W287–294), and particularly criticizes the life-long farming out of taxes (*malikâne*).[83]

Finally, it may be remembered from chapter 8 that reformist tracts and texts of the last decades of the eighteenth century, Westernizing or not, placed emphasis on the individual responsibility of every member of society, thereby implicitly enhancing the absolutist tendencies of the palace. It appears that the janissaries, far from being the political ignoramuses we are used to think of them as being, were perfectly aware of this idea and of its uses; for instance, it appears that they turned against Selim's counsellors, asking for the absolute authority of the sultan, which would in fact restore their own powers.[84] Consequently, they adopted an opposing stance, namely a corporate particularism, claiming that the military should be the only ones entitled to have an opinion about the army. This is what can be made of Kuşmani's remark that some may accuse him of meddling with that which does not concern him, since he is neither a soldier nor a receiver of state salaries. To this, Kuşmani answers with a *coup de force* using religious arguments against those who had appropriated them. He argues that even an itinerant dervish is still a Muslim, and all Muslims are similarly responsible (since the Holy Book was not given in different forms to the travelers or the nomads) for "commanding right and forbidding wrong" (İ15–18); and if one raises the objection that the ulema should know better, Kuşmani maintains that unfortunately they do not care, and all the more so, this neglect to command right and forbid wrong on their part could be disastrous.

83 He describes it as instituted in Süleyman's time (!) and argues that thus the profits of the treasury were not augmented; the new necessary arrangement is that whenever a post falls vacant the revenue is no longer farmed out, but managed by the government instead with the income going to the needs of the *Nizam-i Cedid*. In his memorandum, Mehmed Şerif Efendi had also described the disadvantages of farming out revenues; the remedy was thought to be farming-out for life (*malikâne*), but this also proved disadvantageous as farmers sub-farmed out the revenues. He suggested that the sultan should personally grant state revenues as *malikâne*s to palace officials (Şerif Efendi – Çağman 1999, 225–226). Cf. Menchinger 2017, 181.

84 Cf. Gradeva 2006, 128, on Pasvanoğlu Osman Pasha's proclamations ("1. That the sultan should be the only autocrat and ruler without any councils; 2. That the Janissaries should, according to the ancient usage, be the foremost army in the whole empire; and 3. That all new institutions must be destroyed in the entire empire and the ones of the olden times be restored in their place").

3 The Last Round: from Selim III to Mahmud II

Until 1826, it seemed that the general climate in the Ottoman government had undergone an almost total reversal. Mehmed Said Halet Efendi, an ambassador in Paris from 1802 to 1806 and afterwards a high official of the palace bureaucracy (chancellor of the Imperial Council from 1815 until his execution in 1822) who played a prominent role in decision-making, was known as a conservative thinker who detested European influence and had very close relations with the janissaries.[85] In fact, it seems that Halet Efendi was instead a representative of what was labeled in the previous chapter the "traditionalist" trend of the reformist discourse. Even in his contempt for the Europeans, he essentially repeats Behic Efendi's optimism; indeed, the similarities are striking:[86]

> I am of the opinion that if ... five factories for snuff, paper, crystal, cloth, and porcelain, as well as a school for languages and geography set up, then in the course of five years there will be as good as nothing left for [the Europeans] to hold on to, since the basis of all their current trade is in these five commodities.

What was perhaps more typical of Halet Efendi's views in regard to his era was his marked Khaldunism, which found an impressive moment of glory at the beginning of the Greek War of Independence (1821), when the Ottoman government proclaimed a return to the "nomadic state" as a remedy for military defeats. Indeed, under Halet Efendi's influence an imperial order stated that, although Muslims have turned to a settled way of life (which is "a second nature to man's disposition"), they have now to revert to their ancestors' nomadic (and hence war-like) customs and fight back. A few months later, another decree also urged Muslims to take up arms and abstain from luxury and pomp, "adopting the shape of nomadism and campaign" (*bedeviyyet ve seferiyyet suretini istihsal*). The Muslim inhabitants of Istanbul roamed about in full battle-dress and mounted attacks upon Christians (including foreign subjects) until such behavior was strictly prohibited a few months later.[87] This was the culmination of Ottoman Khaldunism, which had been a recurrent *leitmotif* in a large part of political and historical thought from the mid-seventeenth century

85 See Karal 1940; Lewis 1961, 69 and elsewhere.

86 Karal 1940, 32–33; Lewis 1961, 128.

87 Şânizâde – Yılmazer 2008, 1084, 1169, 1238ff. This rather failed experiment in social engineering was recently studied in detail by Ilıcak 2011. Erdem 2005, 76 notes the measures taken but fails to grasp their Khaldunist underpinnings.

onwards, although during the course of the eighteenth century the emphasis seems to have shifted from the stage theory to the nomadism vs. settled life distinction.

It is usually postulated that the French Revolution played a major role in the advent of the Tanzimat reforms and the introduction of the Ottoman Empire to modernity. This view is based on the identification of modernity with Westernization, on the one hand, and secularization, on the other.[88] Numerous studies have explored the ways in which the notions of liberty and equality (together with nationality) were introduced by various agents, including Ottoman ambassadors, enlightened bureaucrats and intellectuals, foreign officers and refugees, but also Christian subjects of the sultan, and eventually substituted older notions of the religious state. However, the impact of the revolutionary ideas on Ottoman political thought should not be overestimated. As Niyazi Berkes notes, there is "no written document showing a favourable treatment" of these ideas until the 1830s, and even then it is mainly the idea of modernized Europe that served as intermediary;[89] at any rate, viewing the Ottoman late eighteenth and nineteenth centuries as a dualist struggle between the religion-laden *ancien régime* and an enlightened secularism is far too oversimplified a view.[90]

Ottoman authors did not immediately perceive the French Revolution as a major challenge, especially so since a ruler's execution was not in itself something uncommon in Ottoman history. Until the French threat became visible in 1797 (with the occupation of the Ionian islands, and even more so with the invasion of Egypt the next year), the attitude of the Ottoman government towards France remained generally friendly (the reader may remember Selim III's correspondence with Louis XVI and the French translation of Mahmud Raif Efendi's and Seyyid Mustafa's propaganda even as late as 1803).[91] In the dispatches of Ebubekir Ratıb Efendi from Vienna (1792), the revolution is described as "the rising of the rabble"; although Ratıb Efendi attributes it mainly to the bad financial situation of France, he also notes that the insurgents had "tasted freedom" (*serbestiyet*), and even translates Jacobin arguments claiming

88 See Lewis 1953 and 1961, 53–55; Berkes 1964; and cf. the relevant remarks in the introduction of the present book. On the influence of the French Revolution on Ottoman thought see also the studies collected in Baqcué-Grammont – Eldem 1990; ambassadors and other envoys to Europe apart, channels of information also existed within Istanbul itself (Shaw 1971, 195–198). What follows is partly based on Sariyannis 2016, 50–53.

89 Berkes 1964, 83–85.

90 See Hanioğlu 2008, 2; cf. Mardin 1962.

91 Cf. Kuran 1990.

that kings are "human beings like us".[92] The historian Câbî Ömer Efendi gives a rather distorted view of Napoleon executing the French king and declaring that[93]

> kings did not descend from the skies with the angels. I will work and make them recognize me as their Emperor.

Closer to the source, Moralı Ali Efendi, the Ottoman ambassador to Paris from 1797 to 1802, describes in some detail and rather neutrally the function of the Directoire (*müdirân-ı hamse*) and of the Council of Five Hundred (*beşyüz vükela, beşyüz meclisi*); interestingly, he seems to have been more impressed by the new solar calendar and its holidays, which he describes in great detail.[94] Another memorandum, composed in 1798 by the *reisülküttâb* Atıf Efendi, stresses the atheist aspect of the revolution: followers of the well-known atheists (*zındık*) Voltaire and Rousseau, Atıf Efendi writes, introduced to the common people ideas such as the abolition of religions and the sweetness of equality and democracy (*müsavât ve cumhuriyet*), drawing all the people to their cause; thus, they succeeded in persuading the commoners (*avam-ı nas*) that "this equality and freedom" (*serbestiyet*) was the sure means for total worldly happiness. He notes repeatedly that they intend to turn all states into "democracies, i.e. interregna" (*cumhuriyete ya'ni fitret suretine*) and to impose members of the Jacobin sect, known for its tendency to execute and confiscate. As shown by the example of the Ionian islands, which were put "under the regime of freedom" (*serbestiyet sureti*), this could threaten Ottoman lands as well.[95]

It is true that concepts such as "fatherland" (*vatan*), "nation" (*millet*), and "freedom" (*serbestiyyet, hürriyet*) acquired their modern meaning via a gradual process throughout the first half of the nineteenth century, eventually losing

92 Yeşil 2007. Similar observations were made by Vasıf, who wrote that the French rabble "unscrupulously discussed the advantages of independence (*serbestlik*) and being without a ruler", while he also stressed the poor financial situation of pre-revolutionary France: Menchinger 2014a, 210–212.

93 Cabi – Beyhan 2003, 18–19 (*kral olanlar gökden melâike ile inmedi. Ben kendüme imparatorumuzsun* [*dedirtince*] *bu maddede çalışırum*), 503, 831–833.

94 Moralı Ali Efendi – Refik 1911. On Moralı Ali Efendi see Soysal 1999, 338–339.

95 Cevdet 1891/1892, 6:394–401; Arıkan 1990, 88–90. On Âtıf Efendi's biography see Soysal 1999, 339–340; cf. ibid., 206–207 and Lewis 1953, 121–122. The attribution of the Revolution to Voltaire and Rousseau's atheistic ideas also featured in Ratıb Efendi's dispatches: Yeşil 2007, 293. On Ottoman historiography of the French Revolution see also Arıkan 1990; on Vasıf Efendi's account see Menchinger 2017, 191–192.

the religious or legal connotations that once dominated them.[96] On the other hand, Hakan Erdem has argued convincingly that the texts and declarations of the Greek Revolution (or Greek War of Independence), on which the French ideas were undoubtedly a major influence, played a crucial role in shaping Ottoman political ideology during the Tanzimat era.[97] Ataullah Şanizade Efendi, who was studied in chapter 8, offers a useful insight into this interplay between Islamicate tradition, European influences, and the shock of the national dissident movements, which arguably contributed towards shaping Tanzimat thought.

4 The Tanzimat as Epilogue

As stated at the beginning of this chapter, this detailed survey ends with the destruction of the janissaries, arguably the beginning (together with the 1829 clothing laws) of modernity in the Ottoman Empire. Without the janissaries, the main obstacle to the process of modernizing centralization was removed. In the second part of his reign (i.e. after 1826), Mahmud II embarked on a program of reforms far more radical than any applied by his predecessors: aided by his enhanced legitimacy as a desacralized absolute monarch, one who was now visible to the people and who had no need for intermediaries,[98] he effectively reformed the governmental administration towards a more modern system of subordinated ministries, introduced a council with jurisdiction in matters not covered by the Sharia (1838), popularized education and tried to give it a distinctively secular form (apart from primary education and especially in its higher echelons), founded a state newspaper, *Takvîm-i Vekayi* (1831), and initiated a modernized system of population registers focusing on persons rather than households or production (from 1829 on), among many others.[99]

Yet for a time political thought continued along the same lines as it had followed throughout the latter part of the eighteenth century.[100] In some ways, the early Tanzimat was a Selimian-style, Westernizing reform with "tradition-

96 Lewis 1953; 1985; 1988, 38–42, 109–111; Heinzelmann 2002; Erdem 2005, 78–81. For the development of such terms in the Tanzimat period see Doganalp-Votzi – Römer 2008.

97 Erdem 2005, esp. 78ff.

98 Berkes 1964, 94; on the change in Mahmud's public image policies after 1826, as a token of modernity, cf. Stephanov 2014.

99 See Berkes 1964, 97–135; Ortaylı 1995, 37–41 and 77–85; Collective work 1990; Hanioğlu 2008, 60–64.

100 On political thought in the early period of Mahmud's reign see Heyd 1961, 64–65, 74–77; Beydilli 1999b, 57–63; Kapıcı 2013.

alist" reasoning. The works produced to justify Mahmud II's first moves, like Es'ad Efendi's *Üss-i zafer* (1826), kept promoting the concept of "reciprocity" (*mukabele bi'l-misl*) which necessitated the imitation of European military progress in order to fight back against the infidel. Later on, authors such as Ragıb Efendi or Keçecizade İzzet Molla (1785–1829) tried to advocate collective decision-making through a consultative assembly (*meclis-i şura*) composed of peers from the highest echelons of the administration that would discuss matters without the sultan being present. Furthermore, İzzet Molla proposed a fixed salary table for all functionaries (the ulema included), claiming that the bureaucracy should be given a new order just as the army had been. He also argued, as had Penah and Behic Efendi before him, that local production should be encouraged in order to surpass foreign imports. As for his attitude against imitation of the West, he again used the same arguments seen in Selimian times (e.g. in Behic Efendi's work), i.e. that there is no reason the Ottomans cannot excel in terms of progress where not only the infidels, "though deprived of divine support", but also the mediocre men ruling Mehmed Ali's Egypt have succeeded. İzzet Molla thus argued that the "old world" should be arranged into a new order (*eski aleme nizam vermek*), introducing a dynamic dimension in the reform discourse that would flourish in the term "Tanzimat" (reordering) itself. On this issue, as well as in the ultimate emphasis on the sultan's authority, he may be seen as a precursor to the sweeping reforms of the late 1830s:[101]

> We used to be three classes: the ulema, the administrators and scribes (*rical ü ketebe*), and the janissaries (*ocaklu*). We were all three corrupted as time passed; our difference from the janissaries was that we confessed our fault and took refuge with our sultan's forgiveness and clemency.

Indeed, the concentration of power and authority in the person of the sultan was a prerequisite for imposing such a wide reform program, and it seems indeed that Selim III had also initiated such a process. His lack of a strong grand vizier and his being supported by a group of reform-minded statesmen has been blamed for his eventual failure,[102] but, on the other hand, the situation gave him full control of the ultimate decision-making that was necessary for the implementation of such a program.

In fact, if one is determined to find precursors to the Tanzimat reforms in Ottoman texts and practices, we can also mention the "social engineering"

101 Quoted in Kapıcı 2013, 296.

102 See Yıldız 2008, 704–712.

measures taken by Mahmud II following the 1821 Greek revolt, when (as narrated above) he reverted to a peculiar kind of "applied Khaldunism" in order to bring the Muslims back to their nomadic, war-like state. Apart from the order for every Muslim to carry arms, these measures included renouncing luxuries and attempted to impose a simplified way of dressing that would be common for all.[103] After all, Donald Quataert argued convincingly that it is in 1829 that the beginnings of the actual age of reforms in the Ottoman Empire are to be found, since all clothing laws before (and such laws were markedly present throughout the eighteenth century, including the "Tulip Period" and Selim III's era) sought to impose social markers that distinguished along class, gender, and social lines, while Mahmud II tried to create "an undifferentiated Ottoman subjecthood without distinction".[104]

On the other hand, it would be nonsensical to ignore European influences when discussing the origins of the Tanzimat.[105] French observers paralleled the abolition of the janissaries with the French Revolution, and echoes of French revolutionary ideology have been detected in the 1839 Gülhane rescript (*hatt-ı şerif*).[106] However, the majority of scholars agree that the influence of European ideas and institutions did not become pre-eminent until the period after 1839, and that even this first edict was much more traditional than those that followed, or at least that its ideas were (in Niyazi Berkes' words) "a formulation of those that had become more or less crystallized during the latter part of Mahmud's reign".[107] True, Mahmud's reform was a clear attempt at Westernization, and particularly one that, for the first time, "appeared as a formal policy linked to extensive bureaucratic reform and implemented with brutal force".[108] On the intellectual level, however, there is no sign of the direct influence of European ideas: the vocabulary of Mahmud's orders and even of the 1839 edict is still strictly Islamic, even specified (perhaps with a degree of exaggeration) as a Nakşbendi-based emphasis on the Sharia.[109] It seems as if, unlike his unlucky predecessor Selim, Mahmud took great pains

103 Ilıcak 2011. Butrus Abu-Manneh sees a Nakşbendi, Sunna-minded influence, ignoring the Khaldunist ideas strongly prevailing in this policy (Abu-Manneh 1982, 22–23).

104 Quataert 1997; Quataert 2000, 141–148.

105 On this discussion, see Koloğlu 1990; Abu-Manneh 1994, 173–176; Ortaylı 1994a; Findley 2008, 17–18.

106 Koloğlu 1990; Mantran 1990; Hanioğlu 2008, 72–73.

107 Berkes 1964, 144.

108 Hanioğlu 2008, 63.

109 Abu-Manneh 1994, 188ff. and esp. 194–198; cf. the synopsis of Findley 2008, 18, and see also Ortaylı 1995, 86ff. The order announcing the abolition of the janissaries had also been drawn by Pertev Efendi, an official with strong links to the Nakşbendi order, in a similar vocabulary (Abu-Manneh 1982, 21 and 27).

to describe his reform program in strictly non-Westernizing terms, leaving the fully-fledged introduction of European institutions and measures to the next generation, prepared through his educational and centralizing reforms; on this point, Mahmud differed from Peter the Great of Russia, whose reform is often paralleled to the Ottoman "autocratic modernization" of the 1820s and 1830s.[110] Moreover, the initial motives of the nineteenth-century reforms were of a more pragmatic nature than simple admiration for revolutionary and modernist ideas. Donald Quataert has emphasized that the imitation of France was based on its image as "the most powerful nation in continental Europe", with the implication that universal conscription (which presupposed the granting of universal rights) was the basis of that strength.[111] This argument draws a direct line between Mahmud and his successors' reforms on the one hand, and the ideas of eighteenth-century Ottoman authors, both "traditionalist" and "Westernizing", based on the axiom of "reciprocity", on the other.

---

110 See, for example, Ortaylı 1995, 32–35.

111 Quataert 2000, 67. Cf. İlber Ortaylı's remark that "the Ottomans chose Westernization out of necessity, rather than out of admiration for the West" (Ortaylı 1995, 19; see also ibid., 124).

CONCLUSION

Towards an Ottoman Conceptual History

As stated in the introduction, the development of political discourse can be rendered easier to grasp and to comprehend if we study the devopment of its vocabulary; that is to say, the set of concepts and words in whose terms political ideologies, mentalities, and advice are articulated. Given the rough ideological currents described in the previous chapters, we will try to analyze the development of these concepts, i.e. the change—the widening or the narrowing—of their meaning within the relevant discourses.

Before proceeding to the development of Ottoman concepts, however, it might be useful to clarify the meanings associated by the Ottomans with our own modern notions concerning politics; in other words, and following the categorization proposed in the introduction, we will try an "etic" approach before the "emic" one. The reader may recall that on a theoretical level these issues were briefly discussed in the introduction as well; here, we will revert to them in light of the previous chapters.

1 Politics

Firstly, we tried to define the subject of this book as all discourse pertaining to politics and governance, so at least a note should be made here on the various conceptions of "politics" or, as is often said now, "the public sphere".[1] How did Ottomans describe this sphere, and what were the features and sciences considered to be part of it? It is now commonplace that the term used for politics in modern Turkish, *siyaset*, acquired this particular meaning quite recently: medieval Islamic thought used the term as "statecraft", considering it either a branch of Islamic jurisprudence or (for the *falasifa* such as al-Farabi) a product of man's rational thought.[2] For example, al-Ghazali enumerates four forms of profession necessary for humanity, namely those pertaining to nutrition (agriculture etc.), to clothing, to habitation, and finally the science which gives

1 On the definitions of "politics" and the "political" and their application in the Ottoman case, cf. Dağlı 2013, 206ff. For a survey of a relevant discussion about the existence and character of "politics" in cultures that had no relation to ancient Graeco-Roman thought whatsoever, cf. Narayana Rao – Subrahmanyam 2009, 176–179.

2 See e.g. Najjar 1984; Burak 2015.

© KONINKLIJKE BRILL NV, LEIDEN, 2019 | DOI:10.1163/9789004385245_012

people the means of living in society (*majma'*) and in peace, namely *siyasa*. This science is based on both *fikh* and *ahlak*.[3]

Bernard Lewis argued that in Ottoman usage the term mainly meant "punishment", especially when inflicted by the secular branch, or more generally "non-canonical justice".[4] If one has in mind juridical books such as Dede Cöngi's treatise, this would seem to be true, since Ottoman administration also constantly used the adverb *siyaseten* to denote extra-canonical punishment; moreover, Ottoman administrative and historiographical texts abound in terms such as *seyf-i siyaset* ("the sword of punishment"), *siyasetgâh* (place of executions), and so on, where the word clearly means "punishment".[5] However, in its more political meaning the term is certainly not absent from Ottoman literature. It is first seen comparatively early, in Amasi's early fifteenth-century compendium of ethics, where it has the meaning of "government" or "governance" and is defined as the power or measures (*tedbir*) required to keep different people living together in harmony; the term is used in the same sense by Tursun Beg (who speaks of "kingly government or kingly law", *siyaset-i sultanî ve yasağ-ı padişahî*) and Kınalızade, who emphasize that it emanates from the law of God. The same meaning is seen in Celalzade's adaptation of Kashifi's ethics: one must govern oneself (*siyaset-i nefsi*), while an administrator governs the people (*siyaset-i gayri*) by imposing justice. A similar sense is conveyed by Taşköprüzade's definition of the "science of government" (*ilm al-siyâsa*) as pertaining to the government, the administration, and the social assemblies of the cities (*anwâ' al-riyâsât wa'l-siyâsât wa'l-ijtimâ'ât al-madaniyya*) and as concerning kings, judges, ulema, market administrators (*ahl al-ihtisâb*), and administrators of the treasury.[6] Taşköprüzade's description seems to have been particularly influenced by al-Farabi (whom he cites), who speaks of "the royal, political art" and has political science inquiring "into the [various] kinds of actions, and conscious volitional ways of life (*siyar*), and into the habits, *mores*, and natural dispositions which produce these actions and ways of life".[7]

In fact, therefore, all these authors merely translate their Persian prototypes (Tusi, Davvani, and/or Kashifi). Nevertheless, with or without the presence of the specific term (*siyaset*), the Ottomans never neglected the notion of a sphere related to statecraft and which does not belong exclusively to the ruler

3 Laoust 1970, 192–193, 205ff.; Najjar 1984, 98.
4 Lewis 1984.
5 See, for example, Mumcu 1963; Heyd 1973, 192–195; Burak 2015, 20–23.
6 Taşköprüzade – Bakry – Abu'l-Nur 1968, 1:407.
7 See Rosenthal 1958, 119.

himself. Mustafa Ali, for instance, seems to connect equity with government while keeping mildness and punishment (i.e., the administration of justice) separate (*gerek adaletle hükûmetde gerek hüsn-i tedbir ve siyasetde*), while other sixteenth-century authors speak of the "affairs of the kingdom" (*mesalih-i mülk*, Celalzade) or the "affairs of the people" (*masalih-i halk*, Lütfi Pasha). What is translated here as "affairs" is (like *istislah*) a cognate of *maslaha*, a fundamental term of Islamic political vocabulary broadly meaning "the common good" (in al-Ghazali's definition, it is that which allows the acquisition of benefit and the avoidance of harm).[8] The seventeenth-century Ottomans would use a term like "affairs of the state" (or "of the dynasty": *umur-i devlet*) but not necessarily for what we would call "politics" today. Significantly, the term *politika* appears in Behic Efendi's treatise (the scribes have to read "books on politics") with a marginal note explaining it as "a Frankish word used, in our times, to signify falsehood and cheating (*kizb ü hîle*), although its real meaning is political affairs and the government of cities (*umûr-ı siyasiyye ve tedbir-i müdün*)".[9]

Usually, the meaning of such expressions depended on the speaker. When non-ulema elites accused the ulema of becoming involved in "state affairs", they meant non-ulema patronage and appointments;[10] in the same way, the terms *havass* and *avam*, "private" and "public" or "elite" and "commoners", had different connotations depending on their object.[11] For Aziz Efendi in the early seventeenth century, the janissary commander and other officers could be described as "shareholder[s] in this noble state" (*bu devlet-i aliyyeden hıssedâr*). Under all these meanings and nuances, "state affairs", i.e. government issues, formed the object of the "political advice" genre. The audience for such texts was not confined just to rulers or even viziers: it comprised all those termed by Hemdemi "statesmen" (*ehl-i siyaset*), i.e. those who practise good administration (*hüsn-i zabt ile hâkim ve zâbit eyleyüb*).

Thus, there was a sphere of activity that corresponded to our "politics" and whose meaning can best be conveyed as "governance" or "statecraft". This sphere was legitimately shared by all those entitled to a government post, although it was always the sultan who granted such a privilege, at least in theory (one may remember Silahdar's paradoxical praise of the 1656 rebels against the palace eunuchs who had thought "that they could share the power with

8 See Afsaruddin 2014 (and 387 for al-Ghazali's definition); Laoust 1970, 166ff.

9 Behic – Çınar 1992, 37; cf. Beydilli 1999b, 53–54.

10 Zilfi 1988, 112–114.

11 Thus, the term *avam* could mean the rabble, inferior janissary officers, non-dervishes, non-ulema etc.: Sariyannis 2005, 2, fn. 6.

the sultan of the seven regions of the earth"). With Kâtib Çelebi, one may see a widening of the object of "political advice" to the whole of society, as he systematically speaks of "the affairs of the community" (*umur-ı cumhur*) instead of the usual *umur-i devlet*. Rather than from the actual politics of his day and the growing participation of the janissaries in decision-making, this understanding must have come from his Khaldunist conception of history. Indeed, Kâtib Çelebi sees the problems of his day as those of the whole of society rather than of the government, and his definition of *devlet* in terms of society matches this conception. Nevertheless, it would be a gross exaggeration to say that the meaning of politics changed radically from the mid-seventeenth century onwards to encompass a wider strata of the population. Kâtib Çelebi himself continues to use the traditional definitions, such as when he says in his *Takvim* that good politics (*siyaset*) is the prerequisite for the longevity and well-being of a state, and that it can emanate either from reason (*aklî*), in which case it is a branch of philosophy, or from the Sharia.

Furthermore, within the sphere of governance there are different levels of issues, each of which pertains to the competence of different levels of government. Hence the distinction between "important" and trivial affairs of the state, which is also apparent in administrative practice as can be seen from the mere existence of special registers for "important affairs" (*mühimme defterleri*), where the chancellery copied imperial orders related to public order, defence and war, trade regulations, and so forth, excluding (it seems) affairs of a more private nature. In the language of political advice, this distinction is expressed by the terms *külli* and *cüz'i*. There is no unanimity as to which affairs belong in one or the other category: thus, in his second treatise, Koçi Bey describes the inspection of the registers and the knowledge of the situation of the treasury and the army as "the important affairs", noting that all the rest are small (*cüz'iyyât*). Most authors, however, emphasize that market regulation must be considered an important issue to be looked after by the sultan himself: Mustafa Ali claims that if the sultans consider this matter trivial and leave it to the judges, then lower-class people become rich and the army becomes poor, and in almost the same words Hezarfen argues that the regulation of prices is one of the public issues (*umûr-ı külliye*); if the sultan or the viziers consider it a triviality (*cüz'î*) and leave it to a judge, the latter cannot regulate it by himself since it is outside his competence as it is a "matter of politics" (or: of the administrative branch, *emr-i siyaset*). As seen in chapter 8, these terms were current in Ottoman philosophy in many other ways. Vasıf Efendi uses them when defining events with or without a direct connection to God, while they were also used in argumentation and legal theory.

2 State

One cannot examine these notions without mentioning the emergence of the modern concept of the state, i.e. of "an independent political apparatus ... which the ruler may be said to have a duty to maintain", which was recorded in European political theory from the late fifteenth century.[12] In the Ottoman case, Rifaat Abou-El-Haj argued that from the late seventeenth century the Ottoman Empire gradually became an early-modern state, with one of its main features identified as the "progressive separation between the state and the ruling class", as well as the distinction between the ruler and the state apparatus.[13] Indeed, if we were to trace the conceptual change in the meaning of the word (*devlet*), we would trace a transition from an initial meaning of "luck, good fortune" (for instance in the works of Aşıkpaşazade and Ahmedi) through "power" or "dynasty" (e.g. in Lütfi Pasha, Kınalızade, and Mustafa Ali) to the "desacralization" of the term and its modern sense (so in *Kitâb-i müstetâb*, Hezarfen, and Na'ima).[14] The reader may remember how, in the early nineteenth century, Behic Efendi used the strange term "heart of the state" (*kalb-ı devlet*) not for the sultan or even the vizier but for the governmental committee he proposed. A turning point in the history of the term would again be Kâtib Çelebi's definition of the word as both "kingship/kingdom" and "society" or "community", which functions as a bridge between the meanings "power" or "dynasty" and "state apparatus" or "government". A society has to be governed, and its well-being is identified with the good functioning of its government: this line of thought facilitated, it may be said, the semantic transition toward the development of the notion of "state". A similar process, it should be noted, can be discerned in the development of the term *miri*, which would originally be translated as "belonging to the ruler", but which seems to have acquired the meaning of "pertaining to the state" with a gradual distinction between sultanly and state wealth from the mid- or late sixteenth century.[15] On the other hand, the privatization of state assets via tax-farming and other "outsourcing" methods, which prevailed throughout the late seventeenth and eighteenth centuries,[16] was never justified by political writers. They all (from Lütfi Pasha to Ali, Kâtib Çelebi to Hemdemi, Defterdar to Dürri, and Penah Efendi to Sekbanbaşı) suggest the collection of assets by sipahis or state officials (*emanet*); only Canikli

12 Skinner 1978, 2:349–358.

13 Abou-El-Haj 2005, 7.

14 Lewis 1988, 35–37; Sigalas 2007. I tried to trace this development in much more detail in Sariyannis 2013, 87–95. Yılmaz 2015a, 232, fn. 3 places this semantic turn much earlier than I do, "at least by the early sixteenth century if not well before then".

15 Sariyannis 2013, 111–115.

16 See Salzmann 1993; Salzmann 2004.

seems to be more willing to accept the by-then long-established institution and notes that tax-farmers should know the province and its peasants well.

It is interesting to see the different theories put forward on the beginnings of social life and political society.[17] Most Ottoman theories derive from their predecessors and they usually stress the need for cooperation rather than conflict. The main argument is that, as no one can produce all the goods needed for one's own subsistence, people had to live together and, consequently, a ruler had to control and regulate these arrangements. This vision comes from Tusi's philosophy, and thus we see it in Amasi's, Tursun Beg's, and Kınalızade's work, but also in later authors': Ali considers humans "dependent upon one another through the diversity of crafts and abilities", while Akhisari argues that the propagation of mankind comes with social intercourse, which comes with property (*mal*), which comes with custom (*te'amül*), i.e., dealing with each other (*mu'amele ve alış-viriş*). However, here, too, one may discern a change in emphasis from the seventeenth century onwards: Kınalızade had justified governance on the basis of the different wishes of people, which tend to produce fighting and disorder. In later authors, this becomes a commonplace. Hemdemi explains how men formed societies (*cemiyet*) in order to help each other, but then argues that the statesmen's (*ehl-i siyaset*) aim was to prevent people from attacking one another according to their natural faculties of passion and lust. Na'ima stresses that, for their reproductive needs, some men have the natural tendency to dominate others (*re'is bi't-tab olup*) but also claims (and this is the Khaldunian influence) that when they are obliged towards too strict an obeisance their zeal and ardor diminishes. As for Ibrahim Müteferrika, he also began with the need for association in order to secure mankind's sustenance and reproduction but then, like Hemdemi, claims that, due to differences in their dispositions and their customs and opinions (*ihtilaf-ı meşarib ve tebayün-i ayin ve mezahib olmalarıyle*), some men tend to use power and violence in order to take others under their control and make the latter submit to serve them. The need for laws and leaders is based on such injustices and the desire to prevent them. Should we attribute this change to turbulent seventeenth-century Istanbul politics or to the Khaldunist ideas that were increasingly dominant from then on and which emphasized the rise and decline of dynasties as the conflict between the nomadic and the settled state? It is perhaps no coincidence that, throughout the eighteenth century, the image of international politics as a field of natural struggle became prevalent. From Müteferrika and Resmi Efendi, with their emphasis on the necessity of wars from the beginning of history, to Dürri, who argues that greediness and imperialist tendencies are "the natural custom of the states", even authors who

---

17 Cf. Yücesoy 2011, 21–27; Syros 2012a.

advocated peace clearly considered war and conflict as a natural characteristic of humanity (rather than speaking in terms of Holy War).

3 The Ottoman Political Vocabulary and Its Development

Let us now proceed to the concepts used by the Ottomans themselves. The repeated use of an almost settled set of notions by authors writing from the fifteenth to the eighteenth centuries can easily lead a hasty reader to the conclusion that Ottoman political thought is but a series of commonplace assertions and advice that repeated itself in various combinations. And indeed, arguments stating, for instance, that the ruler must practice justice in order to maintain the world order, or that he should prevent bribery and innovation and stick to the old law instead, can be found in most of the authors examined in this book. Yet these very terms ("justice", "bribery", "world order", and so on) did not mean the same for Tursun Beg as they did for Kâtib Çelebi or Penah Efendi; their content was widened, narrowed, or completely changed over the course of time, as was the emphasis given to each in the context of the individual author's argument.[18]

3.1 *Justice* (adalet)

It is quite clear that all Ottoman authors considered justice to be the paramount kingly virtue, usually (but not always) in the context of the famous "circle of justice". Because of its central place in political ideology, justice has been one of the most researched notions in Ottoman studies. It is characteristic that, while Byzantine and Western tradition, following Aristotle, had wisdom as the "most kingly" of kingly virtues, Persian and Ottoman authors substituted justice.[19] As noted in chapter 1, Halil İnalcık argued that it was the Turkic tradition that linked justice to the keeping of law (*törü, yasa*) rather than to the moral perfection of the ruler.[20] This connection of justice with law is reflected in Ottoman administrative texts, such as regulations and "scripts of

18 This approach, of course, is not altogether new: see Ergene 2001; Yılmaz 2002; Hagen 2005; Doganalp-Votzi – Römer 2008; Topal 2017; and cf. Sariyannis 2011a, 140–143.

19 Cf. Panou 2008, 267; among the Western authors, Brunetto Latini in the late thirteenth century follows Aristotle in praising wisdom (prudence), while Francesco Patrizi in the late fifteenth and Sir Thomas Elyot half a century later did give justice a distinct place (Skinner 1978, 1:47–48, 126, 229). There are some Islamic authors, such as Ibn al-Muqaffa' and later "philosophers", in whose work wisdom keeps its pre-eminent place vis-à-vis justice: see Lambton 1962, 98.

20 İnalcık 1967, 269.

justice" (*adaletname*), i.e. circulars against the illegal practices of local officials and notables.[21] But even after justice had taken up a central place in the late Middle Ages, few cared to define it: as Franz Rosenthal notes, "it was taken for granted what justice was, and it was not subjected to searching interpretation".[22] Boğaç Ergene identified two alternative definitions of justice. One was used by the "imperial center" and, following the Persian political tradition, was viewed as the shepherd-like ruler protecting the *reaya* against the abuses of the military elite. Another definition, used by some members of the ruling elite (Ergene traces this definition to some passages by Mustafa Ali, Evliya Çelebi, and Na'ima), understood justice as the recognition of the mutual rights and obligations of the sultan and his servants. According to Ergene, while the first definition was mainly adopted in state documents and regulations, the second seems to have gained weight during the seventeenth and eighteenth centuries. The struggle between the segments of the elite to secure or claim their positions throughout the seventeenth-century crisis of society and state must have been pivotal in this shift.[23] However, as will be analyzed below, political thought insisted (and even became more pronounced) in defining justice in relation to peasants.

In works such as Aşıkpaşazade's history, as seen in chapter 1, justice is generally conceived as the absence of greed, while the identification of justice with generosity can also be seen in Ahmedi. For these early authors, those who should be protected are the warriors rather than the peasants. Although the sixteenth century abounds in texts assuming justice to be a personal characteristic of the sultan, who has to protect the welfare of his flock, it has been noted that the sultan as a person had, by the mid-sixteenth century, "largely retreated from [many authors'] conceptions of justice and the social reality it tendered" and that justice was viewed more as a "generalizable marker of the *status quo*, representing stability via social hierarchy" rather than "a personal quality emanating from the ruler".[24] Indeed, a group of more elaborate texts, mostly based on the *falasifa* tradition, emphasize justice as the maintaining of a balance between the various parts of society. Thus, for the Tusian authors justice has three types, namely equity in distributing property or social rank, justice in financial transactions, and justice in punishment. In all three, justice means knowing and determining the middle way (*evsat*)—or, in Kınalızade's wording, the proportional treatment of all parts. These parts, in fact, are nothing

21 See İnalcık 1965; Abou-El-Haj 1991.

22 Rosenthal 1980, 101.

23 Ergene 2001; cf. Hagen 2005, 66ff.

24 Ferguson 2010, 97–98.

but corporate entities, namely the four social groups (men of the sword, men of the pen, traders, and peasants). The same understanding can be seen in Celalzade's adaptation, although in the preambles to the *kanunname*s, which he seems to have written himself, it is peasants who enjoy the sultan's justice. In other texts from the same period, justice is seen as moderation, in a moral sense or, more particularly, a "judicial" context: for instance, Tursun Beg seems to understand it as fairness in punishment, while the historian Sâfî describes Ahmed I's justice as a "finely defined line between undue severity and unjustified clemency".[25] Together with authors following the Tusian tradition, Lütfi Pasha also conceives of justice as keeping social compartmentalization.

On the other hand, there was an increasing emphasis on the protection of peasants as the explicit aim of justice, although there is no visible shift; this approach instead coexists with that on keeping a just balance among social classes. As early as in Amasi's adaptation of Tusi, one finds the famous circle of justice, repeated by a host of political authors well into the seventeenth century. From the late sixteenth-century *adaletname*s to the early seventeenth-century "declinist" authors, justice was increasingly identified as meaning following the old laws on taxation in order to protect the *reaya*: this was the case with *Kitâb-ı müstetâb*, for example. One might even say that, in this period, the Ottoman administration (and writers associated with the scribal bureaucracy) defined justice as the following of the old laws without any innovations.[26] Although a definition of justice was still elusive, more and more authors made allusions to the excessive tax burdens imposed on the peasants: the "circle of justice" became a recurrent argument for the protection of peasants, from Hasan Dede's treatise to Murad IV—in which the sultan is compared to a shepherd, "his slaves" to lambs, and unjust judges and officers to wolves[27]—to Kâtib Çelebi and Na'ima.[28] At the beginning of the eighteenth century, Defterdar reverted to the old distinction between real and nominal wealth, i.e. between the peasants' welfare and a full treasury. Defterdar argued that the sultans of old managed to have military victories with much less income, as they preferred justice to wealth; this argument, namely that state income should not be sinful and that ultimately one should not place too much importance on the treasury, is found in all "traditionalist" authors of the late eighteenth century, such as Dürri and Canikli Ali Pasha. On the other hand, it

25 Murphey 2005, 9–10.

26 Sariyannis 2011a, 142.

27 Terzioğlu 2010, 295. In the same text, the Circle of Justice is implied by the phrase, "are you then to fill the treasury from the air?" (*hazine'i havadan mı cem' idersin sonra?*).

28 Ayn Ali 1978, 124; Kâtib Çelebi – Gökyay 1968, 156; Na'ima 1864–1866, 1:37; Na'ima – İpşirli 2007, 30. Cf. also Na'ima 1864–1866, 6:152; Na'ima – İpşirli 2007, 1653. On the various formulations of the "circle of justice" in Ottoman literature see also Fleischer 1983, 201.

must have been evident that the place of justice within the system of Ottoman political values gradually waned during the eighteenth century.

3.2 *Law and "The Old Law"*(kanun, kanun-i kadim)

According to the famous thesis promoted first and foremost by Halil İnalcık, the concept of a law that has to be kept, and which is an indispensable part of rulership, was a contribution of Central Asian Turkic tradition to Ottoman political thought and practice. İnalcık remarks that, in the Persian tradition, the ruler's authority is actually above the law, his only limitation being the care for justice.[29] Indeed, authors nearer to this tradition tend to downplay the role of the law: in Ahmedi's famous account of the Mongols, the "law" is something that can be oppressive and may "pass for justice" to some extent; in the same way, justice is more important than a hard law in Şeyhoğlu's work. As for Kınalızade, his criticism of the Mongol *yasa* is almost explicitly an attack on Ebussu'ud and Celalzade's use of sultanly law or *kanun* as a form of legislation *de facto* superior to the Sharia.

The term *kanun* was not an Ottoman invention. Al-Ghazali had written that the *faqih* knows the "political/administrative norms" (*qanun al-siyasa*),[30] while for *siyasa al-shariyya* writers (such as Ibn Taymiyya) this was a concept peculiar to the sultan, who may change the rules *ad libitum* provided they do not contradict (very much) the Sharia. In mid-sixteenth century Ottoman usage, at least, *kanun* seemed arguably to have had the meaning of "lawful", "necessary", and even "permissible" or "habitual".[31] What really distinguishes Ottoman ideas about the "law" from other Islamicate formulations is the glorification of "oldness"; in other words, the idea that the sultan does not grant laws on the basis of his own justice but rather they come from the established laws of his ancestors to which he must abide. In this respect, one should note that the connection of Ottoman law (*yasak/kanun*) with the eponymous dynasty is a recurring feature of both Ottoman statesmen and Arab jurists who opposed them.[32] In *Kitâbu mesâlih* (c. 1560) there is an ambiguous attitude (old laws are not necessarily good, if made by mediocre viziers), but by the end of the sixteenth century (at the latest) *kanun* had become almost identical with "the old law" or *kanun-i kadim*, a kind of constitution set by the great sultans of old.[33] The reader might remember that one of, if not the,

---

29 İnalcık 1967, 267–269. Late Byzantine "mirrors for princes" also stress the need for the monarch to obey the laws (Paidas 2006, 81–83).

30 Laoust 1970, 197.

31 Tezcan 2000, 659–660. This also seems to have been the common meaning of *kanun* in the Mamluk sources: Burak 2015, 7–8.

32 Burak 2015, 15–20.

33 Cf. the general surveys in Öz 2010 and Yılmaz 2015b.

first instances of this reasoning is in Aşıkpaşazade's history, when a reluctant Osman I is finally persuaded to permit a market tax on the grounds that it was an old and established custom. Bitlisi quotes the duty of the sultan to abide by the laws ordained as a manifestation of the virtue of remembrance. Furthermore, as was seen, sultanly decrees around the mid- or late sixteenth century almost identified "the old law" with "justice";[34] in Ahmet Yaşar Ocak's view, the "old law" was considered identical to keeping the "circle of justice" and the proper position of the "four pillars", i.e. the social classes or estates.[35] The law apart, even custom or usage was sanctified in terms of age, as when monasteries or peasant communities claimed privileges arguing that they were "an old custom" (*adet-i kadim*); and, as Nicolas Vatin and Gilles Veinstein argue, by the early eighteenth century even practices such as the dethronement of sultans by rebels or high officials had somehow come to be considered established custom.[36]

Mustafa Ali may, perhaps, be credited as the first to explicitly sanctify the "old law", although in some instances he even criticized Mehmed II's regulations. In chapter 4, we saw how, in his last work, he fell to a characteristic slip of tongue, writing that Mehmed II "promulgated an old law" (meaning, more accurately, "a just law that became old and established"). Later authors took up this perspective: from Akhisari, who argued that the course of things must continue according to "the right manner and the old law" (*uslub-ı kavim ve kanun-i kadim*), to "Sunna-minded" thinkers, such as Münir-i Belgradi or Kadızade Mehmed İlmi, who referred to consultation in the same terms. The apogee of the "old law" concept came with the "declinist" literature of the early seventeenth century, as seen in chapter 5; the 1606 *Kavânîn-i yeniçeriyân* was an explicit attempt to record the "old laws", while the word *kanun* appears in the title of several similar works, such as Aziz Efendi's treatise (*Kânûnnâme-i sultânî*). In the *Kitâb-ı müstetâb*, the "old law" is explicitly inserted into the "circle of justice" since it accompanies justice as a means of maintaining the peasants, the treasury, and the army in a good condition.

As remarked in chapter 7, with Kâtib Çelebi the cult of the old law diminished and the idea of new practices fit for the present times gained weight. True, the former notion continued to be used: for instance, Defterdar mentioned the "old law" when copying Lütfi Pasha and, more emphatically, in his chapter on timars. Yet even the authors described as "traditionalist" gradually ceased to endorse the term, and when they did use it, they modified it along Kâtib Çelebi's

34 İnalcık 1965; Sariyannis 2011a, 142.
35 Ocak 1988, 172.
36 Vatin – Veinstein 2003, 65.

lines. While Penah Efendi proposed the abolition of such paragons of the "old law" as the timar system and the *tapu* landholding, Ratıb Efendi spoke of the need for a renewal of the old laws but admitted that this must be made "according to the nature of this age" (*kavanin-i kadime bu asrın mizac ü tabiatına tatbik ile tecdid*). During the *Nizam-i Cedid* controversy, it seems that the "old law" argument was revived by the janissary opponents of the new army. One may discern it in their Selimian refuters: Sekbanbaşı stressed that the old law on the janissaries has been surpassed due to the rise of prices and the constant need for new troops, while Kuşmani found those claiming that "things must be done as in the time of [their] forefathers" as falling into the sect of fatalism. The very term *Nizam-i Cedid* (probably first coined by Müteferrika, always in the context of military organization) shows very clearly the development; it is quite characteristic that Ömer Faik Efendi named his rather conservative work *Nizâmü'l-atîk* ("The old order").[37]

The influence of Kâtib Çelebi's Khaldunist ideas apart, another factor that contributed to the obsolescence of the "old law" must have been the re-emergence of the *kanun* vs. Sharia conflict: after being the issue of the day in the 1550s and 1560s (as seen in Çivizade's, Birgivi's, and even Kınalızade's work), the conflict seems to have lost its centrality. Although Kadızade Mehmed İlmi criticized judges who declared that they would rule by *yasak* and *kanun* rather than the Sharia, the "Sunna-minded" authors of the seventeenth century, including the Kadızadeli preachers, advocated the Sharia without showing contempt for the *kanun*. Writing sometime between 1623 and 1638, for instance, Üveysî accused the sultan (or his administrators) of observing neither the Sharia nor the *kanun*, as he had abandoned the world to corruption by adopting unholy innovations. In another case, Hemdemi, an author whose influence by Kâtib Çelebi is otherwise evident, complained that canonical punishments such as the cutting off of thieves' hands are neglected. The conflict is usually considered as having culminated, at the other side extreme, with the financial reforms of the early 1690s and the famous 1696 order of Mustafa II that prohibited "the coupling of the [terms] noble Sharia and *kanun*" in favor of the former.[38] It is interesting that the Sharia-minded policy followed by Köprülüzade Fazıl Mustafa Pasha (1689–91) seems to have been termed "new

37 On the shifting uses of the "old custom", especially during the nineteenth century, cf. Karateke 1999.

38 Heyd 1973, 154–155. It may not be a coincidence that, from 1687 onwards, the chief of the descendants of the Prophet takes the primary place in the ceremony of the new sultans' allegiance (*bey'at*), while other symbolic gestures that try to emphasize the caliphal features of the sultans were added in the following decade: Vatin – Veinstein 2003, 286–287, 314.

order" (*nizam-i cedid*) as well:[39] it seems thus that the cult of the "old law" had strong *kanun* connotations.

Throughout the eighteenth century, on the other hand, we often find the two terms coexisting harmoniously, something that might imply that the conflict had finally been resolved or at least supressed. The anonymous "Dialogue between an Ottoman and a Christian officer" joins the rules of the "Sharia" with the "old laws" (the Ottomans had allegedly stopped observing both and thus their superiority waned). Around 1770, Dürri Efendi argued in favor of the "old law" in relation to military regulations while also (like Hemdemi) stressing the Sharia and at the same time adopting Kâtib Çelebi's use of Khaldunism with regard to different measures for different ages, while Canikli frequently mentions "the law, Holy or sultanly" (*gerek şer'i ve gerek kanuni*).

3.3 *Innovation* (bid'at)

While the "old law" was gradually sanctified as a source of authority, innovation (*ihdas, bid'at*) was the subject of criticism from very early, since its negative connotations were present in the Quran; in this, Islamicate thought resembled other medieval cultures (although this is a subject that still has to be thoroughly explored).[40] Of course, the concept did not have any concrete meaning in early Ottoman political thought, i.e. before the concept of the "old law" gained weight or at any rate before Çivizade's and Birgivi's opposition. Rather, it was a standard item in the vocabulary used for criticism, as when Aşıkpaşazade wanted to criticize the decisions of bad counselors.[41] It was in Ebusuud's time that the term began to take on a concrete meaning, namely regulations that contradicted canonical principles. As such, innovation became a standard accusation used by the Kadızadelis against their opponents, and especially the dervish orders; on the other hand, as seen in chapter 6, the latter often used the same argument as well. Sivasi also spoke vehemently against the "people of innovation", although his targets were infidels and heretics rather than women in the palace or dervishes. A usual object of *bid'at* accusations was using tobacco, from Kadızadeli and Halveti preachers alike; an association of this trope with

39 This name is found in Raşid's title of the relevant chapter (*tertib-i nizam-ı cedid be-ahval-ı cizye*), but not in Defterdar's account, which, otherwise, Raşıd copies almost verbatim: Raşid 1865, 2:148; Defterdar – Özcan 1995, 387. The term is not found in Silahdar's history either. Raşid was Defterdar's near-contemporary (he died in 1735), but (until the manuscripts are examined) we cannot exclude the possibility of the title being rewritten after his book was published in 1865.

40 Cf. the remarks on the Byzantine case in Spanos 2014.

41 Aşıkpaşazade – Atsız 1949, 244. The word is used in the same way by Yazıcıoğlu Ahmed Bican (Yerasimos 1990, 195–96) and by contemporaneous ulema-minded authors (e.g. Seyhoğlu: Şeyhoğlu – Yavuz 1991, 54, which has the proviso that there are also "good innovations", *bidat-i hasene*: ibid., 72).

the janissaries (commonly known as heavy smokers) and their political power is tempting, but cannot be established with certainty. On the other hand, Sivasi's disciple Abdulahad Nuri describes the usual course of a new custom in a much more flexible way, one usually attributed to Kâtib Çelebi: something is first prohibited, he maintains, but then takes root in people's customs and, in the end, is declared licit on the grounds of the public good (*istihsan*).

As well as the Sunna-minded condemnation of innovations, the term acquired a specific meaning with the "declinist" authors of the late sixteenth and early seventeenth centuries. Selaniki associates bribery, usury, and corruption with "injustice and innovative practices" (*cevr ü bid'at*), while his contemporary Mustafa Ali has Mehmed II's grand vizier making the grim prophecy that a decline would come if any of the sultan's successors decided to promulgate his own law.[42] In subsequent decades, authors such as Koçi Bey and Aziz Efendi, who glorified the "old law" and lamented departures from it, were fiercely opposed to innovation, which thus acquired a new meaning of deviations from a certain model of landholding and other military and administrative practices. Nowhere is this association clearer than in the anonymous *Kavânîn-i yeniçeriyân*, as the author enumerates those innovations in the corps that are against the (old) law and those that are not (*kanuna muhalif olan bid'atlar ... ve kanun üzere olanlar*).[43] Similar remarks continued to be made even at the beginning of the eighteenth century: let us point to the short note on innovations ("good and bad") that form an appendix in some manuscripts of Defterdar Mehmed Pasha's treatise and to Nahifi's stressing of "the annihilation of innovative and unjust practices", mainly meaning illegal taxes and dues.

Another line of thought, as stressed elsewhere as well, begins with Kâtib Çelebi, who declares clearly that there is no point trying to abolish innovations, even bad ones, once established in a community: "people will not abandon custom" (*halk adeti terk eylemez*), and anyway "scarcely any of the sayings or doings of any age are untainted by innovation". In fact, Kâtib Çelebi favors innovation, in the sense that he theorizes that different times need different measures just as people need different treatment and medicine at different ages; we saw how deeply this concept permeated late seventeenth and eighteenth-century thought, from Hemdemi and Hezarfen to Penah Efendi. Na'ima also systematically inserted such advice, even talking of the Sharia division of state income and expenses, which normally would be considered inviolable. At the beginning of chapter 5 we showed how the justification of innovative practices had already begun by the early seventeenth century; in 1729, Müteferrika could even state that "the ancients always made fine innovations"

42 Selaniki – İpşirli 1999, 458; Ali – Demir 2006, 142–143.

43 Akgündüz 1990–1996, 9:263–268.

in order to argue for the necessity of the printing press. A strange mixed attitude towards the concept of innovation is found in Kuşmani's polemical work: first, he is at pains to show that the alleged innovations of the *Nizam-i Cedid* are not really new, since they were actually used long ago; then, he admits that weapons and tools are generally the innovations of the infidels, who are oriented toward this world, while Muslims neglect worldy affairs as transitory. This argument must be seen in the context of the *mukabele bi'l-misl* concept, i.e. that there must be a spontaneous answer to the Christian advances: in this vein, what Kuşmani really means to say is that in order to respond effectively to the advance of the Europeans, Muslims have to imitate their innovations even if these are not exactly canonically licit.

3.4 *World Order* (nizam-i alem)

Perhaps the most important concept for Ottoman political thought was the need to ensure world order (*nizam-i alem*). Yet however central it may have been, it lacked a clear definition or perhaps even meaning; but even when it was not defined, it is implied as the result of the making of human societies, as described above in the section on state. Most often than not, Ottoman authors described the threats against it without providing a description of its meaning: Ali, for instance, claims that world order is disrupted by neglect of laws and ordinances, while for Kadızade Mehmed İlmi its disruption comes from a lack of will to impose justice, the disobedience of soldiers, and the lack of consultation with the ulema. Modern scholars have alternatively interpreted it as "raison d'état", "unity of the state", "perfect public order", "balanced distribution of prerogatives", and so on.[44] It may be deduced that elements such as the justice of the ruler, balance between the "four pillars", and maintaining the *hadd* or limit between them, among others, were self-evident constituents of the "world order". In the words of Pál Fodor,[45]

> [t]he basic features of the 'good order of the world' as described by the Ottoman mirrors for princes were a just ruler conducting the affairs in person, a functional social stratification in which the norms (*kânûns*) of the early 16th century were observed, the balance between the *kul* and the timariot armies as well as between spending and revenues, and consequently the stable position of the tax-paying *re'âyâ*.

44 See Hagen 2005, 56–57, fn. 7; Berkes 1964, 11; Menchinger 2014a, 163ff.; Menchinger 2017, 84–86.

45 Fodor 1986, 238.

One of the most important consequences of this notion was that small concessions could be made as long as the general idea, i.e. the sultan's power (and, in some cases, the dynasty) was preserved: this is seen in the famous motto "a specific damage is better than a general one" (*zarar-ı ammdan zarar-ı hass yeğdir*), found in quite a few political tracts as well as in chronicles (it is the usual phrase with which a sultan condescends to give the rebels the heads that they are asking for). One of its first instances may be the justification of fratricide by Neşri; significantly, the person to whom the phrase is attributed, on the occasion of the execution of Murad II's brother, notes that this is "an old custom" (*adet-i kadime*), and it is exactly the "world order" that formed the main argument for the legal justification of fratricide.[46] In the same vein, the *fetvas* that were related to the execution of the deposed Ibrahim in 1648 stress both the need to keep the world order and the preference for specific damage to a general one.[47] From another point of view, this is the principle behind *istihsan*, the *fikh* principle of juristic preference that involved a choice between the lesser of two evils.[48]

Gottfried Hagen explored the development of the term "world order" between the fifteenth and eighteenth centuries and found that it had strong overtones of social hierarchies, while it was also conceived of being as something that "can be disrupted but not changed", with the alternative being "not a different order, but chaos" (the latter might take even natural forms, i.e. famine, flood, and other disasters); moreover, as seen in chapter 2, he also showed how the *ahlak* vision of society entailed a static, ahistoric, and universal model of this order, one in which the human agent had only very limited influence.[49] *Ahlak* literature, represented in Ottoman Turkish by Amasi and Kınalızade, seems to have compared the order of the world to the order of one's spiritual life, and its necessary prerequisite, balance between the four classes, to the balance between the various faculties of the soul; and, as moral balance emanates from man's domination over the faculties of his soul, so does social order depend on the ruler's domination and sovereignty.[50] In al-Ghazali's early work, justice is seen as keeping a hierarchical order (*tartib*) among the elements of a city, similar to that governing the elements of the soul.[51] Thus, hierarchy is

46 Neşri – Unat – Köymen 1987, II:573. Cf. Vatin – Veinstein 2003, 149–170; Vatin (forthcoming).

47 Vatin – Veinstein 2003, 203.

48 Cf. Menchinger 2014a, 133.

49 Hagen 2005, 62; Hagen 2013, 437. On the dichotomy of order vs. chaos as a thematic motif with deep roots in Middle Eastern antiquity see Howard 2007, 161–164.

50 Tezcan 1996, 123; Tezcan 2001.

51 Laoust 1970, 74–75. Al-Ghazali proceeds in a partition of the human classes, but which did not find many imitators: those who are served but do not serve themselves, those who

an indispensable element of order.[52] A parallel with the Byzantine notion of *taxiarchia* (*ταξιαρχία*), which combines order and hierarchy with strong connotations of the natural-*cum*-divine order, has already been drawn;[53] and indeed the similarities are quite striking, since these Byzantine concepts could very well be describing a vision of the world and the empire such as, for instance, that expressed by Mustafa Celalzade.

The notion seems to have entered a course of desacralization during the later part of the seventeenth century, as did many others. First, its meaning became narrower: world order now denoted something more akin to state organization or arrangement rather than a cosmic hierarchy. Kâtib Çelebi had spoken of "order" in a more restricted sense, as when he claimed that the only reason for a ruler to interfere in people's lives would be "if there is any general danger for the public affairs or any breach of order" (*emr-i din ü dünyaya zarar-ı am ve nizama muhil ma'naları göreler*). As Hagen again noted, Na'ima "always speaks of *nizam-i devlet* or similar terms, but never uses *nizam-ı 'âlem*".[54] Furthermore, in his second preface Na'ima spoke of "the natural order" (*nizam-ı tabi'i*) of state affairs. Further into the eighteenth century, Resmi Efendi was one of the final authors to have used the concept of a "world order", but with a distinctly different wording: states and dynasties, on whom depend the order of the world (*yeryüzinin nizamını*) and the safety of the people. In the anonymous *Mîzân-ı umûr-ı hâriciyye* (probably Resmi's work, too), it is written that "just like the law provided by Sultan Süleyman to the Exalted State, so other societies (*güruh*) are also bound to arrangements (*nizam*) peculiar and useful for themselves". His contemporary, Dürri Efendi, speaks of order, but never of "world order" (e.g. reordering the army), while Penah mentions the "ordering of the countries" (*nizam-ı ekâlim*).

Ultimately, the notion obtained the even narrower meaning of "military arrangements", while at the same time it acquired the possibility of change, i.e. the possibility that an "old order" may give up its place legitimately and efficiently to a "new" one. The first to introduce this idea, as well as the term "new order" itself, was İbrahim Müteferrika: he maintained that the Ottomans had to learn the methods and innovations used in the new armies, which he names the "new order" (*nizam-ı cedid*), and adds that order (of an army) is a science

serve but are not served, and those who serve and are served.

52 An interesting exception is to be found in Sinan Paşa's work, where (as was seen in chapter 1) the "order and arrangement of the world" is almost completely void of hierarchical connotations: Sinan Paşa – Tulum 2013, 368ff.

53 Oktay 2001. On the Byzantine term cf. Ahrweiler 1975, 134ff.

54 Hagen 2005, 79, fn. 104. On the use of the term in late eighteenth-century texts see Menchinger 2014a, 170ff.; Menchinger 2017, 166–168.

in its own right (*bu fenn-ı garib-i nizam-ı asker zatında ... bir leziz ilm olub*).[55] In the late eighteenth century, this term reemerged: Penah Efendi used the term *nizam-i cedid* for the army, while references to the "new order" in the Austrian army can be found in Ratıb Efendi's account of Austria. Even opponents of the Westernizing reform used the new terms and notions: the title of Ömer Faik's work, *Nizâmü'l-atîk* ("The old order") is, again, quite suggestive. Ömer Faik also speaks of the "apparent order" (*nizam-ı suriyye*), i.e. issues pertaining to the court, economy, and the army, in contrast to spiritual matters such as prayer or the condition of the ulema. As for Şanizade in the early 1820s, he preferred to speak of reordering (*tekmil-i nizam*) the army.

3.5 *Keeping One's Place* (hadd)

At least for the majority of the Ottoman centuries, one of the primary components of what was conceived of as "world order" was the maintainance of a hierarchical society where every "class" or "estate" kept to its place or (to put it as an Ottoman would) knew its limit (*hadd*). As we saw in chapter 2, this emphasis on compartmentalization can be seen in Amasi, who introduced Tusi's theory of the four classes (corresponding to the four elements) and the need for them to be balanced.[56] This theory continued until well into the eighteenth and even the early nineteenth century as a standard form for describing society, especially after Kâtib Çelebi further elaborated on it, and was mostly used as a means to press for stricter control of the army, *recte* a stricter check of the janissaries' power. As a side-effect, one should cite the (not at all unexpected) condemnation of the unemployed, as seen, for example, in Akhisari. On the other hand, what was new in Ottoman political theory and practice was the stress placed on every individual having to keep to their own place, i.e. against crossing class boundaries. This principle took the form of an emphasis on external signs distinguishing not only Muslims from non-Muslims but also rich from poor. The anonymous author of the *Kitâbu mesâlih* (c. 1560) stressed the need for strict sartorial rules along social/religious lines, while only a few decades later Mustafa Ali gave detailed instructions on how everybody should conduct themselves according to their income (on the other hand, he favored mobility, provided it happens at a young age, e.g. in medreses). Clothing restrictions also appear in the first Veliyuddin *telhis*; as for the Sunna-minded authors, Sivasi argues vehemently against the violation of dress codes by non-Muslims.

---

55 Müteferrika – Şen 1995, 191.

56 On the development and the various forms of the four-fold division in Ottoman thought see Sariyannis 2013, 107–111; Yılmaz 1999.

Mustafa Ali's emphasis on social differentiation re-emerges with Kâtib Çelebi, for whom pomp and pageantry, and more generally the imitation of rulers by the middle classes, are harmful aspects associated with the "decline" stages of a society. This Khaldunist view is clearer and further elaborated in Na'ima's writing, where Kâtib Çelebi's medical simile of the body politic is expanded to declare excessive luxury and ease on the part of the peasants a cause of rebellion and strife. In the same vein, he also maintained that merchants should be controlled and avoid greed. On the other hand, he argued that the magnates of the state do need the "signs of splendor and grandeur"; luxury should mark the distinction between the soldiers and the servants of the state, on the one hand, and the commoners, on the other. The emphasis placed on the economic aspect of compartmentalization continued throughout the eighteenth century, such as when Dürri Efendi not only stated that sartorial differentiation should be imposed but also argued against inferiors imitating their superiors on the grounds of private economics (fewer private expenses means a more useful role in war).[57]

In practice, the principle of compartmentalization was mainly directed at peasants entering the *askeri* class, i.e. taxable subjects becoming non-taxable (it should be noted that, in this sense, the *askeri* included the ulema as well). Lütfi Pasha maintained that even in such a case, the transition of a person to non-taxable status should not bring forth the transition of his relatives as well. Within the context of the declinist theory, from the late sixteenth century onwards this principle was turned into a growing emphasis on the destructive role of "strangers" or "intruders" (*ecnebi*) in the army ranks.[58] However commonplace it may seem in a short survey of the sources, this emphasis saw several stages and took different forms even within the same period. More than two decades after Lütfi Pasha was writing, *Kitâbu mesâlih* (c. 1560) spoke of "strangers" in the scribal ranks but has no reference at all to the army; shortly afterwards, the anonymous author of *Hırzü'l-mülûk* mentioned strangers in the *sipahi* corps, while for the janissaries he only lamented their large salaries (not their numbers). The commonly-seen notion of the janissary corps being filled with intruders first appears in Mustafa Ali, who put the beginning of this practice in 1582; his contemporary Akhisari placed it ten years later and described it somewhat differently: peasants and artisans were *forced* to join the army (the emphasis, it must be noted, is on the destruction of the urban economy rather than that of the provinces).

57 On sumptuary laws and sartorial differentiation in practice and in Ottoman mentalities, see Quataert 1997; Murphey 2002, 136–141. On sumptuary laws in pre-modern and early modern Western Europe, cf. Hunt 1996; Muzzarelli – Campanini 2003.

58 On this issue cf. Fodor 1986, 225ff.; Káldy-Nagy 1987; Abou-El-Haj 2005, 38–39, 45.

While Ali and Akhisari lamented the detrimental results of this intrusion for the taxpayers and the state revenue, in the early seventeenth century the stress moved to the harm done to the army itself, i.e. to the increase in the number and the salaries of the troops without any improvement in their effectiveness. Nevertheless, even then there were several stages in how the damage was assessed. In the *Kavânîn-i yeniçeriyân* and in Ayn Ali's treatises, all dated to the first decade of the seventeenth century, the notion of the corrupt janissaries vs. the valiant and virile sipahis is absent; in Ayn Ali's work one may even say that it is the timariot sipahis who are blamed the most. But in works like *Kitâb-ı müstetâb* and Koçi Bey's treatise, janissaries and, more generally, "salaried slaves" are blamed for the decline of the sipahis, especially after the intrusion of strangers.[59] Furthermore, in Koçi Bey the prohibition of mobility works the other way around as well: not only should peasants not enter the military ranks, the sipahis should not do the work of the infantry or peasants. Such views continued to appear, from Kadızade Mehmed İlmi (who lamented the infiltration of peasants into the ranks of both the people of the sword and those of the pen) to the eighteenth-century authors; from the latter, some, like Defterdar, stressed the destruction of the productive base (Dürri even states that the excess of intruders into the *askeri* class now meant the term "taxable peasants" was the same as "non-Muslims"), while others (like Canikli or Penah Efendi) stressed the military effects. Let us note here that we must not necessarily take it at face value when an author laments the ruin of the land due to these practices, as he may only be using a traditional trope (based on the principle of justice) in order to criticize the intrusion of peasants into the army.[60] Clearly, all this criticism targeted the janissaries' increased political power, achieved by their ranks being swelled with the lower urban strata.

At any rate, from the mid-seventeenth century on this understanding of *hadd* gradually lost importance (the main target now being the janissaries as an institution rather than how they were composed—all the more so since, from the mid-eighteenth century, there were increased calls to recruit peasants for a new army) in favor of the moral concept, i.e. the condemnation of luxury and pomp.[61] However, it is interesting that in the eighteenth century such remarks occasionally targeted not only peasants-turned-military but also the blurring of career lines in the administration. Such blurring had begun to be common by the end of the seventeenth century; let us remember Köprülü

59 Cf. Abou Hadj 1988.

60 Gyula Káldy-Nagy notes sarcastically that "tens of thousands of Turkish *re'ayas* could thus be carried off to the galleys of the fleet, but the wise advisors of state administration failed to raise their voice against the decreasing number of agrarians, for they were only concerned when *re'ayas* became *timar*-holders" (Káldy-Nagy 1987, 169).

61 See Sariyannis 2011a, 140–141.

Fazıl Ahmed Pasha's early change of career, from ulema to administrative, and Rami Mehmed's rise from the scribal bureaucracy to the post of grand vizier (see chapter 6). As showed by Norman Itzkowitz, by the eighteenth century the *kalemiyye* career line had gained substantial importance, overshadowing the once omnipotent "palace career".[62] Thus, we see Nahifi arguing against the handling of affairs by tradesmen and men of the market, who should not be allowed in the line of service (*tarik*). Half a century later, Canikli Ali Pasha insisted that one should be promoted along a single career line (*tarik*): for instance, an agha of the janissaries should not become a vizier.

3.6 *Consultation* (meşveret)

A key concept moderating, to some extent, the ruler's absolute power was consultation or *meşveret*, a central notion in the traditional political theories inherited by the Ottomans and, in fact, a central notion in Islamic political thought with its origins in the Quran.[63] One sees consultation praised by authors as diverse as al-Semerkandi, Akhisari, Celalzade, Hasan Dede, and Müteferrika.[64] It is noteworthy that, while all of these writers stressed this need, they also were quite adamant in giving some terms under which consultation should be taken; most of them emphasized experience and piety, with the notable experience of Celalzade, who puts more weight on reason (*akl*). For him, reason is the basis of proper consultation to such a degree that even receiving advice from intelligent non-Muslims could be deemed legitimate. It is clear that, in such a way, he wanted to give the bureaucracy more importance than the ulema: in Bernard Lewis' words, "in general, the ulema urged the need for consultation with the ulema, the bureaucrats were more insistent on the importance of consulting bureaucrats".[65] On the other hand, the struggle over consultation was combined with different views on who and how many would be the sultan's boon companions and favorites, and on how much the sultan should be accessible or secluded, and ultimately on who should have access to the flow of political information in the court.[66]

The emphasis on consultation continued throughout the eighteenth century, both in theory and (as it seems) in practice. Defterdar, for instance, despite stressing that it is a useful practice only with trustworthy men, admitted that sometimes a child or woman could have a sound opinion, while Canikli excluded astrologers and dervishes, but argues that every class should be

62 Itzkowitz 1962.

63 Cf. Ceylan 2005 on the relevant literature; Lewis 1981–1982; Mottahedeh 1989.

64 Cf. Yılmaz 2015a, 255–258.

65 Lewis 1981–1982, 776.

66 See Peksevgen 2004.

consulted concerning its own fields. Şanizade's discussion of consultation, as seen at the end of the previous chapter, shows how, even on the eve of the Tanzimat reforms, the word (*meşveret*) was used in a quite aristocratic way, in contrast to rather than in corroboration with the new ideas favored by the French Revolution.[67] On the other hand, representation among the ruled, with a tradition of unanimous election of notables (albeit by a restricted body, consisting usually of lesser notables), was a common phenomenon in the latter part of the eighteenth century.[68] Furthermore, from 1730 onwards it seems a new model emerged in Ottoman politics, namely contracts or treaties stating mutual rights. An early occurence was the agreement imposed by Murad IV on the rebellious sipahis in 1632;[69] such contract documents were regularly signed throughout the eighteenth century after revolts, both in the provinces and in the capital.[70] This development culminated in 1807 with the *Hüccet-i Şer'iyye* (marking Selim III's fall), and the subsequent year with the famous *Sened-i ittifak*.[71]

4 Some General Remarks

Drawing any general conclusions from the above survey is not an easy task, nor is it obligatory, as there is no reason one should seek a unilinear interpretation of the development of Ottoman political ideas. The grouping of texts into ideological trends, often corresponding to distinct literary genres as well, has perhaps made clear a genealogy of ideas. However, one should not overestimate the relationship between ideological currents and literary genres and sub-genres: such genres co-existed in collections, showing that, even if we can establish currents of thought through the authors' points of view, their audiences were nonetheless more syncretic. This can be seen very clearly in the *mecmua*s (manuscripts with mixed contents), most of which, it seems, belonged to members of the central bureaucracy, and which contain a number of treatises of a general political character. For instance, we read of such a *mecmua* that contained, among histories or lists of officials and fortresses, the early "declinist" treatise *Kitâb-ı müstetâb*, a version of Ayn Ali's much-circulated mid-seventeenth century treatise describing in detail the timar

67 Cf. Hanioğlu 2008, 113.

68 Yaycıoğlu 2008, 144–184; Yaycıoğlu 2012, 444–445; Yılmaz 2015a, 253–255.

69 Na'ima 1864–1866, 3:119–121; Na'ima – İpşirli 2007, 722–723.

70 For such documents of political contracts signed in Crete, see Sariyannis 2008b, 260–263; on the 1730 treaty, see Karahasanoğlu 2009, 211.

71 For the rich literature on the *Hüccet-i Şer'iyye* and the *Sened-i ittifak*, see above, chapter 9. Cf. Sariyannis 2013, 85–86; Yılmaz 2015a, 249–250 and 252–253.

system, and a political essay of the more "traditional" type (*Nesâ'ihü'l-mülûk*) which stressed the need for the sultan to be just and compassionate.[72] Further study of the coexistence of political works in such collections would be very welcome in order to elaborate the ideological conflict and interdependences from the perspectives of not only the authors but also of their readers. Furthermore, political views based on the Persian tradition, religious precepts and dicta, moralist commonplaces, and empirical advice together formed a large inventory of themes and ideas from which authors regularly drew in order to express different agendas for the specific problems of their times. Derin Terzioğlu insightfully remarked that seventeenth-century Kadızadeli preachers had no problem using Ebussu'ud or Dede Cöngi, although one would think the latter would belong to their enemies rather than their precursors.[73]

It may be asked whether this book has offered any new findings, apart from amassing information otherwise scattered. It will be useful to note, therefore, three or four points that earlier surveys either overlooked or did not see and which have become apparent through the method explained in the introduction. For one thing, Tursun Beg and Kınalızade Ali Çelebi were long known as political theorists, but their heavy dependence on earlier models (namely Tusi's and Davvani's reformulation of Aristotelian ethico-political theory) has often been overlooked. On the one hand, this created a sense of originality and Ottoman particularity that was somewhat misleading; on the other, a close comparison of the Iranian sources and their Ottoman imitators highlights some peculiarities in the latter, such as Kınalızade's misunderstood Khaldunist points and his opposition to the Süleymanic legal policies. For subsequent centuries, serial inspection of various authors showed, for instance, that some (such as Hezarfen or Nahifi) merely summarized or copied their friends or predecessors (Ottomanist scholarship tended to see them as original thinkers), while others (like Hemdemi or Penah Efendi) seem to deserve more attention than they have had so far. On the other hand, the same systematic inspection shed light on what constituted Hezarfen's departure from his models, as well as on the context of this departure (in a similar way, Kınalızade's political connotations were hidden in his departures from Devvani's model). Furthermore, in chapter 6, Ekin Tuşalp Atiyas incorporated the "Sunna-minded" authors into the history of Ottoman political thought for the first time and showed what may have been suspected for some time but never seen in detail: namely, that the seventeenth-century Kadızadeli preachers shared a common ground with their Halveti opponents. It also showed that it is possible to discern

72 Ali Çavuş – Şahin 1979, 906–907. On *mecmua*s in general see Aynur – Çakır – Koncu 2012.

73 Terzioğlu 2007, 270–271.

the channels through which this common ground found its way to imperial policy-makers towards the turn of the eighteenth century. Finally, interesting conclusions (and in a similar vein) can be drawn from the study of the eighteenth century as well: we showed that the gap between the "modernist" or "Westernizing" reformers around Selim III and the more "traditionalist" authors writing in the second half of the century was more narrow and blurred than we tend to think, and that these two trends shared some common ideas and prerequisites.

After this study of the conceptual development, we may also try to deduce some turning points in time that constituted "landmarks" for Ottoman thought. One such turning point would be Murad III's reign (1574–95), when the distinctive Ottoman style of institutional advice (initiated some decades earlier by Lütfi Pasha) was combined with the sense of decline; political treatises continued to stress the need for a return to the old values and rules well into the first half of the seventeenth century. We may trace a second turning point to the mid-seventeenth century: starting with Kâtib Çelebi's work, the idea of change as a necessity of the time gradually permeated Ottoman views in order to justify various reformist efforts. In parallel, the so-called "Sunna-minded" authors, whose influence seems to culminate toward the turn of the century, should not be neglected. A final turning point may be located during or soon after the Russian-Ottoman war of 1768–74, when even the more traditionalist authors or administrators felt the urgent need for a Western-style reform of the army.

4.1 *Ottoman Political Ideas in Context*

As stated in the introduction, this book tried to avoid dealing in detail with the Islamicate origins of Ottoman political thought. Yet, after nine chapters of analytical descriptions of Ottoman ideas, a short assessment of the place Ottoman ideas occupy in the history of Islamic political thought should be sketched. For one thing, even if we accept our working hypothesis, i.e. that the Ottoman state followed a trajectory of development similar to those in Western European states, it seems clear that, from the point of view of intellectual history, Ottoman political thought almost never ceased to belong to the broad category of Islamic ideological genealogies. Even works that sought to follow European developments did not depart greatly, neither in form nor categories of thought, from the Islamic tradition: Kâtib Çelebi's conception of historical change and of universal laws was placed in Khaldunist terms, while the "Westernizing" authors of the late eighteenth century used characteristically Islamic concepts such as *mukabele bi'l-misl* and even *emr bi'l-ma'ruf*.

What the Ottomans inherited (and used) as Islamic political thought may be said to have belonged to three main categories: first, the "philosophical" (*falasifa*) or *ahlak* tradition, and more particularly the highly systematized and moralistic form that Avicenna's (Ibn Sina), Averroes' (Ibn Rushd), and especially al-Farabi's systems took in thirteenth- to fifteenth-century Persia within the writings of Nasir al-Din Tusi and Jalal al-Din Davvani, combining Aristotle's ethics with Plato's notion of the ideal state. Secondly, the more "down-to-earth" and concrete *adab* literature, again as it emerged in Seljuk Persia with Nizam al-Mulk and his continuators such as Najm al-Din Razi: these works were founded upon the old idea of justice being the key aspect of successful kingship, with strong Sufi overtones influenced by al-Ghazali. Thirdly, Ibn Taymiyya's early fourteenth-century formulation of the identification of the secular ruler with the imam and his Sharia-based interpretation of al-Mawardi, al-Ghazali, and other theorists of the caliphate.

As seen, the first category, that of the *falasifa* theorists, produced some monumental works, culminating in the 1560s with the example of Kınalızade, before waning, leaving behind a standard model for the description of society (the four "pillars") and an emphasis on the need for balance; the second category produced several works, mostly in the late fifteenth and the early sixteenth centuries, and contributed the "circle of justice" to the standard inventory of Ottoman political ideas, before ceding its place to the typically Ottoman "declinist" advice. As for the third, after giving some weapons to the defenders of the Ebussuudic synthesis, it influenced the Salafist ideas recurrent in the seventeenth century, from the Kadızadeli preachers and their Halveti opponents to the late seventeenth-century bureaucrats. A fourth category, formed of a single author, namely Ibn Khaldun, did not have a marked presence until around a century and a half after his death through the works of Kâtib Çelebi and his continuators, and even more so during the eighteenth century. In this context, the "declinist" *adab* literature, from Lütfi Pasha to Koçi Bey via Mustafa Ali, on the one hand, to Kâtib Çelebi's emphasis on the Khaldunist idea that different times require different measures, on the other, constituted in a way the Ottoman contribution *par excellence* to Islamicate political thought, from whose traditional formulation they depart in both form and content.

Meanwhile, what trajectories had Islamicate thought followed in the other great empires of the region?[74] The Persian lands, where most of the texts

74 Here we will skip the production of Ottoman Arab lands, which may arguably be seen as more than just a "peripheral" Ottoman literature. Both Salafism (in its Wahhabi form) and most of the Sufis examined in the famous "Islamic Enlightenment" debate were a product of these lands (Schulze 1996; Hagen – Seidenstricker 1998; Radtke 2000), while recent research shows that the rational sciences thrived in Ottoman Arabs' works (El-Rouayheb

dominating early Ottoman political thought were born, had found a new stability from the early sixteenth century when Shah Isma'il created the Safavid Empire, for two centuries the Ottomans' threatening neighbor. Safavid state ideology was strongly influenced by Shi'ism, with the shah often seen as the representative of the Hidden Imam. However, following the consolidation of the Safavid state two major schools of Shi'i thought emerged. The first school, the *Usûlî* ("Principled"), arose out of the need to impose the new Shi'ite orthodoxy over a partly Sunni population by establishing a strong clergy. The main exponent of the school, Ali b. al-Husayn al-Karaki (d. 1534), emphasized the obligatory character of Shi'a practices and advocated the legality of Shi'a ulema being remunerated through a land-tax imposed by the imam. It was al-Karaki who formulated the notion of *mujtahid* or "well-qualified jurist", i.e. an ulema who would be the imam's deputy. This idea took the notion of *ijtihad* (independent reasoning) to its extreme limits, considering it to be a kind of charisma concentrated in the leading jurist. With Shah Tahmasp's steady support, this tremendous spiritual authority consolidated the role of the Shi'a ulema in the Empire. Safavid rule was thus conceived as the parallel power of the charismatic shah and the religious leader, with the latter in fact authorizing the former; it was only natural that this would gradually lead to bitter controversies. The main reaction came from the *Akhbarî* ("Traditionist") school, crystallized by Muhammad Amin al-Astarabadi (d. 1627). The Akhbaris considered the Quran and Shi'a *hadith* the only source of law, excluding *ijtihad* and legal reasoning; they concentrated on Sufi gnosis and favored patrimonial rule, while having little interest in government, which they saw as a prerogative of the religious authority as presented in the line of the Safavid dynasty (being descendants of the Prophet through Ali). Anthony Black describes this stance as "political quietism"; other scholars have likened the emergence of the Akhbari Shi'a with the Salafist movements of Sunni Islam or even with Puritanism. Thinkers such as Mir Damad (d. 1631), Molla Sadra (d. 1640), and Molla Kashani (d. 1680) belonged to this trend and tried to reconcile *falasifa* with Sufism. The dispute was resumed with the works of Abdallah al-Samahiji (d. 1723); by the end of the seventeenth century, however, the Usuli jurists' (*mujtahid*) power had increased so much that they eventually took over the whole religious establishment, under Muhammad Baqir Majlisi (d. 1700). Majlisi lay down the theoretic foundations of theocratic rule, where the *mujtahid* would have absolute power to define Shi'a orthodoxy; his political works stressed the authority of kings over their subjects, but with the proviso that the king is "of the right religion" and with the underlying assumption that he follows the *mujtahids*' guidance.

2015). On some aspects of the relationship between the Arab lands and the imperial centre, see the survey by Kechriotis 2013.

It seems that these theoretical foundations of an all-potent ulema clergy survived the upheavals following the fall of the Safavids (in 1722, at the hands of Afghan tribal rulers), although their successors, Nader Shah (d. 1747), Khan Zand (d. 1779), and the Qajar dynasty favored more traditional political ideologies, stressing justice and protection of the peasants; the Akhbari school briefly regained its influence before being definitely crushed in the 1770s by the Usuli scholar Muhammad Baqir Behbahani (d. 1792).[75]

The other great Islamicate empire of the region arose on the Indian subcontinent, under the very strong influence of Persian culture. The rule of the Mughal dynasty began when the Timurid prince Babur (d. 1530) conquered Kabul and then Delhi; of his successors, perhaps the most important was Akbar (r. 1556–1605), whose plan for religious toleration and equality for all his subjects (Muslim—Sunni or Shiʿa—and Hindus) was based on his mystical vision (which also advocated a unification of religious and temporal power under his person). In a sense, Akbar took the Safavid *mujtahid* notion and applied it to the ruler himself, as the ultimate arbitrer of matters, both religious and secular. As expressed by Akbar's vizier and historian, Abu'l-Fazl (d. 1602), the aim of kingship should be "universal peace" (*sulh-e kull*); Akbar even initiated a new religion, the "religion of God" (*din-e illahi*), which would unify all religions and whose spiritual master would be himself. Although Akbar's policy was continued by his successors, his attempt to replace Islam with his own royal religion did not last. The opposition was mainly expressed by Sufi sheikhs, such as Ahmad Sirhindi (d. 1624), a peculiar practitioner of messianism, and more orthodox authors such as Munshi al-Khaqani, Nur al-Din Qazi al-Khaqani, Abd al-Haqq, and Baqir Najm-i Sani, who all wrote *adab*-styled treatises following Davvani's model that emphasized the duty of the king to uphold the Sharia. Finally, Akbar's ideology lost ground to a re-Islamization of the state under Shah Jahan (r. 1628–58) and especially his successor, Aurangzeb (r. 1658–1707), who tried to impose a legal system based on the Sharia and, particularly, the Hanafi school. As the Mughal Empire was disintegrating as a result of the rise of independent Hindu and Sikh polities and Afghan invasions, one should note the Nakshbandi sheikh Shah Wali Allah al-Dihlawi (d. 1762) and his innovative theories: in a manner reminiscent of Kâtib Çelebi's views, he suggested that the Sharia should be adapted to changing conditions, i.e. according to time and place. In this vein (and in the tradition of Akbar's universalism), he strongly advocated the use of balance (*tawazun*) or the middle way as a means of reconciling every conflict in Muslim doctrine, as well as in everyday life. He also formulated a highly original theory of stages (*irtifaqat*) in human history,

---

75 On Safavid and Qajar political ideology and thought see Lambton 1956b; Lambton 1981, 264–287; Arjomand 1984; Newman 1992a and 1992b; Mitchell 2009; Black 2011, 228ff.

encompassing not individual dynasties, as did Ibn Khaldun's earlier work, but the whole moral and social development of humanity.[76]

What parallels can we draw between these developments and the evolution of Ottoman thought? The Usuli school in Iran, and especially al-Karaki's collaboration with Shah Isma'il in order to legitimize the collection of taxes from Muslims, brings to mind Ebussu'ud's legal synthesis, predating it by some decades;[77] on the other hand, the Akhbari renaissance during the seventeenth century has parallels both in time and (to a degree) content with the Ottoman Kadızadelis. The re-emergence of Islam as a state ideology in Mughal India under Aurangzeb, in the same period, cannot be paralleled so easily with Ottoman or Iranian developments since there are many differences between Akbar's universalism and Safavid theocracy, or the *kanun* and *siyasa al-sultaniya* of the Süleymanic era. The "connective systems of learned and holy men", as termed by Francis Robinson, which connected the educational systems of the three empires through shared texts, commentaries, and annotations,[78] can only partly explain these affinities: if Sufi or Salafist texts and ideas did circulate from the Balkans to South Asia, the same cannot be said for their "statist" counterparts. Neither Ebussu'ud's *fetva*s, nor Usuli tracts or Abu'l-Fazl's history seems to have ever passed beyond the borders of each empire; if there is indeed a connection, we have to seek it in a common trajectory of the so-called "tributary empires" of the Islamicate world rather than in the history of ideas.[79] But then, is the Ottoman Empire closer to this type of empire? Or was it closer to being an "early-modern state", especially after the mid-seventeenth century, and should we instead seek affinities with English or French intellectual history? Another fruitful comparison, in this case, might be not with trends in Persian or South Asian intellectual history, but between Kâtib Çelebi and (for instance) Jean Bodin's interest in non-European types

76 On Mughal political practice and thought see Alam 2004; Black 2011, 240ff.; Syros 2012a, 400–404 and 2012b (with a rich bibliography).

77 See Lambton 1981, 268–273; Mitchell 2009, 71ff.

78 Robinson 1997.

79 "Tributary empires" have recently arisen as an analytical tool in comparative history. See the essays collected in Bang – Bayly 2011. For the Ottoman case, an example of the use of this model is Barkey 2008. Another term, that of "gunpowder empires", coined by Marshall Hodgson, has the disadvantage of focusing on a probably minor factor and of leaving non-Islamicate states (such as the Habsburgs' or the Romanovs' empires) outside the paradigm; Linda Darling has tried to use the term, occasionally encompassing developments in England or France (Darling 1998, 232ff.). In an attempt to compare the Ottoman Empire with the Mughals and the Habsburgs, with a special emphasis on "declinist" political literature, see Subrahmanyam 2006.

of government,[80] or between the growing reception of Ibn Khaldun's theories during the eighteenth century and Thomas Hobbes' abstraction on the state.[81] Or, less provocatively and probably more fruitfully, let us consider Kâtib Çelebi's *istihsan* and pragmatism against the Kadızadelis' literal legalism to be a counterpart of Jesuit casuistry against Protestant ethics in Europe—all the more so, to push this argument perhaps a little too far, since the two sides, in both cases, were, to some extent, investing in similar political trends (the Kadızadelis and the Protestants in sorts of constitutionalism, Kâtib Çelebi and the Jesuits in absolutist policies). To put the question another way: are similarities in intellectual history to be attributed to the circulation of ideas, to a common contemporary ground (such as "feudalism" or "modernity"), or to similar types of state formation? And, after all, are such similarities meaningful, or just superficial coincidences? In my opinion, no sound comparison of ideas can be made without a solid foundation of socio-economic and political common ground; and this, in fact, is something we still are far from achieving. For the time being, we can only restrict ourselves to highlighting the different forms Islamicate political thought took in different circumstances.

In fact, to write a history of ideas and of their development and genealogy is not a very difficult task in terms of interpretation. The real difficulties come when one seeks to connect these ideas with their political and social milieus. There are some pioneering studies that have tried to accomplish the task for some late sixteenth and early seventeenth-century authors, as well as for Na'ima, but much more work is needed before we can identify Ottoman groups with a clear political agenda, social interests, and common ideological roots or credos. Indeed, what is really striking in the history of Ottoman political thought is the difficulty of associating ideological currents and trends, as expressed by the relevant literature, to political and social developments. Such questions will undoubtedly form part of the agenda for the future; it is to be hoped that the present book can be a basis for such enquiries.

---

80 One has to note here the nearly contemporaneous systematic endeavor of the Mughal court to gain knowledge of European things: see Lefèvre 2012, 129–137.

81 Recently Vefa Erginbaş suggested "an overwhelming similarity" between Hobbes' ideas on the "state of nature" and İbrahim Müteferrika's views on the beginning of political society: Erginbaş 2014, 86. As we tried to show above, such views (stressing man's oppressive nature, rather than the need for cooperation) were recurrent in Ottoman texts by the mid-seventeenth century.

APPENDIX 1

Historical Timeline

Note: As explained in the Introduction, the structure of this book is not strictly chronological; rather, it tries to follow ideological trends, and as a result the timelines of the various chapters may overlap. This table enables the reader to follow the chronological order of the various works cited in comparison with historical events (first column), at the same time showing the presence of each trend (represented in separate chapters) in every period.

© KONINKLIJKE BRILL NV, LEIDEN, 2019 | DOI:10.1163/9789004385245_013

Historical events	Chapter 1	Chapter 2	Chapter 3
ca. 1299 rise of Osman			
1354 conquest of Gelibolu			
1389 battle of Kosovo, rise of Bayezid I			
1402 battle of Ankara	1401 Şeyhoğlu Mustafa, *Kenzü'l-küberâ* (I)		
		1406 Ahmed Amasi, *Kitâb-ı mir'atü'l-mülûk* (II)	
1413 end of civil war	1411 t.a.q. for Ahmedi's *İskendernâme* (I)		
1451 second reign of Mehmed II			
1453 conquest of Constantinople	Ca. 1453 Yazıcıoğlu Ahmed Bican, *Dürr-i meknûn* (I)		
	Ca. 1478 Aşıkpaşazade's *Tevârîh-i Âl-i Osman* (I)		
1481 Bayezid II	After 1481 Sinan Pasha, *Ma'ârifnâme* (I)		
		After 1488 Tursun Beg, *Târîh-i Ebu'l-feth* (II)	
			1508 Şehzade Korku *Dawat al-nafs* (III)
1512 Selim I			
			1514 Bitlisi, *Risâla f* *al-khilâfa* (III)
1516–17 conquest of Syria and Egypt		Before 1520 Bitlisi, *Qânûn-i shehinshâhî* (II)	
1520 Süleyman I			
1529 siege of Vienna			1529 Hüseyin al-Semerkandi, *Latâ'if al-afkâr* (III)

pter 4	Chapter 5	Chapter 6	Chapter 7	Chapter 8	Chapter 9

(*cont.*)

Historical events	Chapter 1	Chapter 2	Chapter 3
1536 conquest of Baghdad—execution of Ibrahim Pasha			
1545 Ebussu'ud Efendi becomes *şeyhülislam*			
			After 1554 Lütfî Pas *Âsafnâme* (III)
			1557 Taşköprüzade, *Miftâh al-sa'âda* (II,
1559 civil war between Selim and Bayezid			After 1557 Celalzad *Tabakatü'l-memâlik* (III)
			Before 1565 Dede Cöngî Efendi, *Siyase* *şer'iye* (III)
			1564 Celalzade, *Mevâhibü'l-hallâk* (II
		1565 Kınalızade, *Ahlâk-ı Alâî* (II)	
1566 Selim II			Ca. 1566 Birgivi, *Zuh* *al-mulûk* (III)
1571 battle of Lepanto			
1574 Murad III			
			1575 Feridun Bey, *Münşe'âtü's-selâtîn* (
1579 Sokollu Mehmed Pasha's assassination			
1578–1590 war with Iran			
1589 "Beylerbey incident"			

pter 4	Chapter 5	Chapter 6	Chapter 7	Chapter 8	Chapter 9
re 1566 *bu mesâlih*					
4 *Hırzu'l-ûk* (IV)					
ı Ali, *ıatü's-în* (IV)					

(*cont.*)

Historical events	Chapter 1	Chapter 2	Chapter 3
1593–1606 war with the Habsburgs			
1595 Mehmed III			
1596 battle of Mező-Keresztes; beginning of the major Celali rebellions			
1603 Ahmed I			
1609 end of the major Celali rebellions			
1617 Mustafa I's first reign—Osman I			
1622 Osman I's execution			

pter 4	Chapter 5	Chapter 6	Chapter 7	Chapter 8	Chapter 9
6 Kâfî isarî *lü'l-hikem*					
7/8 First pilation Derviş med, *asnâme* (IV)					
o Selaniki, *h* (IV)					
o Ali, *âl-i hall ü* (IV)					
	1606 *Kavânîn-i yeniçeriyân* (V)				
	Ca. 1610 Ayn Ali, *Kavânîn-i Âl-i Osmân* and *Risâle-i vazife-horân* (V)				
	Early 1610s Veysi, *Hab-name* (V)	After 1611 Sivasi, *Dürer-i 'aka'id* (VI)			
		After 1612 Münir-i Belgradi, *Silsiletü'l-mukarrebin* (VI)			
	Ca. 1620 *Kitâb-i müstetâb* (V)				

(*cont.*)

Historical events	Chapter 1	Chapter 2	Chapter 3
1623 Murad IV			
1624 the Persians capture Baghdad			
1638 recapture of Baghdad			
1640 Ibrahim			
1648 Mehmed IV			

pter 4	Chapter 5	Chapter 6	Chapter 7	Chapter 8	Chapter 9
		After 1623 Kadızade Mehmed İlmi, *Nushu'l-hükkâm* (VI)			
veen 4 and 8 Üveysi, *hat-i nbol* (IV)	Ca. 1630 Koçi Bey, first *Risâle* (V)				
	1632 "Veliyüddin *telhis*" (V)				
	1632 Aziz Efendi, *Kânûnnâme-i sultânî* (V)				
	1640 Koçi Bey, second *Risâle* (V)				
	Before 1642 Avni Ömer, *Kânûn-ı Osmanî* (V)				
			1648 Kâtib Çelebi, *Takvîmü't-tevârîh* (VII)		
		1649 Sarı Abdullah, *Nasihatü'l-müluk* (VI)			

(*cont.*)

Historical events	Chapter 1	Chapter 2	Chapter 3
1650–1656 "second wave" of the Kadızadelis (Üstüvanî Efendi)			
1656 "plane-tree incident"; rise of Köprülü Mehmed Pasha			
1661–1676 rise of Köprülü Fazıl Ahmed Pasha; "third wave" of the Kadızadelis (Vanî Efendi)			
1669 fall of Candia			
1683 second siege of Vienna			
1687 Süleyman II			

pter 4	Chapter 5	Chapter 6	Chapter 7	Chapter 8	Chapter 9
			1652 Hemdemî (?), *Nasîhatnâme* (VII)		
			1653 Kâtib Çelebi, *Düstûrü'l-amel* (VII)		
			1655 Kâtib Çelebi, *İrşâdü'l-hayârâ* (VII)		
			1656 Kâtib Çelebi, *Mîzânü'l-hak* (VII)		
	1675 Hezarfen Hüseyin, *Telhisü'l-beyân* (V, VII)		1675 Hezarfen Hüseyin, *Telhisü'l-beyân* (V, VII)		
		1679 Vani Efendi, *Ara'is al-Kur'an* (VI)			
		Before 1683 Rodosizade's translation of *Kitâb al-Kharaj* (VI)			
	After 1688 *Kavânîn-i osmanî ve râbıta-ı Âsitâne* (V)				

(*cont.*)

Historical events	Chapter 1	Chapter 2	Chapter 3
1691 Ahmed II; tax reform (*cizye, malikâne*)			
1695 Mustafa II			
1699 Treaty of Karlowitz			
1703 "Edirne event"; Ahmed III			
1718 Treaty of Passarowitz; Damad İbrahim Pasha's vizierate and "Tulip Period"			
1726 Müteferrika's printing press			
1730 Patrona Halil revolt; Mahmud I			

pter 4	Chapter 5	Chapter 6	Chapter 7	Chapter 8	Chapter 9
					1694, *Risala feva'idü'l-mülûk* (IX)
			1701–2 Nâbî, *Hayriyye* (VII)		
			1704 Na'ima, *Ravzat al-Hüseyin* (VII)		
				Ca. 1715 Defterdar, *Nesâyıhü'l-vüzerâ* (VIII)	
				After 1717 Nahifi, *Nasihatü'l-vüzerâ* (VIII)	
					1718 (?) "Dialogue between a Muslim and a Christian officer" (IX)
			1730 translation of Ibn Khaldun by Pirizade		
					1731 Ibrahim Müteferrika, *Usûlü'l-hikem* (IX)

(*cont.*)

Historical events	Chapter 1	Chapter 2	Chapter 3
1747 death of Humbaracı Ahmed Pasha (Comte de Bonneval)			
1754 Osman III			
1757 Mustafa III			
1757–1763 Ragıb Pasha's vizierate			
1768 end of the "long peace"; Ottoman-Russian war			
1774 Treaty of Küçük Kaynarca; Abdülhamid I			
1782–1785 Halil Hamid Pasha's vizierate; de Tott's military reforms			

…pter 4	Chapter 5	Chapter 6	Chapter 7	Chapter 8	Chapter 9
					1769 Ahmed Resmi, first treatise (IX)
					1772 Ahmed Resmi, second treatise (IX)
				1774 Dürri Mehmed, *Nuhbetü'l-emel* (VIII)	
					1774 Anonymous (Ahmed Resmi?), *Mîzân-ı umûr-ı hâriciyye* (IX)
				1776 Canikli Ali Pasha, *Tedâbîrü'l-gazavât* (VIII)	
				1784 Vasıf Efendi, *Risâle* (VIII)	
				1785 Penah Efendi, *Mora ihtilali tarihi* (VIII)	

(*cont.*)

Historical events	Chapter 1	Chapter 2	Chapter 3
1789 Selim III			
1792 Treaty of Jassy; beginning of the *Nizam-i Cedid* reforms			
1798 Napoleon invades Egypt			
1807 Kabakçı Mustafa's revolt; Mustafa IV			

…pter 4	Chapter 5	Chapter 6	Chapter 7	Chapter 8	Chapter 9
				1787 Ebubekir Ratıb Efendi, plan of Prince Selim's answer to Louis XVI (VIII)	
					1792 memoranda submitted to Selim III; Ebubekir Ratıb Efendi, *Büyük layıha* (IX)
				1802 Behic Efendi, *Sevanihü'l-levayih* (VIII)	
					Ca. 1804 Anonymous (Vasıf Efendi?), *Koca Sekbanbaşı risalesi* (IX)
				1804 Ömer Faik Efendi, *Nizâmü'-atîk* (VIII)	
					1806 Kuşmani, *Zebîre-i Kuşmânî* (IX)

(*cont.*)

Historical events	Chapter 1	Chapter 2	Chapter 3
1808 Mahmud II; Sened-i ittifak			
1826 *Vak'a-i hayriyye*			

pter 4	Chapter 5	Chapter 6	Chapter 7	Chapter 8	Chapter 9
				1825 Şanizade, *Târîh* (VIII)	

APPENDIX 2

Samples of Translated Texts

In order to keep the appendix within reasonable limits, not all the authors mentioned in the book are represented here; instead, we have tried to make a selection that would give a clear idea of the style and arguments of the various ideological trends described above. When not indicated otherwise, translations belong to the author of this book; published translations are occasionally simplified by excluding *termini technici* in parentheses etc.

1 **Aşıkpaşazade** (See Chapter 1)

From *Tevârîh-i Âl-i Osman* ("The histories of the House of Osman"):[1]

> When (Osman) took Karacahisar, the houses of the city remained empty. Many people from the lands of Germiyan came, as well as from other lands. They asked Osman Ghazi for houses, and he gave (some to) them. The town was soon inhabited again. And he also gave (them) some churches to be turned into mosques.
>
> … A judge and a *subaşı* were appointed. A market was founded and common prayers were performed. The people began to ask for laws. Someone from Germiyan came and said: "Sell me the toll of this market!" The community said: "Go to the ruler!" The man went to the ruler and made his request. Osman Ghazi said: "What is this market toll?" The man said: "I am to take money for everything that comes to the market". Osman Ghazi said: "Are the people of the market in debt to you, so that you want (their) money?" The man said: "My lord, it is a custom. In all countries, whoever rules takes money". Osman Ghazi said: "Is this an order of God, or have rulers ordained it themselves?" And again the man said: "It is a custom, my lord. It has been so from olden days". Osman Ghazi was very angry and said: "So one person's gain can belong to another person? No! It is his own property! What have I added to his property so that I may tell him 'give me money'? Go away and do not say such things to me again or you'll regret it". The community said: "My lord, it is a custom that something is given to those who guard this market". Osman Ghazi said: "Well, since you say so as well, everyone who comes and sells something, let him give two aspers. And whoever sells nothing, let him give nothing. And if anybody breaks this law of mine, may God ruin

1 Aşıkpaşazade – Atsız 1949, 103–104.

© KONINKLIJKE BRILL NV, LEIDEN, 2019 | DOI:10.1163/9789004385245_014

his faith and his world. And let nobody take a *timar* without reason from the hands of anybody who has taken it from me. And when he dies, let it pass to his son. Let it be given to him [i.e. the son] even if he is still young. Whenever a campaign is launched, let his servants go on campaign, until he grows to become useful. And may God be pleased with those who guard this law. And if anyone tries to impose a law contrary to this one to my kin, may God not be pleased with whoever made it and whoever applied it".

2 **Ahmedi** (See Chapter 1)

From *Tevârîh-i Mülûk-i Âl-i ʿOsmân* ("History of the rulers of the House of Osman"), translated by Kemal Silay:[2]

Those kings whom I mentioned? I have spoken of their deeds and characters.

Some were infidels, some showed cruelty—more of that in them than kindness.

Concerning the justice of the Mongol Sultans: hear now the explanation of what it was.

They did not mention the fact that Cingiz Han clearly oppressed the people.

They [the Mongol rulers] oppressed them with the law, but they did not paint their hands with blood.

Lawful oppression and confiscation are amenable to the people as a form of justice.

... Orhan was equitable and a dispenser of justice. Because of him, the justice of ʿÖmer was forgotten.

Where the justice of the Ottomans exists, why would the justice of ʿÖmer be mentioned there?

... Since the people received that justice from him [Bayezid I], whether big or small, they became industrious.

No place remained within all of Rum which did not prosper from his justice.

Neither desert nor mountain remained in the land that did not become a sown field, a garden, or an orchard.

... The Ottoman Şah was the ʿÖmer of justice. He knew that the judges were dispensers of injustice.

Their deeds were bribery and corruption of the holy law. They did not even talk of what is cause and effect.

2 Ahmedi – Silay 2004, 1, 5, 20.

… He punished them as necessary. Badness is appropriate for him with bad ways.

3 **Şeyhoğlu Mustafa** (See Chapter 1)

From *Kenzü'l-küberâ ve mehekkü'l-ulemâ* ("Treasure of the great and touchstone of the learned"):[3]

And know that there are three situations for the sultan: the first situation concerns his relation with his soul; the second concerns his relation with his subjects; and the third situation concerns his relation with his God. All three situations have been ordered for the sultans; this means that in each of these situations he must strive for justice, generosity, and granting things to the destitute, while also abstaining from immoral and inappropriate acts and from injustice. For the first situation, i.e. between the ruler and his own soul: it is that he imposes monotheism on himself and keeps his hands and feet and body, which were granted to him (by God), within their limits, carrying out the sacred duties and the well-established practices; for instance, fighting with his (own) self and watching his heart.

The second situation is between the sultan and his subjects … He must show justice and equity amongst the people, not oppress them, and take care so the strong do not oppress the weak; the powerful should not impose weights on the needy … He must help the poor and those who have a family with charity and alimonies; he must take action to do good to those coming and going … He should care for the rights of the peasants, because the subjects are to the sultan like relatives or even his own household.

4 **Sinan Pasha** (See Chapter 1)

From *Ma'ârifnâme* ("The book of knowledge"):[4]

The order of the world and arrangement of the universe is secured by respecting the rights (ordained) among men, so they are always protected from one another. People are joined to each other; and the businesses of some are entrusted to others. Benefits and assistance must be borrowed from each other at all times; one should not prevent another's help. Everybody must strive to benefit from

3 Şeyhoğlu – Yavuz 1991, 66–67, 69–71, 82.

4 Sinan Paşa – Tulum 2013, 368–370 and 724–728. The original is in verse.

the order of the world, a service rendered from either the esoteric or the external (visible) reality. Farmers and weavers, viziers and sultans, judges and teachers, spiritual guides and sheikhs, all serve God according to the capabilities ordained to them. Certainly, all services rendered to sultans cannot be viewed as equal and all posts granted cannot be of the same value; but if one's intentions in rendering a service are pure and clear, one becomes a real man (*merd*).

... (The sultan) should take great care of his soldiers and protect his army: these are the people of honor and zeal who protect the commoners and the peasants ... If one of them is wounded on a day of battle and loses a limb from his body, so that he is useless for the rest of his life, then, again, his name must not be wiped from the registers ... and if one is made a martyr and killed (fighting) with his group, (the sultan) should care for those left behind and protect his children ... True, these soldiers are a good class, and the order of the land finds its arrangement through them, but disciplining them is a difficult task ... They must be divided into several sorts and various classes, so that they are of different opinions and cannot agree; thus, they will not dare to unite and act against the sultan nor gather and associate for great mischief. The mischief of one corps should be prevented through the act of another; in such a way, every class is neutralized through another, and the subjects are safe from all of them. Every group has its bad habits; the soldier's bad habit is his tendency to disobey.

5 **Tursun Beg** (See Chapter 2)

From *Târîh-i Ebu'l-Feth* ("The history of the Conqueror"):[5]

This noble species [mankind], with all these perfect features it has, has by choice as a free agent the tendency to form civilized societies by nature; in other words, it is social in its manner of providing for health and in its ways of making a living: this is society, which, according to our customs, is called town, village, and nomad camp. Man wants this disposition by nature, and (it is) inevitable since all need each other's help; this mutual help cannot be successful unless people gather together in one place ... Yet if people are left to act according to their nature, there is so much quarreling, hostility, conflict, and loathing that mutual help, the real aim of society, cannot be attained; on the contrary, they will be incited against each other and eventually destroy themselves. Thus, it is necessary for man that everybody be placed in a defined position; that one be satisfied with one's position and does not put one's hand upon another's rights; and

5 Tursun Beg – Tulum 1977, 12 and 16–17; cf. the Italian translation in Tursun Bey – Berardi 2007, 14–15 and 19–21.

that everyone be made responsible for a task that is necessary for mutual help, and that everyone be occupied with their task. Arrangements like this are called "government" (*siyaset*). And if this arrangement is made according to the rules of necessity and wisdom—which cause a perfection innate to humanity and allows people to achieve both types of happiness [i.e. of this world and the next]—then wise people call it divine government, and its driving force is the law (*namus*). As for religious people, they call this government Sharia, and its moving force the "Lawgiver", who is the Prophet. Otherwise, that is to say if this arrangement does not reach this degree [of perfection], and is regulated instead solely upon reason in order to achieve the order of the visible world (such as in the case of Jengiz Khan's government), then the name is again related to the cause, and this arrangement is called kingly government, imperial law, or, according to our terms, customary government (*örf*). At any rate, whatever the form of government, its application depends on the existence of a king.

... As for the description of the various kinds of virtues that constitute the beneficences of ethical science, they are written in the philosophical books. As the greatest of the Muslim wise-men, Hoca Nasireddin Tusi, argues in his book *Nasirean Ethics*, the human spirit has three faculties, distinct from one another, that cooperate to cause man to engage in various acts and perform different tasks with the participation of [the divine] will. The first power is the faculty of speech, also called the angel soul; it causes desire for thought, discrimination of things, and seeing the reality of actions. The second is the faculty of wrath, also called the passion soul; it causes desire for anger, heroism, engagement in terrible acts, victory, aggression, and elevation. The third is the faculty of lust, also called the sensual soul, which causes desire for sensual pleasures, for eating and drinking. Now, the number of virtues is proportional to these faculties, so that every time the rational soul [the faculty of speech] is qualified with moderation and desires the knowledge of certainties, then this movement produces the virtue of knowledge, and from this virtue comes naturally the virtue of wisdom. And every time the movement of the passion soul is moderated and obeys the rational soul, being satisfied with the share provided by the rational soul and staying within the limits of necessity and time, then this movement produces the virtue of patience; and from this virtue, the virtue of courage arises naturally. And whenever the sensual soul is moderated and obeys and submits to the rational soul ... then its movements produce the virtue of honesty, which naturally produces generosity. And all these faculties have three situations each, that is excess, deficiency, and moderation; abstaining from excess and deficiency and seeking moderation is another feature, and this feature is called the virtue of justice; with it, all the aforementioned virtues are perfected. That is why the consensus of the wise is that there are four types of virtues: wisdom, courage, honesty, and justice.

6 Kınalızade Ali (See Chapter 2)

From *Ahlâk-ı Alâî* ("Sublime ethics"):[6]

According to its situation, wealth is divided in three ways: first, concerning its acquisition; second, concerning its possession, and third, concerning its spending. Now, as far as is concerns the acquisition of wealth there are again two parts: one is by gain via choice, for instance through trade or a craft, and another is by gain without choice, as in the case of gifts or inheritance. Some have divided the means of the acquisition of wealth into three categories, trade, craftsmanship, and agriculture, while others have divided them into four categories, adding leadership, and since pensions and salaries come from the ruler's rank, this is a true categorization. Now, there is a dispute as to which of these parts is the best. It is related that imam Şafi'î stated that "it is trade, all the more so since it was the glorious occupation of our Prophet Muhammad, peace be upon Him". And imam Maverdi related that Şafi'î considered agriculture the best. Some more recent authors said that "because in these times vicious contracts are abundant, there is suspicion of wealth, but it is possible that in Şafi'î's time commerce was the best, due to the lack of corruption and an abundance of ulema" … They also said that there are three prerequisites for (lawful) gain: that oppression or tyranny are not used, that one abstains from shameful transactions, and that one preserves oneself against vileness and abasement.

… We say that a city can be of two kinds: the virtuous city and the imperfect one. The virtuous city is one where pious deeds and right actions are the cause of association and civilization, while in the imperfect city the cause of association is wickedness and mischief. The virtuous city can only be of one type and no more, because the Highest and Exalted God is only one, pure from any multitude and so one is also the way of God … But the imperfect city is of three kinds: the first comes when the individuals of the city do not use their faculty of reason; instead, it is their other bodily faculties that lie behind their association and gathering. This is called the ignorant city. For instance, it may be driven by the faculty of wrath and so called the irascible ignorant city, or it may be driven by the sensual faculty and thus called the appetitive ignorant city. The second kind

6 Kınalızade – Koç 2007, 335, 451–452, 479–480, 485.

comes when the individuals of the city do use their faculty of reason, but their other faculties prevail; in this case, the faculty of reason obeys the other faculties, which also form the reason for the people's association. This is the vicious city. And the third kind is when the people of the city have deficient rational powers; thus, they imagine that wrong precepts are right and that the corrupt law is correct, taking these as the causes of their association. This is the erroneous city. Now, these imperfect cities, and especially the erroneous one, can be of many sorts, because as we said the ways of ignorance have no end and the types of error are innumerable. It is possible to divide erroneous cities into two kinds: the infidel erroneous city, like the cities of the Franks, the Russians, and the other infidel sections; and the non-infidel erroneous city, such as when corrupt sects of Muslims gather and associate in one place; for instance the Red-Headed People [i.e. the Shiʿa of Iran]. This kind of city may also be described as an ignorant infidel city. It is possible for a virtuous city to change to an imperfect one, and vice versa.

... Let it be known that civilized societies are a general composition and arrangement of various classes and communities. Every class has its appropriate degree (of power) and place, and professes its special activities ... The constitution of the world is based on the equilibrium among these components ... For it is known that, at the beginning of a state [or dynasty], one class is united and its members support and help each other, like the members of a single body, because everyone has power to a limited extent but the power of many gathered together in one place is greater than the power of each individual. A small class, when is united, prevails over a larger but divided one. Is it not clear that any ruling class is not even one-tenth (the number) of its subjects? But they are united and they prevail over their subjects because the latter are not ... Experience has shown that whenever such a ruling class has unity and mutual assistance it is safe from difficulties and deficiencies, but when, later, factions and disagreements appear among this class it starts to weaken and finally ends in ruins.

... The first rule [for the king] is to treat all creatures [i.e. men] as equal because the creatures are for the world like the four elements; and, in the human constitution, if the elements are not equal and in proportion there cannot be health or healing. Similarly, if people are not treated equally the situation of the world cannot be healthy and ordered. Now, the elements of the body of the world are four, like the elements of the human body: firstly the men of the pen, the ulema, the judges, the scribes, the chancellors, the doctors, the poets, the astrologers, and the engineers. They take the place of water, since knowledge is necessary for the life of souls as water is necessary for the life of the world. [As the Quran says,] *We created every living thing from water*. Secondly, the men of the sword, commanders and warriors and sipahis ... This class is like fire, the reason for this analogy being obvious. Thirdly, the class of tradesmen, those who bring merchandise, craftsmen, and artisans ... This class is like the air, from whose movement ease of souls and relaxation of bodies are produced ... The fourth class consists of agriculturers and farmers, who dig and plow arable land ... They are the real earners, since they spend their time and take their sustenance from the black earth, while the other classes take other gains and exchange goods produced by others. This class is like the earth: while they produce many beneficial things, everyone steps on their face and kicks them, yet they, in turn, remain steadfast and endure.

7 **Ebussu'ud Efendi** (See Chapter 3)

From the *fetva* concerning the breaking of the peace treaty with Venice, translated by Colin Imber:[7]

For the Sultan of the people of Islam (may God glorify his victories) to make peace with the infidels is legal only when there is a benefit to all Muslims. When there is no benefit, peace is never legal. When a benefit has been seen, and it is then observed to be more beneficial to break it, then to break it becomes absolutely obligatory and binding. His Excellency [Muhammad] the Apostle of God (may God bless him and give him peace) made a ten-year truce with the Meccan infidels in the sixth year of the Hegira ... Then, in the following year, it was considered more beneficial to break it and, in the eighth year of the Hegira, [the Prophet] attacked [the Meccans], and conquered Mecca the Mighty.

From the preamble to the *kanunname* of Buda and from collections of *fetvas*, translated by Colin Imber:[8]

The inhabitants of the said province [of Hungary] are to remain where they are settled. The moveable goods in their possession, their houses in towns and villages, and their cultivated vineyards and orchards are their property to dispose of as they wish ... The fields which they have from old cultivated and tilled are also confirmed in their possession. However, whereas their goods in the categories mentioned above are their property, their fields are not. [Instead] they belong to the category of royal demesne, known elsewhere in the Protected [Ottoman] Realms as *miri* land. The real substance (*raqaba*) is reserved for the Treasury of the Muslims, and the subjects have the use of it, by way of a loan. They sow and

7 Imber 1997, 84–85.
8 Imber 1997, 122–123 and 127.

> reap whatever cereals and crops they wish, and pay their proportional tribute under the name 'tithe', and benefit from the land however they wish.
>
> ... The peasants do not own the lands in their possession. They are royal demesne. At the time of the conquest, they were not given to anybody as [private] property. It was commanded that [the occupants] should cultivate and till them, and pay proportional tribute under the name of tithe, and fixed tribute under the name of *chift*-tax. The right of the peasants is simply to bear the burden of the land by cultivating and tilling and, after paying the said dues on the produce, to keep the remainder. If they leave the land fallow for three years, it is lawful to take it from them and to give it to someone else.

From a *fetva* answering Çivizade regarding the question of cash-*vakf*, translated by Jon E. Mandaville:[9]

> Although the citations of books seem to be against the permissibility of akçe and filuri awqaf, it is also well known which sources of these books are true and sound. It is recognized absolutely that throughout the lands of the provinces of Rum cash waqf is popular and generally practiced, that most of the awqaf of the mosques and welfare establishments are based on cash, that judges past and present relying on the aforementioned citations have ruled in favor of its permissibility, that up till now military judges and provincial governors have been ruling in favor of its validity and irrevocability, and no one has spoken out against this. The practice is perfectly sound and irrevocable.

8 **Celalzade Mustafa** (See Chapter 3)

From *Tabakâtü'l-memâlik ve derecâtü'l-mesâlik* ("Layers of kingdoms and levels of routes"), translated by Mehmet Şakir Yılmaz:[10]

> The office of drawing the noble, world-adorning signature [i.e. the office of *nişancı*] is the greatest among all offices and the noblest among all services. The supremacy of the *nişancı*'s office over other offices ... is obvious in many respects. First of all, all great Sultans ... needed two types of servants to rule over vast lands; men of pen and men of sword. As a matter of fact, sword and pen are twins; one of them is the soul and the other is the body. However, the pen is

9 Mandaville 1979, 297.

10 Celalzade – Kappert 1981, 259b–260b; trans. based on Yılmaz 2006, 89–90.

above the sword. That happens because the sword aims to destroy, whereas the pen aims to produce … The rule of the sword devastates a country, whereas the rule of the pen causes prosperity … Besides, a lot of people are appropriate to be recruited in the military, but good scribes are very rare. If there is a good scribe in the administration, all other servants can easily be found … Secondly, *nişancıs* are always busy with drawing the noble signature and they always pray for the permanency of the state … Thirdly, all the servants of the Porte receive their salaries from the royal treasury, causing expenditure; whereas *nişancıs* collect revenues from outside, and every year they realize a revenue five to six million aspers. Fourthly, mischief-makers usually depend on Sultanic orders to exploit the tax-paying subjects. If the *nişancı* is careful and cautious, he foresees any undesirable results of a Sultanic order and he prevents it … Justice is the cause of long life and good reputation in this world; it will be rewarded in the other world as well … Therefore, it is obvious that the post of the *nişancı* is the most important rank in the administration.

9 **Lütfi Pasha** (See Chapter 3)

From *Âsafnâme* ("The book of Asaf"):[11]

[On the measures concerning the peasants (*reaya*)]. It is required that the peasants provide men for the irregular cavalry, the paid substitutes (*ellici*), and the raiding forces. True, in the past, Tatars were also obedient to the Ottoman threshold, but they are a rebellious class and cannot be trusted with a campaign … *The registers of the peasants*: it is a law (*kanun*) that these are kept in the imperial council, and that they are drawn up every thirty years, deleting the dead and the sick. But the peasants should not be allowed to wear sumptuous clothes and ride horses like the sipahis. (The vizier) must compare (the new) with the old registers so that peasants are not fewer in number than in the old registers; peasants may have had children, who [have not been registered and thus] will not be included to the peasant class. It is a law that more peasants should be recorded in comparison to the [older] register. And if a peasant leaves where he is (in an attempt) to escape oppression and, God forbid, goes somewhere else, then the judge of his new place must send him back to his old place, so that the lands do not become empty of peasants and ruined. Oarsmen are for the fleet: every four households should send a strong and young oarsman, who will be paid ten aspers a day from the treasury, for as many months as he serves. And if a

11 Akgündüz 1990–1996, 4:275–276 (certain phrases do not exist in all MSS).

peasant performs extraordinary service and out of (the sultan's) abundant grace becomes a sipahi and is endowed with a fief, then his relatives and father and mother are not to follow him; or, if he is a student, he is relieved from his taxable status (*raiyyetlik*), though his family remains taxable. As for the sort of the descendants of the Prophet, they are the sacred Hashimi race but (nowadays) there have been many intruders. A chief (*nakibü's-sâdât*) has been ordained for them; he has to remove those who are not written in their old registers, which contain their pure genealogical trees.

If a peasant rides a horse, he must pay an important fine to his sipahi. Peasants go from one village to another on donkeys. It is not appropriate that peasants are given more licence than this. And it is a law that if a peasant is found with a sword, bow and arrows, a gun or other weapons he must be killed at once. And the inhabitants of his village must pay a full fine. It is a law that if an official (*ehl-i örf*) sees such a weapon, he must ask the people of the village why they did not deliver it [to him] and impose a grave fine upon them. Arms and all necessaries are not for the peasants; the faulty [results] appear even after a hundred years. God knows, license is not good for the peasants; they should not be encouraged. If someone gets wealthy, he must not be oppressed; peasants should be protected.

For **Birgivi Mehmed Efendi**, see below.

10 **Anonymous, Kitâbu mesâlih** (See Chapter 4)

From *Kitâbu mesâlihi'l-müslimîn ve menâfi'i'l-mü'minîn* ("Book on the proper courses for Muslims and on the interests of the faithful").[12]

There is one (mention of the sultan in the) *hutbe* and one coin in all the territories ruled by His Excellency the sultan, the protector of the world. It is appropriate that the *kile* [weight mesure], the ell (*arşun*), the *okka*, and the *dirhem* of every district comply with those of Istanbul. Travelers are helpless in this matter; they arrive in one place and are cheated by words such as "this is the *kile* of Karaman, this is the *okka* of Karaman"; every district has its own type of ells and *kile*s. What is right is that in the happy days of the glorious sultan *kile*, ell, *okka* and the like all be adjusted according to the measures of Istanbul, just like *hutbe* and coinage are the same in every place.

12 Yücel 1988, 94, 98–99, 107–108.

... Moreover, the janissaries should wear something that demonstrates their identity when they do not wear their felt caps, since they fear entering a quarrel or some other problem. It is appropriate that they wear a nightcap (made) from red felt; if they like or if they belong to the elders of the corps, it is fitting that they should also wrap these nightcaps in a short turban. Furthermore, the armorers should wear purple nightcaps and the gunners nightcaps from black felt; thus, when they go out in the streets and in the market without their felt caps they will wear these garments. The same should goes for other militaries, [for instance] the carriers of the cannons should wear blue nightcaps. In this way, they will all be easy to control: no one will start an argument or begin any kind of oppression or mischief. And if they do, they will have no way of denying it; their garments will testify against them and all Muslims will have seen them.

... There is another great and manifest oppression for the peasants, which makes them most unhappy. If, during the winter, a heavenly accident [i.e. a thunderbolt] kills a Muslim's or an infidel's sheep, then the collector of the sheep tax (*koyun hakçısı*) comes and takes the taxes for the dead sheep in full, as he found them in the registers, saying "last year you had so many sheep, you absolutely must give their tax in full". What can the poor man do? He lost his sheep and he gives his money in vain ... Thank God, what need has His Excellency the sultan for this sinful money? All the more so since, from this money, not even a thousandth goes to the treasury: it constitutes the personal income of the tax-collector ... If, in the days of His Excellency the grand vizier this tyranny is abolished, and according to the old law the tax for one's sheep is collected on the basis of their actual number and not according to the old registers, so that no-one is oppressed, this act will be extremely meritorious in God's eyes.

11 Anonymous, *Hırzü'l-mülûk* (See Chapter 4)

From *Hırzü'l-mülûk* ("Stronghold [or, amulet] of the kings"):[13]

Maintaining rulership comes through justice and brave soldiers, and if the soldiers are to be kept obedient, they should be granted fiefs according to their worth. To achieve obedience in such a way, vast territories and a sufficient treasury are needed so that other [soldiers] take salaries and others *zeamet*, timars, and similar high posts. While, for this, most of the towns and villages in the "Protected Domains" should be imperial domains, *zeamet*, and timars, nowadays the majority either belongs to *vakf*s or is private property; nothing has been left

13 Yücel 1988, 176–178.

for *zeamet* or fiefs. Now, concerning the imperial *vakfs*, there is nothing to be said: the great sultans donated to the public kitchens and mosques lands they had conquered by force ... But is it just to grant as private property forty or fifty villages to only one vizier, apart from the other gifts and favors [he is given]? Is not a high post such as that of the vizier sufficient to secure their obedience? And, especially, what need is there to present villages as a gift to a grand vizier? ... Spending so much wealth from the treasury is a deed for which His Excellency the honorable sultan will account for on the Day of Judgment ... It is clear that the purpose of conquering lands and territories is the expansion of the realm and the increase in the wealth of the treasury, not the granting [of lands] to viziers or others. So it is necessary that, from now on, [the sultan] should find it inappropriate to grant to viziers or others anything from the state land, whether villages or arable fields. If villages and fields continue to be granted in such a way for much longer, the revenues will not be sufficient to match the expenses and, moreover, no fief will remain so that if—God forbid!—an enemy moves to attack it will be very difficult to repel him. What is more appropriate is to not grant anything as private property, and even if such has to happen once, it should concern only one village or two, and only to a grand vizier who is devoid of greed and content with the produce of his fiefs, cautious of this world and of the Hereafter, and careful to grant posts only to useful and appropriate people. If a prudent vizier like this wishes to build a mosque and a public kitchen in a suitable place for the sake of the Hereafter, then he should be granted abundant imperial permission; but apart from such a case, he must not be allowed to raise numerous kitchens and mosques.

12 **Mustafa Ali** (See Chapter 4)

From *Nushatü's-selâtîn* ("Counsel for sultans"), translated by Andreas Tietze:[14]

The *sixth* requirement: The dîvân secretaries and the stylists of the high officials at whose fingertips lies the fulfillment of the wishes of the people and in whose lines, that pleasure of the expert beholder, lies the attainment of the aspirations of the century, are in our days for the most part addicted to intoxication by eating *bersh* and opium. As improvement and coming to reason are impossible for their short-sighted minds they undoubtedly neglect their duties, in this way harm and insult the people that come for business. In particular, in unchecked greed they dare to venture certain illegal dispositions; to please someone they write many

14 Ali – Tietze 1979–1982, 1:48–49.

contradictory high orders contrary to the facts, and if they are accountants in the royal treasury they cause with one dot a hundred disorders, perhaps even several thousand finely-spun tricks. By making mistakes in the recording of dates, by entering a date contrary to the truth they certainly cause damage to the superintendants, and these will take care to again indemnify themselves of this loss by taking from the poor population. In this manner constant and concatenated frauds become consolidated like the entries in the register of revenues and interlocked like the figures in the ledger of expenses, and thus lead to decline-bound disintegration.

Therefore, it is incumbent upon the caliph of God and appropriate for his alert statesmen to watch this group carefully as one would inspect a pen-case ... They should not allow them to become as hopelessly confused as the pieces of silk put in the inkstand nor as black and bleak of outlook as their pen-cases are. If the revenues they receive as secretaries do not cover their necessary expenses, one should make all efforts to favor them with certain services and to improve their situation so as to prevent them from greedily writing documents that contradict the truth ... in their urge of acquisition abandoning the straightness of the letter *alif* and bending down to crookedness like the letter *lam*.

[Verses] by the author:

Could the number of the stars be whole
If one left out the dot of the celestial pole?
That dot, the writer of the sky cannot delete
Or else the system remains incomplete.
In the circle of scribes it is the same:
That ominous dot is the center of shame!

From *Mevâidü'n-nefâis fi kavâidi'l-mecâlis* ("Tables of delicacies concerning the rules of social gatherings"), translated by Douglas S. Brookes:[15]

To ensure that the workshop known as the Ottoman state, or the foundation of the Seljuk or Samanid sultanates, should not suffer damage through bribery, and that those great wheels of fortune continue to turn according to their established rules, and that established practice continue to be observed, learned persons have compared this heavy task to that great revolving wheel, which always revoles vigilantly. That is to say, it revolves through an art ... Furthermore, by using intelligent and learned persons, and persons manifesting physical strength, one

15 Ali – Brookes 2003, 59–60.

will ensure that the operation of that workshop and its regular functioning will be secured and guaranteed for months and years.

However, whenever the foundation of a state is damaged so that the great personages turn their thoughts to bribery; whenever kings and ministers toss aside the safeguarding of the law so that their intelligent subjects, who seek their rights without having to pay money, rot in corners, dismissed from office; whenever unworthy and unprincipled low-brows who know only how to count out the coinage of bribery are raised day by day to offices of lofty rank, and so fulfill their every desire—then that waterwheel begins to fall and collapse. Indeed its master even dies, comes to his end. Especially when a capable apprentice, with sufficient strength to repair the waterwheel, does not exist, then on such occasion animals … and even an intelligent and strong-armed human, are too worn out to make that workshop hum …

All in all, when a state or realm is, God forbid, taken over by bribe-takers, its waterwheel is utterly destroyed. Neither does that state endure in order, nor can that realm oppose its seasons, which are like the progression of the days of the months through the year.

13 **Hasan Kâfi Akhisari, Usûlü'l-hikem** (See Chapter 4)

From *Usûlü'l-hikem fi nizâmi'l-âlem* ("Elements of wisdom for the order of the world"):[16]

If you ask whether one may live outside the four classes described as wise and movers (of the world), then (the answer is that), according to wise Muslims, this kind of people should not be left unmolested; on the contrary, they should be constantly pushed and forced to enter one of the four classes … For some philosophers, such jobless people should even be executed instead of being left to wander uselessly … In the times of the sultans of old—God may have mercy on them!—such idle people were inspected once a year and prohibited (from wandering) … But it is against the law if a class neglects its own tasks out of laziness; this results in riots in the realm. Thus, it has become clear that … it is not right if people of one class leave their jobs and are forced to do those of another … Besides, this is the reason for the rebellion and disturbance of recent years. Peasants, villagers, artisans, and inhabitants of the towns were transferred to the border and forced to fight; the [real] soldiers, such as the sipahis, were not cared for during war and lost their means of living because of the officers' negligence; dearth and famine in the land reached such a degree that things that

16 Akhisari – İpşirli 1979–80, 252–253 and 268–269.

previously were bought for one asper could not be found for ten. This recruitment of peasants and town-dwellers for the army by force did not happen in the olden days; it began in A.H. 1001 [1592/3] and continues up to today.

... Now great care must be taken in the matter of inspecting (the army), especially in this period and in these times. We believe that the inability (of our army) to face the infidels in these years, of which we have been witnesses, comes only from the neglect and abandoning of this important matter and this great obligation. We have been experiencing this for 50 years now in our own land, i.e. the Croatian border: our enemies, who are real warriors, start to overpower us every time they create a new type of weapon and start using it. Then, as soon as we begin making and using a similar weapon, we prevail over these accursed ones with God's help, because the Muslim religion is the most powerful. Nowadays, our enemies again use all their strength to make use of some newly-invented weapons, such as guns and cannons: they have invented various sorts of guns and cannons and have begun using them on an excessive scale. But our soldiers have neglected procuring themselves of these weapons and using them; nay, they even neglect using their old weapons. This is the reason that they have reached this point, i.e. that they cannot stand the battle and so flee.

14 Anonymous, Kitâb-i müstetâb (See Chapter 5)

From *Kitâb-i müstetâb* ("The approved [or, agreeable] book"):[17]

... From the happy times of His Excellency the deceased Sultan Murad [III]—may he rest in peace!—the judges and administrators started to exhibit a lack of justice and to make bad decisions in their businesses; the affairs of the Exalted State were neglected and they constantly followed ways contrary to the old law. As a consequence, the villages and the cultivated lands in the "Protected Domains" became ruined, the peasants dispersed, the expenses of the Imperial Treasury surpassed the income and, moreover, janissary corps became corrupted through the entry of strangers into their ranks ... Due to these reasons, the situation of the world became confused and the very foundations of the Exalted State undermined. So, [this treatise] will give answers—God willing—to questions such as: what were the reasons for the appearance of such shameful acts after the aforementioned date, and how can these be mended? ... From among the inappropriate situations that have appeared in these times, the first is that strangers meddled with the class of the sultan's slaves [the janissaries], that the

17 Yücel 1988, 2, 23, 31.

janissaries' numbers increased unnecessarily, that their salaries were also multiplied, and that expenses surpassed income.

... Another issue is that, for 25 or 30 years now, all the official posts in Istanbul have been given through bribery; furthermore, bribery has reached such a degree that, on the pretext of "gifts", bribes are given and taken openly from one household (*kapu*) to another. Among the ulema and state administrators it has been raised now to a pious custom, even being—God forbid!—permissible. For instance, if someone is thought of as pious and sincere, or is not known to associate with young boys or other lustful company, he is not given any post; nay, he is scorned as a useless soul. This is what has become the situation in Istanbul nowadays. In the provinces, too, most of the judges, the governors, the district governors, and the other administrators are addicted to this trouble.

... Thus, the corruption of the state of the world, the interference of strangers with the janissary class, the appearance of robbers and of the Celalis, financial weakness, the scattering of the peasants, the manning of government posts by inappropriate people, the rise of bribery, and, to sum up, all these sinful acts that are contrary to the law are the result of the grand vizier's absence and weakness, and of nothing else.

15 **Koçi Bey, Risâle** (See Chapter 5)

From the first *Risâle* ("Treatise"):[18]

[All the glorious conquests of old] were made by the owners of *zeamet* and timars; this is how tribute was collected from all the neighboring rulers. In the olden days, this class consisted of the selected ones, of the valiant ones who would give their body and soul for the religion and the dynasty, and of the obedient and the superior ones. As long as they were in perfect condition, there was absolutely no need for janissaries for the (various) wars and the battles. They were a pure, disciplined class, well-wishing for the dynasty; not one intruder could be found among their ranks and they were all noblemen (*ocak ve ocakzadeler*) who had owned sultanly fiefs for generations ... It was a sin similar to blasphemy to give a timar to a city lad or a peasant ... The owner of a timar would gain the right to a *zeamet* only if he showed extraordinary courage on an imperial campaign, bringing ten or fiteen enemy heads or prisoners. State officials and soldiers did not use silver harnesses, ornaments, and the like; they all cared only for a good horse, a sharp sword, a humble robe and armor, a spear and, a bow.

18 Koçi Bey – Aksüt 1939, 24–25, 44–46, 51; modern Turkish translation in Koçi Bey – Çakmakcıoğlu 2008, 32–33, 58–61, 67.

... Let it not be a secret for the sultan that the entering of strangers into the janissary corps began in A.H. 990 [1582] ... The nobility and beauty of the corps disappeared; the regulations governing its function declined and became a complete mess. Whereas giving pensions to persons other than the aged and invalids was against the rules, now there are more than 10,000 pensionaries and retired men from among the young and strong. This way, the Muslim treasury perished and was destroyed ... In such a situation, how can the world be restored? How can the treasury be filled? The army consists of soldiers from many generations; of noblemen and the sons of noblemen. The job cannot be done by grocers and the like! To sum up, in the olden days the Muslim army was small in numbers but great in essence, pure and disciplined; it gained victories and conquest via God's order wherever it campaigned ... Now, no army remains: service (*kulluk*) is restricted to salaried slaves, and the seeds of sedition have been sown in the world ... They go to the war whenever they like; there is no obedience, no fear of the sultan. Is that a Muslim army? In our times, these preoccupations have become a duty applicable to all (*farz-i ayn*).

... The [janissary] slaves cannot be controlled by advice; it is impossible to have them reformed with kindness ... In sum, men are controlled by force, not clemency. The great sultans of the past used the salaried cavalry to control the janissary infantry, the janissaries to control the cavalrymen, and the owners of timars and *zeamet* to control both these classes of slaves. Now, the timariots have disappeared completely; (military) service remains restricted to these two classes of slaves, and each one has attained monstrous proportions. If His Excellency the sultan acts carefully, the task is easy: if the *zeamet* and timars attain the perfect state they used to have, and if the numbers of salaried slaves decrease as far as possible, with God's permission the world will find its order once more.

16 **Aziz Efendi** (See Chapter 5)

From *Kânûnnâme-i sultânî* ("Book of sultanly laws and regulations"), translated by Rhoads Murphey:[19]

The same procedure of inspection and investigation would then be carried out for each company one by one recording the town, village and province of each member together with a physical description in an orderly register ... Outsiders who have abandoned their fields and former trade to become Janissaries on the strength of a pay certificate belonging to someone else, not being capable

19 Aziz Efendi – Murphey 1985, 10, 22.

of giving satisfactory answer to the questions about their origins, will remain absent at the time of inspection, and after those pay certificates belonging to pretenders … are excluded, the number of true Janissaries, if God the Almighty wills it, who remain will be only 15,000. If it is the imperial wish of your felicitous majesty that the number of the aforementioned group not become excessively large a law should be put into effect stipulating a maximum size for each of the one hundred and sixty-two companies of the Janissary corps … Furthermore, in accordance with the ancient law, members of the Janissary corps should be resident and present in the barracks in Istanbul which have been assigned to their companies, and not one of them should ever be allowed to reside outside Istanbul. Also, those who are presently bachelors and those who are called to permanent service in regiments of the Porte after the inspections are carried out should not be permitted to marry … At present too warnings and injunctions to this effect should be given, and henceforth the recruitment categories of handpicked assistant to the commander, sons of cavalrymen and place switching should completely abolished. By God the exalted's willing in this manner the desired reforms may be accomplished. Amen.

… In manner mentioned above, the group of salaried servants of the Sultan, from the safe and secure times of your illustrious forefathers until the present day in the era of your majesty's reign, have many times rebelled against the Sultan and laid his well-protected realm to rack and ruin. By their failure to obey their commanders' orders during campaigns they have furthermore been cause for the loss to the enemy of the choice lands and prosperous districts which were brought into Sultanic realm through great pains and difficulties by your venerable ancestors of illustrious descent. Therefore, by carrying out a thorough inspection and investigation of this group and by ousting the illegitimate intruders to rout these brigands and rebels who are more reprehensible than the enemy himself, dispersing a part of them and reducing the remainder to contrition and to reciting constant prayers and praises of God, and by thus doing bringing into being a great victory equal with the conquests of our glorious ancestors, would not this be a miraculous accomplishment vouchsafed by the sanctity of the Caliph Ali Murteza himself?

17 **Anonymous, Kavanin-ı yeniçeriyân** (See Chapter 5)

From *Kavânîn-i yeniçeriyân-ı dergâh-ı âlî* ("Rules of the imperial janissaries"):[20]

20 Akgündüz 1990–1996, 9:263–268.

And the janissaries should not be married from now on. Now there are some married ones among the *acemis*. There must be a strict warning that whoever gets married cannot be a janissary, and he will even be removed from the ranks of the *acemis*. From now on, janissaries must not be given permission to marry; they should not be given permission, according to the old law, unless they have become old and retired and powerless and (this is) told to the sultan. When all the janissaries are bachelors, the post of the *odabaşı* comes late (in one's career): this post belongs to those who are experienced and have understood the laws and regulations of the corps ... Janissaries must not practise any craft; they should not meddle with measures and scales. If they do not obey, they must be punished and turned into timariots.

... The scribes of the janissaries should look after the registers of the corps carefully, and distribute salaries according to the treasury register of the Sultan. And the sultan must show a way for his *silahdar* and *rikabdar* to compare these registers with one another, and to bring in someone experienced so that they can learn (the situation) from him. But whoever (from these experienced people) acts against the law must be punished ... God willing, let the abovementioned law and regulation be applied in the aforementioned way, and with God's permission it is certain that victories and conquests will result. The aforementioned laws are the laws of the Ottoman sultans of the past.

18 **Birgivi Mehmed Efendi** (See Chapter 6)

From *al-Ajwibat al-hâsima li-ʿurûq al-shibhat al-qâsima* ("Zealous answers to the roots of divisive doubts") and from *al-Sayf al-sârim fî ʿadam jawâz waqf al-manqûl wa'l-darâhim* ("The sharp sword for the inadmissibility of movable and cash *vakfs*"), translated by Jon E. Mandaville:[21]

The inadmissibility of the cash waqf is clearly stated in well-known and respected books. The number of scholars who have agreed upon its inadmissibility is well established ... In the established texts, the argument of Zufar [Imam Zufar, a student of Abu Hanifa], which is connected with its permissibility, is a weak one ... [O]f the classical works, neither the Imams Abu Hanifa, Abu Yusuf, Muhammad, nor other masters of the school permit it, clearly they did not accept this aforementioned weak statement. This is why it is not permitted. As for its irrevocability, there is not a single statement to this effect. Zufar says nothing

21 Mandaville 1979, 305–306.

about it. There is nothing in the arguments [of Ebussuud] supporting anything of irrevocability, absolutely nothing …

Thus has the invalidity of the cash waqf been exposed. In it there are the sources of many evils. One is the nonpayment of the ordained *zakat*. A second is the interruption of the regular course of inheritance, an adjudging and execution of testaments involving cash waqf despite suspicions as to its validity, thus withholding truth from the truthful, an ugly oppression. A third, the seizing of the substance of the waqf by its administrators; they carouse, and when they are asked to surrender the waqf the judge prevents this. Or when someone dies and the inheritance is damaged. Verily, there among them children and madmen. As He has said, 'Those who eat the property of orphans, oppressing, will eat and find fire in their stomachs; they will pray burning'. A fourth, the man who makes a cash waqf will become poor, despite what he thinks. Moreover, he believes that he no longer is obliged to celebrate the Day of Sacrifice, or the Breaking of the Fast, or charity to the poor, or the Pilgrimage, or any of those things. He thinks he has the right to take *zakat* and other things forbidden the rich. He is a great offender in this. A fifth, that cash waqf is in little-esteemed books wherein joint partnership, commerce, and the like is mentioned. Now in our day they profit from usury in the very fashion that the Prophet of God censured. The scholars also censured it, made clear its sinfulness. A sixth, that most of the waqf administrators are ignorant and don't recognize the pictures of usury in the Book; they make profit with loans and sale. Any loan from which profit is made is usurious. Some of them lead a dissolute life, taking interest without even going through the motions of using legally permissible devices to do so. They make waqf of usury and the forbidden, pure and simple, giving it to the administrators who consume the usury. They are in the same position as someone struck mad and frenzied by the devil …

19 **Abdülmecid Sivasi** (See Chapter 6)

From *Letâ'ifü'l-ezhâr* ("Smart blossoms and delightful conversations"):[22]

The sultan of the Muslims must abolish the filth that produces immorality, avoiding wealth that comes from things whose unlawfulness has been proven through Quranic verses and the Prophetic tradition. Because, according to the verse "Oh faithful! Really, the polytheists are filthy", this dirty thing [wine] is peculiar to the dirty infidels, so those of a devilish nature who accept the import [of wine] to Muslim lands and argue that they care for the treasury, spending [revenue from

22 From the Turkish translation in Gündoğdu 2000, 77 and 99.

the taxes on it] for the benefit of the sultan's slaves, are in fact driving the sultan down the path of vanity and filling the treasury with such [corrupt] actions. I am confident that they are not sincere in their actions and that this dirty thing does not bring even one *akçe* to the treasury; on the contrary, it ruins it. I say that if our sultan abolished [this tax] and asked from the "Hidden Ones" something less in its place, the treasury would benefit more. His Excellency our Prophet said: "If someone closes a door to the unlawful, God will open to him a door to the lawful".

... If there is a trace of hypocrisy in a behavior, this is a vice or even polytheism [infidelity] according to people of knowledge and of the Sharia. Even if it is taken lightly, as a joke, it is blasphemy; hypocrisy depends on the heart, even if it taken lightly ... Things being thus, and since there is no Quranic verse or Prophetic tradition related to the dance of the dervishes, to say that the *sema* [the dervish dance] is canonically lawful or unlawful, either in order to permit it or to prohibit it, is wrong for people of the external reality, who have avoided the chain of knowledge and do not enter the field of the heart ... So, pronouncing the *sema* lawful is fit for the rule "when there is no Quranic verse stating authoritatively that something is unlawful, this must be rendered lawful". As al-Ghazali has said, "both analogy and [the absence of] an authoritative Quranic verse show that *sema* should be rendered lawful". But if there is carnal desire in the movements of someone performing *sema*, it is unlawful. Perchance someone's ecstacy is genuine and provokes a truthful move, as water turns the water-wheel, making him involuntarily move as if he trembles from cold; then one cannot ask whether these movements are involuntarily and it is not right to act against those who do not know their situation, as if they were sound in mind.

20 Hasan Dede (See Chapter 6)

From *Nasihatnâme* ("Book of advice"):[23]

Two groups of people make this world either destroyed or built. One is oppressive judges, the other oppressive beys. After reforming these two groups, reforming the world is easy. Whenever my sultan wishes, the reform of these groups is at his hand, with God's order, yet on one condition: they must not be dismissed for five or ten years. There is no other solution for the reform of the beys and the judges. If you execute 50 of them everyday, beys and judges who (now) fear dismissal will be reformed and abstain from tyranny.

23 Terzioğlu 2010, 292.

My sultan, you should give all posts to beys or judges with this condition, that "I will not dismiss you. Be safe from the fear of dismissal. But if I perceive any oppression from your part, I will not be satisfied with dismissing you: certainly, I will cut off your head and give your post to someone else. Be aware of this"; warn them like this. The people of our days are sinful Muslims: they do not fear God, they are not ashamed of the Prophet; they always say "today is the day", and know nothing of tomorrow. The tyrants hear of the Afterlife and of the End of Days as if they were legends. That is why they are inclined to oppression and corruption. Most of the people are addicted to their whims: one is a dog of the coffeehouse, another of the tavern. They do not think of the bright-eyed Azrail and do not come around to reason. They follow this custom of the English Franks, tobacco, but forget God's orders and the words of the Prophet. They do not submit to the highest leader; they do not humiliate themselves before the glorious Sharia, they do not keep the laws of the caliph of this era. What has happened to the orders of the religion, to Islam? From the time tobacco appeared, neither is our sword sharp nor does (even) one job go well for us.

21 **Kâtib Çelebi** (See Chapter 7)

From *Düstûrü'l-amel li ıslahi'l-halel* ("Course of measures to redress the situation"):[24]

Let it be known that, according to another view, the state (*devlet*), which means realm and kingdom, consists of human society. Those who discern the secrets of the nature of beings can see that its theoretical and practical situation, if examined carefully, is clearly similar to the individual state of man; these two states are equal to each other … First of all, the natural life of man is measured along three degrees: these are the age of growth, that of stagnation, and that of ageing and decline. The timing of these three stages is appointed according to each individual's realities … Now, the social state of man, which consists of the state (*devlet*), is also divided into three stages: growth, stagnation, and decline. In the same vein, societies differ from one another as far as these three stages are concerned, which is why some past societies passed into decline quickly, while others passed into stagnation because of the disastrous lack of the necessary measures, just like a young man may have an accident. Others, like this great state [of the Ottomans], have a strong disposition and healthy foundations and consequently continue their life with stagnation coming quite late. These stages have specific signs, either in their individual or social form; those who want to

24 From the Turkish translation in Kâtib Çelebi – Gökyay 1968, 155–157.

take measures to readjust public affairs act according to these signs … because the cure applied to an old man cannot be suitable for a child, and vice versa …

Now, the corporeal existence of man is composed of the four humors, which exist in the four elements of nature; by means of the senses and the faculties, human reason controls them all. Likewise, the social existence of man also consists of four elements, which are controlled by the glorious sultan, who is in the place of reason, by means of his senses and faculties, who are his statesmen. These four pillars are the ulema, the military, the merchants, and the peasants. The ulema, this exalted class, corresponds to the blood; the heart, which is the seat of this immaterial jewel, the animal soul, sends this soul, with the blood, to all the limbs of the human body, the legs, the arms, even to its further ends … The military corresponds to phlegm, the merchants to yellow bile, and the peasants to black bile, whose nature is earthly and inferior. These four humors maintain the health of the human disposition, depending on each other to keep their quantities balanced; likewise, the order of societies and the disposition of states are maintained in a similar way. The four humours must be kept balanced, so that the disposition of the body sees no harm. If, for some reason, one of them becomes diminished and damaged or, conversely, stronger than the others, then one needs the appropriate medicine to regain the balance.

From *Mîzânü'l-hak fi ihtiyâri'l-âhak* ("The balance of truth for the selection of the truest [way]"), translated by Geoffrey Lewis:[25]

The ordinances relating to both kinds [of innovation] are set forth explicitly and in detail in the law-books; we do not propose to describe them here. All we wish to say is this: these innovations are all firmly based on custom and habit. Once an innovation has taken root and become established in a community, it is the height of stupidity and ignorance to invoke the principle of 'enjoining right and forbidding wrong' and to hope to constrain the people to abandon it. People will not give up anything to which they have grown accustomed, whether it be Sunna or innovation, unless some man of blood massacre them all … People will not abandon custom. Whatever it is, it will last until God decrees otherwise … The duty of complying belongs to the people; they cannot be forced to comply.

In short, there is no point in conducting profound researches into this subjects, for … if everybody were to carry out an honest self-examination, nothing approaching conformity with the Sunna would be found. Scarcely any of the sayings or doings of any age are untainted by innovation.

… So much for the summary of the treatises [on bribery]. Now for our own view.

25 Kâtib Chelebi – Lewis 1957, 89–90 and 126–127.

It is a widespread belief among the common people that bribery is absolutely unlawful; this is a parrot-cry which they repeat without knowing what class of bribe it is. Even those who do know, say, 'What's the use of arguing? It is unlawful', and they give and take bribes stealthily. Even where there is no earthly reason for payment, no one hesitates to accept bribes. Those who do not take bribes are moved not by piety and fear of God, but by a consideration of the difficulty of hiding it and by fear of gossip, for they regard a bribe as rather a pleasant and agreeable thing. The facts are so; there is no aversion from bribery at the present time.

The best course is this. In bribery of the third and fourth categories [i.e. that given to a ruler to avert harm or secure advantage, and that given to avert the risk of harm to oneself or to one's property, in which cases it is permissible to give but unlawful to receive], the parties should employ the 'oath of hire' for which Ibn Najim quotes Qadikhan, and so save themselves from evil consequences. That is how bribery is conducted nowadays in government departments in all matters except appointments to the office of judge.

Now there is a risk of disruption to the existing order if men persist in nullifying the true and regularising the false ... Now also, compliance with the law is necessary ... It is no use saying 'We have employed a legal device'; there are many actions which can be dressed in the garb of legality but are not acceptable to the reason, because of the manifold corruptions lurking beneath.

22 **Mustafa Na'ima** (See Chapter 7)

From *Ravzat al-Hüseyin fi hulâsât ahbâr al-hâfikayn* ("Huseyin's garden, with a summary of news for East and West"):[26]

Let it be known that the divine custom and God's will have ordained that the situation of every state and community is always settled in a uniform manner; it does not stay perpetually on one path, but instead moves through several periods (from one situation) to a renewed one. The features of one period are different from (those of) another, and the necessities of one stage are unlike those of the preceding one. As for the children of the time [contemporary people], they are in accord with the characteristics of the period in which they live; men of each era are defined according to the circumstances necessary for their era. For it is an innate feature, based on concealed [divine] ordinance, that one conforms

26 Na'ima – İpşirli 2007, 1:26, 37, 39 and 4:1571–1572. For the latter part (on Derviş Pasha's economic views) I use the translation by Metin Kunt (Kunt 1977, 205–206).

and complies to the necessities of the time, that the disposition of the state follows the period, and that it respects the nature of the creatures. Thus, the different periods of a state cannot usually exceed five stages.

... The sword and the pen are most important for rulership and necessary instruments for the foundation of a state. At the beginning of a dynasty there is more need for the sword, in order to secure the fulfilling of its purposes and the application of its orders. In this period, the pen serves to have the ruler's orders achieved. As for the sword, it is appointed to assist in attaining his aims and acquiring his demands. Moreover, during the aforementioned period of weakness and decline of power, which happens in the latter days of a dynasty, imploring assistance from the men of the sword and being in need of them is certain; in these two stages, the superiority of the sword over the pen is obvious ... But in the middle period of a dynasty and during the period of its greatest power, the stabilization of affairs makes it able, up to a point, to do without the sword. In contrast, it is established that there is need for the pen to be used, for tasks such as collecting benefits and revenues, gathering of taxes, controlling the budget, and carrying out orders. Thus, in this period the power of the pen is elevated and the men of the pen are more esteemed than the men of the sword.

... Let it be known that in the last age of every state, that of stagnation, which covers the fourth and fifth stages, expenses always exceed income. In such circumstances, it is imperative that [the state] tries as far as it can simply to increase revenues and decreases expenses, so it reaches a [level of] stability and that completely removes the deficiencies described. At length, the decrease in expenses according to necessity and the ordering of various other issues requires the compelling power of an enforcerer ... In the aforementioned stages, the careful administrators who try to find solutions first must give some breathing space to the treasury by removing the trouble of campaigns until the army regains its power. Then, they should gradually try to reorder the cities and help the people recover.

... The following remarks are derived from ancient philosophers; some wise men are reported to have attributed them to Derviş Paşa. There are three means of gaining wealth: agriculture, commerce, and political authority. Crafts have also been considered by some as a fourth means; nevertheless, it would be proper to limit the means of wealth to the three mentioned above since most artisans are unable to provide for their livingthemselves with a livelihood since they keep of the produce of their crafts barely enough to subsist on while most of the fruit of the labor falls to the rich merchants of that particular commodity. It has been traditionally been the case that agriculture and trade have been the more profitable [to an individual] in direct proportion to [his] power and position in society. This is so because people serve a person of power and high position, work for his gain both with their labor and with their funds, without asking for immediate remuneration, hoping to become closer to him and expecting future benefits. Some others fear his power and oppression and therefore give up an expected share of their profits, or they too may work for him. Thus, in either of these two ways, the payment for the people's services and one-fourth of their labor being due to the person of position, he should amass a huge fortune in a short time.

If a ruler or governor is not able to expand his capital, to increase his income or to obtain necessary supplies through engaging in commerce and agriculture, he is afflicted by two kinds of evil and will be damned in this world and the next. One of these evils is that he will be forced to violate the people's property and seize their money and goods; thus he will become an oppressor. The second evil is that he will not be able to keep the money that he wrongfully seized from the people; he will spend it on necessities like food and clothing and other supplies; this money in the end will fall into the hands of perfidious speculators and usurers while he will fall into shame and ignominy. He will, in effect, have gained for speculators and usurers; he himself will be burdened with the consequences of these evil deeds. Thus, all such a ruler is able to achieve is the destruction of the country and the dispersal of its people.

23 **Defterdar Sarı Mehmed Pasha** (See Chapter 8)

From *Nesâ'ıhü'l-vüzerâ ve'l-ümerâ veya Kitab-ı güldeste* ("Advice for viziers and statesmen, or a book containing a bunch of flowers"), translated by Walter Livingston Wright:[27]

And let not the matter of establishing market prices be passed over with the mere intrusting it to judges and inspectors of weights and measures. It is essential at all times for every ruler to keep track of the small things relating to the general condition of the people. He must set the proper market prices. Every thing must be sold at the price it is worth. For in case the padishah and the vezirs say: "The fixing of market prices, though part of the public business, is insignificant," and are not diligent about it, the city judge alone cannot carry it out. Since he has no connection with matters of policy, he cannot enter upon that path. Under such circumstances, every one buys and sells as he pleases. Through senseless avarice the venom of vipers is added to lawful goods. The most contemptible of the people, useless both for the service of the padishah and for warfare, become

27 Defterdar – Wright 1935, 77–78 and 98–99.

possessors of all the wealth ... The fruiterers and merchants put a double price on provisions and supplies and reap [a harvest of] profits. They rob the people. It is apparent that neglect in this matter redounds to the harm of believers in time of trouble and to the benefit of fruiterers and merchants.

... The sure cause of the augmenting and increase of the Treasury is the certain help of the grand vizier to the defterdars, his allowing their presentation of reports and his paying attention to these. For any matter connected with the public moneys orders must not be given heedlessly, without seeing the account books of the Treasury and investigating its benefit or harm and without referring it to the decision of the defterdar.

Certain tax concessions, instead of being farmed out, should be committed to the charge of trustworthy and upright persons on government account.

Always striving with care to reduce the expenditure and augment the income of the Treasury, he [the defterdar] should especially abstain from waste and spending to no purpose. For the learlend men of the Faith and the great authorities on doctrine have specified that the portion allotted to the venerable judges from the public treasury should be only enough for necessary wants and to avert poverty ... Since the Treasury of the Moslems is the inherited property of no one, it is essential to abstain completely from dissipating and wasting it. Every one must meditate always upon the questioning and answering in this world and that to come, on the punishment and reward, and be on his guard against this.

Let the janissary corps not be increased. Let them be well disciplined, few but élite, and all present in time of need. In this connection also it is fitting to be extremely careful and to be attentive and persevering in keeping their rolls in proper order and in having the soldiers actually present. The late Lütfi Pasha, who was formerly grand vezir, has written in his *Asafnâme*: "Fifteen thousand soldiers are a great many soldiers. It is an heroic deed to pay the wages year by year of fifteen thousand men with no decrease". But under the present conditions the soldiers and pensioned veterans and repeaters of prayers who get pay and rations have exceeded all limits.

24 **Süleyman Penah Efendi** (See Chapter 8)

From *Mora ihtilâli tarihi* ("History of the upheavals in Morea"):[28]

28 Penah Efendi – Berker 1942–1943, 239–240/309–311, 397, 475–476.

Because [the Albanians] have not been given any orderly arrangement, they are a wild and ill-mannered tribe that does not travel through the well-guarded domains and does not know commerce or craftsmanship … In fact, the Albanian language is a rough language … without any degree of subtlety, whereas the good manners of a tribe absolutely depend on its learning the language of its dynasty … There must be a noble sultanly order to the effect that from now on Albanian should not be spoken. After some years they will thus change their language and nobody will speak Albanian; they will speak Turkish instead … One may see that this is possible if one considers that when Spain discovered the New Indias the inhabitants were even worse than the Albanians: they did not discern heaven from earth and had absolutely no knowledge of arts and crafts. The Spanish brought some women from America and married them in Spain; their children spoke the language of both their mothers and their fathers. Then these children were sent back to America as translators, and, shortly after, this tribe forgot the American language and began speaking Frankish … In the same way, some disciples from Delvine and Avlonya should be transferred to Istanbul and settled somewhere outside the walls; rations must be ordained for them and teachers must teach them …

… Another reason for the lack of prosperity in the world is the following: land, whose first cultivator was Adam, cannot be inherited by an imperial permit to (a deceased person's) heirs, as happens with vineyards and gardens. Even officers are helpless against oppressing officers and notables in this respect. The tyranny connected to the title deed (*tapu*) is multiplied (by them) without the slightest gain for the public treasury or the owners of lifelong tax-farms … The Exalted State should show mercy and completely abolish the title deed for the arable lands through a merciful imperial decree; they must belong with full propriety to their masters, just as do orchards and vineyards. If they can be inherited freely, according to the rules laid down by God, to the owners' heirs, this will be an instrument for renewing of the world, without any loss for the treasury or the tax-farmers.

… In the Morea and Rumeli they produce cotton, forty *guruş* an *okka*; an imperial decree should ordain that the inhabitants of both the Protected Domains and of Istanbul use this cotton for their headgear. Undoubtedly, in a very short time headgear similar to the Indian ones will be produced. Because the amount of money going to India is disproportionally large and innumerable, if this continues for some years everybody will be broke … When does a state or a tribe become rich? They become rich whenever they undertake ways to draw wealth from other places with crafts and products other than the money produced in their protected domains, and whenever they produce cloths in their own lands, so their money does not go to other countries.

25 **Ahmed Vasıf Efendi** (See Chapter 8)

From *Risâle* ("Essay"), partly translated by Ethan L. Menchinger:[29]

Let it be known that the infidel kings … have invented a way to achieve great benefits easily; in brief, they build a special place in their capitals, providing it with all the necessary materials and provisions … There they collect children of unknown parents, illegitimate sons of adultery and lust, and they take them to these appointed places … They train the aforementioned children according to the new ways of the science of war, and thus part of their soldiery is arranged and ordered by these Satans; the same is done with part of the peasant subjects of their lands, whom they divide into parts and recruit as if they were their bought slaves … All these groups serve under duress and have to obey orders in every case; certainly this is not something that is unattainable.

… If things have now altered so that our soldiers are denied victory and if the enemy sometimes prevails by land and sea, this is an effect of their faculty of *istidrac* [deceiving temporary success by divine order], produced by Satanic means; and the function of *istidrac* is that it is short and that it is impossible to achieve its aims at all times. Especially in the times when the victorious [Muslim] armies prevail, the weapons of the infidels are still the same: the weapons which they use nowadays being known, their ways of peace are similarly analogous to the rules of war. Whenever the invasion of the Muslim swords into their ranks disperses the measures and arrangements and all the means of intimidation and threatening which they have gathered together, their ill-omened armies are humiliated and scorned, they give up their souls and possessions; who may doubt for this? It is depending on the subtle points of God's will.

Indeed do victory and defeat depend on the will of God. As for Christian nations, their beliefs dispute this. Hence they say, following a group of philosophers, that the circumstances of war are among particular events and that God—Heaven forfend!—has no effect on particular events. They not only ridiculously contend that whichever side can muster superior means of warfare will prevail, but they produce proofs weaker than a spider's web, crediting victory to the perfection of means and necessities and heedless of the sacred import of "Not the least atom is hidden from Him" and "There is no aid but from God the Almighty". In the campaign of Eğri, when the Sultan Mehmed—peace be upon him!—with an innumerable army confronted the enemy, by God's will his regularly and carefully arranged army was dispersed and the enemy prevailed over

29 Vasıf – İlgürel 1978, 150–151; for the translated parts see Menchinger 2014b, 147–150 (additional parts translated by the author).

the Muslim soldiers in most part, but the corps of the *karakulluku*, with the assistance of the valiant Sultan, began fighting without order or weapons and finally destroyed hundreds of thousands of infidels … Ultimately, there is still reason to struggle for the causes at the heart of our discussion; and these, praise to God, are now being readied and gradually brought to completion.

26 **Şanizade** (See Chapter 8)

From *Târîh* ("History"):[30]

The term "noble family" (*hanedan*) is attributed to those who, without oppression and in a habitual manner, sustain themselves and their servants and followers with the properties and lands granted to them by a member of the dynasty and by reason of sultanly authority (*ber cihet-i hakkaniyye ile*), without interfering in the affairs of the kingdom … However, if they usurp public property, kill, and confiscate the goods of the people, raise their own armies and without any rights each one seizes part of the territories of the Exalted State … they thus lead to the imperial territories being expropriated and shared among what they call their noble family (*hanedan*). Now, the suitability of the sultan as a caliph is manifest, as he is the descendant of the House of Osman, who was the chosen heir of the Prophet's family (*muhtar-ı ehl-i İslam olmuş*), and furthermore he is elected (*muhtar*); this document was thus written and signed … in order to cause those who felt estranged from the sultanly power to be partners in the sultanly and imperial orders, which would be issued unanimously with the ministers whom the sultan would choose.

… Some wise men have argued that the proper administration of public affairs needs the consent of all individual men, and in some organized states this wise advice has caused ease and security among subjects and sovereigns. In these countries, and because this practice has been followed to a large degree in their state laws, whenever the need arises two classes of consulting experts, namely state servants and representatives of the subjects, discuss matters in a free manner and proffer their view of the best possible course by way of a petition; their sovereigns either approve it and put it into action or, if they discern any weakness or conceive of any better course, they always have the power to do what they deem best. In the aforementioned states, both important and trivial affairs are conducted this way, without complaints or quarrels; however, to be elected by the people (*muhtâr-ı nâs*), a representative must belong to the experts

30 Şânizâde – Yılmazer 2008, 74–75 (on the signing of the *Sened-i ittifak*) and 1093–1094.

who have knowledge and wisdom, who are literate, and who can discuss affairs, while the right of a representative to enter and serve on the councils of power depends on such qualifications. In the opposite case, there will be no sense whatsoever for the Exalted State–where the sultan has his own independent opinion–except that the high councils of viziers and ulema and the assemblies of the higher notables will fall without reason into the shape of democracy (*cumhûriyyet*), with the vain quest for majority.

27 **İbrahim Müteferrika** (See Chapter 9)

From *Usûlü'l-hikem fî nizâmi'l-ümem* ("Rational bases for the order of the countries"):[31]

Concerning the opinions of the wise on the foundations of the rules of states: it is clear and well-known that sultans and kings of the world, as well as the rulers of men, differ in their religion, sect, custom, and disposition. The same applies for the social forms of humanity, and that is why the structures of states and societies differ from each other. In this matter, the words of all wise men follow the opinions and views of three famous philosophers.

First, there is Plato's view; he said that people must submit and obey to a wise and just king, who has full independence in ruling the affairs of the state and to whose decisions everyone must comply. This kind of state and kingdom became known as "monarchy" (*munarhıyâ*) in the language of the wise men of Ancient Greece, and most of the states in the world are structured along these lines. For a person to be established in this place, a noble lineage is praiseworthy and esteemed.

Secondly, there is Aristotle's view. He said that rulership must be in the hands of the magnates of the state, in the following manner: they should choose a head from among them whom they will obey. In this way, nobody is raised above the rest by lineage, and the head of this government cannot part from justice by acting independently. This form of state is called, in the language of the wise, "aristocracy" (*aristokrâsiyâ*). The word *krâsiyâ* means "government", and thus this means "rule of the magnates". Nowadays, the state of Venice is governed in this manner.

Thirdly, Demokratis' view. He said that administration should be in the hands of the subjects, so that they may avoid oppression by themselves. In this form, government is conducted by election: for instance, people from every village elect one or two whom they deem wise and experienced, and send them as

31 Müteferrika – Şen 1995, 130–131 (copying Kâtib Çelebi); 146–147 (with small abridgements).

representatives to the centre of government where the council is conducted. In their turn, these representatives elect one from among themselves, and in the end a council of ten elected people administers state affairs. These ten people sit on the council for one year and conduct the public affairs. After this term, another ten people are elected in the same way; they inspect the accounts of the previous year's government and punish who that have oppressed people. This form of state is called "democracy" (*dîmukrâsiya*), i.e. Demokratis' opinion, or "rule of the elected"; it is used in England and the Netherlands. All nations and religions are, in general, governed according to one of these three forms of state.

... As for the Muslims, they have complete ignorance of the aforesaid peoples and have not even felt the need of becoming interested in this important task, although they have common borders with the Exalted State and with every opportunity show their enmity and greed towards it. In relation to this, it is imperative that one examines and exposes their state organizations, the rules under which their people settle their affairs, the regulations that ensure the prosperity of their lands, their political laws, their customs, and especially their military ways, which made Europe rise from its small and unimportant state, become dominant where once it was dominated, and expand across the whole world where once it was squeezed into a corner ... Thus, statesmen must learn the situation of the enemy and especially the military manners and the war stratagems recently initiated as a "new order"; in this manner, the Muslim countries will turn away from the sleepiness, bigotry, laziness, and ignorance that cause the surrender of Muslim lands to the infidel, and they will stop the events that open the way to state decline.

28 **Ahmed Resmi** (See Chapter 9)

From *Hülâsatü'l-i'tibâr* ("A summary of admonitions"), translated by Ethan L. Menchinger:[32]

It is impossible to deny that posterity regards the conditions and modes of past history ... Carefully have they studied histories in this fashion, yet heretofore, in every period and in every clime, men have been prey to war and strife ... Reasoned and experienced men, however, who have learned the precept that the prosperity and strength of the worldly realm depend on peace and amity with enemies as circumstances require, know never to glorify battle and act by this logical rule. Preferring peace over war, they have ever bestowed ease and security upon mankind and the state they serve ...

32 Ahmed Resmi – Menchinger 2011, 33, 66–68, 85.

... The goal of peace is desirable and orthodox according to Shari'a and reason. It affords opportunity not only in defeat but even in times of victory. By securing their position, it is known through experience that peacemakers never lose capital but are instead triumphant and enriched with immense profit ... It is said that His Grace Abdurrahman bin 'Avf of the noble elect gained many riches from commerce. To those who inquired, "How did you earn this much wealth?" he supposedly enjoined: "I did not buy or sell living things; I did not sell on credit; in seeing profit I was content with what I received". You see, that there is no greater investment than peace is indubitable. Never has the man been seen who was injured by peace. And when something like this occurs, it has been proven one thousand times that one can mitigate any equivocation or delay when the least opportunity shows itself ... It is plain to reputable men that the adversary's demonstrations, which now assumed the form of goodwill and lenience, were not due to weakness or fear. Rather, it is written in the works of philosophers and especially in the *Nasihatname* Aristotle composed for Alexander that warfare while peace may be feasible is in no way preferable or permissible. In the opinion of Christian states, this rule is at all times held as a guiding principle. They therefore always prefer and promote the way of peace ... It is recorded in popular histories and known in common parlance that in the conflicts between various states for six or seven hundred years, peacemakers have always benefitted ...

... Although it is a difficult matter to winter a year on the Mediterranean Sea, with favorable winds the Russians endured both summer and winter seas for three years ... Such things are the greatest of prodigies, for they are outside the natural conditions of the world. They can occur only once in two or three hundred years, like the campaigns of Sultan Süleyman Khan (Who Resideth in Paradise) to the land of Yemen ... In short, these types of freak occurences appear rarely and subside, like floods or like the great tempests they call hurricanes. They cannot last forever. Consequently, the Russians could turn fortune in their favor because they made such provisions but once in forty years. They cannot always prevail or spoil the general welfare. Ultimately, though, the scoundrels, ignorant of this fine philosophical point, heed not the cosmic prodigies that have occurred in all regions of the world for a thousand years.

29 "Koca Sekbanbaşı" (See Chapter 9)

From *Hulasatü'l-kelam fi reddi'l-avamm* ("The summary of the discourse to refute the rabble"), translated by William Wilkinson:[33]

33 Wilkinson 1820, 240–245.

At the accession to the throne of that flower of Emperors, Sultan Süleyman Cannuni, the science of firing with quickness artillery in position, making use of muskets, and practising such like military exercises, and of defeating large armies with a very small body of troops, was not known amongst the foreign states of Europe and other nations. In this state of things they carried on wars against us; and in such contests the pious enthusiasm of the soldiers of Islam caused the gales of victory and conquest to blow on the side of the Sublime Government. Sometimes, also, they were on that of the enemy. It came to pass by a disposition of Divine Providence, that His Highness Sultan Süleyman having for some years following continually met with bad success in his wars against the Germans, and perceiving that his defeats were owing to the unskilfulness and want of discipline of our soldiers, employed himself in creating a corps of regular troops, and inscribing recruits for that purpose. Immediately a number of idle, and ignorant vagabonds, who disapproved of this institution of troops, quarters, and military regulations, began to murmur, saying, "Was the world originally conquered by the Janissaries? No; it was subdued by the Segbans, and other valiant companies. What sort of corps is this? and what is the meaning of these dresses? What strange things are the water-carriers, cooks, and servants, with their various dresses and titles!" ... Before much time had elapsed, the enemy being broken and routed, and perceiving by experience the advantages of this discipline, obtained peace with a thousand entreaties. Hereupon all the Crals [Christian kings] ... held a council ... They concluded their conference by forming a masterly project, and inventing a method of using with expedition their cannon, muskets, and other instruments of war, and prohibiting their troops from engaging in commerce, they obliged them to pass their whole time in learning military exercises, in which they made such progress that it became at last impossible to break their ranks. In truth, it is well known to those who are acquainted with history, that in the wars which have taken place since the invention of this new system of tactics, the Ottomans have been most frequently worsted, because they found it impossible to make use of their sabres among the infidels as they wished to do; for their regular troops keep in a compact body, pressing their feet together that their order of battle may not be broken ...

By explaining all this, and by giving answers founded on the knowledge of passing events, I have succeeded in convincing many persons, who by falsehood endeavoured to support the unjust opposition of the partisans of the Janissaries.

Bibliography

Primary Sources

Unpublished

Ahmed Resmî Efendi, *Lâyiha*. Istanbul, İstanbul Üniversitesi Kütüphanesi, TY 419, 1b–12a.

Anonymous, *Notitia imperii Othomanici*. London, British Library, Or. MS Harley 3370, ff. 23–79.

Anonymous, *Nizamiyye*. Paris, Bibliothèque nationale, suppl. turc 201.

Anonymous, *Risala feva'idi'l-mülûk*. Paris, Bibliothèque nationale, suppl. turc 221.

Behçetî İbrahim, *Silsiletü'l-Asafiyye fi hakaniyyeti'l-devleti'l-Osmaniye*. Istanbul, Köprülü Kütüphanesi, Hafız Ahmed Paşa, nr. 212.

Beyazizade Ahmed b. Hüsameddin Hasan b. Sinan el-Bosnevi, *al-Tahqiq fi al-redd ala al-zindiq*. Istanbul, Süleymaniye, Esad Efendi, MS 1468.

Beyazizade Ahmed b. Hüsameddin Hasan b. Sinan el-Bosnevi, *al-Usul al-munifa li al-imam Abu Hanifa*. Istanbul, Süleymaniye, Esad Efendi, MS 1140.

Beyazizade Ahmed b. Hüsameddin Hasan b. Sinan el-Bosnevi, *Sak*. Istanbul, Lala İsmail, MS 93.

Derviş Mehmed, *Papasnâme*. Vienna, Österreichische Nationalbibliothek MS Mixt 689; Istanbul, Süleymaniye Kütüphanesi, Saliha Hatun 112/2.

Dürrî Mehmed Efendi, *Nuhbetü'l-emel fî tenkîhi'l-fesâdi ve'l-halel*. Istanbul, Topkapı Sarayı Kütüphanesi, E. H. 1438, ff. 281b–296a.

Hasan Efendi, *Pendnâme-i Hasan* (*Hikâyât-ı makbûle ve nazm-ı mergûb*). Istanbul, Köprülü Kütüphanesi, Ahmed Paşa MS 345.

Hasanbeyzâde Ahmed Paşa, *Usûlü'l-hikem fi nizâmi'l-âlem*. Istanbul, İstanbul Üniversitesi Kütüphanesi, T 6944.

Hemdemî (?), *Nasîhatnâme*. Vienna, Österreische Nationalbibliothek, N.F. 283; Berlin, Staatsbibliothek, Or. Oct. 1598, ff. 125b–172b.

Hezarfen Hüseyin Efendi, *Tenkihü't-tevârîh*. Istanbul, Süleymaniye Kütüphanesi, Hekimoğlu 732.

Kadızâde Mehmed İlmi, *Mesmû'atü'n-nekâyih mecmû'atü'n-nesâyih*. Istanbul, Süleymaniye Kütüphanesi, Hüsrev Paşa, MS 629.

Kadızâde Mehmed İlmi, *Nushü'l-hükkâm sebebü'n-nizâm*. Istanbul, Süleymaniye Kütüphanesi, Aşir Ef. MS 327.

Rodosizade (Rodosluzade) Mehmed, *Terceme-i Kitab-i harac-i Ebu Yusuf*. Istanbul, Süleymaniye Kütüphanesi, Şehid Ali Paşa MS 717; MS 718; Halet Efendi MS 128; Lala İsmail MS 85.

Sarı Abdullah Efendi, *Nasihatü'l-müluk tergiban li-hüsn al-süluk*. Istanbul, Beyazıd Devlet Kütüphanesi, MS 1977.

Saruhanî İbn İsa, *Rümuz-ı kunuz*. Paris, Bibliothèque nationale, suppl. turc 1067.

Seyyid Muhammed b. Seyyid Alâuddin el-Hüseyin er-Razavî, *Miftahü'd-dakaik fi beyani'l-fütüvveti ve'l-hakaik*. Berlin, National Bibliothek, Lanbd. 589; İstanbul Üniversitesi Kütüphanesi, Türkçe Yazmalar, MS 6803.

Sivasî Abdülmecid, *Letâ'ifü'l-ezhâr ve lezâ'izü'l-esmâr* (*Nesâyih-i Mülûk*). Istanbul, Süleymaniye Kütüphanesi, Laleli MS 1613.

Vânî Efendi, *Münşe'ât*. Istanbul, Süleymaniye Kütüphanesi, Ayasofya MS 4308.

Vânî Efendi, *Risâla fî hakk al-farz wa al-sunna wa al-bid'a fî ba'z al-'amal*. Istanbul, Köprülü Kütüphanesi, Lala İsmail 685/1.

Vânî Efendi, *Risâla fî karâhat al-jahr bi al-zikr*. Istanbul, Köprülü Kütüphanesi, Hacı Beşir Ağa 406/3.

Published

Abdi – Unat 1999: Faik Reşit Unat (ed.), *1730 Patrona ihtilâli hakkında bir eser: Abdi tarihi*, Ankara 1999 (1st ed. 1943).

Abu Yusuf – Abbas 1985: Abu Yusuf, *Kitab al-kharaj*, ed. I. 'Abbas, Beirut 1985.

Ahmed Resmi – Menchinger 2011: Ahmed Resmi Efendi, *Hülâsatü'l-i'tibâr. A summary of admonitions: A chronicle of the 1768–1774 Russian-Ottoman War*, Istanbul 2011.

Ahmed Resmi – Parmaksızoğlu 1983: İsmet Parmaksızoğlu (ed.), "Bir Türk diplomatının onsekizinci yüzyıl sonunda devletler arası ilişkilere dair görüşleri", *Belleten* 47 (1983), 527–45.

Ahmedi – Atsız 1949: Nihal Atsız, "Ahmedi ve Dâstân tevârîh-i mülûk-i Âl-i Osman", in Atsız (ed.), *Osmanlı tarihleri I*, Istanbul 1949, 1–35.

Ahmedi – Silay 2004: Kemal Silay (ed.), *Tâce'd-dîn İbrâhîm bin Hızır Ahmedi: History of the kings of the Ottoman lineage and their holy raids against the infidels*, Harvard 2004.

Ahmedi – Ünver 1983: İsmail Ünver, *Ahmedi, İskender-nâme: Inceleme-tıpkıbasım*, Ankara 1983.

Akgündüz 1990–1996: Ahmet Akgündüz, *Osmanlı kanunnâmeleri ve hukukî tahlilleri*, 9 vols, Istanbul 1990–1996.

Akhisari – İpşirli 1979–80: Mehmet İpşirli, "Hasan Kâfî el-Akhisarî ve devlet düzenine ait eseri *Usûlü'l-hikem fî nizâmi'l-âlem*", *Tarih enstitüsü dergisi* 10–11 (1979–80), 239–278.

Akhisari – Karácson 1911: Imre von Karácson – Ludwig von Thalláczy, "Eine Staatsschrift des bosnischen Mohammedaners Molla Hassan Elkjáfi 'über die Art und Weise des Regierens'", *Archiv für slavische philologie* 32 (1911), 139–158.

Akyıldız 1998: Ali Akyıldız, "Sened-i ittifâk'ın tam metni", *İslâm araştırmaları dergisi/Turkish journal of Islamic studies* 2 (1998), 209–222.

Akyıldız – Hanioğlu 2006: Ali Akyıldız – M. Şükrü Hanioğlu, "Negotiating the power of the sultan: The Ottoman *Sened-i ittifak* (Deed of agreement), 1808", in Camron Michael Amin – Benjamin C. Fortna – Elizabeth Frierson (eds), *The modern Middle East: A sourcebook for history*, Oxford 2006, 22–30.

Ali 1860–1868: 'Âlî, *Künhü'l-ahbâr*, 5 vols, Istanbul 1277–85/1860–1868.

Ali – Brookes 2003: Douglas S. Brookes tr., *The Ottoman gentleman of the sixteenth century: Mustafa Âli's* Mevâ'idü'n-nefâ'is fî kavâ'idi'l-mecâlis, "*Tables of delicacies concerning the rules of social gatherings*", Harvard 2003.

Ali – Çerci 2000: Faris Çerçi (ed.), *Gelibolulu Mustafa Âlî ve* Künhü'l-ahbâr*'ında II. Selim, III. Murat ve III. Mehmet devirleri*, 3 vols, Kayseri 2000.

Ali – Demir 2006: Mustafa Demir (ed.), *Gelibolulu Mustafa Âlî, Füsûl-i hall ü akd ve usûl-i harc ü nakd (İslam devletleri tarihi, 622–1599)*, Istanbul 2006.

Ali – Öztekin 1996: Ali Öztekin (ed.), *Gelibolulu Mustafa 'Âlî: Câmi'u'l-buhûr der mecâlis-i sûr. Edisyon kritik ve tahlil*, Ankara 1996.

Ali – Şeker 1997: Mehmet Şeker (intro and ed.), *Gelibolulu Mustafa 'Âlî ve Mevâ'idü'n-nefâis fi-kavâ'ıdi'l-mecâlis*, Ankara 1997.

Ali – Şentürk 2003: M. Hüdai Şentürk (ed.), *Künhü'l-ahbâr c. II: Fâtih Sultân Mehmed devri, 1451–1481*, Ankara 2003.

Ali – Tietze 1975: Mustafa Ali, *Mustafâ 'Âlî's description of Cairo of 1599. Text, transliteration, notes by Andreas Tietze*, Vienna 1975.

Ali – Tietze 1979–1982: Mustafa Ali, *Mustafâ 'Âlî's counsel for sultans of 1581. Text, transliteration, notes by Andreas Tietze*, 2 vols, Vienna 1979–1982.

Ali Çavuş – Şahin 1979: İlhan Şahin, "Timar sistemi hakkında bir risale", *Tarih dergisi* 32 (1979), 905–935.

Ali Cemali Efendi – Kaplan – Yıldız 2013: Mahmut Kaplan – Sümeyye Yıldız, "Ali Cemâlî Efendi'nin *Risale-i nasihat*'i", *Uluslararası sosyal araştırmalar dergisi* 6/27 (2013), 263–278.

Amasi – Coşar 2012: A. Mevhibe Coşar (ed.), *Abdüsselâm el-Amasî: Tuhfetü'l-ümerâ ve minhatü'l-vüzerâ (Siyaset ahlâkı). İnceleme—metin—tıpkıbasım* (2nd ed.), Istanbul 2012.

Amasi – Yılmaz 1998: Mehmet Şakir Yılmaz, "Political thought in the beginning of the Ottoman Empire as expressed in Ahmed bin Husameddin Amasi's *Kitab-ı miratü'l-mülûk* (1406)", unpublished M.A. dissertation, Bilkent University 1998.

Aşık Mehmed – Ak 2007: Mahmut Ak (ed.): *Âşık Mehmed: Menâzırü'l-avâlim*, 3 vols, Ankara 2007.

Aşıkpaşazade – Giese 1929: Friedrich Giese (ed.), *Die altosmanische Chronik des 'Āšikpašazāde*, Leipzig 1929.

Aşıkpaşazade – Atsız 1949: Nihal Atsız ed., *Aşıkpaşaoğlu Ahmed Âşıkî: Tevârih-i Âl-i Osman*, in Atsız (ed.), *Osmanlı tarihleri I*, Istanbul 1949, 77–319.

Âtıf Efendi – Gemici 2009: Nurettin Gemici, "Âtıf Mustafa Efendi ve sıvış yılları sorununun halline dair telhisi", *İslâm araştırmaları dergisi* 21 (2009), 51–74.

Avni Ömer – Uzunçarşılı 1951: İsmail Hakkı Uzunçarşılı, "Kanun-i Osmanı mefhum-i defter-i hakani", *Belleten* 15 (1951), 381–399.

Aydoğdu 2008: Nergiz Aydoğdu, "Makyavelist düşüncenin Türkiye'ye girişi: Onsekizinci yüzyıl Osmanlı siyaset felsefesi", unpublished Ph. D. dissertation, Marmara University 2008.

Ayn Ali – Tuncer 1962: Hadiye Tuncer, *Aynî Ali Efendi: Osmanlı devleti arazi kanunları (Kanunname-i Âl-ı Osman)*, Ankara 1962.

Ayn Ali 1978: Ayn-ı Ali Efendi, *Kavânîn-i Âl-i Osman der hülâsa-i mezâmin-i defter-i divan*, (repr.) Istanbul 1978.

Aziz Efendi – Murphey 1985: Rhoads Murphey (ed.), *Kanûn-nâme-i sultânî li 'Azîz Efendi. Aziz Efendi's Book of sultanic laws and regulations: An agenda for reform by a seventeenth-century Ottoman statesman*, Harvard 1985.

Bacqué-Grammont 1997: Jean-Louis Bacqué-Grammont (ed.), *La première histoire de France en turc ottoman*, Paris 1997.

Bayatlı – Kırzıoğlu 1949: Fahrettin Kırzıoğlu (ed.), *Bayatlı Mahmud Oğlu Hasan: Câm-ı Cem-Âyîn*, in Atsız ed., *Osmanlı Tarihleri I*, Istanbul 1949, 371–403.

Behic – Çınar 1992: Ali Osman Çınar, "Es-Seyyid Mehmed Emin Behic'in *Sevanihü'l-Levayih*'i ve değerlendirilmesi", unpublished M.A. dissertation, Marmara University 1992.

Belgradi – Bitiçi 2001: Taxhidin Bitiçi, "Münîri-i Belgrâdî ve Silsiletü'l-Mukarrebîn Adlı Eseri", unpublished M.A. dissertation, Marmara University 2001.

Beyani – Kutluk 1997: İbrahim Kutluk (ed.), *Beyâni Mustafa bin Carullah: Tezkiretü'ş-şuarâ*, Ankara 1997.

Beydilli 2001: Kemal Beydilli, "Kabakçı isyanı akabinde hazırlanan Hüccet-i Şer'iyye", *Türk kültürü incelemeleri dergisi* 4 (2001), 33–48.

Birgili – Duman 2000: Musa Duman (ed.), *Birgili Muhammed Efendi, Vasiyyet-name: Dil incelemesi, metin, sözlük, ekler indeksi ve tıpkıbasım*, Istanbul 2000.

Bitlisi – Başaran 2000: Orhan Başaran, "İdrîs-i Bitlisî'nin *Heşt Bihişt*'inin Hâtime'si", unpublished Ph. D. dissertation, Atatürk University – Erzurum 2000.

Bitlisi – Tavakkoli 1974: Hasan Tavakkolî, "İdrîs-i Bitlisî'nin *Kanun-ı Şehinşahî*'sinin tenkidli neşri ve türkçeye tercümesi", unpublished Ph.D. dissertation, Istanbul University 1974.

Busbecq – Forster 1927: Edward Seymour Forster (ed.), *The Turkish letters of Ogier Ghiselin de Busbecq, imperial ambassador at Constantinople, 1554–1562. Translated from the Latin of the Elzevir Edition of 1633*, Oxford 1927 (repr. 1968).

Cabi – Beyhan 2003: Mehmet Ali Beyhan (ed.), *Câbî Ömer Efendi: Câbî târîhi (Târîh-i Sultân Selîm-i Sâlis ve Mahmûd-ı Sânî). Tahlîl ve tenkidli metin*, 2 vols, Ankara 2003.

Çağman 1995: Ergin Çağman, "III. Selim'e takdim edilen layıhalara göre Osmanlı Devleti'nde iktisadi değişme", unpublished M.A. dissertation, Marmara University 1995.

Canikli Ali Paşa – Özkaya 1969: Yücel Özkaya, "Canikli Ali Paşa'nın risalesi 'Tedâbîrü'l-ğazavât'", *Ankara Üniversitesi dil-tarih-coğrafya fakültesi tarih bölümü tarih araştırmaları dergisi* 7/12–13 (1969), 119–191.

Cantemir – Tindal 1734: Demetrius Cantemir, *The history of the growth and decay of the Othman Empire*, trans. N. Tindal, London 1734.

Celalzade – Balcı 1996: Mustafa Balcı, "Celalzade'nin *Mevahibü'l-hallak fi meratibi'l-ahlak* isimli eseri", unpublished M.A. dissertation, Harran University 1996.

Celalzade – Kappert 1981: Petra Kappert (ed.), *Geschichte Sultan Süleymân Kânûnîs von 1520 bis 1557, oder* Tabakât ül-Memâlik ve Derecât ül-Mesâlik *von Celâlzâde Mustafâ genannt Koca Nişâncı*, Wiesbaden 1981.

Celalzade – Yılmaz 2011: Ayhan Yılmaz, *Kanunî'nin tarihçisinden Muhteşem Çağ ve Kanunî Sultan Süleyman*, Istanbul 2011.

Cevdet 1891/1892: Ahmet Cevdet Paşa, *Târîh-i Cevdet*, vol. VI, 1309/1891–2.

Dawwani – Deen 1939: S. H. Deen (ed.), *The English translation of "The Akhlak-i-Jalali", a code of morality in Persian composed by Jalal-ud-din Mohammad alias Allama Dawwani*, Lahore 1939.

Dawwani – Thompson 1839: William Francis Thompson (ed.), *Practical philosophy of the Muhammadan people, exhibited in its professed connexion with the European ... being a translation of the Ahklâk-i-Jalâly, the most esteemed ethical work of Middle Asia*, London 1839.

Dede Cöngi – Tuna 2011: A. Sabit Tuna, "Osmanlı siyasetname geleneği içinde Dede Cöngi'nin yeri ve eserinin tahlili", unpublished M.A. dissertation, Istanbul University 2011.

Defterdar – Özcan 1995: Abdülkadir Özcan (ed.), *Defterdar Sarı Mehmed Paşa: Zübde-i vekayiât. Tahlil ve metin (1066–1116/1656–1704)*, Ankara 1995.

Defterdar – Uğural 1990: Hüseyin Ragıp Uğural (ed.), *Defterdar Sarı Mehmed Paşa: Devlet adamlarına öğütler. Osmanlılarda devlet düzeni*, Izmir 1990 (1st ed. Ankara 1969).

Defterdar – Wright 1935: Walter Livingston Wright Jr., *Ottoman statecraft. The book of counsel for vesirs and governors* (Nasâ'ih ül-vüzera ve'l-ümera) *of Sari Mehmed Pasha, the Defterdâr. Turkish text with introduction, translation and notes*, Princeton 1935.

Dımışkî – Dorogi – Hazai 2011–2014: Ilona Dorogi – György Hazai, "Zum Werk von Ebû Bekr b. Bahram Dimişkî über die Geschichte und den Zustand des osmanischen Reiches", *Archivum Ottomanicum* 28 (2011), 49–94; 29 (2012), 193–325; 30 (2013), 303–352; 31 (2014), 167–350.

Ebussuud – Düzdağ 1972: M. Ertoğrul Düzdağ, *Şeyhülislâm Ebussuûd Efendi fetvaları ışığında 16. asır Türk hayatı*, Istanbul 1972.

Esad Efendi – Yılmazer 2000: Ziya Yılmazer (ed.), *Sahhâflar Şeyhi-zâde Seyyid Mehmed Es'ad Efendi: Vak'a-nüvîs Es'ad Efendi tarihi (Bâhir Efendi'nin zeyl ve ilâveleriyle), 1237–1821–1826*, Istanbul 2000.

Evliya Çelebi – Dankoff 1990: Robert Dankoff, *Evliya Çelebi in Bitlis. The relevant section of the Seyahatname*, Leiden 1990.

Eyyubi – Özcan 1994: Abdülkadir Özcan (ed.), *Eyyubî Efendi Kânûnnâmesi. Tahlil ve metin*, Istanbul 1994.

al-Farabi – Walzer 1985: Richard Walzer (ed.), *Al-Farabi on the perfect state. Abû Nasr al-Fârâbî's* Mabâdi' ârâ' ahl al-madîna al-fâdila. *A revised text with introduction, translation, and commentary*, Oxford 1985.

Feridun Bey 1848: Ferîdûn Bey, *Mecmû'a-yı münşe'ât-i Ferîdûn Bey*, 2 vols, Istanbul 1264/1848.

Fodor 1989: Pál Fodor (ed.), *A janicsárok törvényei, 1606*, Budapest 1989.

Gibb 1900–1909: Elias John Wilkinson Gibb, *A history of Ottoman poetry*, 6 vols, London 1900–1909.

Hadžibegić 1947: Hamid Hadžibegić, "Rasprava Ali Čauša iz Sofije o timarskoj organizaciji u XVII stoljeću", *Glasnik zemajskog Muzeja u Sarajevo*, n.s. 2 (1947), 139–205.

Halim Efendi – Şahin 2009: Ayşe Şahin, "Abdullah Halim Efendi'nin *Seyfü'l-izzet ila hazreti sahibi'd-devlet* adlı kitabının çevirim yazısı ve değerlendirilmesi", unpublished M.A. thesis, Marmara University 2009.

Hasan Bey-zâde – Aykut 2004: Hasan Bey-zâde Ahmed Paşa, *Hasan Bey-zâde târîhi*, ed. Şevki Nezihi Aykut, Ankara 2004.

Hezarfen – İlgürel 1998: Hüseyin Hezarfen Efendi, *Telhîsü'l-beyân fî kavânîn-i Âl-i 'Osmân*, ed. Sevim İlgürel, Ankara 1998.

Howard 1996: Douglas A. Howard, "Ottoman administration and the tîmâr system: *Sûret-i Kânûnnâme-i 'Osmânî Berây-ı Tîmâr Dâden*", *Journal of Turkish studies* 20 (1996) [In memoriam Abdülbaki Gölpınarlı, II], 46–125.

Ibn Haldun – Pirizade 2008: Yavuz Yıldırım – Sami Erdem – Halit Özkan – M. Cüneyt Kaya (eds), *İbn Haldun: Mukaddime osmanlı tercümesi. Mütercim Pîrîzâde Mehmed Sâhib*, 3 vols, Istanbul 2008.

Ibn Khaldun – Rosenthal 1958: Franz Rosenthal (ed.), *Ibn Khaldun, The Muqaddimah: An introduction to history*, Princeton 1958.

Ibn Khaldun – Rosenthal – Dawood 1969: Franz Rosenthal (tr.), *Ibn Khaldûn, The Muqaddimah: An introduction to history*, ed. and abridged by N.J. Dawood, Princeton 1969.

Ibn Nüceym – Sahillioğlu 1966: Halil Sahillioğlu, "İbn-i Nüceym'in rüşvet hakkındaki risalesi", *Ankara Üniversitesi hukuk fakültesi dergisi* 22/1 (1966), 691–697.

İbrahim – Acar 2008: Hayrullah Acar, "İbrahim b. Muhammed: *Âdâbu'l-hilâfe ve esbâbu'l-hisâfe*", unpublished Ph.D. dissertation, Ankara University 2008.

İnalcık 1965: Halil İnalcık, "Adâletnâmeler", *Türk tarih belgeleri dergisi*, II-3/4 (1965), 49–145.

İpşirli 1994: Mehmet İpşirli, "Osmanlı devlet teşkilâtına dair bir eser: *Kavânîn-i osmanî ve râbıta-i Âsitâne*", *Tarih enstitüsü dergisi* 14 (1994), 9–35.

İz 1966: Fahir İz, *Eski Türk Edebiyatında Nazım. XIII. yüzyıldan XIX. yüzyıl ortasına kadar yazmalardan seçilmiş metinler*, I. Cild, I. Bölüm, Istanbul 1966.

Kadı Fadlullah – Altay 2008: Ahmet Altay, "Düstûrü'l-mülk vezîrü'l-melik (Metin ve değerlendirme)", unpublished M.A. dissertation, Selçuk University 2008.

Kara Çelebi-zâde – Kaya 2003: Kara Çelebi-zâde Abdülaziz Efendi, *Ravzatü'l-ebrâr zeyli (Tahlîl ve metin)*, ed. Nevzat Kaya, Ankara 2003.

Karal 1941–1943: Enver Ziya Karal, "Nizâm-ı Cedîd'e dâir lâyihalar", *Tarih vesikaları* 1/6 (1941), 414–425; 2/8 (1942), 104–111; 2/11 (1943), 342–351; 2/12 (1943), 424–432.

Kashifi – Keene 1850: Rev. H. G. Keene (ed.), *Akhlâk-i Muhsinî, or The morals of the beneficent, literally translated from the Persian of Husain Vâiz Kâshifî*, Hertford 1850.

Kâtib Çelebi 1733: Kâtib Çelebi, *Takvîmü't-tevârîh*, Istanbul (İbrahim Müteferrika ed.), 1146/1733.

Kâtib Çelebi 1869–1871: Kâtib Çelebi, *Fezleke*, 2 vols, Istanbul 1286–1287/1869–1871.

Kâtib Çelebi 1888/89: Kâtib Çelebi, *Mîzânü'l-Hak fi İhtiyâri'l-Âhak*, Istanbul 1306/1888–1889.

Kâtib Çelebi – Behrnauer 1857: Walter Friedrich Adolf Behrnauer, "Hâğî Chalfa's Dustûru'l-'amal. Ein Beitrag zur osmanischen Finanzgeschichte", *Zeitschrift* der *Deutschen Morgenländischen Gesellschaft* 11 (1857), 111–132.

Kâtib Çelebi – Gökyay 1968: Orhan Şaik Gökyay, *Kâtip Çelebi'den seçmeler*, Istanbul 1968.

Kâtib Çelebi – Yurtoğlu 2012: Bilal Yurtoğlu (ed.), *Katip Çelebi'nin Yunan, Roma ve Hristiyan tarihi hakkındaki risalesi*, Ankara 2012.

Kâtib Chelebi – Lewis 1957: Geoffrey L. Lewis (tr.), *The balance of truth, by Kâtib Chelebi*, London 1957.

Kay Kaus – Birnbaum 1981: Eleazar Birnbaum (ed.), *The book of advice by King Kay Kâ'us ibn Iskander. The earliest Old Ottoman version of his* Kâbûsnâme, Harvard 1981.

Kemalpaşazade – Özcan 2000: Tahsin Özcan, "İbn Kemal'in para vakıflarına dair risalesi", *İslam araştırmaları dergisi* 4 (2000), 31–41.

Kınalızade – Koç 2007: Mustafa Koç (ed.), *Kınalızâde Ali Çelebi: Ahlâk-ı Alâî*, Istanbul 2007.

Kırımlu Hafiz Hüsam – Tekin 2008: Şinasi Tekin (ed.), *Kırımlu Hafiz Hüsam: Teressül (Hacı Selimağa, Nurbanu No:122/5). Edition in transcription, translation into Turkish, notes and facsimile*, Harvard 2008.

Koç – Yeşil 2012: Yunus Koç – Fatih Yeşil (eds), *Nizâm-ı Cedîd kanunları*, Ankara 2012.

Koçi Bey – Aksüt 1939: A. Kemal Aksüt (ed.), *Koçi Bey risalesi*, Istanbul 1939.

Koçi Bey – Behrnauer 1861: Walter Friedrich Adolf Behrnauer, "Koğabeg's Abhandlung über den Verfall des osmanischen Staatsgebäudes seit Sultan Suleiman dem Grossen", *Zeitschrift* der *Deutschen Morgenländischen Gesellschaft* 15 (1861), 272–332.

Koçi Bey – Behrnauer 1864: Walter Friedrich Adolf Behrnauer, "Das Nasîhatnâme. Dritter Beitrag zur osmanischen Finanzgeschichte", *Zeitschrift* der *Deutschen Morgenländischen Gesellschaft* 18 (1864), 699–740.

Koçi Bey – Çakmakcıoğlu 2008: Seda Çakmakcıoğlu (ed.), *Koçi Bey risaleleri*, Istanbul 2008.

Kuşmanî – İşbilir 2006: Ömer İşbilir (ed.), *Nizâm-ı Cedîde dâir bir risâle: Zebîre-i Kuşmânî fî ta'rîf-i nizâm-ı ilhâmî*, Ankara 2006.

Kuşmanî – Yıldız 2007: Aysel Danacı Yıldız (ed.), *Ubeydullah Kuşmanî, Ebubekir Efendi: Asiler ve gaziler; Kabakçı Mustafa risalesi*, Istanbul 2007.

La Croix 1695: Sieur de La Croix, *La Turquie cretienne sous la puissante protection de Louis le Grand, protecteur unique du Cristianisme en Orient, contenant l'état present des nations et des églises grecque, armenienne et maronite, dans l'Empire Otoman*, Paris 1695.

Lami'i-zade – Çalışkan 1997: Yaşar Çalışkan (ed.), *Lâmi'î-zâde Abdullah Çelebi: Latîfeler*, Istanbul 1997.

Latifi – Pekin 1977: Nermin Suner (Pekin) (ed.), *Lâtifî: Evsâf-ı İstanbul*, Istanbul 1977.

Latifi – Yérasimos 2001: Stéphane Yérasimos (ed.), *Éloge d'Istanbul, suivi du Traité de l'invective*, Paris 2001.

Lütfi Pasha – Gibb 1962: H. A. R. Gibb, "Lutfî Paşa on the Ottoman Caliphate", *Oriens* 15 (1962), 287–295.

Lütfî Paşa – Tschudi 1910: Rudolph Tschudi (ed.), *Das Asafname des Lütfi Pascha, nach den Handschriften zu Wien, Dresden und Konstantinopel*, Berlin 1910.

Lütfî Paşa – Kütükoğlu 1991: Mübahat Kütükoğlu, "Lütfî Paşa Âsafnâmesi (Yeni bir metin denemesi)", in *Prof. Dr. Bekir Kütükoğlu'na armağan*, Istanbul 1991, 49–120.

Machiavelli – Thomson 1910: Niccolò Machiavelli, *The Prince*, trans. N. H. Thomson, New York 1910.

Mahmud Efendi – Tunalı 2013: Gülçin Tunalı, "Appropriation of ancient Athens via Greek channels for the sake of good advice as reflected in *Tarih-i medinetü'l-hükemâ*", unpublished Ph.D. dissertation, University of Bochum 2013.

Mahmud Raif Efendi – Beydilli – Şahin 2001: Kemal Beydilli – İlhan Şahin (eds), *Mahmud Râif Efendi ve* Nizâm-ı Cedîd*'e dâir eseri*, Ankara 2001.

Mercator 1610: Gerardus Mercator, *Atlas minor Geradi Mercatoris à I. Hondio plurimis aeneis tabulis auctus atque illustratus*, Amsterdam 1610.

Mesihi – Ménage 1988: Victor L. Ménage, "The *Gül-i sad-berg* of Mesîhî", *Osmanlı araştırmaları/The journal of Ottoman studies* 7–8 (1988), 11–32.

Moralı Ali Efendi – Refik 1911: Ahmed Refik (ed.), "Moralı Esseyid Ali Efendi'nin Sefaretnâmesi", *Tarih-i Osmani encümeni mecmuası* 19–23 (1329/1911), 19:1120–1138, 20: 1246–1259, 21:1333–1343, 22:1378–1390, 23:1458–1466, 24: 1548–1560.

Murad III – Felek 2014: Özgen Felek (ed.), *Kitâbü'l-menâmât. Sultan III. Murad'ın rüya mektupları*, Istanbul 2014.

Müteferrika – Şen 1995: Adil Şen (ed.), *İbrahim Müteferrika ve* Usûlü'l-Hikem fî Nizâmi'l-Ümem, Ankara 1995.

Nabi – Kaplan 2008: Mahmut Kaplan (ed.), *Hayriyye-i Nâbî*, Ankara 2008.

Nabi – Pala 1989: İbrahim Pala (ed.), *Şâir Nâbî: Hayriyye*, Istanbul 1989.

Nahifi – İpşirli 1997: Mehmet İpşirli, "Nahîfî Süleyman Efendi: *Nasihatü'l-vüzera*", *Tarih enstitüsü dergisi* 15 (1997), 15–27.

Na'ima 1864–1866: Mustafa Na'ima, *Târîh-i Nâ'imâ*, 6 vols, Istanbul 1281/1864–66.

Na'ima – İpşirli 2007: Mehmet İpşirli (ed.), *Târih-i Na'imâ (Ravzatü'l-Hüseyn fî hulâsati ahbâri'l-hâfikayn)*, Ankara 2007.

Neşri – Unat – Köymen 1987: Faik Reşit Unat – Mehmed A. Köymen (eds), *Mehmed Neşrî: Kitâb-ı Cihan-nümâ (Neşrî tarihi)*, 2 vols, Ankara 1987 (1st ed. 1949).

Nişancı Mehmed Paşa – Konyalı 1949: İbrahim Hakkı Konyalı (ed.), *Karamanlı Nişancı Mehmed Paşa: Osmanlı sultanları tarihi*, in Atsız (ed.), *Osmanlı tarihleri I*, Istanbul 1949, 321–369.

Nizam al-Mulk – Darke 1960: Hubert Darke (tr.), *The book of government or rules for kings. The* Siyâsat-nâma *or* Siyar al-mulûk *of Nizâm al-Mulk*, New Haven 1960.

Nu'man Efendi – Prokosch 1972: Erich Prokosch, *Molla und Diplomat. Der Bericht des Ebû Sehil Nu'mân Efendi über die österreichisch-osmanische Grenzziehung nach dem Belgrader Frieden 1740/41*, Graz 1972.

Nu'man Efendi – Savaş 1999: Ali İbrahim Savaş (ed.), *Ebû Sehl Nu'mân Efendi: Tedbîrât-ı pesendîde (Beğenilmiş tedbirler)*, Ankara 1999.

Nuri – Akkaya 2003: Hüseyin Akkaya, *Abdülahad Nuri ve divanı*, Istanbul 2003.

Orhonlu 1967: Cengiz Orhonlu, "Osmanlı teşkilâtına aid küçük bir risâle: 'Risâle-i terceme'", *Belgeler* 4/7–8 (1967), 39–50.

Öğreten 1989: Ahmet Öğreten, "Nizâm-ı Cedîd'e dair Islâhât Lâyıhaları", unpublished M.A. dissertation, Istanbul University 1989.

Ömer Faik – Sarıkaya 1979: Ahmet Sarıkaya, "Ömer Fa'ik Efendi, Nizamü'l-Atik", unpublished dissertation, Bitirme Tezi, Istanbul University 1979.

Özcan 2000: Abdülkadir Özcan (ed.), *Anonim Osmanlı tarihi (1099–1116/1688–1704)*, Ankara 2000.

Penah Efendi – Berker 1942–1943: Aziz Berker, "Mora ihtilâli tarihçesi veya Penah Efendi mecmuası, 1769", *Tarih vesikaları* 2 (1942–1943), 63–80, 153–160, 228–240, 309–320, 385–400, 473–480.

Penah Efendi – Sarris 1993: Neoklis Sarris, *Προεπαναστατική Ελλάδα και οσμανικό κράτος: από το χειρόγραφο του Σουλεϋμάν Πενάχ Εφέντη του Μοραΐτη (1785)* [Pre-revolution

Greece and the Ottoman State: From Moreot Süleyman Penah Efendi's Manuscript (1785)], Athens 1993.
Petrossian 1987: A.Y. Petrossian (ed.), *Мебде-и канун-и йеничери оджагы тарихи—Mebde-i kanun-i yeniçeri ocağı tarihi*, Moscow 1987.
Raşid 1865: Raşid Efendi, *Tarih-i Raşid*, 6 vols, Istanbul 1282/1865.
Ratıb Efendi – Arıkan 1996: Sema Arıkan, "Nizam-ı Cedit'in kaynaklarından Ebubekir Ratıb Efendi'nin Büyük Layıhası", unpublished Ph.D. dissertation, Istanbul University 1996.
Ratıb Efendi – Yıldız 2013: Aysel Yıldız, "Şehzadeye öğütler: Ebûbekir Ratıb Efendi'nin Şehzade Selim'e (III) bir mektubu", *Osmanlı araştırmaları/The journal of Ottoman studies* 42 (2013), 233–274.
Razi – Algar 1982: Hamid Algar (ed. – tr.), *The path of God's bondsmen from origin to return (Merşâd al-'ebâd men al-mabdâ' elâ'l-ma'âd). A Sufi compendium by Najm al-Dîn Râzî, known as Dâya*, Delmar NY 1982.
Saruhani – Özgül 2004: Ayhan Özgül, "İlyas b. Îsâ-yı Saruhânî'nin 'Rumûzü'l-künûz' adlı eserin transkripsiyonu ve değerlendirilmesi", unpublished M.A. dissertation, Kırıkkale University 2004.
Selaniki – İpşirli 1999: Selânikî Mustafâ Efendi, *Târih-i Selânikî*, ed. Mehmet İpşirli, 2 vols, Ankara 1999.
Sertoğlu 1992: Midhat Sertoğlu, *Sofyalı Ali Çavuş kanunnâmesi*, Istanbul 1992.
Seyyid Mustafa – Beydilli 1987: Kemal Beydilli, "İlk mühendislerimizden Seyyid Mustafa ve Nizâm-ı Cedîd'e dair risâlesi", *Tarih enstitüsü dergisi* 13 (1983–1987), 387–479.
Shaybani – Khadduri 1966: Majid Khadduri (ed.), *The Islamic law of nations: Shaybani's Siyar*, Baltimore 1966.
Shemesh 1958–1969: Ben Shemesh, *Taxation in Islamic law, Volume I: Yahya b. Adam's Kitab al-Kharaj*, Leiden 1958; *Volume II: Qudama b. Ja'far's Kitab al-Kharaj*, Leiden 1965; *Volume III: Abu Yusuf's Kitab al-Kharaj*, Leiden 1969.
Silahdar – Refik 1928: Silâhdâr Fındıklılı Mehmed Ağa, *Silâhdâr Tarihi*, Ahmed Refik (ed.), 2 vols, Istanbul 1928.
Silahdar – Türkal 2012: Nazire Karaçay Türkal, "Silahdar Fındıklılı Mehmed Ağa, Zeyl-i Fezleke (1065–22 Ca 1106/1654–7 Şubat 1695)", unpublished Ph.D. dissertation, Marmara University, Istanbul 2012.
Sinan Paşa – Ertaylan 1961: İ. Hikmet Ertaylan (ed.), *Sinan Paşa: Maarifnâme*, Istanbul 1961.
Sinan Paşa – Tulum 2013: Mertol Tulum (ed.), *Sinan Paşa: Maârif-nâme. Özlü sözler ve öğütler kitabı*, Ankara 2013.
Solakzade 1879: Mehmed Solakzade, *Tarih-i Solakzade*, Istanbul 1297/1879.
Süreyya – Akbayar 1996: Mehmed Süreyya, *Sicill-i Osmanî*, 6 vols, ed. Nuri Akbayar, Istanbul 1996.

Şânizâde – Yılmazer 2008: Ziya Yılmazer (ed.), *Şâni-zâde Mehmed 'Atâ'ullah Efendi: Şânî-zâde târîhi* [*Osmanlı tarihi* (*1223–1237/1808–1821*)], Istanbul 2008.

Şerif Efendi – Çağman 1999: Ergin Çağman, "III. Selim'e sunulan bir ıslahat raporu: Mehmet Şerif Efendi layihası", *Dîvân—ilmî araştırmalar* 7 (1999/2), 217–233.

Şeyhoğlu – Korkmaz 1973: Zeynep Korkmaz (ed.), *Sadru'd-dîn Şeyhoğlu, Marzubân-nâme tercümesi. İnceleme—metin—sözlük—tıpkıbasım*, Ankara 1973.

Şeyhoğlu – Yavuz 1991: Kemal Yavuz (ed.), *Şeyhoğlu: Kenzü'l-kübera ve mehekkü'l-ulemâ* (*İnceleme, metin, indeks*), Ankara 1991.

Şirazî – Dokuzlu 2012: Emrah Dokuzlu, "Alâî b. Muhibbî eş-Şirâzî'nin "Düstûru'l-vüzerâ" isimli siyasetnâmesinin metin ve tahlili", unpublished M.A. dissertation, Istanbul University 2012.

Taşköprüzade – Bakry – Abu'l-Nur 1968: K. K. Bakry – A. Abu'l-Nur (eds), *Miftâh as-Sa'âdah wa misbâh as-siyâdah fî mawdu'ât al-ulûm, by Ahmad b. Mustafa* (*Tashkupri-zadah*), Cairo 1968.

Tekin 1989: Şinasi Tekin, "XIV. yüzyılda yazılmış gazilik tarikası 'gaziliğin yolları' adlı bir eski Anadolu Türkçesi metni ve gazâ/cihâd kavramları hakkında", *Journal of Turkish studies* 13 (1989), 139–204.

Terzioğlu 2010: Derin Terzioğlu, "Sunna-Minded Sufi preachers in service of the Ottoman state: The *Nasîhatnâme* of Hasan addressed to Murad IV", *Archivum Ottomanicum* 27 (2010), 241–312.

Toroser 2011: Tayfun Toroser (ed.), *Kavanin-i yeniçeriyan—Yeniçeri kanunları*, Istanbul 2011.

Tursun Beg – İnalcık – Murphey 1978: Halil İnalcık – Rhoads Murphey (eds), *The history of Mehmed the Conqueror by Tursun Beg*, Minneapolis – Chicago 1978.

Tursun Beg – Tulum 1977: Mertol Tulum (ed.), *Tursun Bey: Târîh-i Ebü'l-feth*, Istanbul 1977.

Tursun Bey – Berardi 2007: Luca Berardi (tr.), *Tursun Bey: La conquista di Costantinopoli. Introduzione e note di Jean-Louis Bacqué-Grammont e Michele Bernardini*, Milan 2007.

Unat 1941: Faik R. Unat, "Ahmet III devrine ait bir ıslahat takriri", *Tarih vesikaları* 1 (1941), 107–121.

Uşşakizade – Gündoğdu 2005: Uşşakizade Ibrahim Hasib Efendi, *Uşşakîzâde Târîhi* (*Osmanlı ilmiye teşkilatı için mühim bir kaynak*), ed. Raşit Gündoğdu, Istanbul 2005.

Üstüvani – Yurdaydın 1963: Hüseyin Yurdaydın, "Türkiye'nin dini tarihi ile ilgili notlar: I. Üstüvani Risalesi", *Ankara Üniversitesi ilahiyat fakültesi dergisi* 10/1 (1963), 71–78.

Üveysi – von Diez 1811: Heinrich Friedrich von Diez (ed. – tr.), *Ermahnung an Islambol, oder Strafgedicht des turkischen Dichters Uweïssi über die Ausartung der Osmanen*, Berlin 1811.

Vasıf – İlgürel 1978: Ahmed Vâsıf Efendi, *Mehâsinü'l-âsâr ve hakâikü'l-ahbâr*, ed. Mücteba İlgürel, Istanbul 1978.

Veysi – Altun 2011: Mustafa Altun (ed.), *Hâb-nâme-i Veysî*, Istanbul 2011.

Veysi – Salimzjanova 1976: F. A. Salimzjanova, *Вейси. Хаб-Наме. Книга сновидения. Критический текст, перевод с турецкого, введение и примечания*, Moscow 1976.

Wilkinson 1820: William Wilkinson, *An account of the principalities of Wallachia and Moldavia*, London 1820 (repr. New York 1971).

Yahya bin Mehmed – Tekin 1971: Şinasi Tekin (ed.), *Menâhicü'l-inşâ. The earliest Ottoman chancery manual by Yahyâ bin Mehmed el-Kâtib from the 15th Century*, Cambridge MA 1971.

Yazıcıoğlu – Sakaoğlu 1999: Yazıcıoğlu Ahmed Bîcan, *Dürr-i meknun (Saklı inciler)*, ed. Necdet Sakaoğlu, Istanbul 1999.

Yeşil 2012: Fatih Yeşil, *Bir Osmanlı gözüyle Avrupa siyasetinde güç oyunu: Avrupa'ya mensûb olan mîzân-ı umûr-ı hâriciyye beyânındadır*, Istanbul 2012.

Yusuf Khass Hajib – Dankoff 1983: Robert Dankoff (tr. – intro. – notes), *Yûsuf Khâss Hâjib, Wisdom of royal glory (Kutadgu Bilig). A Turko-Islamic mirror for princes*, Chicago – London 1983.

Yücel 1988: Yaşar Yücel (ed.), *Osmanlı Devlet Teşkilâtına dair Kaynaklar: Kitâb-i müstetâb—Kitâbu mesâlihi'l-müslimîn ve menâfi'i'l-mü'minîn—Hırzü'l-mülûk*, Ankara 1988.

Zülfikar – Güler 2007: Mustafa Güler (ed.), *Zülfikar Paşa'nın Viyana sefâreti ve esâreti, 1099–1103/1688–1692: Cerîde-i takrîrât-i Zülfikar Efendi der kal'a-i Beç*, Istanbul 2007.

Secondary Literature

Abou Hadj 1988: Rifaat Abou Hadj, "The Ottoman nasihatname as a discourse over 'morality'", in Abdeljelil Temimi (ed.), *Mélanges Professeur Robert Mantran*, Zaghouan 1988, 17–30.

Abou-El-Haj 1974: Rifaat Ali Abou-El-Haj, "Ottoman attitudes toward peacemaking: The Karlowitz case", *Der Islam* 51 (1974), 131–137.

Abou-El-Haj 1984: Rifa'at Ali Abou-El-Haj, *The 1703 rebellion and the structure of Ottoman politics*, Leiden 1984.

Abou-El-Haj 1991: Rifaat Ali Abou-El-Haj, "Aspects of the legitimization of Ottoman rule as reflected in the preambles of two early *liva kanunnameler*", Turcica 21–23 (1991), 371–383.

Abou-El-Haj 2005: Rifaat Ali Abou-El-Haj, *Formation of the modern state. The Ottoman Empire, sixteenth to eighteenth centuries*, 2nd ed., Syracuse 2005.

Abu-Manneh 1982: Butrus Abu-Manneh, "The Naqshbandiyya-Mujaddidiyya in the Ottoman lands in the early 19th century", *Die Welt des Islams* 22 (1982), 1–36.

Abu-Manneh 1994: Butrus Abu-Manneh, "The Islamic roots of the Gülhane rescript", *Die Welt des Islams* 34 (1994), 173–203.

Afsaruddin 2014: Asma Afsaruddin, "Politics and governance in pre-modern Islamic thought", *Storia del pensiero politico* 3 (2014), 381–398.

Ágoston 2011: Gábor Ágoston, "Military transformation in the Ottoman Empire and Russia, 1500–1800", *Kritika: Explorations in Russian and Eurasian history* 12/2 (2011), 281–319.

Ágoston 2014: Gábor Ágoston, "Firearms and military adaptation: The Ottomans and the European military revolution, 1450–1800", *Journal of world history* 25/1 (2014), 85–124.

Ahmed 2016: Shahab Ahmed, *What is Islam? The importance of being Islamic*, Princeton – Oxford 2016.

Ahrweiler 1975: Hélène Ahrweiler, *L'idéologie politique de l'Empire byzantin*, Paris 1975.

Aigle 2007: Denise Aigle, "La conception du pouvoir dans l'islam. Miroirs des princes persans et théorie sunnite (XIe–XIVe siècles)", *Perspectives médiévales* 31 (2007), 17–44.

Aksan 1993: Virginia Aksan, "Ottoman political writing, 1768–1808", *International journal of Middle East studies* 25 (1993), 53–69.

Aksan 1995: Virginia Aksan, *An Ottoman statesman in war and peace: Ahmed Resmi Efendi, 1700–1783*, Leiden 1995.

Aksan 1998: Virginia Aksan, "Whatever happened to the janissaries? Mobilization for the 1768–1774 Russo-Ottoman war", *War in history* 5 (1998), 23–36.

Aksan 1999: Virginia Aksan, "Locating the Ottomans among early modern empires", *Journal of early modern history* 3 (1999), 103–134.

Aksan 2001: Virginia Aksan, "Enlightening the Ottomans: Tott and Mustafa III", in Ali Çaksu (ed.), *IRCICA international congress on learning and education in the Ottoman world (Istanbul, 12–15 April 1999)*, Istanbul 2001, 163–174.

Aksan 2004: Virginia Aksan, *Ottomans and Europeans: Contacts and conflicts*, Istanbul 2004.

Aksan 2011: Virginia Aksan, "Canikli Ali Paşa (d. 1785): Aa provincial portrait in loyalty and disloyalty", in Eleni Gara – M. Erdem Kabadayı – Christoph K. Neumann (eds), *Popular protest and political participation in the Ottoman Empire. Studies in honor of Suraiya Faroqhi*, Istanbul 2011, 211–224.

Al-Manasir 1992: M. Darwish Al-Manasir, "Abu Yusuf Kitab al-Kharaj", unpublished M.A. dissertation, Amman 1992.

Al-Tikriti 2001: Nabil al-Tikriti, "Şehzade Korkud (c. 1468–1513)", in Kemal Çiçek (ed.), *Pax Ottomanica: Studies in memoriam Prof. Dr. Nejat Göyünç*, Haarlem and Ankara 2001, 659–674.

Al-Tikriti 2004: Nabil al-Tikriti, "Şehzade Korkud (ca. 1468–1513) and the articulation of early 16th century Ottoman religious identity", unpublished Ph.D. dissertation, University of Chicago 2004.

Al-Tikriti 2005a: Nabil Al-Tikriti, "*Kalam* in the service of state: Apostasy and the defining of Ottoman Islamic identity", in Hakan T. Karateke – Maurus Reinkowski (eds), *Legitimizing the Order. The Ottoman rhetoric of state power*, Leiden – Boston 2005, 131–149.

Al-Tikriti 2005b: Nabil Al-Tikriti, "The Hajj as justifiable self-exile: Şehzade Korkud's *Wasîlat al-ahbâb* (915–916/1509–1510)", *al-Masâq* 17/1 (2005), 125–146.

Al-Tikriti 2013: Nabil Al-Tikriti, "Hall ishkâl al-afkâr: An Ottoman royal's sharî'a argument for imperial control over sea ghâzî plunder", in A. Fuess – B. Heyberger – P. Vendrix (eds), *La frontière méditerranéenne du XVe au XVIIe siècle : Échanges, circulations et affrontements*, Turnhout 2013, 125–142.

Al-Tikriti 2017: Nabil Al-Tikriti, "An Ottoman view of world history: Kâtib Çelebi's *Takvimu't-tevarih*", in Turan Gökçe – Mikail Acıpınar – İrfan Kokdaş – Özer Küpeli (eds), *Uluslararası Kâtib Çelebi sempozyumu Bildirileri*, İzmir 2017, 127–149.

Alam 2004: Muzaffar Alam, *The languages of political Islam in India, 1200–1800*, Chicago 2004.

Alexander 1985: John C. Alexander, *Brigandage and public order in the Morea, 1685–1806*, Athens 1985.

Alexander 1997: John C. Alexander (Alexandropoulos), "The Lord giveth and the Lord taketh away: Athos and the Confiscation Affair of 1568–1569", *Mount Athos in the 14th–16th centuries. Athonika symmeikta* 4 (1997), 168–169.

Anastasopoulos 2007: Antonis Anastasopoulos, "Albanians in the eighteenth-century Ottoman Balkans", in Elias Kolovos – Phokion Kotzageorgis – Sophia Laiou – Marinos Sariyannis (eds), *The Ottoman Empire, the Balkans, the Greek lands: toward a social and economic history. Studies in honor of John C. Alexander*, Istanbul 2007, 37–47.

Anastasopoulos 2012: Antonis Anastasopoulos, "The Ottomans and civil society: A discussion of the concept and the relevant literature", in Antonis Anastasopoulos (ed.), *Political initiatives from the BOTTOM-UP in the Ottoman Empire.* (*Halcyon days in Crete VII. A symposium held in Rethymno, 9–11 January 2009*), Rethymno 2012, 435–453.

Anay 1994: Harun Anay, "Celâleddin Devvânî: hayatı, eserleri, ahlâk ve siyaset düşüncesi", unpublished Ph.D. dissertation, Istanbul University 1994.

Andrews – Kalpaklı 2005: Walter G. Andrews – Mehmet Kalpaklı, *The age of beloveds. Love and the beloved in early-modern Ottoman and European culture and society*, Durham 2005.

Anhegger 1953: Robert Anhegger, "Hezarfen Hüseyin Efendi'nin Osmanlı devlet teşkilâtına dair mülâhazaları", *Türkiyat mecmuası* 10 (1951–1953), 365–393.

Apostolopoulos 1976: Dimitris Apostolopoulos, "Quelques hypothèses pour l'étude des origines de la pensée politique grecque post-byzantine (1453–1484). Le processus de transformation du concept de « Bien Commun » en rapport avec l'idéologie née après la prise de Constantinople", unpublished Ph.D. dissertation, Sorbonne University 1976.

Argun 2013: Selim Argun, "Elite configurations and clusters of power: The *ulema, waqf,* and Ottoman state (1789–1839)", unpublished Ph.D. dissertation, McGill University 2013.

Arıkan 1990: Zeki Arıkan, "Fransız İhtilâli ve Osmanlı tarihçiliği", in Jean-Louis Bacqué-Grammont – Edhem Eldem (eds), *De la Revolution Française à la Turquie d'Atatürk : La modernisation politique et sociale. Les lettres, les sciences et les arts. Actes des Colloques d'Istanbul (10–12 mai 1989)*, Istanbul – Paris 1990, 85–100.

Arjomand 1984: Said Amir Arjomand, *The Shadow of God and the Hidden Imam: Religion, political order and societal change in Shi'ite Iran from the beginning to 1890*, Chicago 1984.

Artan 2012: Tülay Artan, "Forms and forums of expression. Istanbul and beyond, 1600–1800", in Christine Woodhead (ed.), *The Ottoman world*, London – New York 2012, 378–406.

Åsard 1987: Erik Åsard, "Quentin Skinner and his critics: Some notes on a methodological debate", *Statsvetenskaplig tidskrift* 90 (1987), 101–116.

Atik 1998: Kayhan Atik, "Kayserili devlet adamı Dürri Mehmed Efendi ve layihası", in Ali Aktan – Ayhan Öztürk (eds), *II. Kayseri ve yöresi tarih sempozyumu bildirileri (16–17 Nisan 1998)*, Kayseri 1998, 69–74.

Aycibin 2011: Zeynep Aycibin, "XVII. yy. sadrazamlarından Köprülüzade Mustafa Paşa döneminde Osmanlı Devleti'nin siyasi ve sosyal durumu", unpublished M.A. dissertation, Mimar Sinan University 2011.

Aydüz 2011: Salim Aydüz, "Nasîr al-Dîn al-Tûsî's influence on Ottoman scientific literature (mathematics, astronomy and natural sciences)", *International journal of Turkish studies* 17/1–2 (2011), 21–38.

Aynur – Çakır – Koncu 2012: Hatice Aynur – Müjgan Çakır – Hanife Koncu (eds), *Mecmûa: Osmanlı edebiyatının kırkambarı*, Istanbul 2012.

Ayoub 2016: Samy Ayoub, "'The Sultân says': State authority in the late Hanafî tradition", *Islamic law and society* 23 (2016), 239–278.

Baer 2008: Marc David Baer, *Honored by the glory of Islam: Conversion and conquest in Ottoman Europe*, Oxford 2008.

Bacqué-Grammont – Eldem 1990: Jean-Louis Bacqué-Grammont – Edhem Eldem (eds), *De la Revolution Française à la Turquie d'Atatürk : La modernisation politique et sociale. Les lettres, les sciences et les arts. Actes des Colloques d'Istanbul (10–12 mai 1989)*, Istanbul – Paris 1990.

Baldwin 2015: James E. Baldwin, "The deposition of Defterdar Ahmed Pasha and the rule of law in seventeenth-century Egypt", *Osmanlı araştırmaları/The journal of Ottoman studies* 46 (2015), 131–161.

Balivet 1993: Michel Balivet, "Culture ouverte et échanges inter-religieux dans les villes ottomanes du XIVe siècle", in Elizabeth A. Zachariadou (ed.), *The Ottoman emirate (1300–1389). Halcyon days in Crete I: A symposium held in Rethymno, 11–13 January 1991*, Rethymnon 1993, 1–6.

Ball 2007: Terence Ball, "Professor Skinner's visions", *Political studies review* 5 (2007), 351–364.

Balta 2006: Fider Balta, "Evliya Çelebi *Seyahatnamesi*'nde siyasal kültür unsurları", unpublished M.A. dissertation, Cumhuriyet University-Sivas 2006.

Bang – Bayly 2011: Peter Fibiger Bang – C. A. Bayly (eds), *Tributary empires in global history*, Basingstoke 2011.

Barbarics-Hermanik 2013: Zsusza Barbarics-Hermanik, "İbrahim Müteferrika als transkultureller Vermittler im osmanischen Reich", in Arno Strohmeyer – Norbert Spannenberger (eds), *Frieden und Konfliktmanagement in interkulturellen Räumen. Das Osmanische Reich und die Habsburgermonarchie in der Frühen Neuzeit*, Stuttgart 2013, 283–308.

Barkey 1994: Karen Barkey, *Bandits and bureaucrats. The Ottoman route of state centralization*, Ithaca – London 1994.

Barkey 2008: Karen Barkey, *Empire of difference. The Ottomans in comparative perspective*, Cambridge 2008.

Barnes 1987: John Robert Barnes, *An introduction to religious foundations in the Ottoman Empire*, Leiden 1987.

Başaran 2014: Betül Başaran, *Selim III, social control and policing in Istanbul at the end of the eighteenth century: Between crisis and order*, Leiden 2014.

Başaran – Kırlı 2015: Betül Başaran – Cengiz Kırlı, "Some observations on Istanbul's artisans during the reign of Selim III (1789–1808)", in Suraiya Faroqhi (ed.), *Bread from the lion's mouth: Artisans struggling for a livelihood in Ottoman cities*, New York 2015, 259–277.

Bejczy – Nederman 2007: István Bejczy – Cary Nederman (eds), *Princely virtues in the middle ages, 1200–1500*, Turnhout 2007.

Bekar 2011: Cumhur Bekar, "A new perception of Rome, Byzantium and Constantinople in Hezarfen Huseyin's universal history", unpublished M.A. dissertation, Boğaziçi University 2011.

Belhaj 2013: Abdessamad Belhaj, "Law and order according to Ibn Taymiyya and Ibn Qayyim al-Jawziyya: A re-examination of *siyâsa shar'iyya*", in Birgit Krawietz and Georges Tamer, in collaboration with Alina Kokoschka (eds), *Islamic theology, philosophy and law: Debating Ibn Taymiyya and Ibn Qayyim al-Jawziyya*, Berlin – Boston 2013, 400–421.

Berkes 1962: Niyazi Berkes, "İlk Türk matbaası kurucusunun dinî ve fikrî kimliği", *TTK Belleten* 26/104 (1962), 715–737.

Berkes 1964: Niyazi Berkes, *The development of secularism in Turkey*, London 1964 (repr. in facsimile 1998).

Berkey 2001: Jonathan P. Berkey, *Popular preaching and religious authority in the medieval Islamic Near East*, Seattle 2001.

Beydilli 1984: Kemal Beydilli, "İgnatius Mouradgea D'Ohsson (Muradcan Tosunyan). Ailesi hakkında kayıtlar, 'Nizâm-ı Cedîd'e dâir Lâyihası ve Osmanlı İmparatorluğundaki siyâsî hayatı", *İstanbul Üniversitesi edebiyat fakültesi tarih dergisi* 34 (1983–1984) [Prof. Dr. M. C. Şehâbeddin Tekindağ hatıra sayısı], 247–314.

Beydilli 1999a: Kemal Beydilli, "Dış politika ve siyasî ahlâk", *Dîvân—ilmî araştırmalar* 7 (1999), 47–56.

Beydilli 1999b: Kemal Beydilli, "Kücük Kaynarca'dan Tanzimât'a ıslâhât düşünceleri", *Dîvân—ilmî araştırmalar* 8 (1999), 25–64.

Beydilli 2001: Kemal Beydilli, "From Küçük Kaynarca to the collapse", in Ekmeleddin İhsanoğlu (ed.), *History of the Ottoman state, society and civilisation*, Istanbul 2001, 63–131.

Beydilli 2005: Kemal Beydilli, "Sekbanbaşı risalesinin müellifi hakkında", *Türk kültürü incelemeleri dergisi* 12 (2005), 221–24.

Beyhan 2003: Mehmet Ali Beyhan, "Islahatlar ve buhranlar literatürü: III. Selim ve II. Mahmud dönemi", *Türkiye araştırmaları literatür dergisi* 1/2 (2003), 57–99.

Binbaş 2011: İ. Evrim Binbaş, "Structure and function of the genealogical tree in Islamic historiography (1200–1500)", in İ. E. Binbaş – N. Kılıç-Schubel (eds), *Horizons of the world. Festschrift for İsenbike Togan*, Istanbul 2011, 465–544.

Bingöl 1988: Abdulkuddüs Bingöl, *Gelenbevî İsmail*, Ankara 1988.

Birinci 1996: Ali Birinci, "Birgivi Risalesi: Ilk dini kitap niçin ve nasıl basıldı?", *Türk yurdu* 112 (1996), 13–14.

Black 2011: Anthony Black, *The history of Islamic political thought. From the Prophet to the present*, 2nd ed., Edinburgh 2011.

Boarini 2009: Serge Boarini (ed.), *La casuistique classique: genèse, formes, devenir*, Saint-Étienne 2009.

Bombaci 1965–1966: Alessio Bombaci, "Qutluɣ bolzun! A contribution to the history of the concept of 'fortune' among the Turks", *Ural-Altaische jahrbücher* 36 (1965), 284–291, and 38 (1966), 13–43.

Boroujerdi 2013: Mehrzad Boroujerdi (ed.), *Mirror for the Muslim prince. Islam and the theory of statecraft*, Syracuse 2013.

Bouquet 2015: Olivier Bouquet, "Is it time to stop speaking about Ottoman modernisation?", in Marc Aymes – Benjamin Gourisse – Élise Massicard (eds), *Order and compromise: Government practices in Turkey from the late Ottoman Empire to the early 21st century*, Leiden – Boston 2015, 45–67.

Brummett 2015: Palmira Brummett, *Mapping the Ottomans: Sovereignty, territory, and identity in the early modern Mediterranean*, Cambridge 2015.

Burak 2013: Guy Burak, "The second formation of Islamic law: The post-Mongol context of the Ottoman adoption of a school of law", *Comparative studies in society and history* 55/3 (2013), 579–602.

Burak 2015: Guy Burak, "Between the *Kânûn* of Qâytbây and Ottoman *yasaq*: A note on the Ottomans' dynastic law", *Journal of Islamic studies* 26/1 (2015), 1–23.

Burak 2016: Guy Burak, "Evidentiary truth claims, imperial registers, and the Ottoman archive: Contending legal views of archival and record-keeping practices in Ottoman Greater Syria (seventeenth-nineteenth centuries)", *Bulletin of the School of Oriental and African Studies* 79/2 (2016), 233–254.

Buzov 2005: Snjezana Buzov, "The lawgiver and his lawmakers: The role of legal discourse in the change of Ottoman imperial culture", unpublished Ph.D. dissertation, University of Chicago 2005.

Calder 1993: Norman Calder, *Studies in early Muslim jurisprudence*, Oxford 1993.

Ceylan 2005: Ayhan Ceylan, "Osmanlı'da Meşrutiyet öncesi merkezî meclisler literatürü", *Türkiye araştırmaları literatür dergisi* 3/5 (2005), 623–646.

Cezar 1986: Yavuz Cezar, *Osmanlı maliyesinde bunalım ve değişim dönemi* (*XVIII. yy. 'dan Tanzimat'a malî tarih*), Istanbul 1986.

Clayer 1994: Nathalie Clayer, *Mystiques, état et société. Les Halvetis dans l'aire balkanique de la fin du XVe siècle à nos jours*, Leiden 1994.

Clayer 2002: Nathalie Clayer, "Münîrî Belgrâdî. Un représentant de la *'ilmiyye* dans la région de Belgrade, fin XVIe-début XVIIe siècle", in S. Praetor – C. K. Neumann (eds), *Frauen, Bilder und Gelehrte. Studien zu Gesellschaft und Künsten im osmanischen Reich = Arts, women and scholars: Studies in Ottoman society and culture. Festschrift Hans Georg Majer*, Istanbul 2002, 549–568.

Collective work 1990: *Sultan II. Mahmud ve reformları semineri, 28–30 Haziran 1989. Bildiriler*, Istanbul 1990.

Cook 2000: Michael Cook, *Commanding right and forbidding wrong in Islamic thought*, Cambridge 2000.

Cook 2002: David Cook, *Studies in Muslim apocalyptic*, Princeton 2002.

Costache 2010–2011: Ştefania Costache, "Loyalty and political legitimacy in the Phanariots' historical writing in the eighteenth century", *Südost-Forschungen* 69/70 (2010/2011), 25–50.

Curry 2010: John J. Curry, *The transformation of Muslim mystical thought in the Ottoman Empire. The rise of the Halveti order, 1350–1650*, Edinburgh 2010.

Cvetkova 1975: Bistra A. Cvetkova, "To the prehistory of the Tanzimat: An unknown Ottoman political treatise of the 18th century", *Etudes historiques*, vol. VII, Sofia 1975, 133–146.

Çavuşoğlu 1990: Semiramis Çavuşoğlu, "The Kâdîzâdeli movement: An attempt of Şeriat-minded reform in the Ottoman Empire", unpublished Ph.D. dissertation, Princeton University 1990.

Çelebi 1998: İlyas Çelebi, "XVII. Yüzyıl Osmanlı Kelamcıları ve Beyazızade Ahmed Efendi'nin Kelam İlmindeki Yeri," *Kuran mesaji ilmi araştirmalar dergisi* 10–12 (1998), 104–112.

Çıpa 2014: H. Erdem Çıpa, "Sultan of a golden age that never was: The image of Selîm I (r. 1512–1520) in Ottoman advice literature", *Archivum Ottomanicum* 31 (2014), 129–155.

Çolak 2003: Orhan M. Çolak, "İstanbul kütüphanelerinde bulunan siyasetnâmeler bibliyografisi", *Türkiye araştırmaları literatür dergisi* 1/2 (2003), 339–378.

Dağlı 2013: Murat Dağlı, "The limits of Ottoman pragmatism", *History and theory* 52 (2013), 194–213.

Dakhlia 2002: Jocelyne Dakhlia, "Les Miroirs des princes islamiques : une modernité sourde?", *Annales. Histoire, sciences sociales* 2002/5, 57e année, 1191–1206.

Dankoff 2006: Robert Dankoff, *An Ottoman mentality. The world of Evliya Çelebi*, rev. edition, Leiden 2006.

Darling 1996: Linda T. Darling, *Revenue-raising and legitimacy: Tax collection and finance administration in the Ottoman Empire, 1560–1660*, Leiden – New York 1996.

Darling 1997: Linda T. Darling, "Ottoman fiscal administration: Decline or adaptation?", *The Journal of European economic history* 26/1 (1997), 157–179.

Darling 1998: Linda T. Darling, "Rethinking Europe and the Islamic world in the age of exploration", *Journal of early modern history* 2/3 (1998), 221–246.

Darling 2002: Linda T. Darling, "Another look at periodization in Ottoman history", *The Turkish Studies Association journal* 26/2 (2002), 19–28.

Darling 2006: Linda T. Darling, "Public finances: The role of the Ottoman centre", in Suraiya Faroqhi (ed.), *The Cambridge history of Turkey, vol. 3: The later Ottoman Empire, 1603–1839*, Cambridge 2006, 118–131.

Darling 2008: Linda T. Darling, "Political change and political discourse in the early modern Mediterranean world", *Journal of interdisciplinary history*, 38/4 (2008), 505–531.

Darling 2011: Linda T. Darling, "Reformulating the *Gazi* narrative: When was the Ottoman state a *gazi* state?", *Turcica* 43 (2011), 13–53.

Darling 2013a: Linda T. Darling, "Ottoman Turkish: Written language and scribal practice, 13th to 20th centuries", in B. Spooner – W. L. Hanaway (eds), *Literacy in the Persianate world. Writing and the social order*, Philadelphia 2012, 171–195.

Darling 2013b: Linda T. Darling, "*Mirrors for Princes* in Europe and the Middle East: A case of historiographical incommensurability", in A. Classen (ed.), *East meets West in the middle ages and early modern times: Transcultural experiences in the premodern world*, Berlin – Boston 2013, 223–242.

Darling 2013c: Linda T. Darling, *A history of social justice and political power in the Middle East: The circle of justice from Mesopotamia to globalization*, New York 2013.

Darling 2014: Linda T. Darling, "Nasihatnameler, İcmal defterleri, and the timar-holding Ottoman elite in the late sixteenth century", *Osmanlı araştırmaları/The journal of Ottoman studies* 43 (2014), 193–226.

Darling 2015: Linda T. Darling, "Nasihatnameler, İcmal defterleri, and the timar-holding Ottoman elite in the late sixteenth century. Part II, including the seventeenth century", *Osmanlı araştırmaları/The journal of Ottoman studies* 45 (2015), 1–23.

Dikici 2006: A. Ezgi Dikici, "Imperfect bodies, perfect companions? Dwarfs and mutes at the Ottoman court in the sixteenth and seventeenth centuries", unpublished M.A. dissertation, Sabancı University 2006.

Dikici 2013: A. Ezgi Dikici, "The making of Ottoman court eunuchs: Origins, recruitment paths, family ties, and 'domestic production'", *Archivum Ottomanicum* 30 (2013), 105–136.

Diriöz 1994: Meserret Diriöz, *Eserlerine göre Nâbî*, Istanbul 1994.

Doganalp-Votzi – Römer 2008: Heidemarie Doganalp-Votzi – Claudia Römer, *Herrschaft und Staat: politische Terminologie des Osmanisches Reiches der Tanzimatzeit*, Vienna 2008.

Doğan 2013: Cem Doğan, "16. ve 17. yüzyıl Osmanlı siyasetnâme ve ahlâknâmelerinde İbn Haldûnizm: Kınalızâde Ali Efendi, Kâtip Çelebi ve Na'îmâ örnekleri", *Uluslararası sosyal araştırmalar dergisi* 6/27 (2013), 197–214.

Donaldson 1963: Dwight M. Donaldson, *Studies in Muslim ethics*, London 1963.

Duman 2006: Mahmut Duman, "Köprülü Mehmed Paşa. Hayatı, şahsiyeti ve faaliyetleri", unpublished M.A. dissertation, Selçuk University 2006.

Dunn 1996: John Dunn, "The history of political theory", in John Dunn, *The history of political theory and other essays*, Cambridge 1996, 11–38.

Dursteler 2004: Eric R. Dursteler, "Education and identity in Constantinople's Latin rite community, c. 1600", *Renaissance studies* 18 (2004), 287–303.

Duţu 1971: Alexandru Duţu, *Les livres de sagesse dans la culture roumaine. Introduction à l'histoire des mentalités sud-est européennes*, Bucharest 1971.

Eisenstadt 2000: Shmuel N. Eisenstadt, "Multiple modernities", *Daedalus* 12 (2000), 1–29.

Eldem 2014: Edhem Eldem, "Début des lumières ou simple plagiat? La très voltairienne préface de l'histoire de Şanizade Mehmed Ataullah Efendi", *Turcica* 45 (2014), 269–318.

El-Rouayheb 2008: Khaled El-Rouayheb, "The myth of the triumph of fanaticism in the seventeenth-century Ottoman Empire", *Die Welt des Islams* 48 (2008), 196–201.

El-Rouayheb 2010: Khaled El-Rouayheb, "From Ibn Hajar al-Haytami (d.1566) to Khayr al-Din al-Alusi (d.1899): Changing views of Ibn Taymiyya amongst Sunni Islamic scholars", in S. Ahmed – Y. Rapoport (eds.), *Ibn Taymiyya and his times*, Oxford 2010, 269–318.

El-Rouayheb 2015: Khaled El-Rouayheb, *Islamic intellectual history in the seventeenth century: Scholarly currents in the Ottoman Empire and the Maghreb*, Cambridge 2015.

Emecen 2001a: Feridun Emecen, "Osmanlı hanedanına alternatif arayışlar üzerine bazı örnekler ve mülahazalar", *İslam araştırmaları dergisi* 6 (2001), 63–76.

Emecen 2001b: Feridun Emecen, "From the founding to Küçük Kaynarca", in Ekmeleddin İhsanoğlu (ed.), *History of the Ottoman state, society and civilisation*, Istanbul 2001, 3–62.

Emecen 2010: Feridun Emecen, *Zamanın İskenderi, şarkın fatihi: Yavuz Sultan Selim*, Istanbul 2010.

Emecen 2014: Feridun Emecen, "İhtirasın gölgesinde bir Sultan: Yıldırım Bayezid", *Osmanlı araştırmaları/The journal of Ottoman studies* 43 (2014), 67–92.

Emrence 2007: Cem Emrence, "Three waves of late Ottoman historiography", *MESA bulletin* 41/2 (2007), 137–151.

Erdem 2005: Hakan Erdem, "'Do not think of the Greeks as agricultural labourers': Ottoman responses to the Greek War of Independence", in Faruk Birtek – Thaleia Dragonas (eds), *Citizenship and the nation-state in Greece and Turkey*, London 2005, 67–84.

Ergene 2001: Boğaç A. Ergene, "On Ottoman justice: Interpretations in conflict (1600–1800)", *Islamic law and society* 8/1 (2001), 52–87.

Erginbaş 2014: Vefa Erginbaş, "Enlightenment in the Ottoman context: İbrahim Müteferrika and his intellectual landscape", in Geoffrey Roper (ed.), *Historical aspects of printing and publishing in languages of the Middle East. Papers from the third symposium on the history of printing and publishing in the languages and countries of the Middle East, University of Leipzig, September 2008*, Leiden – Boston 2014, 53–100.

Erimtan 2007: Can Erimtan, "The perception of Saadabad: The 'Tulip Age' and Ottoman-Safavid rivalry", in Dana Sajdi (ed.), *Ottoman tulips, Ottoman coffee. Leisure and lifestyle in the eighteenth century*, London – New York 2007, 41–62.

Ermiş 2014: Fatih Ermiş, *A history of Ottoman economic thought. Developments before the nineteenth century*, London – New York 2014.

Eryılmaz 2010: Fatma Sinem Eryılmaz Arenas-Vives, "The *Shehnamecis* of Sultan Süleyman: 'Arif and Eflatun and their dynastic project", unpublished Ph.D. dissertation, University of Chicago 2010.

Essid 1995: Yassine Essid, *A critique of the origins of Islamic economic thought*, Leiden 1995.

Evstatiev 2013: Simeon Evstatiev, "The Qadizadeli movement and the spread of Islamic revivalism in the seventeenth and eighteenth century Ottoman Empire", Center for Advanced Studies Sofia, *Working paper series* 5 (2013), 1–34.

Fakhry 1994: Majid Fakhry, *Ethical theories in Islam*, 2nd ed., Leiden 1994.

Fakhry 2000: Majid Fakhry, *Islamic philosophy, theology and mysticism. A short introduction*, Oxford 2000.

Faroqhi 1994: Suraiya Faroqhi, "Part II: Crisis and change, 1590–1699", in Halil İnalcık – Donald Quataert (eds), *An economic and social history of the Ottoman Empire, 1300–1914*, Cambridge 1994, 411–636.

Faroqhi 1998: Suraiya Faroqhi, "Migration into eighteenth-century 'Greater Istanbul' as reflected in the kadı registers of Eyüp", *Turcica* 30 (1998), 163–183.

Faroqhi 2002: Suraiya Faroqhi, "Ottoman attitudes towards merchants from Latin Christendom before 1600", *Turcica* 35 (2002), 69–104.

Faroqhi 2006: Suraiya Faroqhi, "Presenting the sultans' power, glory and piety: A comparative perspective", in Zeynep Tarım Ertuğ (ed.), *Prof. Dr. Mübahat Kütükoğlu'na Armağan*, Istanbul 2006, 169–206.

Faroqhi 2008: Suraiya Faroqhi, *Another mirror for princes. The public image of the Ottoman sultans and its reception*, Istanbul 2008.

Fazlıoğlu 2003: İhsan Fazlıoğlu, "Osmanlı düşünce geleneğinde 'siyasî metin' olarak kelâm kitapları", *Türkiye araştırmaları literatür dergisi* 1/2 (2003), 379–398.

Felek 2012: Özgen Felek, "(Re)creating image and identity: Dreams and visions as a means of Murad III's self-fashioning", in Özgen Felek – Alexander Knysh (eds), *Dreams and visions in Islamic societies*, New York 2012, 249–272.

Ferguson 2008: Heather L. Ferguson, "Reading kanunname: Law and governance in sixteenth-century Ottoman Empire", *The international journal of the humanities* 6/8 (2008), 75–82.

Ferguson 2009: Heather L. Ferguson, "The circle of justice as genre, practice, and objectification: A discursive re-mapping of the early modern Ottoman Empire", unpublished Ph.D. dissertation, University of California 2009.

Ferguson 2010: Heather L. Ferguson, "Genres of power: Constructing a discourse of decline in Ottoman nasihatname", *Osmanlı araştirmalari* 35 (2010), 81–116.

Fındıkoğlu 1953: Z. Fahri Fındıkoğlu, "Türkiyede İbn Haldunizm", *60. doğum yılı münasebetiyle Fuad Köprülü armağanı*, Istanbul 1953, 153–164.

Findley 1980: Carter Vaughn Findley, *Bureaucratic reform in the Ottoman Empire. The Sublime Porte, 1789–1922*, Princeton 1980.

Findley 1995: Carter Vaughn Findley, "Ebu Bekir Ratib's Vienna embassy narrative: Discovering Austria or propagandizing for reform in Istanbul?", *Wiener Zeitschrift für die Kunde des Morgenlandes* 85 (1995), 41–80.

Findley 2008: Carter Vaughn Findley, "The Tanzimat", in Reşat Kasaba (ed.), *The Cambridge history of Turkey. Vol. 4: Turkey in the modern world*, Cambridge 2008, 11–37.

Fleet 2002: Kate Fleet, "Early Ottoman self-definition", *Journal of Turkish studies* 26/I (2002) [Essays in Honor of Barbara Flemming I], 229–238.

Fleet 2003: Kate Fleet, "Tax-farming in the early Ottoman state", *The medieval history journal* 6/2 (2003), 249–258.

Fleischer 1983: Cornell H. Fleischer, "Royal authority, dynastic cyclism, and "Ibn Khaldûnism" in sixteenth-century Ottoman letters", *Journal of Asian and African studies* 18/3–4 (1983), 198–220.

Fleischer 1986a: Cornell H. Fleischer, *Bureaucrat and intellectual in the Ottoman Empire: The historian Mustafa Âli (1541–1600)*, Princeton 1986.

Fleischer 1986b: Cornell H. Fleischer, "Preliminaries to the study of the Ottoman bureaucracy", *Journal of Turkish studies* 10 (1986) [*Raiyyet rüsûmu: Essays presented to Halil İnalcık*], 135–141.

Fleischer 1990: Cornell H. Fleischer, "From Şeyhzade Korkud to Mustafa Âli: Cultural origins of the Ottoman *nasihatname*", H.W. Lowry – R.S. Hattox (eds), *IIIrd Congress on the social and economic history of Turkey. Princeton University, 24–26th August 1983*, Istanbul – Washington – Paris 1990, 67–77.

Fleischer 2007: Cornell H. Fleischer, "Shadows of shadows: Prophecy in politics in 1530s Istanbul", *International journal of Turkish studies* 13/1–2 (2007), 51–62.

Flemming 1968: Barbara Flemming, *Türkische Handschriften* (Verzeichnis der orientalischen Handschriften in Deutschland, Vol. XIII/1), Wiesbaden 1968.

Flemming 1987: Barbara Flemming, "Sâhib-kırân und Mahdî: Türkische Endzeiterwartungen im ersten Jahrzehnt der Regierung Süleymâns", in György Kara (ed.), *Between the Danube and the Caucasus. A collection of papers concerning oriental sources on the history of the peoples of Central and South-Eastern Europe*, Budapest 1987, 43–62.

Flemming 1988: Barbara Flemming, "Political genealogies in the sixteenth century", *Osmanlı araştırmaları/The journal of Ottoman studies* 7–8 (1988), 123–137.

Flemming 1994: Barbara Flemming, "The sultan's prayer before battle", in Colin Heywood – Colin Imber (eds), *Studies in Ottoman history in honour of Professor V. L. Ménage*, Istanbul 1994, 63–75.

Fodor 1984: Pál Fodor, "Ahmedi's Dasitan as a source of early Ottoman history", *Acta Orientalia Academiae Scientiarum Hungaricae* 38 (1984), 41–54.

Fodor 1986: Pál Fodor, "State and society, crisis and reform, in 15th–17th century Ottoman mirror for princes", *Acta Orientalia Academiae Scientiarum Hungaricae* 40/2–3 (1986), 217–40.

Forster 2006: Regula Forster, *Das Geheimnis der Geheimnisse: Die arabischen und deutschen Fassungen des pseudo-aristotelischen Sirr al-asrar/Secretum Secretorum*, Wiesbaden 2006.

Fortna 2000: Benjamin C. Fortna, "Islamic morality in late Ottoman 'secular' schools", *International journal of Middle East studies* 32/3 (2000), 369–393.

Fotić 1994: Aleksandar Fotić, "The official explanations for the confiscation and sale of monasteries (churches) and their estates at the time of Selim II", *Turcica* 26 (1994), 33–54.

Fotić 2005: Aleksandar Fotić, "Belgrade: A Muslim and non-Muslim cultural centre (sixteenth-seventeenth centuries)", in Antonis Anastasopoulos (ed.), *Provincial elites in the Ottoman Empire. Halcyon days in Crete V. A symposium held in Rethymno, 10–12 January 2003*, Rethymno 2005, 51–75.

Fouchécour 1986: Charles-Henri de Fouchécour, *Moralia. Les notions morales dans la littérature persane du 3e/9e au 7e/13e siècle*, Paris 1986.

Frazee 1983: Charles A. Frazee, *Catholics and sultans. The Church and the Ottoman Empire, 1453–1923*, Cambridge 1983.

Gardet – Anawati 1970: Louis Gardet – M.-M. Anawati, *Introduction à la théologie musulmane. Essai de théologie comparée*, Paris 1970.

Geertz 1983: Clifford Geertz, "'From the native's point of view': On the nature of anthropological understanding", in C. Geertz (ed.), *Local knowledge: Further essays in interpretive anthropology*, New York 1983, 55–72.

Gel 2010: Mehmet Gel, "XVI. yüzyılın ilk yarısında Osmanlı toplumunun dinî meselelerine muhalif bir yaklaşım: Şeyhülislam Çivizâde Muhyiddin Mehmed Efendi ve fikirleri üzerine bir inceleme", unpublished Ph.D. dissertation, Gazi University 2010.

Gel 2013a: Mehmet Gel, "Kanûnî devrinde 'Müftî' ile Rumeli kazaskeri arasında bir 'hüccet-i şer'iyye' ihtilafı yahut Kemalpaşazâde-Fenârîzâde hesaplaşması", *Osmanlı araştırmaları/The journal of Ottoman studies* 42 (2013), 53–91.

Gel 2013b: Mehmet Gel, "Kanûnî devrinde vüzerâ gölgesinde 'vakfa ilâve mülkün satışı' üzerine bir hukukî tartışma: 'Da'vâ-yı âsiyâb'", *Belleten* 77 (2013), 927–953.

Gelder 1987: Geert Jan van Gelder, "The conceit of pen and sword: On an Arabic literary debate", *Journal of Semitic studies* 32/2 (1987), 329–360.

Genç 2000: Mehmet Genç, "Esham: Iç borçlanma", in *Osmanlı İmparatorluğunda devlet ve ekonomi*, Istanbul 2000, 186–195.

Gerber 1994: Haim Gerber, *State, society and law in Islam: Ottoman law in comparative perspective*, Albany 1994.

Gerber 2013: Haim Gerber, "An early eighteenth-century theory of the Ottoman caliphate", *Journal of Turkish studies* 40 (2013) [Defterology: Festschrift in honor of Heath Lowry], 119–125.

Gerçek 1939: Selim Nüzhet Gerçek, *Türk matbaacılığı: I—Müteferrika matbaası*, Istanbul 1939.

Goto-Jones 2008: Christopher Goto-Jones, "The Kyoto School and the history of political philosophy: Reconsidering the methodological dominance of the Cambridge School", in Christopher Goto-Jones (ed.), *Re-politicising the Kyoto School as philosophy*, London 2008, 3–25.

Gökbilgin 1971: M. Tayyip Gökbilgin, "Kâtip Çelebi, interprète et rénovateur des traditions religieuses au XVIIe siècle", *Turcica* 3 (1971), 71–79.

Gökbilgin 1975–1976: M. Tayyip Gökbilgin, "Taşköprü-zâde ve ilmî görüşleri", I: *İslam Tetkikleri Enstitüsü dergisi* 6/1–2 (1975), 127–138; II: *İslam Tetkikleri Enstitüsü dergisi* 6/3–4 (1976), 169–182.

Gökbilgin 1978: M. Tayyip Gökbilgin, "Ayn-ı Ali risalesi ve Osmanlı İmparatorluğu teşkilat ve müesseselerini aydınlatmadaki büyük önemi", introduction to Ayn-ı Ali Efendi, *Kavânîn-i Âl-i Osman der hülâsa-i mezâmin-i defter-i divan*, repr. Istanbul 1978, 3–40.

Gökbilgin 1991: M. Tayyip Gökbilgin, "XVII. Asırda Osmanlı devletinde ıslâhat ihtiyaç ve temayülleri ve Kâtip Çelebi", in *Kâtip Çelebi. Hayatı ve eserleri hakkında incelemeler*, Ankara 1991 (1st ed. 1957), 197–218.

Gökyay 1991: Orhan Şaik Gökyay, "Kâtip Çelebi: Hayatı, şahsiyeti, eserleri", in *Kâtip Çelebi. Hayatı ve eserleri hakkında incelemeler*, Ankara 1991 (1st ed. 1957), 3–90.

Görgün 2014: Tahsin Görgün, "Fatih dönemi İstanbul'unda bazı felsefi tartışmalar ve siyaset teorisi", in Feridun Emecen – Emrah Safa Gürkan (eds), *Osmanlı İstanbulu I (I. Uluslararası Osmanlı İstanbulu Sempozyumu Bildirileri, 29 Mayıs – 1 Haziran 2013, İstanbul 29 Mayıs Üniversitesi)*, Istanbul 2014, 407–417.

Gradeva 2006: Rossitsa Gradeva, "Osman Pazvantoglu of Vidin: Between old and new", in Frederick F. Anscombe (eds), *The Ottoman Balkans, 1750–1830*, Princeton 2006, 115–161.

Greene 1996: Molly Greene, "An Islamic experiment? Ottoman land policy on Crete", *Mediterranean historical review* 11/1 (1996), 60–78.

Greene 2000: Molly Greene, *A shared world. Christians and Muslims in the early modern Mediterranean*, Princeton 2000.

Grehan 2006: James Grehan, "Smoking and 'early modern' sociability: The great tobacco debate in the Ottoman Middle East (seventeenth to eighteenth centuries)", *American historical review* 111/5 (2006), 1352–1377.

Griffel 2017: Frank Griffel, "Contradictions and lots of ambiguity: Two new perspectives on premodern (and postclassical) Islamic societies", *Bustan: The Middle East book review* 8/1 (2017), 1–21.

Grignaschi 1976: Mario Grignaschi, "L'origine et les metamorphoses du 'Sirr al-asrar'", *Archives d'histoire doctrinale et littéraire du Moyen Âge* 43 (1976), 7–112.

Grunebaum 1962: Gustav E. von Grunebaum, "The concept and function of reason in Islamic ethics", *Oriens* 15 (1962), 1–17.

Gülsoy 2001: Ersin Gülsoy, "Osmanlı tahrir geleneğinde bir değişim örneği: Girit eyaleti'nin 1650 ve 1670 tarihli sayımları", in Kemal Çiçek (ed.), *Pax Ottomana. Studies in memoriam Prof. Dr. Nejat Göyünç*, Haarlem – Ankara 2001, 197–200.

Günay 2010: Vehbi Günay, "Osmanlı nasihat ve ıslahatname geleneğinde Veysi ve Habname'sinin yeri", in Ekrem Čaušević – Nenad Moačanin – Vjeran Kursar (eds), *Perspectives on Ottoman studies: Papers from the 18th symposium of the international committee of pre-Ottoman and Ottoman studies (CIEPO)*, Berlin 2010, 303–313.

Gündoğdu 2000: Cengiz Gündoğdu, *Bir Türk mutasavvıfı: Abdülmecîd Sivâsî (971/1563–1049/1639). Hayatı, eserleri ve tasavvufî görüşleri*, Ankara 2000.

Gündoğdu 2012: Birol Gündoğdu, "Ottoman constructions of the Morea rebellion, 1770s: A comprehensive study of Ottoman attitudes to the Greek uprising", unpublished Ph.D. dissertation, University of Toronto 2012.

Gündoğdu 2016: Hüseyin Gündoğdu, "Genres in the Ottoman political thought during the classical age (1400s–1700s)", unpublished Ph.D. dissertation, Fatih University 2016.

Hadjikyriacou – Lappa (unpublished): Antonis Hadjikyriacou – Daphne Lappa, "Beyond fluidity: Conversion and religious identity in eastern mediterranean 'contact zones'", unpublished conference paper presented at the "Rethinking early modernity: Methodological and critical innovation since the ritual turn" Conference, Victoria University in the University of Toronto, 25–27 June 2014.

Hagen 1995/96: Gottfried Hagen, "Überzeitlichkeit und Geschichte in Kâtib Čelebis Ğihânnümâ", *Archivum Ottomanicum* 14 (1995/96), 133–159.

Hagen 2000: Gottfried Hagen, "Some considerations on the study of Ottoman geographical writing", *Archivum Ottomanicum* 18 (2000), 183–193.

Hagen 2003a: Gottfried Hagen, *Ein osmanischer Geograph bei der Arbeit. Entstehung und Gedankenwelt von Katib Celebis Ğihannüma*, Berlin 2003.

Hagen 2003b: Gottfried Hagen, "Translations and translators in a multilingual society: A case study of Persian-Ottoman translations, late fifteenth to early seventeenth century", *Eurasian studies* 2/1 (2003), 95–134.

Hagen 2005: Gottfried Hagen, "Legitimacy and world order", in Hakan T. Karateke – Maurus Reinkowski (eds), *Legitimizing the order. The Ottoman rhetoric of state power*, Leiden – Boston 2005, 55–83.

Hagen 2006: Gottfried Hagen, "Afterword: Ottoman understandings of the world in the seventeenth century", in Robert Dankoff, *An Ottoman mentality. The world of Evliya Çelebi*, rev. edition, Leiden 2006, 215–256.

Hagen 2013: Gottfried Hagen, "The order of knowledge, the knowledge of order: Intellectual life", in Suraiya Faroqhi – Kate Fleet (eds), *The Cambridge history of Turkey. Vol. 2: The Ottoman Empire as world power, 1453–1603*, Cambridge 2013, 407–456.

Hagen – Seidenstricker 1998: Gottfried Hagen – Tilman Seidenstricker, "Reinhard Schulze's Hypothese einer islamischen Aufklärung: Kritik einer historiographischen Kritik", *Zeitschrift der Deutschen Morgenländischen Gesellschaft* 148 (1998), 83–110.

Hallaq 2001: Wael B. Hallaq, *Authority, continuity and change in Islamic law*, Cambridge 2001.

Hallaq 2002: Wael B. Hallaq, *A history of Islamic legal theories: An introduction to Sunnî* usûl al-fiqh, Cambridge 2002 (1st ed. 1997).

Hamadeh 2008: Shirine Hamadeh, *The city's pleasures: Istanbul in the eighteenth century*, Seattle 2008.

Hammer 1963: Joseph von Hammer-Purgstall, *Geschichte des osmanischen Reiches*, ed. H. Duda, Graz 1963 (2nd ed.; first published 1827–1835).

Hanioğlu 2008: Mehmet Şükrü Hanioğlu, *A brief history of the late Ottoman empire*, Princeton – Oxford 2008.

Hathaway 1996: Jane Hathaway, "Problems of periodization in Ottoman history: The fifteenth through the eighteenth centuries", *The Turkish Studies Association bulletin* 20/2 (1996), 25–31.

Hathaway 2003: Jane Hathaway, "Exiled chief harem eunuchs as proponents of the Hanafî madhhab in Ottoman Cairo", *Annales islamologiques* 37 (2003), 191–199.

Hathaway 2004: Jane Hathaway, "Rewriting eighteenth-century Ottoman history", *Mediterranean historical review* 19/1 (2004), 29–53.

Hathaway 2013: Jane Hathaway, "Households in the administration of the Ottoman Empire", *Journal of Turkish studies* 40 (2013) [Defteroloji: Heath Lowry Armağanı], 127–149.

Heck 2002: Paul L. Heck, *The construction of knowledge in Islamic civilization: Qudâma b. Ja'far and his* Kitâb al-kharâj wa-sinâ'at al-kitâba, Leiden 2002.

Heinzelmann 2002: Tobias Heinzelmann, "Die Konstruktion eines osmanischen Patriotismus und die Entwicklung des Begriffs *vatan* in der ersten Hälfte des 19. Jahrhunderts", in H. L. Kieser (ed.), *Aspects of the political language in Turkey (19th–20th Centuries)*, Istanbul 2002, 41–51.

Hellmuth – von Ehrenstein 2001: Eckhart Hellmuth – Christoph von Ehrenstein, "Intellectual history made in Britain: Die *Cambridge School* und ihre Kritiker", *Geschichte und Gesellschaft* 27 (2001), 149–172.

Herzog 1999: Christoph Herzog, "Zum Niedergangsdiskurs im Osmanischen Reich und in der islamischen Welt", in Stephan Conermann (ed.), *Mythen, Geschichte(n), Identitäten: Der Kampf um die Vergangenheit*, Hamburg 1999, 69–90.

Heyd 1961: Uriel Heyd, "The Ottoman 'ulema and Westernization in the time of Selim III and Mahmud II", in Uriel Heyd (ed.), *Studies in Islamic history and civilization. Scripta Hierosolymitana* 9 (1961), 63–96.

Heyd 1973: Uriel Heyd, *Studies in old Ottoman criminal law*, ed. V. L. Ménage, Oxford 1973.

Holbrook 1999: Victoria R. Holbrook, "The intellectual and the state: Poetry in Istanbul in 1790s", *Oriente moderno* XVIII (LXXXIX), n.s. 1 (1999), 233–51.

Howard 1988: Douglas A. Howard, "Ottoman historiography and the literature of 'decline' of the sixteenth and seventeenth centuries", *Journal of Asian history* 22 (1988), 52–77.

Howard 1995/96: Douglas A. Howard, "Historical scholarship and the classical Ottoman kânûnnâmes", *Archivum Ottomanicum* 14 (1995/96), 79–109.

Howard 2007: Douglas A. Howard, "Genre and myth in the Ottoman advice for kings literature", in Virginia Aksan – Daniel Goffman (eds), *The early modern Ottomans: Remapping the empire*, Cambridge 2007, 137–166.

Howard 2008: Douglas A. Howard, "From manual to literature: Two texts on the Ottoman timar system", *Acta Orientalia Acad. Sc. Hung.* 61/1–2 (2008), 87–99.

Hunt 1996: Alan Hunt, *Governance of the consuming passions. A history of sumptuary law*, New York 1996.

Ilıcak 2011: Şükrü Ilıcak, "A radical rethinking of Empire: Ottoman state and society during the Greek War of Independence, 1821–1826", unpublished Ph.D. dissertation, Harvard University 2011.

Işıksel 2010: Güneş Işıksel, "II. Selim'den III. Selim'e Osmanlı diplomasisi: Birkaç saptama", in Seyfi Kenan (ed.), *Nizâm-ı Kâdîm'den Nizâm-ı Cedîd'e: III. Selim ve dönemi*, Istanbul 2010, 315–338.

Işıksel 2014: Güneş Işıksel, "Méandres d'une pratique peu institutionnalisée : la diplomatie ottomane, XVᵉ–XVIIIᵉ siècle", *Monde(s)* 5 (2014), 43–55.

Ibrahim 2015: Ahmed Fekry Ibrahim, *Pragmatism in Islamic law: A social and intellectual history*, Syracuse 2015.

Iggers 1995: Georg Iggers, "Zur 'linguistischen Wende' im Geschichtsdenken und in der Geschichtsschreibung", *Geschichte und Gesellschaft* 21 (1995), 557–570.

İhsanoğlu 1995/96: Ekmeleddin İhsanoğlu, "Genesis of learned societies and professional associations in Ottoman Turkey", *Archivum Ottomanicum* 14 (1995/96), 161–189.

Imber 1987: Colin Imber, "The Ottoman dynastic myth", *Turcica* 19 (1987), 7–27.

Imber 1992: Colin Imber, "Süleymân as a caliph of the Muslims: Ebû's-Su'ûd's formulation of Ottoman dynastic ideology", in Gilles Veinstein (ed.), *Soliman le Magnifique et son temps. Actes du Colloque de Paris*, Paris 1992, 179–184.

Imber 1993: Colin Imber, "The legend of Osman Gazi", in Elizabeth A. Zachariadou (ed.), *The Ottoman emirate (1300–1389). Halcyon days in Crete I: A symposium held in Rethymno, 11–13 January 1991*, Rethymnon 1993, 67–75.

Imber 1994: Colin Imber, "Canon and apocrypha in early Ottoman history", in Colin Heywood – Colin Imber (eds), *Studies in Ottoman history in honour of Professor V. L. Ménage*, Istanbul 1994, 117–137.

Imber 1995: Colin Imber, "Ideas and legitimation in early Ottoman history", in Metin Kunt – Christine Woodhead (eds), *Süleyman the Magnificent and his age: The Ottoman Empire in the early modern world*, London – New York 1995, 138–153.

Imber 1997: Colin Imber, *Ebu's-su'ud. The Islamic legal tradition*, Edinburgh 1997.

Imber 2009: Colin Imber, *The Ottoman Empire, 1300–1650. The structure of power*, 2nd edition, New York 2009.

Imber 2011: Colin Imber, *Warfare, law and pseudo-history*, Istanbul 2011.

İnalcık 1955: Halil İnalcık, "Land problems in Turkish history", *The Muslim world* 45 (1955), 221–228 (also in İnalcık, *The Ottoman Empire: Conquest, organization and economy. Collected studies*, London 1978).

İnalcık 1962: Halil İnalcık, "The rise of Ottoman historiography", in B. Lewis – P. M. Holt (eds), *Historians of the Middle East*, London 1962, 152–167.

İnalcık 1965: Halil İnalcık, "Adâletnâmeler", *Türk tarih belgeleri dergisi* 11/3–4 (1965), 49–145.

İnalcık 1967: Halil İnalcık, "Kutadgu Bilig'de Türk ve İran siyaset nazariye ve gelenekleri", *Reşit Rahmeti Arat İçin*, Ankara 1967, 259–271.

İnalcık 1969a: Halil İnalcık, "Suleiman the Lawgiver and Ottoman law", *Archivum Ottomanicum* 1 (1969), 105–138 (also in İnalcık, *The Ottoman Empire: Conquest, organization and economy. Collected studies*, London 1978).

İnalcık 1969b: Halil İnalcık, "Capital formation in the Ottoman Empire", *The Journal of economic history* 19 (1969), 97–140 (also in İnalcık, *The Ottoman Empire: Conquest, organization and economy. Collected studies*, London 1978).

İnalcık 1969–1970: Halil İnalcık, "The policy of Mehmed II toward the Greek population of Istanbul and the Byzantine buildings of the city", *Dumbarton Oaks Papers* 23/24 (1969–1970), 231–249 (also in İnalcık, *The Ottoman Empire: Conquest, organization and economy. Collected studies*, London 1978).

İnalcık 1972: Halil İnalcık, "The Ottoman decline and its effects upon the *reaya*", in Henrik Birnbaum – Speros Vryonis, Jr. (eds), *Aspects of the Balkans: Continuity and change*, The Hague 1972, 338–354 (also in İnalcık, *The Ottoman Empire: Conquest, organization and economy. Collected studies*, London 1978).

İnalcık 1973: Halil İnalcık, "Application of the Tanzimat and its social effects", *Archivum Ottomanicum* 5 (1973), 97–128 (also in İnalcık, *The Ottoman Empire: Conquest, organization and economy. Collected studies*, London 1978).

İnalcık 1977: Halil İnalcık, "Tursun Beg, historian of Mehmed the Conqueror's time", *Wiener Zeitschrift für die Kunde des Morgenlandes* 69 (1977), 55–71.

İnalcık 1980: Halil İnalcık, "Military and fiscal transformation in the Ottoman Empire, 1600–1700", *Archivum Ottomanicum* 6 (1980), 283–337 (also in İnalcık, *Studies in Ottoman social and economic history*, London 1985).

İnalcık 1992a: Halil İnalcık, "Islamization of Ottoman laws on land and land tax", in Ch. Fragner – K. Schwarz (eds), *Festgabe an Josef Matuz: Osmanistik – Turkologie – Diplomatik*, Berlin 1992, 101–118.

İnalcık 1992b: Halil İnalcık, "Comments on 'Sultanism': Max Weber's typification of the Ottoman polity", *Princeton papers in Near Eastern studies* 1 (1992), 49–73.

İnalcık 1993: Halil İnalcık, "Dervish and sultan: An analysis of the *Otman Baba vilâyetnâmesi*", in Grace Martin Smith – Carl W. Ernst (eds), *Manifestations of sainthood in Islam*, Istanbul 1993, 209–223.

İnalcık 1994a: Halil İnalcık, "The Ottoman state: Economy and society, 1300–1600", in Halil İnalcık – Donald Quataert (eds), *An economic and social history of the Ottoman Empire, 1300–1914*, Cambridge 1994.

İnalcık 1994b: Halil İnalcık, "How to read 'Âshık Pasha-zâde's history", in Colin Heywood – Colin Imber (eds), *Studies in Ottoman history in honour of Professor V. L. Ménage*, Istanbul 1994, 139–156.

İnan 2003: Kenan İnan, "The incorporation of writings on periphery in Ottoman historiography: Tursun Bey's comparison of Mehmed II and Bayezid II", *International journal of Turkish studies* 9/1–2 (2003), 105–117.

İnan 2006: Kenan İnan, "On the sources of Tursun Bey's *Târih-i Ebü'l-Feth*", in Eugenia Kermeli – Oktay Özel (eds), *The Ottoman Empire: Myths, realities and 'black holes'. Contributions in honour of Colin Imber*, Istanbul 2006, 75–109.

İnan 2009: Kenan İnan, "Remembering the good old days: The Ottoman *nasihatname* [advice letters] literature of the 17th century", in Andreas Gémes – Florencia Peyrou – Ioannis Xydopoulos (eds), *Institutional change and stability conflicts. Transitions and social values*, Pisa 2009, 111–127.

İnanır 2008: Ahmet İnanır, "İbn Kemal'in fetvaları ışığında Osmanlı'da İslâm hukuku", unpublished Ph.D. dissertation, Istanbul University 2008.

Itzkowitz 1962: Norman Itzkowitz, "Eighteenth century Ottoman realities", *Studia Islamica* 16 (1962), 73–94.

Ivanyi 2012: Katharina A. Ivanyi, "Virtue, piety and the law: A study of Birgivî Mehmed Efendî's *al-Tarîqa al-Muhammadiyya*", unpublished Ph.D. dissertation, Princeton University 2012.

Janssen 1985: Peter L. Janssen, "Political thought as traditionary action: The critical response to Skinner and Pocock", *History and theory* 24 (1985), 115–146.

Jobst 1980: Wolfgang Jobst, "Der Gesandtschaftsbericht des Zülfiqâr Efendi über die Friedensverhandlungen in Wien 1689", unpublished Ph.D. dissertation, Vienna University 1980.

Johansen 1988: Baber Johansen, *The Islamic law on land tax and rent. The peasants' loss of property rights as interpreted in the Hanafite legal literature of the Mamluk and Ottoman periods*, London – New York – Sydney 1988.

Jones 2012: Linda G. Jones, *The power of oratory in the medieval Muslim world*, Cambridge 2012.

Kafadar 1986: Cemal Kafadar, "When coins turned into drops of dew and bankers became robbers of shadows: The boundaries of Ottoman economic imagination at the end of the sixteenth century", unpublished Ph.D. dissertation, McGill University 1986.

Kafadar 1989: Cemal Kafadar, "Self and others: The diary of a dervish in seventeenth century Istanbul and first-person narratives in Ottoman literature", *Studia Islamica* 69 (1989), 121–150.

Kafadar 1991: Cemal Kafadar, "Les troubles monétaires de la fin du XVIe siècle et la prise de conscience ottomane du déclin", *Annales. Économies, sociétés, civilisations* 46/2 (1991), 381–400.

Kafadar 1993: Cemal Kafadar, "The myth of the Golden Age: Ottoman historical consciousness in the post-Süleymânic era", in Halil İnalcık – Cemal Kafadar (eds), *Süleymân the Second and his time*, Istanbul 1993, 37–48.

Kafadar 1995: Cemal Kafadar, *Between two worlds. The construction of the Ottoman state*, Berkeley – Los Angeles – London 1995.

Kafadar 2001: Cemal Kafadar, "Osmanlı siyasal düşüncesinin kaynakları üzerine gözlemler", in M. Ö. Alkan (ed.), *Modern Türkiye'de siyasi düşünce. Vol. I, Cumhuriyet'e devreden düşünce mirası: Tanzimat ve meşrutiyet'in birikimi*, Istanbul 2001, 24–28.

Kafadar 2007: Cemal Kafadar, "Janissaries and other riffraff of Ottoman Istanbul: Rebels without a cause?", *International journal of Turkish studies* 13/1–2 (2007), 113–134.

Kaldellis 2013: Anthony Kaldellis, "How to usurp the throne in Byzantium: The role of public opinion in sedition and rebellion", in D. G. Angelov – M. Saxby (eds), *Power and subversion in Byzantium*, Farnham – Burlington 2013, 43–56.

Kaldellis 2015: Anthony Kaldellis, *The Byzantine Republic: People and power in New Rome*, Cambridge MA. 2015.

Káldy-Nagy 1987: Julius Káldy-Nagy, "The 'strangers' (*ecnebiler*) in the 17th century Ottoman military organization", in György Kara (ed.), *Between the Danube and the Caucasus. A collection of papers concerning oriental sources on the history of the peoples of Central and South-Eastern Europe*, Budapest 1987, 165–169.

Kapıcı 2013: Özhan Kapıcı, "Bir Osmanlı mollasının fikir dünyasından fragmanlar: Keçecizâde İzzet Molla ve II. Mahmud dönemi Osmanlı siyaset düşüncesi", *Osmanlı araştırmaları/The journal of Ottoman studies* 42 (2013), 275–315.

Karabela 2010: Mehmet Kadri Karabela, "The development of dialectic and argumentation theory in post-classical Islamic intellectual history", unpublished Ph.D. dissertation, McGill University 2010.

Karahasanoğlu 2009: Selim Karahasanoğlu, "A Tulip Age legend: Consumer behavior and material culture in the Ottoman Empire (1718–1730)", unpublished Ph.D. dissertation, Binghampton University 2009.

Karal 1940: Enver Ziya Karal, *Halet Efendinin Paris büyük elçiliği, 1802–6*, Istanbul 1940.

Karal 1960: Enver Ziya Karal, "Ebubekir Ratıb Efendi'nin Nizam-ı Cedid Islahatı'ndaki rolü", *Türk tarih kongresi (Ankara 1956). Kongreye sunulan tebliğler*, Ankara 1960, 347–355.

Karal 1988: Enver Ziya Karal, *Selim III'ün Hatt-ı Hümayunları—Nizam-ı Cedit (1789–1807)*, Ankara 1988 (1st ed. 1946).

Karataş 2010: Hasan Karataş, "The cash waqfs debate of 1545–1548: Anatomy of a legal debate at the age of Süleyman the Lawgiver", *İnsan ve toplum* 1/1 (2010), 45–66.

Karataş 2014: Hasan Karataş, "The Ottomanization of the Halveti Sufi order: A political story revisited", *Journal of the Ottoman and Turkish studies association* 1:1–2 (2014), 71–89.

Karatay 1961: Fehmi Edhem Karatay, *Topkapı Sarayı Müzesi Kütüphanesi: Türkçe yazmalar kataloğu*, 2 vols, Istanbul 1961.

Karateke 1999: Hakan Karateke, "Osmanlı devletinde 'adet-i kadime' üstüne", *Journal of Turkish studies* 23 (1999), 117–133.

Karateke 2005: Hakan Karateke, "Legitimizing the Ottoman Sultanate: A framework for historical analysis", in Hakan T. Karateke – Maurus Reinkowski (eds), *Legitimizing the order. The Ottoman rhetoric of state power*, Leiden – Boston 2005, 13–52.

Karateke 2012: Hakan Karateke, "'On the tranquillity and repose of the sultan': The construction of a topos", in Christine Woodhead (ed.), *The Ottoman world*, London 2012, 116–129.

Karateke – Reinkowski 2005: Hakan T. Karateke – Maurus Reinkowski (eds), *Legitimizing the order. The Ottoman rhetoric of state power*, Leiden – Boston 2005.

Kastritsis 2007: Dimitris Kastritsis, *The sons of Bayezid. Empire building and representation in the Ottoman civil war of 1402–13*, Leiden 2007.

Kastritsis 2013: Dimitris Kastritsis, "Ferîdûn Beg's *Münşe'âtü's-selâtîn* ('Correspondence of sultans') and late sixteenth-century Ottoman views of the political world", in S. Bazzaz – Y. Batsaki – D. Angelov (eds), *Imperial geographies in Byzantine and Ottoman space*, Washington 2013, 91–110.

Kastritsis 2016: Dimitri Kastritsis, "The Alexander Romance and the rise of the Ottoman Empire", in Andrew C. S. Peacock – Sara Nur Yıldız (eds), *Islamic literature and intellectual life in fourteenth- and fifteenth-century Anatolia*, Würzburg 2016, 243–283.

Kavak 2012: Özgür Kavak, "Bir Osmanlı kadısının gözüyle siyaset: *Letâifü'l-efkâr ve kâşifü'l-esrâr* yahut Osmanlı saltanatını fıkıh diliyle temellendirmek", *Marmara Üniversitesi ilâhiyat fakültesi dergisi* 42/1 (2012), 95–120.

Kaya 2014: M. Cüneyt Kaya, "In the shadow of 'prophetic legislation': The venture of practical philosophy after Avicenna", *Arabic sciences and philosophy* 24 (2014), 269–296.

Kaylı 2010: Ahmet Kaylı, "A critical study of Birgivi Mehmed Efendi's (d. 981/1573) works and their dissemination in manuscript form", unpublished M.A. dissertation, Boğaziçi University 2010.

Kechriotis 2013: Vangelis Kechriotis, "Postcolonial criticism encounters late Ottoman studies", *Historein* 13 (2013), 39–46.

Kenan 2010: Seyfi Kenan (ed.), *Nizâm-ı Kâdîm'den Nizâm-ı Cedîd'e: III. Selim ve dönemi*, Istanbul 2010.

Kermeli 1997: Eugenia Kermeli, "Ebû's Su'ûd's definitions of church *vakfs*: Theory and practice in Ottoman law", in Robert Gleave – Eugenia Kermeli (eds), *Islamic Law. Theory and practice*, London – New York 1997, 141–156.

Kermeli 2008: Eugenia Kermeli, "Caught in between faith and cash: The Ottoman land system of Crete, 1645–1670", in Antonis Anastasopoulos (ed.), *The Eastern Mediterranean under Ottoman rule: Crete, 1645–1840*, Rethymno 2008, 17–48.

Kermeli-Ünal 2013: Eugenia Kermeli-Ünal, "17. Yüzyılda bir kültürel rastlaşma: Vani Efendi ile Panagiotakis Nikousios'un söyleşi", in Ümit Ekin (ed.), *Prof. Dr. Özer Ergenc'e armağan*, Istanbul 2013, 446–457.

Kermeli 2014: Evgenia Kermeli, "The tobacco controversy in early modern Ottoman Christian and Muslim discourse", *Hacettepe Üniversitesi Türkiyat araştırmaları dergisi* 21 (2014), 121–135.

Khismatulin 2015: Alexey Khismatulin, "Two mirrors for princes fabricated at the Seljuq court: Nizâm al-Mulk's *Siyar al-mulûk* and al-Ghazâlî's *Nasîhat al-mulûk*", in Edmund Herzig – Sarah Stewart (eds), *The idea of Iran, vol. VI: The age of the Seljuqs*, London – New York 2015, 94–130.

Khoury 2001: Dina Rizk Khoury, "Administrative practice between religious law (shari'a) and state law (kanun) on the eastern frontiers of the Ottoman Empire", *Journal of early modern history* 5/4 (2001), 305–330.

Kırlı 2010: Cengiz Kırlı, "Devlet ve istatistik: Esnaf kefalet defterleri ışığında III. Selim iktidarı", in Seyfi Kenan (ed.), *Nizâm-ı Kâdîm'den Nizâm-ı Cedîd'e: III. Selim ve dönemi*, Istanbul 2010, 183–212.

Kiraz 2013: Celil Kiraz, "Gelenbevi'nin En'âm 158. Ayetle ilgili risâlesine göre imanın son kabul zamanı ve iman-amel ilişkisi", *Uludağ Üniversitesi ilahiyat fakültesi dergisi* 22/2 (2013), 33–54.

Klein 2006: Yaron Klein, "Between public and private: An examination of *hisba* literature", *Harvard Middle Eastern and Islamic review* 7 (2006), 41–62.

Koloğlu 1990: Orhan Koloğlu, "Fransız Devrimi ile II. Mahmut reformları arasında ilk paralellik kurma çabaları", in Jean-Louis Bacqué-Grammont – Edhem Eldem (eds), *De la Revolution Française à la Turquie d'Atatürk: La modernisation politique et sociale. Les lettres, les sciences et les arts. Actes des Colloques d'Istanbul (10–12 mai 1989)*, Istanbul – Paris 1990, 113–123.

Kolovos 2007: Elias Kolovos, "Beyond 'classical' Ottoman *defter*ology: A preliminary assessment of the *tahrir* registers of 1670/71 concerning Crete and the Aegean islands", in Elias Kolovos – Phokion Kotzageorgis – Sophia Laiou – Marinos Sariyannis (eds), *The Ottoman Empire, the Balkans, the Greek lands: Toward a social and economic history (Studies in honor of John C. Alexander)*, Istanbul 2007, 201–35.

Korkut 2003: Hasan Korkut, "Osmanlı sefaretnâmeleri hakkında yapılan araştırmalar", *Türkiye araştırmaları literatür dergisi* 1/2 (2003), 491–511.

Koselleck 1979: Reinhart Koselleck, "Begriffsgeschichte und Sozialgeschsichte", in Reinhart Koselleck, *Vergangene Zukunft. Zur Semantik geschichtlicher Zeiten*, Frankfurt 1979, 107–129.

Koselleck 2002: Reinhart Koselleck, *The practice of conceptual history. Timing history, spacing concepts*, tr. Todd Samuel Presner et al., Stanford 2002.

Kömbe 2013: İlker Kömbe, "Dünya düzeninin temelleri: Adalet dairesi literatürüne giriş", *Dîvân: Disiplinerarası çalışmalar dergisi* 18/35 (2013), 139–198.

Krstić 2011: Tijana Krstić, *Contested conversions to Islam. Narratives of religious change in the early modern Ottoman Empire*, Stanford 2011.

Kunt 1971: İ. Metin Kunt, "The Köprülü years, 1656–1661", unpublished Ph.D. dissertation, Princeton University 1971.

Kunt 1973: İ. Metin Kunt, "Naima, Köprülü and the grand vizierate", *Boğaziçi Üniversitesi dergisi* 1 (1973), 57–62.

Kunt 1977: İ. Metin Kunt, "Derviş Mehmed Paşa, vezir and entrepreneur: A study in Ottoman political-economic theory and practice", *Turcica* 9 (1977), 197–214.

Kunt 1983: İ. Metin Kunt, *The sultan's servants. The transformation of Ottoman provincial government, 1550–1650*, New York 1983.

Kunt 1994: İ. Metin Kunt, "The waqf as an instrument of public policy: Notes on the Köprülü family endowments", in Colin Heywood – Colin Imber (eds), *Studies in Ottoman history in honour of Professor V. L. Ménage*, Istanbul 1994, 189–198.

Kunt 2012: Metin Kunt, "Royal and other households", in Christine Woodhead (ed.), *The Ottoman world*, London – New York 2012, 103–115.

Kunt – Woodhead 1995: Metin Kunt – Christine Woodhead (eds), *Süleyman the Magnificent and his age: The Ottoman Empire in the early modern world*, London 1995.

Kuran 1990: Ercüment Kuran, "III. Selim zamanında Türkiye'nin çağdaşlaşması ve Fransa", in Jean-Louis Bacqué-Grammont – Edhem Eldem (eds), *De la Revolution Française à la Turquie d'Atatürk : La modernisation politique et sociale. Les lettres, les sciences et les arts. Actes des Colloques d'Istanbul (10–12 mai 1989)*, Istanbul – Paris 1990, 51–56.

Kurz 2011: Marlene Kurz, *Ways to heaven, gates to hell. Fazlîzâde 'Alî's struggle with the diversity of Ottoman Islam*, Berlin 2011.

Küçük 2012: Bekir Harun Küçük, "Early enlightenment in Istanbul", unpublished Ph.D. dissertation, University of California 2012.

Küçük 2013: Bekir Harun Küçük, "Natural philosophy and politics in the eighteenth century: Esad of Ioannina and Greek Aristotelianism at the Ottoman court", *Osmanlı araştırmaları/The journal of Ottoman studies* 41 (2013), 125–158.

Küçük 2017: Bekir Harun Küçük, "Early modern Ottoman science: A new materialist framework", *Journal of early modern history* 21 (2017), 1–13.

Lambton 1954: Ann K. S. Lambton, "The theory of kingship in the *Nasîhat ul-mulûk* of Ghazâlî", *The Islamic quarterly* 1 (1954), 47–55 (also in Lambton, *Theory and practice in medieval Persian government*, London 1980).

Lambton 1956a: Ann K. S. Lambton, "*Quis custodiet custodes*. Some reflections on the Persian theory of government", *Studia Islamica* 5 (1956), 125–148 (also in Lambton, *Theory and practice in medieval Persian government*, London 1980).

Lambton 1956b: Ann K. S. Lambton, "*Quis custodiet custodes*. Some reflections on the Persian theory of government (*cont.*)", *Studia Islamica* 6 (1956), 125–146 (also in Lambton, *Theory and practice in medieval Persian government*, London 1980).

Lambton 1962: Ann K. S. Lambton, "Justice in the medieval Persian theory of kingship", *Studia Islamica* 17 (1962), 91–119 (also in Lambton, *Theory and practice in medieval Persian government*, London 1980).

Lambton 1971: Ann K. S. Lambton, "Islamic mirrors for princes", *La Persia nel medioevo: Atti del Convegno internazionale, Roma, 1970*, Rome 1971, 419–442 (also in Lambton, *Theory and practice in medieval Persian government*, London 1980).

Lambton 1974: Ann K. S. Lambton, "Islamic political thought", in Joseph Schacht – C. E. Bosworth (eds), *The legacy of Islam*, Oxford 1974, 404–424 (also in Lambton, *Theory and practice in medieval Persian government*, London 1980).

Lambton 1980: Ann K. S. Lambton, *Theory and practice in medieval Persian government*, London 1980.

Lambton 1981: Ann K. S. Lambton, *State and government in medieval Islam. An introduction to the study of Islamic political theory: The jurists*, Oxford 1981.

Laoust 1970: Henri Laoust, *La politique de Gazâlî*, Paris 1970.

Lauzière 2010: Henri Lauzière, "The construction of Salafiyya: Reconsidering Salafism from the perspective of conceptual history," *International journal of Middle East studies* 42/3 (2010), 369–389.

Le Gall 2004: Dina Le Gall, "Kadızadelis, Nakşbendis, and intra-Sufi diatribe in seventeenth-century Istanbul," *The Turkish Studies Association journal* 28/1–2 (2004), 1–28.

Leder 1999: Stefan Leder, "Aspekte arabischer und persischer Fürstenspiegel. Legitimation, Fürstenethik, politische Vernunft", in Angela de Benedictis with Annamaria Pisapia (eds), *Specula principum*, Frankfurt-am-Main 1999, 21–50.

Lefèvre 2012: Corinne Lefèvre, "Europe-Mughal India-Muslim Asia: Circulation of political ideas and instruments in early modern times", in Antje Flüchter – Susan Richter (eds), *Structures on the move: Technologies of governance in transcultural encounter*, Berlin – Heidelberg 2012, 127–145.

Lekesiz 2007: M. Hulusi Lekesiz, "XVI. yüzyıl Osmanlı düzenindeki değişimin tasfiyeci (püritanist) bir eleştirisi: Birgivi Mehmet Efendi ve fikirleri", unpublished Ph.D. dissertation, Hacettepe University 2007.

Lelić 2017: Emin Lelić, "Physiognomy (*ʿilm-i firâsat*) and Ottoman statecraft: Discerning morality and justice", *Arabica* 64 (2017), 609–646.

Levend 1962: Agâh Sırrı Levend, "Siyaset-nameler", *Türk dili araştırmaları yıllığı—belleten* (1962), 167–194.

Levend 1963: Agâh Sırrı Levend, "Ümmet çağında ahlâk kitaplarımız", *Türk dili araştırmaları yıllığı-belleten* (1963), 89–115.

Lewis 1953: Bernard Lewis, "The impact of the French Revolution in Turkey. Some notes on the transmission of ideas", *Journal of world history* 1 (1953), 105–125.

Lewis 1961: Bernard Lewis, *The emergence of modern Turkey*, London 1961.

Lewis 1962: Bernard Lewis, "Ottoman observers of Ottoman decline", *Islamic studies* 1 (1962), 71–87.

Lewis 1981–1982: Bernard Lewis, "Meşveret", *Tarih enstitüsü dergisi* 12 (1981–1982), 775–782.

Lewis 1984: Bernard Lewis, "Siyâsa", in A. H. Green (ed.), *In quest of an Islamic humanism: Arabic and Islamic studies in memory of Mohamed al-Nowaihi*, Cairo 1984, 3–14.

Lewis 1985: Bernard Lewis, "Serbestiyet", *İstanbul Üniversitesi iktisat fakültesi mecmuası* 41 (1985) [Ord. Prof. Ömer Lütfi Barkan'a Armağan], 47–52.

Lewis 1986: Bernard Lewis, "Ibn Khaldūn in Turkey", in Moshe Sharon (ed.), *Studies in Islamic history and civilization*, Jerusalem 1986, 527–530.

Lewis 1988: Bernard Lewis, *The political language of Islam*, Chicago – London 1988.

Lindner 1983: Rudi P. Lindner, *Nomads and Ottomans in medieval Anatolia*, Bloomington 1983.

Lindner 2007: Rudi P. Lindner, *Explorations in Ottoman prehistory*, Ann Arbor 2007.

Lindner 2009: Rudi P. Lindner, "Anatolia, 1300–1451", in Kate Fleet (ed.), *The Cambridge history of Turkey. Vol. 1: Byzantium to Turkey, 1071–1453*, Cambridge 2009, 102–137.

Lowry 2003: Heath W. Lowry, *The nature of the early Ottoman state*, Albany NY 2003.

Lowry 2011: Heath W. Lowry, *Hersekzâde Ahmed Paşa: An Ottoman statesman's career and pious endowments*, Istanbul 2011.

Madelung 1985: Wilfred Madelung, "Nasir al-Din Tusi's ethics: Between philosophy, Shi'ism, and Sufism", in R. G. Hovannisian (ed.), *Ethics in Islam*, Malibu 1985, 85–101.

Majer 1980: Hans Georg Majer, "Die Kritik aus den Ulema in den osmanischen politischen Traktaten des 16–18 Jahrhunderts", in O. Okyar – H. Inalcik (ed.), *Social and economic history of Turkey (1071–1920). Papers presented to the first international congress on the social and economic history of Turkey*, Ankara 1980, 147–155.

Mandaville 1979: Jon E. Mandaville, "Usurious piety: The cash waqf controversy in the Ottoman Empire", *International journal of Middle East studies* 10 (1979), 289–308.

Mantran 1989: Robert Mantran (ed.), *Histoire de l'Empire ottoman*, Paris 1989.

Mantran 1990: Robert Mantran, "La déclaration des droits de l'homme et les édits sultaniens de 1839 et de 1856", in Jean-Louis Bacqué-Grammont – Edhem Eldem (eds), *De la Revolution Française à la Turquie d'Atatürk : La modernisation politique et sociale. Les lettres, les sciences et les arts. Actes des Colloques d'Istanbul (10–12 mai 1989)*, Istanbul – Paris 1990, 141–147.

Manzalaoui 1974: Mahmoud Manzalaoui, "The pseudo-Aristotelian *Kitâb sirr al-asrâr*: Facts and problems", *Oriens* 23–24 (1974), 147–257.

Mardin 1962: Şerif Mardin, *The genesis of Young Ottoman thought: A study in the modernization of Turkish political ideas*, Princeton 1962.

Mardin 1969a: Şerif Mardin, "Power, civil society and culture in the Ottoman Empire", *Comparative studies in society and history* 11/3 (1969), 258–281.

Mardin 1969b: Şerif Mardin, "The mind of the Turkish reformer, 1700–1900", in Sami Ayad Hanna – George H. Gardner (eds), *Arab socialism*, Salt Lake City 1969, 24–48.

Marlow 2009: Louise Marlow, "Surveying recent literature on the Arabic and Persian mirrors for princes genre", *History compass* 7/2 (2009), 523–538.

Martı 2008: Huriye Martı, *Birgivi Mehmed Efendi*, Ankara 2008.

Matuz 1970: Joseph Matuz, "Über die Epistolographie und İnša-Literatur der Osmanen", in *Deutscher Orientalistentag 1968* (*Zeitschrift der Deutschen Morgenländischen Gesellschaft* Supplement), Wiesbaden 1970, 574–594.

McGowan 1994: Bruce McGowan, "The age of the *ayans*, 1699–1812", in Halil İnalcık – Donald Quataert (eds), *An economic and social history of the Ottoman Empire, 1300–1914*, Cambridge 1994, 637–758.

Ménage 1962: Victor L. Ménage, "The beginnings of Ottoman historiography", in B. Lewis – P. M. Holt eds, *Historians of the Middle East*, London 1962, 168–179.

Ménage 1964: Victor L. Ménage, *Neshrî's history of the Ottomans. The sources and development of the text*, London 1964.

Ménage 1971: Victor L. Ménage, "Three Ottoman treatises on Europe", in C. E. Bosworth (ed.), *Iran and Islam. In memory of the late Victor Minorsky*, Edinburgh 1971, 421–433.

Menchinger 2010: Ethan L. Menchinger, "'Gems for royal profit': Prefaces and the practice of eighteenth-century Ottoman court history", *History studies: Uluslararası tarih araştırmaları dergisi* 2:2 (2010), 127–151.

Menchinger 2014a: Ethan L. Menchinger, "An Ottoman historian in an age of reform: Ahmed Vâsıf Efendi (ca. 1730–1806)", unpublished Ph.D. dissertation, University of Michigan 2014.

Menchinger 2014b: Ethan L. Menchinger, "A reformist philosophy of history: The case of Ahmed Vâsıf Efendi", *Osmanlı araştırmaları/The journal of Ottoman studies* 44 (2014), 141–168.

Menchinger 2017: Ethan L. Menchinger, *The first of the modern Ottomans. The intellectual history of Ahmed Vâsıf*, Cambridge 2017.

Mengüç 2013: M. Cem Mengüç, "Histories of Bayezid I, historians of Bayezid II: Rethinking late-fifteenth century Ottoman historiography", *Bulletin of the School of Oriental and African Studies* 76/3 (2013), 373–389.

Mitchell 2003: Colin P. Mitchell, "To preserve and protect: Husayn Va'iz-i Kashifi and Perso-Islamic chancellery culture", *Iranian studies* 36/4 (2003), 485–507.

Mitchell 2009: Colin P. Mitchell, *The practice of politics in Safavid Iran. Power, religion and rhetoric*, London – New York 2009.

Mottahedeh 1989: Roy Mottahedeh, "Consultation and the political process in the Islamic Middle East of the 9th, 10th and 11th centuries", in Moawiyah M. Ibrahim (ed.-in-chief), *Arabian studies in honour of Mahmoud Ghul: Symposium at Yarmouk University, December 8–11, 1984*, Wiesbaden 1989, 83–88.

Mottahedeh – Stilt 2003: Roy Mottahedeh – Kristen Stilt, "Public and private as viewed through the work of the *muhtasib*", *Social research: An international quarterly of the social sciences* 70/3 (2003), 735–748.

Moustakas 2011: Konstantinos Moustakas, "Byzantine 'visions' of the Ottoman Empire: Theories of Ottoman legitimacy by Byzantine scholars after the fall of Constantinople", in A. Lymberopoulou (ed.), *Images of the Byzantine world: Visions, messages and meanings. Studies presented to Leslie Brubaker*, Aldershot 2011, 215–219.

Moustakas 2012: Konstantinos Moustakas, "Idealizing themes of Osmanli origins in the historical texts of the 15th and early 16th centuries", *Ariadni* 18 (2012), 151–170.

Mumcu 1963: Ahmet Mumcu, *Osmanlı devletinde siyaseten katl*, Ankara 1963.

Mundy – Saumarez Smith 2007: Martha Mundy – Richard Saumarez Smith, *Governing property, making the modern state: Law, administration and production in Ottoman Syria*, London 2007.

Murphey 1981: Rhoads Murphey, "Dördüncü Sultan Murad'a sunulan yedi telhis", *VIII. Türk tarih kongresi, Ankara: 11–15 Ekim 1976. Kongreye sunulan bildiriler*, Ankara 1981, 2:1095–1099.

Murphey 1989: Rhoads Murphey, "Review Article: Mustafa Ali and the politics of cultural despair", *International journal of Middle East studies* 21 (1989), 243–255.

Murphey 1993: Rhoads Murphey, "Continuity and discontinuity in Ottoman administrative theory and practice during the late seventeenth century", *Poetics today 14/2: Cultural processes in Muslim and Arab societies: Medieval and early modern periods* (1993), 419–443.

Murphey 1996: Rhoads Murphey, "An Ottoman view from the top and rumblings from below: The sultanic writs (*hatt-ı hümayun*) of Murad IV (r. 1623–1640)", *Turcica* 28 (1996), 319–338.

Murphey 1999: Rhoads Murphey, "Westernization in the eighteenth-century Ottoman Empire: How far, how fast?", *Byzantine and modern Greek studies* 23 (1999), 116–139.

Murphey 2002: Rhoads Murphey, "Forms of differentiation and expression of individuality in Ottoman society", *Turcica* 34 (2002), 135–170.

Murphey 2005: Rhoads Murphey, "Mustafa Safi's version of the kingly virtues as presented in his *Zübdet'ül Tevarih*, or Annals of Sultan Ahmed, 1012–1023 A.H./1603–1614 AD", in C. Imber – K. Kiyotaki (eds.), *Frontiers of Ottoman studies, vol. I*, London – New York 2005, 5–24.

Murphey 2008: Rhoads Murphey, *Exploring Ottoman sovereignty. Tradition, image and practice in the Ottoman imperial household, 1400–1800*, London 2008.

Murphey 2009a: Rhoads Murphey, "The Veliyyuddin Telhis: Notes on the sources and interrelations between Koçi Bey and contemporary writers of advice to kings", *Belleten* 43/171 (1979), 547–571; repr. with revisions in Rhoads Murphey, *Essays on Ottoman historians and historiography*, Istanbul 2009, 121–142.

Murphey 2009b: Rhoads Murphey, "Solakzade's treatise of 1652: A glimpse at operational principles guiding the Ottoman state during times of crisis", *Beşinci milletlerarasi Türkiye sosyal ve iktisat tarihi kongresi tebliğleri*, vol. 1, Ankara 1990, 27–32; repr. in Rhoads Murphey, *Essays on Ottoman historians and historiography*, Istanbul 2009, 43–48.

Mustafayev 2013: Shahin Mustafayev, "Views on supreme power and law in medieval nomadic society (case of "Oghuzname" by Yazicioglu Ali)", *Studia et documenta turcologica* 1 (2013), 277–286.

Muzzarelli – Campanini 2003: Maria Giuseppina Muzzarelli – Antonella Campanini (eds), *Disciplinare il lusso. La legislazione suntuaria in Italia e in Europa tra medioevo ed età moderna*, Rome 2003.

Nagata 2005: Yuzo Nagata, "*Ayan* in Anatolia and the Balkans during the eighteenth and nineteenth centuries: A case study of the Karaosmanoğlu family", in Antonis Anastasopoulos (ed.), *Provincial elites in the Ottoman Empire. Halcyon days in Crete V: A symposium held in Rethymno, 10–12 January 2003*, Rethymno 2005, 269–294.

Naguib 2013: Shuruq Naguib, "Guiding the sound mind: Ebu's-su'ûd's *Tafsir* and rhetorical interpretation of the Qur'an in the post-classical period", *Osmanlı araştırmaları/ The journal of Ottoman studies* 42 (2013), 1–52.

Najjar 1984: Fauzi M. Najjar, "*Siyasa* in Islamic political philosophy", in Michael E. Marmura (ed.), *Islamic theology and philosophy: Studies in honor of George F. Hourani*, Albany 1984, 92–111.

Narayana Rao – Subrahmanyam 2009: Velcheru Narayana Rao – Sanjay Subrahmanyam, "Notes on political thought in medieval and early modern South India", *Modern Asian studies* 43/1 (2009), 175–210.

Necipoğlu 1992: Gülru Necipoğlu, "A kânûn for the state, a canon for the arts: Conceptualizing the classical synthesis of Ottoman art and architecture", in Gilles Veinstein (ed.), *Soliman le Magnifique et son temps. Actes du colloque de Paris*, Paris 1992, 195–216.

Neumann 2000: Christoph Neumann, *Araç tarih, amaç Tanzimat: Tarih-i Cevdet'in siyasi anlamı*, Istanbul 2000.

Newman 1992a: Andrew J. Newman, "The nature of the Akhbârî/Usûlî dispute in late-Safawid Iran, part one: 'Abdallâh al-Samâhijî's *Munyat al-mumârisîn*", *Bulletin of the School of Oriental and African Studies* 55/1 (1992), 22–51.

Newman 1992b: Andrew J. Newman, "The nature of the Akhbârî/Usûlî dispute in late-Safawid Iran, part two: The conflict reassessed", *Bulletin of the School of Oriental and African Studies* 55/2 (1992), 250–261.

Nizri 2014: Michael Nizri, *Ottoman high politics and the ulema household*, Basingstoke 2014.

Nutku 1987: Özdemir Nutku, *IV. Mehmet'in Edirne şenliği (1675)*, Ankara 1987.

Ocak 1979–1983: A. Yaşar Ocak, "XVII. yüzyılda Osmanlı İmparatorluğu'nda dinde tasfiye (puritanizm) teşebbüslerine bir bakış: Kadızâdeliler hareketi", *Türk kültürü araştırmaları*, 17–21/1–2 (1979–1983), 208–225.

Ocak 1988: A. Yaşar Ocak, "Osmanlı siyasi düşüncesi", in Ekmeleddin İhsanoğlu (ed.), *Osmanlı devleti ve medeniyeti tarihi*, Istanbul 1988, 2:164–174.

Ocak 1991: A. Yaşar Ocak, "Les réactions socio-religieuses contre l'idéologie officielle ottomane et la question de *zendeqa ve ilhâd* (hérésie et athéisme) au XVIe siècle", *Turcica* 21–23 (1991), 71–82.

Ocak 1993a: A. Yaşar Ocak, "Les milieux soufis dans les territoires du beylicat ottoman et le problème des 'Abdalan-i Rum' (1300–1389)", in E. A. Zachariadou (ed.), *The Ottoman emirate (1300–1389). Halcyon days in Crete I: A symposium held in Rethymno, 11–13 January 1991*, Rethymnon 1993, 145–158.

Ocak 1993b: A. Yaşar Ocak, "Kalenderi dervishes and Ottoman administration from the fourteenth to the sixteenth centuries", in Grace Martin Smith – Carl W. Ernst (eds), *Manifestations of sainthood in Islam*, Istanbul 1993, 239–255.

Ocak 1998 : A. Yaşar Ocak, *Osmanlı toplumunda zındıklar ve mülhidler (15.–17. yüzyıllar)*, Istanbul 1998.

Ocak 2009: A. Yaşar Ocak, "Social, cultural and intellectual life, 1071–1453", in Kate Fleet (ed.), *The Cambridge history of Turkey. Vol. I: Byzantium to Turkey, 1071–1453*, Cambridge 2009, 353–422.

Odorico 2009: Paolo Odorico, "Les miroirs des princes à Byzance. Une lecture horizontale", in Paolo Odorico (ed.), *"L'éducation au gouvernement et à la vie". La tradition des « règles de vie » de l'antiquité au Moyen-Âge. Actes du colloque international (Pise, 18 et 19 mars 2005)*, Paris 2009, 223–246.

Oktay 2001: Cemil Oktay, "Bizans siyasî ideolojisi'nden Osmanlı siyasî ideolojisi'ne", in M. Ö. Alkan (ed.), *Modern Türkiye'de siyasi düşünce. Vol. 1, Cumhuriyet'e devreden düşünce mirası: Tanzimat ve meşrutiyet'in birikimi*, Istanbul 2001, 29–36.

Oktay 2002: Ayşe Sıdıka Oktay, "Kınalızâde Ali Efendi'nin hayatı ve *Ahlâk-ı Alâî* isimli eseri", *Dîvân—disipliner arası çalışmalar dergisi* 12 (2002), 185–233.

Olson 1977: Robert W. Olson, "Jews, janissaries, esnaf and the revolt of 1740 in Istanbul: Social upheaval and political realignment in the Ottoman Empire", *Journal of the economic and social history of the orient* 20/2 (1977), 185–207.

Ortaylı 1994a: İlber Ortaylı, "Le *Tanzimat* et le modèle français: Mimétisme ou adaptation?", in İlber Ortaylı, *Studies on Ottoman transformation*, Istanbul 1994, 107–116.

Ortaylı 1994b: İlber Ortaylı, "Reforms of Petrine Russia and the Ottoman mind", in İlber Ortaylı, *Studies on Ottoman transformation*, Istanbul 1994, 217–222.

Ortaylı 1995: İlber Ortaylı, *İmparatorluğun en uzun yüzyılı*, Istanbul 1995 (1st ed. 1983).

Ortaylı 2001: İlber Ortaylı, "Osmanlı'da 18. yüzyıl düşünce dünyasına dair", in M. Ö. Alkan (ed.), *Modern Türkiye'de siyasi düşünce. Vol. I, Cumhuriyet'e devreden düşünce mirası: Tanzimat ve meşrutiyet'in birikimi*, Istanbul 2001, 37–41.

Öz 2010: Mehmet Öz, "Kânûn-i kadîm: Osmanlı gelenekçi söyleminin dayanağı mı, ıslahat girişimlerinin meşrulaştırma aracı mı?", in Seyfi Kenan (ed.), *Nizâm-ı Kâdîm'den Nizâm-ı Cedîd'e: III. Selim ve dönemi*, Istanbul 2010, 59–77.

Özcan 1982: Abdülkadir Özcan, "Şeḥid Ali Paşa'ya izafe edilen *Ta'limât-nâme*'ye dair", *Tarih enstitüsü dergisi* 12 (1982), 191–202.

Özdemir 2013: Lale Özdemir, *Ottoman history through the eyes of Aşıkpaşazade*, Istanbul 2013.

Özel 1999: Oktay Özel, "Limits of the Almighty: Mehmed II's 'land reform' revisited", *Journal of the economic and social history of the Orient* 42/2 (1999), 226–246.

Özel 2005: Ahmet Özel, "İslam hukuku ve modern devletler hukukunda mukabele bilmisl/misilleme/karşılıklılık", *İslam hukuku araştırmaları dergisi* 5 (2005), 49–66.

Özel 2012: Oktay Özel, "The reign of violence: The *celali*s, c. 1550–1700", in Christine Woodhead (ed.), *The Ottoman world*, London – New York 2012, 184–202.

Özkan 2006: Selim Hilmi Özkan, "Amcazade Hüseyin Paşa'nın hayatı ve faaliyetleri (1644–1702)", unpublished Ph.D. dissertation, Süleyman Demirel University 2006.

Özkul 1996: Osman Özkul, "III. Selim döneminde Osmanlı ulemâsı ve yenileşme konusundaki tutumları (1789–1807)", unpublished Ph.D. dissertation, Istanbul University 1996.

Öztürk 1981: Necati Öztürk, "Islamic orthodoxy among the Ottomans in the seventeenth century: With special reference to the Qadi-Zade movement", unpublished Ph.D. dissertation, University of Edinburgh 1981.

Paidas 2006: Konstantinos D. S. Paidas, *Τα βυζαντινά « κάτοπτρα ηγεμόνος » της ύστερης περιόδου (1254–1403). Εκφράσεις του βυζαντινού βασιλικού ιδεώδους*, Athens 2006.

Palonen 2006: Kari Palonen, "Two concepts of politics: Conceptual history and present controversies", *Distinktion: Scandinavian journal of social theory* 12 (2006), 11–25.

Panou 2008: Nikolaos Panou, "How to do kings with words: Byzantine imperial ideology and the representation of power in pre-Phanariot admonitory literature", unpublished Ph.D. dissertation, Harvard University 2008.

Pazarbaşı 1997: Erdoğan Pazarbaşı, *Vânî Mehmed Efendi ve Araisü'l-Kur'an*, Ankara 1997.

Peacock 2016: Andrew C. S. Peacock, "Advice for the sultans of Rum: The "mirrors for princes" of early thirteenth-century Anatolia", in Bill Hickman – Gary Leiser (eds), *Turkish language, literature, and history: Travelers' tales, sultans, and scholars since the eighth century*, London – New York 2016, 276–307.

Peacock – Yıldız 2016: Andrew C. S. Peacock – Sara Nur Yıldız (eds), *Islamic literature and intellectual life in fourteenth- and fifteenth-century Anatolia*, Würzburg 2016.

Peirce 1993: Leslie Peirce, *The imperial harem. Women and sovereignty in the Ottoman Empire*, Oxford 1993.

Peirce 2003: Leslie Peirce, *Morality tales: Law and gender in the Ottoman court of Aintab*, Berkeley 2003.

Peksevgen 2004: Sefik Peksevgen, "Secrecy, information control and power building in the Ottoman Empire, 1566–1603", unpublished Ph.D. dissertation, McGill University 2004.

Pektaş 2015: Nil Pektaş, "The beginnings of printing in the Ottoman capital: Book production and circulation in early modern Constantinople", *Osmanlı bilimi araştirmalari* 16.2 (2015).

Petrosjan 1987: Irina E. Petrosjan, "The *mabda-i kanun-i yeniçeri ocağı tarihi* on the system of *devşirme*", in György Kara (ed.), *Between the Danube and the Caucasus. A collection of papers concerning oriental sources on the history of the peoples of Central and South-Eastern Europe*, Budapest 1987, 217–228.

Philliou 2011: Christine M. Philliou, *Biography of an empire: Governing Ottomans in an age of revolution*, Berkeley – Los Angeles 2011.

Piterberg 2003: Gabriel Piterberg, *An Ottoman tragedy: History and historiography at play*, Berkeley – Los Angeles 2003.

Plessner 1928: Martin Plessner, *Der Oikonomikos des Neupythagoreers "Bryson" und sein Enfluss auf die Islamische Wissenschaft*, Heidelberg 1928.

Pocock 1987: J. G. A. Pocock, "The concept of a language and the *métier d'historien*: Some considerations on practice", in Anthony Pagden (ed.), *The languages of political theory in early-modern Europe*, Cambridge 1987, 21–25.

Pocock 1988: J. G. A. Pocock, "What is intellectual history?", in Juliet Gardiner (ed.), *What is history today?*, London 1988, 114–116.

Pocock 1996: J. G. A. Pocock, "Concepts and discourses: A difference in culture? Comment on a paper by Melvin Richter", in H. Lehmann – M. Richter (eds), *The meaning of historical terms and concepts. New studies on* Begriffsgeschichte, Washington 1996, 47–58.

Pollock 2008: Sheldon Pollock, "Is there an Indian intellectual history? Introduction to 'Theory and method in Indian intellectual history'", *Journal of Indian philosophy* 36 (2008), 533–542.

Pollock 2009: Sheldon Pollock, "Future philology? The fate of a soft science in a hard world", *Critical inquiry* 35 (2009), 931–961.

Pourjavady – Schmidtke 2006: Reza Pourjavady – Sabine Schmidtke, "Some notes on a new edition of a medieval philosophical text in Turkey: Shams al-Dîn al-Shahrazûrî's *Rasâ'il al-shajara al-ilâhiyya*", *Die Welt des Islams* 46 (2006), 76–85.

Quataert 1993: Donald Quataert, "Janissaries, artisans and the question of Ottoman decline, 1730–1826", in Donald Quataert (ed.), *Workers, peasants and economic change in the Ottoman Empire, 1730–1914*, Istanbul 1993, 197–203.

Quataert 1997: Donald Quataert, "Clothing laws, state and society in the Ottoman Empire, 1720–1829", *International journal of Middle East studies* 29 (1997), 403–425.

Quataert 2000: Donald Quataert, *The Ottoman Empire, 1700–1922*, Cambridge 2000.

Quataert 2003: Donald Quataert, "Ottoman history writing and changing attitudes towards the notion of 'decline'", *History compass* 1 (2003), 1–10.

Radtke 1994: Bernd Radtke, "Warum ist der Sufi orthodox?", *Der Islam* 71 (1994), 302–307.

Radtke 2000: Bernd Radtke, *Autochthone islamische Aufklärung im 18. Jahrhundert: Theoretische und filologische Bemerkungen. Fortführung einer Debatte*, Utrecht 2000.

Radtke 2002: Bernd Radtke, "Birgiwîs *Tarîqa Muhammadiyya*. Einige Bemerkungen und Überlegungen", *Journal of Turkish studies* 26/II (2002) [Essays in Honour of Barbara Flemming, II], 159–174.

Rahimguliyev 2007: Bayram Rahimguliyev, "Osmanlı edebiyatında dönüşümün şiiri: Sülhiyyeler", unpublished M.A. dissertation, Bilkent University, Ankara 2007.

Reindl-Kiel 2002: Hedda Reindl-Kiel, "Fromme Helden, Wunder, Träume: Populäre Geschichtsauffassung im Osmanischen Reich des 18. und frühen 19. Jahrhunderts", *Journal for Turkish studies* 26/II (2002) [Essays in Honour of Barbara Flemming, II], 175–181.

Reindl-Kiel 2003: Hedda Reindl-Kiel, "The tragedy of power: The fate of grand vezirs according to the *Menakıbname-i Mahmud Paşa-i Veli*", *Turcica* 35 (2003), 247–256.

Repp 1986: Richard C. Repp, *The müfti of Istanbul. A study in the development of the Ottoman learned hierarchy*, London 1986.

Richter 1987: Melvin Richter, "*Begriffsgeschichte* and the history of ideas", *Journal of the history of ideas* 48 (1987), 247–263.

Riedlmayer 2008: Andras J. Riedlmayer, "Ottoman copybooks of correspondence and miscellanies as a source for political and cultural history", *Acta orientalia Hung.* 61 (2008), 201–14.

Robinson 1997: Francis Robinson, "Ottomans-Safavids-Mughals: Shared knowledge and connective systems", *Journal of Islamic studies* 8 (1997), 151–184.

Rodinson 1966: Maxime Rodinson, *Islam et capitalisme*, Paris 1966.

Rosenthal 1958: Erwin I. J. Rosenthal, *Political thought in medieval Islam. An introductory outline*, Cambridge 1958.

Rosenthal 1980: Franz Rosenthal, "Political justice and the just ruler", *Israel oriental studies* 10 (1980), 92–101.

Ruiu 2014: Adina Ruiu, "Conflicting visions of the Jesuit missions to the Ottoman Empire, 1609–1628", *Journal of Jesuit studies* 1/2 (2014), 260–280.

Rüstem 2016: Ünver Rüstem, "The spectacle of legitimacy: The dome-closing ceremony of the Sultan Ahmed mosque", *Muqarnas* 33 (2016), 253–344.

Sabev 2006: Orlin Sabev (Orhan Salih), *İbrahim Müteferrika ya da ilk Osmanlı matbaa serüveni (1726–1746). Yeniden değerlendirme*, Istanbul 2006.

Sabev 2014: Orlin Sabev (Orhan Salih), "Portrait and self-portrait: İbrahim Müteferrika's mind games", *Osmanlı araştırmaları/The journal of Ottoman studies* 44 (2014), 99–121.

Sajdi 2007: "Decline, its discontents and Ottoman cultural history: By way of introduction", in Dana Sajdi (ed.), *Ottoman tulips, Ottoman coffee. Leisure and lifestyle in the eighteenth century*, London – New York 2007, 1–40.

Sahillioğlu 1968: Halil Sahillioğlu, "Sıvış yılı buhranları", *İstanbul Üniversitesi iktisat fakültesi mecmuasi* 27/1–2 (1968), 89–100.

Sahillioğlu 1970: Halil Sahillioğlu, "*Sıvış* year crises in the Ottoman Empire", in M. A. Cook (ed.), *Studies in the economic history of the Middle East: From the rise of Islam to the present day*, London – New York – Toronto 1970, 230–252.

Sahillioğlu 1985: Halil Sahillioğlu, "1524–1525 Osmanlı bütçesi", *İstanbul Üniversitesi iktisat fakültesi mecmuasi* 41 (1985) [Ord. Prof. Ömer Lütfi Barkan'a Armağan], 415–452.

Salgırlı 2003: Saygın Salgırlı, "Manners and identity in late seventeenth century Istanbul", unpublished M.A. dissertation, Sabancı University 2003.

Salzmann 1993: Ariel Salzmann, "An ancient regime revisited: "Privatization" and political economy in the eighteenth-century Ottoman Empire", *Politics and society* 21/4 (1993), 393–423.

Salzmann 2000: Ariel Salzmann, "The Age of Tulips: Confluence and conflict in early modern consumer culture (1550–1730)", in Donald Quataert (ed.), *Consumption studies and the history of the Ottoman Empire, 1550–1922*, New York 2000, 83–106.

Salzmann 2004: Ariel Salzmann, *Tocqueville in the Ottoman Empire. Rival paths to the modern state*, Leiden – Boston 2004.

Salzmann 2012: Ariel Salzmann, "The old regime and the Ottoman Middle East", in Christine Woodhead (ed.), *The Ottoman world*, London – New York 2012, 409–422.

Sarıcaoğlu 2001: Fikret Sarıcaoğlu, *Kendi kaleminden bir padişahın portresi: Sultan I. Abdülhamid (1774–1789)*, Istanbul 2001.

Sarıkaya 2010: M. Saffet Sarıkaya, "Nisabu'l-İntisab'da esnaf teşkilatı ve fütüvvetnamelere yönelik eleştiriler", *E-Makâlât. Mezhep araştırmaları* 3/1 (2010), 43–64.

Sariyannis 2005: Marinos Sariyannis, "'Mob', 'scamps' and rebels in seventeenth-century Istanbul: Some remarks on Ottoman social vocabulary", *International journal of Turkish studies* 11/1–2 (2005), 1–15.

Sariyannis 2005–2006: Marinos Sariyannis, "Aspects of 'neomartyrdom': Religious contacts, 'blasphemy' and 'calumny' in seventeenth-century Istanbul", *Archivum Ottomanicum* 23 (2005/06), 249–262.

Sariyannis 2007: Marinos Sariyannis, "Law and morality in Ottoman society: The case of narcotic substances", in Elias Kolovos, Phokion Kotzageorgis, Sophia Laiou, Marinos Sariyannis (eds), *The Ottoman Empire, the Balkans, the Greek lands: Toward a social and economic history. Studies in honor of John C. Alexander*, Istanbul 2007, 307–321.

Sariyannis 2008a: Marinos Sariyannis, "Ottoman critics of society and state, fifteenth to early eighteenth centuries: Toward a corpus for the study of Ottoman political thought", *Archivum Ottomanicum* 25 (2008), 127–150.

Sariyannis 2008b: Marinos Sariyannis, "Rebellious janissaries: Two military mutinies in Candia (1688, 1762) and their aftermaths", in Antonis Anastasopoulos (ed.), *The eastern Mediterranean under Ottoman rule: Crete, 1645–1840* (*Halcyon Days in Crete VI. A symposium held in Rethymno, 13–15 January 2006*), Rethymno 2008, 255–274.

Sariyannis 2011a: Marinos Sariyannis, "The princely virtues as presented in Ottoman political and moral literature", *Turcica* 43 (2011), 121–144.

Sariyannis 2011b: Marinos Sariyannis, "Notes on the Ottoman poll-tax reforms of the late seventeenth century: The case of Crete", *Journal of the economic and social history of the Orient* 54 (2011), 39–61.

Sariyannis 2012: Marinos Sariyannis, "The Kadızadeli movement as a social and political phenomenon: The rise of a 'mercantile ethic'?", in Antonis Anastasopoulos (ed.), *Political initiatives from the bottom-up in the Ottoman Empire.* (*Halcyon Days in Crete VII. A symposium held in Rethymno, 9–11 January 2009*), Rethymno 2012, 263–289.

Sariyannis 2013: Marinos Sariyannis, "Ruler and state, state and society in Ottoman political thought", *Turkish historical review* 4 (2013), 83–117.

Sariyannis 2015: Marinos Sariyannis, "*Ajâ'ib ve gharâ'ib*: Ottoman collections of *mirabilia* and perceptions of the supernatural", *Der Islam* 92/2 (2015), 442–467.

Sariyannis 2016: Marinos Sariyannis, "Ottoman ideas on monarchy before the Tanzimat reforms: Toward a conceptual history of Ottoman political notions", *Turcica* 47 (2016), 33–72.

Sariyannis (forthcoming): Marinos Sariyannis, "Ottoman Ibn Khaldunism revisited: The pre-Tanzimat reception of the *Muqaddima*, from Kınalızade to Şanizade", in Marinos Sariyannis (ed.), *Political thought and practice in the Ottoman Empire.* (*Halcyon days in Crete IX. A symposium held in Rethymno, 9–11 January 2015*), Rethymno.

Savage-Smith 2013: Emilie Savage-Smith, "Were the four humours fundamental to medieval Islamic medical practice?", in Elisabeth Hsu – Peregrine Horden (eds), *The body in balance: Humoral theory in practice*, Oxford 2013, 89–106.

Sawyer 1997: Caroline Goodwin Sawyer, "Alexander, history, and piety: A study of Ahmedi's 14th-century *Iskendernâme*", unpublished Ph.D. dissertation, Columbia University 1997.

Schacht 1964: Joseph Schacht, *An introduction to Islamic law*, Oxford 1964.

Schaendlinger 1992: Anton C. Schaendlinger, "Reformtraktate und -vorschläge im Osmanischen Reich im 17. und 18. Jahrhundert", in Ch. Franger – K. Schwarz (eds), *Festgabe an Josef Matuz. Osmanistik—Turkologie—Diplomatik*, Berlin 1992, 239–253.

Schmidt 1991: Jan Schmidt, *Pure water for thirsty Muslims. A study of Mustafâ 'Âlî of Gallipoli's* Künhü'l-ahbâr, Leiden 1991.

Schulze 1996: Reinhard Schulze, "Was ist die islamische Aufklärung?", *Die Welt des Islams* 36 [Islamic Enlightenment in the 18th Century?]-3 (1996), 276–325.

Shapiro 2014: Henry R. Shapiro, "Legitimizing the Ottoman sultanate in early modern Greek", *Journal of Turkish studies* 42 (2014), 285–316.

Shaw 1971: Stanford J. Shaw, *Between old and new: The Ottoman Empire under Sultan Selim III, 1789–1807*, Cambridge MA 1971.

Shaw 1976: Stanford J. Shaw, *History of the Ottoman Empire and modern Turkey. Vol. 1: Empire of the Gazis: The rise and decline of the Ottoman Empire, 1280–1808*, Cambridge 1976.

Shefer-Mossensohn 2009: Miri Shefer-Mossensohn, *Ottoman medicine: Healing and medical institutions, 1500–1700*, Albany NY 2009.

Sheikh 2016: Mustapha Sheikh, *Ottoman puritanism and its discontents: Aḥmad al-Rūmī al-Āqḥiṣārī and the Qāḍīzādelis*, Oxford 2016.

Sievert 2013: Henning Sievert, "Eavesdropping on the Pasha's salon: Usual and unusual readings of an eighteenth-century Ottoman bureaucrat", *Osmanlı araştırmaları/The Journal of Ottoman studies* 41 (2013), 159–195.

Sigalas 2007: Nicos Sigalas, "Devlet et Etat: Du glissement sémantique d'un ancien concept du pouvoir au début du XVIIIe siècle ottoman", in G. Grivaud – S. Petmezas (eds), *Byzantina et Moderna: Mélanges en l'honneur d'Hélène Antoniadis-Bibicou*, Athens n.d. (2007), 385–415.

Silay 1992: Kemal Silay, "Ahmedi's history of the Ottoman dynasty", *Journal of Turkish studies* 16 (1992), 129–200.

Sivers 1971: Peter von Sivers, "Die Imperialdoktrin des osmanischen Reiches 1596–1878", in Friedemann Büttner (ed.), *Reform und Revolution in der islamischen Welt. Von der osmanischen Imperialdoktrin zum arabischen Sozialismus*, Munich 1971, 17–48.

Skinner 1969: Quentin Skinner, "Meaning and understanding in the history of ideas", *History and theory* 8 (1969), 3–53.

Skinner 1978: Quentin Skinner, *The foundations of modern political thought*, 2 vols, Cambridge 1978.

Soyer 2007: Emel Soyer, "XVII. yy. Osmanlı divan bürokrasisi'ndeki değişimlerin bir örneği olarak Mühimme Defterleri", unpublished M.A. dissertation, Istanbul University 2007.

Soysal 1999: İsmail Soysal, *Fransız ihtilâli ve Türk-Fransız diplomasi münasebetleri (1789–1802)*, Ankara 1999 (1st ed. 1964).

Sönmez 2012: Ebru Sönmez, *Idris-i Bidlisi. Ottoman Kurdistan and Islamic legitimacy*, Istanbul 2012.

Spanos 2014: Apostolos Spanos, "Was innovation unwanted in Byzantium?", in Ingela Nilsson – Paul Stephenson (eds), *Byzantium wanted: The desire for a lost empire*, Uppsala 2014, 43–56.

Spencer 1970: Martin E. Spencer, "Weber on legitimate norms and authority", *The British journal of sociology* 21/2 (1970), 123–134.

Stavrakopoulou 2012: Anna Stavrakopoulou (ed.), *Georgios N. Soutsos: Alexandrovodas the unscrupulous (1785)*, Istanbul 2012.

Stavrides 2001: Theoharis Stavrides, *The sultan of vezirs. The life and times of the Ottoman grand vezir Mahmud Pasha Angelović (1453–1474)*, Leiden 2001.

Stein 1985: Joshua M. Stein, "Habsburg financial institutions presented as a model for the Ottoman Empire in the *Sefaretname* of Ebu Bekir Ratib Efendi", in Andreas Tietze (ed.), *Habsburgisch-osmanische Beziehungen, Beihefte zur Wiener Zeitschrift für die Kunde des Morgenlandes* 13 (1985), 233–241.

Stephanov 2014: Darin Stephanov, "Sultan Mahmud II (1808–1839) and the first shift in modern ruler visibility in the Ottoman Empire", *Journal of the Ottoman and Turkish studies association* 1:1–2 (2014), 129–148.

Stuurman 2000: Siep Stuurman, "The canon of the history of political thought: Its critique and a proposed alternative", *History and theory*, 39/2 (2000), 147–166.

Subrahmanyam 2006: Sanjay Subrahmanyam, "A tale of three empires: Mughals, Ottomans, and Habsburgs in a comparative context", *Common knowledge* 12/1 (2006), 66–92.

Subtelny 2013: Maria E. Subtelny, "A late medieval Persian *Summa* on ethics: Kashifi's *Akhlâq-i Muhsinî*", *Iranian studies* 36/4 (2003), 601–614.

Sunar 2006: Mehmet Mert Sunar, "Cauldron of dissent: A study of the janissary corps, 1807–1826", unpublished Ph.D. dissertation, Binghampton University 2006.

Sunar 2010: Mehmet Mert Sunar, "Ocak-ı âmire'den ocak-ı mülgâ'ya doğru: Nizâm-ı Cedîd reformları karşısında yeniçeriler", in Seyfi Kenan (ed.), *Nizâm-ι Kâdîm'den Nizâm-ι Cedîd'e: III. Selim ve dönemi*, Istanbul 2010, 497–527.

Swain 2013: Simon Swain, *Economy, family, and society from Rome to Islam: A critical edition, English translation, and study of Bryson's* Management of the estate, Cambridge 2013.

Syros 2010: Vasileios Syros, "Between Chimera and Charybdis: Byzantine and post-Byzantine views on the political organization of the Italian city-states", *Journal of early modern history* 14 (2010), 451–504.

Syros 2011: Vasileios Syros (ed.), *Well begun is only half done: Tracing Aristotle's political ideas in Medieval Arabic, Syriac, Byzantine, and Jewish sources*, Tempe 2011.

Syros 2012a: Vasileios Syros, "Shadows in heaven and clouds on earth: The emergence of social life and political authority in the early modern Islamic empires", *Viator* 43/2 (2012), 377–406.

Syros 2012b: Vasileios Syros, "An early modern South Asian thinker on the rise and decline of empires: Shâh Walî Allâh of Delhi, the Mughals, and the Byzantines", *Journal of world history* 23/4 (2012), 793–840.

Syros 2013: Vasileios Syros, "Galenic medicine and social stability in early modern Florence and the Islamic empires", *Journal of early modern history* 17 (2013), 161–213.

Şahin 2013: Kaya Şahin, *Empire and power in the reign of Süleyman. Narrating the sixteenth-century Ottoman world*, Cambridge 2013.

Şakul 2005: Kahraman Şakul, "Nizâm-ı Cedid düşüncesinde batılılaşma ve İslami modernleşme", *Dîvân—ilmî araştırmalar* 19 (2005), 117–150.

Şakul 2014a: Kahraman Şakul, "Ottoman perceptions of the military reforms of Tipu Sultan and Şahin Giray", in Marinos Sariyannis (ed.-in-chief), *New trends in Ottoman studies. Papers presented at the 20th CIEPO Symposium, Rethymno, 27 June–1 July 2012*, Rethymno 2014, 655–662 [e-book: http://anemi.lib.uoc.gr/metadata/7/8/e/metadata-1412743543-919456-15948.tkl].

Şakul 2014b: Kahraman Şakul, "The evolution of Ottoman military logistical systems in the later eighteenth century: The rise of a new class of military entrepreneur", in Jeff Fynn-Paul (ed.), *War, entrepreneurs, and the state in Europe and the Mediterranean, 1300–1800*, Leiden – Boston 2014, 307–327.

Şeker 1995: Mehmet Şeker, "Political view of 'Âlî: Evaluation of the work of 'Âlî so-called 'Fusul-i harj u naqd'", in Daniel Panzac (ed.), *Histoire économique et sociale de l'Empire ottoman et de la Turquie (1326–1960). Actes du sixième congrès international tenu à Aix-en-Provence du 1er au 4 juillet 1992*, Paris 1995, 855–864.

Şen 2011: Ahmet Tunç Şen, "A mirror for princes, a fiction for readers: The *Habname* of Veysi and dream narratives in Ottoman Turkish literature", *Journal of Turkish literature* 8 (2011), 41–65.

Şen 2017: Ahmet Tunç Şen, "Reading the stars at the Ottoman court: Bâyezîd II (r. 886/1481–918/1512) and his celestial interests", *Arabica* 64 (2017), 557–608.

Şeşen 2004: Ramazan Şeşen, "Lale Devrinde yenileşme hareketleri ve tercüme edilen eserler", *Journal of Turkish studies* 28/II (2004) [Kaf dağının ötesine varmak: Festschrift in honor of Günay Kut], 47–57.

Tabakoğlu 1985: Ahmet Tabakoğlu, "XVII. ve XVIII. yüzyıl Osmanlı bütçeleri", *İstanbul Üniversitesi iktisat fakültesi mecmuası* 41 (1985) [Ord. Prof. Ömer Lütfi Barkan'a Armağan], 389–414.

Taştan 2012: Yahya Kemal Taştan, "Evliya Çelebi's views on the Ottoman dynasty", in Nuran Tezcan – Semih Tezcan – Robert Dankoff (eds), *Evliya Çelebi. Studies and essays commemorating the 400th anniversary of his birth*, Istanbul 2012, 242–262.

Telci 1999: Cahit Telci, "Bir Osmanlı aydınının XVIII. yüzyıl devlet düzeni hakkındaki görüşleri: Penah Süleyman Efendi", in Kemal Çiçek (ed.-in-chief), *Osmanlı. Vol. 7: Düşünce*, Ankara 1999, 178–188.

Terzioğlu 1999: Derin Terzioğlu, "Sufi and dissident in the Ottoman Empire: Niyazi Misri (1618–1694)", unpublished Ph.D. dissertation, Harvard University 1999.

Terzioğlu 2007: Derin Terzioğlu, "Bir tercüme ve bir intihal vakası: Ya da İbn Teymiyye'nin *Siyâsetü'ş-şer'iyye*'sini Osmanlıcaya kim(ler), nasıl aktardı?", *Journal of Turkish studies* 31/II (2007) [In memoriam Şinasi Tekin, II], 247–275.

Terzioğlu 2010: Derin Terzioğlu, "Sunna-minded Sufi preachers in service of the Ottoman state: The *nasîhatnâme* of Hasan addressed to Murad IV", *Archivum Ottomanicum* 27 (2010), 241–312.

Terzioğlu 2012: Derin Terzioğlu, "Sufis in the age of state-building and confessionalization", in Christine Woodhead (ed.), *The Ottoman world*, London – New York 2012, 86–99.

Terzioğlu 2013: Derin Terzioğlu, "Where *ilmihal* meets catechism: Islamic manuals of religious instruction in the Ottoman Empire in the age of confessionalization", *Past and present* 220 (2013), 79–114.

Tezcan 1996: Baki Tezcan, "The definition of sultanic legitimacy in the sixteenth century Ottoman Empire. The *Ahlâk-ı Alâ'î* of Kınalızâde Alî Çelebi (1510–1572)", unpublished M.A. dissertation, Princeton University 1996.

Tezcan 2000: Baki Tezcan, "The 'Kânûnnâme of Mehmed II': A different perspective", in Kemal Çiçek (ed.-in-chief), *The great Ottoman-Turkish civilisation. Vol. 3, Philosophy, science and institutions*, Ankara 2000, 657–665.

Tezcan 2001: Baki Tezcan, "Ethics as a domain to discuss the political: Kınalızâde Ali Efendi's *Ahlâk-i Alâî*", in Ali Çaksu (ed.), *IRCICA international congress on learning and education in the Ottoman World (Istanbul, 12–15 April 1999)*, Istanbul 2001, 109–120.

Tezcan 2010a: Baki Tezcan, *The second Ottoman Empire: Political and social transformation in the early modern world*, Cambridge – New York 2010.

Tezcan 2010b: Baki Tezcan, "Some thoughts on the politics of early modern Ottoman science", in Donald Quataert – Baki Tezcan (eds), *Beyond dominant paradigms in Ottoman and Middle Eastern/North African studies. A tribute to Rifa'at Abou-El-Haj*, Istanbul 2010, 135–156.

Tezcan 2013: Baki Tezcan, "Erken Osmanlı tarih yazımında Moğol hatıraları", *Journal of Turkish studies* 40 (2013) [Defterology: Festschrift in honor of Heath Lowry], 385–399.

Tezcan 2014: Baki Tezcan, "İbrâhîm Müteferrika ve Risâle-i İslâmiyye", in Hatice Aynur – Bilgin Aydın – M. Birol Ülker (eds), *Kitaplara vakfedilen bir ömre tuhfe. İsmail E. Erünsal'a Armağan*, Istanbul 2014, 515–556.

Tezcan (forthcoming): Baki Tezcan, "From Veysî (d. 1628) to Üveysî (fl. ca. 1630): Ottoman advice literature and its discontents", forthcoming in Sina Rauschenbach – Christian Windler (eds), *The Castilian "Arbitristas" and the cultural and intellectual history of early modern Europe*, Wiesbaden (Wolfenbütteler Forschungen 143).

Thomas 1972: Lewis V. Thomas, *A study of Na'ima*, ed. N. Itzkowitz, New York 1972.

Thys-Senocak 1998: Lucienne Thys-Senocak, "The Yeni Valide mosque complex at Eminönü", *Muqarnas* 15 (1998), 58–70.

Tietze 1982: Andreas Tietze, "Mustafâ Âlî on luxury and the status symbols of Ottoman gentlemen", *Studia turcologica memoriae Alexii Bombaci dicata*, Napoli 1982, 577–590.

Topal 2017: Alp Eren Topal, "From decline to progress: Ottoman concepts of reform, 1600–1876", unpublished Ph.D. dissertation, Bilkent University 2017.

Toutant 2016: Marc Toutant, "Le premier roman d'Alexandre versifié en ottoman ou les fondements d'une didactique princière", *Turcica* 47 (2016), 3–31.

Treiger 2011: Alexander Treiger, "Al-Ghazâlî's classifications of the sciences and descriptions of the highest theoretical science", *Dîvân: disiplinerarası çalışmalar dergisi* 16/30 (2011), 1–32.

Tuck 2001: Richard Tuck, "History of political thought", in Peter Burke (ed.), *New perspectives on historical writing*, 2nd ed., Cambridge 2001, 218–232.

Tunalı Koç 2006: Gülçin Tunalı Koç, "Osmanlı Atinası ve düşünce tarihi ekseninde Kadı Mahmud Efendi'nin *Tarih-i Medinetü'l-Hükemâ* adlı eseri", *Dîvân—ilmî araştırmalar* 20 (2006), 169–184.

Tunalı 2014: Gülçin Tunalı, "'Seseya'. Representation of Theseus by the Ottoman mufti of Athens at the beginning of the eighteenth century", in Andreas Helmedach – Markus Koller – Konrad Petrovszky – Stefan Rohdewald (eds), *Das osmanische Europa. Methoden und Perspektiven der Frühneuzeitforschung zu Südosteuropa*, Leipzig 2014, 487–506.

Turna 2009: B. Babür Turna, "Perception of history and the problem of superiority in Ahmedi's *Dastân-ı tevârih-i mülûk-i Âl-i Osman*", *Acta orientalia* 62/3 (2009), 267–283.

Tuşalp Atiyas 2013: E. Ekin Tuşalp Atiyas, "Political literacy and the politics of eloquence: Ottoman scribal community in the seventeenth century", unpublished Ph.D. dissertation, Harvard University 2013.

Uğur 1995: Ahmet Uğur, "Osmanlı siyaset-namelerine göre hazine ve bununla ilgili hususlar", in H.G. Majer – R. Motika (eds), *Türkische Wirtschafts- und Sozialgeschichte von 1071 bis 1920, Akten des IV. Internationalen Kongresses, München 1986*, Wiesbaden, 1995, 337–342.

Uğur 2001: Ahmet Uğur, *Osmanlı siyâset-nâmeleri*, Istanbul 2001 (1st ed. Kayseri 1987).

Uluçay 1950–1955: M. Çağatay Uluçay, "Koçi Bey'in Sultan İbrahim'e takdim ettiği Risale ve arzları", *Zeki velidi togan armağanı*, Istanbul 1950–1955, 177–199.

Unan 1997: Fahri Unan, "Taşköprülü-zâde'nin kaleminden XVI. yüzyılın ilim ve âlim anlayışı", *Osmanlı araştırmaları* 17 (1997), 149–264.

Unan 2004: Fahri Unan, *İdeal cemiyet, ideal hükümdar, ideal devlet. Kınalı-zâde Ali'nin* Medîne-i fâzıla'*sı*, Ankara 2004.

Unat 1968: Faik Reşit Unat, *Osmanlı sefirleri ve sefaretnâmeleri*, Ankara 1968.

Ursinus 2012: Michael Ursinus, "The transformation of the Ottoman fiscal regime, c. 1600–1850", in Christine Woodhead (ed.), *The Ottoman world*, London – New York 2012, 423–435.

Uzunçarşılı 1936: İ. Hakki Uzunçarşılı, "Sadrazam Halil Hamid Paşa", *Türkiyat mecmuası* 5 (1936), 213–267.

Uzunçarşılı 1938: İ. Hakki Uzunçarşılı, "Selim III'ün veliaht iken Fransa kralı Lüi XVI ile muhabereleri", *Belleten* 2.5–6 (1938), 191–246.

Uzunçarşılı 1949: İ. Hakkı Uzunçarşılı, *Osmanlı tarihi*, vol. 2, Ankara 1949.

Uzunçarşılı 1975: İ. Hakkı Uzunçarşılı, "Tosyalı Ebubekir Ratıb Efendi", *Belleten* 39/153 (1975), 49–76.

Uzunçarşılı 1978: İ. Hakki Uzunçarşılı, "Osmanlı devleti maliyesinin kuruluşu ve Osmanlı devleti İç Hazinesi", *Belleten* 42 (1978), 67–93.

Uzunçarşılı 1988: İ. Hakki Uzunçarşılı, *Osmanlı devleti teşkilâtından kapukulu ocakları. Vol. I: Acemi ocağı ve yeniçeri ocağı*, Ankara 1988.

Varlık 1979: M. Çetin Varlık, "Şeyhoğlu'nun *Kenzü'l-küberâ ve mahakkü'l-ulemâ* adlı tercüme eseri", *I. milletlerarası Türkoloji kongresi, Istanbul 15–20 X 1973*, vol. 2, Istanbul 1979, 544–552.

Vatin 2010: Nicolas Vatin, *Ferîdûn Bey. Les plaisants secrets de la campagne de Szigetvár. Edition, traduction et commentaire des folios 1 à 147 du* Nüzhetü'l-esrâri-l-ahbâr der sefer-i Sigetvâr (*ms. H 1339 de la Bibliothèque du Musée de Topkapı Sarayı*), Vienna 2010.

Vatin 2012: Nicolas Vatin, "Sur l'emploi des mots dans le récit de la prise de Constantinople par les auteurs ottomans du XVe et du début du XVIe siècle", in François Georgeon (ed.), *Documents de travail du CETOBAC, 2/1: Les mots du politique—fascicule 1 : L'Empire ottoman*, 2012 (http://cetobac.ehess.fr/docannexe/file/1354/mots_du_politique_1.pdf), 5–14.

Vatin (forthcoming): Nicolas Vatin, "How to date the law of fratricide? A hypothesis", unpublished paper.

Vatin – Veinstein 2003 : Nicolas Vatin – Gilles Veinstein, *Le Sérail ébranlé. Essai sur les morts, dépositions et avènements des sultans ottomans, XIVe–XIXe siècle*, Paris 2003.

Veinstein 1988: Gilles Veinstein, "Du marché urbain au marché du camp: L'institution ottomane des *orducu*", in A. Temimi (ed.), *Mélanges Prof. R. Mantran*, Zaghouan 1988, 299–327.

Veinstein 2004: Gilles Veinstein, "Le législateur ottoman face à l'insularité : L'enseignement des *kânûnnâme*", in Nicolas Vatin – Gilles Veinstein (eds), *Insularités ottomanes*, Paris 2004, 101–106.

Veinstein 2008: Gilles Veinstein, "Les règlements fiscaux ottomans de Crète", in Antonis Anastasopoulos (ed.), *The eastern Mediterranean under Ottoman rule: Crete, 1645–1840*, Rethymno 2008, 3–16.

Vryonis 1971: Speros Vryonis Jr., *The decline of medieval Hellenism in Asia Minor and the process of Islamization from the eleventh through the fifteenth century*, Berkeley 1971.

Weber 1978: Max Weber, *Economy and society. An outline of interpretive sociology*, translation ed. by Guenther Roth and Claus Wittich, 2 vols, Berkeley – Los Angeles – London 1978.

Weber 1985: Max Weber, "Die drei reinen Typen der legitimen Herrschaft", now in Max Weber, *Gesammelte Aufsätze zur Wissenschaftslehre*, ed. J. Winckelmann, 6th ed., Tübingen 1985, 474–487 (tr. by H. Gerth as "The three types of legitimate rule", *Berkeley publications in society and institutions* 4/1 [1958], 1–11).

Welle 2014: Jason Welle O.F.M., "The status of monks in Egypt under early Mamlûk rule: The case of Ibn Taymiyya (with an annotated translation of Ibn Taymiyya's *Fatwâ* on the status of monks)", *Logos: A journal of Eastern Christian studies* 55 (2014), 41–67.

Wittek 1925: Paul Wittek, "Der Stammbaum der Osmanen", *Der Islam* 14 (1925), 94–100.

Woodhead 1988: Christine Woodhead, "Ottoman *inşa* and the art of letter-writing: Influences upon the career of the *nişancı* and prose stylist Okçuzade (d. 1630)", *Osmanlı araştırmaları/The Journal of Ottoman studies* 7–8 (1988), 143–159.

Woodhead 1995: Christine Woodhead, "Perspectives on Süleyman", in Metin Kunt – Christine Woodhead (eds), *Süleyman the Magnificent and his age: The Ottoman Empire in the early modern world*, London 1995, 164–190.

Woodhead 2006: Christine Woodhead, "Scribal chaos? Observations on the post of *re'isülküttab* in the late sixteenth century", in Eugenia Kermeli – Oktay Özel (eds), *The Ottoman Empire: Myths, realities and 'black holes'. Contributions in honour of Colin Imber*, Istanbul 2006, 155–172.

Wurm 1971: Heidrun Wurm, *Der osmanische Historiker Hüseyn b. Ğa'fer, genannt Hezârfenn, und die Istanbuler Gesellschaft in der zweiten Hälfte des 17. Jahrhunderts*, Freiburg im Breisgau 1971.

Yakubovych 2017: Mykhaylo M. Yakubovich, "Crimean scholars and the Kadızadeli tradition in the 18th century", *Osmanlı araştırmaları/The Journal of Ottoman studies* 49 (2017), 155–170.

Yapp 1992: Malcolm Edward Yapp, "Europe in the Turkish mirror", *Past and Present* 137 (1992), 134–155.

Yavari 2014: Neguin Yavari, *Advice for the sultan. Prophetic voices and secular politics in medieval Islam*, Oxford 2014.

Yaycıoğlu 2008: Ali Yaycıoğlu, "The provincial challenge: Regionalism, crisis, and integration in the late Ottoman Empire (1792–1812)", unpublished Ph.D. dissertation, Harvard University 2008.

Yaycıoğlu 2010: Ali Yaycıoğlu, "Sened-i ittifak (1808): Osmanlı İmparatorluğu'nda bir ortaklık ve entegrasyon denemesi", in Seyfi Kenan (ed.), *Nizâm-ı Kâdîm'den Nizâm-ı Cedîd'e: III. Selim ve dönemi*, Istanbul 2010, 667–709.

Yaycıoğlu 2012: Ali Yaycıoğlu, "Provincial power-holders and the empire in the late Ottoman world: Conflict or partnership?", in Christine Woodhead (ed.), *The Ottoman world*, London – New York 2012, 436–452.

Yérasimos 1990: Stéphane Yérasimos, *La fondation de Constantinople et de Sainte-Sophie dans les traditions turques*, Paris 1990 [For the Ottoman texts, see the Turkish translation by Ş. Tekeli: S. Yerasimos, *Konstantiniye ve Ayasofya efsaneleri*, Istanbul 1993].

Yeşil 2007: Fatih Yeşil, "Looking at the French Revolution through Ottoman eyes: Ebubekir Ratib Efendi's observations", *Bulletin of the School of Oriental and African Studies* 70/2 (2007), 283–304.

Yeşil 2011a: Fatih Yeşil, *Aydınlanma çağında bir Osmanlı kâtibi: Ebubekir Ratıb Efendi (1750–1799)*, Istanbul 2011.

Yeşil 2011b: Fatih Yeşil, "Bir Fransız maceraperestin savaş ve diplomasiye dair görüşleri: Humbaracı Ahmed Paşa'nın (Kont Alexander Bonneval) lâyihaları", *Hacettepe Üniversitesi Türkiyat araştırmaları dergisi* 15 (2011), 205–228.

Yeşil 2014: Fatih Yeşil, "How to be(come) an Ottoman at the end of the eighteenth century", *Osmanlı araştırmaları/The Journal of Ottoman studies* 44 (2014), 123–139.

Yıldırım 2011: Rıza Yıldırım, "Inventing a Sufi tradition: The use of the *futuwwa* ritual gathering as a model for the Qizilbash *djem*", in John Curry – Erik S. Ohlander (eds), *Sufism and society: Arrangements of the mystical in the Muslim world, 1200–1800*, New York 2011, 164–182.

Yıldırım 2013: Riza Yıldırım, "Shīʿitisation of the Futuwwa Tradition in the Fifteenth Century", *British Journal of Middle Eastern Studies* 40 (2013), 53–70.

Yıldız 2008: Aysel Yıldız, "Vaka-yı Selimiyye or the Selimiyye incident: A study of the May 1807 rebellion", unpublished Ph.D. dissertation, Sabancı University 2008.

Yıldız 2012: Aysel Yıldız, "The anatomy of a rebellious social group: The *yamak*s of the Bosporus at the margins of Ottoman society", in Antonis Anastasopoulos (ed.), *Political Initiatives from the Bottom-Up in the Ottoman Empire (Halcyon Days VII: A Symposium held in Rethymno, January 9–11, 2009)*, Rethymno 2012, 291–324.

Yıldız 2016: Aysel Yıldız, "Osmanlı tarihinde bir ordu boykotu: Maçin bozgunu (1791) akabinde yaşanan tartışmalar", *Cihannüma. Tarih ve coğrafya araştırmaları dergisi* 2/2 (2016), 123–162.

Yılmaz 1999: Coşkun Yılmaz, "Siyasetnameler ve Osmanlılarda sosyal tabakalaşma", in G. Eren (ed.), *Osmanlı, 4: Toplum*, Ankara 1999, 69–81.

Yılmaz 2000a: Coşkun Yılmaz, "Hezarfen bir şahsiyet: İbrahim Müteferrika ve siyaset felsefesi", *İstanbul armağanı 4: Lale devri*, Istanbul 2000, 259–333.

Yılmaz 2000b: Fehmi Yılmaz, "The life of Köprülüzade Fazıl Mustafa Paşa and his reforms (1637–1691)", *The Journal of Ottoman studies* 20 (2000), 165–221.

Yılmaz 2002: Coşkun Yılmaz, "Osmanlı siyaset düşüncesinde kavramlar", in Hasan Celal Güzel – Kemal Çiçek – Salim Koca (eds), *Türkler*, vol. 11, Ankara 2002, 34–44.

Yılmaz 2003a: Coşkun Yılmaz, "Osmanlı siyaset düşüncesi kaynakları ile ilgili yeni bir kavramsallaştırma: Islahatnâmeler", *Türkiye araştırmaları literatür dergisi* 1/2 (2003), 299–338.

Yılmaz 2003b: Hüseyin Yılmaz, "Osmanlı tarihçiliğinde Tanzimat öncesi siyaset düşüncesine yaklaşımlar", *Türkiye araştırmaları literatür dergisi* 1/2 (2003), 231–298.

Yılmaz 2005: Hüseyin Yılmaz, "The sultan and the sultanate: Envisioning rulership in the age of Süleymân the Lawgiver (1520–1566)", unpublished Ph.D. dissertation, Harvard University 2005.

Yılmaz 2006: Mehmet Şakir Yılmaz, "'Koca Nişancı' of Kanuni: Celalzade Mustafa Çelebi, bureaucracy and 'kanun' in the reign of Süleyman the Magnificent (1520–1566)", unpublished Ph.D. dissertation, Bilkent University 2006.

Yılmaz 2007: Mehmet Şakir Yılmaz, "Crime and punishment in the imperial historiography of Süleyman the Magnificent: An evaluation of Nişancı Celâlzâde's view", *Acta Orientalia Academiae Scientiarum Hungaricae* 60 (2007), 427–445.

Yılmaz 2008: Hüseyin Yılmaz, "Osmanlı devleti'nde Batılılaşma öncesi meşrutiyetçi gelişmeler", *Dîvân. Disiplinlerarası çalışmalar dergisi* 13/24 (2008), 1–30.

Yılmaz 2015a: Hüseyin Yılmaz, "Containing Sultanic authority: Constitutionalism in the Ottoman Empire before modernity", *Osmanlı Araştırmaları/The Journal of Ottoman Studies* 45 (2015), 231–264.

Yılmaz 2015b: Çoşkun Yılmaz, "Osmanlı siyasi düşüncesinde kânûn-ı kadîm", in Azmi Bilgin et al. (eds), *XI. Milli Türkoloji Kongresi Bildirileri. 11–13 Kasım 2014*, Istanbul 2015, 2:101–117.

Yılmaz Diko 2015: Gülay Yılmaz Diko, "Blurred boundaries between soldiers and civilians: Artisan janissaries in seventeenth-century Istanbul", in Suraiya Faroqhi (ed.), *Bread from the lion's mouth: Artisans struggling for a livelihood in Ottoman cities*, New York 2015, 175–193.

Yi 2004: Eunjeong Yi, *Guild dynamics in seventeenth-century Istanbul: Fluidity and leverage*, Leiden 2004.

Yi 2011: Eunjeong Yi, "Artisans' networks and revolt in late seventeenth-century Istanbul: An examination of the Istanbul artisans' rebellion of 1688", in Eleni Gara – M. Erdem Kabadayı – Christoph K. Neumann (eds), *Popular protest and political participation in the Ottoman Empire. Studies in honor of Suraiya Faroqhi*, Istanbul 2011, 105–126.

Yurtoğlu 2009: Bilal Yurtoğlu, *Kâtip Çelebi*, Ankara 2009.

Yurtoğlu 2014: Bilal Yurtoğlu, "Kınalızade'de meratibü'l-kainat ve insanın evrendeki yeri", *Dört Öğe* 5 (2014), 149–175.

Yücesoy 2011: Hayrettin Yücesoy, "Justification of political authority in medieval Sunni thought", in Asma Afsaruddin (ed.), *Islam, the state, and political authority: Medieval issues and modern concerns*, New York 2011, 9–33.

Yüksel 1972: Emrullah Yüksel, "Les idées religieuses et politiques de Mehmed al-Birkewi, 929–981/1523–1573", unpublished Ph.D. dissertation, Sorbonne University, 1972.

Yürük 2014: Ali Yücel Yürük, "Lütfî Paşa'nın (ö. 970/1563) Osmanlı haberleşme ve ulaşım sistemine ulak zulmü bağlamında getirdiği yenilikler", in Hatice Aynur – Bilgin Aydın – M. Birol Ülker (eds), *Kitaplara vakfedilen bir ömre tuhfe. İsmail E. Erünsal'a Armağan*, Istanbul 2014, 597–626.

Zachariadou 1992: Elizabeth A. Zachariadou, "Religious dialogue between Byzantines and Turks during the Ottoman expansion", in B. Lewis – F. Niewöhner (eds), *Religionsgespräche im Mittelalter*, Wiesbaden 1992, 289–304 (also in Zachariadou, *Studies in pre-Ottoman Turkey and the Ottomans*, Aldershot 2007).

Zachariadou 1995: Elizabeth A. Zachariadou, "Histoires et légendes des premiers Ottomans", *Turcica* 27 (1995), 45–89.

Ze'evi 2004: Dror Ze'evi, "Back to Napoleon? Thoughts on the beginning of the modern era in the Middle East", *Mediterranean Historical Review* 19/1 (2004), 73–94.

Zervos 1992: Sokratis K. Zervos, "À la recherche des origines du phanariotisme: Panayote Nikoussios, le premier grand drogman grec de la Sublime-Porte", *Epeteris kentrou epistemonikon ereunon* 19 (1992), 307–25.

Zilfi 1986: Madeline C. Zilfi, "The Kadizadelis: Discordant revivalism in seventeenth-century Istanbul", *Journal of Near Eastern studies* 45/4 (1986), 251–269.

Zilfi 1988: Madeline C. Zilfi, *The politics of piety: The Ottoman ulema in the postclassical age (1600–1800)*, Minneapolis 1988.

Zilfi 1999: Madeline C. Zilfi, "Hâkim's chronicle revisited", *Oriente moderno* n.s. 18 (79)/1 (1999) ["The Ottoman Empire in the eighteenth century", ed. K. Fleet], 193–2

Indices

Personal Names

Place Names, Subjects, Terms

Titles of Works*

* See also individual authors in the Index of Personal Names.